THE STATE OF THE WORLD'S CHILDREN 2019

CHILDREN, FOOD AND NUTRITION

Growing well in a changing world

CONTENTS

PERSPECTIVES

SPOTLIGHTS

TEXT BOXES

GRAPHICS

FIGURES

STATISICAL TABLES

Foreword

In the spoonful a mother or father feeds to a toddler, food is love. In the feast a family cooks for a child's coming of age, food is community. In the shouts and laughter of teenagers sharing snacks after school, food is joy. And for every child and young person everywhere, food is life – a fundamental right and a foundation of healthy nutrition and sound physical and mental development.

Sadly, as this *State of the World's Children* report shows, far too many of our children and young people are not getting the diets they need, which is undermining their capacity to grow, develop and learn to their full potential. That hurts not just individual children and young people, it hurts us all.

This situation forces us to ask some difficult questions: How is it in the 21st century that we still have 149 million children under 5 with stunting and almost 50 million with wasting? How is it possible that overweight and obesity in children and young people are continuing to rise, and increasingly among the poor? And why are healthy diets becoming more expensive while unhealthy, non-nutritious diets are becoming cheaper?

Nutrition has long been at the core of UNICEF's work. In 2018, we helped provide life-saving therapeutic feeding for 4.1 million children with severe acute malnutrition; we improved the quality of diets for over 15.6 million children through home-based fortification; we supported programmes to prevent anaemia and other forms of malnutrition for 58 million adolescent girls and boys; and we ensured that over 300 million children received services for the prevention of stunting and other forms of malnutrition.

Nutrition has also long been key to our thought leadership. In 1990, our pioneering malnutrition framework broke new ground in setting out the multiple causes of poor nutrition. In 2019, we have rethought our framework to emphasize what creates good nutrition – from the diets of children and women to the care they benefit from, the food environments in which they live, and the ways in which our societies underpin the right to adequate nutrition through our values and political commitment. Each of these determinants presents an opportunity to improve the nutrition of our children, young people and women.

As Executive Director of UNICEF and Chair of the Lead Group of the Scaling Up Nutrition Movement, I want to emphasize again my commitment, and the commitment of UNICEF, to use all of these opportunities to work for better nutrition for every child, especially in the crucial first 1,000 days – from conception to age two years – and during adolescence, the two unparalleled windows of opportunity. We are underscoring this commitment by launching this report along with UNICEF's new nutrition strategy, which sets out our priorities and plans to improve the nutrition of children, young people and women, in the years to come.

We already know so much of what works to prevent malnutrition in all its forms, from conception, through early childhood and into adolescence. But this is a battle we cannot win on our own. It needs the political determination of national governments, backed by clear financial commitments, as well as policies and incentives that encourage the private sector's investment in nutritious, safe and affordable food for children, young people, women and families. And, increasingly, it needs a determination to make children's nutrition a priority across not just the food system but also in the health, water and sanitation, education and social protection systems. Success in each of these supports success in all.

Young people and women know the value of good nutrition and eating well. "Eating healthily is being responsible for your own health," said a 16-year-old girl in China during one of more than 70 workshops organized for this report. In India, a 13-year-old girl told us that "food is important for us so that we are able to study well." They are clear, too, on the barriers to healthy nutrition: "I don't have enough money to buy food for me and my baby," a 20-year-old mother said in Guatemala; "I lack knowledge about what kinds of food are healthy," an 18-year-old girl said in Zimbabwe.

Good nutrition paves the way for a fair chance in life. Let us work together to lower these barriers and to ensure that every child, young person and woman has the nutritious, safe, affordable and sustainable diets they need at every moment of life to meet their full potential.

Henrietta H. Fore
UNICEF Executive Director

A child sells snacks to other children outside a clinic in Gaza City, State of Palestine. © UNICEF/UN068011/El Baba

Children, food and nutrition | Growing well in a changing world
Key Messages

At least 1 in 3 children under 5 is undernourished or overweight and 1 in 2 suffers from hidden hunger, undermining the capacity of millions of children to grow and develop to their full potential.

➤ Globally, at least 1 in 3 children under 5 is not growing well due to malnutrition in its more visible forms: stunting, wasting and overweight.

➤ Globally, at least 1 in 2 children under 5 suffers from hidden hunger due to deficiencies in vitamins and other essential nutrients.

➤ Undernutrition continues to exert a heavy toll. In 2018, almost 200 million children under 5 suffered from stunting or wasting while at least 340 million suffered from hidden hunger.

➤ Overweight and obesity continue to rise. From 2000–2016, the proportion of overweight children (5 to 19 years old) rose from 1 in 10 to almost 1 in 5.

➤ The number of stunted children has declined in all continents, except in Africa while the number of overweight children has increased in all continents, including in Africa.

The triple burden of malnutrition – undernutrition, hidden hunger and overweight – threatens the survival, growth and development of children, young people, economies and nations.

➤ Stunting – a clear sign that children in a country are not developing well – is both a symptom of past deprivation and a predictor of future poverty.

➤ Wasting can be lethal for children, particularly in its most severe forms. Contrary to common belief, most wasted children around the world live in Asia and not in emergency settings.

➤ Hidden hunger harms children and women. Iron deficiency reduces children's ability to learn and iron deficiency anaemia increases women's risk of death during or shortly after childbirth.

➤ Child overweight can lead to early onset of type-2 diabetes, stigmatization and depression, and is a strong predictor of adult obesity, with serious health and economic consequences.

➤ The greatest burden of all forms of malnutrition is shouldered by children and young people from the poorest and most marginalized communities, perpetuating poverty across generations.

The triple burden of malnutrition is driven by the poor quality of children's diets: 2 in 3 children are not fed the minimum recommended diverse diet for healthy growth and development.

➤ Only 2 in 5 infants under six months of age are exclusively breastfed, as recommended. Breastfeeding could save the lives of 820,000 children annually worldwide.

➤ Use of breastmilk substitutes is of concern. Sales of milk-based formula grew by 41 per cent globally and by 72 per cent in upper middle-income countries such as Brazil, China and Turkey from 2008–2013.

➤ Poor diets drive malnutrition in early childhood: 44 per cent of children aged 6 to 23 months are not fed fruits or vegetables and 59 per cent are not fed eggs, dairy, fish or meat.

➤ Only 1 in 5 children aged 6 to 23 months from the poorest households and rural areas is fed the minimum recommended diverse diet for healthy growth and brain development.

➤ Many school-going adolescents consume highly processed foods: 42 per cent drink carbonated soft drinks at least once a day and 46 per cent eat fast food at least once a week.

Globalization, urbanization, inequities, humanitarian crises and climate shocks are driving unprecedented negative changes in the nutrition situation of children around the world.

➤ Globalization is shaping food options and choices: 77 per cent of processed food sales worldwide are controlled by just 100 large firms.

➤ In cities, many poor children live in 'food deserts', facing an absence of healthy food options, or in 'food swamps', confronted with an abundance of high-calorie, low-nutrient, processed foods.

➤ Poor families tend to select low-quality food that costs less. Because of poverty and exclusion, the most disadvantaged children face the greatest risk of all forms of malnutrition.

➤ Climate shocks, loss of biodiversity, and damage to water, air and soil are worsening the nutritional prospects of millions of children and young people, especially among the poor.

➤ UNICEF and its partners treated more than 3.4 million children with severe malnutrition in humanitarian settings in 2018, from Afghanistan and Yemen to Nigeria and South Sudan.

Improving children's nutrition requires food systems to deliver nutritious, safe, affordable and sustainable diets for all children.

➤ Millions of children are eating too little of what they need, and millions are eating too much of what they don't need: poor diets are now the main risk factor for the global burden of disease.

➤ National food systems must put children's nutrition at the heart of their work because their nutritional needs are unique and meeting them is critical for sustainable development.

➤ Financial incentives should be used to reward actors who increase the availability of healthy and affordable foods in markets and other points of sale especially in low-income communities.

➤ Financial disincentives on unhealthy foods can improve children's diets. For example, taxes on sugary foods and beverages can reduce their consumption by children and adolescents.

➤ Fortification of complementary foods and staple foods with micronutrients can be a cost-effective intervention to combat hidden hunger in children, young people and women.

Food environments are crucial. When healthy options are affordable, convenient and desirable, children and families make better food choices

➤ Children, adolescents, young people, parents and families need support to demand nutritious foods, but food environments need to promote and support healthy diets.

➤ Innovative, fun, memorable and engaging communication strategies to promote healthy eating can leverage the cultural and social aspirations of children, adolescents and families.

➤ Legislation plays a key role in promoting good diets for children, such as by regulating the marketing of breastmilk substitutes to mothers and families, and of unhealthy food to children.

➤ The marketing of unhealthy foods and sugar-sweetened beverages is directly linked to growing overweight and obesity in children.

➤ Front of package labelling – visible, accurate and easy to understand – helps children, young people and families make healthier food choices and incentivizes suppliers to deliver healthy food.

➤ Governments need to promote healthy food environments in schools, including healthy meals and limiting the sale and advertising of 'junk food' in proximity to schools and playgrounds.

➤ The health, water and sanitation, education and social protection systems also have crucial roles to play in promoting and supporting good nutrition for children, adolescents and women.

Improving children's nutrition requires food systems to deliver nutritious, safe, affordable and sustainable diets for all children.

➤ Investing in child nutrition is key to human capital formation because nutrition is central to children's growth, cognitive development, school performance and future productivity.

➤ A large and young labour force – with a great creativity and productivity potential – is emerging in Africa and Asia. However, malnutrition risks limiting this demographic dividend.

➤ Returns from investment in nutrition are high. For example, every dollar invested in reducing stunting generates an economic return equivalent to about US$18 in high-burden countries.

One word must be at the heart of our response to children's malnutrition – action. We need action that reflects the core role of food systems, that strengthens the supply of – and demand for – better food, that improves children's food environments, and leverages the role of key supportive systems.

With action comes another imperative: accountability. Progress must be measured, shared, acted on and celebrated. Sound nutrition is fundamental to children's well-being and the achievement of the Sustainable Development Goals. It needs to be put at the heart of government policy and supported by key stakeholders, including civil society and the private sector.

The State of the World's Children 2019 report concludes with the following **Agenda to Put Children's Nutrition Rights First**:

1 Empower families, children and young people to demand nutritious food.

2 Drive food suppliers to do the right thing for children.

3 Build healthy food environments for all children.

4 Mobilize supportive systems – health, water and sanitation, education and social protection – to scale up nutrition results for all children.

5 Collect, analyse and use good-quality data and evidence regularly to guide action and track progress. ∎

Girl , 8, enjoys a fizzy drink just purchased from a local street vendor in Pretoria, South Africa. © UNICEF/UN0343581/Hearfield

How the triple burden of malnutrition harms children, adolescents and women

● Undernutrition: stunting and wasting

- Poor growth, infection and death
- Poor cognition, school-readiness and school performance
- Poor earning potential later in life

● Hidden hunger: deficiencies in micronutrients

- Poor growth and development
- Poor immunity and tissue development
- Poor health and risk of death

● Overweight (including obesity)

- Short-term: cardiovascular problems, infections and poor self-esteem
- Long-term: obesity, diabetes, and other metabolic disorders

CHILDREN AND ADOLESCENTS

Undernutrition: stunting and underweight

- Perinatal complications
- Prematurity and low birth weight
- Chronic diseases for child in later life

Hidden hunger: deficiencies in micronutrients

- Maternal mortality and morbidity
- Neural tube defects in newborns
- Prematurity, low birth weight and impaired cognitive development in newborns

Overweight (including obesity)

- Gestational diabetes and pre-eclampsia
- Obstetric complications
- Overweight and chronic disease for child in later life

PREGNANT WOMEN

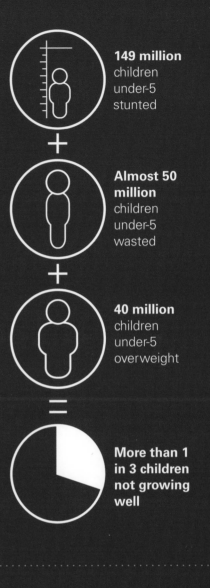

149 million children under-5 stunted

+

Almost 50 million children under-5 wasted

+

40 million children under-5 overweight

=

More than 1 in 3 children not growing well

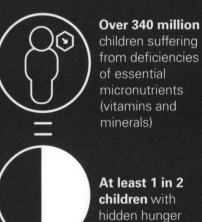

Over 340 million children suffering from deficiencies of essential micronutrients (vitamins and minerals)

=

At least 1 in 2 children with hidden hunger

GROWING WELL IN A CHANGING WORLD

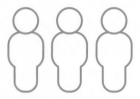

At least one in three children is not getting the nutrition they need to grow well, particularly in the crucial first 1,000 days – from conception to the child's second birthday – and often beyond. An increasing number of children and young people are surviving, but far too few are thriving because of malnutrition. To meet the challenges of the 21st century, we need to recognize the impact of forces like urbanization and globalization on nutrition, and focus increasingly on using local and global food systems to improve the diets of children, young people and women.

➤ Globally, at least 1 in 3 children is not growing well due to malnutrition in its more visible forms: stunting, wasting and overweight. At least 1 in 2 suffers from hidden hunger due to deficiencies – often not visible – in essential nutrients.

➤ This triple burden of malnutrition – undernutrition, hidden hunger and overweight undermines children's health and physical and cognitive development.

➤ Food systems are key: They need to provide children and young people with diets that are nutritious, safe, affordable and sustainable.

A mother prepares food in Korhogo, in the North of Côte d'Ivoire. © UNICEF/UN0241733/Dejongh

mal·nu·tri·tion
/, maln(y)o͞o'triSH(ə)n/
noun

lack of proper nutrition, caused by not having enough to eat, not eating enough of the right things, or being unable to use the food that one does eat

Bad diets across the population are now the leading cause of death worldwide

A changing world

It is 20 years since *The State of the World's Children* report last examined children's nutrition. In that time, much has changed.

We have changed where we live: more and more families have left the farm and the countryside behind and have moved to cities, a global shift that will only grow in the years to come.

We have changed our roles. In societies around the world, women are increasingly joining the formal workforce, balancing work responsibilities with their role as primary caregivers, and often with little support from families, employers or society at large.

The conditions of life on our planet have changed. The crisis of climate change, the loss of biodiversity, and the damage done to water, air and soil, now raise concerns over whether we can feed this generation of children sustainably, never mind the generations to come.

Finally, we have changed what we eat. We are leaving behind traditional and indigenous diets and embracing modern diets that are frequently high in sugars and fats, low in essential nutrients and fibre, and often highly processed.

This is the backdrop to children's malnutrition today. As with so much else, it, too, is changing. A word once inextricably linked in the public's mind with images of hunger and famine, malnutrition must now be used to describe a much broader swathe of children – children with stunting and wasting, but also those suffering from the hidden hunger of deficiencies in essential vitamins and minerals, as well as the growing numbers of children and young people who are overweight or obese.

These are the children who are not growing well.

Their numbers are worryingly high (*see Figure A.1*). Globally, at least one in three children under the age of 5 is stunted, wasted or overweight and, in some cases, suffers from a combination of two of these forms of malnutrition. Further, at least one in two children suffers from hidden hunger due to deficiencies – often not visible – in vitamins and essential nutrients, which can harm survival, growth and development at every stage of life.

Malnutrition – a triple burden

The children who are not growing well are the victims of the three strands of the triple burden of malnutrition that is rapidly emerging in communities around the world, including in some of the world's poorest countries.

The first strand is **undernutrition**. Despite some declines, undernutrition continues to affect tens of millions of children. Its presence is visible in the stunted bodies of children deprived of adequate nutrition in the crucial first 1,000 days – from conception to the child's second birthday – and often beyond. These children may carry the burden of early stunting for the rest of their lives and may never meet their full physical and intellectual potential. Undernutrition is also evident in the wasted bodies of children at any stage of life when circumstances such as food shortages, poor feeding practices and infection, often compounded by poverty, humanitarian crises and conflict, deprive them of adequate nutrition and, in far too

Where are children not growing well?

FIGURE A.1 | **Prevalence of children under 5 who are not growing well (stunted, wasted or overweight), 2018**

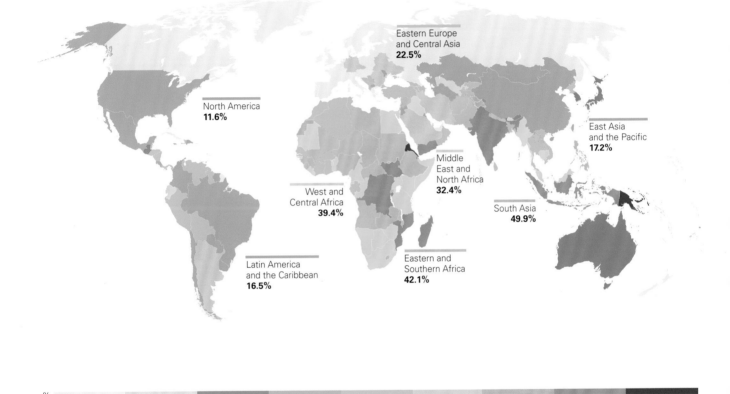

**Eastern Europe
and Central Asia
22.5%**

**North America
11.6%**

**East Asia
and the Pacific
17.2%**

**Middle
East and
North Africa
32.4%**

**West and
Central Africa
39.4%**

**South Asia
49.9%**

**Latin America
and the Caribbean
16.5%**

**Eastern and
Southern Africa
42.1%**

%								
No data	No recent data	Less than 10.0	10.0–19.9	20.0–29.9	30.0–39.9	40.0–49.9	50.0–59.9	Greater than 60

1 in 3 children
worldwide under
the age of 5 is not
growing well

Note: Country data are the most recent available estimate between 2006 and 2018; where only data prior to 2000 are available, the dark grey color denoting no recent data is used. The designations employed in this publication and the presentation of the material do not imply on the part of the United Nations Children's Fund (UNICEF) the expression of any opinion whatsoever concerning the legal status of any country or territory, or of its authorities or the delimitations of its frontiers.

'Growing well' is defined as free from stunting, wasting and overweight. See Note on Figures on p. 179 for more information.

Source: UNICEF analysis of UNICEF/World Health Organization/World Bank Group Joint Malnutrition Estimates, 2019 edition. *Levels and trends in child malnutrition: Key findings of the 2019 edition of the Joint Child Malnutrition Estimates.*

many cases, result in death. In 2018, 149 million children under 5 were stunted and almost 50 million were wasted.

The second strand of malnutrition is **hidden hunger**. Deficiencies of essential vitamins and minerals – often referred to as micronutrients – rob children of their vitality at every stage of life and undermine the health and well-being of children, young people and women. This heavy toll is made all the more insidious by the fact that hidden hunger is rarely noticed until it is too late to do anything. The numbers of children affected by hidden hunger are striking. Based on the most recent data available, UNICEF estimates that at least 340 million children under 5 suffer from micronutrient deficiencies.[1]

The third strand is **overweight** and, in its more severe form, obesity. The numbers of obese girls and boys between the ages of 5 and 19 have soared since the mid-1970s, rising by between 10- and 12-fold globally.[2] Overweight, long thought of as a condition of the wealthy, is now increasingly a condition of the poor, reflecting the greater availability of 'cheap calories' from fatty and sugary foods in almost every country in the world. It brings with it a heightened risk of non-communicable diseases, such as type 2 diabetes and coronary heart disease. Analysis carried out as part of the Global Burden of Disease study suggests that diets lacking adequate nutrition are now the leading cause of death worldwide.[3]

Behind all these numbers are the real lives of the children and women. They are the toddlers like Moteab, who, like hundreds of thousands of other children in Yemen, has had to fight for his life from severe wasting. Moteab survived, but many other children living through

conflicts and humanitarian crises around the world have not. They are the infants like Joemar in the Philippines, who live far from warzones but who also suffer from severe wasting. They are the children of mothers like Uruma in Tanzania, who go to school on an empty stomach because their parents cannot afford to buy food. They are the teens like Zahfa in Indonesia, who get too little time to exercise and who are surrounded by unhealthy food options. And they are the mothers like Xaiathon in rural Laos, who must balance breastfeeding her child and feeding her family with the demands of working on a farm.

Surviving, but not thriving

The state of children's malnutrition in the 21st century can be summed up like this: more children and young people are surviving, but far too few are thriving. They are not thriving in the crucial first 1,000 days, when the foundations for healthy, lifelong physical growth and mental development are laid. And they are not thriving at other crucial development stages of life across childhood and into adolescence.

Malnutrition has many causes. A mother's nutritional status, for example, profoundly affects her child's survival, growth and development, as does the child's feeding in the first hours and days of life. For far too many children, the causes of malnutrition also include poor access to essential health services and to clean water and adequate sanitation, which can lead to illnesses that prevent the child from absorbing nutrients (*see Chapter 3*).

But to understand malnutrition, there is an increasing need to focus on food and diet, and at every stage of the child's and young person's life. The picture that emerges is a troubling one: **far too many children and young people are eating too little healthy food and too much unhealthy food**.

These problems start early on. In their first six months, only two out of five children are being exclusively breastfed, depriving them of the best food a baby can get. When it comes to the 'first foods' (or complementary foods) that infants should start consuming at around the age of 6 months, these too are, in far too many cases, not meeting children's needs. Fewer than one in three children between 6 and 23 months is eating the diverse diet that can support their rapidly growing bodies and brains. For the poorest children, the proportion falls to only one in five. Among older children, low consumption of fruits and vegetables is widespread.[4] This is true, too, of many adolescents, many of whom also regularly miss or skip breakfast and consume soft drinks and fast food.[5]

The diets of children today increasingly reflect the global 'nutrition transition', which is seeing communities leave behind often more healthy, traditional diets in favour of modern diets.[6] For many families, especially poorer families, this means an increasing reliance on highly processed foods, which can be high in saturated fat, sugar and sodium and low in essential nutrients and fibre, as well as on 'ultra-processed' foods, which have been characterized as formulations containing little or no whole food and which are extremely palatable, highly energy dense, and low in essential nutrients.[7] Often missing from these diets are whole grains, fruit, nuts and seeds, vegetables, and omega-3 fatty acids.[8]

There is increasing concern about the impact of these diets on human health. Much of the focus is on rising overweight and obesity, but modern diets are also implicated in undernutrition. In Nepal, a recent study suggested that children under 2 may be getting on average a quarter of their energy intake from items such as biscuits, instant noodles and juice drinks, which is lowering their intake of essential vitamins and minerals. Children eating the most of these sorts of snacks and beverages were shorter than their peers.[9]

A greater focus on food systems

Health impacts are not the only concern around modern diets. In a world facing multiple environmental crises, there is also concern about the sustainability of these diets. Food production accounts for almost a third of greenhouse gas emissions and 70 per cent of fresh water use, and current modes of food production are the leading cause of environmental change.[10] Climate-related shocks, such as flooding, are already challenging the capacity of some communities to feed themselves and are exposing children to increased risk from waterborne diseases. If current trends continue, the impact of food production on the environment will only grow, with food demand set to increase by at least half by mid-century.[11] This demand will have to be satisfied against the backdrop of a world that, after decades of decline, is seeing a slow rise in hunger, with 820 million people suffering from undernourishment in 2018.[12]

In response to these challenges, and in this UN Decade of Action on Nutrition,

Far too many children and young people are eating too little healthy food and too much unhealthy food

To make food systems work better for children, we need to understand the unique nutritional needs of children at every stage of life

there is a growing focus on the role of **food systems** – all the elements and activities involved in the "production, processing, distribution, preparation and consumption of food" as well as the outcomes of these activities, including nutrition and health.[13] In other words, everything and everyone involved in bringing food 'from farm to mouth'.

Food systems are becoming more complex. More food now crosses borders, and production is concentrated in the hands of a relatively small number of businesses – just 100 large firms account for 77 per cent of processed food sales worldwide.[14] For families around the world, business is playing a growing role in providing the food they eat and, through marketing, in shaping what they want to eat and their aspirations. Understanding how food systems work is essential to improving our diets.

Far too often, the interests of a very important group of people are left out of food systems analysis – children. This is a dangerous omission. Children are a unique group. Poor diets have lifelong impacts on their physical growth and brain development. That is why they must be at the heart of our thinking about food systems. **If food systems deliver for children, they are delivering for us all.**

Making food systems work for children

Thirty years ago, the Convention on the Rights of the Child spoke of the need to provide children with "adequate nutritious foods" to combat malnutrition and disease. That goal has not changed. What has changed are the contexts in which this needs to happen, and the realization that food systems are a key – and underappreciated – part of the puzzle.

To make food systems work better for children, we need to understand the **unique nutritional needs of children** at every stage of life, particularly in the first 1,000 days – but also on day 1,001, and then on through the school years, when a well-nourished child can focus better and learn more in the classroom, and throughout the vital years of adolescence, when physical and mental development again speeds up and when lifelong eating habits are established.

To make food systems work better for children, we need to understand the rapidly evolving contexts that are shaping and reshaping children's diets. Climate change, urbanization and globalization are profoundly altering how and what children eat, as well as the social and cultural values we attach to food.

To make food systems work better for children, we need to respond to the challenges children, young people, women and families are facing around the world – food deserts, the high cost of healthy foods, time pressures, the limited availability of nutrient-rich foods, including fruits and vegetables – and the pressure many children, adolescents and families feel from marketing and advertising.

To make food systems work better for children, we need to address the scandal of child labour in agriculture and food production, much of which is hazardous. In 2016, 108 million

children aged between 5 and 17 were engaged in agricultural labour, accounting for 71 per cent of all child labour.[15]

And to make food systems work better for children, we need to ensure food systems work with, and are not undermined by, all the other systems that affect children's lives. The health, water and sanitation, education and social protection systems must all work together to provide children and their families with the knowledge, support and services they need to ensure that nutritious diets translate into better growth and development.

When food systems work better for children, we all benefit. Good nutrition can break the vicious intergenerational cycles through which malnutrition perpetuates poverty, and poverty perpetuates malnutrition. Children who are well nourished have a firm foundation from which they can develop to their full potential. When children do that, societies and economies develop better, too.[16, 17]

Our goal must be to give children diets that are **nutritious**, **safe, affordable** and **sustainable.** ■

A father carries his daughter of 7 months through a grocery store in Maitland, Cape Town, South Africa.
© UNICEF/UN0315717/Sokol

Good nutrition can break the vicious intergenerational cycles through which malnutrition perpetuates poverty, and poverty perpetuates malnutrition

About this report

This edition of *The State of the World's Children* report examines children, food and nutrition. It seeks to deepen understanding around the causes and consequences of children's malnutrition in all its forms and to highlight how governments, business, families and other stakeholders can best respond.

Chapter 1 examines the changing face of children's malnutrition. It sets out the current state of undernutrition, hidden hunger and overweight worldwide, explores the lives of children affected by severe acute malnutrition, and investigates the cost to children and to us all of malnutrition. It also introduces in greater detail some of the main ideas around food systems.

Chapter 2 investigates malnutrition across the life of the child, from development in the womb to the point where a young person is entering adulthood. It explores the developmental impacts of malnutrition and the unique nutritional needs and influences at each stage of childhood.

Chapter 3 explores malnutrition in a changing world. Globalization and urbanization are changing children's diets while disasters and conflict worsen nutritional prospects for millions of poor and excluded children. Without transformation of today's food systems, healthy diets will remain out of reach for the most vulnerable children, perpetuating intergenerational cycles of disadvantage.

Chapter 4 examines the current state of responses to children's malnutrition, including the increased attention – at the global and national level – to the importance of addressing malnutrition across multiple systems, with particular emphasis on the food system in synergy with the health, water and sanitation, education and social protection systems, and on how different stakeholders are responding.

Finally, **Chapter 5** sets out an agenda to put children's nutrition rights first (*see opposite page*). This agenda is driven by two imperatives. First, children have unique nutritional needs and can suffer unique harm from malnutrition. Putting children's needs first is key to ensuring that every child and young person has the nutrition they need to get the best start in life. Second, all children and young people will need nutritious, safe, affordable and sustainable diets if societies are to meet the economic, social and environmental challenges of our changing world in the 21st century.

Put children's nutrition first

1. Empower families, children and young people to demand nutritious food

Demand affects supply as food producers respond to consumers' behaviours and aspirations. When healthy options are affordable, convenient and desirable, parents and caregivers make better food choices for children. As children grow older, knowledge and information can make them powerful agents of change. Stimulating demand for nutritious foods means not only educating consumers on the benefits of healthy diets, but also leveraging cultural and social aspirations.

2. Drive food suppliers to do the right thing for children

Demand alone is not enough: healthy food must be available, affordable, safe and convenient. Food producers and suppliers have a key role to play, and so do governments, which must create a level playing field for all producers and suppliers and help ensure that their actions align with children's best interests. Food systems are diverse, and so are the solutions, but all food production and consumption must become sustainable if we are to protect children's nutrition today and tomorrow.

3. Build healthy food environments for all children

The personal and external food environments are where children and their caregivers interact with the food system. While the forces of supply and demand shape food environments, context-appropriate actions such as mandatory front-of-pack labelling and protection against exploitative marketing practices can help create food environments that are conducive to nutritious diets for children.

4. Mobilize supportive systems to scale up nutrition results for every child

As well as food systems, four other key systems must be mobilized to deliver nutrition services, improve nutrition practices and achieve nutrition outcomes at scale. The health, water and sanitation, education and social protection systems must all deliver interventions in a coordinated fashion. A systems approach to children's nutrition can help ensure that children and families have access to healthy diets and that children receive the nutrition services they need to develop to their full potential.

5 | Collect, analyse and use good-quality data and evidence regularly to guide action and track progress

Lack of adequate data prevents governments from responding with effective policies, strategies and programmes. Accurate and timely data are needed to understand malnutrition, take coordinated, evidence-based action, and to hold all actors to account. Data collection methods and frequency must be transformed to expand what we know about the diets and nutrition of children, adolescents and women at every stage of life. Data systems must become responsive and a culture of data-sharing and transparency must be developed.

What do young people think about food and nutrition?

More than **150,000 adolescents** and young people in over **35 countries** told UNICEF's U-Report about their attitudes towards food, nutrition and body image.

U-Report is an innovative social messaging tool used by more than 7 million young people around the world to share their views on a range of common concerns.

All numbers refer to the percentage of respondents.
(Numbers may not add up to 100% due to rounding)

Do you eat healthily?

Most U-Reporters, especially in low-income countries, say they eat healthily

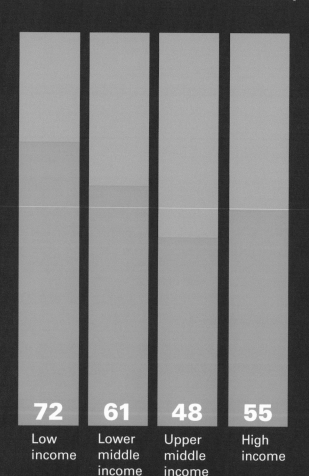

72	**61**	**48**	**55**
Low income	Lower middle income	Upper middle income	High income

Where do you mostly eat?

U-Reporters mostly eat at home with family

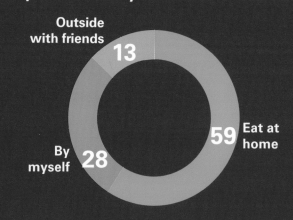

Outside with friends **13**

By myself **28**

59 Eat at home

Older U-Reporters are more likely to eat alone

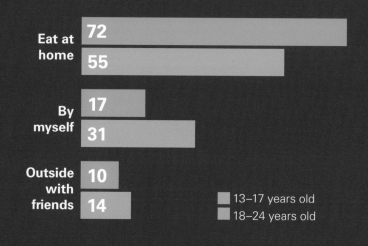

Eat at home **72** / **55**

By myself **17** / **31**

Outside with friends **10** / **14**

■ 13–17 years old
■ 18–24 years old

Eating with the family means eating healthier

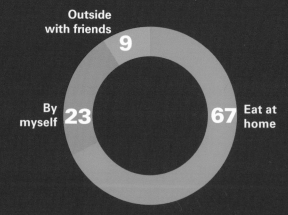

Outside with friends **9**

By myself **23**

67 Eat at home

Of U-Reporters who say they eat healthily more than 2 out of 3 say they mostly eat at home with their families

What is the most important factor when deciding what to eat?

Healthiness is the main concern in low- and lower-middle-income countries

Cost **11**

Convenience **13**

Taste **26**

50 Healthy

But taste comes first in upper-middle and high-income countries

Bodyweight is also a concern in food choices

13–17 years old
18–24 years old

Females **15**

Males **8**

Females **45**

Males **50**

Older U-Reporters are more likely to say weight is a relevant factor in food choices

In high-income countries, weight is a concern for around 3 out of 5 females but only for around 1 in 2 males.

What's stopping you from eating healthier?

"Healthier food is often expensive, so my family can't afford it."
Female, 16, Eswatini

"Because my father has no means and I am a student of the 11th grade sciences."
Male, 17 Mali

"Nutritious food is quite costly and scarce."
Female, 23, India

"Can't buy healthy food because I can't afford it. We'll eat vegetables and fruits sometimes but it's just so expensive to buy it every day."
Female, 21, Philippines

"Not enough time to cook, lack of really fresh and useful products on store shelves."
Female, 19, Ukraine

"Unhealthy foods are unfortunately tasty."
Male, 16, Brazil

"Because of the appearance and taste of [healthy] food. It does not look colorful and is tasteless."
Male, 18, Thailand

What do young people think about healthy eating?

More than 450 young people in 18 countries took part in **The State of the World's Children 2019 workshops** *to talk about what they eat and why. The workshops were held along with similar events for mothers (see page 29). For a note on the workshop methodology, see page 178. Here we present an initial analysis of what participants in 12 countries said about the obstacles to eating healthily and how they try to improve their diets. A full analysis will be published in 2020. Responses have been translated and edited for clarity where necessary.*

Do young people know which foods are healthy?

Overall, the adolescents who participated in the workshops reported making more healthy than unhealthy food choices.[115] After describing what they ate over a 24-hour period, they were asked to rate whether the items were healthy or unhealthy. Their assessments were accurate for around half of the items, but inaccurate for about a fifth. For just under a third of the items, they were unable to say whether the choice was healthy or unhealthy. Overall, adolescents appear to have a limited understanding of the nutritional qualities of over half the foods they commonly encounter.

What prevents young people from eating healthily?

Adolescents said they faced significant barriers to healthy eating. Cost and taste were top of the list:

"We lack money here to stay healthy … Our family is unable to find good jobs." *Girl, 16, India*

"Some of the food is hard to afford." *Boy, 16, Zimbabwe*

Many perceived healthy foods to be more expensive:

"Cheap food is not healthy, and healthy food is not cheap." *Girl, 13, China*

Taste was another barrier:

"I really like junk food." *Girl, 14, Guatemala*

"Healthy food is mainly not delicious." *Girl, 14, Kyrgyzstan*

Taste was a particularly relevant factor for urban participants. Some suggested that their food preferences had been affected by the ready availability of junk food:

"We are not able to eat healthy food because we have already tasted junk food and are now attracted to that only." *Boy, 14, India*

Many adolescents reported that nutritious foods were not sold near their homes:

"Meat is not available. We have money to buy meat, but the place is too far away." *Girl, 14, Ghana*

"Unhealthy food is easier to come by." *Boy, 17, USA*

Access and affordability were acute issues for some. In the Sudan, adolescents in a refugee camp were nearly three times more likely than rural participants to identify cost as a barrier to healthy eating. Lack of access to healthy food was also a key barrier.

The workshop participants pointed to the role of parents and caregivers in determining what they eat. They also highlighted time constraints for both themselves and their parents:

"My choice of food is not prepared for me. My parents decide what we will eat." *Girl, 15, Ghana*

"Sometimes, there is no time to cook so I eat fast food." *Girl, 15, Guatemala*

"Mothers do not have time." *Boy, 14, Mexico*

How do adolescents try to improve their own diets?

Young people from all the countries surveyed reported taking personal action to eat better. Many said they valued eating well and set themselves personal goals:

"I remind myself to prioritize my health for at least one meal a day." *Girl, 18, USA*

"I try to make a better plan of what I'm going to do during the day to avoid those types of [unhealthy] food." *Girl, 15, Serbia*

Adolescents generally understood that some foodstuffs are not healthy, and took active steps to eat less unhealthy food:

"I avoid the things that will affect me too much … junk food and street food." *Philippines, age and gender not indicated*

"I arrange time properly to have enough time to eat and start cooking for myself." *Girl, 13, China*

Sometimes they avoid unhealthy food by distracting themselves:

"If I get tempted to binge, I'll go for a walk, take a nap, or call a friend or talk to my mom. I think about how I'm going to feel later." *Girl, 17, USA*

Some said they ate foods they regarded as healthy even if they were not very tasty:

"I can tolerate the bad taste for the sake of my health." *Girl, 17, Egypt*

In lower-middle-income countries, gaining work was an important response to the high cost of food:

"Since there is no money to buy food, I have to … work … in order to get the money to buy it." *Boy, 14, Ghana*

"If I work … to have money, then I will buy food for my family." *Boy, 13, the Sudan*

Saving money and eating home-grown and home-cooked food were other solutions:

"Sometimes I save some money during the week so that I can buy healthy food." *Girl, 16, Serbia*

"I … plant fruits and vegetables." *Boy, 15, Guatemala*

©UNICEF/China/2019/Ma Yuyuan

Summary
Large numbers of adolescents value healthy eating and go to some lengths to improve their own diets. However, many face significant obstacles, notably cost and access to healthy food.

What ideas do young people have to improve nutrition?

Workshop participants highlighted the need for increased knowledge and awareness about diet and nutrition:

"Educate people. Urge people to eat healthy meals. Hold meetings at the village library." *Group response, Egypt*

"Become informed through newspapers and the internet and purchase food accordingly." *Boy, 13, China*

They said governments, institutions and community leaders had a big role to play ...

"We need community leaders to talk to parents." *Group response, Ghana*

"Prevent [the] selling of unsafe food." *Group response, Serbia*

... as do young people:

"Form cooperative youth groups that deal with food issues and health." *Group response, Zimbabwe*

"We can spread ... the awareness necessary to solve problems. And write banners. We can create WhatsApp groups dedicated to solving problems." *Group response, Egypt*

What feeding challenges do mothers face?

More than 320 women in 18 countries took part in **The State of the World's Children 2019 workshops** *to talk about how they feed their babies and themselves. The workshops, organized with UNICEF country offices and national committees and Western Sydney University (WSU), were held along with similar events for young people (see page 26). For a note on the workshop methodology, see page 178. Here we present an initial analysis of what participants in 12 countries said about their infant feeding practices and the barriers they face in feeding their children and themselves well. A full analysis will be published in 2020. Responses have been translated and edited for clarity where necessary.*

What are mothers' infant-feeding practices?

The World Health Organization recommends that babies be exclusively breastfed for their first 6 months of life, and then introduced to first (or complementary) foods, which gradually replace breastmilk between the ages of 6 and 23 months. Results from the workshop suggest that feeding practices in many instances are not optimal.

Almost all of the women breastfed either from birth or within the first 10 days after birth.[116] However, around two out of five mothers introduced breastmilk substitutes (BMS) by the time their baby was 8 weeks old, and most were combining breastmilk and BMS (and, often, other liquids) before their baby reached 6 months of age.

Most mothers introduced first foods at 6 months of age, but a fifth started before their baby was 5 months old. Some waited until the baby was between 7 and 9 months.

What barriers do mothers face in feeding their babies well?

Overwhelmingly, the main barrier to feeding babies healthily was financial:

"I cannot even afford to give my baby unhealthy foods as I do not have the money." *Age 20, Zimbabwe*

"Money. I am not able to buy food to feed the child." *Age 25, India*

"There is no money at home." *Age 24, Ghana*

Mothers often echoed the perception of a 38-year-old workshop participant in the United States, who said, "Healthy food is expensive."

"In Australia, many things are expensive, like fish … vegetables and meat. It should be cheap so that anyone can buy it." *Age 29, Australia*

"Sometimes, some foods are expensive." *Age 22, Mexico*

Access and availability are also obstacles:

"Sometimes healthy food is not available in the house." *Age 28, Egypt*

"It is difficult to get a vehicle to go … to buy food." *Age 30, Ghana*

"It is hard to get fruits and vegetables, melon, watermelon, cucumber, carrot." *Age 22, Guatemala*

Mothers reported feeding challenges when babies disliked certain foods, or were 'fussy' or sickly.

"My baby doesn't like healthy food." *Age 24, Egypt*

"Children do not want to eat healthy food – they pester us, they start crying." *Age 25, India*

"[I find it difficult to find] food that my child wants; my child does not accept a particular type of food." *Age 29, Sudan*

© UNICEF/Baddoo/2019

"My child does not like to suck my nipple."
Age 29, China

"When baby is not feeling well, when the baby is teething, it makes it difficult to feed."
Age 20, Ghana

Mothers also reported having to cope with unwanted family advice:

"My mother-in-law wants to feed my 8-month-old congee [a type of rice porridge] every day because these are easy-to-digest foods. I want the child to have all kinds of food." *Age 27, China*

"My husband's grandmother tells me what to feed him [my baby]." *Age not specified, Mexico*

What barriers do mothers face in feeding themselves well?

Mothers identified a range of creative workarounds to the barriers they face in feeding babies and themselves, including earning extra income and growing food themselves:

"Lack of money ... if I had money, I would purchase and prepare food as a mother [should]."
Age 25, Guatemala

"Sometimes I am short of money to buy some healthy foods." *Age 25, Kyrgyzstan*

"I eat healthy food when it is available. When it's not, I eat whatever is available." *Age 20, Zimbabwe*

"It is easier to acquire other foods [as opposed to healthy foods]." *Age 19, Mexico*

"It's a long distance from market to house."
Age 26, the Sudan

What are mothers' solutions to the barriers they face?

Just as with their babies, mothers reported cost as the biggest barrier to their own efforts to eat healthily, followed by accessibility and availability:

"We can farm maize and sell it to get money; grow vegetables and sell to get money; sell cell phones for money; sell clothes for money." *Age 20, Zimbabwe*

"We can grow the food." *Age 26, Zimbabwe*

To overcome children's food preferences and 'fussiness', they described a range of creative solutions:

"I let her watch cartoons, rattle with toys, try to amuse her during the feeding." *Age 34, Serbia*

"I put mashed vegetables in the porridge and feed when the child talks." *Age 35, China*

"I blend the fruit and put it in the cake... I mix it with some food that she likes." *Age 25, Serbia*

To cope with unwanted advice from members of the family, women mostly said they tried to just ignore it, although this was not always possible:

"My mother told me to give my one-week-old baby some porridge, but I ignored her." *Age not specified, Australia*

"My mother-in-law constantly said I did not have enough milk, and in the end I stopped breastfeeding." *Age not specified, Australia*

Summary
Cost is by far the biggest obstacle to feeding and eating healthily for mothers, followed by a lack of availability and access to healthy foods. Many mothers described a range of other challenges, including babies' dislike of certain foods, 'fussy' eaters and family pressure.

PERSPECTIVE
Upholding a child's right to food and nutrition

Hilal Elver
United Nations
Special Rapporteur
on the
Right to Food

Since 2014, Hilal Elver has served as the Special Rapporteur on the right to food, responsible for carrying out the right to food mandate, as prescribed by the United Nations Human Rights Council. Hilal Elver is an international law professor and a Global Distinguished Fellow at the UCLA Law School's Resnick Center for Food Law and Policy; she is also a research professor at the UC, Santa Barbara, where she has been Distinguished Visiting Professor since 2002.

It should concern us all that so many children around the world suffer from malnutrition in all its forms. This situation demands a determined and effective policy response – a response that can only come about if there is political will to protect and respect children's human rights, notably the right to adequate food, which guarantees freedom from hunger, and includes nutrition as a critical element. Safeguarding this right requires states to ensure that everyone – including children – has access to food that, at the very least, meets their basic nutritional needs and is culturally appropriate and safe.

States also need to respond to the structural and root causes of hunger and malnutrition from a human rights perspective. This should be guided by the principle that children's economic, social and cultural rights are indivisible, a principle that underpins the Convention on the Rights of the Child (CRC), which marks its 30th anniversary this year. Nowhere is this indivisibility more relevant than in nutrition: the rights to clean water, health and an adequate standard of living, for example, are preconditions for the full realization of the right to food.

Similarly, the CRC extends additional protections to children to ensure their right to enjoy the highest attainable standard of health. For example, it calls on states to take measures to combat disease and malnutrition by, among other actions,

providing adequate nutritious foods, as well as nutrition information and education. Children also have rights to social protection, to an adequate standard of living, and to non-discrimination. This last principle is especially important for protecting adolescent girls from gender discrimination and violence, and for preventing discrimination against children of indigenous and rural communities.

Even short-term hunger can harm a child's development. The CRC recognizes this unique vulnerability across the life course: it refers to the need to support those responsible for children's care and to provide appropriate ante- and post-natal healthcare for mothers. This is supplemented by the Convention on the Elimination of All Forms of Discrimination Against Women, which promulgates rights for women during pregnancy and lactation. Unfortunately, that Convention falls short of protecting women's individual right to adequate food and nutrition beyond their capacity as mothers. Granting women the autonomy to make everyday choices and the freedom to enjoy fundamental rights has been proven to improve reproductive health, family nutrition and child welfare.

Over the years, the Committee on the Rights of the Child has issued several General Comments to help states implement policies. General Comment No. 15, for example, emphasizes social protection,

school-feeding programmes and preventive measures to avoid all forms of malnutrition. It also calls upon states to limit children's exposure to harmful food advertisements, and calls upon private companies to comply with the International Code of Marketing of Breast-milk Substitutes and relevant World Health Assembly resolutions.

In considering the importance of breastfeeding, General Comment No. 7 advocates its promotion and protection, endorsing the World Health Organization's recommendations on exclusive breastfeeding. Nevertheless, many working mothers still face considerable obstacles in fulfilling this, in part because governments often fail to provide adequate maternity leave to protect both mothers and children.

Other General Comments cover the impact of private sector activities on the natural resources required to produce adequate food (No. 16), and the particular risks of malnutrition among children who are living with HIV/AIDS (No. 3). Also worth noting is General Comment No. 11, which, along with the Declaration on the Rights of Indigenous Peoples, focuses on indigenous children, for whom the

cultural significance of traditional land and the quality of the natural environment are intrinsically linked to the right to life and survival. A human-rights-based approach to child nutrition requires a clear understanding of the link between environmental degradation, access to natural resources and the rights of children to food and nutrition.

Integrating these human rights instruments and soft law documents, such as the Voluntary Guidelines to Support the Progressive Realization of the Right to Adequate Food in the Context of National Food Security, into policymaking will ensure that rural children, children of migrants, refugees, and internally displaced peoples, as well as children affected by conflict and climate change, are not forgotten, and will help states to guarantee the right to food and nutrition in even the most marginalized communities. Applying a human-rights-based approach to the child's right to food and nutrition in a holistic manner requires good governance and political will at national and international levels. Once this political will is garnered, improving participation, accountability, monitoring and transparency are the first steps to implementing human rights principles effectively.■

01 CHILD MALNUTRITION TODAY

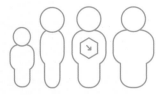

Globally, almost 200 million children under 5 suffer from stunting, wasting, or both and at least 340 million from the hidden hunger of vitamin and mineral deficiencies. At the same time, 50 million children under 5 are overweight and the toll from overweight and obesity keeps rising, even in lower-income countries. These patterns reflect a profound triple burden of malnutrition that threatens the survival, growth and development of children and of nations.

➤ Far too many children continue to be affected by undernutrition and hidden hunger, while the numbers who are overweight are rising rapidly.

➤ Malnutrition is both a result, and a significant cause, of poverty and deprivation.

➤ Food systems offer a range of significant entry points to improve children's nutrition.

➤ Investment in nutrition brings high returns and is key to meeting the SDGs.

A village health worker feeds micronutrients powder to a child in Liping County, Guizhou Province, China.
©UNICEF/China/2016/Xia Yong

All three strands
of malnutrition
– undernutrition,
hidden hunger and
overweight – are
interwoven

Introduction

In the 21st century, children's malnutrition has three key strands. The first is the continuing scourge of undernutrition. Despite declines in some parts of the world, undernutrition deprives far too many children of the energy and nutrients they need to grow well and is linked to just under half of all deaths of children aged under 5 each year.[1] The second strand is hidden hunger – deficiencies in essential vitamins and minerals such as vitamins A and B, and iron and zinc. Unseen, and all too often ignored, hidden hunger robs children of their health and vitality and even their lives. The third strand is overweight and, in its more severe form, obesity. Once regarded as a condition of the rich, overweight now afflicts more and more children, even in some of the world's least-developed countries. It is also fuelling a rise in diet-related non-communicable diseases (NCDs) later in life, such as heart disease, which is the leading cause of death worldwide.[2]

All three strands of malnutrition – undernutrition, hidden hunger and overweight – are interwoven. They can affect children, families and communities simultaneously and over the course of a single lifetime. The consequences are profound, not just for the child's own prospects – in childhood itself and on into adulthood – but also for national economic development and the attainment of the Sustainable Development Goals (SDGs).

These forms of malnutrition also share many common causes. These begin with the diets of children and mothers, and stretch out to the ways in which access, affordability and decision-making power are distributed across our societies. Increasingly, we cannot think about the roots of these three strands of malnutrition without talking about food systems – everything that happens to bring food 'from farm to mouth'. Children's malnutrition in the 21st century increasingly reflects the reality that too many food systems provide children with too little of the food they do need, and too much of the food they don't need.

Child malnutrition today

Undernutrition – stunting and wasting

Undernutrition profoundly affects how children survive, grow and develop. Two of its most important forms are stunting and wasting.

Stunting

Stunting is used to describe populations of children who are too short for their age. But stunting is about far more than the height of an individual child – every community has shorter and taller children. Rather, it is a stark sign that children in a community are not developing well, physically and mentally, particularly in the first 1,000 days. Stunting has been described as not just the "best overall indicator" of children's well-being, but also an "accurate reflection" of inequality in societies.[3] As one report has noted, stunting "is both a symptom of past deprivation and a predictor of future poverty."[4]

Sadly, in many communities, especially where short stature is common, the extent to which children are stunted is not fully recognized.[5] Because of its lifelong consequences for children's development, such failures are serious, not just for the well-being of individual children, but for broader economic and social development.

Where do stunted children live?

FIGURE 1.1 | **Percentage of stunted children under 5, 2018**

**GLOBAL TOTAL STUNTED
21.9% (149 million)**

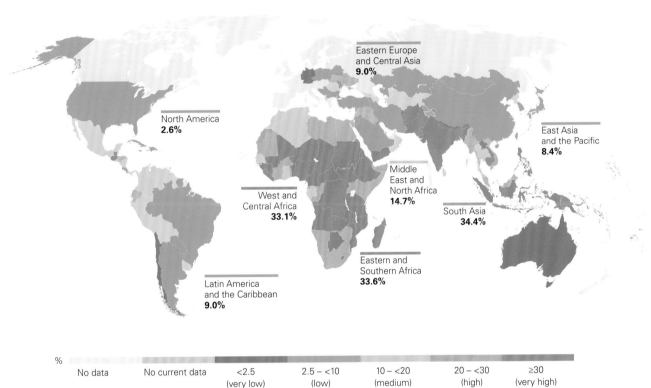

Eastern Europe
and Central Asia
9.0%

North America
2.6%

East Asia
and the Pacific
8.4%

Middle
East and
North Africa
14.7%

West and
Central Africa
33.1%

South Asia
34.4%

Eastern and
Southern Africa
33.6%

Latin America
and the Caribbean
9.0%

%					
No data	No current data	<2.5 (very low)	2.5 – <10 (low)	10 – <20 (medium)	20 – <30 (high)	≥30 (very high)

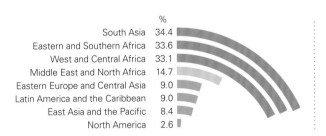

	%
South Asia	34.4
Eastern and Southern Africa	33.6
West and Central Africa	33.1
Middle East and North Africa	14.7
Eastern Europe and Central Asia	9.0
Latin America and the Caribbean	9.0
East Asia and the Pacific	8.4
North America	2.6

In South Asia and sub-
Saharan Africa, **1 in 3
children under five
is stunted**

Note: Country data are the most recent available estimate between 2000 and 2018; where only data prior to 2000 are available, the dark grey color denoting no recent data is used. The designations employed in this publication and the presentation of the material do not imply on the part of the United Nations Children's Fund (UNICEF) the expression of any opinion whatsoever concerning the legal status of any country or territory, or of its authorities or the delimitations of its frontiers.

Source: UNICEF/World Health Organization/World Bank Group Joint Malnutrition Estimates, 2019 edition.

Despite the encouraging declines in stunting, most parts of the world are currently not on course to meet targets for the SDG era

As with other forms of malnutrition, the causes of stunting start with the nutritional status of the mother. Mothers who suffered stunting in childhood are at greater risk of having stunted children. Women who are short of stature are also at greater risk of giving birth to pre-term children or children of low birthweight, who are, in turn, more likely to go on to be stunted. In 2015, an estimated 14.6 per cent of newborns had low birthweight, and about 9 out of 10 of these infants were in low- and middle-income countries.[6] Stunting can thus be perpetuated across generations and, because of its close link to deprivation, can transmit poverty from one generation to the next.

This cycle can be broken. In just a single generation, women malnourished in childhood but who subsequently experience substantial improvements in their health, nutrition and living environment before conceiving can have children who are close to normal height.[7] Evidence such as this underscores the importance of investing in maternal nutrition, not just to raise the life prospects of women, but also those of the next generation.

After a child is born, the nutritional status of the mother continues to be a factor through breastfeeding (see Chapter 2). Other factors also influence the child's development, including the extent to which a child's family has the resources to offer adequate food and care and its access to health services and clean water and sanitation. Repeated infections and gut inflammation can trap a child in a vicious cycle of disease and malnutrition: for example, a child with an inflamed gut finds it harder to absorb adequate nutrition, which weakens the child's resistance to illness. It is estimated that a quarter of all cases of stunting in children aged 2

and under can be attributed to the child having experienced five or more cases of diarrhoea.[8] Combating stunting thus requires investments in improving the quality of children's diets and related nutrition practices and services.

Globally, the proportion and number of stunted children under 5 has been declining (see Figure 1.2). It fell by a quarter between 2000 and 2018 to 149 million children. In broad terms, this reflects rising incomes and improvements in governance in many countries.[9] However, despite worldwide declines, progress in reducing stunting in much of Africa has been slow. Indeed, reflecting strong population growth, two UNICEF regions in the continent actually saw increases in the numbers of children affected between 2000 and 2018: the number of children under 5 with stunting rose by 1.4 million in Eastern and Southern Africa and by 6.5 million in West and Central Africa. The implications of this continuing burden of stunting for Africa's human capital development are serious.

Despite the encouraging declines in stunting, most parts of the world are currently not on course to meet targets for the SDG era. Similarly, targets for wasting and overweight risk not being met without a sustained effort. The global reductions in stunting can also mask the reality that, in many countries, huge proportions of children still suffer from stunting – around 38 per cent of under-5s in India and Pakistan and 43 per cent in the Democratic Republic of the Congo.[10] Even these national statistics paint only a partial picture. Within countries, there can be major differences between regions. In India, for example, almost half of children are stunted in the worst-affected state compared with a fifth in the least-affected state.[11]

In Pakistan, six-year-old Mudassir's height is measured in a nutrition screening session.
© UNICEF/UN048378/Pirozzi

FIGURE 1.2 | **Projections for malnutrition in children under 5 compared to 2030 targets**

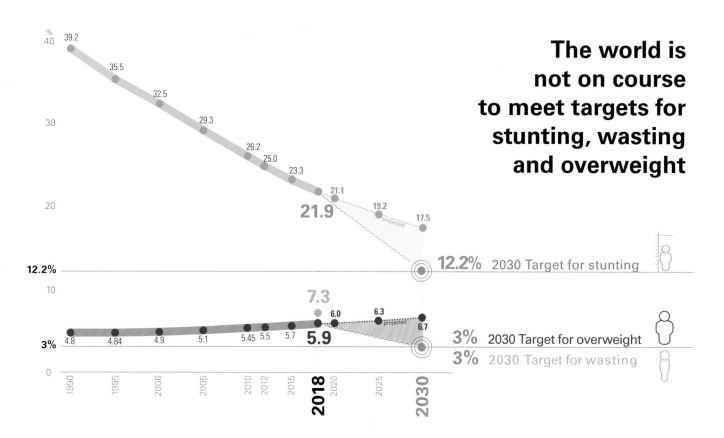

Notes: WHA 2030 targets are a) 50% reduction in the number of children under-5 who are stunted, b) Reduce and maintain childhood overweight to less than 3% and c) Reduce and maintain childhood wasting to less than 3%. Wasting is an acute condition that can change frequently and rapidly over the course of a calendar year. This makes it difficult to generate reliable trends over time with the input data available and, therefore, this report provides only the most recent global and regional estimates. https://data.unicef.org/resources/who-unicef-discussion-paper-nutrition-targets/

Source: UNICEF/World Health Organization/World Bank Group Joint Malnutrition Estimates, 2019 edition. Projections are based on analyses conducted by the UNICEF/World Health Organization/World Bank Income Group Joint Malnutrition Estimates Working Group.

Wasting

Wasting describes a child who is too thin for his or her height. With important exceptions, it often reflects a *recent* loss of weight arising from severely poor nutrient intake, illness or both. Globally, wasting threatens the lives of 7.3 per cent of the world's under-5s, or around 50 million children. In 2013, wasting led to around 13 per cent

of worldwide deaths among under-5s representing 875,000 child deaths that could have been prevented.[12]

Trends in wasting can shift rapidly and frequently in response to factors like the seasonal availability of food and disease patterns for diarrhoea and malaria. Nevertheless, there is concern that the global declines seen in child stunting have not been seen in wasting.

Globally, wasting threatens the lives of 7.3 per cent of the world's under-5s, or around 50 million children

This seems to be particularly true in South Asia, a global epicentre for wasting, where 15.2 per cent of under-5s are affected, a proportion that international agencies class as 'high'[13] (other hotspots include sub-Saharan Africa, Southeast Asia and Oceania – *see Figure 1.3*), and where rates of wasting have shown little improvement.[14] South Asia is also notable for when wasting occurs in a child's life. Wasting in the region is most widespread in the first year of the child's life, and less so in later childhood. In effect, many wasted children appear to be born wasted.[15] This has important implications for solving the problem of wasting (as well as stunting) in the region: it clearly supports a strong prevention approach, particularly in supporting the nutrition of adolescent girls and mothers, and encouraging improved infant feeding and hygiene practices in the first two years of life (*see Chapter 3*).[16]

Wasting – the more widespread form of acute malnutrition – can be devastating for children, particularly in its most serious forms. Left untreated, children with severe acute malnutrition (SAM) are nearly 12 times more likely to die than a healthy child.[17] SAM often results from a rapid deterioration in nutritional status, and is typically characterized by wasting, extreme thinness, or the swelling that is typical of nutritional oedema.[18, 19] While the risk of death associated with SAM is highest for under-5s, school-age children and adolescents are also at risk. Children who appear to recover from SAM can still suffer cognitive impairments and other developmental problems, especially if they have stunted growth.[20]

Global rates of severe wasting remain high: in 2018, around 16.6 million children under 5 were estimated to suffer from it.[21] As with other forms of

> Wasting can be devastating for children, particularly in its most severe forms

BOX 1.1 | Caring for wasted children at home

Recent years have brought significant breakthroughs in the treatment of SAM, notably with the rolling out of community management of acute malnutrition (CMAM) in many countries. Before CMAM, children with SAM were typically referred for lengthy and expensive in-patient hospital stays, a burden on many families that contributed to low rates of treatment. The CMAM approach instead empowers families to treat SAM at home, usually with ready-to-use therapeutic foods (RUTF) for children without medical complications, which comprise the majority of cases.

This approach has improved survival rates and has proved highly cost-effective, although more needs to be done to lower costs, for example through local production of RUTF).[27] While management of SAM is among the 10 highest impact nutritional interventions to reduce child mortality,[28] this impact can potentially be boosted still further: For example, health services that provide early detection of both SAM and HIV can be critical in improving survival rates among children by facilitating interventions at a critical point in disease progression and child development.■

August 13, 2016 Weight: 3.3 kg   September 20 2016 Weight: 4.6 kg   December 2016 Weight: 6+ kg   September 2017 Weight: 9 kg

Born in the rural Philippine province of Palawan, Joemar comes from a deprived family in which both parents have suffered health problems. The family's ethnic community has limited access to services and understanding of malnutrition. As a result, and despite showing clear symptoms, Joemar was not immediately diagnosed as suffering from severe acute malnutrition. Once treatment began, he made swift progress, doubling his weight in just a few months. Just like Joemar, more Filipino children are now getting a second chance: Supported by UNICEF, the Philippines is scaling up services and capacities to prevent and treat acute malnutrition and, by 2022, aims to put in place a nationwide programme of interventions, with a strategic focus on the first 1,000 days.
© UNICEF/Philippines/2016

Where do wasted children live?

FIGURE 1.3 | **Percentage of wasted children under 5, 2018**

GLOBAL TOTAL WASTED
7.3% (49.5 million)

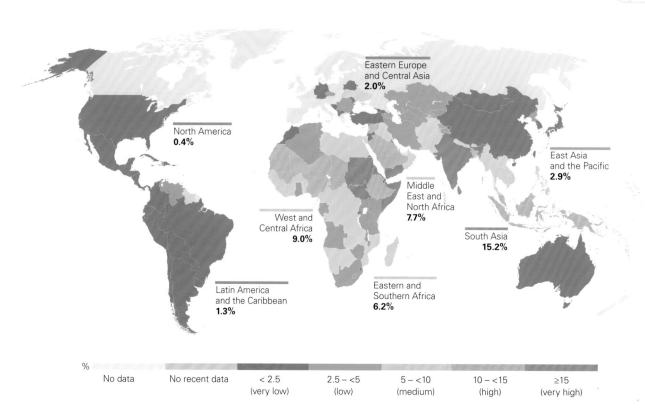

Eastern Europe
and Central Asia
2.0%

North America
0.4%

East Asia
and the Pacific
2.9%

Middle
East and
North Africa
7.7%

West and
Central Africa
9.0%

South Asia
15.2%

Latin America
and the Caribbean
1.3%

Eastern and
Southern Africa
6.2%

| % | No data | No recent data | < 2.5 (very low) | 2.5 – <5 (low) | 5 – <10 (medium) | 10 – <15 (high) | ≥15 (very high) |

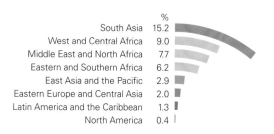

	%
South Asia	15.2
West and Central Africa	9.0
Middle East and North Africa	7.7
Eastern and Southern Africa	6.2
East Asia and the Pacific	2.9
Eastern Europe and Central Asia	2.0
Latin America and the Caribbean	1.3
North America	0.4

In **South Asia** more than **1 in 7
children** under 5 **is wasted**

Note: Country data are the most recent available estimate between 2000 and 2018; where only data prior to 2000 are available, the dark grey color denoting no recent data is used. The designations employed in this publication and the presentation of the material do not imply on the part of the United Nations Children's Fund (UNICEF) the expression of any opinion whatsoever concerning the legal status of any country or territory, or of its authorities or the delimitations of its frontiers.

Source: UNICEF/World Health Organization/World Bank Group Joint Malnutrition Estimates, 2019 edition.

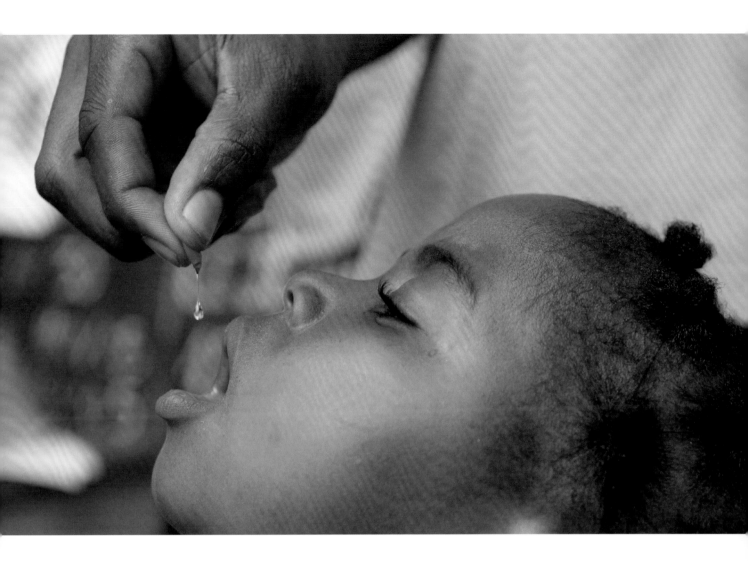

malnutrition, poverty is often at the heart of SAM. Seasonal fluctuations matter, too: the rainy season is often the pre-harvest period when food stocks are low, roads are cut off, and the incidence of waterborne disease increases. Children who are ill are also at particular risk: those with HIV are three times as likely to die from SAM as their counterparts. [22, 23, 24] HIV together with malnutrition among infants is particularly fatal.

Although children suffering SAM are often the face of humanitarian emergencies, most SAM cases actually occur in non-emergency settings. The mistaken assumption that SAM mainly occurs in emergencies – and is the responsibility of the humanitarian community – has hampered effective prevention and treatment of SAM globally.

Overall, far too few children with SAM are being treated. Despite global progress in the number of children reached (from 1.1 million children in 2009 to 4.4 million in 2017), only about one in four children receives treatment. [25] Scaling up successful approaches requires supportive national policies, dedicated government resources and integration into routine national services. In countries where this has been achieved, efficiency and scale-up have been greatly increased. [26] Even so, although treatment saves lives, it does not address the underlying and basic causes that are key to ensuring the long-term prevention of wasting.

A girl receives Vitamin A drops at Mont Ngafula Health Centre in Kinshasha, Democratic Republic of Congo. Vitamin A deficiency is the leading cause of preventable childhood blindness and increases the risk of death from common childhood illnesses such as diarrhoea. Despite the increasing availability of fortified foods, about one in five children is deficient in vitamin A. [41] © UNICEF/ UNI44415/Pirozzi

Where do children with hidden hunger live?

FIGURE 1.4 | **Percentage of children under 5 with hidden hunger**

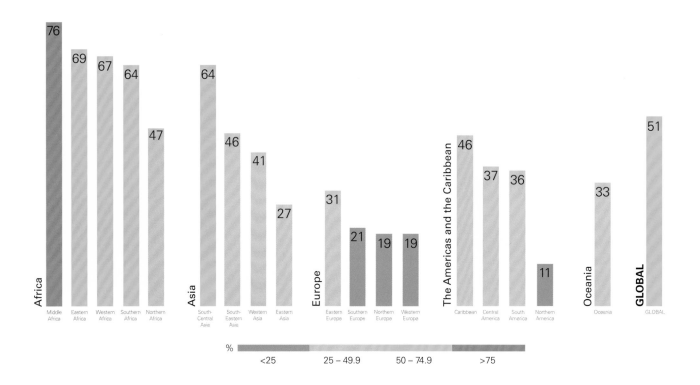

Source: UNICEF estimates, 2019 based on Black et al, 2013 and Stevens et al, 2015. See Note on Figures on p. 179 for more information.

> At least 340 million children under 5 (one in two) suffer from hidden hunger

Hidden hunger

Children and mothers who are deficient in micronutrients – the vitamins and minerals that are essential for survival, growth and development – can suffer devastating consequences. Some examples: vitamin A deficiency is the main cause of blindness in children.[29] Women with severe anaemia (often, although not exclusively, linked to a lack of iron in the diet) have double the risk of dying during or shortly after childbirth (*see Figure 1.4*).[30] Iodine deficiency, even in its mild forms, can harm a child's

ability to learn.[31] UNICEF estimates that globally, at least one in two children under 5 – or 340 million – suffers from hidden hunger due to deficiencies in vitamins and other essential nutrients.[32]

Often, however, the effects are invisible or may appear too late for anything to be done. That's why these deficiencies are often referred to as 'hidden hunger'. Hidden or not, the impact is very real. As UNICEF's Kul C. Gautam said in 2004, "You might not feel it in the belly, but it strikes at the core of your health and vitality."[33]

As with all forms of malnutrition, poor diets play a major role in hidden hunger. Indeed, dietary diversity is used as a measure of whether or not children and mothers are meeting their micronutrient needs.[34] These measures paint a worrying picture (*see Chapter 2*). But children and mothers also need to be physically able to absorb vitamins and minerals. Conditions such as diarrhoea and chronic gut inflammations can prevent that from happening, as can other factors, for example whether a micronutrient comes from an animal- or plant-source food.

More broadly, hidden hunger can exist with both traditional and modern diets. Some communities in low-income countries, for example, depend heavily on just a few staples, such as grains and tubers, and may only very occasionally eat more nutrient-rich items such as fruit, vegetables, meat, fish, eggs and dairy. Modern diets, too, are implicated. Processed and ultra-processed foods can be fortified with essential vitamins and minerals, and in many parts of the world this helps meet children's micronutrient needs (*see Chapter 4*). However, ultra-processed foods and drinks can also be deficient in essential vitamins and minerals.[35, 36] And because some of these foods, such as cheap instant noodles and biscuits, can be very filling, they can reduce children's appetite for more nutrient-dense fruits and vegetables.[37]

Precise and up-to-date estimates of the extent of hidden hunger are lacking, reflecting the challenge, cost and time-consuming nature of measuring it. Given the seriousness of hidden hunger's impact on children, there is an urgent need to improve understanding of the problem through the development of inexpensive and effective forms of testing. UNICEF's recent global estimate – of at least 340 million children under 5 – is a conservative figure as it only reflects the estimated number of children who suffer from vitamin A and iron deficiencies.[38] In both high- and low-income countries, children are at greatest risk of hidden hunger and frequently suffer multiple deficiencies simultaneously, a reflection of their poor diet overall.[39, 40]

Overweight and obesity

Overweight and obesity matter for children, both in childhood and in later life. In childhood, they can lead to a number of medical conditions, including gastrointestinal, musculoskeletal and orthopaedic complications, as well as the early onset of type 2 diabetes and behavioural and emotional problems, including depression and stigmatization. Childhood obesity is also a strong predictor of adult obesity, which can have serious health and economic consequences.[42]

The number of overweight children has increased in every continent (*see Figure 1.5*). Based on recent trends, the number of overweight under-5s will rise from 40 million children to 43 million by 2025.[43]

Overweight is sometimes seen as a problem only in wealthy countries, but it is striking just how much it now also affects low- and middle-income countries and how rapidly the problem is growing (*see Figure 1.6*). In 2018, almost half the world's overweight under-5s lived in Asia and a quarter in Africa; in Africa, the number of overweight under-5s rose by just under 44 per cent between 2000 and 2018.[44]

These data tell only part of the story, however. Estimates for older children help indicate the true scale of the overweight challenge. According to the NCD Risk Factor Collaboration, the

Overweight is sometimes seen as a problem only in wealthy countries, but it is striking just how much it now also affects low- and middle-income countries

Where do overweight children live?

FIGURE 1.5 | **Percentage of overweight children under 5, 2018**

GLOBAL TOTAL OVERWEIGHT
40.1 million (5.9%)

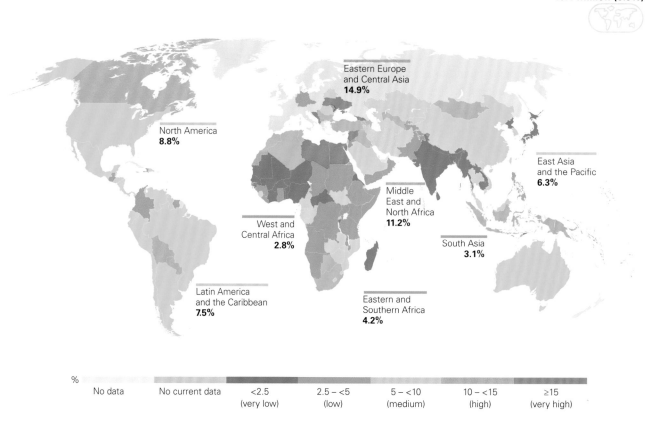

Eastern Europe
and Central Asia
14.9%

North America
8.8%

East Asia
and the Pacific
6.3%

Middle
East and
North Africa
11.2%

West and
Central Africa
2.8%

South Asia
3.1%

Latin America
and the Caribbean
7.5%

Eastern and
Southern Africa
4.2%

%						
No data	No current data	<2.5 (very low)	2.5 – <5 (low)	5 – <10 (medium)	10 – <15 (high)	≥15 (very high)

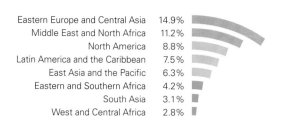

Eastern Europe and Central Asia	14.9%
Middle East and North Africa	11.2%
North America	8.8%
Latin America and the Caribbean	7.5%
East Asia and the Pacific	6.3%
Eastern and Southern Africa	4.2%
South Asia	3.1%
West and Central Africa	2.8%

In **Eastern Europe and Central Asia,** almost **1 in 7 children** under 5 **is overweight**

Note: Country data are the most recent available estimate between 2000 and 2018; where only data prior to 2000 are available, the dark grey color denoting no recent data is used. The designations employed in this publication and the presentation of the material do not imply on the part of the United Nations Children's Fund (UNICEF) the expression of any opinion whatsoever concerning the legal status of any country or territory, or of its authorities or the delimitations of its frontiers.

Source: UNICEF/World Health Organization/World Bank Group Joint Malnutrition Estimates, 2019 edition.

FIGURE 1.6 | **Trend in percentage of countries by World Bank income group where at least 10 per cent of children aged 5–19 years are overweight**

FIGURE 1.7 | **Increase in overweight among under-5 and 5–19-year-old children and young people**

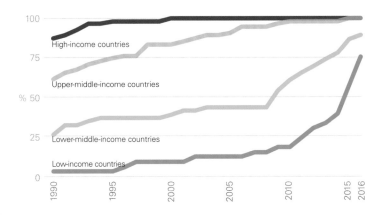

Low- and lower middle-income countries have seen a significant rise in overweight over the past decade.

Note: Income classifications are based on World Bank FY19 classifications.

Source: NCD Risk Factor Collaboration (NCD-RisC) (2017). 'Worldwide trends in body-mass index, underweight, overweight, and obesity from 1975 to 2016: A pooled analysis of 2416 population-based measurement studies in 128·9 million children, adolescents, and adults', *The Lancet*, 390(10113), pp. 2627–2642

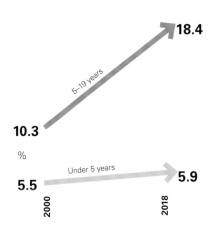

Source: UNICEF/World Health Organization/World Bank Group Joint Malnutrition Estimates and NCD Risk Factor Collaboration (2017).

proportion of overweight children aged between 5 and 19 rose from around 1 in 10 (10.3 per cent) in 2000 to a little under 1 in 5 (18.4 per cent) in 2016 (*see Figure 1.7*).

What's driving these increases? Research points to a few key factors. A rising intake of calories, a shift in what children are eating from traditional to modern diets, urbanization and falling levels of physical activity all play a part.[45] Some research also suggests that changes in the gut microbiome may be a factor.

Where are childhood trends going? There are signs that overweight has been levelling off in high-income

countries, albeit at very high levels – around a third of children aged 2 to 15 in the United Kingdom, for example.[46] However, this trend is not being seen in poorer communities, resulting in widening inequalities in rates of obesity between high- and low-income social groups. Children from poorer backgrounds also tend to have more severe forms of overweight.[47, 48] In low- and middle-income countries, and especially in much of Asia, rates of overweight look likely to go on rising. Strikingly, there is little or no consistent evidence of countries achieving and sustaining a decline in obesity across the population since the 1980s,[49] underlining the need to focus on prevention.

Overweight is no longer a problem just for wealthier countries and is rising faster among older children

SPECIAL SECTION

Overweight and obesity in OECD and EU countries

A century ago, overweight and obesity were linked to wealth. Not anymore. In wealthy counties, poor children are often the most likely to be overweight or obese.[50]

Although rates of overweight in children have plateaued in many high-income countries, they have nevertheless settled at levels that put millions of children's lives, health and futures at risk.[51] Among 41 countries in the OECD and EU, not one has fewer than one in five children (aged 5–19 years) overweight, except for Japan (*see Figure 1.8*).

Overweight and disadvantage

The children who suffer overweight are usually from socio-economically disadvantaged families. In the United States, for example, overweight in children decreases as families' education and income levels increase.[53] The link between obesity and socio-economic disadvantage has also been demonstrated in Europe.[54] A study using data from the 2008 WHO Childhood Obesity Surveillance Initiative in Europe linked parental socio-economic status and lack of education with obesity in children in Czechia, Portugal and Sweden.[55]

The impact of overweight on lives and economies offers a cautionary tale as these health risks rapidly expand into low- and middle-income countries.[56] The effects are also economic. In Germany, the lifetime cost of overweight and obesity – due to factors including lost productivity and illness – is about 145 billion euros (about US$162 billion).[58] In the United States, US$190 billion a year is spent on treating obesity and obesity-related conditions – about a fifth of the country's healthcare expenditures. In Brazil's public hospitals, the estimated direct costs of diseases related to overweight and obesity were US$2.1 billion annually.[58]

Response

Despite growing awareness of the dangers of overweight, efforts to address the issue have not been systematic.[59] In recent years, however, countries including Belgium, Chile, Finland, France, Hungary and Mexico have begun to establish policies to address obesity, including taxes and easy-to-understand nutrition labels such as front-of-pack warning labels. These and other efforts are guided by WHO recommendations aimed at providing a holistic approach to addressing childhood obesity.[60, 61, 62]

Globally, there is little information on government spending to address obesity and diet-related NCDs, such as diabetes, cardiovascular disease and some cancers.[63] In 2015, only about 0.01 per cent of global development assistance was spent on preventing and treating obesity- and diet-related NCDs.[64] As low- and middle-income countries begin to deal with the complex consequences of growing rates of overweight, the costs of prevention and treatment risk exceeding the capabilities of healthcare systems to respond. ■

The children who suffer from overweight are usually from socio-economically disadvantaged families

FIGURE 1.8 | **Percentage of children and adolescents 5–19 years who are overweight in 41 OECD and EU countries**

Country	Prevalence (%) 2016	% increase since 1990	Country	Prevalence (%) 2016	% increase since 1990
United States	41.86	49.7	Croatia	28.00	160.0
New Zealand	39.46	44.6	Republic of Korea	27.63	94.9
Greece	37.26	48.9	Norway	27.47	42.1
Malta	37.11	20.1	Czechia	27.19	81.2
Italy	36.87	39.1	Slovenia	27.18	168.8
Chile	35.54	61.1	Finland	26.81	35.7
Mexico	35.51	76.0	Austria	26.68	48.8
Israel	34.80	18.2	Germany	26.58	37.0
Australia	34.11	35.1	Luxembourg	26.33	29.3
Spain	33.80	38.4	Poland	25.72	131.1
Cyprus	33.47	50.6	Denmark	25.11	13.6
Portugal	32.57	86.2	Netherlands	24.77	61.9
Canada	32.15	45.1	Romania	24.56	171
United Kingdom	31.12	33.1	Belgium	23.93	-1.8
Ireland	30.86	84.4	Sweden	23.62	24.6
France	30.09	38.7	Slovakia	23.36	157.0
Turkey	29.55	151.1	Switzerland	21.87	39.4
Bulgaria	28.47	120.6	Latvia	21.33	75.9
Hungary	28.45	117.3	Lithuania	20.58	84.2
Iceland	28.33	15.3	Estonia	20.46	68.0
			Japan	14.42	14.3

Source: NCD Risk Factor Collaboration (2017).[52]

Undernutrtion, hidden hunger and overweight share common causes, notably the poor quality of children's diets

Pulling the strands of malnutrition together

As noted earlier, the various strands of malnutrition – undernutrition, hidden hunger and overweight – are interwoven in many different ways. For example, two or three forms of malnutrition may strike children simultaneously or across the course of their lives. In addition, two, or increasingly all three, are simultaneously present in growing numbers of countries and communities – a **triple burden of malnutrition** (*see Figure 1.9*)**.** Finally, all three share many common causes, notably the poor quality of children's diets.

Coexistence in individuals

One of the most common ways in which a child can suffer multiple forms

of malnutrition is the coexistence of stunting and wasting. As one group of experts puts it, "a wasted child is more likely to become stunted and a stunted child is more likely to become wasted."[65] Such children are likely to have experienced "an early environment characterized by harsh deprivation," as one study notes.[66] This combination of stunting and wasting increases the risk of death, even compared with children who are severely wasted.[67] Given these links, there have been growing calls in recent years for nutrition programmes to address stunting and wasting simultaneously. Failure to do so risks undermining the effectiveness of programmes.[68]

Other forms of coexistence also exist. For example, 8.2 million children under 5 are estimated to suffer from both stunting and overweight globally while stunting,

FIGURE 1.9 | Number of countries with overlapping forms of childhood stunting, wasting, overweight and anaemia

How many countries face a triple burden of malnutrition?

101 countries had at least a medium **stunting** prevalence

77 countries had at least a medium **overweight** prevalence

124 countries had moderate *anaemia* prevalence

62 countries had at least a medium **wasting** prevalence

Note: A medium stunting prevalence is defined as >10%; a medium overweight prevalence is defined as >5%; a medium wasting prevalence is defined as >5%; a moderate anaemia prevalence is defined as >20%. Analysis is based on 134 countries with recent estimates for at least three indicators.

Source: UNICEF, WHO, World Bank Group (2019). *Joint Child Malnutrition Estimate*s. WHO, Geneva. Source for anaemia data: Global Health Observatory, World Health Organization (2019). *Anaemia in children <5 years – Estimates by country* [Data table]. Retrieved from http://apps.who.int/gho/data/view.main. ANEMIACHILDRENREGv.

wasting and overweight often coexist with different forms of hidden hunger.[69] Individuals can also suffer from different forms of malnutrition across their lives: for example, stunting in early childhood may raise the risk of overweight in later life.[70]

The triple burden of malnutrition

Many parts of the world are now facing the triple burden of malnutrition, which is evident in countries, communities and even individual families. One regularly cited example is where a family has an overweight mother and a stunted child. In India, analysis of 2011–2012 data suggests this may be the case in 5 per cent of rural and 8 per cent of urban households. For Egypt, the figure is 5.6 per cent of households, according to analysis of 2008 data. In both countries, the problem appears to be growing.[71] In Egypt, researchers attribute part of the rise to families' increased consumption of sugary snacks, which fail to provide children with the nutrients they need for healthy growth and provide excess calories to the mother.[72] These examples highlight the need to consider children's malnutrition in the wider family and household context.

More broadly, many low- and middle-income countries are now facing the challenge of coping with the continuing burden of stunting and wasting, various forms of hidden hunger and rising rates of overweight (*see Figure 1.9*). For many, these multiples challenges risk outpacing their capacity to respond.

Poverty, exclusion and malnutrition

Poverty is often at the heart of malnutrition. According to a 2016 UNICEF and World Bank Study, of the 385 million children living in extreme poverty around the world in 2013, half lived in sub-Saharan Africa and just over a third in South Asia. More than four out of five of these children lived in rural areas. They are more likely to be underfed and malnourished, get sick, not complete school and fall back into poverty in the aftermath of drought, disease or economic instability. Poor children are also least likely to have access to safe water and adequate sanitation, to receive preventative healthcare such as vaccinations, and when ill are less likely to get adequate medical care. These problems are experienced even more intensely by children living through emergencies and other crises (*see Special section: Nutrition in emergencies*).

Poverty is about more than just financial resources. For many children and families, it is intertwined with social exclusion, discrimination and marginalization driven by gender, disability, ethnicity, geographic remoteness and displacement. At the individual level, such exclusion and inequity determine local access to goods and services, including healthy foods. At the societal level, they can mean that the voices and needs of poor and marginalized communities are not heard in broader decision-making.

The impact of **gender** is evident in every facet of malnutrition and its causes (*see Chapter 3, Special section: Girls and women need stronger support for better nutrition*). Research and programmatic experience show that women's empowerment is associated with better nutrition for children and women, yet in far too many places, women are still served last (and least) at mealtimes and have very limited autonomy, which can mean having limited or no control over their own and their family's income and being excluded from making decisions.

Poverty is often at the heart of malnutrition ... poor children are more likely to be underfed and malnourished, get sick, not complete school and fall back into poverty in the aftermath of drought, disease or economic instability

Stigma around disability can result in newborns not being breastfed or children being given less nutritious or smaller portions of food

Disability can be both a cause and consequence of malnutrition. A lack of nutrients, vitamins and minerals, or exposure to high levels of toxins, for example, can lead to blindness or neurological damage. At the same time, some disabilities – such as intellectual and developmental disabilities or a cleft palate – can lead to a reduced nutrient intake or failure to meet increased nutritional needs. Stigma around disability can result in newborns not being breastfed or children being given less nutritious or smaller portions of food, or even not being fed at all.

Indigenous people and other disadvantaged **ethnic groups** also

face greater risk of malnutrition. In Brazil, for example, the rate of stunting among indigenous groups in 2013 was two to five times higher than among non-indigenous groups. Explanations for this difference include poorer nutrient intake, poorer sanitation and less access to primary healthcare services.[73]

Geographical remoteness can also determine whether a family has access to essential foods and healthcare and nutrition services. Compared with their urban counterparts, children living in rural areas of Burundi, Honduras and Mali are twice as likely to be stunted, which rises to three times as likely in Peru.[74]

FIGURE 1.10 | **Percentage of stunted children in poorest vs. richest households in low-, lower-middle-, upper-middle- and high-income countries**

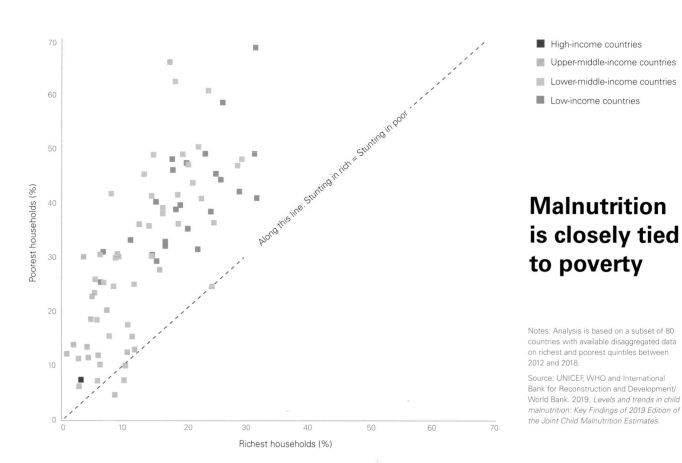

Malnutrition is closely tied to poverty

Notes: Analysis is based on a subset of 80 countries with available disaggregated data on richest and poorest quintiles between 2012 and 2018.

Source: UNICEF, WHO and International Bank for Reconstruction and Development/ World Bank. 2019. *Levels and trends in child malnutrition: Key Findings of 2019 Edition of the Joint Child Malnutrition Estimates.*

SPOTLIGHT
United Kingdom: Poorest children at greater risk of overweight and food insecurity

One in three children in England is overweight or obese by the time they leave primary school.[114] Overweight and obesity prevalence is more than twice as high in the poorest areas, and the gap is widening as obesity continues to rise in the most deprived areas.[115] The picture is similar for children elsewhere in the United Kingdom.[116]

Children's diets are heavily influenced by the environments in which they live. England's poorest areas are fast-food hotspots, with five times more outlets than in the most affluent areas.[117] Children from poorer areas are disproportionately exposed to takeaways selling fried chicken, burgers and pizzas, and poorer areas also have more visible advertising for unhealthy foods than wealthier areas.[118]

The UK food retail environment encourages unhealthy foods consumption. Up to 40 per cent of foods purchased in supermarkets are on promotion, and unhealthy foods are more likely to be promoted.[119] Promotions have been shown to increase the amount people buy, and locations such as end-of-aisle displays and checkouts are frequently used to promote unhealthy foods.[120]

At the same time, nearly 2 million children in England live in food poverty,[121] and less than one-fifth of 5-to-15-year-olds eat five portions of fruits and vegetables a day.[122] In an affluent city like London, almost 1 in 10 children reports going to bed hungry.[123]

The UK faces the dual challenge of confronting 'food swamps' in poor areas, by restricting the promotion of unhealthy food, while ensuring that retailers in poor areas offer affordable healthy food.

© iStock.com/Bea Kiss

The UK Government has pledged to halve childhood obesity and reduce the obesity gap between children from the richest and poorest areas by 2030.[124] The UK introduced a sugary drinks levy and the world's first sugar reduction programme aimed at a 20 per cent reduction in the most popular products consumed by children.[125] The UK is also consulting on new legislation to ban unhealthy foods at checkout areas, store entrances and the end of aisles, as well as price promotions encouraging over-consumption of these products, such as 'buy one, get one free', multi-buy offers or unlimited refills.[126]

Local authorities have been encouraged to use their planning powers to limit the opening of additional fast-food outlets close to schools, while the Mayor of London has banned advertising for unhealthy foods on the Transport for London network.[127]

Recognizing that infancy and early childhood are critical times for establishing food preferences and dietary patterns, the UK has recently called for action to reduce sugar in commercial baby foods and end misleading labelling practices. Public Health England found that some sweet snacks marketed as suitable for babies and toddlers contain as much sugar as confectionery.[128]

In parallel, the UK Government set up the Healthy Start Scheme to provide fruit and vegetable vouchers to low-income families with young children, which has helped increase these families' spending on fresh fruit and vegetables by 15 per cent.[129]

Even though much remains to be done to tackle childhood obesity, the UK is paving the way to ensure that all children grow up in a healthy food environment. ∎

The role of food systems

The trends in children's nutrition are clear: on the one hand, there have been some declines in undernutrition, notably in stunting, albeit at far too slow a rate to meet globally agreed targets. There is also evidence of some reductions in hidden hunger, but again at far too slow a rate. On the other hand, the proportion of children who are overweight is rising rapidly, even in countries that still struggle with undernutrition.

What explains these trends? In part, they reflect a world where children are increasingly able to satisfy their energy needs but not their *nutritional* needs. As part of the global nutrition transition described by Barry Popkin,[75] more and more people are moving towards modern diets high in saturated fats, trans-fats, sugar and salt. This transition is linked to a rising prevalence of diet-related NCDs. Low-quality diets are now believed to be the single biggest risk factor for the global burden of disease.[76]

The result is that more children are surviving, but far too few are thriving – failing to develop to their full physical and mental potential. In such a world, we need increasingly to focus on the quality of children's diets and ask this question: **Why are so many children eating too little of what they need, while an increasing number of children are consuming too much of what they don't need?**

To answer this question requires getting to grips with **food systems** – everything that happens to bring food 'from farm to mouth'. As work by numerous international experts – including the FAO, IFAD, the Global Panel on Agriculture and Food Systems for Nutrition, and the High Level Panel of Experts on Food Security and Nutrition – has demonstrated, the processes and activities that shape what we eat today are becoming increasingly complex.[77, 78, 79]

To better explain how these processes affect children, UNICEF worked with international experts to develop the Innocenti Framework on Food Systems for Children and Adolescents (*see below*).[80] This framework puts children's diets at the heart of food-system analysis for two reasons: first, because children's nutritional requirements are unique and critical; and second, because there are no 'magic bullet' solutions to improving children's nutrition over the long term, other than having food systems that deliver nutritious, safe, affordable and sustainable diets for all children. Action is needed at different points in the food system – with synergistic actions in the health, water and sanitation, education, and social protection systems – (*see Chapter 4*) to both increase the supply of, and demand for, nutritious foods.

The Innocenti Framework has three main components – **drivers, determinants and interactions.**

Drivers

The ways in which societies supply and distribute food to children, the range of choices available to caregivers and consumers and the decisions that they take can all be affected by drivers that, at first glance, may appear distant from food systems. In recent decades, for example, factors such as rising incomes, technological innovation, marketing and globalization have all helped to transform food systems and the diets they deliver to children and adolescents.

Why are so many children eating too little of what they need, while an increasing number are consuming too much of what they don't need?

Determinants

The core of the Innocenti Framework consists of four determinants that

describe the processes, conditions and actors most directly involved in the production and consumption of food for and by children.

The processes and activities that shape what children eat today are becoming increasingly complex

---

BOX 1.2 | How can agriculture better support nutrition?

Agriculture is the foundation of all food systems and key to providing children with nutritious, safe, affordable and sustainable diets. However, the interaction between agriculture and children's nutrition is far from straightforward.

At one level, this reflects the reality that child nutrition goals may conflict with economic and political goals.[82] For example, while investment in agriculture has improved productivity, food diversity has declined: just three crops (rice, wheat and maize) now account for nearly two thirds of the world's calorie intake.[83] At another level, this reflects the wide variety of food production systems globally – urban and rural, small and large, traditional and modern – all of which may affect nutrition outcomes in different ways.

Modern and industrialized food systems offer production efficiency gains and year-round access to low-cost foods, but they are increasingly oriented toward producing animal feed, industrial inputs for processed foods, and biofuels rather than food for primary consumption. This has both dietary and environmental impacts, including loss of biodiversity, soil and water contamination, and the production of greenhouse gases.[84]

Smallholder opportunities

The dynamics are different in traditional food systems, where food safety and food loss are greater concerns.[85] Around four out of five of the world's rural poor make some or all of their living from agriculture,[86] many as smallholders – a loosely defined term that can be thought of as referring to small family-run holdings that produce a subsistence crop and one or two cash crops. The decisions taken by – and options available to – smallholders can have major effects on the nutrition of some of the world's most disadvantaged children.

Smallholders face choices over whether to produce a more nutritious and diverse array of foodstuffs for the family's own consumption, or whether to sell what they produce to provide extra income. This income can be increased further if the family processes food before selling it; however, they may only be able to do this if they can access functioning markets and transportation.[87]

Another way in which smallholder agriculture can affect children's nutrition is if it leads to the empowerment of women, who play a major role in farm work, food processing and child feeding. Women's participation in agriculture has the potential to help shift control of household resources to them, which then become more likely to be directed toward child feeding and care.[88] However, programmes aimed at strengthening the role of women can unintentionally harm children's nutrition if they compete with child feeding and care – including breastfeeding – or impair women's own health and nutrition.[89] This underlines the need for initiatives for women in agriculture to be accompanied by other interventions, such as in nutrition counselling and support, behaviour change communication, and providing access to water, sanitation and health services.

While more work is needed to demonstrate how agriculture can best improve children's nutrition, the potential is clear, as is the certainty that fundamental change in children's nutrition cannot happen without the support of agriculture. ∎

The Innocenti Framework on Food Systems for Children and Adolescents

The Innocenti Framework identifies some of the key points in food systems where action can be taken to increase both the supply of, and demand for, nutritious foods for children and young people.

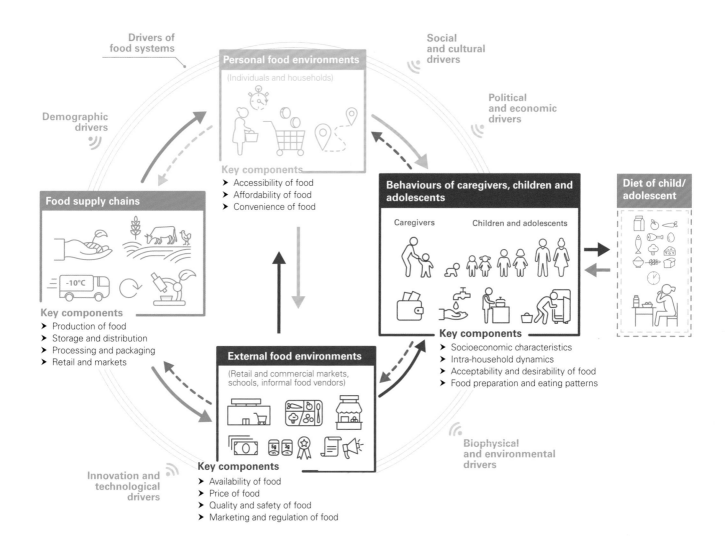

Drivers of food systems

Demographic drivers

Social and cultural drivers

Political and economic drivers

Personal food environments

(Individuals and households)

Key components
- Accessibility of food
- Affordability of food
- Convenience of food

Food supply chains

Key components
- Production of food
- Storage and distribution
- Processing and packaging
- Retail and markets

External food environments

(Retail and commercial markets, schools, informal food vendors)

Key components
- Availability of food
- Price of food
- Quality and safety of food
- Marketing and regulation of food

Behaviours of caregivers, children and adolescents

Caregivers   Children and adolescents

Key components
- Socioeconomic characteristics
- Intra-household dynamics
- Acceptability and desirability of food
- Food preparation and eating patterns

Diet of child/ adolescent

Innovation and technological drivers

Biophysical and environmental drivers

Source: UNICEF, 2019[81]

The Innocenti Framework puts children's diets at the heart of food-system analysis

Food supply chains comprise all the actors and activities involved in producing, processing and distributing food (and, ultimately, to disposal or use of waste). Agricultural production is still the source of most of what children eat, and offers key opportunities for improving children's nutrition, for example by researching and developing more nutritious crops. Other interventions can include equipping smallholders and women to grow nutritious vegetables and to raise short-cycle livestock, such as poultry and goats, and developing mixed farming and cropping systems and aquaculture for fish production. There are also opportunities along the length of food chains to support better nutrition for children, such as fortifying foods with essential micronutrients, and reducing the use of saturated fats, trans-fats, sugar and salt. Improved food storage and management can reduce food safety risks and contaminants, while minimizing food loss and spoilage.

External food environments describe, firstly, all the physical places where caregivers, children and adolescents go to purchase or consume food. What foods and food items are on offer in stores and markets do much to determine the accessibility, affordability and convenience of food choices. For families living in 'food deserts', for example, fresh produce may simply not be available (*see Chapter 3*). Also important in external food environments are marketing and advertising, which help to shape tastes and influence purchasing decisions.[90] Key interventions in external food environments to improve children's

Nutritional education and information are an important response to influence lifelong behaviour for healthier food choices, habits and overall nutrition

Traditional staples are the foundation of Uruma and her family's diet in Tanzania. She often struggles to find enough to feed her family. "The children sometimes go to school in the morning without eating anything," she says. When her husband earns a little extra, "I may return with meat, so the children can enjoy eating meat."

Produced/photographed by MAKMENDE

nutrition can include enforcing standards on food fortification. In addition, a mix of taxes and tax incentives can lower demand for unhealthy foods and encourage the supply of healthy foods. Other actions can include regulation of packaging and labelling and of marketing, especially of foods targeted at children and young people (*see Chapter 4*).

Personal food environments represent the factors that help determine and, in many cases, limit the dietary choices of families and children. These include families and children's access to shops and markets and their purchasing power, which will determine the affordability and convenience of food (*see Chapter*

3). As well as a lack of income, lack of time is a significant burden. Rural women in particular must often balance unpaid farm work with their role as primary caregivers.[91] Important responses can include providing families with cash transfers that, with appropriate nutrition counselling and support, can offer extra resources and desire to purchase nutritious food for children.[92] There is also scope to address time poverty by reducing the burden of women's farm and domestic work. For example, improving access to household water sources can cut the amount of time women spend collecting water, and likewise, better tools can speed up planting and weeding, while day-care centres can support childcare.[93]

In Mexico, Gabriela tries to feed her family healthy foods, such as salad at lunchtime, but six-year-old Ikal has other ideas. "Mom, can I have a candy?" he begs. Gabriela finds it overwhelming: "They're just children," she says, "Everything has pretty pictures on it. Everything … has sugar. They're still kids, so they want sweets all the time."

Produced/photographed by MAKMENDE

Like many young people, Indonesian teenager Rafsi is taking more of his own decisions about what to eat, especially when he hangs out with friends in the mall. Rafsi is trying to lose weight: "I go to the gym," he says, "I hope I will lose more because still right now I'm overweight." But it's not easy: "It's difficult to eat healthy when our friends are eating more delicious foods than healthy foods."

Produced/photographed by MAKMENDE

The behaviours of caregivers, children and adolescents – or how families, children and young people procure and prepare food and how children are fed and supervised – is influenced by many factors. These include eating patterns, nutritional knowledge, taste preferences, appetite and levels of physical activity. Also important are socio-economic factors, such as food and dietary taboos, and the tendency in some cultures to prioritize boys and men over girls and women at mealtimes. Nutrition information, education and counselling are an important response to influence lifelong behaviour for healthier food choices, habits and overall nutrition.

Interactions

None of these four determinants stands completely alone. As the arrows in the framework indicate, they interact with each other, shaping and reinforcing each other in ways that can both help and harm children's nutrition. For example, while the food offered in local markets helps shape the diets of children and families, it is in turn influenced by demand from children and families. These interactions show the importance of ensuring that policies to improve the supply of nutritious foods must also strengthen demand.

Malnutrition can harm a child's economic prospects and, as a consequence, broader socio-economic development in numerous ways

What are the economic impacts of children's malnutrition?

The coming decades will see a dramatic shift in the contours of the world's population – one that will see Africa become the centre of global population growth. By 2050, the population of Africa is forecast to have doubled since 2017, reaching a total of 2.5 billion people. In short, the future of humanity will be increasingly African. As populations age in much of the rest of the world, Africa over the coming decades will still be a young continent; in 2050, it will be the place where just over two out of five of the world's children are born.[94]

The emergence of a large and young labour force in such a short period of time will provide Africa – as well as India and some other countries in South and Southeast Asia – with the chance to harness their demographic dividend. But that potential will be realized only with improvements in human capital – people's education, training, skills and health.[95] Malnutrition stands in the way of that happening.

The impact on children

There are numerous ways in which malnutrition can harm a child's economic prospects and, as a consequence, broader socio-economic development. Stunting in the first 1,000 days is associated with poorer cognitive development and lower educational outcomes.[96] Evidence from a number of countries indicates that malnourished children spend less time in school, typically because of poorer brain development and school readiness, illness or because they start school

later in life and are more likely to have to repeat grades. In sub-Saharan Africa, for example, research has shown that children lost up to 2.5 years of schooling if there was a famine while they were in utero and during their childhood.[97]

By contrast, there are also numerous examples of how better nutrition is associated with improvements in children's school performance. In the 1940s, for example, the United States Government required bread to be fortified to help overcome widespread iron deficiency. Subsequent analysis showed improved rates of school enrolment.[98] Similarly, Tanzanian children who received intensive iodine supplementation in the late 1980s and 1990s spent up to around an extra half-year in school compared with children who had not been treated.[99] Studies on supplementation programmes in Guatemala[100] and in China[101] also suggest that children improved their performance in areas such as mathematics and reading.

Perhaps the most direct way of demonstrating malnutrition's effects on an individual's economic prospects is to look at its association with reduced earnings – in effect, the impact of malnutrition on productivity. Available research indicated that the average lifetime lost earnings associated with stunting is US$1,400 per child, ranging from under US$300 in Tajikistan to over US$30,000 in wealthier countries such as the Bahamas, United Arab Emirates, Kuwait and Qatar.[102] Studies have also suggested that stunting is linked to lower earnings: according to one, an increase of one centimetre in height in adulthood was associated with a 4 per cent increase in wages for men and 6 per cent for women.[103]

An additional, and easily overlooked, way in which malnutrition can affect children's social and economic prospects is by fuelling conflict. There is growing evidence that poor economic and health status, including malnutrition, is associated with higher rates of armed conflict. According to one analysis in 2008, lowering the prevalence of under-5 malnutrition by 5 percentage points was associated with a decrease in the likelihood of conflict of up to 3.5 percentage points.[104] The reasons for this are not fully clear, but as John Boyd Orr, first Director-General of the FAO, once said, "We cannot build peace on empty stomachs."[105]

All these impacts on the individual serve to undermine the ability of countries to develop their human capital, defined as the "aggregate levels of education, training, skills, and health in a population".[106] This loss is significant. According to the African Union's Cost of Hunger in Africa study, child malnutrition costs African economies between 1.9 per cent and 16.5 per cent of GDP every year.[107] More recent studies indicate that malnutrition continues to exert a heavy burden on Africa's economies.[108]

Much less work has been done on estimating the cost of childhood obesity, especially in low- and middle-income countries. Overweight can have an impact on the broader economy by making individuals less productive – through lower levels of physical activity and higher rates of NCDs – and by raising the cost of healthcare to treat conditions such as hypertension, diabetes and stroke. According to estimates prepared for WHO, if current trends continue, economic losses in low- and middle-income countries from heart disease, cancer, diabetes and chronic respiratory disease will reach more than US$7 trillion over the period 2011–2025, equivalent to about 4 per cent of these countries' annual output.

Investing in nutrition

Nutrition must be seen as a cornerstone investment if the world is to achieve the Sustainable Development Goals by 2030. According to estimates by the World Bank and others, it would cost just an additional US$8.50 per child per year to meet global targets for under-5 child stunting.[109] That's equivalent to just US$5 billion a year. Two numbers help put that figure in perspective: it's a little less than the combined annual spend on advertising of around US$7.2 billion a year by three of the world's largest food and restaurant multinationals in the early 2010s.[110] It's equivalent to just under 1 per cent of the US$620 billion that high-income and emerging economies spend each year on agriculture support[111] (which includes direct payments to farmers as well as tariff barriers and export subsidies).

Such investments have an impressive rate of return. Every dollar invested in reducing stunting generates estimated economic returns equivalent to about US$18 in high-burden countries.[112] Even without these returns, investment in children's nutrition must be at the heart of any equity agenda. "Everyone puts all their eggs in the equality of opportunity basket," the former President of The World Bank, Jim Yong Kim, has said, "But we're essentially lying when 25% of children in the world are stunted. Inequality is baked into the brains of 25% of all children before the age of five. So the only way that we can realistically say there is equality of opportunity is if we bring stunting down to zero."[113] ■

Every dollar invested in reducing stunting generates estimated economic returns equivalent to about US$18 in high-burden countries

PERSPECTIVE

Why is addressing children's nutrition important for a country's broader economic development?

Dr. Sania Nishtar
Special Assistant
to the Prime
Minister on
Poverty Alleviation
and Social
Protection,
Pakistan

Dr Sania Nishtar is Special
Assistant to the Prime
Minister of Pakistan on
Poverty Alleviation and
Social Protection and Federal
Minister in the Government
of Pakistan. She is also
Chair of the Benazir Income
Support Programme, and
Co-chair of the WHO High
Level Commission on NCDs.
Dr Nishtar founded the non-
profit, non-governmental
thinktank Heartfile. In
2017, she was Pakistan's
candidate for WHO Director
General and was among the
three shortlisted finalists.

After years of brutal conflict, Yemen has become one of the world's worst humanitarian crises and is descending into famine. Even if the conflict ends tomorrow, the consequences of this crisis will be long-lasting, not least because of the impact of malnutrition on brain development, which in turn shapes the cognitive abilities of future workforces. Today's food insecurity is starving Yemen of its future talent.

Unfortunately, malnutrition is not isolated to extreme hunger in warzones. Children around the world contend with multiple forms of malnutrition that go beyond undernutrition.

Many countries are grappling with the double burden of malnutrition. Undernutrition in young children and overweight later in life lead to higher risk of costly diseases, such as hypertension and diabetes. Both sides of the same coin of malnutrition can be on painful display within one country – quite feasibly within the same homes, classrooms and playgrounds.

Major diabetes epidemics in China, Cambodia and Ukraine have been linked to famines and starvation 40–50 years earlier. Severe food shortages in the Second World War could be an explanation for the current high rate of diabetes in Nauru, Singapore and Malaysia. This raises the possibility of future 'hotspots' of diabetes in regions that have droughts and famine or internal and regional fighting (e.g., the Horn of Africa and Yemen), once socio-economic conditions improve.

Malnutrition does not just lead to deaths and disease. It also undermines the human right to a healthy life, and negatively affects economic development by escalating healthcare costs and incurring productivity losses.

In the case of undernutrition, productivity losses are due to decreased physical and intellectual capacity, whereas in the case of obesity, lost workdays, lower productivity at work, mortality and permanent disability come into play.

The impact of these costs on a country's gross domestic product (GDP) can be massive. In Asia, the annual GDP losses from low weight, poor childhood growth and micronutrient deficiencies average 11 per cent. The global economic impact of obesity is estimated to be US$2 trillion or 2.8 per cent of global GDP – roughly the same economic cost as smoking or armed conflict. Cumulatively, the estimated impact on the global economy of different forms of malnutrition could be as high as US$3.5 trillion a year, or US$500 for each individual.

Perhaps the most compelling association of nutrition with a country's economic development is seen in human capital. In 2018, the World Bank launched a Human Capital Index, emphasizing that this digital age requires countries to urgently invest in their people if they hope to compete in the economy of the future.

The Human Capital Index is a composite measure, factoring in child survival, years of

© UNICEF/UN0281635/Dejongh

schooling and stunting. It has enabled the insight that malnutrition is therefore directly responsible for the loss of human capital.

Individuals who have had stunted growth may lose schooling and experience delayed entry into the labour force, meaning that 43 per cent of children aged under 5 in low- and middle-income countries are at elevated risk of poverty because of stunting.

Investing in child nutrition would produce a long-term impact on development. The Copenhagen Consensus has indicated that for every dollar spent on nutrition in the first 1,000 days of a child's life, the benefit could be an average of US$45.

An average annual investment of US$7 billion over the next 10 years would be sufficient to achieve the global nutrition targets to reduce child wasting and stunting and maternal anaemia and to improve breastfeeding rates. With this investment, 3.7 million children's lives could be saved by 2025, with at least 65 million fewer stunted children, 105 million more children exclusively breastfed and 265 million fewer women suffering from anaemia compared to 2015. Without this investment, development opportunities will be missed.

Costly as malnutrition is, the solutions do not need to be. *The Lancet* estimates that over 820,000 children's lives could be saved through measures such as breastfeeding babies exclusively immediately after birth, and continuing to feature breastmilk as part of their diet up to 2 years of age and beyond.

However, the usefulness of free measures should not be used to understate how effective cash can be in the hands of those at the sharp end of malnutrition. Following the Pakistan Government's new prioritization of nutrition, I have been invited to lead the Benazir Income Support Programme (BISP), which is a national cash transfer system.

The US$1.15 billion programme currently gets money into the hands of over 5.6 million poor and marginalized families. Independent evaluation has shown that the programme empowers women in particular, changing how they are viewed in their communities. I look forward to integrating a new nutrition-centred initiative within its framework in order to address malnutrition further.

There is increasing awareness and evidence that investments to reduce malnutrition do pay off and are much needed. For the sake of our health and economies, both now and in the future, countries need to take on the many-headed hydra that is malnutrition.■

02 FEEDING A CHILD FOR LIFE

From the womb to adolescence, children at every stage of life have unique nutritional needs, eating behaviours and dietary influences, and are harmed in different ways by malnutrition. Early childhood is a time of rapid growth and nutritional vulnerability. School-age children are exposed to broader influences that affect their diets and food choices. Adolescence presents a window of opportunity for establishing healthy, lifelong nutrition.

➤ Malnutrition during pregnancy and early childhood can adversely affect brain development.

➤ Generally, school-age children around the world are eating too little nutrient-rich foods and too many unhealthy snacks.

➤ Obesity in adolescence can have lifelong negative effects on the brain, contributing to early onset of cognitive dysfunction during ageing.

A family in Kang Maes District, Cambodia sits outside their home as the younger children eat their meal and the eldest child helps prepare ingredients. © UNICEF/UN074041/Pirozzi

Food and nutrition across childhood

At all ages, children are not eating diets with enough nutrients or diversity, and they are eating too much sugar, salt and fat. The risks at each age can lead to one or more forms of malnutrition: stunting, wasting, hidden hunger or overweight and obesity. These conditions can affect school performance and lifelong economic opportunities, and present health risks into adulthood.

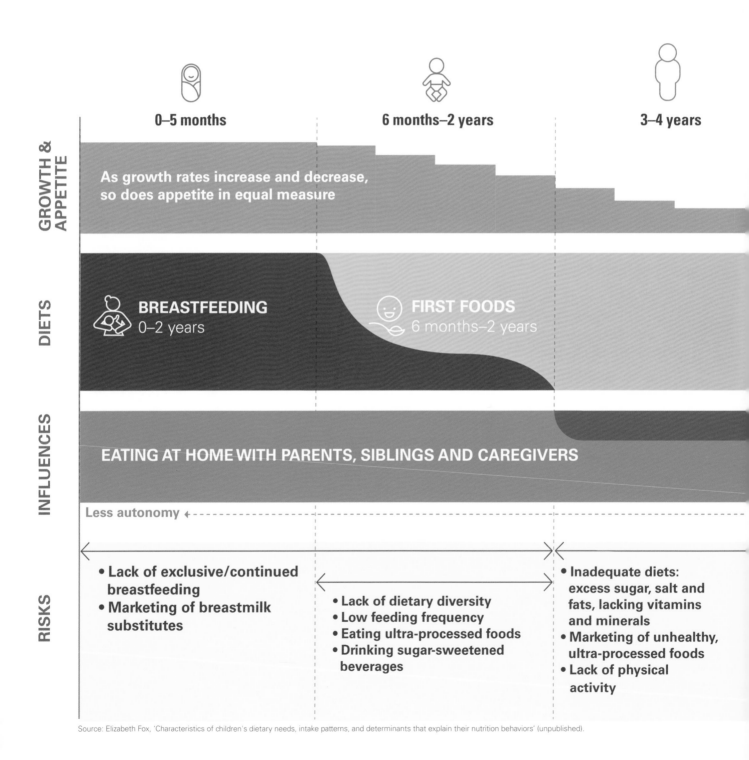

0–5 months

6 months–2 years

3–4 years

GROWTH & APPETITE

As growth rates increase and decrease, so does appetite in equal measure

DIETS

BREASTFEEDING
0–2 years

FIRST FOODS
6 months–2 years

INFLUENCES

EATING AT HOME WITH PARENTS, SIBLINGS AND CAREGIVERS

Less autonomy ←

RISKS

- Lack of exclusive/continued breastfeeding
- Marketing of breastmilk substitutes

- Lack of dietary diversity
- Low feeding frequency
- Eating ultra-processed foods
- Drinking sugar-sweetened beverages

- Inadequate diets: excess sugar, salt and fats, lacking vitamins and minerals
- Marketing of unhealthy, ultra-processed foods
- Lack of physical activity

Source: Elizabeth Fox, 'Characteristics of children's dietary needs, intake patterns, and determinants that explain their nutrition behaviors' (unpublished).

At every stage of childhood, children have unique nutritional needs, risks and eating behaviours

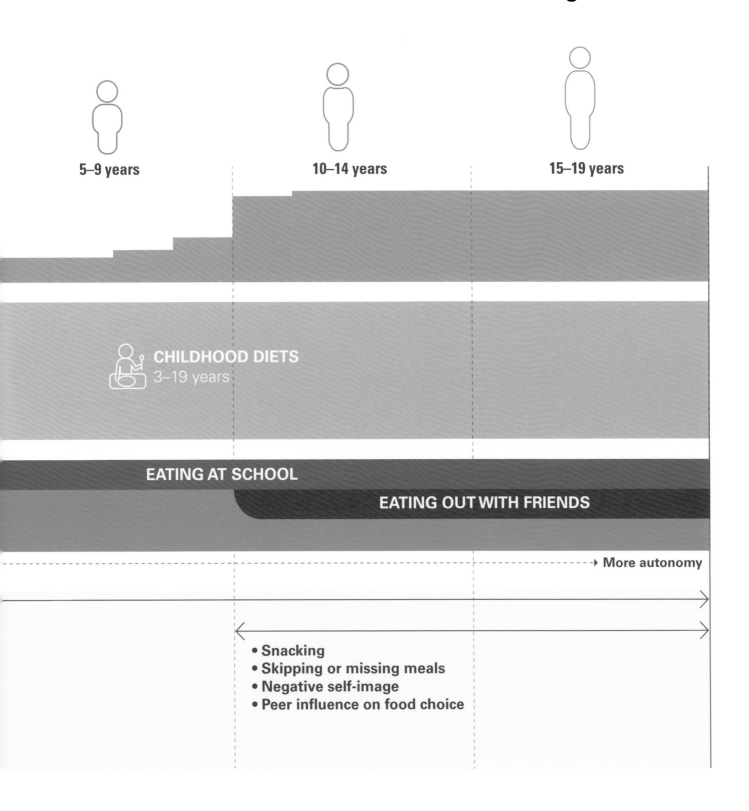

5–9 years

10–14 years

15–19 years

CHILDHOOD DIETS
3–19 years

EATING AT SCHOOL

EATING OUT WITH FRIENDS

→ **More autonomy**

- Snacking
- Skipping or missing meals
- Negative self-image
- Peer influence on food choice

Lack of proper nutrition during the early years can have lifelong consequences

Introduction

Across every stage of childhood – from the womb until adulthood – a child's nutritional needs, and the behaviours and influences on diet evolve and change. An infant undergoes vast physiological changes week by week. As children start school, eating patterns and diet can change drastically. Later, adolescents have opportunities to establish lifelong healthy eating habits, yet are vulnerable to the long-term effects of overweight and obesity. Proper maternal and child nutrition in the early stages of life lead to lower health risks across the life course and the prevention of non-communicable diseases (NCDs).[1] An understanding of these differences across childhood is important for the design of policies and programmes that support child nutrition effectively.

As a child grows, the main influencers on diet shift gradually from mainly parents and other caregivers in the early years to the staff of day-care centres and schools and, finally, to peers and friends in the school-age years and adolescence. Food marketing and broader social forces affect what parents and caregivers feed their children, and act more directly on children's food choices as they grow older.

Early years: Vulnerability and opportunity (the first five years of life)

Early childhood is a time of rapid physical growth and brain development. Lack of proper nutrition and exposure to illness and infection during these early years can have lifelong consequences on educational attainment and health and economic outcomes, especially for children from the poorest and most marginalized communities.

The first 1,000 days – from the point of conception to around the child's second birthday – are especially crucial. Poor maternal nutrition before conception and while the child is in the womb, the absence of exclusive breastfeeding in the first six months, and the inability of caregivers to provide a diverse and nutritious range of 'first foods' can lead to stunting, wasting and micronutrient deficiencies. For children and their communities, the consequences can be profound and lifelong.

Impact of maternal malnutrition and malnutrition in early childhood

Good nutrition starts even before birth. Poor maternal nutrition affects the child while in the womb and during childbirth.

Maternal malnutrition, in the form of underweight and anaemia, increases the risk of pre-term birth and low birthweight, which in turn increase the risk of neonatal death, stunting and wasting. In addition, maternal overweight is a common complication of pregnancy:[2] it increases the risk of gestational diabetes and pre-eclampsia, a potentially life-threatening complication, and can lead to difficulties in labour and higher rates of post-partum haemorrhage. There are risks for the child too, including pre-term birth,[3] low birthweight, not initiating breastfeeding, and an increased risk of overweight later in life.[4]

The developmental demands of the foetus increase micronutrient requirements; many pregnant women experience hidden hunger or micronutrient deficiencies (see Chapter 1). Iron deficiency can lead

How breastfeeding helps the mother and child

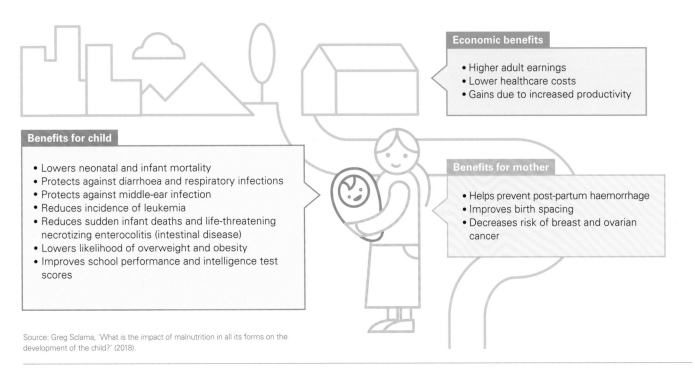

Economic benefits
- Higher adult earnings
- Lower healthcare costs
- Gains due to increased productivity

Benefits for child
- Lowers neonatal and infant mortality
- Protects against diarrhoea and respiratory infections
- Protects against middle-ear infection
- Reduces incidence of leukemia
- Reduces sudden infant deaths and life-threatening necrotizing enterocolitis (intestinal disease)
- Lowers likelihood of overweight and obesity
- Improves school performance and intelligence test scores

Benefits for mother
- Helps prevent post-partum haemorrhage
- Improves birth spacing
- Decreases risk of breast and ovarian cancer

Source: Greg Sclama, 'What is the impact of malnutrition in all its forms on the development of the child?' (2018).

to anaemia. In fact, iron deficiency is the most frequent cause of nutritional anaemia.[5] Folate prevents neural-tube defects such as spina bifida in the foetus.[6] Calcium reduces the risk of pre-eclampsia and pre-term birth.[7] Vitamin A supports immune function and foetal development, especially during the third trimester.[8] Finally, a lack of zinc in mothers is associated with low birthweight, poor foetal neural developments, pre-term delivery and increased neonatal mortality.[9]

While the effects of nutrition on the brain vary across childhood, brain development is fastest during the early years. Malnutrition during pregnancy and early childhood can adversely affect brain development, affecting cognition, school readiness, behaviour and productivity into the school-age years and beyond. Providing essential energy, protein, fatty acids and micronutrients to a child during this period can establish lifetime brain function. A well-nourished child can interact with the environment and caregivers in a way that supports further healthy brain development.[10]

The power of breastfeeding

The wide-ranging benefits of breastfeeding – for a child's healthy immune system, brain development and microbiome – are well documented and reflected in a global consensus within the nutrition community. UNICEF and WHO recommend exclusive breastfeeding for the first six months and continued breastfeeding up to two years old or beyond. As the World Bank's Keith Hansen memorably wrote in *The Lancet* in 2016, "If breastfeeding did not already exist, someone who invented it today would deserve a dual Nobel Prize in medicine and economics."[11]

Breastmilk is not just food – it's a powerful medicine tailored to the infant's needs

Only 2 out of 5 newborns begin breastfeeding in the first hour of life

Breastfeeding has profound benefits for the child, especially in the first hour of life. Colostrum, the first milk produced by a mother, protects an infant's immature immune system against infection and inflammation.[12] Babies who begin breastfeeding in their first hour have a much lower risk of dying, even compared with babies who begin breastfeeding later on in their first day.[13]

Breastmilk is not just food – it's a powerful medicine tailored to the infant's needs that can significantly reduce the risk of death.[14] Universal breastfeeding could save the lives of 820,000 children under 5 annually worldwide. Breastfed children also have much lower rates of diarrhoea and

respiratory-related disease. Other benefits include improved school performance[15] and higher adult earnings, as well as improved physical well-being. Growing evidence also points to breastfeeding reducing overweight, obesity and chronic diseases such as diabetes later in life.[16]

The dividends from breastfeeding are particularly high in lower-income countries, where families are often unable to access clean water and healthcare. Even in high-income countries, breastfeeding is still important for health and healthy growth and development. For example, it reduces sudden infant deaths and life-threatening necrotizing enterocolitis, a potentially fatal inflammation of the gut that affects mostly premature infants.

FIGURE 2.1 | **Percentage of infants aged 0–5 months fed infant formula, by UNICEF region, 2018**

The rise in use of breastmilk substitutes is an area of growing concern

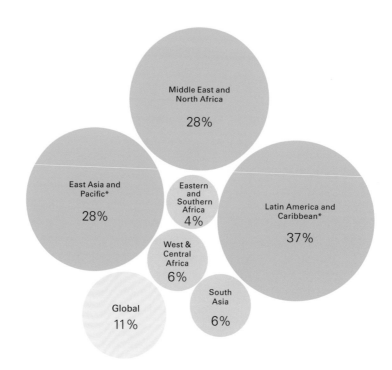

Middle East and North Africa
28%

East Asia and Pacific*
28%

Eastern and Southern Africa
4%

Latin America and Caribbean*
37%

West & Central Africa
6%

South Asia
6%

Global
11%

Notes: Between 2008 and 2013, sales of (typically cow's) milk-based formula grew by 41 per cent globally and by 72 per cent in upper middle-income countries such as Brazil, China, Peru and Turkey. Analysis based on a subset of 73 countries with available data between 2013–2018, covering 61 percent of the global population. Regional estimates are presented only where available data represents at least 50 percent of the region's population.

*To meet adequate population coverage, East Asia and Pacific does not include China and Latin America and Caribbean does not include Brazil. Data not available for Europe and Central Asia and North America.

Source: UNICEF global databases, 2019.

FIGURE 2.2 | Trends in percentage of infants aged 0–5 months exclusively breastfed, by UNICEF region, around 2005 and around 2018

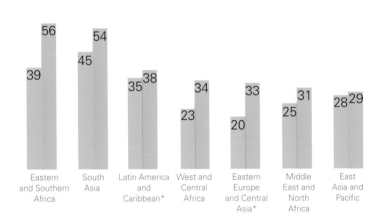

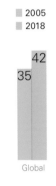

Many regions have made gains in exclusive breastfeeding

Notes: Analysis based on a subset of 80 countries with comparable trend data covering 74 per cent of the global population for around 2005 (2003–2008) and for around 2018 (2013–2018). Regional estimates are presented only where available data represents at least 50 percent of the region's population.

*To meet adequate population coverage, Latin America and Caribbean does not include Brazil and Eastern Europe and Central Asia does not include Russian Federation.

Source: UNICEF global databases, 2019.

Mothers benefit from breastfeeding too. It helps prevent heavy bleeding after birth and accelerates the contraction of the uterus. In addition, because lactating mothers are less likely to ovulate while breastfeeding, it improves birth spacing. There is also robust evidence of protection against breast and ovarian cancer,[17] some evidence of a reduced risk of type 2 diabetes, and a reduction of hypertension and lower cardiovascular risk among mothers who breastfeed.[18]

Why are so many children not breastfed?

Despite these benefits, far too many babies are not breastfeeding optimally. Only just over two out of five (44 per cent) of newborns begin breastfeeding in the first hour of life and around the same proportion (42 per cent) of children under six months are exclusively breastfed. Why?

The answer is complex, but it includes factors such as the promotion of breastmilk substitutes, social and cultural taboos against breastfeeding, the struggle many women face to balance work with childcare, and lack of support for breastfeeding.

Breastmilk substitutes

In the first three days of life, 43 per cent of newborns worldwide are given liquids or foods other than breastmilk, most commonly sugar water, honey, tea, animal milk, infant formula or plain water.[19] In West and Central Africa, water is the most common liquid given to infants in the first three days after birth, potentially exposing them to pathogens and other life-threatening substances. Elsewhere, many infants in Latin America and the Caribbean do not receive breastmilk at all and receive breastmilk substitutes – in Mexico, 48

SPOTLIGHT
A day is (almost) never enough: The daily life of a breastfeeding working mother in rural Laos

Xaiathon lives in Houychengkao Village in rural Laos. At 33 years old, she has four sons ranging in age from 2 months to 15 years. Together with her husband, she farms a small lot and maintains a home with their children.

"My day starts very early, because of the long walk to the farm," she says. Because of this, her breastfeeding practice is not as regular as her doctor has advised. In addition to farm work and preparing meals for the boys, Xaiathon gathers firewood, feeds the hog and cattle, does the laundry, cleans the house, and helps out at a neighbour's farm to augment their barely-enough harvest.

She's usually only able to breastfeed Kaka (her youngest son) when she's at home in the morning before going to the farm (which is an hour's walk from their home), and again in the evening when she's back. "It is a challenge to keep up because of the farm work. Sometimes when it rains, I can't go back home to breastfeed them, so in the rainy season I make sure there's rice porridge left at home. A few times I've had my fellow mothers in the neighbourhood breastfeed my boys," she says.

To make up for the lack of breastmilk during the day, she chews pieces of meat and mixes them with the rice porridge that she has prepared for Kaka in the morning. Her heavy workload means Xaiathon is also unable to follow through with her visits to the health centre in town. "I would rather just spend the time at the farm instead," she says, adding that their meagre harvest is the only source of income for their family of six.

As the sun sets and her husband approaches their home, the boys run to greet him, eager to see what fruits he has got for them along the way. For Xaiathon, the day is only halfway done: she still has to prepare dinner, do the dishes and feed her little son. She will try to get some rest as soon as the boys are back from evening playtime with their neighbours, mindful of another early start the next day.■

Before heading out to the farm, Xaiathon gathers and cuts the fire wood, and clears their backyard garden of bushes. "I also consider this a bit of warm-up, before the real hard work at the farm awaits," she says with a smile. © UNICEF/Laos/2018

per cent of infants 0–5 months and 33 per cent of children 6–11 months consume infant formula, while only 35 per cent of children under 2 consume breastmilk.[20]

The rise in the promotion, sales and use of breastmilk substitutes, including follow-on formulas and toddler milks, is an area of growing concern. These products are often marketed with misleading claims that they improve young children's IQ and immune systems, or are necessary for healthy growth. Between 2008 and 2013, sales of (typically cow's) milk-based formula grew by 41 per cent globally and by 72 per cent in upper middle-income countries such as Brazil, China, Peru and Turkey.[21]

The fastest growing category of formula milk is toddler milks, marketed for children aged between 13 and 36 months. Global sales grew by 53 per cent between 2008 and 2013.[22] Unnecessary for healthy growth, these drinks may also increase the child's preference for sweet tastes.[23] Compared with formulas, which contain added sugars, breastmilk exposes children to a broader range of tastes and flavours from the mother's diet, thus preparing children for a more diverse diet as they grow older. Most toddler milks contain a combination of powdered milk without its natural fats, and corn syrup and other added sweeteners and vegetable oil.

Public health professionals have raised concerns about the rise in the use of toddler milks. "My view is that these companies created a fake feeding period that they filled with this new product," New York University's Jennifer L. Pomeranz has said. "We're adding in now another few years of processed food consumption that didn't previously exist."[24]

Social norms and healthcare

Social norms, taboos and traditional practices significantly influence feeding behaviours. For example, many cultures believe babies should not consume colostrum and should be fed another liquid, such as sugar water, honey or animal milk, before beginning breastfeeding.

To begin breastfeeding immediately after childbirth, mothers need support from health professionals. However, a 2018 UNICEF report found that the presence of a medical doctor, nurse or midwife at the time of delivery did not necessarily support the early initiation of breastfeeding.[25] Only 34 per cent of newborns delivered by a skilled birth attendant began breastfeeding within the first hour of birth in South Asia, while the rates are only 45 per cent in Middle East/North Africa, 47 per cent in Latin America and Caribbean, and 48 per cent in East Asia and Pacific. Another emerging concern is the rise of caesarean delivery. Research in South Asia has found that caesarean delivery is a significant predictor of delayed initiation of breastfeeding.[26] Across 51 countries, early initiation rates among newborns delivered by vaginal birth were more than twice as high as initiation rates among newborns delivered by caesarean section.[27]

Mothers living with HIV can breastfeed without negative consequences for their own health and the health of their children. When these mothers take antiretroviral medicine consistently throughout the breastfeeding period, the risk of transmitting HIV to their children is extremely low. To achieve safe breastfeeding among mothers living with HIV, scaling up treatment services and adherence counselling and support within health facilities at the community level are required.

Social norms, taboos and traditional practices significantly influence feeding behaviours

What are young children eating?
The importance of first foods

FIGURE 2.3 | **Percentage of children aged 6–23 months fed food groups, by type, global, 2018***

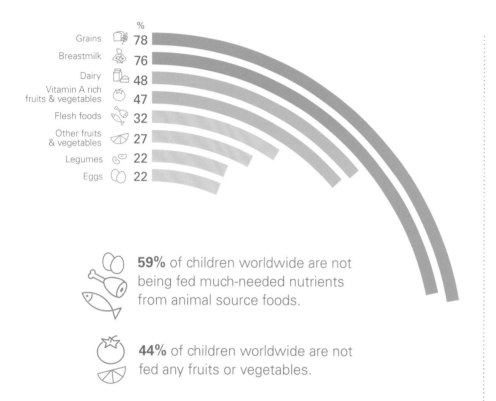

%
Grains 78
Breastmilk 76
Dairy 48
Vitamin A rich fruits & vegetables 47
Flesh foods 32
Other fruits & vegetables 27
Legumes 22
Eggs 22

59% of children worldwide are not being fed much-needed nutrients from animal source foods.

44% of children worldwide are not fed any fruits or vegetables.

When children start eating soft, semi-solid or solid foods at 6 months old, they need nutritious and safe diets with a range of nutrients to grow well.

Without enough diversity in children's diets, they may not get enough nutrients to grow well, which can take a devastating toll on children's bodies and brains. **UNICEF and WHO recommend that children at this age eat a minimum of five of eight food groups.**

FIGURE 2.4 | **Percentage of children aged 6–23 months eating at least 5 of 8 food groups (Minimum Dietary Diversity), by UNICEF region, 2018****

Fewer than **1 in 3 children** eats foods from the minimum number of food groups

% 29 20 24 25 36 40 60

Global | South Asia | Eastern and Southern Africa | West and Central Africa | Middle East and North Africa | East Asia and Pacific | Latin America and the Caribbean

FIGURE 2.5 | **Percentage of children aged 6–23 months eating at least 5 of 8 food groups by wealth quintile and place of residence, global, 2018*****

Only **1 in 5 children from the poorest households and rural areas** eats foods from the minimum number of food groups

% 21 38 23 39

Poorest | Richest | Rural | Urban

* Analysis based on a subset of 71 countries with data available between 2013–2018 covering 61 per cent of the global population.
** Regional and global estimates based on the most recent data for each country between 2013–2018.
*** Analysis based on a subset of 74 countries with disaggregated data available between 2013–2018.

Source for all figures pages 60–61: UNICEF Global Databases, 2019.

2 in 3 children aged 6–23 months are not eating foods from the minimum number of food groups

FIGURE 2.6 | **Percentage of children aged 6–23 months fed food groups, by type, by World Bank income group, 2018**

While the vast majority of young children consume breastmilk, they are not eating enough animal source foods, fruits, legumes or vegetables and rely too heavily on grains.

Except for breastmilk, the percentage of young children consuming any of the other 7 food groups is systematically higher in upper-middle-income countries than in low- and lower-middle-income countries.

The percentage of children consuming non-dairy animal source foods such as eggs, meat, poultry and fish in upper-middle-income countries is nearly twice as high as those in low- and lower-middle-income countries.

FIGURE 2.7 | **Percentage of children aged 6–23 months fed food groups, by type and age, global, 2018**

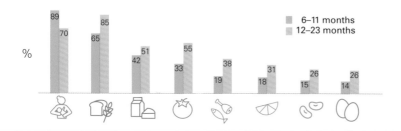

Younger children are eating less diverse diets compared to children 1–2 years of age.

Note for Figure 2.7: Analysis based on a subset of 71 countries with data available between 2013–2018 covering 61 percent of the global population. Income groupings are based on the FY19 World Bank income classification. Estimates by World Bank income groups are only displayed if available data represents at least 50 percent of the population.

*To meet adequate population coverage, upper-middle-income countries do not include Brazil, China and the Russian Federation.

Children aged 6–23 months can suffer lifelong consequences if they eat unhealthy diets that lack diversity and rely on foods high in sugar and fat and low in essential nutrients

Balancing work with childcare

Unfortunately, working mothers worldwide face barriers to breastfeeding. Mothers in the workforce need a supportive environment, including paid maternity and parental leave and breastfeeding breaks for working mothers. In a 2015 study involving 11,025 participants from 19 countries, maternal employment was the most frequently cited barrier to exclusive breastfeeding.[28] Attention paid at a national level to supporting working mothers in the workplace can have significant effects. Viet Nam, for example, extended paid maternity leave in 2012 from four to six months – a bold departure from other maternity leave policies in Southeast Asia. Since then, the government has mandated all workplaces with a substantial female workforce to offer childcare facilities and lactation spaces.[29]

The importance of complementary foods and why children are not getting them

When children are around 6 months old, breastmilk is insufficient to provide all the energy and nutrients they need. Their nutritional needs for growth and development between 6 and 23 months are greater per kilogram of bodyweight than at any other time of life, making them especially vulnerable to nutritional deficiencies and growth faltering. Introducing a healthy and diverse range of complementary foods along with breastfeeding can help protect against illness and death, while also ensuring healthy growth and development and preventing overweight/obesity later in life. Equally, children between 6 and 23 months can suffer lifelong consequences if they

eat unhealthy diets that lack diversity and rely on foods that are high in sugar and fat and low in essential nutrients.

It is recommended that infants start eating complementary foods at 6 months, but globally only over two thirds of infants aged 6–8 months are eating complementary foods. However, far too many begin much earlier. Nearly half of children 4–5 months of age and around 15 per cent of infants 2–3 months of age are already eating foods in Latin America and Caribbean and East Asia and Pacific regions.[30] In the United States, 21 per cent of infants 0–5 months of age consume grains, and this is higher among African-American infants (34 per cent).[31]

Starting from 6 months of age, children benefit especially from foods of animal origin, including meat, fish, eggs and dairy products, which are effective in providing them with essential nutrients and vitamin A, iron, zinc and calcium that are so needed between the ages of 6 and 23 months. Animal-source food (ASF) supports growth and physical activity and strengthens cognitive performance. ASF is densely packed with a range of essential micronutrients, well suited to the smaller stomachs of younger children. Stunting in early childhood is also associated with low consumption of ASF.[32] But ASF – especially eggs and dairy – are expensive in low-income, rural areas, and consumption is lower (*see Chapter 3*). Globally, only two in five children are being fed ASF. Fish – which is relatively cheap and protein-dense with micronutrients – is a major part of young children's ASF diets in lowland areas of Africa and Asia.[33]

SPOTLIGHT
Complementary feeding and behaviour change in Rwanda

Denise is a voluntary community health worker in Akabacuzi Village, where the legendary 1,000 hills of Rwanda begin to slide into the drier, flatter savannahs. Twenty-two children in her village used to suffer from undernutrition, but today, not a single child is considered either severely or moderately undernourished. Much of this improvement is due to Denise's efforts to ensure parents know what and how to feed their youngest children and put that knowledge into practice.

Through cooking sessions in her home, Denise demonstrates techniques to prepare nutritious food. Recently, she showed other mothers how to make beet juice, which is rich in vitamins and minerals. Moth-ers with children in their arms gath-ered to share the juice, poured into plastic cups. Previously, parents in this community would have thought it natural to feed young children a diet heavy in carbohydrates such as potatoes. Now they know this is not enough: diverse fruits, legumes, grains, vegetables, and sources of protein such as eggs, fish, meat and dairy products need to be a regular part of their diet.

Denise and her fellow community health workers across Rwanda are in the vanguard of the fight against undernutrition, for which prompting behaviour change is a core strate-gy. To encourage better use of local resources, the government rolled out the '1,000 Days for 1,000 Hills' campaign, which pushed out mes-sages across various channels, in-cluding community radio stations, community health workers (who hold monthly growth-monitoring sessions and cooking demon-strations), agricultural technicians (who teach communities to create kitchen gardens), and members of village savings and loans groups. Parliamentarians, religious leaders and journalists also helped spread campaign messages.

"At first, people did not think about feeding children vegetables and other healthy foods," Denise says. "Now we know what a balanced diet is. As long as we keep informing and encouraging people, no more children here will be malnourished." ■

During a nutrition session, Denise, a Community Health Worker, demonstrates how to prepare beet juice for a group of women in Gatsibo District, Rwanda. © UNICEF/UN0301144/Noorani

Fruits, vegetables, legumes, nuts and seeds are also important, not only as good sources of vitamins, minerals and fibre, but also because children who learn to enjoy eating a variety of fruits, vegetables, legumes, nuts and seeds are likely to go on eating them into adulthood.

Fortification

In many parts of the world, local foods alone cannot meet young children's high nutrient requirements. Fortified complementary foods or multiple micronutrient powders can help close these gaps. Around the world, a range of fortified blended foods high in proteins and micronutrients are distributed through social protection and supplementary feeding programmes, to provide extra food and nutrients beyond what is normally provided at home.[34]

For instance, fortification products such as micronutrient powders enable caregivers to add essential vitamins and minerals to foods prepared at home for young children, reducing forms of hidden hunger, such as iron deficiency and anaemia. As of 2017, programmes providing micronutrient powders had been implemented in at least 47 countries, reaching over 16 million children aged 6–59 months. Infants and young children also benefit from eating large-scale, centrally processed fortified foods such as iodized salt, iron-fortified flours and vitamin-A-fortified oil. For example, in Nairobi, Kenya, such products meet around a quarter of the vitamin A requirement and half the iron requirement of children between 6 and 23 months of age.[35]

Finally, biofortification – the process of breeding staple food crops with

higher micronutrient content – can reach vulnerable young children living in rural areas with limited access to diverse diets and commercially marketed fortified foods.[36] In 2017, an estimated 5 million under-5s in 14 countries in Africa, Asia and Latin America were consuming biofortified staple foods, including iron-rich beans, provitamin-A-rich maize, cassava and sweet potato, and zinc-rich wheat and rice.

Influences on young children

As any parent knows, infants and toddlers can be fussy eaters. Taste and food preferences can change from week to week and parents often offer what the child prefers. Young children's innate preference for sweet foods is helping to drive the increase in the consumption of commercial snack foods such as cookies, cakes and sweets and sugar-sweetened beverages in low-income countries.[38] A 2016 study of feeding practices among young children in Dakar, Dar es Salaam, Kathmandu and Phnom Penh found that the biggest reason for mothers feeding their children chocolates, sweets, cookies, chips or crisps, and cakes was that "the child likes it", far outweighing other factors such as affordability, convenience or perceptions that the foods were healthy.[39] The study found that, in all four cities, young children were more likely to eat commercially produced snack foods than foods rich in micronutrients, such as leafy green and orange-fleshed vegetables.

At the same time, a growing body of evidence from high-income countries indicates that commercial foods available on the market do not always deserve the 'healthy halo' that they tend to have among parents. Evidence of widespread inappropriate promotion of commercial

Children who are hungry at school struggle to pay attention and complete tasks and score worse on cognitive tests

SPOTLIGHT
Mothers' clubs take a stand against malnutrition in Haiti

Jacqueline Saintil is determined to breastfeed her 3-month-old baby James exclusively until he is 6 months old and then to give complementary food in addition to breastmilk to keep him healthy. "My 5-year-old Ervens was not exclusively breastfed. After three months, I gave him water and food almost every day. He was not a very strong baby," she explains.

The 25-year-old mother, who sold second-hand clothes before she gave birth to James, grows beans in a small garden that she can now harvest and sell because of the training in nutrition she has received. "I will make vegetable soup, with corn and dry fish, to feed my son when he's six months," she adds.

Jacqueline acquired her nutritional knowledge from the local Paillant Mothers' Club in her town of Les Nippes. Thanks to a set of cards with simple drawings, she and 29 other women were taught how to help prevent their children catching diseases or suffering from malnutrition. They learned that breastmilk contains all the nutrients required by babies and no other food or liquid is necessary until the age of 6 months. They were also shown how to make nutrient-dense meals of purees using local ingredients.

In mothers' clubs, community counsellors advise parents and caretakers of children aged under 5. Each week, mothers meet to discuss one theme on child well-being and development.

A total of 411 women have been trained in 20 clubs in Les Nippes. The club is participative, interactive and joyful. The training raises women's self-esteem and social status within their communities. Women were so proud of their achievements that they organized a graduation ceremony at their own expense. According to Beatrice Rubin of the Paillant health centre, vaccine coverage is nearly 100% for ante- and post-natal consultations as women from the club educate their peers. Referrals of malnourished children are more numerous since the course started.

Prevention of malnutrition is key in Haiti, which is characterized by chronic poverty coupled with a deep socio-economic crisis. Only 40% of infants aged under 6 months are exclusively breastfed, 11% of 6–23-month-old children are fed following minimum acceptable feeding practices, and more than 1 in 5 children aged under 5 years is stunted.[37] ∎

Jacqueline breastfeeds 3-month-old James. © UNICEF/Haiti/2019/Seck

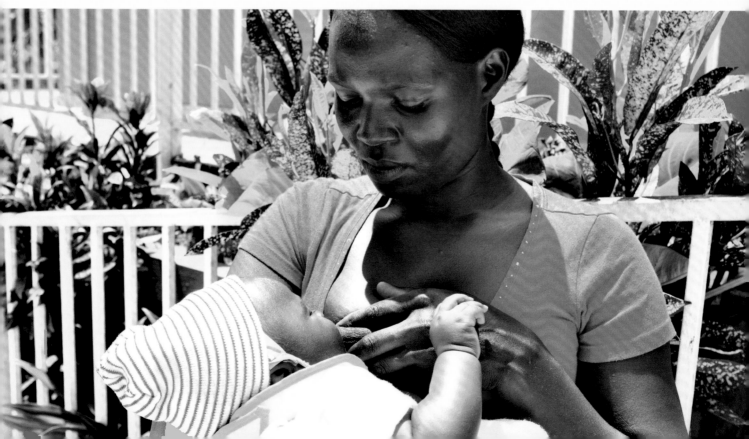

As children grow into toddlerhood, they start to choose their own food and are exposed to new influences aside from their parents and caregivers

foods includes labelling that encourages early introduction, products with high amounts of sugar, use of artificial flavours, inappropriate consistency for developing eating behaviours, and various nutritional and health claims.[40]

As children grow into toddlerhood, from the ages of 2 to 4 years, they start to choose their own food and, in many instances, eat outside the home, opening them to new influences aside from their parents and caregivers. At this age, positive models of eating from parents, caregivers, siblings, educators and peers become more important and influential.[41]

Health professionals also play a major role in influencing parents through information, support, counselling and

care (*see Chapter 3*). With three quarters of all newborns delivered with the help of a skilled birth attendant, these providers have a significant impact on breastfeeding uptake and practices.

In many parts of Africa, Asia and Latin America, mothers-in-law and grandmothers are especially influential on how infants and young children are fed. However, their advice can often be inappropriate – insisting, for example, that colostrum is 'dirty' and urging mothers to hold off feeding animal-source foods until the child is 18 months of age.[42] Grandmothers can negatively influence exclusive breastfeeding either through providing advice on early introduction of water and/or foods or actively feeding the infant themselves during the first six months.[43]

BOX 2.1 | Responsive feeding

How a caregiver and child interact helps to shape long-term behaviours and attitudes toward food. Responsive feeding – the process of recognizing cues for hunger and fullness and responding to them appropriately – helps develop healthy eating habits beginning in infancy and limits child underweight and obesity.

Responsive feeding is grounded in several key principles for caregivers:
- ➤ Attend to the child's signals of hunger and satiety
- ➤ Recognize and respond to the child's feeding needs in a prompt, emotionally supportive and developmentally appropriate manner
- ➤ Ensure the availability of healthy food
- ➤ Create a safe and comfortable eating environment with few distractions.[46]

Non-responsive feeding is characterized by a lack of reciprocity between the caregiver and child. It can reflect situations where the caregiver takes control and

dominates the feeding situation; where the child controls the situation; or where the caregiver ignores the child. When caregivers dominate feeding, they can not only override the child's internal hunger and satiety cues, but also interfere with the child's development of autonomy and independence.

According to a 2011 study, responsive feeding promotes a child's acceptance of food and adequate intake.[47] Feeding infants and young children in response to hunger and satiety cues, instead of using food as a soothing strategy, can improve sleep behaviours, which can then help the child to be more physically active when awake and to better self-regulate their appetite.[48] A 2015 review concluded that responsive feeding interventions are the most promising obesity prevention measures for children under 2 years of age.[49] Lack of responsive feeding increases the risk of suboptimal growth and development in environments where undernutrition is prevalent. ■

Finally, the modern food system exerts a significant influence on young children's diets. The retail sector determines the availability of and access to breastmilk substitutes, toddler drinks and other foods specifically targeted at young children, while advertising, packaging and placement of unhealthy snacks in supermarkets can make it difficult for parents and children to make healthy food choices.[44] The private sector can contribute in positive ways when it increases the availability, affordability and quality of complementary foods and supplements, distributing these products through channels such as retail markets, public health systems and social marketing, and generating demand for them among consumers (see Special Section 'Influence of food marketing on children's diets', Chapter 4).[45]

Middle childhood: A time of transition (ages 5–9)

When children start going to primary school, lifelong dietary habits continue to be developed. A child's family, school and broader social forces all affect food availability and food choices, but children also start taking some responsibility for their own diets. This period of transition is important for establishing healthy eating habits. At this age, traditional gender roles and expectations begin to take hold for many children in low- and middle-income settings, with girls often helping out in the kitchen and caring for younger siblings, and boys assisting in income generation.[50]

This period of childhood is marked by continued, steady growth. How much children eat during this phase

can vary widely. Appetites and food intake can increase before growth spurts and decrease during slower growth periods.[51]

Research also shows the potential for children to catch up during this age after early stunting. One study conducted in 2010 in Peru found that stunted children who caught up by the age of 6 years did as well in cognitive tests as non-stunted children.[52]

Nutritional needs and patterns

Far too many school-age children around the world are eating too little fruits and vegetables and too many unhealthy snacks that are high in sugar, saturated fat, sodium and salt, for example in bread, cookies, sweets, ice cream and sweetened beverages that are often marketed to and popular among school-age children. Low consumption of fruits and vegetables is common – a worrying phenomenon given that children who eat fruits and vegetables in childhood are more likely to continue doing so into adulthood.[53] Many government departments of health recommend five portions of fruit and vegetables a day, but it is clear that many children are not getting anywhere close to these amounts. In a Brazilian study, for example, no children aged 7–8 years met the diet quality index for vegetables. Children in developing countries, especially in poorer households and rural areas, tend to have diets made up of a few staples such as cereals, roots or tubers with little protein.[54]

Across higher and lower income countries and across food systems, there is a clear relationship between diet, cognitive development and academic achievement.[55]

© UNICEF/UN0283275// Frank Dejongh

Overweight and obesity in middle childhood has both short- and long-term effects

Hunger is an important factor. Energy is essential for concentration and participation in school activities, so children who have an empty stomach and feel hungry at school – from skipping breakfast or not eating enough – struggle to pay attention and complete tasks.

Hidden hunger also impairs school performance; certain micronutrient deficiencies affect learning. According to research, iron deficiency is linked with lower test scores.[56] Anaemia can cause fatigue and prevent children from paying attention in class. Eating an adequate diet regularly (in particular at breakfast) has been associated with higher academic achievement, while ultra-processed snacks and fast food may have negative associations.[57]

The effects of **early malnutrition** have long-term consequences. The impacts of nutrient deficiencies in utero or in early childhood affect school performance: for example, stunting serves as a predictor of poor educational outcomes throughout childhood.[58]

Reflecting the link between diet and school performance, some school-feeding programmes emphasize a diverse diet in foods that provide a range of nutrients. For example, Bhutan's school-feeding programme benefits around 45 per cent of the country's total student population. Micronutrient deficiencies are a major challenge – one in three adolescent girls in Bhutan is anaemic, and iron deficiency is thought to be a major cause. In 2017, a government analysis revealed that Bhutan's school menus were deficient in many micronutrients, particularly iron, B vitamins and zinc, and did not provide adequate dietary diversity. Recognizing

these challenges, several initiatives have been launched. Rice, the Bhutanese staple food, has been fortified and is now supplied to all schools. School menus are also reviewed to increase diversity and nutrition in meals.

School-age nutritional risks and concerns

Overweight (and obesity) in middle childhood has both short- and long-term effects. In the short term, it can raise cardiovascular risk factors, including type 2 diabetes, high blood pressure, high LDL cholesterol, and even atherosclerosis, and may also be linked to illnesses including asthma and low-grade systemic inflammation.[59] Through its impact on the immune and pulmonary systems, overweight and obesity raise the risk of infections,[60] an impact that may be particularly severe for hospitalized children.[61] Childhood obesity is also linked to psychological and social problems, including low self-esteem, self-image and behavioural problems. Girls appear to be at greater risk, and the risk increases with age.[62] In the long term, childhood overweight and obesity increase the risk of adult overweight five-fold[63] and is associated with a range of metabolic disorders in adulthood, including diabetes, stroke, high triglycerides, heart disease and hypertension.[64]

Research has found that children in sub-Saharan Africa, especially in urban areas and among higher-income households, are sitting more and exercising less, which has implications for their health and nutrition.[65] In this, they are following the example of children in high-income countries, who now spend more than half their school day sitting in classrooms,[66] and are spending more time sitting watching television or other screens at home.

Missing breakfast

Despite the clear evidence of its benefits, school-age children around the world commonly miss or skip breakfast, depriving them of a meal that particularly supports cognition, especially among undernourished children.[67] The reasons vary, but far too many children from poorer backgrounds have no choice – their families simply lack the resources or time to feed them in the morning. Many must rely on food provided or acquired at school instead. According to a WHO report, two-thirds of countries in Africa, the Americas and Southeast Asia provide school meals, but meal provision is less common in Europe and the Western Pacific.[68] For many children, therefore, the evening meal is the main meal, meaning they spend much of the day feeling hungry, which interferes with their attention in class and affects school performance, an effect recorded, for example, among children in Ghana and Uganda.[69]

It may seem counter-intuitive, but in some settings, children who miss or skip breakfast have a higher BMI than their peers who do not. According to research conducted in New Zealand in 2007, this is because children who miss or skip breakfast subsequently eat more snacks – cookies, sweets, chips or crisps, and sweetened carbonated drinks that are high in calories but low in nutrients – between meals.[70]

It is important to note that data on what school-age children eat are limited. In many studies, children complete questionnaires at schools without the involvement of their parents, while younger children have trouble self-reporting their food intake – overestimation of food intake is common.[71] Among older students, body image concerns can result in less accurate reporting, and under-reporting is likely especially among those who are overweight or perceive themselves to be overweight.[72]

The school environment

In many countries, the school food environment promotes the consumption of unhealthy foods and overweight and obesity. Ultra-processed foods and sugar-sweetened beverages are often sold to children in school cafeterias or at convenience stores and street stalls outside schools.

Changing the food environment to provide healthier foods is not easy. For example, Mexico has taken action in recent years to reduce the availability of unhealthy foods in schools, but it continues to face challenges. In 2010, the government established food and beverage guidelines for elementary schools. However, in 2017, a study of 39 schools showed that energy-dense foods prohibited in the guidelines were still widely available, while vegetables, fruits, and plain water accounted for less than 7 per cent of the foods and drinks available in schools.[73] In addition, advertisements for sugar-sweetened beverages, pastries and sweets, many featuring gifts or special promotions, remain common outside schools, particularly state schools, and can influence food and drink choices among children.[74]

In many countries, the school food environment promotes the consumption of unhealthy foods and overweight and obesity

> Adolescents are especially vulnerable to undernutrition, in part because their rapid physical growth and development during puberty raises their nutritional needs

Padma, 17, chats with members of the Adolescent Girls' Club at Muttock Tea Estate, Dibrughar district, Assam, India. The club raises local awareness about the risks of drinking salt tea.
© UNICEF/UN0324156/Boro

Adolescence: Crucial years for lifelong nutrition (ages 10–19)

Adolescence is a time of rapid physical and psychosocial development and changes that accompany puberty. Boys have higher nutrient requirements due to a faster growth rate and greater gain in bone growth and muscle mass; girls are especially vulnerable to malnutrition, and gendered cultural norms mean they often lack access to nutritious food, education and economic opportunity.[75] Adolescent girls also have higher iron requirements than boys because of growth spurts and the onset of menstruation.

With an estimated 1.25 billion people aged between 10 and 19 in 2020, there will be 250 million more adolescents compared with just 30 years ago. Proper nutrition for this large cohort is important for both their current and future well-being. Yet around the world, adolescents routinely fail to consume diets that would give them the foundation for long, healthy and productive adult lives. In rural areas, they often have limited food options and are susceptible to seasonal food shortages. In urban areas, they are surrounded by fast food and nutrient-poor snacks and drinks. In all settings, unhealthy snacks tend to be eaten. Hidden hunger affects tens of millions.

Adolescent dietary habits and risks

As with younger children, the diets of adolescents in low- and middle-income countries are generally nutritionally poor. Among school-going adolescents, 34 per cent consume fruit and 21 per cent vegetables less than once a day, but 42 per cent drink carbonated soft drinks at least once a day. Just under half (46 per cent) consume fast food at least once a week. Half of adolescent girls in low-income and rural settings in low- and middle-income countries eat fewer than three meals a day, with most missing or skipping breakfast. Snacking is common during school hours, and lunch is usually eaten outside the home.[76]

Adolescent dietary habits vary across country income groups

FIGURE 2.8 | **Adolescent diets based on World Bank income group, 2008–2015**

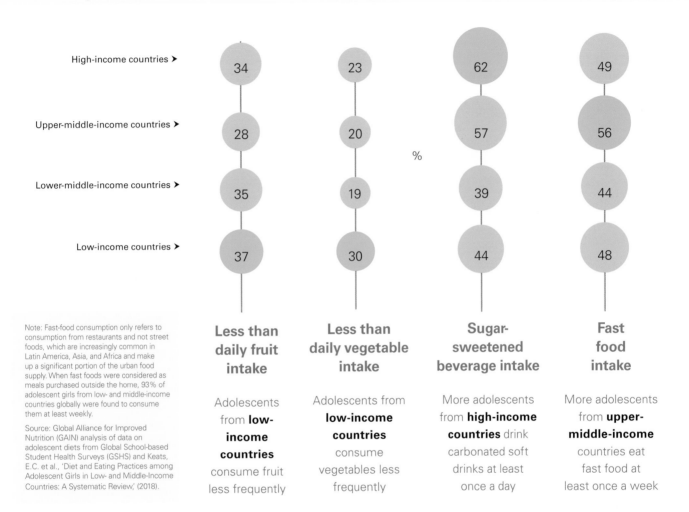

High-income countries ➤

Upper-middle-income countries ➤

Lower-middle-income countries ➤

Low-income countries ➤

	Less than daily fruit intake	Less than daily vegetable intake	Sugar-sweetened beverage intake	Fast food intake
High-income	34	23	62	49
Upper-middle-income	28	20	57	56
Lower-middle-income	35	19	39	44
Low-income	37	30	44	48

%

Less than daily fruit intake

Adolescents from **low-income countries** consume fruit less frequently

Less than daily vegetable intake

Adolescents from **low-income countries** consume vegetables less frequently

Sugar-sweetened beverage intake

More adolescents from **high-income countries** drink carbonated soft drinks at least once a day

Fast food intake

More adolescents from **upper-middle-income** countries eat fast food at least once a week

Note: Fast-food consumption only refers to consumption from restaurants and not street foods, which are increasingly common in Latin America, Asia, and Africa and make up a significant portion of the urban food supply. When fast foods were considered as meals purchased outside the home, 93% of adolescent girls from low- and middle-income countries globally were found to consume them at least weekly.

Source: Global Alliance for Improved Nutrition (GAIN) analysis of data on adolescent diets from Global School-based Student Health Surveys (GSHS) and Keats, E.C. et al., 'Diet and Eating Practices among Adolescent Girls in Low- and Middle-Income Countries: A Systematic Review,' (2018).

Nutrient deficiencies, overweight/obesity and pregnancy

Adolescents are especially vulnerable to undernutrition, in part because their rapid physical growth and development during puberty raises their nutritional needs. The absence of adequate nutrition risks undermining this crucial period of growth and development, an impact that is compounded for the 16 million girls between 15 and 19 years old and the 2.5 million girls under age 16 in developing countries who give birth each year.[77]

Diet and nutrition play a key role in brain development right into adulthood. Undernutrition in adolescence is associated with impaired cognitive function, school absenteeism and psychological stress.[78] As Dr Neville Golden, a member of the American Academy of Pediatrics Committee on Nutrition and chief of adolescent medicine at Stanford University School of Medicine in California, has said, "If [teens] don't eat right, they can become irritable, depressed [and] develop problems such as obesity and eating disorders – and those have a whole host of psychological morbidities."[79]

While prevention of stunting in the first 1,000 days remains a priority, adolescence provides a second window of opportunity for high return on investment with nutritional interventions

There is evidence that sugar is particularly harmful for the adolescent brain, which is especially responsive to rewarding behaviours. The consumption of tasty foods high in sugar, salt and/or fat is hard to resist, but research in animal models indicates that individuals who drank sugar water during adolescence showed less motivation and pursued rewards as adults, behaviours that signify depression and other mood disorders.[80]

Iron deficiency is a particular area of concern. To support their rapid growth and physical development, adolescents need sharp increases in the intake of certain vitamins and minerals, especially iron and especially for girls. Iron deficiency and iron deficiency anaemia are the leading causes of adolescent disability-adjusted life years (DALY) lost by girls aged 10–19 and boys ages 10–14 (one DALY can be thought of as one lost year of 'healthy' life). Despite improvements in South Asia, rates of iron deficiency and associated anaemia there remain the highest in the world, followed by sub-Saharan Africa.[81]

After iron deficiency, iodine deficiency is the second most common form of hidden hunger among adolescents. Global iodine status improved between 2003 and 2017, with the number of iodine-deficient countries decreasing from 54 to 19 and the number of countries with adequate iodine intake increasing from 67 to 111.[82] Although the DALY rate has gone down across regions from 1990 to 2015, progress has slowed in recent years.

Overweight, obesity and associated NCDs are increasing among adolescents in most regions of the world.[83] While rising trends have plateaued in many

high-income countries, although at high levels, they have accelerated in parts of Asia. Losing weight is hard. A child who becomes obese during adolescence is likely to remain so into adulthood and to face higher risks of NCDs such as type 2 diabetes. There is some evidence that obesity in adolescence can have lifelong negative effects on the brain, contributing to early onset of cognitive dysfunction during ageing.[84]

Pregnancy brings its own set of nutritional vulnerabilities. Each year, around 16 million adolescent girls aged 15–19 give birth. Most come from disadvantaged backgrounds and, as such, often have inadequate nutritional status before conception; as nutrient requirements increase during pregnancy, these risks are compounded.[85] Pregnant adolescents are at increased risk of malnutrition due to the competing growth and needs of the foetus.[86] Studies have shown that adolescent pregnancy carries a greater risk of complications and stunting of a girl's growth while also leading to a higher risk of health complications around the time of childbirth.[87] Negative consequences for offspring are much greater for early adolescent pregnancies (younger than age 16) than for late adolescent pregnancies (aged 16–24).[88]

Catch-Up Growth

The rate of physical growth during adolescence is rapid, second only to that in early childhood.[91] Healthy nutrition is vital in this period, and some evidence suggests that rapidly growing teens can even gain back some of the linear growth deficits suffered in early childhood, a phenomenon known as 'catch-up growth'. Typically, stunting prevalence decreases with age – that is,

SPOTLIGHT
In search of healthy habits in Indonesia

It's 8am and the sun is already scorching the sports yards in front of a high school in Klaten District, Central Java, Indonesia. There's basketball practice on one side and tennis on the other, but not everyone is joining in. "I don't like doing sports outside, there's so much dust, and it's hot!" Zahfa giggles. Judging by the number of her classmates chatting in the shade, she's not alone.

For many of the students, this sports class is the only physical activity they do all week. Their school day is long and does not give them time to exercise. Nor does it encourage healthy eating habits – students arrive at 6.45am and classes continue, with a few rest breaks, until late afternoon, which partly explains why missing breakfast is so common.

According to a 2017 UNICEF study, around half of Indonesian teenagers miss or skip daily breakfast at home, so their first meal of the day is made up of whatever they can get at school.[89] There's typically no regulation on what can be sold in school canteens, so what's available is largely left to the discretion of the school or vendors. Typically, the school curriculum also includes little about nutrition and healthy activities.

Factors such as these, as well as wider changes in diets (such as increased consumption of unhealthy foods) and industrialization have helped double rates of overweight in adolescents between 2004 and 2013. Indonesia has traditionally focused on reducing undernutrition, which remains a major problem – around 30 per cent of children under 5 have stunted growth.[90] Nevertheless, amid rising overweight, there's increasing awareness of the need to improve the knowledge, attitudes and behaviours of adolescents, their families and communities on healthy eating and physical activity.

That also means integrating nutrition and physical education messages into the school curriculum for students like Zahfa. "At home, I just watch TV," she says, "or I hang out with my friends, eating and chatting in the café." Although she does try to get to the gym once or twice a week, it's a challenge to fit it into her day. "School finishes at 4pm, so if I go to the gym, I don't get home until 6pm. It's tiring." ■

Zahfa at school in Klaten District, Central Java, Indonesia. © UNICEF/Indonesia/2018

To a teenager, the future can seem too abstract and far away to worry about the long-term effects of what they eat

some children who were stunted early achieve normal stature by adulthood.[92]

The potential for catch-up growth depends on many factors, including the severity of stunting experienced and the external environment during adolescence. Some evidence suggests that children who experience catch-up growth perform better on cognitive tests than their stunted peers who do not catch up.[93] Despite these promising findings, the physiological mechanisms underlying catch-up growth are complex, and measurement is difficult.[94] More evidence is needed on the extent to which physical and cognitive deficiencies can be eliminated.

While adolescence may provide an opportunity to catch up, gaining weight too rapidly in this period also poses

risks. Children who are undernourished usually reach puberty at a later age, as the body delays sexual maturation, allowing more time for growth.[95] Yet studies from Kenya and Senegal have found that when a stunted teen gains weight quickly, for example after moving from a rural area to a city or being adopted into an affluent environment, it triggers earlier puberty, so closing the 'window' for growth.[96]

Good nutrition is critical to support the increased biological demands of adolescence. While prevention of stunting in the first 1,000 days remains a priority, adolescence provides a second window of opportunity for a high return on investment with nutritional interventions. For some children, catch-up growth means a second, and perhaps final, chance to overcome the deficits suffered in early life.

BOX 2.2 | Eating disorders, diet and adolescent mental health

Concern over body size and physical appearance, rapid bodily changes, societal pressure for thinness, dieting and peer pressure all make adolescence a time of increased vulnerability to eating disorders.

The risk of developing an eating disorder is influenced by both genetic and environmental factors. Eating disorders run in families, and over 50 per cent of liability of developing an eating disorder is due to genetic factors.[97] Societal pressures to be thin in girls, and to have low body fat and high muscularity in boys, can lead to behaviours that may be the first step in a slippery slope toward eating disorders.[98] Other mental health problems seen in adolescence such as depression, anxiety and low self-esteem are also associated with eating disorders.[99] Eating disorders are more common in girls, but in part this is because they may be under-detected in boys.[100] Healthcare professionals may fail to recognize the symptoms of eating disorders in boys because they assume they are female-only disorders.

In addition to eating disorders, both healthy diets and food availability play a role in adolescent mental health. According to a study in the United States, among mothers, past-year food insecurity – lacking access to enough food for a healthy, active lifestyle – increases the risk for childhood behavioural problems (aggressive behaviours, anxiety/depression, and inattention/hyperactivity).[101] Mental health outcomes associated with food insecurity are not limited to childhood. Multiple US studies have reported an increased risk of past-year diagnoses of mood, anxiety and substance misuse disorders among adolescents reporting past-year food insecurity, independent of other aspects of socio-economic status.[102] Indeed, these associations have been reported in other countries, continuing in college and through young adulthood, highlighting the global importance of having adequate, healthy food available across all phases of development for both physical and mental well-being.[103] ■

Adolescent food choices

To a teenager, the future can seem too abstract and far away to worry about the long-term nutritional and health effects of what they eat. Health and nutrition are simply not a major influence on the diets of many adolescents.[104] Instead, external factors, such as disposable income to spend on snacks and fast food, peer pressure and the social desire to fit in among friends, body image issues, and food marketing can all play a role in influencing what adolescents eat.

Casual work and pocket money from parents provides irregular income, particularly in middle- and high-income countries, and is often used to buy unhealthy snacks.[105] As one teen in Iran says, "Sometimes I decide to start eating healthy, but then in the morning I see my mom hasn't prepared me a healthy snack and instead gives me money to buy snacks. Then it is natural that I go for buying things such as crisps and puffed cheese."[106]

Body image affects food choices as well. Depending on the local context, many adolescent boys want to gain weight and muscle mass, while many girls can be concerned about either excess weight or gaining weight as a sign of well-being and attractiveness. Eating disorders are not limited to high-income countries. Among young Tanzanian women aged 15–23, eating disorder symptoms increased with media exposure.[107]

Marketing, packaging and aspirational status symbols have a seductive pull on all consumers, but adolescents are especially influenced by these factors. Fast food and prepared snacks are widely available in urban areas worldwide and can be especially appealing to young people. Fast food restaurants, with their clean, bright interiors, are places where teens can hang out with friends.

For example, in Guatemala, the consumption of fast food and soft drinks is a sign of higher social status and upward mobility: "Being able to eat fast food was perceived as a sign that a family had middle- or upper-class status. Adolescents in … rural areas 'dreamt' of eating fried chicken in fast food restaurants, and adolescents from poorer economic backgrounds looked forward to consuming soft drinks on special occasions … They indicated that they purchased snacks because of the taste ('it just tastes good'), notions about the food ('it gives us energy'), and peer pressure and social acceptance ('we all buy it')."[108]

Conclusion

Each stage of childhood produces specific nutritional needs, eating behaviours and influences on diet. But whether it's not breastfeeding exclusively in the first few months, not eating a diverse diet in the early years, or consuming too much sugar, salt and fat during the adolescent years, children are not eating the diets they need in order to grow healthy, and this has lifelong consequences. The reasons why children are malnourished at different ages reflect a combination of drivers at the individual, family and broader societal levels. Widening our lens of analysis beyond each stage of childhood reveals the many causes of malnutrition. ■

The reasons why children are malnourished at different ages reflect a combination of drivers at the individual, family and broader societal levels

SPECIAL SECTION

What is a healthy diet?

What should children eat? It's a simple question, but for many parents and caregivers, and even children themselves, the answer is not straightforward. The exact make-up of a healthy diet depends on each individual and local contexts, but the basic principle of a healthy diet is one that contains fruits and vegetables, whole grains, fibres, nuts and seeds, and during the complementary feeding phase, animal source foods. Healthy diets limit free sugars, sugary snacks and beverages, processed meats, saturated and industrially produced trans-fats and salt.[109]

Ninety countries have developed food-based dietary guidelines, often based on recommendations from international organizations, into clear, understandable dietary advice that can also be visualized to aid communication.[110] However, these guidelines are often not specific to the different phases of children's development and rely on recommendations that are not harmonized globally. Countries also struggle to provide clear guidance in the context of rapidly changing modern food environments, with ultra-processed, packaged foods taking up more of children's daily diet. Dietary recommendations can also become politicized, with food producers pushing back if government recommendations urge the public to eat less of their products. We have remarkably little data on dietary intakes and food consumption patterns over time, which also affect the design and updates of such guidelines.

Most national dietary guidelines advise eating a varied diet of four to five food groups:

➤ fruits and vegetables (up to half of daily diets in many cases)

➤ whole grains and starchy foods

➤ healthy, lean proteins and dairy foods

➤ limited intake of sugar, fat and salt.

Across all child age groups, energy intake should be in balance with energy expenditure to prevent overweight and obesity. While a common guideline of an adequate diet applies throughout childhood, there are specific recommendations for birth to age 2:

➤ Exclusive breastfeeding from the first hour of life until 6 months of age, and continued breastfeeding until age 2

➤ Nutritious and safe complementary (soft, semi-solid and solid) foods should be progressively introduced starting at 6 months, with a particular emphasis on a diverse range of iron-rich, nutrient-dense foods without added salt, sugar or fat, such as lean animal-source foods (including eggs, meat, fish and dairy), fruits and vegetables, and legumes, nuts and seeds.

Debates about public health nutrition in the media and among policymakers have often been influenced by controversies, fads and lobbying by business-interest groups, with arguments often based only loosely on the scientific evidence, or misinterpretation or over-simplifying of the evidence. This can result in a muddying of the evidence that undermines policymakers' confidence to take action. Controversies over conflicts of interest in nutrition research funding, especially when provided by the food industry, have added to the public's confusion over what makes up a healthy diet. For example, industry-funded research investigating the health impact of sugar-sweetened beverages is overwhelmingly and consistently more likely to reach 'weak/null' conclusions compared with independent studies.[111] A lack of conflict-free funding to implement evidenced-based dietary recommendations and nutritional interventions limits the broad impact of dietary guidelines. Past nutrition policy and programmes have often relied on 'knowledge' as the driver of behaviour change, assuming that better dietary choices will be made through education and dietary guidelines. Knowledge alone is not enough to improve dietary intake, however, and broader policy, behaviour change and environmental strategies are needed, especially given low investment by governments

Cooked rice, vegetables, meat and beans are portioned for children into small bowls at the 'Baby Café' in Pandas Village in Klaten District, Central Java Province. Parents and grandparents come to the Café each morning to buy food prepared by 'cadres' (volunteer community health workers). 'Cadres' help improve children's nutrition by providing information and counselling to their mothers. © UNICEF/UN04263/Estey

in public education and communications campaigns compared to the food industry's investment in marketing. Even if they have nutritional information, consumers may choose unhealthier but tastier, less expensive or more convenient foods that are marketed to them.[112]

In recent years, Brazil has provided some common-sense public recommendations based on what and how people actually eat on a daily basis. Researchers looked at the available data and saw that people were cooking less at home and eating more processed, packaged foods, leading to nutritional problems such as overweight, obesity and diet-related NCDs. According to the University of Sao Paulo's Carlos Monteiro, whose Center for Epidemiological Studies in Health and Nutrition helped develop the guidance, "the more people used the ready-to-consume products, the more problems they had with the diet ... people

who preserve that pattern of having freshly prepared dishes had the best diet. The good news is that these people are not the richest. They have lower income, many of them live in isolated places in Brazil." The recommendations provide guidance on what and how to eat (encouraging more cooking and eating with others at home) with one 'golden rule': always prefer natural or minimally processed foods and freshly made dishes and meals to ultra-processed foods.[113, 114]

While our understanding of what makes up a healthy diet for children has advanced in recent years, gaps remain in defining the optimal intake for children at specific ages and for those living in different geographic regions and in different food environments. Unlocking further understanding through funding and research can put in place better evidence-based dietary recommendations and effective nutritional interventions at scale.■

PERSPECTIVE

Women lead the way in community-based child nutrition in rural Tanzania

Scholastica Nguli
Founder,
Rondo Women's
Development
Organization,
Tanzania

Scholastica Nguli, the founder of the Rondo Women's Development Organization (ROWODO), has worked since 2011 to reduce child deaths caused by malnutrition in the Rondo area of Lindi region, Tanzania. ROWODO is a member of the Partnership for Nutrition in Tanzania (PANITA), a collection of 300 civil society organizations.

In Africa, rural, remote villages are often synonymous with poverty and malnutrition, but this is not the case for the small village of Rondo in south-eastern Tanzania, where women have simply refused to watch their children die or suffer from stunting. Instead, they have been educating their communities to adopt a lifestyle of healthy eating. They walk up to 7 kilometres conducting door-to-door calls on families or to give talks at health centres where women usually congregate. These women are undertaking these life-changing activities in addition to their demanding daily chores such as tilling the land, fetching firewood, preparing food for their families and taking care of their children.

Because a lack of awareness of breastfeeding is one of the factors behind the burden of child malnutrition in the Rondo area, Rondo Women's Development Organization (ROWODO) decided to spread their knowledge to healthcare facilities through household visits and public meetings to ensure that nutrition is placed high on the agenda – and ultimately to end hunger, achieve food security, improve nutrition and promote sustainable agriculture.

ROWODO faces a range of challenges that impair efforts to stop malnutrition. The first is cultural beliefs. Most communities in Rondo restrict breastfeeding soon after their child is born, throwing out breastmilk because they believe it is dangerous to their babies. This restricts babies' intake of important vitamins from their mother's first milk after birth.

Another challenge is the lack of gender equality. Since most of the men do not participate in domestic duties, mothers have a heavy workload, for example going to the well to fetch water, going to the forest to find firewood, preparing food for the family and cleaning the household. Because these mothers are so busy, child feeding is negatively affected.

There is also a problem of giving children food other than breastmilk before the age of 6 months. When a child cries repeatedly, many women believe they are crying because of hunger and that they are not satisfied with breastmilk. They start to give them porridge made from cassava flour, which is not suitable. Many families also go to traditional healers when their child is suffering instead of the hospital. This exacerbates malnutrition and the increasing incidence of deaths among children aged under 5 years.

© UNICEF/UNI197919/Schermbrucker

To fight malnutrition in Rondo ward, ROWODO:

➤ educates mothers, either one-on-one by visiting families or by hosting talks at maternal clinics, on the importance of exclusive breast-feeding after giving birth, at least until the baby is up to 6 months old

➤ teaches parents about the dangers of feeding babies under six months old foods other than their mother's milk

➤ provides information on the importance of feeding infants up to 2 years old with nutrient-rich food, such as cassava, lentils, beans and grains such as ulezi (millet) that are grown locally

➤ breaks old myths, for example one that says a pregnant woman should not eat eggs.

The women of Rondo have become the epitome of taking action at a time when most of society waits for government to fight malnutrition alone. Often, communities see malnutrition as too big a problem and feel that there is nothing they can do to change it. Yet the action by the women in Rondo demonstrates that there are solutions within the reach of communities to end malnutrition.

All interventions count, whether it is breastfeeding, washing hands before eating, keeping a clean environment, or drinking clean, safe water. There is no one specific approach that communities must adopt to help them accomplish significant change. The example of Rondo shows that collective action has a significant effect on bringing malnutrition in a community to an end. ■

03 MALNUTRITION IN A CHANGING WORLD

Globalization, urbanization, climate shocks and emergencies are worsening the nutritional prospects of millions of poor and excluded children. For many, lack of access to nutritious, safe, affordable and sustainable food is compounded by the threat of disease from poor water and sanitation. We need a nutrition transformation to ensure these children get the chance to fulfil their potential and to help end the flow of poverty across generations.

➤ Globalization has changed everything from crop harvesting to supermarket food displays. 77% of processed food sales worldwide are controlled by just 100 large firms.

➤ By 2050, 70% of the world's adolescents will live in cities, more exposed to the marketing of unhealthy foods and more vulnerable to diet-related diseases.

➤ Without action, future generations will likely face increased food insecurity and malnutrition brought on by climate change.

Ruma, 10, picks spinach on the roof of her family's shelter in the Kutupalong refugee camp in southeastern Bangladesh. "We will eat it tonight for dinner," she says. Her family receives food rations of rice and dal, but no fresh vegetables. "My two favourite things right now are studying and playing. I am a good student. Now, I can read. My dream is to become a language teacher." © UNICEF/UN0331082/Nybo

Because of poverty and exclusion, the greatest risk of all forms of malnutrition is shouldered by the most disadvantaged children

Introduction

Across urban and rural contexts, poor-quality diets threaten the survival, physical growth, brain development and life potential of poor and excluded children, setting them up to pass disadvantage down to the next generation. Even in an ever-changing world, this is as – if not more – accurate today as it was decades ago.

The world has undeniably changed. A growing body of evidence about nutrition – on the importance of maternal nutrition before and during pregnancy, on exclusive breastfeeding and diverse first foods, and on good care and hygiene practices in early childhood – is providing crucial insights to pave the way for good nutrition from the first 1,000 days into middle childhood, adolescence and adulthood and on to new generations.

Globalization, unplanned urbanization and climate shocks are also driving dietary changes, both positive and negative, and these changes are shaping families' food options and choices. Those who can afford it may have greater access to diverse and nutritious food, but for far too many, these benefits remain out of reach. Because of poverty and exclusion, the greatest risk of all forms of malnutrition, and, consequently, the heaviest non-communicable disease (NCD) risk burden is shouldered by the most disadvantaged children.

Emerging science

Nutritious food is necessary to ensure children grow well, but it's not sufficient. Around the world, diarrhoeal and other diseases undermine the nutrition of tens of millions of children, as do less well understood conditions such as chronic inflammations of the gut. Increasing evidence shows that poor diets are harming children's gut flora, raising their risk of infection, and that intergenerational cycles of malnutrition can also be the outcome of both maternal underweight and overweight.

Greater knowledge in areas such as hygiene and sanitation, the microbiome and epigenetics has the potential to prevent disease and poor nutritional outcomes from the first 1,000 days into adulthood.

Hygiene and sanitation

Malnutrition underlies 45 per cent of deaths in children under 5 years of age. Diarrhoea is particularly deadly when children are undernourished, killing over 700 children under 5 every day in 2016.[1] Most childhood cases can be traced back to unsafe drinking water, foods contaminated in the home, or faecal contamination from poultry and livestock. Improper sanitation helps spread infectious diseases and intestinal worms and encourages the development of conditions such as environmental enteric dysfunction.

Our understanding of the role of hygiene and sanitation in malnutrition is evolving. For example, recent research suggests that much higher levels of hygiene and sanitation are needed to safeguard children from stunting than was previously thought: "Conventional thinking is that improving access to food and educating families about hygiene will prevent childhood malnutrition, but these interventions keep failing," according to the lead author of a study

BOX 3.1 | Conceptual Framework of the Determinants of Maternal and Child Nutrition

When children and women eat well, everyone benefits. Children provided with a nutritious, safe and diverse diet are equipped for the physical and cognitive development, school performance and healthy life that awaits them.

For children to eat well at each stage of growth, not only must food be of good quality and consistently available, accessible and affordable, but several other factors must be in place. Their families need resources. These include money, but also knowledge of how to access and provide a healthy diet. They need support in the face of financial stress and time pressure. They need access

to quality health services and a healthy environment, free of disease and unsanitary conditions.

Children's diets are also determined by broader forces at play, such as political commitment, economic priorities and social norms.

To better understand and address these complex and far-reaching challenges, UNICEF has developed the 2020 Conceptual Framework of the Determinants of Maternal and Child Nutrition. It builds on UNICEF's 1990 framework on the causes of child undernutrition, acknowledges the evolving and multiple nature of maternal and child malnutrition, and

incorporates new knowledge on the drivers of malnutrition.

The Conceptual Framework uses a positive narrative about what contributes to improving maternal and child nutrition and preventing malnutrition in all its forms in children, adolescents and women. It provides conceptual clarity about the enabling, underlying and immediate determinants of maternal and child nutrition, and about the outcomes resulting from improved nutrition in children, adolescents and women (*see below*). The Framework guides UNICEF's 2020–2030 Global Strategy for Maternal and Child Nutrition.■

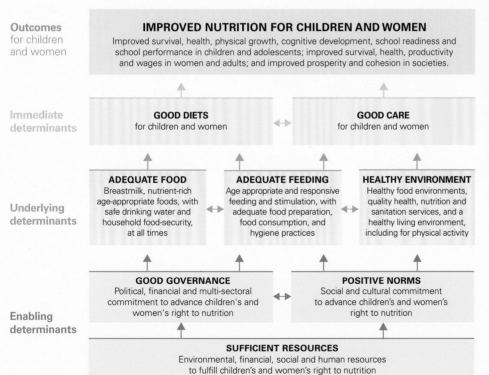

Children's diets are also determined by political commitment, economic priorities and social norms

Source: UNICEF. Maternal and Child Nutrition UNICEF Strategy 2020–2030. UNICEF: New York; 2019

Children washing their hands in a refugee camp in Betou, Republic of the Congo. © UNICEF/UN0327817/Diefaga

in rural Gambia.[7] "There's a very high threshold of hygiene necessary to allow children to grow properly – communities need improved living conditions and access to clean water piped into their homes. These findings should redirect governments' priorities, shifting efforts to providing drastically better housing, and better access to clean water."[8]

Food safety

Contamination of food – whether from the environment or from microorganisms – has dire implications for children's health. Infants and children are especially vulnerable to such threats because their metabolic system is still developing and key organ maturation is susceptible to permanent and lifelong disruption.[9]

BOX 3.2 | Environmental enteric dysfunction

The deleterious effects of acute diarrhoea on health are well known, yet in otherwise healthy populations, and those in which interventions have reduced diarrhoea, many children still do not achieve normal growth.[2] The exact cause of this growth failure is unknown, but there's increasing interest in the possible role of environmental enteric dysfunction (EED).

EED is a subclinical disorder where chronic exposure to faecal pathogens inflames and damages the intestines, reducing the body's ability to absorb nutrients. It is strongly associated with stunting and iron deficiency.[3] The condition is highly prevalent among people living in conditions of poverty.[4] Biomarkers for EED are found in children living in unsanitary household environments and are associated with high levels of stunting.[5]

EED may also play a role in poor cognitive development and educational achievement among children. A longitudinal study in eight low- and middle-income countries found an association between a higher number of enteric infections and poorer cognitive scores at 2 years of age, independent of diarrhoea.[6] ■

The best preventative measure for infants, who are especially vulnerable to foodborne and waterborne disease, is breastfeeding.

Parasites, viruses and bacteria – such as *Salmonella* and *E. coli* – naturally inhabit the surfaces of raw food and can cause serious illness. Without good hygiene practices such as regular handwashing with soap, the improper handling of food in preparation or storage can result in foodborne illness.

The impacts of contamination via water, air or soil and exposure to antibiotics and pesticides have been well documented in recent years and, in high-income countries in particular, have resulted in a demand for organic and pesticide-free foods. Researchers and the scientific community are also examining the effects of exposure to food additives and substances in contact with foods in its packaging, for example, plastics.

The microbiome

Often called the body's 'second brain', the gut microbiota has been the subject of growing research and attention in recent years. Its powerful effects on physical and mental health are becoming increasingly clear, as is its role in enhancing immune system functions.

Our bodies are home to trillions of microbes that play an instrumental role in nutrition and healthy growth. These tiny intestinal guests not only metabolize the food we eat and affect our weight and cognitive development,[11] but also strengthen our immune systems. They even predict our vulnerability to developing diseases, including obesity.[12]

By the age of 3, children have established most of their microbiome for life.[13] Whether the microbiome begins to develop during pregnancy or childbirth is still a matter of debate, but the first hours, days and years of life are critical. In childbirth, microbes from the birth canal and vagina are passed to the baby, inducing an important immune response. Breastfeeding and skin-to-skin contact starting in the first hour help create a healthy microbiome. Breastmilk contains proteins, human

Contamination of food has dire implications for children's health

Microbes tell the body whether it needs a particular type of food, through what's known as the 'gut–brain axis'

milk oligosaccharides and probiotics that improve health and brain development. Breastmilk has been called "probably the most specific personalised medicine that the child is likely to receive, given at a time when gene expression is being fine-tuned for life."[14]

Threats to this development include: exposure to antibiotics (in utero or in early life), birth by caesarean section, formula feeding and lack of diversified first foods. These disrupt microbiome establishment and can adversely affect nutrition and health,[15] for example by increasing a child's vulnerability to allergies and asthma.[16]

Adding diversified first foods to an infant's diet after the first six months of life adds bacterial variety that helps digest fibre, starch and proteins. A more diverse diet helps the microbiome perform a greater set of metabolic tasks. Adequate, largely plant-based diets high in fibres and proteins create healthy microbiomes.

By the same token, eating processed foods that are high in sugar, salt, fat and additives affects the microbiome in ways that can encourage obesity, diabetes and inflammatory bowel disease.[17] For example, some additives in foods such as mayonnaise and ice cream break down the protective barrier of mucus in the gut that separate microbes from the intestinal lining and produce proteins that inflame the gut.[18]

The gut microbiome also influences our food choices. Research shows that microbes communicate with the brain, telling the body whether it needs a particular type of food, through what's known as the 'gut–brain axis'. This might start even in breastfeeding, when the infant's needs are communicated to the mother via contact between saliva and the nipple in a feedback loop.[19]

There is still much to learn about the microbiome's role and development during the early years. For example, little is known about the gut microbiota of children in the first two years of life in low- and middle-income countries. More research is needed also on links between mothers' microbiomes during pregnancy and childbirth and infant stunting.[20]

BOX 3.3 | Additives

In the United States, an estimated 10,000 chemicals are allowed in food and its packaging, yet considerable knowledge gaps exist on the safety of these chemicals. The American Academy of Pediatrics (AAP) released a policy statement in 2018 asking for reforms to how food additives are regulated. It highlighted concerns over bisphenol A (BPA), phthalates, perfluoroalkyl substances, perchlorate, artificial food colours and nitrates/nitrites, given their links to endocrine disruption, attention-deficit hyperactivity disorder (ADHD), and chronic conditions such as cancer, type 2 diabetes and obesity.

In addition to better testing, closing data gaps and labelling additives, the AAP also recommend reducing exposure by eating more fresh or frozen fruits and vegetables, avoiding processed meats, handwashing with soap before handling food, washing fruits and vegetables, and avoiding putting plastic in a microwave or dishwasher.[10] ∎

BOX 3.4 | Epigenetics

Epigenetics is the study of changes in organisms brought about by modifications in gene expression. It is a change in phenotype (observable physical and biochemical traits) without a change to genotype (the inherited genetic composition of a cell, i.e. DNA). In other words, a person's environment or lifestyle can change which genes in their DNA sequence are expressed or not expressed, and that change can be passed down to their children.

For example, maternal micronutrient deficiencies can alter foetal metabolism and organ development, resulting in epigenetic changes in the child. This epigenetic adaptation puts children at increased risk of childhood overweight or obesity, and chronic diseases in adulthood, including obesity, coronary heart disease, stroke and type 2 diabetes.[22]

How does this happen? Put simply, the baby of an undernourished mother 'expects' a low-nutrient world. However, fed a diet high in calories (and low in nutrients), the child becomes predisposed to some forms of disease.[23] ∎

Intergenerational cycles of malnutrition

A mother's health and nutritional status is key to determining that of her child (*see Chapter 2*). Both maternal undernutrition and maternal overweight affect children's development, including that of their metabolism, "fueling an intergenerational cycle of malnutrition."[21] Much more research is needed on the complex impacts of maternal – and paternal – nutrition on children, especially in emerging areas such as epigenetics.

Amid growing global rates of obesity, increasing attention is being paid to the negative effects of maternal overweight and diabetes on health and nutrition outcomes for the mother herself and for her child and future generations.[24] Today, maternal overweight[25] is the most common risk factor of pregnancy.[26]

The association between maternal overweight and a child's risk of metabolic disease is remarkably strong across the life course. Studies from around the world have shown an association between maternal overweight and overweight in the next generation at the ages of 21, 32 and even – according to the Helsinki Birth Cohort Study – 62. That same study also found links between maternal overweight and children's physical and psychosocial functioning in late adulthood. [27, 28]

At the same time, examples of rapid improvements in tackling undernutrition – from Japan, South Korea and more recently Brazil[29] and Peru[30] – show that nutritional status can dramatically improve even within a single generation. A 2013 study of children in their first two years from Brazil, Ghana, India, Norway, Oman and the United States also concluded that, with adequate care and nutrition, children of parents who experienced adverse nutritional conditions can still attain optimum height.[31] To ensure that happens, women and girls – and especially adolescent mothers – need support and guidance on nutrition before pregnancy, for their own well-being and so as not to miss the window of opportunity of the first 1,000 days.

Both maternal undernutrition and overweight fuel the intergenerational cycle of malnutrition

SPECIAL SECTION

Girls and women need stronger support for better nutrition

As primary caregivers, women play a pivotal – if not the most crucial – role in whether children are eating well, yet far too many women are excluded from decision-making. They face early marriage and early pregnancy as girls, intrahousehold discrimination and domestic violence, restrictions to their education and employment opportunities, and gender-biased laws that limit their access to land and financing. What is more, far too many girls and women struggle with malnutrition themselves.

Poor diets are amplifying gender imbalances by reducing learning potential, increasing reproductive and maternal health risks and lowering productivity. These impacts are perpetuating intergenerational cycles of malnutrition and inequity: the children of malnourished mothers are more likely to suffer stunting, cognitive impairments, weakened immunity and a higher risk of disease and death.

Adolescent girls are especially vulnerable to malnutrition because they are experiencing their fastest physical growth since the first years of life. With menstruation, their bodies require more iron. Adolescent pregnancy – a major contributor to maternal and child mortality – presents particular risks because girls' bodies have not finished growing and the foetus might compete for nutrients.

Women are more vulnerable to micronutrient deficiencies, particularly iron deficiency anaemia. This unmet nutritional need for iron is linked to the greater likelihood of being poor, and lacking power and access to resources. Malnourished mothers confront major risks. These include a compromised immune system, greater risk of dying in childbirth, lower productivity and capacity to generate income, and greater difficulty in caring for their families.

When girls and women are denied the right to food, nutrition and health, children, households, communities and economies suffer. Conversely, when they are empowered to achieve higher levels of education, control more income, bring assets home and to make decisions, nutrition improves and everyone benefits, setting a virtual cycle in motion.

Women face a disproportionate work burden. While more likely than men to work as unpaid family labourers or in the informal sector, they also make up nearly 40 per cent of the world's formal labour force.[115] Yet, almost everywhere, mothers remain responsible for most child feeding and care.

As mothers increasingly take on new roles – as entrepreneurs, academics and community leaders, for example – many grapple with time poverty. The time and energy demands of multiple roles can make for a stressful, if not impossible, challenge to feed their children, and themselves, well. Without the support of their partner or family network – and without access to affordable, healthy foods – they may rely on the convenience of processed foods or fast foods.

Along the same lines, without the right workplace practices or national policies in place, mothers

Chantal, a tea plucker on the Rutsiro Tea Plantation in Rwanda, has four children. Before the plantation's early childhood development centre was built, Chantal would carry her daughter, Umuhoza, now 3, on her back all day when she worked. "It was very uncomfortable to pluck tea while carrying our children. We were also very unproductive because we had to stop and breastfeed and care for our children. We knew we were not giving them the best opportunities, but we had no choice. After the centre was built, we had more time. Our children are now doing well and we are more productive." In 2017, UNICEF Rwanda partnered with the National Agricultural Export Development Board to help tea plantations and factories be more family-friendly work environments. This includes advocating for paid maternity leave and breastfeeding breaks, flexible working hours for new parents and affordable child care options. © UNICEF/UN0308986/Rudakubana

might not be able to exclusively breastfeed or continue breastfeeding. Despite three ILO Conventions on Maternity Protection – the first was 100 years ago – most countries have made only slow progress in adopting policies to support breastfeeding.

To address this requires raising women's social status, autonomy and decision-making power. It requires enabling girls to stay in school longer to achieve better livelihoods and independence. It also requires investing in adolescent girls' and women's nutrition and health, with a particular focus on the pre-pregnancy, pregnancy and lactation periods.

To make the right nutrition decisions, women and mothers need adequate information, counselling, support and access to nutritious, safe, affordable and sustainable foods. They need maternity protection policies so that workplaces support exclusive and continued breastfeeding, and enough paid parental leave. A recent study recommends a minimum of six months' paid leave to ensure the best outcomes for mothers and children (this aligns with the WHO recommended duration for exclusive breastfeeding).[116] Gender-equitable parental leave policies that encourage fathers to use leave are also associated with reduced family stress, more involved parenting and more stable relationships. ■

77 per cent of processed food sales worldwide are controlled by just 100 large firms

Globalization

Globalization – the flow of goods, technologies, information, capital and more across country borders – has overtaken food systems. It has changed everything from the harvesting of crops to the way food is displayed in a supermarket to what children eat.

On the one hand, families who can afford it have access to a greater availability and diversity of food – quinoa, kimchi or year-round strawberries. On the other hand, with the expansion of ultra-processed and fast foods and the impact of marketing, multinational and transnational corporations are making it increasingly hard for children to eat well.

The rise of supermarkets, convenience stores and fast-food chains around the world reflects changes in both consumer demand and the supply of low-nutrient foods to consumers, including children and their caregivers. A quarter of a century ago, food supplies tended to be under the control of national governments, which focused heavily on food security. However, from the mid-1990s, food was included in world trade agreements. The result is that food systems are now exposed to business forces that have changed the availability, price and marketing of foods.

While there are millions of farmers, food producers and consumers, there are only a few large processors and marketers: 77 per cent of processed food sales worldwide are controlled by just 100 large firms.[32]

As the High Level Panel of Experts on Food Security and Nutrition points out in its 2017 report, "The progressive concentration of much of the economic power in the hands of transnational food corporations over the past decades has limited the domestic policy space and political power of local and national governments. In turn, this has reduced governments' ability to protect and promote the right to adequate food of their people."[33] The same report highlights that "those most impacted by inequitable, dysfunctional food systems and unhealthy food environments include

---

BOX 3.5 | Ultra-processed foods

Processing of food is not in and of itself undesirable. Many popular, traditional and nutritious foods are 'processed' – think of drying wheat or fruit or making yoghurt. However, not all food processing is the same, and nutrition specialists typically make a distinction between 'processed' and 'ultra-processed' foods. The latter have been defined as "industrial formulations"[36] containing little or no whole foods, but rather substances extracted from whole foods, for example "hydrogenated oils and fats, flours and starches, variants of sugar, and cheap parts or remnants of animal foods usually with little nutritional value compared to the original whole food."[37] These foods are energy dense, high in fat, sugar and sodium, and low in fibre and micronutrients – think of burgers, nuggets, cookies and sugary drinks.

Avoiding ultra-processed foods is not easy; nor are they designed for moderate consumption. Thanks to their high levels of fat, sugar, salt and other flavours, many ultra-processed foods taste delicious and feel satisfying in the mouth. Also, taking into account their heavy marketing – often aimed at children (see Chapter 4) – and wide availability, it is easy to see why such ultra-processed items displace fresh or minimally processed foods.■

low-income consumers, the rural and urban poor, smallholder and subsistence farmers and indigenous peoples."[34]

On the demand side, economic and climate forces are moving people to urban areas where lifestyle, socio-cultural pressures and marketing are changing diets (*see 'Urbanization' below*). The increasing availability and growing market share of ultra-processed foods, for example, presents a tremendous loss for traditional food markets, small-scale farmers and rural populations who can't compete with the big businesses or supermarket chains. In some cases, this is pushing rural families to move to urban areas in search of better livelihoods.

For some children, this means greater access to education, healthcare services and diverse foods. For others, urban life means dietary threats (greater exposure to fats, sugars, salt, etc.), sedentarism, environmental pollution and unsanitary or overcrowded living conditions.

Ultra-processed foods are at the heart of the globalization of food markets. As markets in high-income countries have matured, global or transnational food and beverage businesses have increasingly sought out new markets in low- and middle-income countries, including sub-Saharan Africa, which represents an "amazing opportunity", as the head of one fast-food business has said.[35]

Many of these businesses focus on ultra-processed food items because their low production cost, long shelf-life and high retail value make them highly profitable.

A street lined with market stalls in Freetown, Sierra Leone.
© UNICEF/UN072187/Phelps

The lack of public spaces drives adolescents to meet at fast-food chains instead

As a result, such foods are now almost ubiquitous, and found even in remote areas of Ethiopia and Nepal, where a choice of vegetables, fruits and fish is not.[38]

Some experts have argued that because the distribution chains of transnational food companies now reach so far into rural areas, urbanization is no longer the main factor in determining whether or not people, including children, have access to unhealthy foods.[39]

A recent global analysis of trends in mean body mass index (BMI) segregated by rural and urban areas from 1985 to 2017 found that in low- and middle-income regions (and with the exception of women in sub-Saharan Africa), adult BMI is increasing at the same rate or faster in rural areas than in cities. The authors cite the possible reasons as less energy spent on daily work and domestic chores, and, with increased incomes and a widening availability of food products high in fat, salt or sugar, increased consumption of low-quality calories[40] – in short, what has been called "the urbanization of rural life."[41]

Urbanization

Since the mid-20th century, the share of the world's population living in cities has risen from 30 per cent to more than half. Urban dwelling is only set to grow, significantly affecting children and young people. In 2009, around half the world's adolescents lived in cities; by 2050, that proportion is forecast to rise to 70 per cent.[42]

A common narrative is that dietary changes are happening first in urban areas, as are the consequent nutritional outcomes and increase in NCDs.[43] One reason for this is the change in lifestyle and environment. Compared to those in rural areas, urban residents rely less on starchy carbohydrates and tend to consume more meat and other proteins, more fruits and vegetables (among richer households), more food outside the home, and more ultra-processed foods.[44] The result is a higher prevalence of overweight and obesity among city dwellers. From Sri Lanka to India, from China to Benin, urbanization is also associated with high rates of diabetes, hypertension and cardiovascular disease.[45]

City life accounts for some of these trends: more sedentary jobs, less time and energy spent on domestic chores and greater use of public transport to get around, which can mean reduced physical activity.

For children living in cities, spaces for outdoor play might be hard to find or unsafe. This is important because children who get more exercise are less likely to be obese,[46] not only because exercise burns calories, but also because it changes how the body processes glucose and also likely benefits mental health and helps combat depression. The lack of public spaces for children to play or for adolescents to convene also drives them to meet at fast-food chains instead.

Buying food

Families living in cities typically buy their food, so income is a key factor in what they eat. They are more likely to buy their food from large retailers, such as supermarkets, and much of it is packaged and processed or ultra-processed.[47] Research from Kenya shows that people shopping in supermarkets buy fewer unprocessed staples (fresh fruits and vegetables, etc.) and more processed

SPOTLIGHT
Child nutrition in poor urban areas of Kuala Lumpur

In the low-cost flats of Kuala Lumpur, Rohana, Noor and Siti Fatimah are three mothers with a common struggle: providing their children with a nutritious diet. During a focus group discussion held for the SOWC report, they shared their main challenges.

Malaysia bears a significant double burden of malnutrition: while 20.7 per cent of children under five suffer from stunting and 11.5 per cent from wasting, 12.7 per cent of children (5–19-year-olds) are obese.[118] This reality is more complex in poor urban areas, where malnutrition rates tend to be higher than the national average.[119]

Affordability is a common problem. While all three mothers understand the importance of eating nutritious food, cost constraints determine what they can feed their children, regardless of its nutritional value. The cheapest and most typical meal consists of fried eggs, rice and soy sauce. Noor, mother of four explained, "I do not think about that thing [healthy and balanced food)]. Others are eating fish, but I am able to provide only rice. I know it's not good, but that's all I can provide."

Poor-quality diets are both physically damaging and psychologically distressing. One mother said that she might only have the chance to serve chicken once a year. Another mother acknowledged that eggs are easy to obtain, but one of her children is allergic to them, so she is obliged to find alternatives. A third mother received a report that her child attempted self-harm because the child was not able to eat at a famous fast-food chain.

Meal frequency is also a major concern. Sometimes, they must purchase their groceries on credit at the nearby shop. Noor and Siti Fatimah explained that they ration the food among their children throughout the day. Otherwise, they will finish the food too quickly.

Balancing work and household activities is also an important issue. While two of the three mothers were able to achieve flexible working arrangements with their employers, Noor has to take her infant with her to work. This slows her down and impedes her work performance, ultimately affecting her income.

All three mothers expressed a strong desire to escape poverty. To develop her business, Rohana explained, she would benefit from policies that provide support to single mothers. Noor and Siti Fatimah agreed. With access to start-up capital, they too would like to open a business of their own. ■

Siti Fatimah peels boils eggs to put in curry at her home in Desa Rejang, Setapak, Kuala Lumpur. © UNICEF/Zahri 2019

Television commercials for snacks and sugary drinks target children

and ultra-processed food items.[48] This is also seen in Thailand, where supermarket shopping is associated with consumption of soft drinks, snack foods, processed meats and instant foods.[49]

Children and caregivers in cities also experience more exposure to the marketing of processed foods, which can influence food choices.[50] Such marketing is seen in public city spaces – including near schools – and in television commercials for snacks and sugary drinks, for example, that target children.

For the urban poor, such as those living in slums, eating well proves even more challenging as access to nutritious foods narrows. Many rely heavily on street food, which is often high in fat and salt. Street food accounts for about a quarter of household food spending in low- and middle-income countries.[51] Food-insecure households in urban areas of Malawi, for instance, were more likely to consume processed foods from street vendors. One study concluded that "Food insecure urban residents may be especially vulnerable to poor health outcomes associated with both poor access to nutrient-dense foods and diets high in refined and processed foods."[52]

Cities are taking action to address these challenges. As of July 2019, 198 cities around the world signed the Milan Urban Food Policy Pact with the aim to "develop sustainable food systems that are inclusive, resilient, safe and diverse, that provide healthy and affordable food to all people".[53] The NOURISHING Framework also brings together policy action across food environments, food systems and behaviour change. From Curitiba,[54] Amsterdam, Daegu and Dakar to London,[55] city-level action includes improving access to healthy foods for

poor households, introducing school-based advocacy and learning, urban farming, and enforcing restrictions on the marketing of unhealthy foods.

Access to healthy food

Not everyone has access to healthy foods. For families in rural and remote areas, or areas with poor infrastructure, limited physical access to healthy food outlets can be compounded by issues around access to farmland as well as climate and seasonal fluctuations, which can threaten food security and diet diversity.[56]

In our increasingly urbanized world, families in cities also face major challenges in finding healthy foods. Many live in 'food deserts' – mostly urban neighbourhoods where residents have little or no access to healthy food markets.[57] In these communities, people may buy food from fast-food outlets and unexpected places such as petrol (gas) stations, barber shops, gyms, discount stores, hardware stores, local general shops and laundromats.[58] The abundance of high-calorie, low-nutrient, processed foods in these areas has also led to the more descriptive term 'food swamp.'[59]

Because they offer an abundance of nutrient-poor, ultra-processed, fatty and sugar-sweetened foods (and limited or no options for healthy food), food deserts and swamps are by their nature obesogenic environments and have been found to strongly predict obesity rates.[60, 61] The high prevalence of food deserts in low-income, minority and underserved neighbourhoods[62] also means that the already vulnerable and disadvantaged children living in these areas face increased risks of suffering overweight, obesity and the lifelong burden of NCDs.

SPOTLIGHT
Childhood obesity: An urgent concern for China

Amid rapid economic growth and urbanization, China has experienced a remarkable shift in malnutrition since 1985. While the rate of stunting among school children declined from 16 per cent in 1985 to 2 per cent in 2014, rates of overweight and obesity increased from 1 to 20 per cent.[68]

China is now home to one of the largest groups of obese children worldwide.[69] In 2015, the Global Burden of Disease reported over 15 million obese children (aged 2–19) in China.[70] The Chinese Center for Disease Control and Prevention put the total number of both overweight and obese children at 120 million in 2012.[71]

Boys are at greater risk of suffering overweight and obesity than girls:[73] 21 versus 12 per cent, according to a 2018 study among 9–11-year-olds.[74] Overweight and obesity are also more prevalent in wealthy households,[75, 76, 77] and rates are significantly higher among schoolchildren in urban areas, although this disparity is narrowing and has even converged in some affluent areas.[78, 79] Overall, the children at greatest risk of being overweight or obese are only-sons from wealthy, urban households.

Why is this happening?

Many factors have led to the rise in overweight in China. Rapid economic development, urbanization and technological advancement have brought changes in lifestyle and behaviour. These are evident in decreased physical activity among children, together with a shift in diet away from the traditional cuisine that is rich in plant foods and grains prepared at home, to a modern diet high in meat, sugar and fried foods, and often consumed in snacks or away from home.[80, 81] Consumption of sugar-sweetened beverages (SSB) also plays a role.[82]

Decreased physical activity – without decreased food intake – puts children at risk of overweight. In 2006, the Chinese Government launched a national programme, Hundreds of Millions of Teenagers Sunshine Sports, which aims to provide 85 per cent of schoolchildren with more opportunities for exercise and physical activity. In line with the WHO recommendation of at least 60 minutes of moderate-to-vigorous physical activity each day,[83] physical education was added as one of four components of a students' 'all-round' development.

However, a 2010 analysis of students aged 9–18 years old showed that only 23 per cent were meeting the WHO recommendation. Physical activity was lowest among children with a heavy homework burden,[84] possibly reflecting a traditional idea in Chinese culture that 'to be a scholar is to be the top of society'.[85] This means that children routinely sacrifice play in favour of academic study.[86]

Another cultural idea at play is the tendency to perceive plumpness as a symbol of wealth, high social status and good health. Providing food is a family's top priority and children are likely to be overfed, especially in families where grandparents play a major role as caregivers.[87]

In response to the alarming rates of overweight and obesity among children in China, China Central Government has emphasized the urgent need for interventions and actions in their National Nutrition Plan (2017–2030) and Healthy China Action (2019–2030). ■

FIGURE 3.1 | **Prevalence of stunting, thinness and overweight among children (7–18 years old) in China, 1985–2014**[72]

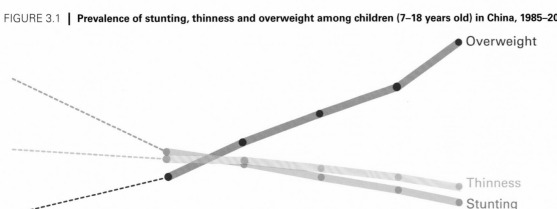

Note: Stunting, thinness and overweight are defined according to WHO anthropomorphic definitions.

As children grow, they develop lifelong eating habits

Although food deserts and swamps have typically been identified in high-income countries, they are increasingly found in low- and middle-income countries experiencing rapid urbanization and food-systems transformation. For example, in urban parts of Brazil, Honduras, Peru[63] and South Africa, food deserts are seen in communities facing a high degree of poverty, and racial, ethnic and income inequality.[64] In Mexico, where obesity prevalence ranks among the highest globally, food swamps are a bigger problem than deserts.[65]

Growing up in a food desert has serious implications for a child's nutrition and well-being. First, if families have less access to fruits and vegetables, young children may have no choice but to eat diets lacking in diversity during a period of critical development. Second, as children grow, they develop lifelong eating habits. This means that even if access to healthy food improves, diets may not: in the United States, for example, the opening of a new grocery store in a Philadelphia food desert increased awareness, but did not alter dietary intake or obesity in the community.[66]

In countries such as South Africa, Botswana and Zimbabwe, the urban dynamics are very different, with large numbers of highly mobile residents as well as informal economies and prominent gender disparities. Yet while the dynamics differ, evidence supports

---

BOX 3.6 | Food prices and nutrition

A recent study of global food prices indicates that healthy, nutrient-dense foods, especially animal-source food (ASF) and fortified infant cereals, are much more expensive (on a per-calorie basis) than starchy staples and unhealthy processed foods in low-income countries.

This global study, led by the International Food Policy Research Institute, set out to discover how relative prices differ across countries and regions, and whether these differences explain child feeding practices and stunting prevalence.

The study compared the *relative caloric price* of a wide range of healthy and unhealthy foods to the *caloric cost* of the cheapest staple food in each country (e.g. rice, wheat, cassava or maize). For example, a *relative caloric price of 5* for eggs implies that it costs five times more to obtain a calorie from an egg than to obtain a calorie from rice.

In high-income countries, ASFs are relatively cheap, at only one to four times more expensive than starchy staples. By contrast, in low-income regions of Asia and sub-Saharan

Africa, which have the highest rate of stunting, ASFs can be very expensive. In sub-Saharan Africa, calories from eggs, milk and fortified infant cereals are around nine to ten times more expensive than starchy staples.

The study findings indicate that countries with higher relative prices of ASF and fortified infant cereals have much lower consumption of those foods by infants and young children, and much higher stunting rates. This suggests that improving the affordability of these foods is a key pathway to addressing the global burden of undernutrition.

The study also sheds light on why obesity rates increase with national income. Oils/fats and sugar are very cheap in all regions. However, sugar- and fat-rich processed foods are often expensive in low-income countries, but their prices decline rapidly as countries reach middle- and upper-income levels. Unhealthy processed foods are also cheaper sources of calories than healthy foods in many poor countries, which may explain the dual-burden phenomenon of rising obesity in the midst of persistent undernutrition.[91] ∎

a similar conclusion: the mere presence of a supermarket may be insufficient to improve nutrition if other aspects of the food environment are not adequate.[67]

Cost

Cost is a contentious issue. There is debate, for example, over whether healthy foods are more expensive than unhealthy foods – healthy foods can cost less in purely price terms, but that advantage can be outweighed by things such as the time costs of preparing food from scratch.

Despite this, it's clear that cost is a real obstacle that prevents many families from eating a diverse range of nutrient-dense foods. This is especially true for the poorest families, who have to spend a bigger share of their income on food. In the Democratic Republic of the Congo, for example, research shows

that the cost of nutrient-dense foods is a significant barrier to diversifying young children's diets,[88] while in Ghana, foods rated as healthiest by caregivers are generally also rated the least accessible due to their cost.[89] In the United States, higher costs (both in terms of price and preparation time) and less access to healthy foods in the neighbourhood help drive differences between richer and poorer families' consumption of fruit and vegetables.[90]

Overall, poorer families tend to select low-quality food that costs less.[92] This might suggest that as incomes rise, families eat better. Unfortunately, this is not always the case. Research shows that when families – urban or rural – spend more money on food, it is for both healthy and unhealthy foods,[93] and that a rise in income produces increased spending on convenience foods.[94]

A girl crosses a puddle on a flooded road in Maputo, Mozambique. Yvonne, whose home is pictured here, lives with fourteen family members and makes a living selling vegetables from the stall.
© UNICEF/UN0139437/Prinsloo

The impacts of climate shocks fall heaviest on the poorest families, who are both the worst affected and least able to cope

There may be several explanations for this counter-intuitive result.[95] Factors beyond affordability and price – such as convenience, exposure to marketing, physical access to healthy food, level of nutritional knowledge and cultural factors – may make obesogenic foods more desirable. Also, if women do not control the additional income, it may not be directed to the needs of the family or child. Alternatively, other underlying determinants of child malnutrition – such as food safety – may remain unchanged.

As food systems continue to transform, increasing income alone will not be enough to address today's triple burden of malnutrition. Knowledge constraints, gender inequities, unfair marketing practices and other elements of the food environment and food supply – together with finding ways to reduce the cost of healthy foods – will all need to be addressed.

Climate shocks

Children disproportionately suffer the impacts of climate change and environment degradation. In the immediate aftermath of a flood or typhoon, for example, children are the most at-risk group for waterborne diseases, such as those accompanied by diarrhoea, and which heighten their risks of malnutrition and death.

Sustained undernutrition and loss of agricultural productivity, together with families' livelihoods, also threaten children's growth, development and learning, and can lead to 'distress migration'.[96] These impacts fall heaviest on children from the poorest families, who are both the worst affected and least able to cope.[97] The cumulative effects of prolonged or recurrent climate-related disasters and variability are often passed to the next generation of children, perpetuating and deepening cycles of intergenerational inequality.

Floods, storms, drought and extreme heat around the world have collectively doubled in number since 1990, with devastating results.[98] New crises, floods and drought have resulted in an increase of 11 per cent in people facing food insecurity since 2016.[99]

Climate-related disasters cause severe food crises: drought is responsible for 80 per cent of damage and losses in agriculture,[100] dramatically altering what food is available to children and families, as well as its quality and price. This is true in both rural areas – for small-scale food producers, agricultural labourers and families who buy their food – and urban areas, where resulting food price hikes determine what food is accessible.

Impacts of food production on the environment and on children

Industrial food production plays a major role in the environmental effects of climate change and environmental degradation because of its tremendous ecological footprint and contribution to emissions and pollution. In addition, the heavy use of fresh water, fertilizers and pesticides also presents risks to children's nutrition and well-being.

Greenhouse gas emissions

Food systems account for up to one-third of greenhouse gas (GHG) emissions globally, according to a 2012 study.[101] For example, the increasing production of meat is one of the largest sources of methane.[102] If current trends towards meat-heavy diets continue,

SPOTLIGHT
Climate change threatens child nutrition in Bangladesh

Over 19 million children spread across Bangladesh are at the frontline of climate change disasters, a quarter of them under 5 years old. Floods and riverbank erosion are driving families to city slums, where they face overcrowding and a lack of access to healthy food, education, adequate health services, sanitation and safe water. In slums, children must often fend for themselves and are at greater risk of malnutrition, child labour, child marriage and exposure to pollution, violence and abuse.

Extreme climatic events such as drought and flash floods cause severe agricultural losses. In a country where over 60 per cent of the population depend on agriculture for their livelihood, this means that children from the poorest families are most likely to go hungry. Reductions in production also lead to an increase in food prices, hitting the poorest families hardest.

A rise in communicable and non-communicable diseases linked to changing climate conditions and unplanned urbanization also threaten children and their families. These include hepatitis A, cholera, dysentery, typhoid, dengue and chikungunya fever.[117]

Ruma, her husband, Ali Akbar, and their two children, Sunjida, 3, and Shahaun, 9, moved to the Chalantika slum of Dhaka after their home was repeated flooded by the Meghna River. "At least we can stand on dry ground here even if we struggle with the cost of living," Ruma says.

"My husband earns about 7,000 Taka [US$83] a month. By the time we have paid our rent and bought our groceries, there is very little left over. But at least we are able to earn here, which we often weren't able to do when we lived in the countryside."

Ruma shares a small kitchen – a few planks of wood atop bamboo poles set in a swamp – with at least 10 other families. While they initially used butane gas, this proved impossible to share equitably. Wood is now preferred, further worsening the slum's air quality. Her family eats rice and lentils most days, she says, and can occasionally afford meat or fish. Her son, Shahaun, is showing signs of malnourishment.

In addition to the arduous challenge of trying to provide her family with healthy food, Ruma describes an unhealthy environment with no access to safe water, basic toilets or adequate hygiene. Electricity in the slum is irregular, and rodents and insects in their single room "make our lives an absolute misery," she says.

The Government of Bangladesh will begin the second phase of its Climate Change Strategy and Action Plan this year, placing greater emphasis on the needs of the poorest and most vulnerable, and demanding more attention and resources to ensure that child nutrition, health, education, sanitation and water, and social protection services are shielded from the effects of climate change. ■

A child wades through flood waters on her way to school in Kurigram district, Bangladesh. © UNICEF/UN0286416/Akash

A chemical pesticide is up to 10 times more toxic to a child than to an adult

the environmental impacts of food production on GHG emissions are estimated to increase by 87 per cent.[103]

To benefit both people and the planet, the EAT-Lancet Commission recently proposed a dietary shift that doubles the consumption of healthy foods such as fruits, vegetables, legumes and nuts, and halves that of less healthy foods such as red meat and added sugar. The authors note that given the unique dietary needs of children, including for high-quality protein, this "universal healthy reference diet" is for children aged 2 and above.[104]

Food production also demands significant use of fresh water, with water scarcity already affecting children in every continent.[105] Further, fertilizers put aquatic systems at risk of contamination, and pesticides pose direct risks to children.[106] In addition to ingesting food with pesticide residue, many children are exposed to pesticides while working in agriculture, which accounts for 71 per cent of child labour.[107]

Pre-natal exposure to pesticides can increase the risk of foetal death and birth defects, while exposure in childhood can disrupt the endocrine system, cause cancer and delay neurodevelopment. A chemical pesticide is up to 10 times more toxic to a child than to an adult, and acute poisoning usually results in death.[108]

Biodiversity loss

Together with climate change and pollution, food production is also implicated in the loss of biodiversity. A recent UN report sounded the alarm on the scale of the problem: nearly 1 million species are threatened with extinction due to human activities.[109] Changes in land and water use – for example, clearing forests for large-scale crop or livestock production systems – is recognized as a major driver of biodiversity loss.[110]

Biodiversity is not only essential for healthy ecosystems; it also directly affects food security and nutrition.[111] Children's dietary diversity is also at stake.[112] With less diversity in crop production, diets are becoming increasingly homogenous around the world (*see Chapter 1*).[113] Just three crops – rice, wheat and maize – now make up nearly two-thirds of the global caloric intake.[114]

Without improvements to today's dietary patterns and food production, children, their families and future generations are likely to face greater risk of food insecurity and malnutrition brought on by climate shocks and environmental degradation.

Conclusion

The causes of child malnutrition are more complex and far-reaching today than they were in 1990. Sweeping changes, seen in globalization, unplanned urbanization and climate change, are exacerbating already unfair outcomes for the poorest and most excluded children and their families. Worldwide crises threaten to halt or reverse progress in reducing child undernutrition.

At the same time, there is greater acknowledgement that the exclusion of certain groups from essential foods, services, resources and decision-making is unfair and avoidable – and that children are paying the price.

Researchers, experts and practitioners also recognize and are expanding the evidence-base on the causes and risks of malnutrition being passed from one generation to the next. This knowledge and attention have the potential to make interventions more effective and to drive action. Even so, more is needed in research and practice to fully understand the particular circumstances of children from different population groups. For example, few empirical studies exist on aspects beyond poverty and gender. For a larger, more sustainable impact, practitioners will need to pay explicit attention to addressing marginalization and gender inequities that underpin disparities in the longer term.

If food systems are to transform and deliver better diets for children, the broader forces that affect children's diets, growth and development – resources, governance and norms – will also require more attention (*see Chapter 4*). They can be broken down, examined and understood. Such analysis reveals power structures in food systems and where power is exerted, which allows the nutrition community and the public to leverage and exploit spaces for change.

Such change is already happening in many countries (*see Chapter 4*). With greater coordination and implementation of policies and programmes across the food, health, water and sanitation, education and social protection systems, it can be transformative.■

A girl carries a bucket of water collected from a nearby dry river bed in northern Kenya. Turkana is one of the districts hardest hit by prolonged drought and recurrent cholera. © UNICEF/UN0275168/ Njuguna

SPECIAL SECTION

Nutrition in emergencies

UNICEF and its partners treated more than 3.4 million children with severe acute malnutrition (SAM) in emergency contexts around the world in 2018. The greatest numbers of children were treated in Afghanistan, Chad, the Democratic Republic of the Congo, Ethiopia, Nigeria, Niger, Somalia, South Sudan, Sudan and Yemen. Almost 90 per cent of the children recovered.[120]

In Sudan, as of April 2019, 11 of 18 states have global acute malnutrition rates above the Integrated Food Security emergency threshold of 15 per cent. While 2.4 million children under 5 suffer from wasting a year, close to one third (700,000) of those suffer from SAM, with high rates in Eastern Sudan and among South Sudanese refugees.[121]

Historically, efforts to address nutrition in emergencies focused largely on identifying cases of wasting – a visual indication of severe acute malnutrition.[122] However, the complexity and protracted nature of crises have led to a global recognition that many forms of malnutrition occur in emergency settings. New evidence shows that these forms can include stunting and micronutrient deficiencies.[123] In protracted humanitarian crises, the prevalence of stunting is increasing, while rates of wasting continue to be high.[124] As a result, global nutrition leaders are turning to approaches that combine short- and long-term solutions to the problems of malnutrition.

These efforts focus on preventing avoidable deaths and promoting growth. UNICEF and its partners conduct nutrition assessments, identify and treat children, and provide fortified foods and supplements to prevent nutrient deficiencies. They also promote breastfeeding and provide guidance on feeding infants and young children, which can save lives in emergency situations.

Addressing nutritional needs in complex and protracted emergencies involves partnerships around the world that work to save lives and provide local and national governments with the assistance they need to address malnutrition in communities and to develop emergency response plans during crises.

While 86 per cent of international humanitarian assistance is distributed in countries experiencing long- and medium-term crises, emphasis is increasingly placed on resilience planning.[125] Between 2005 and 2017, the average length of crises that received an inter-agency funding appeal rose from 4 to 7 years.[126]

Yemen

In Yemen, home to Moteab and his family, protracted conflict, economic crisis and the dismantling of essential services, including those for health and water and sanitation, turned daily life into a "living hell".[127] His father's job, transporting goods in a wheelbarrow, provided the family with the bare minimum of food – bread for breakfast, vegetables, usually potatoes, for lunch and anything left over for dinner.

By the time Moteab turned 2 years old, the combination of poverty and protracted conflict left him in a struggle for his life. "He would throw up whatever he ate or drank," his mother said. After seven months of repeated

illnesses with vomiting, diarrhoea and weight loss, his mother was directed to a free health centre in Abs, where her son was diagnosed with SAM.

Moteab is just one of the 400,000 children in Yemen who suffered from SAM in 2018.[128] The humanitarian crisis is one of the worst in recent history.[129]

In emergencies around the world, treating children like Moteab involves tools and approaches to providing a combination of routine medication, therapeutic foods, individualized care and links to other social services such as for hygiene and sanitation.[130]

Tsahara holds her son, Moctar, 2, who is suffering from severe acute malnutrition. They have just visited the UNICEF-supported health centre in the village of Sarkin Yamma Saboua, Niger, about 6 kilometres from their home village. © UNICEF/UNI122685/Asselin

For example, in Yemen, partners employ the Standardized Monitoring and Assessment of Relief and Transitions (SMART), a methodology that allows for systematic collection of reliable information that can be used to make decisions and allocate resources to priority needs.

Community management of acute malnutrition (CMAM) is also an important approach for addressing SAM in emergencies around the world. In Yemen, by 2018, UNICEF and its partners were supporting more than 3,300 outpatient therapeutic feeding programmes, such as the one in Abs where Moteab received treatment.[131]

Though most children can be treated at home with ready-to-use therapeutic foods (RUTF), Moteab's condition required treatment at a stabilization centre in Aslam, one of 69 centres for children who experience health complications in addition to SAM. However, as fighting closed in on the area, Moteab was moved to Sana'a, where he and his family were provided with the support necessary for treatment in a therapeutic feeding centre at a hospital.

For Moteab, the life-saving nutrition services he needed were provided free to his family. They are services that have set him on the path to recovery. "I can see improvement since his admission to Al-Sabeen Hospital," his mother says. "He has been receiving very good healthcare. He now finishes the entire feed of the specialized milk that is given to him and interacts with people around him."

"I am happy," she adds, "but I am worried about the other children in our district that might reach my son's situation if they do not receive support and care quickly."

Niger

In Niger, where the prevalence of stunting for children under 5 is 41 per cent and anaemia is 77 per cent,[132] doctors often treat SAM that is linked to preventable disease. Dr Abale Laoali at the Intensive Nutritional Rehabilitation Centre in Diffa explains, "Throughout the country, the children who are severely wasted and do not have access to adequate healthcare experience higher rates of malarial infections. We've also observed that children affected by malaria experience a decrease of defences in their immune system. This makes them lose their appetite, and to suffer from vomiting, pneumonia or severe diarrhoea. At this point, the risk of severe malnutrition is very high due to the lack of food, the diseases, the poor health and hygiene conditions – and displacement."

One of Dr Laoali's patients is 3-month-old Sani, diagnosed with SAM, pneumonia, malaria and a congenital heart disease. Two years ago, his mother Fatima fled Damasak, Nigeria, a town held by Boko Haram, with her three children. They have since been continuously displaced. During her pregnancy with Sani, Fatima was anaemic and suffered food insecurity and high levels of stress. After arriving at the temporary site for displaced people in Chetimari, Fatima brought Sani to the nearest health centre. "The nurses told me that my little baby was in danger because, in addition to malnutrition, he had contracted malaria and pneumonia," she says. "He didn't tolerate my breastmilk, he didn't have any appetite and he vomited a few times. I began to fear for Sani's life."

After 20 days of hospitalization and thanks to the guidance of healthcare workers and support from partners, Sani is breastfeeding again and has regained weight. His malaria symptoms are gone and he is breathing without the help of an oxygen machine. ■

PERSPECTIVE

Sesame Workshop's Raya teaches children healthy habits

Sherrie Westin
President,
Social Impact and
Philanthropy,
Sesame Workshop

and Raya
Global Health
Ambassador

For 50 years, Sesame Workshop has focused on a whole-child curriculum – not only delivering the academic and socio-emotional lessons children need to thrive, but also teaching critical skills in health and resilience.

Many children around the world suffer from malnutrition, which can be caused by a lack of access to healthy food and by childhood illness. In fact, malnutrition and preventable and treatable illnesses such as pneumonia and diarrhoea are the leading causes of death for children under the age of 5.

We also know that our characters have a great potential to talk to children, model behaviours and provide the language to talk about tough topics. That's why we created Raya, a special Sesame Street Muppet. She's 6 years old, with long braids and a beaming smile – and she teaches children in 11 countries, and 30 languages life-saving lessons about water, sanitation and hygiene (WASH) through our WASH UP! initiative, in partnership with World Vision.

We've seen encouraging results. Independent research conducted with support from the Gates Foundation found that our programme led to measurable improvements in WASH knowledge, attitudes and behaviours among children in Bangladesh, India and Nigeria. Raya and WASH UP! continue to inspire tens

of thousands of children to bring positive change to their homes, schools and communities.

As our 'global health ambassador', Raya was the perfect companion to help me with this piece. Thanks for chatting with me today, Raya. I know you know a lot about how to stay healthy!

Raya
I sure do! Like how important it is to make sure water is clean before drinking it. I tell my friends that one way you can get sick is from tiny germs you can't even see. And how we all get germs on our hands, so it's important to wash them for 20 seconds with soap and water after we use the bathroom and before we eat food, to scrub those germs away!

Sherrie
What about your friends living where there is no clean running water?

Raya
Lots of my friends around the world do not have running water, but they still have to wash the germs off. One fun thing we make together is called a tippy tap. It's a hand-washing station people can build anywhere – they're easy to make and use! And if you do have to go to the bathroom outside, it's really important to wear sandals or shoes to the latrine to protect your feet from germs too, because that's another way you can get sick.

Sherrie

That's right, Raya. And when children get sick, illness can prevent their bodies from absorbing the nutrients they need to get well, stay healthy and grow properly. That can cause something called malnutrition.

Raya

So getting sick is the same thing as *malnutrition*?

Sherrie

Getting sick is one of many reasons for malnutrition. Malnutrition can also mean not having enough food to eat, or not eating enough of the kinds of nutrient-rich foods that help children grow into healthy adults.

Raya

I think I get it! I have a friend who taught me about different kinds of food. You know him too!

Sherrie

Are you talking about a certain blue, fuzzy monster named …

Raya

Cookie Monster!

Sherrie

He does know a lot about his favourite subject. What did Cookie Monster teach you?

Raya

He taught me and my friends on Sesame Street about the difference between 'sometimes foods' and 'anytime foods'. Cookies are a 'sometimes food', because they're something we should eat only once in a while as a treat. But an apple is an 'anytime food' because it's full of vitamins and an important part of a healthy diet. I can eat a delicious apple any time!

Sherrie

I love that Cookie Monster taught you something important about nutrition, and you're telling other people like me about it. Just like when you show children that washing up is easy to learn. Children who learn life-saving behaviours from you then teach their families.

Raya

Right! Healthy habits are contagious!

Sherrie

So you're making an important difference in the world by helping so many children stay healthy. Keep up the great work!

Raya

Thanks! I will!■

Sherrie Westin is President of Social Impact and Philanthropy for Sesame Workshop, the non-profit educational organization behind Sesame Street. Westin leads the Workshop's efforts to serve vulnerable children through mass media and targeted initiatives. She serves as Sesame Workshop's chief mission ambassador, raising awareness, developing strategic partnerships and cultivating philanthropic support to further the Workshop's mission to help children everywhere grow smarter, stronger and kinder.

Sesame Workshop's global health ambassador, Raya, is an energetic 6-year-old who's guiding conversations all over the world about clean water, handwashing and proper latrine use. Raya always remembers to wash her hands with soap and water and to wear her sandals in the latrine to avoid contracting illness. She encourages children to share what they learn with friends and family, making good habits contagious.

04 RESPONSES TO MALNUTRITION

The evolving nature of global child malnutrition demands a new response: one that can deliver nutrition-specific interventions and nutrition-sensitive development in a more coordinated fashion. The response must acknowledge the central role and responsibility of the food system, and work together with the health, water and sanitation, education and social protection systems to provide better diets for children.

➤ A systems approach to nutrition reflects the reality that child nutrition has multiple determinants and the shared responsibilities of multiple sectors and stakeholders, public and private

➤ Recent years have brought growing momentum to improve food systems, but the unique needs of children have been ignored. Children's needs must be at the heart of food systems.

➤ Nutrition-specific approaches are also needed in four key supporting systems – health, water and sanitation, education and social protection.

Tuyisenge holds her 11-month-old daughter, Fabiola, while a community health worker measures her mid-upper arm circumference at a UNICEF-supported care group growth monitoring session in Musanze District, Rwanda. "Before I used only potato and beans, no other vegetables," Tuyisenge says. "Now I use all kinds of vegetables as well as small fish. I see the difference in the growth of my children."
© UNICEF/UN0301162/Noorani

Introduction

For too long, nutrition was on the periphery of the global development agenda. In recent years, however, it has gained greater attention, reflecting growing recognition of the social and economic benefits of investing in nutrition. As the body of research on effective interventions has expanded, global policy discussions increasingly focus on evidence-based approaches.[1]

The list of interventions is long, and growing: from promoting breastfeeding, to better supporting the poorest families; from making labelling clearer and more informative, to tackling iron deficiency anaemia and other forms of hidden hunger; from improving children's food environments, to making safe drinking water available everywhere – a huge array of actions can be taken (and in many cases, are being taken) to improve children's nutrition.

A baby eats a piece of bread while being carried in the Hanaq Chuquibamba community in Peru.
© UNICEF/ Vilca 2019

Clearly, much more needs to be done. Nevertheless, there are causes for hope. More and more governments are laying out strategies to improve nutrition. In many countries, these represent an important first step that can be built on in the years to come. For these approaches to make a real difference, governments need to recognize three key realities.

- First, there are **no easy fixes if nutrition goes wrong in childhood**. The nutritional needs of children are unique, and uniquely important. That's why children and young people must be at the heart of thinking around food and nutrition.

- Second, **we need to meet malnutrition challenges by working across all relevant systems** and sectors. Food systems need to better serve children's needs, but other systems – notably, those for health, water and sanitation,

Nutrition and the Sustainable Development Goals

Source: www.un.org/sustainabledevelopment/hunger/

education and social protection – also have crucial roles to play as part of a coordinated and systemic approach.

- Third, while **governments may be at the forefront in setting policies, strategies and programmes, they cannot do it alone**. Business and civil society groups, as well as families, children and young people themselves, all have important roles to play.

How governments are responding to a growing momentum

In 2008, the Copenhagen Consensus concluded that nutrition interventions were among the most cost-effective in development.[2] That same year, *The Lancet* published its landmark series on Maternal and Child Undernutrition, which highlighted the 'golden window' for nutrition in the first 1,000 days after conception[3] (later followed by an examination of the growing problem of overweight).[4] The momentum from these critical conversations catalysed nutrition as a global development priority, leading to a number of global initiatives, including the creation of the Scaling up Nutrition (SUN) movement, a multi-stakeholder, multi-sectoral approach to support country-level strategies to combat malnutrition.

Building on the World Health Assembly's Global Nutrition targets, the UN Sustainable Development Goals (SDGs) cast nutrition as a central input and outcome of sustainable

We need to meet child malnutrition challenges by working across all relevant systems

163 countries now have comprehensive or topic-specific policies, strategies and plans that are relevant to nutrition and the promotion of healthy diets

development. Goal 2 specifically calls on Member States to "end hunger, achieve food security, improve nutrition, and promote sustainable agriculture." Indeed, 12 of the 17 SDGs contain indicators that are crucial for nutrition.[5] Adding to this global ambition, the United Nations General Assembly proclaimed the Decade of Action on Nutrition (2016–2025), enhancing the global commitment to eradicating hunger and preventing all forms of malnutrition.

This growing global momentum has spurred many governments to update or develop new approaches to nutrition. According to WHO, 163 countries now have comprehensive or topic-specific policies, strategies and plans that are relevant to nutrition and the promotion of healthy diets.[6]

These signs of commitment are welcome: however, there are reasons to be cautious. First, many of these policies are still nascent – one third date from 2015 or later – so it will take time to assess their impact. Second, national nutrition policies do not always fully incorporate goals, targets and indicators related to the World Health Assembly's Global Nutrition Targets. The incorporation of targets and SMART commitments[7] is fundamental to ensuring that governments are held accountable and that nutrition interventions are effectively monitored.[8] Finally, there is evidence that nutrition policies and programmes are still often fragmented and uncoordinated.[9]

Scaling-up nutrition results

National approaches have increasingly addressed nutrition concerns through interventions in a number of traditionally defined sectors, such as health and

education. Some of these interventions can be thought of as direct, or nutrition-specific, because they directly address the immediate and some underlying causes of malnutrition, particularly in the most disadvantaged populations, for example in breastfeeding counselling or the early detection and treatment of severe acute malnutrition (SAM). Others can be thought of as indirect, or nutrition-sensitive, because they aim to address the basic and some underlying causes of malnutrition, such as through promoting social safety nets, education and empowerment of women.

Nutrition-sensitive interventions boost the effectiveness of nutrition-specific interventions. In Brazil, for example, a nutrition-sensitive social protection programme utilizing conditional cash transfers has reduced malnutrition-related child mortality. Pregnant and lactating women receive cash transfers on condition that they attend pre- and post-natal appointments and participate in educational activities on nutrition and health.[10] Likewise, the education sector provides a compelling entry point for governments to address malnutrition using a nutrition-sensitive approach, particularly among the most vulnerable. Pathways include helping children develop healthy dietary habits from an early age and improving the nutrition literacy of adolescent girls.

The benefits of mixing nutrition-specific and nutrition-sensitive approaches across a range of sectors are clear.[11] However, many actors remain focused exclusively on nutrition-specific approaches.[12] And because of a lack of coordination among actors and sectors, efforts to promote better diets for children and prevent all forms of malnutrition are often falling short.

It is clear, then, that translating political commitment to tackle malnutrition into action requires more than just increased attention; it also requires the mobilization of government systems, institutions and resources, and coordinated strategies.[13] Success requires more than isolated sectoral results – it requires a coordinated systems approach in which food systems themselves are transformed and other key systems work together with the food system to deliver nutrition results at scale.

Multiple responses to a multifaceted challenge: A systems approach

Why take a systems approach? First, it better captures the importance of the interactions and interconnections across different areas, such as food, health and education, and crystallizes a common purpose: better diets and better nutrition for children, adolescents and women. Second, a systems approach avoids the simplistic thinking that malnutrition has straightforward determinants that operate along linear pathways. Instead, it puts the focus on multiple, interconnected determinants, and recognizes shared responsibility, and the need to mobilize attention and resources from a wider variety of societal and governmental institutions.

Five systems in particular have crucial roles to play. The food system must respond and provide better dietary choices for children, adolescents and women. The health, water and sanitation, education and social protection systems are also fundamental in driving transformation, particularly in the personal and external food environments, and delivering the necessary services to support better diets, practices and nutrition outcomes. Achieving results at scale depends on the robustness of these five leading systems to implement nutrition-specific and nutrition-sensitive interventions at every stage of life (see Figure 4.1).

This is not to say that other systems cannot also play a part. Information systems, for example, are fundamental to the collection, analysis and interpretation of nutrition-related data, and can provide the basis for timely and effective decisions to improve nutritional outcomes among children. Many countries have different forms of information systems in place to support nutrition interventions.

A systems approach targets the key systems that have the ability to deliver nutrition interventions at scale, making them more accountable for nutrition results beyond their sectoral objectives. To give an example, in many countries, nutrition is viewed as being within the remit of the health sector, which is given the main responsibility for delivering nutrition interventions. However, although the health system is clearly an important pathway for scaling up certain nutrition interventions, many crucial determinants of child malnutrition, such as diet diversity, are well beyond its normal scope. Instead, action is needed across multiple systems to ensure quality coverage.

How and where this happens will vary according to the context. Innovative approaches to mobilizing systems for improved nutrition are certainly needed. As the examples in this chapter show (see Special Section), there is no shortage of success stories and lessons learned that can help to show the way forward.

A systems approach targets the key systems that have the ability to deliver nutrition interventions at scale

Multiple responses to a multifaceted challenge: A systems approach to nutrition

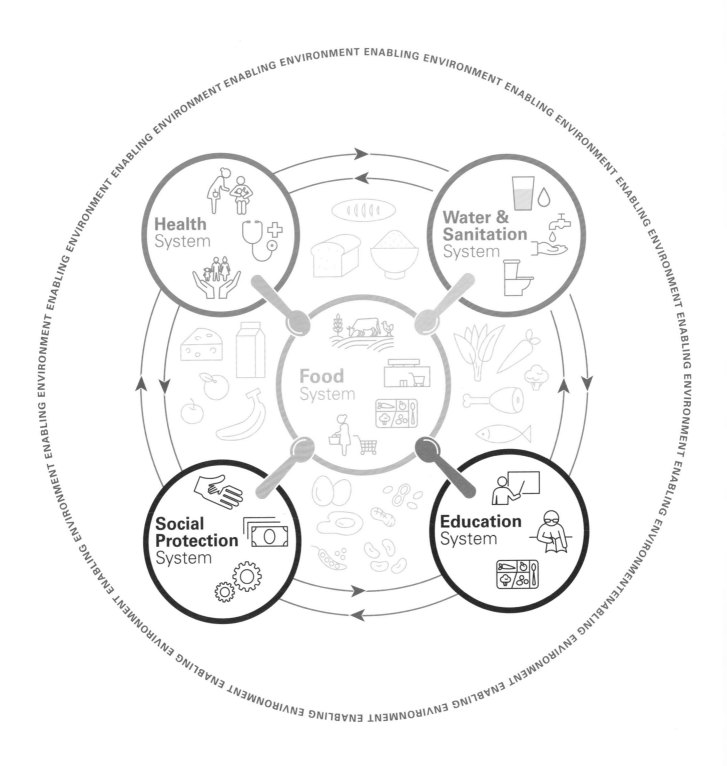

Source: UNICEF. Maternal and Child Nutrition UNICEF Strategy 2020–2030. UNICEF: New York; 2019

A systems approach makes multiple systems accountable for nutrition results beyond sectoral objectives

The food system

includes all of the activities and actors involved in bringing food from production to consumption and through to disposal (*see Chapter 1*). This system includes intermediate steps, such as processing, distribution, marketing and retail. It is organized into four main parts: food supply chains, external food environments, personal food environments and the behaviours of caregivers and consumers with respect to food.

The health system

includes preventive services as well as curative care. It is more than just service delivery: governance, financing, supplies and equipment, workforce and information systems are all integral parts of the health system. A strong health system supports family practices, and produces equitable survival, growth and development outcomes for children, adolescents and women.

The water and sanitation system

comprises the policies, programmes, services, facilities and actors involved in providing safe drinking water and safe sanitation infrastructure. Policies often target the most vulnerable populations to address their basic needs. A strong water and sanitation system is essential to ensuring safe food, safe drinking water, and clean and healthy environments for children, adolescents and women.

The education system

refers to formal and informal institutions designed to educate children, from basic kindergarten to secondary school. While public schools are often the primary consideration of education system policy, private schools can also follow national education guidance. A strong education system has trained teachers, sound pedagogy, solid infrastructure and resources, and should be used as a delivery system to improve nutrition outcomes.

The social protection system

comprises a set of public and private policies and programmes that aims to prevent, reduce and eliminate economic and social vulnerabilities to poverty and deprivation. Nutrition-sensitive social protection programmes can mitigate the effects of poverty on the nutrition of children, adolescents and women. A strong system combines different programmes, often focusing on the protection of vulnerable groups, and breaking the cycle of poverty.

SPECIAL SECTION

What does a systems approach to nutrition look like in practice?

Meeting the malnutrition challenge requires action across five key systems: those for food, health, water and sanitation, education and social protection. There are already many examples from around the world of how each of these systems is helping to support improvement in maternal and child nutrition.

Food system

Commercial fortification of staple foods with micronutrients is one of the most successful and cost-effective interventions to combat hidden hunger. In the 1920s, Switzerland and the United States started adding iodine to salt, virtually eliminating goitre and cretinism – the most severe forms of iodine deficiency disorders – and paving the way for subsequent fortification initiatives.[14] Today, many countries routinely fortify refined cereal grains with micronutrients.[15]

While technically simple, commercial fortification requires cooperation between government agencies and a mature food industry with centralized and specialized processing and an adequate distribution infrastructure. It also requires monitoring and quality control and is more effective when paired with consumer education campaigns to promote consumption. Commercial fortification has been widely successful in urban areas, where people typically purchase food in central markets and stores. It is more challenging in rural areas, where the distribution infrastructure may be more patchy.

Universal salt iodization and large-scale food fortification

Universal salt iodization is one of the great global nutrition success stories. Today, iodized salt is available to 86 per cent of world's households. The result is that, between the early 1990s and 2016, the number of countries in which iodine deficiency is a public health problem fell from 113 to just 19.[16] This progress has led to a major decline in iodine deficiency disorders and has contributed to improving the intellectual development of millions of children. Salt iodization is also highly cost-effective, costing only about US$0.05 per person per year.[17]

Following the success of salt iodization in developed countries, momentum gathered to scale it up globally. In 1994, WHO and UNICEF endorsed universal salt iodization as a safe, effective and sustainable way to address iodine deficiency.[18] However, salt iodization has made slow progress in Southeast Asia and sub-Saharan Africa, especially in rural areas with poor infrastructure and in countries that rely on small-scale salt processors. As with any form of food fortification, successful scale-up requires political commitment, engagement from the food industry, and links with national nutrition programmes and other development priorities. Programmes also need to align with changing dietary patterns. For example, the increased consumption of salt through processed foods, rather than as table salt, means that food industries should ensure they use iodized salt. Salt iodization is also compatible with WHO's recommendation to reduce salt intake to less than 5g a day. By ensuring that all food-grade salt is iodized, this limit can be safely met.[19]

Large-scale food fortification

The success of salt iodization paved the way for subsequent fortification initiatives around the world. In the United States, for example, salt iodization was followed in 1933 by the fortification of milk with vitamin D to prevent rickets and, in 1942, with the requirement to add thiamine, riboflavin and iron to flour.[20] In 1996, the government mandated the addition of folic acid to flour to reduce the prevalence of neural tube defects, the most common of which are spina bifida and anencephaly, a fatal condition. Subsequent assessments demonstrated that the prevalence of neural tube defects had decreased by 19–32 per cent. Numerous other countries have seen similar improvements.[21] New national flour fortification programmes are being considered, including in high-income settings such as the United Kingdom, where folic acid fortification is under review.[22]

Currently 81 countries – from South Africa, Morocco and Jordan, to Indonesia, to Mexico and Uruguay – mandate fortification of wheat flour alone or in combination with maize flour and rice.[23] Even so, significant untapped potential remains: if all countries worldwide fortified flour with folic acid, this could prevent an estimated 230,000 cases of neural tube defects a year.[24] Other obstacles include the reality that national flour fortification standards do not always meet minimal requirements for key nutrients such as iron, zinc and vitamin B12.[25]

As set out in the 2015 Arusha Statement on Food Fortification,[26] critical actions are still needed. These include improved oversight and enforcement of food fortification standards and regulations, better evidence to guide policy and programme design, stronger accountability and global reporting, continued advocacy, and additional (albeit modest) investment.

Health system

Health facilities can play a major role in improving nutrition outcomes, but all too often, these opportunities are missed. For national health systems to meet their full potential, they need to deliver preventive services and curative care, but also to foster positive family practices, such as breastfeeding, that can significantly scale up nutrition results. Cambodia, Rwanda and India are three examples of countries where the health system is taking on this role.

Cambodia has invested substantially in awareness-raising in communities, as well as in improved quality of care around the time of delivery. As a result the percentage of deliveries by a skilled birth attendant doubled between 2005 and 2014 to 89 per cent in 2014, while institutional deliveries increased from 22 per cent to 83 per cent. Importantly, rates of early initiation of breastfeeding rose more than tenfold between 1998 and 2014 to 63 per cent.[27] The programme has also helped stop the rise of breastmilk substitute use among newborns.[28]

Rwanda has also made significant progress. It implemented an intensive and sustained communication campaign around feeding practices, including early initiation of breastfeeding, and the Baby-Friendly Hospital Initiative. By 2014, skilled birth attendants assisted at 91 per cent of deliveries, up from 39 per cent in 2005, including at nearly all births in health facilities. The rates of early initiation of breastfeeding also increased, from 64 per cent in 2005 to 81 per cent in 2014.[29] Rwanda now has 45,000 community health workers who counsel mothers about adequate feeding practices and safe deliveries.

In India, national and state governments implemented a multi-pronged strategy to support breastfeeding, including large-scale programmes, effective capacity-building initiatives, strong partnerships, community-based action, and communications campaigns. As a result, early initiation of breastfeeding rose from 24.5 per cent in 2006 to 44.6 per cent in 2014. The increase was even greater – from 12.5 per cent in 2006 to 34.4 per cent in 2014 – in the seven states with the highest rates of newborn deaths.[30, 31]

These examples demonstrate how countries can integrate and improve the quality of breastfeeding counselling within the health system to achieve results at scale. All three countries were able to strengthen the capacity of health workers and health facilities to deliver nutrition interventions. These positive results demonstrate the benefits of institutionalization, protection, promotion and support of breastfeeding in maternity facilities, particularly in the first days of life.

Water and sanitation system

By causing conditions such as diarrhoea and dysentery, which prevent children from absorbing nutrients, poor water and sanitation are major factors in malnutrition. Improvements in the water, sanitation and hygiene (WASH) system, combined with nutrition interventions, can therefore play a critical role in preventing stunting and other forms of malnutrition. Such approaches have been adopted in Pakistan and Ethiopia, which both suffer high rates of stunting – more than one third of children aged under 5 are affected – and where access to basic sanitation services is still a major national concern.

In Pakistan's Sindh province, UNICEF Pakistan and its partners implemented an integrated package of WASH and nutrition interventions focused on the crucial first 1,000 days. The WASH activities focused on reducing the incidence and severity of infection and controlling environmental enteropathy, a chronic inflammation of the gut. Interventions included maintaining safe water supplies, encouraging community-based approaches to eliminate open defecation, improving hygiene behaviour, and developing service provider capacity. Challenges remain, but there has been significant progress. Community health workers have been mobilized, and WASH clubs have been formed in schools to empower children to promote positive practices. In total, an estimated 922,000 children aged under 5 and women have been reached with packages of nutrition services, including micronutrient supplementation.

In Ethiopia, UNICEF implemented a Baby WASH programme in 2017, with the aim of protecting babies and young children from microbial infections during play and feeding. The programme includes interactive communication for development tools and materials, including a radio drama series, public service announcements (PSAs), and discussion groups with mothers.

The intervention has helped change behaviours. According to an internal evaluation report, almost three quarters of those who listened to the radio programmes and PSAs said they had made changes. Around half said they were washing their hands more often and using soap, while around a quarter had stopped open defecation. Work has already begun with the Ministry of Health to scale up the approach across the country, including the development of national guidelines and a training manual, and the launch of a national training initiative for trainers who will implement the Baby WASH approach in the regions.[32]

Education system

School-based food and nutrition interventions can play a key role in creating an environment that provides and promotes healthy diets and nutrition among children and adolecents.[33] By educating and influencing children (and their parents) to make healthy food choices, education systems can deliver not only nutrition-specific interventions but also ensure nutrition-friendly environments.

In India, the adolescent anaemia control programme shows how the education system can work to scale up nutrition-specific results. The programme began in 2000 with the launch of a pilot targeting adolescent girls in 2,000 public schools across five states. The pilot delivered three main interventions: weekly iron–folic acid supplementation, monthly nutrition and education, and twice-yearly deworming. It benefited 8.8 million girls aged 10–19. After a year, the programme reported a significant decrease in the prevalence of moderate to severe anaemia.[34]

Based on the positive outcomes and lessons learned, the Government of India launched the national weekly iron and folic acid supplementation programme in 2012, targeting 116 million adolescents aged 10–19, across 32 states. For the first time, almost 40 million boys were also in-corporated in the programme. By 2016–2017, the national programme was reaching 36 per cent of the targeted adolescents, and all states had taken key steps to maintain the sustainability of the programme. Co-led by the Ministry of Health and Family Welfare, the Ministry of Education and the Ministry of Women and Child Development, the programme is a promising example of the sort of coordination among different government institutions that is fundamental to building an effective education-system approach to improving nutrition.

Social protection system

Social protection programmes are a powerful instrument to not only lift families and children out of poverty, but also to promote maternal and child nutrition. A range of interventions, such as conditional and unconditional cash transfers, food rations and school feeding, can all help limit the long-term effects of deprivation and provide communities with the means to access and afford nutritious food. Cash-transfer programmes, in particular, have proven benefits for the nutritional status and health outcomes of children.[35]

Social protection programmes have been widely implemented in Latin America, and have helped countries reduce poverty, promote food security and improve nutritional outcomes for children, young people and families. In Brazil, for example, the Bolsa Familia ('family allowance') programme launched in 2003 reached more than 13 million families in its first decade of implementation, and contributed significantly to social and public health improvements.[36] Specifically focused on nutrition, the programme played a vital role in helping low-income families to purchase food, thus enhancing their dietary quality and diversity.[37] Among children aged under 5, the programme was crucial to reducing child mortality, which is closely linked to malnutrition. A study published by *The Lancet* showed that Bolsa Familia was crucial to reducing child mortality among children aged 5, by incentivizing pre- and post-natal care and supporting immunization campaigns and health and nutrition activities for mothers and children.[38]

Similarly, Mexico's conditional cash-transfer programme, Prospera, has benefited around 7 million families.[39] Child nutrition has been a major component of the programme from its inception. Families included in the programme benefit from regular maternal and child services where children's nutritional status is monitored. Nutrition services aim to improve families' capacity to eat healthily and feed their children a nutritious, safe and affordable diet. As studies have shown, the programme has helped to promote nutrition and optimum growth, and has also enhanced dietary diversity among families and children.[40, 41]

These large-scale interventions prove the importance of nutrition-sensitive social protection systems, helping countries not only to mitigate the effects of poverty, but also to strengthen families in their childcare role, which is a fundamental aspect of ensuring healthy eating habits and better child nutrition. ◼

Food systems need to be reshaped from simply feeding people to nourishing people – especially children – well

Putting children at the heart of food systems

Effective food systems (*see Chapter 1*) are fundamental to securing nutritious, safe, affordable and sustainable diets for all children, everywhere. Despite their central role, however, food systems have been largely absent in policy and programming for maternal and child nutrition. Fortunately, attitudes and approaches are changing. There is growing recognition in the international community that food systems need to be reshaped from simply feeding people to nourishing people – especially children – well.

An important early step in this thinking came with the Rome Declaration on Nutrition in 2014. Since then, reports and studies have shed light on particular aspects of food systems.[42] For example, a report by the High Level Panel of Experts on nutrition and food systems dives deeper into the crucial role of food environments in shaping dietary choices, as well as the potential pathways in all food systems – whether traditional, modern or mixed – towards more sustainable and healthier diets.[43]

Among other insights, the role of key stakeholders has been emphasized by the Global Panel on Agriculture and Food Systems for Nutrition,[44] while the Global Nutrition Report has underlined the role of government and business in ensuring that food systems and food environments support healthy diets.[45] Most recently, in early 2019, the EAT-Lancet Commission highlighted the need to accelerate the transformation of food systems to achieve not only the SDGs, but also climate goals.[46]

This momentum needs now to extend to ensure that food systems meet the needs of children and young people. Given children's unique nutritional requirements, there is an urgent need to put their needs at the heart of food systems. Among key issues that need to be considered are interventions to improve dietary choices in food environments, i.e., the points at which children, young people and caregivers interact with the wider food system, such as stores, markets, restaurants and fast-food outlets and marketing and advertising. The roles of legislation and regulation, and how business and the private sector can better support nutritious diets for children, are also vital components of a systems approach.

Supporting food system transformation through legislation

Legislation can play a fundamental role in promoting better dietary choices for children and young people at various points in the food system, such as by regulating the marketing of unhealthy food to children and of breastmilk substitutes to caregivers, by levying taxes on unhealthy foods to create price disincentives, and by increasing demand for and access to nutritious foods. It also creates a level playing field for all companies.

The International Code of Marketing of Breast-milk Substitutes (BMS), for example, is a well-established regulatory framework that protects and promotes breastfeeding, while ensuring the proper use of breastmilk substitutes, when necessary, by prohibiting their promotion and ensuring adequate product labelling.[47] (Nevertheless, according to the Access to Nutrition Foundation,

Shirin, 16, in her grocery store in Bangladesh. © UNICEF/UN066971/ Mawa

"The world's six largest baby food companies continue to market BMS using marketing practices that fall considerably below the standards of the Code".)[48] As of April 2018, 136 of 194 countries had at least some form of legal measure in place to address the provisions of the Code. Several countries have also made significant efforts to address inappropriate marketing practices of commercial complementary foods.[49] Despite these efforts, most countries still lack an effective and sustained response to tackling the marketing of BMS and other non-appropriate foods for infants and young children.

Sugar taxes

In response to rapid rises in overweight and obesity, several countries have applied taxes on sugary foods, with sugar-sweetened beverages (SSBs) the most common target. Consumption of such drinks is increasing in most countries, particularly among children and adolescents, and over-consumption contributes to unhealthy diets and weight gain.[50] According to the Global Nutrition Report, 59 countries have some sort of tax on SSBs in place.[51]

Most recently, Malaysia, for example, has started taxing two categories of beverages in 2019: drinks containing more than 5 grams of added sugar/ sweeteners per 100 ml and fruit and vegetable juices containing more than 12 grams of sugar per 100 ml. Comparing sugar taxes across countries is complicated, since they may be levied on different products, at different levels and for different purposes. It is too soon to properly assess and analyse the impact and effectiveness of this new tax.[52]

The private sector has tremendous potential to improve children's nutrition

More broadly, a recent published UNICEF review highlights positive effects in several countries on the consumption of taxed products. In Mexico, for example, consumption of taxed beverages decreased by 5.5 per cent in 2014 and 9.7 per cent in 2015,[53] while in France the demand for colas decreased by 6.7 per cent and 6.1 per cent in the first two years of implementation.[54] The Global Nutrition Report 2018 also reported that some observational studies confirm that SSB taxes are achieving positive results.[55]

Labelling and nutrition information

Legislation to place nutrition information on the front of food packages is another policy response that some countries have used. Such labelling lets caregivers and consumers – including children and young people – make informed choices and drives product reformulation. While the evidence continues to build, it suggests that food labelling can help consumers overcome barriers to meeting healthy preferences caused by inadequate information.[56] The ultimate effect on consumers' behaviour depends on their existing food preferences and level of nutrition knowledge, as well as the type of food. When the label is visible, easy to understand and not misleading, it can positively affect consumer choices. Evidence shows that well-designed labels positively affect all consumers regardless of whether they're rich or poor, and highly educated or not.[57] Nutritional labelling can potentially create incentives for manufacturers to reformulate their products to make them healthier.[58]

There are several different approaches to food labelling (*see Spotlight 'A pioneering effort in food labelling'*). Systems that enable an easy, evaluative judgement about a product's healthiness and wholesomeness (or otherwise) appear particularly effective in helping caregivers and consumers choose nutritionally favourable products. For example, colour-coded labels are more effective than plain-text labels in steering consumers toward wholesome foods.[59] Among the most common, the Multi-Traffic Light (MTL) system is often preferred by consumers for its ease. However, more recent evidence finds that warning labels and summary indicator approaches (e.g. Nutri Score) are more strongly associated with healthier purchases.[60] Warning labels in particular may be a simpler and more direct way of transmitting important nutritional information to consumers.[61, 62]

There is a strong case for adopting such labelling. Perhaps as importantly, a recent study across Latin America confirmed that when buying foods for their children, parents do consider front-of-package (FOP) information to compare the nutritional value of products, and they look for systems that are easy to understand and interpret.[63]

Role of the private sector

The private sector has tremendous potential to improve children's nutrition. Private sector actors – from smallholders to small-and medium-sized enterprises (SMEs), through to multinational food corporations – all have a role to play in transforming the world's increasingly complex global and local food systems. Private sector capacity and actions along the value chain, such as cold storage, improved packaging, fortification and some forms of processing, can reduce nutrient loss, improve food safety and deliver more nutrient-dense foods to families.[69] This is especially important in low- and middle-income countries,

SPOTLIGHT
A pioneering effort in food labelling

Faced with a rapid increase in overweight, which affects almost half of its children today, Chile has launched a comprehensive programme to try to improve children's food environments, with the aim of encouraging and supporting children, young people and caregivers to make healthier decisions.

Key initiatives include a National Food and Nutrition Policy, which outlines the right to good-quality, culturally appropriate food that supports good health and well-being.[64] Other actions include a new and innovative food labelling law that aims to protect children's nutrition by modifying food environments, promoting informed decisions on food, and decreasing consumption of excess sodium, sugar and saturated fats.

The law addresses five main areas: new front of package (FOP) warning labels; restrictions on food advertising, especially that directed towards children aged under 14; incorporation of messages promoting healthy lifestyle habits in food advertising; restrictions on the sale of food with excess sodium, sugar and saturated fats in schools; and incorporation of activities in all schools that contribute to developing healthy eating habits and an active lifestyle.[65]

The new warning labels have a striking format: white letters on a black octagon, warning consumers that a product is high in calories, sodium, sugar and/or saturated fat (*see below*).

Evaluations of the law and its implementation indicate that the public, especially children, support and easily understand these new messages.[66] Most consumers take the warning labels on food products seriously and prefer to buy foods with fewer or no labels. Also, the majority of schools comply with the regulations, generating healthier environments without advertising or marketing for inappropriate foods, and the presence of healthier food with critical nutrients, and more spaces for physical activities.[67] A number of industries have reformulated the composition of their food products in order to stay below the established limits of unhealthy ingredients.[68] ∎

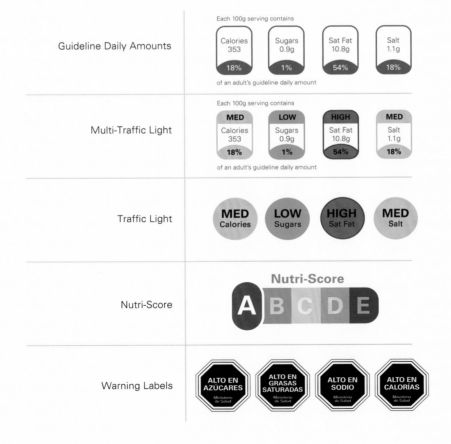

The failure of the food system to deliver healthy food for children represents a collective failure

where SMEs are numerous, and sanitation and food loss are primary concerns.[70]

In many settings, large private sector players command an increasing share of the market, giving them a tremendous ability to either enhance or reduce the nutritional value of foods. Processing is key to this. The processing of food is not inherently bad – human societies have used it for millennia to improve the safety and nutritional value of food and reduce perishability. However, processing can also remove essential nutrients and add harmful saturated fats, trans-fats, sugar and salt.[71] As noted in Chapter 3, there are reasons to be particularly concerned about the rapid growth in consumption of ultra-processed foods, which, in far too many cases, simply fail to meet the nutritional needs of children.

Commitments and accountability

The failure of the food system to deliver healthy food for children represents a collective failure. Correcting it will require collective action by, among others, governments, families, civil society and the private sector. As the role of large businesses grows in global food systems, there is a need to ensure they play a positive role in promoting nutritious, safe, affordable and sustainable foods and meet their obligations to the world's children and their families.

Engaging with business

Various governance mechanisms have emphasized the need for private sector engagement to promote better nutrition in recent years, and for clearly defined rules of engagement for improving nutritional outcomes for children. As early as 2004, the WHO World Health Assembly endorsed the Global Strategy

on Diet, Physical Activity and Health, which noted that the private sector can be a significant player in promoting healthy diets. It also highlighted the important role of the food industry in reducing the fat, sugar and salt content of processed foods, reviewing marketing practices and introducing healthier and more nutritious choices for consumers.[72]

In 2015, the United Nations Secretary General launched the Global Strategy for Women's, Children's and Adolescents' Health to strengthen the potential impact of the SDGs. The strategy highlights the importance of the business community in promoting better nutrition and healthier foods.[73] The Independent Accountability Panel created to support this strategy, however, recommends that governments regulate the food and beverage industry and adopt a binding global convention to encourage the production of healthier foods, reduce unhealthy content and control the marketing of unhealthy food for children.[74] Similarly, the Report of the Commission on Ending Childhood Obesity calls for a governance structure in which the private sector is actively engaged and held accountable in the implementation of interventions.[75]

The food industry itself has previously expressed a formal commitment to working towards better diets, nutrition and health outcomes. For example, in May 2018, the International Food Beverage Alliance formally expressed commitment to align with the WHO target to eliminate industrially produced trans-fat from the global food supply by 2023.[76]

Holding food and beverage businesses accountable to their commitments, and monitoring their progress toward stated goals, have proved challenging in the past. For example, previous experience in areas such as food marketing to children indicates that the food industry's commitments are patchy, lack ambition and are not always strictly observed.[77, 78]

Ensuring accountability requires strong coordination between the public and private sectors. Achieving better diets for children is a shared responsibility in which stakeholders not only recognize their responsibility to work for better nutrition for children, but also review current practices that may be blocking progress. Legislation and regulation have an important role, but governments can also provide incentives for businesses to increase the demand for, and to provide healthy food.[79] Businesses usually prefer the latter approach, and there is evidence that such carrot-and-stick approaches work.[80]

There are numerous challenges to mobilizing action and accountability from the private sector. Nutritional goals for children and young people compete with vested commercial interests to create strong barriers for significant transformation. A recent *Lancet* study on obesity points out that even though many evidence-based actions and policy recommendations have been identified, they have not translated into meaningful action due to vested commercial interests and insufficient public demand. The Lancet Commission has emphasized the need to reduce the influence of large commercial interests in policy development, allowing governments to implement effective policies.[81]

Public and private sectors have the shared responsibility to respond and create new avenues to deliver healthy diets and good nutrition for children: this response must be sustainable and drive profound change in the current system.

A girl at Hua Ngai Primary School, in Muong Cha, Dien Bien, Vietnam holds up a lunch tray she has washed after a nutritious school lunch. © UNICEF/ UN043574/Lister

PERSPECTIVE

The food industry must accelerate action to tackle the global nutrition crisis

Inge Kauer
Executive
Director,
Access to
Nutrition
Foundation

As Executive Director of the Access to Nutrition Foundation, Inge oversees all aspects of ATNF, including collaboration with external partners and stakeholders. She is also member of the board of ATNF. Prior to joining ATNF, Inge was a partner at Boer & Croon, a Dutch-based management consulting firm. She also worked in senior management positions with Porter Novelli, a global, full-service communications agency, and has advised various companies within the food and beverage industry on socially responsible practices and issues of corporate reputation.

What children eat and drink affects their health and well-being in the short and long term. Poor nutrition causes obesity and diet-related diseases at one end of the spectrum, and stunting, wasting and vulnerability to infection at the other. The global nutrition crisis is placing a huge burden on healthcare services and threatening the achievement of the UN's Sustainable Development Goals. The private sector can make a pivotal contribution to addressing this global problem.

Food and beverage (F&B) manufacturers have a huge influence on the diets of consumers. As incomes rise, so consumers tend to eat and drink more packaged foods and beverages. This is driving growth in the F&B industry, particularly in emerging markets, where economic growth has been almost five times faster than in mature markets. The 22 largest F&B manufacturers worldwide assessed in the 2018 Global Access to Nutrition Index operate in over 200 countries and generate approximately US$500 billion in sales.

At the Access to Nutrition Foundation (ATNF), we believe that these companies have a vital role to play in addressing the world's nutrition challenges and the

diseases caused by poor diets. Moreover, ATNF is convinced that companies that adopt comprehensive global nutrition strategies will perform better in the long term.

The Global Access to Nutrition Index is designed to track the contribution being made by F&B manufacturers to addressing global nutrition challenges and to encourage them to do more.

We see evidence of impact: since the 2016 assessment, many companies have stepped up their efforts to encourage better diets, largely through better policies and disclosure of information. Some have also increased efforts to address undernutrition, either philanthropically or through their core business, by, for example, fortifying certain foods.

While the results of the 2018 Global Index are heartening, they also show that much more progress still needs to be made. The average score overall, although still quite low, rose from 2.5 to 3.3 out of 10, and nine companies scored 5 or more, compared with only two in 2016. Even so, the 2018 Index shows there is still considerable room for improvement in the nutritional quality of companies' products.

© UNICEF/UNI183010/Quintos

The Product Profile, which assessed the healthiness of companies' products in nine countries, revealed that less than one-third of the 23,000 products surveyed can be classified as healthy.

If we zoom in on what companies are doing to ensure good nutrition for children, the 2018 Index raises some specific concerns. Only 14 per cent of the products meet the WHO's European Region dietary guidelines for marketing to children. None of the companies' portfolios comprises more than 50 per cent of products that meet the healthy standard suitable to be marketed to children. Furthermore, most companies' policies on responsible marketing to children still fall short. For example, they do not cover all media, including digital, nor apply to children over the age of 13. Only one company extends its policy on responsible marketing to 18-year-olds, which is considered best practice. The 2018 Index recommends companies stop on- and offline marketing of products to children that do not meet WHO recommendations.

The marketing of breastmilk substitutes is another area where companies need to take action. Companies publicly state their adherence to the International Code of Marketing of Breast-milk Substitutes and a few companies have strengthened their policies in response to the 2016 Index, but the 2018 Global Index found that all baby food companies that we assessed continue to contravene its guidance. Our in-depth research in Thailand and Nigeria, for example, found a high incidence of non-compliance with the code, mostly through point-of-sale promotions offered by major online retailers. Baby food companies must ensure that their marketing policies align fully with the code, are applied completely and consistently around the world – in developing as well as developed countries – and to all products, including toddler milks. Companies can also support breastfeeding mothers in their workplaces by offering flexible and supportive working arrangements, stronger maternity leave arrangements and appropriate facilities to express and store breastmilk.

To support good nutrition for children, food companies need to step up their efforts to market healthy products and make more products suitable for consumption by children. Only then can they fulfil the enormous potential they have to contribute to the aims of ending hunger and promoting healthy lives that are incorporated within the Sustainable Development Goals.■

Interventions to promote healthy eating and lifestyles are more effective and sustainable when they encourage community engagement

Civil society and community responses

Local communities and civil society organizations (CSOs) can play a significant role in promoting better child nutrition, including by representing the voices of marginalized groups (such as smallholders, indigenous children, and women), holding government and business accountable, and directly serving the nutritional needs of their communities.[82, 83]

Specifically, four key roles for CSOs were identified by *The Lancet* series on Maternal and Child Nutrition (2013):

➤ They can advocate nationally and globally for nutritional priorities and actions.

➤ They can ensure accountability for the coverage and quality of nutrition services (similar to health services or education services).

➤ They can generate context-specific knowledge on the causes of malnutrition and possible solutions.

➤ They can implement nutritional programmes and platforms for delivery.[84]

One concern over the role of CSOs is the evidence that, in some cases, special interest groups have been founded to set up false CSOs – a practice called 'astroturfing'. These groups present the appearance of a grassroots effort that supports corporate agendas, for example by challenging soda taxes.[85]

Top-down and bottom-up change

Community-based responses to malnutrition are either top down or bottom up. In a top-down response, local groups are mobilized to implement community-based interventions, such as education and behaviour change campaigns, and emergency responses. In many cases, these interventions are planned and designed at a national level, but their implementation by local groups enhances their legitimacy and transparency. There is evidence to suggest that interventions to promote healthy eating and lifestyles are more effective and sustainable when they encourage community engagement and consider the specificities of the local context.[86]

Bottom-up responses can include advocacy by grassroots CSOs for systemic and fundamental change to the food system. Among the causes taken up by grassroots CSOs are hunger and malnutrition, particularly in children, soil and water conservation, food-waste reduction, the right to food, local food production, urban agriculture, regulation of genetically modified organisms, reform of trade practices, and the rights of youth, women and indigenous peoples. In the global south, 'food sovereignty' has emerged as a key issue for grassroots CSOs. Its core principle is that "communities have the right to define their own food and agriculture policy."[87]

Numerous other grassroots CSOs and social movements are working to reform the food system and improve nutrition. For example, the Pakistan Fisherfolk Forum promotes the rights and empowerment of fishing communities and works to protect their livelihoods

SPOTLIGHT
Surviving and thriving in Peru

When they were born in 2000 in the Hanaq Chuquibamba community, located in the Peruvian Andes, Josué Abdías and Josué Abraham were both undernourished. Today, the twins are healthy adolescents and both are preparing to go to university. The twins' turnaround mirrors Peru's broader success in combating undernutrition. In 2000, almost one in three children in Peru was stunted; today, thanks in part to interventions such as the Good Start Programme[95], from which the twins benefited, the prevalence is just 12.9 per cent.

Peru's success in fighting undernutrition reflects a determined national political effort, coordination between sectors, and an effective results-based budgeting and monitoring system. Community leadership has also been key. In Hanaq Chuquibamba, local leader and father of the twins, Igidio Sataraura, emphasized the centrality of the community's work to monitor children's nutritional status, ensure access to health and nutrition services, and disseminate knowledge about feeding and other caring practices.

However, Peru's fight against malnutrition is not over. There is concern over the continuing prevalence of forms of hidden hunger, particularly iron deficiency anaemia, and, increasingly, overweight. A stakeholder consultation organized by UNICEF Peru in November 2018 brought together government representatives, academia and CSOs to reflect on strategies to continue the fight against all forms of malnutrition. Participants recognized the new challenges posed by persistent undernutrition and rising overweight and emphasized the role of the public sector in coordinating policies, strategies and programmes, as well as the need for continued inter-sectoral coordination and adequate funding. ∎

Josué Abdías and Josué Abraham with their parents in the Hanaq Chuquibamba community in Peru. © UNICEF/ Vilca 2019

through sustainable fishing policies and practices.[88] The Movimento dos Trabalhadores Rurais Sem Terra (MST; 'Landless Workers Movement') is the largest social movement in Latin America. It has worked for over 30 years for the principles of agrarian reform and food sovereignty in Brazil.[89] Local CSOs are working for reform in modern food systems in high-income countries as well. In the UK, for example, CSOs have been successful in promoting Fair Trade, organic certification, ecological approaches, permaculture, and local and slow food movements.[90]

CSOs can play a key role in promoting nutrition in non-food systems too. For example, in the education system, CSOs may shape policy around obesogenic school environments, school feeding and nutrition education. In the social protection sector, they may work to ensure that children from marginalized communities receive essential services. CSOs have also advocated for community-led plans for improved water and sanitation.

Despite their potential to contribute to improving children's nutrition, CSOs have encountered difficulties in participating in policy formulation and have enjoyed relatively little success in holding governments and the private sector to account.[91, 92] Nevertheless, there are instances of where CSOs have been included in national and international dialogues to shape nutritional priorities and policies. The SUN Movement includes a Civil Society Network of over 2,000 local member organizations, to foster alliances and promote nutrition actions in SUN member countries.[93] The UN Committee on World Food Security also has a civil society mechanism that provides an inclusive space to ensure civil society is represented in wider policy debates.[94]

Conclusion

The evidence in this chapter is clear: all over the world, there are countless examples of initiatives both big and small that are helping to improve children's nutrition. However, as the continuing toll of stunting, wasting and hidden hunger, and the rising toll of overweight, also make clear, much remains to be done. If we are to meet the malnutrition challenge full on, we need a scaled-up approach that puts children's nutritional rights at the heart of food systems and prioritizes nutrition outcomes in other key systems. The next, and final, chapter of this report identifies how this can be done by identifying five key principles to mobilize government, business and civil society to transform children's nutrition in the 21st century. ∎

Mother breastfeeding her baby girl in the family yurta in Kyrgyzstan. © UNICEF/UN0151410/Voroni

SPECIAL SECTION

Influence of food marketing on children's diets

Far from being a matter of simple personal preference, individual food choices and eating habits are largely influenced by the food environment – a mix of factors that includes food availability, accessibility, affordability and preference. **One important influence in the food environment on consumer behaviour and a child's diet is food marketing.**

Across high-, middle- and low-income countries, children are becoming increasingly subjected to ubiquitous marketing strategies that have a powerful effect. Advertisements, food packaging that attracts children and digital campaigns all stimulate a preference for, and consumption of unhealthy food – particularly fast food, ultra-processed foods high in salt, sugar and/or fat, and sugar-sweetened beverages. All these conspire to increases the risk of overweight among children.

According to the WHO Commission on Ending Childhood Obesity (the ECHO Commission), food marketing is directly linked to growing overweight and obesity and related harms to children's health and nutrition: "There is unequivocal evidence that the marketing of unhealthy foods and sugar-sweetened beverages is related to childhood obesity."[96] For example, a survey of Australian children aged 10–16 showed that those who engaged with more food content online, especially video ads, were more likely to consume unhealthy food.[97] Several other systematic reviews have determined the extent, nature and impact of food marketing on children and subsequent reviews have reaffirmed these findings.[98]

Efforts by governments and civil society to promote healthy diets in high-income countries face a steep challenge. The marketing of unhealthy food outstrips spending on healthier food or healthy food promotion in North America and Western Europe. In 2012, the amount spent on fast-food advertising in the United States was over 12 times the total spent on milk, water, vegetables and fruit combined.[99] In the UK, unhealthy food advertising spending is 30 times greater than spending by the government on healthy eating habits.[100] A recent study conducted across 22 countries found that for every one advert for healthy foods, there were four promoting foods high in fats, sugar and salt – and marketing of these unhealthy products was most frequent during children's peak viewing time.[101] Globally, children are exposed to a huge volume of marketing for unhealthy foods and beverages, despite the implementation of self-regulatory initiatives by industry.

In-store marketing (*retail marketing*) also represents a major threat to children. A recent study in Mexico shows that in-store techniques are used with the specific aim of attracting children to unhealthy foods, including, for example, the placement of products at children's eye-level, promotions with prizes, and the use of licensed movie and cartoon characters.[102]

Lower-income countries represent an unprecedented opportunity to the manufacturers and marketers of ultra-processed foods, fast food and sugar-sweetened beverages. From 2011 to 2016, fast-food sales grew by 254 per cent in Argentina, 113 per cent in India, 83 per cent in Viet Nam and 64 per cent in Egypt.[103] Digital marketing is both more effective and pervasive than traditional methods using TV and print, raising concerns about the effects of food marketing. An analysis in Europe found that combining online marketing with other media increased the returns on TV and cinema advertising by around 70 per cent.[104] Globally, one in three internet users is estimated to be a child. In less developed countries, the internet

Aleksa, 8, and Kosta, 12, play games on their mobile phones in Belgrade, Serbia. Digital media magnify the reach and impact of marketing unhealthy foods to children. © UNICEF/UN040855/Bicanski

is often predominantly accessed through smart-phones, giving food marketers a channel for adver-tising that is available to children almost all of the time.[105]

There are psychological, technical and structural rea-sons why digital media multiplies the channels for marketing, magnifying its reach and impact. First, digital media allows for 'micro-targeting' of mar-keting messages, reaching those most vulnerable. Second, digital media allows for ever-evolving, novel and creative approaches such as games, and peer photo- and video-sharing that creates immersive, en-gaging techniques that magnify their appeal. Third, invasive, immersive, entertaining, high-engaging and data-driven techniques are widely shared by children with their peers.

In response to the growing influence of food market-ing, in May 2010, the 63rd World Health Assembly unanimously endorsed the WHO recommendations on the marketing of foods and non-alcoholic bever-ages to children.[106] WHO urges Member States to restrict the marketing of unhealthy food to children, to promote better nutrition, and to contribute to the commitments to end childhood obesity. As opposed to voluntary self-regulation by the food industry, WHO recommends legally binding rules through legislation.

A recent study evaluated food marketing policies and sales in 79 countries. Assessing regulations in force up to 2014, and food sales between 2002 and 2016, it found that unhealthy food sales increased where countries did not have unhealthy food marketing regulations, whereas unhealthy food sales reduced after such policies were implemented. Notably, countries with industry self-regulation policies also saw an increase in unhealthy food sales, whereas sales decreased where regulation was statutory.[107]■

PERSPECTIVE

Grassroots activism in Mexico battles childhood obesity

Alejandro Calvillo Unna
Director General,
El Poder del
Consumidor,
Mexico

Alejandro Calvillo Unna was part of the group that founded Greenpeace Mexico. He worked for 12 years at Greenpeace, with five of those as Executive Director. He founded the Mexican civil society association El Poder del Consumidor (EPC) ('Consumer Power') in 2006, where he serves as Director. EPC has been a central actor in obtaining a soda tax, mandatory regulation of food and beverages in schools, and the implementation of a regulation on marketing that targets children. Alejandro is a member of The Lancet Commission on Obesity and has contributed to the WHO's advisory groups.

An epidemic of childhood obesity is sweeping the world. Consensus in the scientific community and among international organizations points to the mass introduction of ultra-processed food and sugar-sweetened beverages (SSBs) into our diets as the main reason. Yet scientific data revealing the damage to health caused by ultra-processed foods and recommendations by the World Health Organization (WHO) to reduce consumption of these products have been vigorously contested by major multinational food and beverage corporations.

Non-profit organizations play a vital role in encouraging policies that take on these powerful forces to battle the global obesity epidemic. Academic institutions that generate research and evidence often do not have a prominent impact on influencing public policy. Research is published in scientific journals and often remains hidden from the legislative sphere. An alliance between academia and civil society can unlock change, with the latter lobbying for public policies based on evidence generated by the former.

Non-profit organizations that fight for public health policies to combat obesity and regulations to create healthier environments for children are crucial for building discussion in the media and generating public opinion that is favourable to anti-obesity policies.

Public campaigns, while lacking the vast funding that goes into advertising junk food and SSBs, provide information capable of generating a shift in public awareness and a sense of urgency to act to protect health, especially for children.

In Mexico, we created a simple campaign in 2013 to show how much sugar there was in a single 600-ml bottle of SSB, the most popular container size. As of 2011, Mexico was the world's largest consumer of SSBs. The campaign presented the viewer with two images. In one ad, the caption read: "Would you drink 12 spoonfuls of sugar? Soda is sweet, diabetes isn't." In the second ad, which showed an adult hand offering a soft drink to a boy and a girl, the text read: "Would you give them 12 spoonfuls of sugar? Why do you give them soda?" With billboards on the street and advertising in city metro stations, the information had a strong impact on a population that had no idea how much sugar these beverages contained.

The campaign, which was accompanied by data on the growing consumption of SSBs and the rising number of diabetes-related deaths enabled us to present a proposal on levying a tax on these drinks. In 2014, we succeeded in having a special tax of about 10 per cent imposed on SSBs as part of Mexico's federal tax reform.

¿Les darías **12** cucharadas de azúcar?

¿POR QUÉ LES DAS REFRESCO?

© El Poder del Consumidor, Mexico

The demand for extra taxes on SSBs has been accompanied by a proposal for regulations to change the obesogenic environment for children, such as banning unhealthy food and beverage advertising to children and removing these products from schools. In 2014, we successfully advocated for legislation making school food and beverage guidelines mandatory, although the political will needed to enforce them has been lacking. Laws prohibit the advertising of these products to children on television and movies during certain hours and require food and beverage containers to bear front-of-pack (FOP) labels.

However, these regulations are developed by an institution with a profound conflict of interest, and are influenced by the interests of the food industry. Thus, the FOP label, designed by the industry itself, is hard for consumers to understand, and the sugar criterion it recommends is actually a risk to health. Regulations on advertising to children are, in practice, a simulation: they do not cover the shows and times that children watch the most TV, and nor do they control advertising on the street, on the internet or other media, or the use of gifts and promotions that encourage children to consume unhealthy products.

In response, we filed multiple cases against the FOP label. Two of these cases were ruled in our favour, establishing that the FOP label was a violation to the right to healthy food, information and the best interests of the child. In parallel, the scientific community proposed a FOP warning label for unhealthy foods and beverages that clearly alerts the consumer if a product is high in sugar, fats or sodium.

We also conducted a study to show that Mexican schools remain obesogenic environments, that the guidelines are not enforced, and that educational authorities must fulfil their obligation to guarantee a healthy environment for children.

In some cases, such as in Chile, health authorities and legislators committed to the common good have pushed policies to battle the obesity epidemic without broad-based movement from civil society. However, in most cases, the actions of these organizations remain crucial in driving change. The partnership between civil society and academia requires a third partner who is essential to achieving the common goal – legislators and public officials who are committed to public health and who are willing to face down the powerful vested interests that stand in their way. ∎

Some innovations in nutrition

NEW AND IMPROVED DIGITAL HEIGHT BOARDS

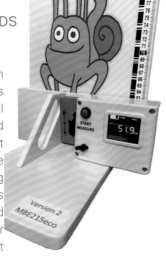

Collecting accurate data on young children's height is challenging. A new digital height board, designed for children's comfort and to yield more precise measurements, is now being tested. Improved estimates will provide governments and practitioners with a better understanding of the rate at which children are growing. © UNICEF, 2019

BETTER TASTING THERAPEUTIC FOOD FOR CHILDREN IN CAMBODIA

One in three children under five in Cambodia is stunted or underweight, but only 6 per cent of children suffering from severe acute malnutrition receive treatment. To make therapeutic food more appealing and less expensive than imported milk-based products, the Cambodian Government's Department of Fisheries, France's Institut de Recherche pour le Développement and UNICEF developed Nutrix. Filled with micronutrients and designed to appeal to Cambodian children in taste, it is locally produced and made from fish, rice and beans.

A NEW APPROACH TO PREVENTING CHILDHOOD OBESITY THROUGH AN INNOVATIVE PARTNERSHIP

Any parent knows how difficult it can be to get children to eat healthy food. In 2018, Beko, the leading home appliance brand in Europe, launched #EatLikeAPro, a global initiative to help families encourage their children to eat better and prevent childhood obesity. Beko enlisted the help of star players from its partner FC Barcelona to share the stars' favourite healthy eating stories and recipes on the #EatLikeAPro website to inspire parents to prepare healthier meals for their children. The campaign captured worldwide attention, generating 28 million views with a reach of over 140 million people.

To amplify global awareness about the importance of healthy eating and introduce on-the-ground impact, Beko joined forces with UNICEF, which has been working with FC Barcelona since 2006 to promote children's rights and education through sport. To raise funds, Beko and FC Barcelona took advantage of the more than 650 million viewers of an El Clasico match and launched the #EatLikeAPro hashtag-sharing campaign. For every hashtag used, Beko donated 1 euro to UNICEF. The fund reached 1 million euros in 11 days, with hashtag shares taking place in 167 countries. The funds are being used to support UNICEF programmes in six Latin American countries to address the root causes of the emerging overweight and obesity epidemic.

© Marc Ensenyat

In May 2019, with UNICEF's technical input and FC Barcelona and Barça Foundation collaboration, Beko surveyed over 13,500 children between the ages of 6 and 10 in 18 countries, to find out whether they would eat healthier food if they knew their hero or role model did. An overwhelming 80 per cent of the children said they would. The consequent #EatLikeAPro online campaign features FC Barcelona player Gerard Piqué promoting healthy eating to primary-school children. The campaign registered over 15 million views in its first month.* Through this unique tripartite partnership, #EatLikeAPro has developed into an award-winning social campaign with global reach and importance.

*Social monitoring statistics supplied by Beko.

USING AI-DRIVEN PHOTOGRAPHY TO DETERMINE MALNUTRITION

The traditional approach of measuring a child's upper-arm circumference and weight–height ratio requires time, equipment and trained staff. Using new facial recognition and machine learning technologies, the Method for Extremely Rapid Observation of Nutritional Status assesses

© Kimetrica

malnutrition in children aged 6–59 months in emergency settings without human assessment – or error. The algorithm estimates body mass index (BMI) by analysing a digital image of the child. (For their safety, the actual image is not stored.) This rapid and less intrusive tool is intended to complement rather than replace other measurements.

WHAT'S IN THIS? SCAN THE BARCODE AND FIND OUT

From Australia to India to France, customers are using their smartphones to scan barcodes on packaged foods to find out how much sugar, salt and fat they contain. Nutritional information collected through the FoodSwitch app for over 34,000 packaged foods was used to improve Australia's Health Star Rating food labelling system for sugary packaged foods. In India, FoodSwitch was used to evaluate the healthiness of the packaged foods sold by the largest food manufacturers.

Open Food Facts, an open-source platform that has nutritional information on over 75,000 products, entered by volunteers in 150 countries, was used by the French National Nutrition and Health Programme to validate its nutrition grading scoring. These consumer-generated databases are proving to be a more cost-effective alternative to purchasing data from market research companies.

A DATA-DRIVEN RESPONSE TO THE TRIPLE BURDEN IN INDIA

India's Comprehensive National Nutrition Survey (CNNS), which ran from 2016 to 2018 across all states, was the biggest ever nationwide effort to paint a detailed picture of the nutritional status of pre-schoolers, school-age children and adolescents up to 19 years old.

For the first time, the extent and severity of micronutrient deficiencies, information on fat distribution and nutritional risk factors for non-communicable diseases (NCDs) and links between children's nutritional status and their cognitive development were assessed in a single survey. As well as being unprecedented in scale, the CNNS used innovative data quality assurance measures, including SMS-based monitoring and gold-standard methods for biological sample collection and laboratory testing.

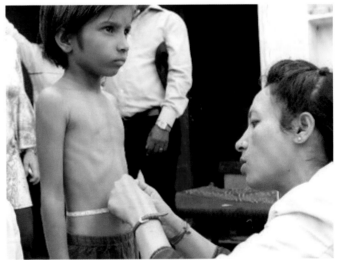

© UNICEF/UN052963/Matta

Notable findings from the survey, which was made possible through a philanthropic partnership with Megha and Aditya Mittal, included seasonal variations in vitamin A deficiency, a large disparity in anaemia prevalence between girls and boys, and evidence that overweight and obesity, as well as the threat of diabetes, are on the rise among school-age children.

These findings have informed India's ambitious child nutrition programmes. They also provide the basis for potential new policy recommendations, including scaling up dietary diversification and food fortification to address vitamin A deficiency, tackling the triple burden of malnutrition and starting programmes in the early years to instil healthy lifelong eating habits.

05 AN AGENDA TO PUT CHILDREN'S NUTRITION RIGHTS FIRST

One word must be at the heart of our response to children's malnutrition – action. We need action that reflects the core role of food systems, that strengthens the supply of – and demand for – better food, that improves children's food environments, and that reflects the role of key supportive systems: health, water and sanitation, education and social protection. With action comes another imperative: accountability. Progress must be measured, shared, acted on and celebrated.

These five key responses are essential to improve children's nutrition:

➤ Empower families, children and young people to demand nutritious food

➤ Drive food suppliers to do the right thing for children

➤ Build healthy food environments for all children

➤ Mobilize supportive systems to scale up nutrition results for all children

➤ Collect, analyse and use good-quality data and evidence regularly to guide action and track progress

Two girls buy guava fruits at Honiara Central Market, Guadalcanal, Solomon Islands. © UNICEF/UN0343034/Naftalin

Put children's nutrition first

**1 in 3 children
is not growing well**
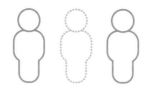
**For every child
to grow well**

1 Empower families, children and young
people to demand nutritious food

Drive food suppliers to do
the right thing for children **2**

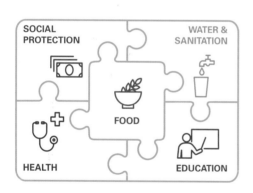

4 Mobilize supportive systems to scale up
nutrition results for all children

Build healthy food environments
for all children **3**

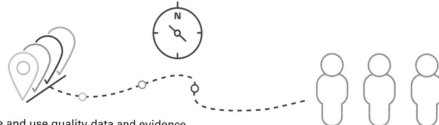

5 Collect, analyse and use quality data and evidence
regularly to guide action and track progress

Introduction

Nutrition is a basic building block in a child's life. Every aspect of childhood – from development in the womb, to playing and exploring in infancy and early childhood, and from learning in school, to preparing for adulthood and employment – is built on a foundation of good nutrition. For those suffering from malnutrition, every challenge in life becomes more difficult and every opportunity harder to grasp. Amid growing concern about how the world is feeding itself, this report proposes an agenda for every child to eat well.

This report began by defining malnutrition as "lack of proper nutrition, caused by not having enough to eat, not eating enough of the right things, or being unable to use the food that one does eat." Globally, one in three children under 5 is not growing well because of malnutrition and two in three are at risk of malnutrition because of the poor quality of their diets.

The nature of malnutrition is also evolving as family diets become determined by ever more globalized and commercialized food systems. Food systems are failing children and urgent transformation is needed. Children's unique nutritional needs during the various stages of life must be at the heart of the food system transformation and a priority for all actors involved in the provision of nutritious, affordable, safe and sustainable diets.

This report comes at a time of concern not only about the ability of the world to produce enough nutritious food for everyone, but also about its capacity to do so sustainably in ways that protect the planet. This report is unique in its call to put children first, at the centre of the world's food and nutrition challenge. However, amid this wave of interest, we would do well to remember a proverb from Nigeria: Fine words do not produce food. Words aren't enough. Our response to children's malnutrition must be grounded in action.

First, our response must recognize the right of children to food and nutrition as a human right. Thirty years ago, with the signing of the Convention on the Rights of the Child, world leaders came together to commit to the right of every child to enjoy a full childhood. Still today, far too many children are robbed of their present and their future because of malnutrition. UNICEF calls on all actors to put children first and combat malnutrition by recommitting to the right of all children – without exception – to food and nutrition as a human right.

Second, women and children's well-being must be at the heart of government policy. When it comes to ensuring healthy diets, governments have a critical role to play through policy, regulation, quality assurance and effective programmes. These commitments – and the financial investments associated with them – should be grounded in evidence and linked to a set of clear targets and accountability metrics for each stakeholder. Progress towards food and nutrition targets should be regularly tracked, shared, acted on and celebrated.

Third, putting children at the centre of food systems requires a multi-pronged approach: stimulating demand for healthy options, strengthening the supply of nutritious foods, and improving children's food environments. Experiences from

Fine words do not produce food. Words aren't enough. Our response to children's malnutrition must be grounded in action

Dr. Pakirova prepares dinner for her family in Kyrgyzstan's Chon Alai district.
© UNICEF/UN0146971/Voronin

an increasing number of countries provide examples of what works, but better data and evidence are needed to monitor performance, document lessons and improve actions at scale.

Finally, our response must go beyond the food system itself and be supported through the efforts of other systems. We have seen how four systems – health, water and sanitation, education, and social protection – can work together with the food system to support children's nutrition in diverse contexts. It's time to

enhance these interventions to scale up the impact for nutrition. The importance of nutrition to children's development and well-being, and the growth and development of national economies and human capital, mean that we must put nutrition at the core of how we address wider challenges such as in health, education, poverty reduction and equity.

To guide the response to children's malnutrition, this report proposes the following **Agenda to Put Children's Nutrition Rights First**.

1 | Empower families, children and young people to demand nutritious food

Demand affects supply because food producers respond to consumer behaviours and aspirations. When healthy options are affordable, convenient and desirable, parents and caregivers make better food choices for children. As children grow older, they make more food choices, so knowledge and information can make them powerful agents of change. Stimulating demand for nutritious foods means not only educating consumers on the benefits of a healthy diet, but also leveraging cultural and social aspirations to change behaviours and practices.

➤ **Understand and leverage family and community dynamics.** Family and community dynamics, including intrahousehold distribution and the utilization of foods, can vary greatly. Evidence consistently shows that when women have more education, decision-making power and control over the household's income, they tend to choose healthier foods and feeding practices for their children. One area of constraint is that food preparers in households can lack the skills to create meals that meet the nutritional needs of children. It is also important to engage fathers and the extended family to support women's multiple roles, especially women in the formal and informal workforces.

➤ **Improve nutrition education to enable better lifelong dietary habits.** Nutrition education starts at home, continues in school, and should be reinforced by public communication campaigns. It should also be incorporated in the health and social protection systems. Parents need to be educated about nutritious foods and healthy feeding practices for their children and the risks of over-consumption of unhealthy foods. Education should extend beyond the benefits of healthy foods to behaviour change and empowerment, especially for school-age children and adolescents, who are themselves agents of change.

➤ **Improve the desirability of healthy foods.** Innovative, fun, memorable and engaging communication strategies to promote healthy eating – including but not limited to campaigns – can leverage the social and cultural aspirations of children, adolescents and parents. These strategies should capture parents' interests and aspirations, such as physical growth, brain development and school performance, as well as the interests and aspirations of school-age children and adolescents, such as sport, appearance, strength, pop culture, social media and more.

➤ **Use proven legislation to reduce demand for unhealthy foods.** In certain circumstances, specific taxes on unhealthy foods, such as sugar-sweetened beverages, can reduce demand for these products by making them relatively more expensive than healthier alternatives. Combined with nutritional education, these tools have proved effective drivers towards more nutritious diets for children. ∎

2 | Drive food suppliers to do the right thing for children

It's not enough that children and families demand healthy food – it must also be available, affordable, safe and convenient. Food producers and suppliers have a key role to play, and governments can set standards to create a level playing field for all producers and suppliers, ensuring that their actions align with children's best interests. Food systems are diverse, and so are the solutions. In non-industrialized food systems, for example, smallholders can be supported to raise their productivity; in industrialized food systems, stronger market linkages and incentive structures can improve the availability and affordability of fresh and healthy foods. All food systems need to move towards environmentally sustainable production and consumption to protect children's nutrition today and in future generations.

➤ **Provide economic incentives, and eliminate disincentives, for producers to supply more nutritious children's foods.** Policymakers can incentivize food producers to supply nutritious, safe and affordable foods to children while eliminating subsidies for sugar, refined grains and processed oils. As the complementary feeding period (6–23 months) is particularly important for children's growth and development, food producers should be discouraged from marketing nutrient-poor, sugar-rich and highly processed foods as suitable for this age group. Incentives should also seek to increase the proportion of fresh fruits and vegetables available at markets, supermarkets and other points of sale, especially in low-income communities and food deserts. Business-friendly policies, such as reduced rents, tariffs and utilities, can be used to reward companies that produce and market healthy foods.

➤ **Invest in the modernization of infrastructure and transport chains to reduce food and nutrient losses and improve food safety, especially in rural areas.** Many of the foods that children need most, including fruits, vegetables, and foods of animal origin such as fish, eggs, milk and dairy, are also highly perishable. Where infrastructure is poor, much is lost to spoilage and contamination, driving up the price and reducing availability and affordability. Children's diets often then turn to highly processed foods, which are less expensive and have a longer shelf-life. Investments by the food industry and governments in storage, packaging, processing, cold-chain logistics and other infrastructure to bring healthy foods to market can reduce both the costs to producers and the prices faced by families.

➤ **Strengthen policies, strategies and programmes to enhance the resilience of the food supply in crisis-prone areas and fragile contexts.** In humanitarian settings, children always suffer the most. Appropriately formulated, ready-to-prepare fortified complementary foods have a critical role to play in supporting optimal growth and development in infants and young children, as do ready-to-use therapeutic foods (RUTF) for the treatment of acute malnutrition in children. Governments of crisis-hit areas should ensure that such foods are readily available through either facilitating local production or removing barriers to import. Investment in well-designed social protection programmes can ensure that women and children living in vulnerable households have access to more nutritious and diverse diets.

> **Reduce the environmental impact of food production for today's and tomorrow's children.** There are clear linkages between food production and consumption, environmental sustainability, and the impact on children's nutrition and health. Robust interventions are needed to reduce the environmental impact of food production and consumption in ways that evidence shows are harmful to children, including greenhouse gas emissions, fossil fuel use, pesticide use and fertilizer run-off. Production systems such as agroecology, agroforestry, intercropping and integrated crop-livestock management can enhance the sustainability and biodiversity of food systems for generations to come.■

3 | Build healthy food environments for all children

The personal and external food environments are where children and their caregivers interact with the food system. While the forces of supply and demand shape food environments, context-appropriate actions such as protection against exploitative marketing and mandatory labelling can help create food environments that are conducive to nutritious diets for children.

> **Create environments conducive to healthy breastfeeding and complementary feeding practices.** Strictly enforce the International Code of Marketing of Breast-milk Substitutes and hold violators accountable. Promote supportive policies for mothers, parents and families, including maternity leave and the provision of time and spaces for breastfeeding in the workplace and in public places. Stimulate the availability, accessibility and affordability of easy-to-prepare complementary foods at points of sale, particularly in low- and middle-income countries.

> **Enhance the transparency of nutritional information through front-of-package food labelling.** Governments should mandate front-of-package food labelling, especially for foods that are marketed to children or marketed as suitable for children. Labelling can raise awareness of the nutritional value of foods, promote behaviour change among parents, adolescents and children, and stimulate businesses to work towards product transformation by adding healthier ingredients and removing unhealthy ingredients. To be effective, such labels need to be prominent and instantly readable. Quality seals and similar highly visible certifications can also be awarded to vendors that provide healthy options and food choices for children.

> **Regulate the marketing of unhealthy foods to children.** Children everywhere should be protected against the impact of harmful and exploitative marketing and advertising of unhealthy foods. Regulations should target advertising on television, and in games, movies, books and social media for all age groups, as well as businesses and restaurants that give away toys to market unhealthy foods.

> **Reduce obesogenic influences around places designed for children, particularly schools.**

For many children, schools provide their first regularly consumed meals outside the home. Governments and ministries of education need to take steps to combat obesogenic food environments, including ensuring that school meals are nutritious and diverse, limiting the sale and advertising of sugar-sweetened beverages and foods high in unhealthy fats, sugar and salt in proximity to schools and playgrounds, and ensuring that adequate time during the school day is set aside for active play in safe recreational spaces. ■

---

4 | Mobilize supportive systems to scale up nutrition results for all children

While the food system is a critical pillar for the provision of healthy diets for children, four other key systems must be mobilized to deliver nutrition services, improve nutrition practices and achieve nutrition outcomes at scale. In addition to the food system, the health, water and sanitation, education and social protection systems must all deliver interventions in a coordinated fashion. A systems approach ensures that children and families have access to healthy diets and receive the nutrition services children need to grow and develop to their full potential.

> **The health system.** Actions need to be integrated into the health system to ensure that children survive, grow and

develop to their full potential. Investment in the nutritional knowledge and skills of health workers, the frontline between the health system and families, is particularly important. Preventive care against malnutrition, such as early initiation of breastfeeding, counselling and support for exclusive breastfeeding, complementary feeding and maternal nutrition, are essential services that should be delivered during pre- and post-natal healthcare visits. Screening and treatment for anaemia, vitamin A deficiency, growth failure and excessive weight gain also require health system skills, support and supplies. Finally, given the high mortality risk associated with wasting, governments should systematically integrate into routine services the early detection and treatment of children with life-threatening wasting.

> **The water and sanitation system.** The water and sanitation system is critical to ensuring children have access to safe drinking water and safe sanitation. Such access is essential to ensure a healthy diet, protect children from infection and enteropathy to ensure their bodies can utilize nutrients, and to prevent stunting, wasting and other forms of malnutrition. Governments should support the construction of improved latrines and reduce the distance that women and children must travel to access safe drinking water and toilets. While investments in infrastructure are important, behaviour change communication for optimal feeding, safe food handling and handwashing with soap at critical times should be mainstreamed in communities and schools, targeting parents and children from a young age.

> **The education system.** The education system can deliver a number of nutrition interventions to support healthy diets and good nutrition for children and adolescents. In both formal and informal education settings, nutrition education from as early an age as possible should ensure that children and their caregivers are empowered to make healthy food choices. Schools should create healthy food environments for children and adolescents,

which includes ensuring the availability of safe drinking water and limiting the availability of obesogenic influences within schools and school zones. In some contexts, school feeding programmes may be useful in providing nutritious meals to vulnerable children. The education system can play a key role in the delivery of integrated programmes for the prevention of iron deficiency and anaemia through the provision of micronutrient supplements, deworming prophylaxis and counselling on healthy eating, for example.

> **The social protection system.** The social protection system forms a crucial safety net to protect the nutrition and well-being of children and women from the most vulnerable families in society and those suffering from social exclusion and poverty. In a direct way, the social protection system can ensure children's access to nutritious and diverse diets through food transfers, food vouchers or cash transfers. Social protection programmes can also secure access to nutrition services through the health system, such as pre- and post-natal care and nutritional counselling to mothers (including those of malnourished children) and through the education system using school-feeding vouchers, for example. In addition, the social protection system is essential to support children's and households' food security by preventing the depletion of productive assets in emergencies, such as livestock and seeds.

5 | Collect, analyse and use good-quality data and evidence regularly to guide action and track progress

Accurate and timely data are required to understand the malnutrition problem, to take coordinated, evidence-based action, and to hold all actors – public and private – to account. Yet the scarcity of data remains a major barrier that is preventing governments from responding with effective policies, strategies and programmes. Data collection methods and frequency must be transformed to expand what we know about the diets and nutrition of children, adolescents and women across the lifecycle, extending beyond the traditional focus on the first 1,000 days. Action to improve malnutrition requires responsive data systems and a culture of data-sharing and transparency.

➤ **Set targets for, and track progress on, complementary feeding for infants and young children.**
It is vital to address the absence of global targets for improving the diets of children and feeding practices in the crucial complementary feeding period. Global and national targets for continued breastfeeding, complementary feeding and healthy diets should be set. These targets should use standardized indicators that can be regularly collected in national nutrition data and information systems and surveys. Indicators and targets should focus on improving positive practices, such as increasing the consumption of fruits and vegetables and achieving minimum dietary diversity, as well as reducing negative behaviours such as the consumption of ultra-processed foods. Tracking both healthy and unhealthy feeding

patterns is essential to assess how well the food system is delivering for children.

➤ **Improve metrics, data collection and targets for children's diets and nutrition during the school-age years and through adolescence.**
Data on older children and adolescents are scarce and often of poor quality. Addressing this knowledge gap demands increased attention. Dietary and nutritional data for school-age children and adolescents are important not only to understand the geographic and socio-economic distribution of eating patterns and different forms of malnutrition in middle childhood and adolescence, but also to understand who and what influences dietary choices – if choices do exist – in this age group and to design effective interventions that target school-age children and adolescents. As is the case with complementary feeding, global and national targets for the nutrition of school-age children and adolescents are imperative if progress is to take place.

➤ **Support the development of novel analytical tools and methodologies for studying dynamic food systems and identifying the factors affecting children's diets and nutrition.**
Industrialized food systems are characterized by complexity and rapid change. Putting children at the centre of food systems requires a new set of analytical tools and methodologies to understand how production and consumption

choices are made, how children's food environments are shaped, and how different actors and stakeholders – public and private – interact. A range of established and innovative tools – including household surveys, food mapping and food system dashboards – can enable policymakers to compare their food system with those of other similar countries and identify key challenges and prioritize actions.

➤ **Set targets and improve data collection to measure the coverage and equity of essential nutrition services delivered through the health, water and sanitation, education and social** **protection systems.** Globally, much of the data in the area of children's nutrition relate to services delivered through health system interventions and contacts. Given the important role of other systems in supporting children's nutrition, improved monitoring is needed of the interventions and actions delivered through all programmes and delivery platforms. Data systems and capacities should be strengthened to monitor newly developed indicators and targets for the coverage and equity of essential nutrition interventions. This is an essential step in ensuring that a transparent public accountability system is put in place.■

A child is weighed during a routine growth monitoring session at the Centre for the Protection of Mother & Child Health. Tunis, Tunisia.
© UNICEF/UN0212543/Noorani

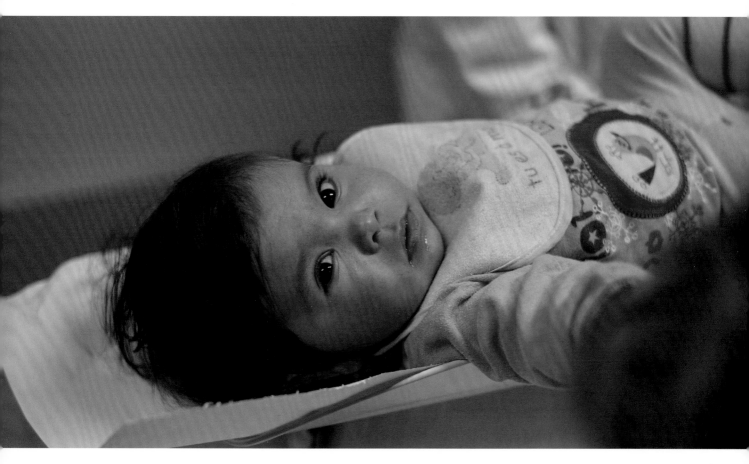

SPECIAL SECTION

Better data, better diets

Like the challenge of malnutrition itself, data on child nutrition – what is tracked, analysed and compared across geographies and populations – are evolving. The global dietary shift and the triple burden of malnutrition are increasing the need for more data, while technologies are opening opportunities for new understanding. **As addressing malnutrition becomes more holistic, with a focus on systems that cut across sectors and take into account food environments and consumer behaviour, a wider range of actionable data is needed.**

Using data and evidence to shape decision-making for policies and programming is crucial to improving the lives of children. Unfortunately, current data gaps, particularly on the nature and quality of children's diets around the world and across the life course, make the prevalence, nature and scope of malnutrition difficult to understand. The broader food environment in which dietary decisions are made is also poorly understood, highlighting the need for new tools to better understand children's diets. Methods to measure food availability, access, affordability, demand and use as a set of inter-related factors that influence children's diets are needed, along with tracking and understanding the nutrition transition as unhealthy diets become more prevalent worldwide.

However, the potential impact and effectiveness of data do not lie only in tracking more indicators or producing more surveys: the analysis and use of existing data to drive policy advocacy and programme design and implementation is vital. This effort must also be linked to the development of global and national targets for improving children's diets and feeding practices.

Data on children under 5

Most data on nutrition for low- and middle-income countries relate to children under 5. Given the influence of the first 1,000 days on lifelong nutrition, health and economics and the amount of programming on early childhood

nutrition globally, this isn't surprising. Indicators for this age group include:

➤ prevalence of low birthweight, stunting, wasting, and overweight

➤ rates of early, exclusive and continued breast-feeding

➤ timely introduction of complementary foods

➤ minimum meal frequency

➤ minimum diet diversity and minimum acceptable diet for ages 6–23 months

➤ vitamin A supplementation coverage, among others.

In low- and middle-income countries, stunting and overweight among children under 5 are tracked closely at the national level, albeit with varying frequency. Some countries invest in annual data collection, while others collect data every three to five years. Wasting, on the other hand, is a condition that can change seasonally and rapidly, so trends over time can be difficult to identify, although snapshot data are tracked through Multiple Indicator Cluster Surveys (MICS) and Demographic and Health Surveys (DHS), among others. With current data, countries and regions can be compared, but sub-national data by household wealth and geographic and sex differentials, available in some countries, can reveal important disparities that inform policy and local implementation. In high-income countries, on the other hand, these nutrition indicators tend to be lacking for children under 5 since they are either not collected systematically or not routinely reported in a comparable way.

Data gaps on the nutritional status of school-age and adolescent children

The nutritional status of older children is less well understood and tracked. The WHO/CDC Global School-Based Student Health Survey asks adolescents aged 13–17 about some aspects of their dietary behaviour (consumption of fruits, vegetables, soft drinks and fast food) and physical activity (physical education and cycling/walking to school), and indicators on overweight and thinness are tracked. However, these data are based on self-reported height and weight in European countries, which could underestimate obesity rates because of social desirability bias.[1] Additionally, the overarching gap is that a child's nutritional well-being throughout the life course is not tracked systematically. There is currently no standardized set of recommended indicators to be collected routinely through administrative systems, and no surveys at the country level.

Dietary habits and food intake

Another major gap is the lack of whole-of-diet data on what children, adolescents and women actually eat, and a dearth of data on micronutrient malnutrition. Without more knowledge on patterns and distributions of dietary habits, it is difficult to establish dietary priorities and goals.

Feeding practices for young children and mothers are tracked through household surveys, with the indicators for minimum dietary diversity (percentage of children 6–23 months of age who received foods from five or more food groups the previous day) and minimum acceptable diet

(number of children aged 6–23 months of age who had at least the minimum dietary diversity and meal frequency the previous day).

However, including diet diversity indicators – tracking how much and how often foods of various kinds are consumed, weighted by nutritional value – in more surveys for a broader range of children would provide a better understanding of malnutrition. These indicators have been found to be powerful predictors of economic status and malnutrition (both stunting and wasting).

Gathering reliable information on what children, adolescents and women eat is fraught with challenges. One example in data collection among school-age children is their limited cognitive ability to self-report their food intake. Some questionnaires can also be quite long, straining children's shorter attention spans. Many studies rely on questionnaires completed at school by children with little involvement of their parents. School-age children have been known to under-report or over-report their dietary intake, limiting the reliability of some data.

Surveys of adolescents are hampered by their lack of motivation to respond to voluntary questionnaires and body image issues. Under-reporting and misreporting of food intake are common among overweight and obese adolescents.

Finally, food composition databases, which give (not always accurate) estimates for energy and macro- and micronutrient levels in common local foods, are either unavailable at the country level or not uniform across countries, making cross-country comparisons difficult. They do not adequately address the special needs of young children. In many studies, global food composition databases are modified to accommodate country-specific foods, again making comparisons unreliable.■

PERSPECTIVE

Working together to deliver healthy people and a healthy planet

Peter Bakker
President and CEO, World Business Council for Sustainable Development

Peter Bakker is President and Chief Executive Officer (CEO) of the World Business Council for Sustainable Development (WBCSD), a global, CEO-led organization of over 200 leading businesses working together to accelerate the transition to a sustainable world. WBCSD member companies come from all business sectors and all major economies, representing a combined revenue of more than US$8.5 trillion and with 19 million employees. Mr Bakker is a distinguished business leader who, until June 2011, served as Chief Finance Officer and then CEO of TNT NV, the global transport and logistics company.

It is painfully visible that our food system is broken. Our future depends on our ability to create a food system that supports healthy people and a healthy planet. Current food systems are outstripping the resources of the planet, while diets are resulting in global health crises of both over- and undernutrition. All this will be amplified by continued population growth and changes in dietary habits.

The private sector is often seen as part of the problem, but I believe it can play a pivotal role in providing solutions. Take food processing for example: it can deliver high-quality food that extends the life of fruit and vegetables, thus reducing food waste. It can make healthy foods available all year round in environmentally challenged communities such as the Sahel region. In addition, when food is produced responsibly, the environmental impact of agricultural practices can be kept to a minimum or even be regenerative.

Nearly all food consumed around the world is produced, processed or supplied by business, ranging from smallholder farmers and family farms to large, multinational companies. This provides business with a unique opportunity and ability to improve children's health and quality of life by creating more healthy, enjoyable food for all, that is produced responsibly and sustainably.

There is a clear business imperative to help meet the nutritional needs of children: malnutrition contributes to reduced productivity, and rising health, insurance and environmental costs, as well as vulnerable supply chains, which all have a direct impact on the bottom line. As populations grow and diets evolve, there are growth opportunities for companies that move first and create new markets for healthy food.

Food companies can help nudge parents and children towards healthy and sustainable food options. For example, advertising and in-store marketing are powerful tools that affect consumer behaviour. At the same time, business also needs to show restraint in advertising directly to children, because they are particularly susceptible to commercial messages. At the World Business Council for Sustainable Development (WBCSD), we are helping businesses to accomplish this, for example by developing a country-level project that includes a toolkit on marketing and advertising products containing less sugar.

Public education campaigns play an important role as well. A combination of policy, information and community engagement is required to reach everyone, including those living in disadvantaged communities.

We must also focus more on the environmental impact of food production. As we move towards the limits of the natural resources our planet can provide, diets need to be adjusted. Initiatives such as the EAT-Lancet Commission report, the FABLE Consortium's national country modelling, the Food Systems Dialogues, and the Food and Land Use Coalition are at the forefront of solving this challenge. Many leading businesses

© UNICEF/UN016877/Noorani

support and encourage their evidence-based work, using it to inform business strategy and actions.

Finally, healthy and sustainable food must be accessible and affordable. We cannot reinforce socio-economic inequities in feeding our children. Unfortunately, even in areas where food is widely available, healthier and more sustainable options are often more expensive. Moreover, many smallholder farmers don't have sufficient food remaining from their harvest, or enough money to purchase diverse healthy foods.

From a business perspective, today's children are tomorrow's farmers and company workers. Failing them is not an option, yet we are on a path to do so. We need to react urgently, and business must make bold strides to contribute to finding solutions.

At WBCSD, we're bringing together companies that are taking a leadership role to explore, develop and scale up solutions. Many of our member companies, individually and through WBCSD programmes and projects, are innovating to shift towards healthy diets Our organization calls on business to transform the food system to achieve a vision of healthy people and a healthy planet, by:

➤ ensuring food and nutrition security in the supply chain

➤ making healthy, nutritionally appropriate and sustainably produced foods accessible and affordable to children and their families

➤ using the power of marketing responsibly by rebalancing marketing spending on healthy offerings, providing actionable information and making healthy options easily accessible

➤ engaging in platforms that convene business, government, science and civil society to transform the food system.

There is no silver bullet to solve malnutrition and only a collaborative and holistic approach will successfully transform the food system.

There is a massive urgency to act NOW: we have to build momentum for our children and our planet. Research published by the EAT-Lancet Commission has provided targets against which we can take aligned action. Let's work together to transform the food system and achieve our vision for healthy people and a healthy planet. ■

Endnotes

INTRODUCTION: GROWING WELL IN A CHANGING WORLD

1 UNICEF estimates, 2019 based on Black et al, 2013 and Stevens et al, 2015. See Methodology on p. 178 for more information.

2 NCD Risk Factor Collaboration (2017). 'Worldwide trends in body-mass index, underweight, overweight, and obesity from 1975 to 2016: A pooled analysis of 2416 population-based measurement studies in 128.9 million children, adolescents, and adults', *The Lancet*, 390(10113), pp. 2627–2642.

3 Ashkan, A., et al. (2017). 'Health effects of dietary risks in 195 countries, 1990–2017: A systematic analysis for the Global Burden of Disease Study 2017', *The Lancet*, 393(10184), pp. 1958–1972.

4 ibid.

5 Keats, E. C., et al (2018). *Diet and eating practices among adolescent girls in low- and middle-income countries: A systematic review*. Strengthening Partnerships, Results, and Innovations in Nutrition Globally (SPRING) project, Arlington, VA.

6 FAO, IFAD, UNICEF, WFP and WHO (2019). *The State of Food Security and Nutrition in the World 2019: Safeguarding against economic slowdowns and downturns*. Food and Agriculture Organization, Rome.

7 Monteiro, C. A., et al (2013). 'Ultra-processed products are becoming dominant in the global food system', *Obesity Review*s, 14(Supplement 2), pp. 21–28.

8 Ashkan, A., et al. (2017). 'Health effects of dietary risks in 195 countries, 1990–2017: A systematic analysis for the Global Burden of Disease Study 2017', *The Lancet*, 393(10184), pp. 1958–1972.

9 Pries, A.M., et al (2019). 'Unhealthy snack food and beverage consumption is associated with lower dietary adequacy and length-for-age Z-scores among 12–23-month-olds in Kathmandu Valley, Nepal', *Journal of Nutrition*, nxz140.

10 Willett, W., et al. (2019). 'Food in the Anthropocene: the EAT–Lancet Commission on healthy diets from sustainable food systems', *The Lancet*, 393(10170), pp. 447–492.

11 Searchinger, T., et al (2018). *World Resources Report: Creating a sustainable food future*. World Resources Institute, Washington DC.

12 FAO, IFAD, UNICEF, WFP and WHO (2019). *The State of Food Security and Nutrition in the World 2019: Safeguarding against economic slowdowns and downturns*. Food and Agriculture Organization, Rome.

13 HLPE (2017). *Nutrition and food systems. A report by the High Level Panel of Experts on Food Security and Nutrition*. Committee on World Food Security, Rome.

14 Hossain, N. (2017). 'Inequality, hunger and malnutrition: Power matters'. In K. Von Grebmer (ed.), *2017 global hunger index: The inequalities of hunger*, International Food Policy Research Institute, Washington DC, pp. 25–29.

15 ILO (2017). *Global estimates of child labour: Results and trends, 2012–2016*. International Labour Office (ILO), Geneva.

16 United Nations (undated). Sustainable Development Goals Knowledge Platform. United Nations, New York.

17 Webb, P. (2014). *Nutrition and the Post-2015 Sustainable Development System. A Technical Note*. United Nations Standing Committee on Nutrition, New York.

CHAPTER 1: CHILD MALNUTRITION TODAY

1 Black, R. et. al, "Maternal and child undernutrition and overweight in low-income and middle-income countries," *The Lancet* 382: 427-51 (2013).

2 WHO (2018).'Top 10 causes of death'. <https://www.who.int/gho/mortality_burden_disease/causes_death/top_10/en/>, retrieved 22 July 2019.

3 de Onis, M. and Branca, F. (2016). 'Childhood stunting: A global perspective', Maternal & Child Nutrition 12 (Supplement 2), pp. 12–26.

4 Development Initiatives (2017). *The P20 initiative: Data to leave no one behind, Baseline report March 2017.* Development Initiatives, Washington DC.

5 de Onis, M. and Branca, F. (2016). 'Childhood stunting: A global perspective', Maternal & Child Nutrition 12 (Supplement 2), pp. 12–26.

6 Blencowe, H. el al. (2019). 'National, regional, and worldwide estimates of low birthweight in 2015, with trends from 2000: A systematic analysis', *The Lancet Global Health*, 7(7), e849-e860.

7 de Onis, M. and Branca,F. (2016). 'Childhood stunting: A global perspective', *Maternal & Child Nutrition* 12 (Supplement 2), pp. 12–26.

8 Walker, C. L. F., et al. (2013). 'Global burden of childhood pneumonia and diarrhoea', *The Lancet*, 381(9875), pp. 1405–1416.

9 Smith, L. C. and Haddad, L. (2015). 'Reducing child undernutrition: Past drivers and priorities for the post-MDG era', *World Development*, 68, pp. 180–204.

10 UNICEF (2018). New expanded databases for malnutrition, infant and young child feeding and iodized salt. <https://data.unicef.org/resources/nutrition-data/>, retrieved 22 July 2019.

11 UNICEF, WHO and World Bank (2019). Joint child malnutrition estimates expanded database: stunting.

12 Black, R. E., et al. (2013). 'Maternal and child undernutrition and overweight in low-income and middle-income countries', *The Lancet*. 382(9890), pp. 427–451; Harding, K. L., Aguayo, V. M. and Webb, P (2018). 'Factors associated with wasting among children under five years old in South Asia: Implications for action', *PLoS ONE* 13(7), e0198749.

13 de Onis, M., et al. (2018). 'Prevalence thresholds for wasting, overweight and stunting in children under 5 years,' *Public Health Nutrition* 22(1), pp. 175–179.

14 Harding, K. L., Aguayo, V. M. and Webb, P (2018). 'Factors associated with wasting among children under five years old in South Asia: Implications for action', *PLoS ONE* 13(7), e0198749.

15 Myatt, M., et al. (2018). 'Children who are both wasted and stunted are also underweight and have a high risk of death: a descriptive epidemiology of multiple anthropometric deficits using data from 51 countries,' *Archives of Public Health* 76(28).

16 Harding, K. L., Aguayo, V. M. and Webb, P (2018). 'Factors associated with wasting among children under five years old in South Asia: Implications for action', *PLoS ONE* 13(7), e0198749.

17 Olofin, I., et al. for the Nutrition Impact Model Study (anthropometry cohort pooling). (2013). 'associations of suboptimal growth with all-cause and cause-specific mortality in children under five years: A pooled analysis of ten prospective studies', *PLoS ONE*, 8(5), e64636.

18 USAid (2016). 'Community-based management of acute malnutrition: Technical guidance brief'. <https://www.usaid.gov/global-health/health-areas/nutrition/technical-areas/community-based-management-acute-malnutrition>, retrieved 22 July 2019.

19 <https://www.unicef.org/nutrition/index_sam.html>, retrieved 22 July 2019.

20 Khara, T. and Dolan, C. (2014). *Technical briefing paper: Associations between wasting and stunting, policy, programming and research implications*. Emergency Nutrition Network, Oxford.

21 No Wasted Lives Coalition (undated). 'State of acute malnutrition'. <https://www.acutemalnutrition.org/en/countries>, retrieved 22 July 2019; UNICEF, WHO and World Bank Group (2019). *Joint Child Malnutrition Estimates*. WHO, Geneva.

22 Jesson, J., et al. (2015). 'Prevalence of malnutrition among HIV-infected children in Central and West-African HIV-care programmes supported by the Growing Up Programme in 2011: A cross-sectional study', *BMC Infectious Diseases* 15, p. 216.

23 Muenchhoff, M., et al. (2018). 'Malnutrition in HIV-infected children is an indicator of severe disease with an impaired response to antiretroviral therapy', AIDS Research and Human Retroviruses, 34(1), pp. 46–55.

24 Rose, A. M., et al. (2014). 'Aetiology and management

of malnutrition in HIV-positive children', *Archives of Disease in Childhood*, 99, pp. 546–551.

25 No Wasted Lives Coalition (undated). 'State of acute malnutrition'. <https://www.acutemalnutrition.org/en/countries>, retrieved 22 July 2019;

26 UNICEF Evaluation Office (2013). *Evaluation of community management of acute malnutrition (CMAM): Global Synthesis Report (Evaluation Report)*. UNICEF, New York.

27 WHO, UNICEF, WFP and UN System Standing Committee on Nutrition (2007). *Community-based management of severe acute malnutrition: A joint statement*. WHO, Geneva.

28 Bhutta, Z. A., et. al. (2013). 'Evidence-based interventions for improvement of maternal and child nutrition: what can be done and at what cost?' *The Lancet*, 382(9890), pp. 452–477.

29 Gillespie, S., et al (eds) (2016). *Nourishing Millions: Stories of change in nutrition*. International Food Policy Research Institute, Washington, DC, p. 35.

30 Daru, J., et al. (2018). 'Risk of maternal mortality in women with severe anaemia during pregnancy and post partum: A multilevel analysis', *The Lancet Global Health*, 6(5), e548–e554.

31 UNICEF (2018). 'Globally, 86 per cent of the population has access to iodized salt', UNICEF, New York, July 2018.

32 UNICEF estimates, 2019 based on Black et al, 2013 and Stevens et al, 2015. See Methodology on p. 178 for more information.

33 UNICEF (2004). 'The hidden hunger of the vitamin and mineral deficient child', UNICEF, New York, March 2004.

34 Kennedy, G. Ballard, T. and Dop, M. (2013). *Guidelines for measuring household and individual dietary diversity*. Food and Agriculture Organization and European Union, Rome and Brussels.

35 Louzada, M., at al. (2018). 'The share of ultra-processed foods determines the overall nutritional quality of diets in Brazil', *Public Health Nutrition*, 21(1), pp. 94–102.

36 Martínez Steele, E., et al. (2017). 'The share of ultra-processed foods and the overall nutritional quality of diets in the US: Evidence from a nationally representative cross-sectional study', *Population Health Metrics*, 15(6).

37 Swinburn, B. A., et al. (2019). 'The Global Syndemic of Obesity, Undernutrition, and Climate Change: The Lancet Commission report,' *The Lancet* 393(10173), pp. 791–846.

38 UNICEF estimates, 2019 based on Black et al, 2013 and Stevens et al, 2015. See Methodology on p. 178 for more information.

39 Bird, J. K., et al. (2017). 'Risk of deficiency in multiple concurrent micronutrients in children and adults in the United States', Nutrients, 9, p. 655.

40 Riaz, M., et al. (2018). 'Maternal nutrition during early pregnancy and cardiometabolic status of neonates at birth', Journal of Diabetes Research, Article ID 7382946, 8 pages.

41 National Nutrition Agency (NaNA) Gambia, UNICEF, Gambia Bureau of Statistics (GBOS) and GroundWork (2019). *Gambia National Micronutrient Survey* 2018. Banjul, Gambia.

42 WHO (2016). *Report of the commission on ending childhood obesity*, WHO, Geneva.

43 UNICEF, WHO, International Bank for Reconstruction and Development and World Bank (2019). *Levels and trends in child malnutrition: Key findings of the 2019 Edition of the Joint Child Malnutrition Estimates*, WHO, Geneva.

44 ibid.

45 Ng, M., et al. (2014). 'Global, regional, and national prevalence of overweight and obesity in children and adults during 1980–2013: A systematic analysis for the Global Burden of Disease Study 2013', *The Lancet*, 384(9945), pp. 766–781.

46 van Jaarsveld, C. H. M. and Gulliford, M. C. (2015). 'Childhood obesity trends from primary care electronic health records in England between 1994 and 2013: Population-based cohort study', *Archives of Disease in Childhood*, 100, pp. 214–219.

47 Manios, Y., et al. (2018). 'Prevalence and sociodemographic correlates of overweight and obesity in a large Pan-European cohort of preschool children and their families. The Toy Box study', *Nutrition*, 55–56, pp. 192–198.

48 Spinelli, A., et al. (2019). 'Prevalence of severe obesity among primary school children in 21 European countries', *Obesity Facts*, 12, pp. 244–258.

49 Ng, M., et al. (2014). 'Global, regional, and national prevalence of overweight and obesity in children and adults during 1980–2013: A systematic analysis for the Global Burden of Disease Study 2013', *The Lancet*, 384(9945), pp. 766–781.

50 Manios, Y., et al. (2018). 'Prevalence and sociodemographic correlates of overweight and obesity in a large Pan-European cohort of preschool children and their families. The Toy Box-study', *Nutrition*, 55–56, pp. 192–198.

51 NCD Risk Factor Collaboration (2017). 'Worldwide trends in body-mass index, underweight, overweight, and obesity from 1975 to 2016: A pooled analysis of 2416 population-based measurement studies in 128·9 million children, adolescents, and adults', *The Lancet*, 390(10113), pp. 2627–2642.

52 ibid.

53 Department of Health and Human Services Centers for Disease Control and Prevention (2018). 'Prevalence of obesity among youths by household income and education level of head of household – United States 2011–2014', *Morbidity and Mortality Weekly Report*, 67(6), pp. 186–189.

54 Lissner, L., et al. (2016). 'Socio-economic inequalities in childhood overweight: Heterogeneity across five countries in the WHO European Childhood Obesity Surveillance Initiative (COSI-2008)', *International Journal of Obesity*, 40(5), pp. 796–802.

55 ibid.

56 Kraak, V.I., at al. (2016). 'Progress achieved in restricting the marketing of high-fat, sugary and salty food and beverage products to children', *Bulletin of the World Health Organization*, 94(7), pp. 540–548.

57 Development Initiatives (2017). *Global Nutrition Report 2017: Nourishing the SDGs*. Development Initiatives, Bristol, UK, p. 52.

58 Hruby, A. and Hu, F. B. (2015). 'The epidemiology of obesity: A big picture', *Pharmacoeconomics*, 33(7), pp. 673–689.

59 NCD Risk Factor Collaboration (2017). 'Worldwide trends in body-mass index, underweight, overweight, and obesity from 1975 to 2016: A pooled analysis of 2416 population-based measurement studies in 128·9 million children, adolescents, and adults', *The Lancet*, 390(10113), pp. 2627–2642, p. 2640.

60 OECD (2017). Obesity Update 2017, The Organisation for Economic Co-operation and Development, Paris, p. 9.

61 ibid.

62 WHO (2016). *Report of the Commission on Ending Childhood Obesity*. WHO, Geneva, pp. vii–xi.

63 Development Initiatives (2017). *Global Nutrition Report 2017: Nourishing the SDGs*. Development Initiatives, Bristol, UK, p. 76.

64 ibid., p. 62.

65 Wasting–Stunting Technical Interest Group (WaSt TIG) (2018). *Child wasting and stunting: Time to overcome the separation: A briefing note for policymakers and programme implementers*. Emergency Nutrition Network, Oxford, UK.

66 McDonald, C. M., et al. (2013). 'The effect of multiple anthropometric deficits on child mortality: Meta-analysis of individual data in 10 prospective studies from developing countries', *American Journal of Clinical Nutrition*, 97(4), pp. 896–901.

67 Khara, T. and Dolan, C. (2014). *Technical Briefing Paper: Associations between Wasting and Stunting, policy, programming and research implications*. Emergency Nutrition Network, Oxford, UK.

68 Harding, K. L., Aguayo, V. M. and Webb, P. (2018). 'Factors associated with wasting among children under five years old in South Asia: Implications for action', *PLoS ONE* 13(7), e0198749.

69 Development Initiatives (2018). *2018 Global Nutrition Report: Shining a light to spur action on nutrition*. Development Initiatives, Bristol, UK, p. 14.

70 De Lucia Rolfe, E., et al. (2018). 'Associations of stunting in early childhood with cardiometabolic risk factors in adulthood', *PLoS One*, 13(4), e0192196.

71 Dang, A. and Meenakshi, J. V. (2017). 'The nutrition transition and the intra-household double burden of malnutrition in India', *ADBI Working Paper* 725, Asian Development Bank Institute, Tokyo.

72 Aitsi-Selmi, A. (2014). 'Households with a stunted child and obese mother: trends and child feeding practices in a middle-income country, 1992–2008', *Maternal & Child Health, 19(6), pp. 1284–1291*.

73 Horta, B. L., et al. (2013). 'Nutritional status of indigenous children: Findings from the First National Survey of Indigenous People's Health and Nutrition in Brazil, *International Journal of Equity in Health*, 12(23).

74 UNICEF, WHO and World Bank (2019). Joint child malnutrition estimates expanded database: stunting.

75 Popkin, B. M., Adair and Ng, S. W. (2012). 'Global nutrition transition and the pandemic of obesity in developing countries', *Nutrition Reviews*, 70(1), pp. 3–21.

76 Hawkes, C., Harris, J. and Gillespie, S. (2017). 'Changing diets: Urbanization and the nutrition transition'. In IFPRI, Global Food Policy Report, International Food Policy Research Institute, Washington DC, p. 35.

77 FAO (2013). *The State of Food and Agriculture: Food systems for better nutrition*, Food and Agriculture Organization of the United Nations, Rome.

78 Global Panel on Agriculture and Food Systems for Nutrition (2016). *Food systems and diets: Facing the challenges of the 21st century*, Global Panel on Agriculture and Food Systems for Nutrition, London.

79 HLPE (2017). *Nutrition and food systems*. High Level Panel of Experts on Food Security and Nutrition of the Committee on World Food Security, Rome.

80 This section draws on UNICEF, GAIN (2018). 'Food systems for children and adolescents', *Interim Summary Report*, of event at UNICEF Office of Research, Innocenti Florence, Italy, 5–7 November 2018.

81 UNICEF, GAIN (2019). 'Food systems for children and adolescents', *Final Report*, of event at UNICEF Office of Research, Innocenti Florence, Italy, 5–7 November 2018.

82 Pinstrup-Andersen, P. (2013). Nutrition-sensitive food systems: From rhetoric to action. *The Lancet*, 382(9890), pp. 375–376.

83 Jones, A. D. and Ejeta, G. (2015). 'A new global agenda for nutrition and health: The importance of agriculture and food systems', *Bulletin of the World Health Organization* 94(3), pp. 228–229.

84 Gillespie, S. and van den Bold, M. (2017). 'Agriculture, food systems, and nutrition: Meeting the challenge', *Global Challenges* 1(3), 1600002.

85 FAO (2013). *The State of Food and Agriculture: Food systems for better nutrition*, Food and Agriculture Organization of the United Nations, Rome.

86 Ruel, M. T. and Alderman, H. (2013). 'Nutrition-sensitive interventions and programmes: How can they help to accelerate progress in improving maternal and child nutrition?' *The Lancet*, 382(9891), pp. 536–551.

87 Herforth, A. and Harris, J. (2014). 'Understanding and applying primary pathways and principles', *Brief 1: Improving Nutrition through Agriculture Technical Brief Series*. USAID and Strengthening Partnerships, Results, and Innovations in Nutrition Globally (SPRING) Project, Arlington, VA.

88 Ruel, M. T. and Alderman, H. (2013). 'Nutrition-sensitive interventions and programmes: How can they help to accelerate progress in improving maternal and child nutrition?' *The Lancet*, 382(9891), pp. 536–551; Gillespie, S. and van den Bold, M. (2017). 'Agriculture, food systems, and nutrition: Meeting the challenge', *Global Challenges* 1(3), 1600002.

89 Gillespie, S. and van den Bold, M. (2017). 'Agriculture, food systems, and nutrition: Meeting the challenge', *Global Challenges* 1(3), 1600002.

90 WHO Regional Office for Europe (2018). *Evaluating implementation of the WHO Set of Recommendations on the marketing of foods and non-alcoholic beverages to children. Progress, challenges and guidance for next steps in the WHO European Region*, WHO, Geneva; WHO Regional Office for the East Mediterranean (2018). *Implementing the WHO recommendations on the marketing of food and non-alcoholic beverages to children*.

91 Grassi, F., Landberg, J. and Huyer, S. (2015). *Running out of time: The reduction of women's work burden in agriculture production*. Food and Agriculture Organization of the United Nations, Rome.

92 Rasella, D., et al. (2013). 'Effect of a conditional cash transfer programme on childhood mortality: A nationwide analysis of Brazilian municipalities', *The Lancet*, 382(9886), pp. 57–64.

93 Grassi, F., Landberg, J. and Huyer, S. (2015). *Running out of time: The reduction of women's work burden in agriculture production*. Food and Agriculture Organization of the United Nations, Rome

94 UNICEF (2018). *Generation 2030: Africa 2.0*. UNICEF, New York.

95 Lim, S. S., et al. (2018). 'Measuring human capital: a systematic analysis of 195 countries and territories, 1990–2016', *The Lancet*, 392(10154), pp. 1217–1234.

96 Black, R. E., et al. (2013). 'Maternal and child undernutrition and overweight in low-income and middle-income countries', *The Lancet*, 382(9890), pp. 427–451; WHO (2018). *Malnutrition factsheet*, WHO, Geneva.

97 Agbor, J. A. and Price, G.N. (2014). 'Does famine matter for aggregate adolescent human capital acquisition in Sub-Saharan Africa?', *African Development Review*, 26(3), pp. 454–467.

98 Niemesh, G. T. (2015). Ironing out deficiencies: Evidence from the United States on the economic effects of iron deficiency', *Journal of Human Resources*, 50(4), pp. 910–958.

99 Field, E., Robles, O. and Torero, M. (2009). 'Iodine deficiency and schooling attainment in Tanzania', *American Economic Journal: Applied Economics*, 1(4), pp. 140–169.

100 Maluccio, J. A., et al. (2009). The impact of improving nutrition during early childhood on education among Guatemalan adults', *The Economic Journal*, 119, pp. 734-763.

101 Wong, H. L., et al. (2014). 'Improving the health and education of elementary schoolchildren in rural China: Iron supplementation versus nutritional training for parents', *Journal of Development Studies*, 50(4), pp. 502–519.

102 Fink, G., et al. (2016). 'Schooling and wage income losses due to early-childhood growth faltering in developing countries: National, regional, and global estimates', *American Journal of Clinical Nutrition*,104(1), pp. 104–112.

103 McGovern, M. E., et al. (2017). 'A review of the evidence linking child stunting to economic outcomes', *International Journal of Epidemiology*, 46(4), pp. 1171–1191.

104 Pinstrup-Andersen, P. and Shimokawa, S. (2008). 'Do poverty and poor health and nutrition increase the risk of armed conflict onset?', *Food Policy*, 33(6), pp. 513–520.

105 House of Commons (1946). 31 May Debate, 5(423), col 1544.

106 Lim, S. S., et al. (2018). 'Measuring human capital: a systematic analysis of 195 countries and territories, 1990–2016', *The Lancet*, 392(10154), pp. 1217–1234

107 African Union Commission, NEPAD Planning and Coordinating Agency, UNECA and WFP (2014). *The cost of hunger in Africa: Social and economic impact of child undernutrition in Egypt, Ethiopia, Swaziland and Uganda*. United Nations Economic Commission for Africa, Addis Ababa.

108 1Hoddinott, J. (2016). 'The economics of reducing malnutrition in Sub-Saharan Africa', Working paper for Global Panel on Agriculture and Food Systems for Nutrition (unpublished).

109 World Bank Group (2013). 'Reaching the global target to reduce stunting: How much will it cost and how can we pay for it?', World Bank Group

110 Garde, A. and Murphy, B. (2018). *A child rights-based approach to food marketing: A guide for policy makers*. UNICEF, New York, p. 13.

111 OECD (2018). *Agricultural Policy Monitoring and Evaluation 2018*. Organisation for Economic Co-operation and Development, Paris.

112 World Bank Group (2013). 'Reaching the global target to reduce stunting: How much will it cost and how can we pay for it?', World Bank Group, citing Hoddinott, J., et al. (2013). 'The economic rationale for investing in nutrition', *Maternal & Child Nutrition*, 9 (Supplement 2), pp. 69–82. Median estimate for a sample of 17 high-burden countries used by the authors.

113 Boseley, S. (2016). 'World Bank to name and shame countries that fail to prevent stunting in children', *The Guardian*, London, 30 September

114 UK Government (2018). *Childhood obesity: A plan for action*. HM Government, London, ch. 2.

115 NHS Digital (2018). *National Child Measurement Programme, England: 2017/18 School Year* [PAS]. Department for Health and Social Care, London.

116 RCPCH (2017). *State of Child Health Report 2017*. Royal College of Paediatrics and Child Health, London.

117 Public Health England (2018). England's poorest areas are fast-food hotspots. Press release 29 June.

118 Adams, J., Ganiti, E. and White, M. (2011). 'Socio-economic differences in outdoor food advertising in a city in Northern England', *Public Health Nutrition*, 14(6), pp. 945–950.

119 Public Health England (2015). *Sugar Reduction: The evidence for action*. Public Health England, London.

120 Winkler, L., et al., (2016). 'Substituting sugar confectionery with fruit and healthy snacks at checkout – a win-win strategy for consumers and food stores? a study on consumer attitudes and sales effects of a healthy supermarket intervention', *BMC Public Health*, 16(1184).

121 Children's Commissioner for England (2019). *Childhood vulnerability in England 2019*. Children's Commissioner for England, London.

122 NHS Digital (2017). Healthy Survey for England < https://digital.nhs.uk/data-and-information/publications/statistical/health-survey-for-england> retrieved 31 July 2019.

123 Smith, A. (2018). *Food poverty in Camden and*

Islington, January 2018: Understanding the local picture. Islington and Camden Public Health.

124 UK Government (2018). *Childhood obesity: A plan for action.* HM Government, London, ch. 2

125 UK Government (2017). *Childhood obesity: a plan for action*

126 UK Government (2019). *Government Response to* the House of Commons Health and Social Care Select Committee report on 'Childhood obesity: Time for action', Eighth Report of Session 2017–19. HM Government, London.

127 Office of the Mayor on London and the London Assembly (2018). Mayor confirms ban on junk food advertising on transport network. Press release 23 November.

128 Public Health England (2019). *Foods and drinks aimed at infants and young children: Evidence and opportunities for action.* Public Health England, London.

129 Griffith, R., von Hinke, S. and Smith, S. (2018). 'Getting a healthy start: The effectiveness of targeted benefits for improving dietary choices', *Journal of Health Economics*, 58, pp. 176–187.

CHAPTER 2: FEEDING A CHILD FOR LIFE

1 Baird, J., Jacob, C., Barker, M., Fall, C., Hanson, M., Harvey, N., Inskip, H., Kumaran, K. and Cooper, C. (2017). 'Developmental origins of health and diseases: a lifecourse approach to the prevention of non-communicable diseases', *Healthcare*, 5(14).

2 Catalano, P. M. and Kartik, S. (2017). 'Obesity and pregnancy: mechanisms of short-term and long-term adverse consequences for mother and child', *BMJ*, 356, j1.

3 McDonald, S. D., Han, Z., Mulla, S., Beyene, J. and Knowledge Synthesis Group (2010). 'Overweight and obesity in mothers and risk of preterm birth and low birthweight infants: systematic review and meta-analyses', *BMJ* (Clinical Research ed.), 341, c3428.

4 Poston, L., Caleyachetty, R., Cnattingius, S., Corvalán, C., Uauy, R., Herring, S. and Gillman, M. W. (2016). 'Preconceptional and maternal obesity: epidemiology and health consequences', *The Lancet. Diabetes & Endocrinology*, 4(12), pp. 1025–1036.

5 Darnton-Hill, I. and Mkparu, U. C. (2015). 'Micronutrients in pregnancy in low- and middle-income countries', *Nutrients*, 7(3), pp. 1744–1768; Stevens, G. A., Finucane, M. M., De-Regil, L. M., Paciorek, C. J., Flaxman, S. R., Branca, F. et al. (2013). 'Global, regional, and national trends in haemoglobin concentration and prevalence of total and severe anaemia in children and pregnant and non-pregnant women for 1995–2011: a systematic analysis of population-representative data', *The Lancet Global Health*, 1(1), e16–25.

6 De-Regil, L. M., Pena-Rosas, J. P., Fernandez-Gaxiola, A. C. and Rayco-Solon, P. (2015). 'Effects and safety of periconceptional oral folate supplementation for preventing birth defects', *Cochrane Database of Systematic Reviews*, 12, CD007950.

7 Mackillop, L. (2015). 'Pre-eclampsia: reducing the risk with calcium supplements', *BMJ Clinical Evidence*, 1402.

8 McCauley, M. E., Broek, N., Dou, L. and Othman, M. (2015). 'Vitamin A supplementation during pregnancy for maternal and newborn outcomes', *Cochrane Database of Systematic Reviews*, 10, CD008666.

9 Chaffee, B. W. and Kinga, J. C. (2012). 'Effect of zinc supplementation on pregnancy and infant outcomes: A systematic review', *Paediatratric Perinatal Epidemiology*, 2(1), pp. 118–137.

10 Prado, E. L. and Dewey, K. G. (2014). 'Nutrition and brain development in early life', *Nutrition Reviews*, 72(4), pp. 267–284.

11 Hansen, K. (2016). 'Breastfeeding: A smart investment in people and in economies', *The Lancet*, 387(10017), p. 416.

12 Ballard, O. and Morrow, A. L. (2013). 'Human milk composition nutrients and bioactive factors', *Pediatric Clinics of North America*, 60(1), pp. 49–74.

13 Smith, E. R., Hurt, L., Chowdhury, R., Sinha, B., Fawzi, W. and Edmond, K. M. (2017). 'Delayed breastfeeding initiation and infant survival: A systematic review and meta-analysis', *PLoS ONE*, 12(7).

14 ibid.

15 Lancet Breastfeeding Series Group (2016). 'Breastfeeding in the 21st century: Epidemiology, mechanisms, and lifelong effect', *The Lancet*, 387(10017), pp. 475–490.

16 ibid; Ballard, O. and Morrow, A. L. (2013). 'Human milk composition nutrients and bioactive factors', *Pediatric Clinics of North America*, 60(1), pp. 49–74.

17 Chowdhury, R., Sinha, B., Sankar, M. J., Taneja, S., Bhandari, N., Rollins, N., et al. 2015). 'Breastfeeding and maternal health outcomes: A systematic review and meta-analysis'. *Acta Paediatrica*, 104, pp. 96–113.

18 Bonifacino, E., SchwartzE. B., Jun, H., Wessel, C.B. and Corbelli, J. A. (2018). 'Effect of lactation on maternal hypertension: A systematic review', *Breastfeeding Medicine*, 13(9), pp. 578–588.

19 UNICEF (2018). *From the First Hour of Life*, UNICEF, New York

20 Rodríguez-Ramírez, S., Muñoz-Espinosa, A., Rivera, J. A., González-Castell, D. and González de Cosío, T. (2016). 'Mexican children under 2 years of age consume food groups high in energy and low in micronutrients', *Journal of Nutrition*, 146 (Supplement), pp. 1916S–19123S.

21 Baker, P., Smith, J., Salmon, L., Friel, S., Kent, G., Iellamo, A. at al. (2016). 'Global trends and patterns of commercial milk-based formula sales: Is an unprecedented infant and young child feeding transition under way?' *Public Health Nutrition*, 19(14), pp. 2540–2550.

22 ibid.

23 Pomeranz, J. L., Romo Palafox, M. J. and Harris, J. L. (2018). 'Toddler drinks, formulas, and milks: Labeling practices and policy implications', *Preventive Medicine*, 109, pp. 11–16.

24 Wilhelm, M. (2018). 'Toddler Milks: Filling a nutritional need or a marketing niche?' *The Salt*, National Public Radio, 20 February.

25 UNICEF (2016). *From the First Hour of Life*, UNICEF, New York.

26 Benedict, R., Hope, C., Torlesse, H. and Stoltzfus, R. J. (2018). 'Trends and predictors of optimal breastfeeding among children 0–23 months: South Asia: Analysis of national survey data', *Maternal & Child Nutrition*, 14(S4), e12698.

27 UNICEF, *Capture the Moment*, 2018, p. 16.

28 Balogun, O. O., Dagvadorj, A., Anigo, K. M., Ota, E. and Sasaki, S. (2015). 'Factors influencing breastfeeding exclusivity during the first 6 months of life in developing countries: A quantitative and qualitative systematic review', *Maternal & Child Nutrition*, 11(4), pp. 433–451.

29 UNICEF (2017). *The Baby-friendly Hospital Initiative in Viet Nam: Enhancing healthcare quality criteria.* UNICEF, New York.

30 White, J. M., Bégin, F., Kumapley, R., Murray, C. and Krasevec, J. (2017). 'Complementary feeding practices: Current global and regional estimates', *Maternal & Child Nutrition*, 13 (Supplement 2), e12505.

31 Hamner, H. C., Perrine, C. G., Gupta, P. M., Herrick, K. A. and Cogswell, M. E. (2017). 'Food consumption patterns among US children from birth to 23 months of age, 2009–2014', *Nutrients*, 9(9), pp. 2009–2014.

32 Headey, D., Hirvonen, K. and Hoddinott, J. (2018). 'Animal-sourced foods and child stunting', *American Journal of Agricultural Economics*, 100(5), pp. 1302–1319.

33 International Food Policy Research Institute (IFPRI) (2019). 'Food markets and nutrition in the developing world: Results from ARENA II', Policy Seminar < http://www.ifpri.org/event/food-markets-and-nutrition-developing-world-results-arena-ii> retrieved 18/7/19.

34 Pérez-Expósito, A. B. and Klein, B. P. (2009). 'Impact of fortified blended food products on nutritional status of infants and young children in developing countries', *Nutrition Reviews*, 67(12), pp. 706–718.

35 Leyvraz, M., David-Kigaru, D. M., Macharia-Mutie, C., Aaron, G. J., Roefs, M. and Tumilowicz, A. (2018). 'Coverage and consumption of micronutrient powders, fortified staples, and iodized salt among children aged 6 to 23 months in selected neighborhoods of Nairobi County, Kenya', *Food and Nutrition Bulletin*, 39(1), pp. 107–115.

36 Bouis, H. E. and Saltzman, A. (2017). 'Improving nutrition through biofortification: A review of evidence from HarvestPlus, 2003 through 2016', *Global Food Security*, 12, pp. 49–58.

37 Institut Haïtien de l'Enfance (IHE) et ICF (2018). *Enquête Mortalité, Morbidité et Utilisation des Service*s (EMMUS-VI 2016–2017), IHE et ICF, Pétion-Ville, Haïti et Rockville, Maryland, USA

(Haiti Demography and Health Study (DHS), 2016–2017); UNICEF data on malnutrition <https://data.unicef.org/topic/nutrition/malnutrition/>; UNICEF data on infant and young child feeding <https://data.unicef.org/topic/nutrition/infant-and-young-child-feeding/>.

38 Kavle, J. A., Mehanna, S., Saleh, G., Fouad, M. A., Ramzy, M., Hamed, D et al. (2015). 'Exploring why junk foods are "essential" foods and how culturally tailored recommendations improved feeding in Egyptian children', *Maternal & Child Nutrition*, 11(3), pp. 346–370; Pries, A. M., Huffman, S. L., Champeny, M., Adhikary, I., Benjamin, M., Coly, A. N. et al. (2017). 'Consumption of commercially produced snack foods and sugar-sweetened beverages during the complementary feeding period in four African and Asian urban contexts', *Maternal & Child Nutrition*, vol. 13 (Supplement 2).

39 ibid.

40 Elliott, C. D. and Conlon, M. J. (2015). 'Packaged baby and toddler foods: Questions of sugar and sodium', *Pediatric Obesity*, 10, pp. 149–55; Cogswell, M. E., Gunn, J. P., Yuan, K., Park, S. and Merritt, R. (2015). 'Sodium and sugar in complementary infant and toddler foods sold in the United States', Pediatrics, 135, pp. 416–423; Crawley, H. and Westland, S. (2017). *Baby foods in the UK: A review of commercially produced jars and pouches of baby foods marketed in the UK*, First Steps Nutrition Trust, London; WHO (2019). Improving the nutritional quality of commercial foods for infants and young children in the WHO European Region, WHO, Copenhagen, Denmark, p. 24.

41 De Cosmi, V., Scaglioni, S. and Agostoni, C. (2017). 'Early taste experiences and later food choices', *Nutrients*, 9(2), p. 107.

42 Manikam, L., Prasad, A., Dharmaratnam, A., Moen, C., Robinson, A., Light, A. et al. (2018). 'Systematic review of infant and young child complementary feeding practices in South Asian families: The India perspective', *Public Health Nutrition*, 21(4), pp. 637–654.

43 Kavle, J. A., Lacroix, E., Dau, H. and Engmann, C. (2017). 'Addressing barriers to exclusive breast-feeding in low- and middle-income countries: A systematic review and programmatic implications', *Public Health Nutrition*, 20(17), pp. 3120–3134.

44 Mazarello Paes, V., Ong, K. K. and Lakshman, R. (2015). 'Factors influencing obesogenic dietary intake in young children (0–6 years): A systematic review of qualitative evidence', *BMJ Open*, 5(9), e007396.

45 van Liere, M. J., Tarlton, D., Menon, R., Yellamanda, M.and Reerink, I. (2017). 'Harnessing private sector expertise to improve complementary feeding within a regulatory framework: Where is the evidence?' *Maternal & Child Nutrition*, 13 (Supplement 2), e12429.

46 Black, M. M. and Aboud, F. E. (2011). 'Responsive feeding is embedded in a theoretical framework of responsive parenting', *Journal of Nutrition*, 141(3); Saltzman, J.A., Pineros-Leano, M., Liechty, J.M., Bost, K.K., Fiese, B. H. et al. (2016). 'Eating, feeding, and feeling: Emotional responsiveness mediates longitudinal associations between maternal binge eating, feeding practices, and child weight', *International Journal of Behavioral Nutrition and Physical Activity*, 13(89).

47 Bentley, M. E., Wasser, H. M. and Creed-Kanashiro, H. M. (2011). 'Responsive feeding and child

undernutrition in low- and middle-income countries', *Journal of Nutrition*, 141, pp. 502–507.

48 Pérez-Escamilla, R., Segura-Pérez, S. and Lott, M. (2017). *Feeding Guidelines for Infants and Young Toddlers: A responsive parenting approach*, Robert Wood Johnson Foundation, Princeton, NJ.

49 Redsell, S. A., Edmonds, B., Swift, J. A., Siriwardena, A. N., Weng, S., Nathan, D. and Glazebrook, C. (2016). 'Systematic review of randomised controlled trials of interventions that aim to reduce the risk, either directly or indirectly, of overweight and obesity in infancy and early childhood', *Maternal & Child Nutrition*, 12(1), pp. 24–38.

50 Fox, E. 'Characteristics of children's dietary needs, intake patterns, and determinants that explain their nutrition behaviors' (unpublished).

51 Brown, J. E. (2002) 'Child and preadolescent nutrition'. In *Nutrition Through the Lifecycle*, pp. 310–337. Cengage Learning, Boston, Mass.

52 Prentice, A. M., Ward, K. A., Goldberg, G. R., Jarjou, L. M., Moore, S. E., Fulford, A. J. and Prentice, A. (2013). 'Critical windows for nutritional interventions against stunting', *American Journal of Clinical Nutrition*, 97(5), pp. 911–918; Crookston, B. T., Schott, W., Cueto, S., Dearden, K. A., Engle, P., Georgiadis, A. et al. (2013). 'Postinfancy growth, schooling, and cognitive achievement: Young lives', *American Journal of Clinical Nutrition*, 98(6), pp. 1555–1563; Gandhi, M., Ashorn, P., Maleta, K., Teivaanmäki, T., Duan, X. and Cheung, Y. B. (2011). 'Height gain during early childhood is an important predictor of schooling and mathematics ability outcomes', *Acta Paediatrica*, 100(8), pp. 1113–1118; Crookston, B. T., Penny, M. E., Alder, S. C., Dickerson, T. T., Merrill, R. M., Stanford, J. B. et al. (2010). 'Children who recover from early stunting and children who are not stunted demonstrate similar levels of cognition', *Journal of Nutrition*, 140, pp. 1996–2001.

53 Craigie, A. M., Lake, A. A., Kelly, S. A., Adamson, A. J. and Mathers, J. C. (2011). 'Tracking of obesity-related behaviours from childhood to adulthood: A systematic review', *Maturitas*, 70(3), pp. 266–284.

54 Ochola, S. and Masibo, P. K. (2014). 'Dietary intake of schoolchildren and adolescents in developing countries', *Annals of Nutrition & Metabolism*, 64(2), pp. 4–40.

55 Burrows, T., Goldman, S., Pursey, K. and Lim, R. (2017). 'Is there an association between dietary intake and academic achievement? A systematic review', *Journal of Human Nutrition and Dietetics*, 30(2), pp. 117–140.

56 Halterman, J. S., Kaczorowski, J. M., Aligne, C. A., Auinger, P. and Szilagyi, P. G. (2001). 'Iron deficiency and cognitive achievement among school-aged children and adolescents in the United States', *Pediatrics*, 107(6), pp. 1381–1386; Walter, T. (2003). 'Effect of iron-deficiency anemia on cognitive skills and neuromaturation in infancy and childhood', *Food Nutrition Bulletin*, 24 (Supplement 4), S104–S110.

57 Adolphus, K., Lawton, C. L., Champ, C. L. and Dye, L. (2016). 'The effects of breakfast and breakfast composition on cognition in children and adolescents: A systematic review', *Advances in Nutrition*, 7(3), 590S–612S; Kim, S. Y., Sim, S., Park, B., Kong, I. G., Kim, J. H. and Choi, H. G. 'Dietary habits are associated with school performance in adolescents', *Medicine* (Baltimore), 95(12), e3096.

58 Woldehanna, T., Behrman, J. and Araya, M. (2017). 'The effect of early childhood stunting on children's cognitive achievements: Evidence from Young Lives Ethiopia', *Ethiopia Journal of Health and Development*, 31(2), pp.74–85; Walker, S., Chang, S., Powell, C. and Grantham-McGregor, S. (2005). 'Effects of early childhood psychosocial stimulation and nutritional supplementation on cognition and education in growth-stunted Jamaican children: Prospective cohort study', *The Lancet*, 366(9499), pp. 1804–1807.

59 Chung, S. T., Onuzuruike, A. U. and Magge, S. N. (2018). 'Cardiometabolic risk in obese children', *Annals of the New York Academy of Sciences*, 1411(1), pp. 166–183; Reilly, J. J., Methven, E., McDowell, Z. C., Hacking, B., Alexander, D., Stewart, L. and Kelnar, C. J. H. (2003). 'Health consequences of obesity', *Archives of Disease in Childhood*, 88(9), pp. 748–752.

60 Rodriguez-Morales, A. J., Bolivar-Mejía, A., Alarcón-Olave, C. and Calvo-Betancourt, L. S. (2016). 'Nutrition and infection', In *Encyclopedia of Food and Health*, Elsevier, pp. 98–103.

61 Bechard, L. J., Rothpletz-Puglia, P., Touger-Decker, R., Duggan, C. and Mehta, N. M. (2013). 'Influence of obesity on clinical outcomes in hospitalized children: A systematic review', *JAMA Pediatrics*, 167(5), pp. 476–482.

62 Reilly, J. J., Methven, E., McDowell, Z. C., Hacking, B., Alexander, D., Stewart, L. and Kelnar, C. J. H. (2003). 'Health consequences of obesity', *Archives of Disease in Childhood*, 88(9), pp. 748–752.

63 Chung, S. T., Onuzuruike, A. U. and Magge, S. N. (2018). 'Cardiometabolic risk in obese children', *Annals of the New York Academy of Sciences*, 1411(1), pp. 166–183.

64 Reilly, J. J. and Kelly, J. (2011). Long-term impact of overweight and obesity in childhood and adolescence on morbidity and premature mortality in adulthood: Systematic review. *International Journal of Obesity*, 35(7), pp. 891–898; Umer, A., Kelley, G. A., Cottrell, L. E., Giacobbi, P., Innes, K. E. and Lilly, C. L. (2017). 'Childhood obesity and adult cardiovascular disease risk factors: A systematic review with meta-analysis', *BMC Public Health*, 17(1), p. 683.

65 Muthuri, S. K., Wachira, L. J. M., Leblanc, A. G., Francis, C. E., Sampson, M., Onywera, V. O. and Tremblay, M. S. (2014). 'Temporal trends and correlates of physical activity, sedentary behaviour, and physical fitness among school-aged children in Sub-Saharan Africa: A systematic review', *International Journal of Environmental Research and Public Health*, 11(3), pp. 3327–3359.

66 Minges, K. E., Chao, A. M., Irwin, M. L., Owen, N., Park, C., Whittemore, R. and Salmon, J. (2016). 'Classroom standing desks and sedentary behavior: A systematic review', *Pediatrics*, 137(2), e20153087–e20153087.

67 Adolphus, K., Lawton, C. L., Champ, C. L. and Dye, L. (2016). 'The effects of breakfast and breakfast composition on cognition in children and adolescents: a systematic review. *Advances in Nutrition*, 7(7), 590S-612S .

68 Global nutrition policy review 2016-2017: country progress in creating enabling policy environments for promoting healthy diets and nutrition. Geneva: World Health Organization; 2018. Licence: CC BY-NC-SA 3.0 IGO.

69   Ochola, S. and Masibo, P. K. (2014). 'Dietary intake of schoolchildren and adolescents in developing countries', *Annals of Nutrition & Metabolism*, 64, pp. 24–40.

70   Utter, J., Scragg, R., Mhurchu, C. N. and Schaaf, D. (2007). 'At-home breakfast consumption among New Zealand children: Associations with body mass index and related nutrition behaviors', *Journal of the American Dietetic Association*, 107(4), pp. 570–576.

71   Ochola, S. and Masibo, P. K. (2014). 'Dietary intake of schoolchildren and adolescents in developing countries', *Annals of Nutrition & Metabolism*, 64, pp. 24–40.

72   Livingstone, M. B. E. and Robson, P. J. (2000). 'Measurement of dietary intake in children', *Proceedings of the Nutrition Society*, 59(2), pp. 279–293.

73   Jimenez, A., Morales-Ruán, M del C, López-Olmedo, N., Théodore, F., Moreno-Saracho, J., Tolentino-Mayo, L., Bonvecchio, A. et al. (2017).'The fight against overweight and obesity in school children: Public policy in Mexico', *Journal of Public Health Policy*, 38(4), pp. 407–428.

74   Barquera, S., Hernández-Barrera, L., Rothenberg, S. J. and Cifuentes, E. (2018). 'The obesogenic environment around elementary schools: Food and beverage marketing to children in two Mexican cities', *BMC Public Health*, 18(1), p.461.

75   Ivers, L. C. and Cullen, K. A. (2011). 'Food insecurity: Special considerations for women'. *American Journal of Clinical Nutrition* 94(6), 1740S–1744S; Spear, B. A. (2002). 'Adolescent growth and development', *Journal of the American Dietetic Association*, 102(3) (Supplement), S23–S29.

76   Keats, E. C., Rappaport, A. I., Jain, R., Oh, C., Shah, S. and Bhutta, Z. A. (2018). 'Diet and eating practices among adolescent girls in low- and middle-income countries: a systematic review.' *Nutrients*, 10(12), e1978.

77   The World Health Organization, "Adolescent Pregnancy Key Facts" (2018)

78   Patton, G. C., Sawyer, S. M., Santelli, J. S., Ross, D. A., Afifi, R., Allen, N. B. et al. (2016). 'Our future: A Lancet commission on adolescent health and wellbeing', *The Lancet* 387(10036), pp. 2423–2478; Cusick, S. E. and Kuch, A. E. (2012). 'Determinants of undernutrition and overnutrition among adolescents in developing countries', *Adolescent Medicine: State of the Art Reviews*, 23(3), pp. 440–456; Belachew, T., Hadley, C., Lindstrom, D., Gebremariam, A., Lachat, C. and Kolsteren, P. (2011). 'Food insecurity, school absenteeism and educational attainment of adolescents in Jimma Zone Southwest Ethiopia: A longitudinal study', *Nutrition Journal*, 10(29).

79   Costa, S. (2016). 'Teens, Your Brain Needs Real Food', U.S. News and World Report, 5 January 2016, <https://health.usnews.com/health-news/health-wellness/articles/2016-01-05/teens-your-brain-needs-real-food>, retrieved 16/7/19.

80   The Conversation, 'Why Sugar is so much worse for teenagers' brains,' RMIT University, <https://theconversation.com/why-sugar-is-so-much-worse-for-teenagers-brains-67238> retrieved 16/7/19.

81   Akseer, N., Al-Gashm, S., Mehta, S., Mokdad, A. and Bhutta, Z. A. (2017). 'Global and regional trends in the nutritional status of young people: A critical and neglected age group', *Annals of the New York Academy of Sciences*, 1393, pp. 3–20.

82   Gizak, M., Rogers, L., Gorstein, J., Zimmerman, M. and Andersson, M. (2018). 'Global iodine status in school-age children, women of reproductive age and pregnancy women in 2017', Iodine Global Network.

83   NCD Risk Factor Collaboration (NCD-RisC). (2017). 'Worldwide trends in body-mass index, underweight, overweight, and obesity from 1975 to 2016: A pooled analysis of 2416 population-based measurement studies in 128·9 million children, adolescents, and adults', *The Lancet*, 390(10113), pp. 2627–2642.

84   Wang, J., Freire, D., Knable, L., Zhao, W., Gong, B., Mazzola, P. et al. (2015). 'Childhood and adolescent obesity and long-term cognitive consequences during aging', *Journal of Comparative Neurology*, 523(5), pp. 757–768.

85   Williamson, N. (2013). 'Motherhood in childhood: Facing the challenge of adolescent pregnancy'. *State of World Population 2013*. United Nations Population Fund (UNFPA), New York.

86   Scholl, T. O., Hediger, M. L., Schall, J. I., Khoo, C. S. and Fischer, R. L. (1994). 'Maternal growth during pregnancy and the competition for nutrients', *American Journal of Clinical Nutrition*, 60(2), pp. 183–188.

87   Bearinger, L. H., Sieving, R. E., Ferguson, J. and Sharma, V. (2007) 'Global perspectives on the sexual and reproductive health of adolescents: Patterns, prevention, and potential'. *The Lancet*, 369, pp. 1220–1231.

88   Restrepo-Méndez, M del C., Lawlor, D. A., Horta, B. L., Santos, I. S., Menezes, A.M., Barros, F. C. and Victora, C. G. (2015). 'The association of maternal age with birthweight and gestational age: A cross-cohort comparison', *Paediatric and Perinatal Epidemiology*, 29(1), pp. 31–40.

89   UNICEF (2016). *Reality Check Approach. Perspectives and experiences of adolescents on eating, drinking and physical activity*. UNICEF, Jakarta, Indonesia.

90   National Institute of Research and Development and Ministry of Health (2018) Basic health research survey (Riset Kesehatan dasar). Ministry of Health, Jakarta.

91   Christian, P. and Smith, E. R. (2018). 'Adolescent undernutrition: Global burden, physiology, and nutritional risks', *Annals of Nutrition and Metabolism*, 72(4), pp. 316–328.

92   Prentice, A. M., Ward, K. A., Goldberg, G. R., Jarjou, L. M., Moore, S. E., Fulford, A. J. and Prentice, A. (2013). 'Critical windows for nutritional interventions against stunting', *American Journal of Clinical Nutrition*, 97(5), pp. 911–918.

93   Georgiadis, A. and Penny, M. E. (2017). 'Child undernutrition: opportunities beyond the first 1000 days', *The Lancet Public Health*, 2(9), e399.

94   Handa, S. and Peterman, A. (2016). 'Is there catch-up growth? Evidence from three continents', *Oxford Bulletin of Economics and Statistics*, 78(4), pp. 470–500.

95   McIntyre, M. H. (2011). 'Adult stature, body proportions and age at menarche in the United States National Health and Nutrition Survey (NHANES) III', *Annals of Human Biology*, 38(6), pp. 716–720; Willemsen, R. H. and Dunger, D. B. (2015). 'Normal variation in pubertal timing: Genetic determinants in relation to growth and adiposity. In J.-P. Bourguignon and A.-S. Parent (eds), *Endocrine Development*, 29, pp. 17–35, S. Karger AG, Basel.

96   Leenstra, T., Petersen, L. T., Kariuki, S. K., Oloo, A. J., Kager, P. A., and ter Kuile, F. O. (2005). 'Prevalence and severity of malnutrition and age at menarche: cross-sectional studies in adolescent schoolgirls in western Kenya', *European Journal of Clinical Nutrition*, 59(1), pp. 41–48; Coly, A. N., Milet, J., Diallo, A., Ndiaye, T., Bénéfice, E., Simondon, F. et al. (2006). 'Preschool stunting, adolescent migration, catch-up growth, and adult height in young Senegalese men and women of rural origin', *Journal of Nutrition*, 136(9), pp. 2412–2420.

97   Yilmaz Z., Hardaway A. and Bulik, C. (2015). 'Genetics and epigenetics of eating disorders', *Advances in Genomics and Genetics*, 5, pp. 131–150.

98   Striegel-Moore, R. H. and Bulik, C. M. (2007). 'Risk factors for eating disorders', *American Psychologist*, 62(3), pp. 181–198.

99   O'Brien, K.M. and Vincent, N.K. (2003). 'Psychiatric comorbidity in anorexia and bulimia nervosa: Nature, prevalence, and causal relationships', *Clinical Psychologial Review*, 23(1), pp. 57–74.

100 Limbers, C. A., Cohen, L. A. and Gray, B. A. (2018). 'Eating disorders in adolescent and young adult males: Prevalence, diagnosis, and treatment strategies', *Adolescent health, medicine and therapeutics*, 10(9), pp. 111–116.

101 Whitaker, R. C., Phillips, S. M. and Orzol, S. M. (2006). 'Food insecurity and the risks of depression and anxiety in mothers and behavior problems in their preschool-aged children', *Pediatrics*, 118(3), e859–868.

102 Darling, K. E., Fahrenkamp, A. J., Wilson, S. M., D'Auria, A. L. and Sato, A. F. (2017). 'Physical and mental health outcomes associated with prior food insecurity among young adults', *Journal of Health Psychology*, 22(5), pp. 572–581; Bruening, M., van Woerden, I., Todd, M. and Laska, M. N. (2018). 'Hungry to learn: The prevalence and effects of food insecurity on health behaviors and outcomes over time among a diverse sample of university freshmen' *International Journal of Behavioral Nutrition and Physical Activity*, 15(1).

103 Rani, D., Singh, J. K., Acharya, D., Paudel, R., Lee, K. and Singh, S. P. (2018). 'Household food insecurity and mental health among teenage girls living in urban slums in Varanasi, India: A cross-sectional study', *International Journal of Environmental Research and Public Health*, 15(8) e1585; McIntyre, L., Williams, J. V. A., Lavorato, D. H. and Patten, S. (2013). 'Depression and suicide ideation in late adolescence and early adulthood are an outcome of child hunger', *Journal of Affective Disorders*, 150, pp. 123–129; Belsky, D. W., Moffitt, T. E., Arseneault, L., Melchior, M. and Caspi, A. (2010). 'Context and sequelae of food insecurity in children's development', *American Journal of Epidemiology*, 172(7), pp. 809–818; Jebena, M. G., Lindstrom, D., Belachew, T., Hadley, C., Larchat, C., Verstraeten, R., De Cock, N. and Kolsteren, P. 'Food insecurity and common mental disorders among Ethiopian youth: Structural equation modeling', *PLoS ONE* 11(11), e0165931.

104 Story, M., Neumark-Sztainer, D. and French, S. (2002). 'Individual and environmental influences on adolescent eating behaviors', *Journal of the American Dietetic Association*, 102(3), (Supplement), S40–S51.

105 Anthrologica and World Food Programme (2018).

Bridging the Gap: Engaging adolescents for nutrition, health and sustainable development. World Food Programme, Rome.

106   Karimi-Shahanjarini, A., Omidvar, N., Bazargan, M., Rashidian, A., Majdzadeh, R. and Shojaeizadeh, D. (2010). 'Iranian female adolescents' views on unhealthy snacks consumption: A qualitative study', *Iranian Journal of Public Health*, 39(3), pp. 92–101.

107   Eddy, K. T., Hennessey, M. and Thompson-Brenner, H. (2007). 'Eating pathology in East African Women: The role of media exposure and globalization', *Journal of Nervous and Mental Disease*, 195(3), p. 196–202.

108   Anthrologica and World Food Programme (2018). *Bridging the Gap: Engaging adolescents for nutrition, health and sustainable development.* World Food

109   WHO (undated). Healthy Diet < https://www.who.int/behealthy/healthy-diet>, retrieved 14/7/19.

110   Herforth, A., Arimond, M., Álvarez-Sánchez, C., Coates, J., Christianson, K., and Muehlhoff, E. (2019). 'A global review of food-based dietary guidelines', *Advances in Nutrition*, 10(4), pp. 590–605.

111   Litman, E. A., Gortmaker, S. L., Ebbeling, C. B. and Ludwig, D. S. (2018). 'Source of bias in sugar-sweetened beverage research: A systematic review', *Public Health Nutrition*, 21(12), pp. 2345–2350; Bes-Rastrollo, M. (2016). 'Impact of sugars and sugar taxation on body weight control: A comprehensive literature review', *Obesity*, 24(7),

Programme, Rome

pp. 1410–1426.

112   Guthrie, J., L. Mancino and C.T.J. Lin (2015). 'Nudging consumers toward better food choices: Policy approaches to changing food consumption behaviors,' *Psychology & Marketing*, 32(5), pp. 501–511.

113   Johnson, N. (2015). 'Brazil's nutrition wisdom: No junk food, no eating alone,' Grist, 2 March, <https://grist.org/food/brazils-nutrition-wisdom-no-junk-food-no-eating-alone/> retrieved 14/7/19.

114   Belluz, J. (2015). 'Brazil has the best nutritional guidelines in the world', *Vox*, 20 February, <https://www.vox.com/2015/2/20/8076961/brazil-food-guide> retrieved 14/7/19.

CHAPTER 3: MALNUTRITION IN A CHANGING WORLD

1   Analysis based on CHERG estimates presented in UNICEF (2015). *Committing to Child Survival – A Promise Renewed: Progress Report 2015.*

2   Lunn, P.G., Northrop-Clewes, C. A. and Downes, R. M. (1991). 'Intestinal permeability, mucosal injury and growth faltering in Gambian infants', *The Lancet*, 338, pp. 907–910; Humphrey, J. H. (2009). 'Child undernutrition, tropical enteropathy, toilets, and handwashing', *The Lancet,* 374, pp. 1032–1035; Pickering, A. J., Djebbari, H., Lopez, C., Coulibaly, M. and Alzua, M. L. (2015). 'Effect of a community-led sanitation intervention on child diarrhoea and child growth in rural Mali: A cluster-randomised controlled trial', *The Lancet Global Health*, 3(11), e701–e711.

3   Fahim, S. M., Das, S., Sanin, K. I., Gazi, M. A., Mahfuz, M., Islam, M. M. and Ahmed, T. (2018). 'Association of fecal markers of environmental enteric dysfunction with zinc and iron status among children at first two years of life in Bangladesh', *American Journal of Tropical Medicine and Hygiene*, 99(2), pp. 489–494.

4   Prendergast, A. J., Humphrey, J. H., Mutasa, K., Majo, F. D., Rukobo, S., Govha, M. et al. (2015). 'Assessment of environmental enteric dysfunction in the SHINE Trial: Methods and Challenges', *Clinical Infectious Diseases*, 61 (Suppl 7), pp. S726–732.

5   Lin, A., Arnold, B. F., Afreen, S., Goto, R., Huda, T. M. N., Haque, R. et al. (2013). 'Household environmental conditions are associated with enteropathy and impaired growth in rural Bangladesh', *American Journal of Tropical Medicine and Hygiene*, 89(1), pp. 130–137.

6   MAL-ED Network Investigators (2018). 'Early childhood cognitive development is affected by interactions among illness, diet, enteropathogens and the home environment: findings from the MAL-ED birth cohort study', *BMJ Global Health*, 3(4), e000752.

7   Husseini, M., Darboe, M. K., Moore, S. E., Nabwera, H. M. and Prentice, A. (2018). 'Thresholds of socio-economic and environmental conditions necessary to escape from childhood malnutrition: a natural experiment in rural Gambia', *BMC Medicine*, 16 (1), p. 199.

8   LSHTM (2018). 'Good housing with indoor plumbing may be key to eliminating childhood malnutrition and stunting'. Press release 1 November, London School

of Hygiene and Tropical Medicine.

9   Trasande, L., Shaffer, R. M., Sathyanarayana, S. and Council on Environmental Health (2018). 'Food Additives and Child Health', *Pediatrics*, 142(2), e20181408.

10   ibid

11   Carlson, A., Xia, K., Azcárate-Peril, M., Goldman, B., Ahn, M., Styner, M., Thompson, A., Geng, X., Gilmore, J., and Knickmeyer, R. (2017). 'Infant gut microbiome associated with cognitive development', *Biological Psychiatry*, 83(2), pp. 148–159; Davis, C. D. (2016). 'The gut microbiome and its role in obesity', *Nutrition Today*, 51(4), pp. 167–174.

12   ibid.

13   Tanaka, M. and Nakayama, J. (2017). 'Development of the gut microbiota in infancy and its impact on health in later life', *Allergology International*, 66(4), pp. 515–522.

14   Lancet Breastfeeding Series Group (2016). 'Breastfeeding in the 21st century: Epidemiology, mechanisms, and lifelong effect', *The Lancet*, 387(10017), pp. 475–490.

15   Bokulich, N. A., Chung, J., Battaglia, T., Henderson, N. et al. (2016). 'Antibiotics, birth mode, and diet shape microbiome maturation during early life', *Science translational medicine*, 8(343), pp. 343ra82.

16   Francino, M. P. (2016). 'Antibiotics and the human gut microbiome: Dysbioses and accumulation of resistances', *Frontiers in Microbiology*, 6(1543).

17   Zinöcker, M. K. and Lindseth, I. A. (2018). 'The Western diet–microbiome–host interaction and its role in metabolic disease', *Nutrients*, 10(3), pp. e365.

18   Velasquez-Manoff, M. (2018). 'The germs that love diet soda', *The New York Times*, 6 April.

19   Victora, C. (2017). 'Breastfeeding as a biological dialogue', *Archivos Argentinos de Pediatría*, 115(5), pp. 413–414; UNICEF (2018). *From the First Hour of Life*, UNICEF, New York, p. 30.

20   Kane, A. V., Dinh, D. M. and Ward, H. D. (2015). 'Childhood malnutrition and the intestinal microbiome', *Pediatric Research*, 77(1), pp. 256–262.

21   FAO, IFAD, UNICEF, WFP and WHO (2018). *The State of Food Security and Nutrition in the World 2018:*

Building climate resilience for food security and nutrition. Food and Agriculture Organization of the United Nations, Rome.

22   Godfrey, K. M., Reynolds, R. M., Prescott, S. L., Nyirenda, M., Jaddoe, V. W. V., Eriksson, J. G. and Broekman, B. F. P. (2017). 'Influence of maternal obesity on the long-term health of offspring', *The Lancet Diabetes & Endocrinology*, 5(1), pp. 53–64; Christian, P. and Stewart, C. P. (2010). 'Maternal micronutrient deficiency, fetal development, and the risk of chronic disease', *Journal of Nutrition*, 140(3), pp. 437–445; Krikke, G. G., Grooten, I. J., Vrijkotte, T. G. M., van Eijsden, M., Roseboom, T. J. and Painter, R. C. (2016). 'Vitamin B12 and folate status in early pregnancy and cardiometabolic risk factors in the offspring at age 5–6 years: Findings from the ABCD multi-ethnic birth cohort', *British Journal of Obstetrics and Gynaecology (BJOG)*, 123(3), pp. 384–392.

23   Vaag, A. A., Grunnet, L. G., Arora, G. P. and Brøns, C. (2012). 'The thrifty phenotype hypothesis revisited'. *Diabetologia*, 55(8), pp. 2085–2088.

24   Hanson, M., Gluckman, P. and Bustreo, F. (2016). 'Obesity and the health of future generations', *The Lancet Diabetes & Endocrinology*, 4(12), pp. 966–967.

25   Chen, C., Xu, X. and Yan, Y. (2018). 'Estimated global overweight and obesity burden in pregnant women based on panel data model', *PLoS ONE*, 13(8), e0202183.

26   Poston, L., Caleyachetty, R., Cnattingius, S., Corvalán, C., Uauy, R., Herring, S. and Gillman, M. W. (2016). 'Preconceptional and maternal obesity: Epidemiology and health consequences', *The Lancet Diabetes & Endocrinology*, 4(12), pp. 1025–1036.

27   Mamun, A. A., O'Callaghan, M., Callaway, L., Williams, G., Najman, J. and Lawlor, D. A. (2009). 'Associations of gestational weight gain with offspring body mass index and blood pressure at 21 years of age: Evidence from a birth cohort study', *Circulation*, 119(13), pp. 1720–1727; Hochner, H., Friedlander, Y., Calderon-Margalit, R., Meiner, V., Sagy, Y., Avgil-Tsadok, M. et al. (2012). 'Associations of maternal prepregnancy body mass index and gestational weight gain with adult offspring cardiometabolic risk factors: the Jerusalem Perinatal Family Follow-up Study', *Circulation*, 125(11), pp. 1381–1389.

28   Eriksson, J. G., Sandboge, S., Salonen, M., Kajantie, E. and Osmond, C. (2015). 'Maternal weight in pregnancy and offspring body composition in late adulthood: Findings from the Helsinki Birth Cohort Study (HBCS)', *Annals of Medicine*, 47(2), pp. 94–99; Westberg, A. P., Salonen, M. K., von Bonsdorff, M., Kajantie, E. and Eriksson, J. G. (2016). 'Maternal body mass index in pregnancy and offspring physical and psychosocial functioning in older age: Findings from the Helsinki Birth Cohort Study (HBCS)', *Annals of Medicine*, 48(4), pp. 268–274.

29   Monteiro, C. A., Benicio, M. H. and Conde, W. L. et al. (2009), 'Narrowing socioeconomic inequality in child stunting: The Brazilian experience, 1974–2007', *Bulletin of the World Health Organization*, 88(4), pp. 305–311.

30   Huicho, L., Segura, E. R., Huayanay-Espinoza, C. A., Niño de Guzman, J., Restrepo-Méndez, M. C., Tam, Y., Barros, A. J. D. and Victora, C. G. (2016). 'Child health and nutrition in Peru within an antipoverty political agenda: A countdown to 2015 country case study', *The Lancet Global Health*, 4(6), e414–e426.

31   Garza, C., Borghi, E., Onyango, A. W. and de Onis, M. (2013). Parental height and child growth from birth to 2 years in the WHO Multicentre Growth Reference Study. 8 September.

32   Hossain, N. (2017). 'Inequality, hunger and malnutrition: Power matters'. In K. Von Grebmer (ed.), *2017 Global hunger index: The inequalities of hunger*, International Food Policy Research Institute, Washington DC, pp. 25–29.

33   HLPE (2017). *Nutrition and food systems. A report by the High Level Panel of Experts on Food Security and Nutrition.* Committee on World Food Security, Rome, pp. 112.

34   ibid.

35   Gray, A., Fontanella-Khan, J. and Munshi, N. (2018). 'Burger King looks to expand in sub-Saharan Africa', *The Financial Times*, 9 October <https://www.ft.com/content/57407046-cc0a-11e8-b276-b9069bde0956>.

36   Ministry of Health of Brazil (2014). *Dietary Guidelines for the Brazilian Population.* Ministry of Health of Brazil.

37   Replace trans fat: an action package to eliminate industrially-produced trans-fatty acids. WHO/NMH/NHD/18.4 [internet]. Geneva: World Health Organization; 2018.

38   Global Panel on Agriculture and Food Systems for Nutrition (2018). 'Improving diets in an era of food market transformation', Policy Brief No. 11, London.

39   Stuckler, D., McKee, M., Ebrahim, S. and Basu, S. (2012) 'Manufacturing epidemics: The role of global producers in increased consumption of unhealthy commodities including processed foods, alcohol, and tobacco', *PLoS Med* 9(6), e1001235.

40   NCD Risk Factor Collaboration (NCD-RisC) (2019). 'Rising rural body-mass index is the main driver of the global obesity epidemic in adults', *Nature*, 569(7755), pp. 260–264.

41   Popkin, B. M. (2006). 'Global nutrition dynamics: The world is shifting rapidly toward a diet linked with noncommunicable diseases', *American Journal of Clinical Nutrition*, 84(2), pp. 289–298.

42   UNICEF (ed.) (2011). *Adolescence: an age of opportunity.* UNICEF, New York.

43   Kennedy, G., Nantel, G. and Shetty, P., (2004). *Globalization of food systems in developing countries: Impact on food security and nutrition.* Food and Agriculture Organization of the United Nations, New York, p. 11.

44   Hawkes, C., Harris, J. and Gillespie, S. (2017). 'Changing diets: Urbanization and the nutrition transition'. In *2017 Global Food Policy Report*, pp. 34–41, International Food Policy Research Institute (IFPRI), Washington DC.

45   ibid.

46   *The Lancet Diabetes & Endocrinology* (2017). (Editorial) 'Tackling childhood obesity: a step in the right direction', 6, February <https://www.thelancet.com/action/showPdf?pii=S2213-8587%2818%2930005-6>, retrieved 14/7/19.

47   Popkin, B. M. (2014). 'Nutrition, agriculture and the global food system in low and middle income countries', *Food Policy*, 47, 91–96.

48   Demmler, K. M., Ecker, O. and Martin, Q. (2017). 'Supermarket shopping and nutritional outcomes: A panel data analysis for urban Kenya', *World Development*, 102, February, pp. 292–303.

49   Kelly, M, Seubsman, S.-a., Banwell, C., Dixon, J. and Sleigh, A. (2014). 'Thailand's food retail transition: Supermarket and fresh market effects on diet quality and health', *British Food Journal* 116(7).

50   Global Panel on Agriculture and Food Systems for Nutrition (2016). *Food systems and diets: Facing the challenges of the 21st century*, London.

51   Hawkes, C., Harris, J. and Gillespie, S. (2017). 'Changing diets: Urbanization and the nutrition transition'. In 2017 *Global Food Policy Report*, pp. 34–41, International Food Policy Research Institute (IFPRI), Washington DC, p. 38.

52   Jones, A. D. (2015). 'Household food insecurity is associated with heterogeneous patterns of diet quality across urban and rural regions of Malawi', *World Medical & Health Policy*, 7(3), pp. 234–254.

53   Milan Urban Food Policy Pact. <http://www.milanurbanfoodpolicypact.org/>

54   FAO, EStà and City of Curitiba (2018). *Curitiba: facilitating access of low-income households to healthy food.* Food and Agriculture Organization of the United Nations.

55   Forster, T., Egal, F., Escaduro, A. G., Dubbeling, M and Renting, H. (2015). *Milan Urban Food Policy Pact: Selected Good Practices from Cities*, Fondazione Giangiacomo Feltrinelli, Milan.

56   FAO, IFAD, UNICEF, WFP and WHO (2018). *The State of Food Security and Nutrition in the World 2018: Building climate resilience for food security and nutrition.* Food and Agriculture Organization of the United Nations, Rome; Hirvonen, K., Taffesse, A. S. and Worku Hassen, I. (2016). 'Seasonality and household diets in Ethiopia', *Public Health Nutrition*, 19(10), pp. 1723–1730; Oduor, F. O., Boedecker, J., Kennedy, G., Mituki-mungiria, D. and Termote, C. (2018). 'Caregivers' nutritional knowledge and attitudes mediate seasonal shifts in children's diets', *Maternal & Child Nutrition*, 15(1), e12633.

57   HLPE (2017). *Nutrition and food systems. A report by the High Level Panel of Experts on Food Security and Nutrition.* Committee on World Food Security, Rome.

58   Lucan, S. C., Maroko, A. R., Seitchik, J. L., Yoon, D. H., Sperry, L. E. and Schechter, C. B. (2018). 'Unexpected neighborhood sources of food and drink: implications for research and community health', *American Journal of Preventive Medicine*, 55(2), e29–e38. https://doi.org/10.1016/j.amepre.2018.04.011

59   HLPE (2017). *Nutrition and food systems. A report by the High Level Panel of Experts on Food Security and Nutrition.* Committee on World Food Security, Rome.

60   Odoms-Young, A., Singleton, C.R., Springfield, S. et al. (2016). 'Retail environments as a venue for obesity prevention', Current Obesity Reports, 5(2), pp. 184–191; Hilmers, A., Hilmers, D. C. and Dave, J. (2012). 'Neighborhood disparities in access to healthy foods and their effects on environmental justice', *American Journal of Public Health*, 102(9), pp. 1644–1654.

61   Gartin, M. (2012). 'Food deserts and nutritional risk in Paraguay', *American Journal of Human Biology*, 24, pp. 296–301.

62   Walker, R. E., Keane, C. R. and Burke, J. G. (2010). 'Disparities and access to healthy food in the United States: A review of food deserts literature', *Health & Place*, 16(5), pp. 876–884.

63   Gartin, M. (2012). 'Food deserts and nutritional risk in Paraguay', *American Journal of Human Biology*, 24, pp. 296–301.

64   HLPE (2017). *Nutrition and food systems. A report by the High Level Panel of Experts on Food Security and Nutrition.* Committee on World Food Security, Rome.

65   Bridle-Fitzpatrick, S. (2015). 'Food deserts or food swamps? A mixed-methods study of local food environments in a Mexican city', *Social Science & Medicine*, 142, pp. 202–213.

66   Cummins, S., Flint, E. and Matthews, S. A. (2014). 'New neighborhood grocery store increased awareness of food access but did not alter dietary habits or obesity', *Health Affairs (Project Hope)*, 33(2), pp. 283–291.

67   Battersby, J. and Crush, J. (2014). 'Africa's urban food deserts', *Urban Forum*, 25(2), pp. 143–151.

68   Song, Y., Agardh, A., Ma, J., Li, L., Lei, Y., Stafford, R. S. and Prochaska, J. J. (2018). 'National trends in stunting, thinness and overweight among Chinese school-aged children, 1985–2014', *International Journal of Obesity*, 43(2), pp. 402–411.

69   GBD 2015 Obesity Collaborators. (2017). 'Health effects of overweight and obesity in 195 countries over 25 years', *New England Journal of Medicine*, 377, pp. 13–27.

70   GBD Collaborative Network (2017). *Global Burden of Disease Study 2015 (GBD 2015) Obesity and Overweight Prevalence 1980–2015.*, Institute for Health Metrics and Evaluation (IHME), Seattle, US.

71   Li, P. (2012). 'Obesity is a growing concern in China', China.org.cn <http://www.china.org.cn/china/2012-09/14/content_26521029.htm>, retrieved 14/7/19.

72   Song, Y., Agardh, A., Ma, J., Li, L., Lei, Y., Stafford, R. S. and Prochaska, J. J. (2018). 'National trends in stunting, thinness and overweight among Chinese school-aged children, 1985–2014', *International Journal of Obesity*, 43(2), pp. 402–411.

73   Wang, H., Xue, H., Du, S., Zhang, J., Wang, Y. and Zhang, B. (2017). 'Time trends and factors in body mass index and obesity among children in China:

1997–2011', *International Journal of Obesity*, 41(6), p. 964–970.

74 Zhang, J., Zhai, Y., Feng, X., Li, W., Yue, B., Astell-burt, T., Zhao, P and Shi, X. (2018). 'Gender differences in the prevalence of overweight and obesity, associated behaviors, and weight-related perceptions in a national survey of primary school children in China', *Biomedical and Environmental Sciences*, 31(1), pp. 1–11.

75 GBD 2015 Obesity Collaborators. (2017). 'Health effects of overweight and obesity in 195 countries over 25 years', *New England Journal of Medicine*, 377, pp. 13–27.

76 Ji, C. Y. and Chen, T. J. (2013). 'Empirical changes in the prevalence of overweight and obesity among Chinese students from 1985 to 2010 and corresponding preventive strategies', *Biomedical and Environmental Sciences*, 26(1), pp. 1–12.

77 He, W., James, S. A., Merli, M. G. and Zheng, H. (2014). 'An increasing socioeconomic gap in childhood overweight and obesity in China', *American Journal of Public Health*, 104(1), e14–e22.

78 Zhang, Y. X., Wang, Z. X., Zhao, J. S. and Chu, Z. H. (2016). 'Prevalence of overweight and obesity among children and adolescents in Shandong, China: Urban–rural disparity', *Journal of Tropical Pediatrics*, 62(4), pp. 293–300.

79 Song, Y., Wang, H. and Dong, B. et al. (2016). '25-year trends in gender disparity for obesity and overweight by using WHO and IOTF definitions among Chinese school-aged children: a multiple cross-sectional study', *BMJ Open*, 6, e011904.

80 Zhai, F. Y., Du, S. F., Wang, Z. H., Zhang, J. G., Du, W. W. and Popkin, B. M. (2014). 'Dynamics of the Chinese diet and the role of urbanicity, 1991–2011', *Obesity Review*, 15,(Supplement 1), pp. 16–26.

81 Mroz, T. A., Zhai, F. and Popkin, B.M. (2004). 'Rapid income growth adversely affects diet quality in China-particularly for the poor!', *Social Science and Medicine*, 59(7), pp. 1505–1515.

82 Ma, G. S. (2018). Report on the consumption of Sugar-Sweetened Beverages of Children in China. The Population Publishing House, Beijing, p. 12.

83 WHO (2010). *Global Recommendations on Physical Activity for Health*.

84 Zhang, X., Song, Y., Yang, T. B. et al. (2012). 'Analysis of current situation of physical activity and influencing factors in Chinese primary and middle school students in 2010', *Chinese Journal of Preventive Medicine*, 46(9), pp. 781–788.

85 Yang, C. (2009). 'Social justice, stratification, and college access: Examining higher education expansion in Taiwan'. Paper presented at the annual meeting of the 53rd Annual Conference of the Comparative and International Education Society, Francis Marion Hotel, Charleston, South Carolina, <http://citation.allacademic.com/meta/p298842_index.html> retrieved 14/7/19.

86 Wang, H. and Zhai, F. (2013). 'Programme and policy options for preventing obesity in China', *Obesity Review* 14, (Supplement 2), pp. 134–140.

87 Wei, X., Ma, Y., Hu, J., Lin, W., Zhao, Z. and Wen, D. (2018). 'Predicting weight status in Chinese pre-school children: independent and interactive effects of caregiver types and feeding styles', *Public Health Nutrition*, 21(6), pp. 1123–1130.

88 Burns, J., Emerson, J. A., Amundson, K., Doocy, S., Caulfield, L. E. and Klemm, R. D. W. (2016). 'A qualitative analysis of barriers and facilitators to optimal breastfeeding and complementary feeding practices in South Kivu, Democratic Republic of Congo', *Food and Nutrition Bulletin*, 37(2), pp. 119–131.

89 Armar-Klemesu, M., Osei-Menya, S., Zakariah-Akoto, S., Tumilowicz, A., Lee, J. and Hotz, C. (2018). 'Using ethnography to identify barriers and facilitators to optimal infant and young child feeding in rural Ghana: Implications for programs', *Food and Nutrition Bulletin*, 39(2), pp. 231–245.

90 Johnson, S. L. (2016). 'Developmental and environmental influences on young children's vegetable preferences and consumption', *Advances in Nutrition: An International Review Journal*, 7(9), 220S–231S.

91 Headey, D. D. and Alderman, H. H. (forthcoming). 'The relative caloric prices of healthy and unhealthy foods differ systematically across income levels and continents', *The Journal of Nutrition*.

92 Darmon, N. and Drewnowski, A. (2015). 'Contribution of food prices and diet cost to socioeconomic disparities in diet quality and health: A systematic review and analysis', *Nutrition Reviews*, 73(10), pp. 643–660.

93 Hawkes, C., Harris, J. and Gillespie, S. (2017). 'Changing diets: Urbanization and the nutrition transition'. In *2017 Global Food Policy Report*, pp. 34–41, International Food Policy Research Institute (IFPRI), Washington DC. p. 37.

94 Muhammad, A., Seale, J. L., Meade, B. and Regmi, A. (2011). 'International evidence on food consumption patterns: An update using 2005 international comparison program data', *USDA Economic Research Service Technical Bulletin*, 1929, US Department. of Agriculture, Economic Research Service, March.

95 Herforth, A., & Ahmed, S. (2015). The food environment, its effects on dietary consumption, and potential for measurement within agriculture-nutrition interventions. Food Security, 7(3), 505–520. https://doi.org/10.1007 /s12571-015-0455-8.

96 FAO, IFAD, UNICEF, WFP and WHO (2018). *The State of Food Security and Nutrition in the World 2018: Building climate resilience for food security and nutrition*. Food and Agriculture Organization of the United Nations, Rome.

97 Food Security Information Network (FSIN) (2019). *2019 Global report on food crises: Joint analysis for better decisions*, Food and Agriculture Organization of the United Nations, Rome, Italy and Washington DC; World Food Programme (WFP); International Food Policy Research Institute (IFPRI). <http://fsinplatform.org/>

98 FAO, IFAD, UNICEF, WFP and WHO (2018). *The State of Food Security and Nutrition in the World 2018: Building climate resilience for food security and nutrition*. Food and Agriculture Organization of the United Nations, Rome.

99 Food Security Information Network (FSIN) (2018). *Global report on food crises 2018*.

100 FAO (undated). T*he impact of disasters on agriculture and food security*. Food and Agriculture Organization of the United Nations, Rome.

101 Vermeulen, S. J., Campbell, B. M. and Ingram, J. S. I (2012). 'Climate change and food systems', *Annual Review of Environmental Resources*, 37, pp. 195–222.

102 Gerber, P.J., Steinfeld, H., Henderson, B., Mottet, A., Opio, C., Dijkman, J., Falcucci, A. and Tempio, G. (2013).

Tackling climate change through livestock: A global assessment of emissions and mitigation opportunities. Food and Agriculture Organization of the United Nations (FAO), Rome, p. 15.

103 Springmann, M., Clark, M., Mason-D'Croz, D., Wiebe, K., Bodirsky, B. L. et al. (2018). 'Options for keeping the food system within environmental limits', *Nature*, 562, pp. 519–525.

104 Willett, W., Rockström, J., Loken, B., Springmann, M. et al. (2019). 'Food in the Anthropocene: the EAT–Lancet Commission on healthy diets from sustainable food systems', *The Lancet*, 393(10170), pp. 447–492.

105 UN Water (undated). Water scarcity. <http://www.unwater.org/water-facts/scarcity/>, retrieved 14/7/19.

106 UNICEF (2018). *Understanding the Impacts of Pesticides on Children: A discussion paper*. UNICEF, New York.

107 International Labour Office (2017). *Global Estimates of Child Labour: Results and trends, 2012–2016*, International Labour Organization, Geneva, p. 9.

108 UNICEF (2018). *Understanding the Impacts of Pesticides on Children: A discussion paper*. UNICEF, New York.

109 Brondizio, E. S., Settele, J., Díaz, S. and Ngo, H. T. (eds) (2019). *Global Assessment Report on Biodiversity and Ecosystem Services: Summary for policymakers of the global assessment report on biodiversity and ecosystem services*, IPBES Secretariat, Bonn, Germany.

110 Bélanger, J. and Pilling, D. (eds). (2019). *The State of the World's Biodiversity for Food and Agriculture*. Commission on Genetic Resources for Food and Agriculture, FAO, p. 95.

111 Collette, L., Hodgkin, T., Kassam, A., Kenmore, P., Lipper, L., Nolte, C., Stamoulis, K. and Steduto, P. (2011). *Save and grow: a policymaker's guide to sustainable intensification of smallholder crop production*. FAO, Rome.

112 Remans, R., Flynn, D. F. B., DeClerck, F., Diru, W., Fanzo, J., Gaynor, K., Lambrecht, I., Mudiope, J., Mutuo, P. K., Nkhoma, P. et al. (2011). 'Assessing nutritional diversity of cropping systems in African villages', *Plos One*, 6(6); DeClerck, F. A. J., Fanzo, J., Palm, C. and Remans, R. (2011). 'Ecological approaches to human nutrition', *Food and Nutrition Bulletin*, 32(1), pp. S41–S50; Herrero, M., Thornton, P. K., Power, B., Bogard, J. R., Remans, R., Fritz, S. et al. (2017). 'Farming and the geography of nutrient production for human use: a transdisciplinary analysis', *The Lancet Planetary Health*, 1(1), e33–e42; Remans, R., DeClerck, F.A., Kennedy, G. and Fanzo, J. (2015). 'Expanding the view on the production and dietary diversity link: Scale, function, and change over time', *Proceedings of the National Academy of Sciences of the United States of America*, 112(45), E6082–E6082; Lachat, C., Raneri, J. E., Walker Smith, K., Kolsteren, P., Van Damme, P., Verzelen, K., Penafiel, D., Vanhove, W. et al. (2017). 'Dietary species richness as a measure of food biodiversity and nutritional quality of diets', *Proceedings of the National Academy of Sciences*, 115(1), pp. 127–132.

113 Khoury, C.K., Bjorkman, A. D., Dempewolf, H., Ramirez-Villegas, J., Guarino, L., Jarvis, A., Rieseberg, L. H. and Struik, P. C. (2014). 'Increasing homogeneity in global food supplies and the implications for food security', *Proceedings of the National Academy of Sciences of the United States of America*, 111(11), pp. 4001–4006.

114 Jones, A. D. and Ejeta, G. (2015). 'A new global agenda for nutrition and health: the importance of agriculture and food systems', *Bulletin of the World Health Organization*, 94(3), pp. 228–229.

115 World Bank data <https://data.worldbank.org/indicator/SL.TLF.TOTL.FE.ZS>

116 Schulte, B., Durana, A., Stout, B. and Moyer, J. (2017). *Paid family leave: How much time is enough?* New America, Washington DC.

117 UNICEF (2019). *A Gathering Storm: Climate change clouds the future of children in Bangladesh.* UNICEF, New York.

118 WHO (undated). Global Health Observatory data repository. WHO, Geneva, Switzerland.

119 UNICEF Malaysia and DM Analytics (2018). *Children Without: A study of urban child poverty and deprivation in low-cost flats in Kuala Lumpur.* UNICEF Malaysia, Putrajaya, Malaysia.

120 UNICEF (2019). *Annual results report 2018: Humanitarian action* (draft). UNICEF, New York.

121 UN OCHA (2018). *Humanitarian needs overview: Sudan.* United Nations Office for the Coordination of Humanitarian Affairs, New York.

122 Fanzo, J. and Hawkes, C. (2018). *2018 Global nutrition report: Shining a light to spur action on nutrition.* Independent Expert Group of the Global Nutrition Report, p. 15.

123 ibid.

124 Mates, E., Shoham, J., Khara, T. and Dolan, C. (2017). *Stunting in humanitarian and protracted crises: Discussion paper.* Emergency Nutrition Network, Oxford, UK.

125 ibid., p. 63.

126 UN OCHA (2018). World humanitarian data and trends 2018 <http://interactive.unocha.org/publication/datatrends2018/> retrieved 30 July 2019.

127 UNICEF (2018). 'Conflict in Yemen: A living hell for children', News note, 4 November.

128 UNICEF (2018). *Yemen humanitarian situation report (December 2018).* UNICEF, New York.

129 ibid.

130 UNICEF (2019). *Annual results report 2018: Humanitarian action* . UNICEF, New York, p. 32 .

131 SOWC submission from Yemen Country Office.

132 World Bank (2017). Prevalence of anemia among children (% of children under 5) <https://data.worldbank.org/indicator/SH.ANM.CHLD.ZS> retrieved 30 July 2019.

CHAPTER 4: RESPONSES TO MALNUTRITION

1 Nomura, M. Takahashi, K and Reic, M. R. (2015). 'Trends in global nutrition policy and implications for Japanese development policy', *Food and Nutrition Bulletin*, 36(4), pp. 493–540.

2 Copenhagen Consensus Center (2008). Copenhagen Consensus 2008: Results. Copenhagen Consensus Center, Copenhagen, Denmark.

3 The lancet (2008–). Maternal and Child Undernutrition Series. <https://www.thelancet.com/series/maternal-and-child-undernutrition> retrieved 25 July 2019.

4 ibid.

5 UN Standing Committee on Nutrition (2014). Nutrition and the Post-2015 Sustainable Development System. A Technical Note. United Nations, New York.

6 WHO (2017). *Global Nutrition Policy Review 2016-2017.* WHO, Geneva, Switzerland, p11.

7 'SMART' is generally accepted to represent 'Specific, Measurable, Achievable, Relevant and Time-bound', or minor variations thereof.

8 IFPRI (2016). *Global Nutrition Report 2016: From promise to impact: Ending malnutrition by 2030.* International Food Policy Research Institute, Washington DC, p.134.

9 Reich, M. R. and Balarajan, Y. (2012). *Political economy analysis for food and nutrition security.* World Bank, Washington DC.

10 Rasella, D., Aquino, R., Santos, Carlos A. T., Paes-Sousa, R. and Barreto, M. L. (2013). 'Effect of a conditional cash transfer programme on childhood mortality: A nationwide analysis of Brazilian municipalities', *The Lancet*, 382(9886), pp. 57–64.

11 Ruel, M. T. and Alderman, H. (2013). 'Nutrition-sensitive interventions and programmes: How can they help to accelerate progress in improving maternal and child nutrition?' *The Lancet*, 382(9891), pp. 536–551.

12 United Nations System Standing Committee on Nutrition (2017). Global Governance for Nutrition and the role of UNSCN. Discussion Paper. United Nations, New York.

13 Baker, P., Hawkes, C., Wingrove, K., Demaio, A. R., Parkhurst, J., Thow, A. M. and Walls, H. (2018). 'What drives political commitment for nutrition? A review and framework synthesis to inform the United Nations Decade of Action on Nutrition', *BMJ Global Health*, 3(1), e000485.

14 Miller, B. D. D. and Welch, R. M. (2013). 'Food system strategies for preventing micronutrient malnutrition', *Food Policy*, 42, pp. 115–128.

15 Backstrand, J. R. (2002). 'The history and future of food fortification in the United States: A public health perspective', *Nutrition Reviews*, 60, pp. 15–26.

16 Iodine Global Network (2016). Global Iodine Nutrition Scorecard 2016, Iodine Global Network, Zurich.

17 Horton, S. et al. (2008). Best Practice Paper: Food Fortification with Iron and Iodine. Copenhagen Consensus Center, Denmark, p.21.

18 UNICEF and WHO Joint Committee on Health Policy (1994). World Summit for Children Mid-Decade Goal: Iodine deficiency disorders (IDD), UNICEF and WHO Joint Committee on Health Policy Special Session, 27–28 January 1994 (JCHPSS/94/2.7), WHO, Geneva.

19 WHO (2014). Guideline: Fortification of food-grade salt with iodine for the prevention and control of iodine deficiency disorders. WHO, Geneva.

20 Dwyer, J. T., Wiemer, K. L., Dary, O., Keen, C. L., King, J. C., Miller, K. B. et al. (2015). 'Fortification and health: Challenges and opportunities', *Advances in Nutrition*, 6(1), pp. 124–31.

21 Crider, K. S., Bailey, L. B. and Berry, R. J. (2011). 'Folic acid food fortification: Its history, effect, concerns, and future directions', *Nutrients*, 3(3), pp. 370–84.

22 UK Government and devolved administrations (2019). Proposal to add folic acid to flour: Consultation document. UK Government, London.

23 Global Fortification Data Exchange (undated). Map: Fortification Legislation. <http://www.fortificationdata.org> retrieved 25 July 2019.

24 Kancherla, V., Wagh, K., Johnson, Q. and Oakley, G. P. Jr. A. (2018). 'A 2017 global update on folic acid-preventable spina bifida and anencephaly', *Birth Defects Research*, 110(14), pp. 1139–1147.

25 Bobrek, K., Broersen. B., Aburto, N., Garg, A., Serdula, M., Velazquez, F. B. et al. (2019). 'National wheat and maize flour fortification standards and their comparison with international guidelines in countries with mandatory fortification', *Current Developments in Nutrition,* 3 (Supplement 1).

26 Government of Tanzania and the Global Alliance for Improved Nutrition (GAIN) (2015). Arusha Statement on Food Fortification, at the Global Summit on Food Fortification, 9–11 September, Arusha, Tanzania.

27 UNICEF and WHO (2018). *Capture the Moment: Early initiation of breastfeeding: The best start to every newborn.* UNICEF, New York.

28 Prak, S., Dahl, M. I., Oeurn, S., Conkle, J., Wise, A. and Laillou, A. (2014). 'Breastfeeding trends in Cambodia and the increased use of breastmilk substitutes – why is it a danger?' *Nutrients*, 6(7), pp. 2920–2930.

29 UNICEF and WHO (2018). *Capture the Moment: Early initiation of breastfeeding: The best start to every newborn.* UNICEF, New York.

30 UNICEF (2016). Annual Results Report – Nutrition 2015. UNICEF, New York, p. 16.

31 Aguayo, V. M., Gupta, G., Singh, G. and Kumar, R. (2016). 'Early initiation of breast feeding on the rise in India', *BMJ Global Health* 1(2), e000043.

32 Federal Democratic Republic of Ethiopia-Ministry of Health (2017). Baby and mother WASH: Implementation Guideline. UNICEF Ethiopia, Addis Ababa, Ethiopia.

33 UNSCN (2017). Schools as a system to improve nutrition: A new statement for school-based food and nutrition interventions. United Nations System Standing Committee on Nutrition, Washington DC.

34 UNICEF (2018). 'Forging an anaemia-free future: The path to India's nationwide adolescent anaemia control programme', Field Reports: Lessons from improving nutrition at scale. UNICEF, New York, p. 3.

35 Gaarder, M. M., Glassman, A. and Todd, J. E. (2010). 'Conditional cash transfers and health: Unpacking the causal chain', *Journal of Development Effectiveness*, 2(1), pp. 6–50; Ranganathan, M. and Lagarde, M. (2012). 'Promoting healthy behaviours and improving health outcomes in low- and middle-income countries: A review of the impact of

conditional cash-transfer programmes', *Preventive Medicine*, 55 (Supplement), S95–105.

36   Instituto de Pesquisa Econômica Aplicada (IPEA) (2013). Programa Bolsa Familia: Uma decada de inclusão e cidadania. IPEA, Brasília, p. 29.

37   Bortoletto Martins, A. P. and Monteiro, C. (2016). 'Impact of the Bolsa Família program on food availability of low-income Brazilian families: a quasi-experimental study', *BMC Public Health*, 16, p. 827.

38   Rasella, D., Aquino, R., Santos, Carlos A. T., Paes-Sousa, R. and Barreto, M. L. (2013). 'Effect of a conditional cash transfer programme on childhood mortality: A nationwide analysis of Brazilian municipalities', *The Lancet*, 382(9886), pp. 57–64.

39   Government of Mexico (undated). ¿Qué es PROSPERA Programa de Inclusión Social?. <https://www.gob.mx/prospera/documentos/que-es-prospera> retrieved 26 July 2019.

40   Hoddinott, J., Skoufias, E. and Washburn, R. (2000). The Impact of PROGRESA on Consumption: A final report', International Food Policy Research Institute, Washington DC.

41   Fernald, Lia C. H., Gertler, P. J. and Neufeld, L. M. (2008). 'Role of cash in conditional cash transfer programmes for child health, growth, and development: An analysis of Mexico's opportunities', *The Lancet* 371(9615), pp. 828–837.

42   FAO and WHO (2014). Conference Outcome Document: Rome Declaration on Nutrition. Food and Agriculture Organization of the United Nations and World Health Organization, Rome, p.2.

43   HLPE (2017). *Nutrition and food systems.* A report by the High-Level Panel of Experts on Food Security and Nutrition of the Committee on World Food Security, Committee World Food Security, Rome.

44   Global Panel on Agriculture and Food Systems for Nutrition (2016). *Food systems and diets: Facing the challenge of the 21st Century.* Global Panel on Agriculture and Food Systems for Nutrition, London.

45   Fanzo, J. and Hawkes, C. (2018). *2018 Global Nutrition Report: Shining a light to spur action on nutrition.* Development Initiatives, Bristol, UK.

46   EAT–Lancet Commission (2019). Food in the Anthropocene: the EAT–Lancet Commission on healthy diets from sustainable food systems. <https://www.thelancet.com/commissions/EAT> retrieved 26 July 2019.

47   WHO (1981). *International Code of Marketing of Breast-milk Substitutes.* WHO, Geneva.

48   Access to Nutrition Foundation (2018). *Access to Nutrition Index Global Index 2018.* Access to Nutrition Foundation, Utrecht.

49   WHO, UNICEF and IBFAN (2018). Marketing of Breast-Milk Substitutes: National Implementation of the International Code Status Report. WHO, Geneva.

50   WHO (2015). *Guideline: Sugars intake for adults and children.* WHO, Geneva.

51   Fanzo, J. and Hawkes, C. (2018). *2018 Global Nutrition Report: Shining a light to spur action on nutrition.* Development Initiatives, Bristol, UK, p. 94.

52   KPMG (2018). Budget 2019 Of Sugar Tax and the Digital Economy. KPMG, Malaysia.

53   Colchero, M. A., Rivera-Dommarco, J., Popkin, B. M. and Ng, S.W. (2017). 'In Mexico, evidence of sustained consumer response two years after implementing a sugar-sweetened beverage tax', *Health Affairs*, 36(3), pp. 564–571.

54   UNICEF (2018). Review of sugar taxes: Case studies on the implementation of sugar taxes in various jurisdictions. UNICEF, New York.

55   Fanzo, J. and Hawkes, C. (2018). *2018 Global Nutrition Report: Shining a light to spur action on nutrition.* Development Initiatives, Bristol, UK, p.16.

56   Hawkes, C., Smith, T.G., Jewell, J., Wardle, J. Hammond, R. A., Friel, S. et al. (2015). 'Smart food policies for obesity prevention', *The Lancet*, 385(9985), pp. 2410–2421.

57   Kanter, R., Vanderlee, L. and Vandevijvere, S. (2018). 'Front-of-package nutrition labelling policy: Global progress and future directions', *Public Health Nutrition*, 21(8), pp.1399–1408.

58   Hawley, K. L., Roberto, C. A., Bragg, M. A., Liu, P.J., Schwartz, M. B. and Brownell, K. D. (2013). 'The science on front-of-package food labels', *Public Health Nutrition*, 16(3), pp. 430–439.

59   Hersey, J. C., Wohlgenant, K. C., Arsenault, J. E., Kosa, K. M. and Muth, M. K. (2013). 'Effects of front-of-package and shelf nutrition labeling systems on consumers', *Nutrition Reviews*, 71(1), pp.1–14.

60   Egnell, M. Talati, Z., Hercberg, S., Pettigrew, S. and Julia, C. (2018). 'Objective understanding of front-of-package nutrition labels: An international comparative experimental study across 12 countries', *Nutrients*, 10(10), p. 1452.

61   Neal, B. Crino, M., Dunford, E., Gao, A., Greenland, R., Li, N., Ngai, J., Ni Mhurch,C. et al. (2017). 'Effects of different types of front-of- packing labelling information on the healthiness of food purchases: A randomized controlled trial', *Nutrients*, 9(12), p. 1284.

62   Hawley, K. L., Roberto, C. A., Bragg, M. A., Liu, P. J., Schwartz, M. B. and Brownell, K. D. (2013). 'The science on front-of-package food labels', *Public Health Nutrition*, 16(3), pp. 430–439.

63   INSP-UNICEF (2016). Review of current labelling regulations and practices for food and beverage targeting children and adolescents in Latin America countries (Mexico, Chile, Costa Rica and Argentina) and recommendations for facilitating consumer information. UNICEF, New York, p.23.

64   Ministerio de Salud (2017). Gobierno de Chile. Política Nacional de Alimentación y Nutrición. <http://www.bibliotecaminsal.cl/politica-nacional-de-alimentacion-y-nutricion/> retrieved 26 July 2019.

65   Osiac, L. R. and Quevedo, T. P. (2018). 'Ley de Etiquetado y Publicidad de Alimentos: Chile innovando en nutrición pública una vez más' ('Law of food labelling and advertising: Chile innovating in public nutrition once again'), *Revista Chilena de Pediatría*, 89(5),pp. 579–581.

66   Correa, T., Fierro, C., Reyes, M., Dillman Carpentier, F. R., Taillie, L. S. and Corvalán, C. (2019). 'Responses to the Chilean law of food labeling and advertising: Exploring knowledge, perceptions and behaviors of mothers of young children', *International Journal of Behavioral Nutrition and Physical Activity* 16(1), p.21.

67   ibid.

68   Kanter, R., Reyes, M., Swinburn, B., Vandevijvere, S. and Corvalán, C. (2019). 'The food supply prior to the implementation of the Chilean law of food labeling and advertising', *Nutrients* 11(1), p. 52.

69   Downs, S. and Fanzo, J. (2016). 'Managing value chains for improved nutrition'. In M. Eggersdorfer, K. Kraemer, J. B. Cordaro, J. Fanzo, M. Gibney, E. Kennedy, A. Labrique and J. Steffen. *Good nutrition: perspectives for the 21st century*, pp. 45–59. Krager Publications, Basel.

70   FAO (2013). *The State of Food and Agriculture 2013: Food Systems for Better Nutrition.* Food and Agriculture Organization, Rome.

71   HLPE (2017). Nutrition and food systems. A report by the High-Level Panel of Experts on Food Security and Nutrition of the Committee on World Food Security, Committee World Food Security, Rome.

72   WHO (2004). Global Strategy on Diet, Physical Activity and Health. WHO, Geneva, p.13.

73   United Nations (2016). The Global Strategy for Women's, Children's and Adolescents' Health (2016–2030). United Nations, New York.

74   Independent Accountability Panel for Every Woman, Every Child, Every Adolescent (IAP) (2018). Private Sector: Who is Accountable? Summary Report. WHO, Geneva, p.5.

75   WHO (2017). Report of the Commission on Ending Childhood Obesity. Implementation plan: Executive summary. WHO, Geneva, p. 9.

76   International Food and Beverage Alliance (2019). Enhanced commitment to phase out industrially produced trans-fatty acids, Press Release (undated). <https://ifballiance.org/uploads/press/pdf/5ccc4b8061475_IFBA%20iTFA%20Enhanced%20Commitment%2002.05.2019.pdf> retrieved 26 July 2019.

77   WHO Regional Office for Europe (2018). Evaluating Implementation of the WHO Set of Recommendations on the Marketing of Foods and Non-Alcoholic Beverages to Children. WHO, Geneva.

78   Kelly, B., Vandevijvere, S., Ng, S., Adams, J., Allemandi, L., Bahena-Espina, L., Barquera, S., et al. (2019). 'Global benchmarking of children's exposure to television advertising of unhealthy foods and beverages across 22 countries', *Obesity Reviews*, https://doi.org/10.1111/obr.12840.

79   Haddad, L. (2018). 'Reward food companies for improving nutrition', *Nature*, 556(7699),pp.19–22.

80   Afshin, A., Peñalvo, J. L., Del Gobbo, L., Silva, J., Michaelson, M., O'Flaherty, M. et al. (2017). 'The prospective impact of food pricing on improving dietary consumption: A systematic review and meta-analysis', *PloS One*, 12(3), e0172277.

81   Swinburn, B. A., Kraak, V.I., Allender, A., Atkins, V.J., Baker, P. I., Bogard, J. R., Brinsden, H., Calvillo, A., De Schutter, O., Devarajan, R., Ezzati, M., Friel, S., Goenka, S., Hammond, R. A., Hastings, G., Hawkes, C. et al. (2019). 'The global syndemic of obesity, undernutrition, and climate change: The Lancet Commission report', The *Lancet*, 393(10173), pp.791–846.

82   HLPE (2017). *Nutrition and food systems. A report by the High-Level Panel of Experts on Food Security and Nutrition of the Committee on World Food Security*, Committee World Food Security, Rome.

83   Swinburn, B., Kraak, V., Rutter, H., Vandevijvere, S., Lobstein, T., Sacks, G. et al. (2015). 'Strengthening of accountability systems to create healthy food environments and reduce global obesity', *The Lancet*, 385(9986), pp.2534–2545.

84   Gillespie, S., Haddad, L., Mannar, V., Menon, P.

and Nisbett, N. (2013). 'The politics of reducing malnutrition: Building commitment and accelerating progress', *The Lancet*, 382(9891), pp. 552–569.

85 Yanamadala, S. Bragg, M. A., Roberto, C. A. and Brownell K. A. (2012). 'Food industry front groups and conflicts of interest: the case of Americans Against Food Taxes', *Public Health Nutrition*, 15(8). pp. 1331–1332.

86 King, L., Gill, T., Allender, S. and Swinburn, B. (2011). 'Best practice principles for community-based obesity prevention: Development, content and application', *Obesity Reviews*, 12(5), pp. 329–338.

87 Patel, R. C. (2012). 'Food sovereignty: Power, gender, and the right to food', *PLoS Medicine*, 9(6), e1001223.

88 Pakistan Fisher Folk Forum <http://pff.org.pk/>

89 Movimento dos Trabalhadores Rurais Sem Terra (MST) <https://www.mstbrazil.org/content/what-mst>

90 Durrant, R. (2014). Civil society roles in transition: towards sustainable food? Briefing Paper. Food Research Collaboration, Centre for Food Policy, City, University of London.

91 Swinburn, B., Kraak, V., Rutter, H., Vandevijvere, S., Lobstein, T., Sacks, G. et al. (2015). 'Strengthening of accountability systems to create healthy food environments and reduce global obesity', *The Lancet*, 385(9986), pp.2534–2545.

92 HLPE (2017). *Nutrition and food systems. A report by the High Level Panel of Experts on Food Security and Nutrition of the Committee on World Food Security*. Rome.

93 SUN Civil Society Network <https://scalingupnutrition.org/sun-supporters/sun-civil-society-network/>

94 Civil Society and Indigenous Peoples' Mechanism for relations with the UN Committee on World Food Security <http://www.csm4cfs.org/the-csm/>

95 Launched by the Ministry of Health and UNICEF with support from USAID in 1999, the programme promoted growth and development for young children (from conception to 3 years of age) in rural communities in Andean and Amazon regions. The programme promoted health, nutrition, caring and hygiene practices with an emphasis on local and community involvement.

96 World Health Assembly (2016). 'Report of the Commission on Ending Childhood Obesity', Resolution A69/8, 24 March 2016, WHO, Geneva, p. 19.

97 Baldwin, H. L., Freeman, B. and Kelly, B. (2018). 'Like and share: Associations between social media engagement and dietary choices in children', *Public Health Nutrition* 21(17), pp. 3210–3215.

98 For summaries of existing evidence, see Cairns, G., Angus, K., Hastings, G. and Caraher, M. (2013). 'Systematic reviews of the evidence on the nature, extent and effects of food marketing to children: A retrospective summary', *Appetite* 62, pp. 209–215; Boyland, E. and Tatlow Golden, M. (2017). 'Exposure, power and impact of food marketing on children: Evidence supports strong restrictions', *European Journal of Risk Regulation* 8(2), pp. 224–236.

99 Harris, J. L., Schwartz, M. B., Munsell, C. R. et al. (2015). Fast Food Facts 2013: Measuring progress in nutrition and marketing to children and teens. UConn Rudd Center for Food Policy and Obesity, Hartford, CT.

100 O'Dowd, A. (2017). 'Spending on junk food advertising is nearly 30 times what government spends on promoting healthy eating', *BMJ*, 359, j4677.

101 Kelly, B., Vandevijvere, S., Ng, S., Adams, J., Allemandi, L., Bahena-Espina, L., Barquera, S., et al. (2019). 'Global benchmarking of children's exposure to television advertising of unhealthy foods and beverages across 22 countries', *Obesity Reviews*, <https://doi.org/10.1111/obr.12840>.

102 UNICEF Regional Office for Latin America and the Caribbean, 'Childhood Overweight and the Retail Environment in Latin America and the Caribbean: Synthesis report', United Nations Children's Fund, Panama City, September 2019.

103 Euromonitor International data, cited in D. Searcey and M. Richtel (2017). 'When KFC Came to Ghana', *New York Times*, 2 October, p. A1.

104 WHO (2016). Tackling food marketing to children in a digital world: Trans-disciplinary perspectives. WHO, Geneva.

105 UNICEF (2017). *The State of the World's Children Report. Children in a Digital World*. UNICEF, New York.

106 World Health Assembly Resolution 63.14: Marketing of foods and non-alcoholic beverages to children.

107 Kovic, Y., Noel, J. K., Ungemack, J. A. and Burleson, J. A. (2018). 'The impact of junk food marketing regulations on food sales: An ecological study', *Obesity Reviews*, 19(6), pp. 761–769.

CHAPTER 5: AN AGENDA TO PUT CHILDREN'S NUTRITION RIGHTS FIRST

1 Elgar, F. J. and Stewart, J. M. (2008). 'Validity of self-report screening for overweight and obesity: Evidence from the Canadian Community Health Survey', *Canadian Journal of Public Health*, 99(5), pp. 423–427; Stommel, M. and Schoenborn, C. A. (2009). 'Accuracy and usefulness of BMI measures based on self-reported weight and height: Findings from the NHANES & NHIS 2001–2006', *BMC Public Health*, 9, p. 421.

METHODOLOGIES FOR THE STATE OF THE WORLD'S CHILDREN 2019 WORKSHOPS

1 US Department of Agriculture and US Department of Health and Human Services (2015). *Dietary guidelines for Americans 2015–2020*, 8th ed. US Government Printing Office, Washington DC.

2 Australian National Health Medical Research Council (2013). *Eat for health: Australian dietary guidelines*. Australian Government, National Health and Medical Research Council and Department of Health and Ageing.

3 Krasevec, J., An, X., Kumapley, R., Bégin, F. and Frongillo, E. A. (2017). 'Diet quality and risk of stunting among infants and young children in low-and middle-income countries', *Maternal & Child Nutrition*, 13 (Supplement 2), e12430.

NOTE ON FIGURES

1 Black, R.E., et al., Maternal and child undernutrition and overweight in low-income and middle-income countries. *The Lancet*, 2013. 382(9890): p. 427-51.

2 WHO, Iron deficiency anemia. Assessment, Prevention and Control. A guide for programme managers. WHO (Geneva): 2001.

3 Williams, A.M., et al., Data needed to respond appropriately to anemia when it is a public health problem. Ann N Y Acad Sci, 2019. 1450(1): p. 268-280.

4 Stevens, G.A., et al., Trends and mortality effects of vitamin A deficiency in children in 138 low-income and middle-income countries between 1991 and 2013: a pooled analysis of population-based surveys. *The Lancet Global Health*, 2015. 3: p. e528–36.

5 United Nations, Department of Economic and Social Affairs, Population Division (2019). World Population Prospects 2019, Online Edition. Rev. 1.

Methodologies for *The State of the World's Children 2019* workshops

Methodology

The State of the World's Children 2019 workshops used a distributed data-gathering process to collect adolescents' and mothers' insights, perceptions and experiences of food and nutrition. This process was co-designed by a team at Western Sydney University (WSU) and UNICEF and has been used previously in a range of international, child-centered research and child consultation projects, including for *The State of the World's Children 2017* report.

The process engaged representatives from UNICEF country offices and national committees to deliver five-hour, face-to-face workshops with adolescents aged between 14 and 16 (although a number of participants were older or younger than this), and with mothers of babies and infants who were still receiving complementary feeding. The workshops used a range of creative activities to elicit responses from participants. These focused on themes identified by UNICEF, WSU and an advisory board (*see Table A1*).

Before organizing the workshops, facilitators received a detailed guide and participated in a 90-minute training webinar to learn about workshop recruitment, content and administrative processes.

By the end of July 2019, workshops had been held in 18 countries: Afghanistan, Australia, Bangladesh, China, Egypt, Ethiopia, Ghana, Guatemala, India, Indonesia, Kyrgyzstan, Mexico, Nigeria, the Philippines, Serbia, the Sudan, the United States and Zimbabwe.

With one exception, each country hosted four workshops, and in total, 48 workshops were hosted for 464 adolescents and 328 mothers (five countries are missing from this analysis). The average workshop size was 16.5 participants. Participating country offices and national committees recruited a diverse sample of participants, and some also ran workshops with specific groups, for example, internally displaced refugees in the Sudan.

The research received ethics approval from Western Sydney University's Human Research Ethics Committee (Approval No. H11101).

Support for the project was provided by the Government of Norway.

Data collection and analysis

Data and analysis from the workshops are not statistically representative. Rather, the aim was to enable adolescents and new mothers to describe in their own words their perceptions and experiences of the foods they eat and their ideas about nutrition.

The bulk of the data collected was qualitative. Participants worked individually and in groups to complete surveys, short-answer questions, creative exercises (e.g., drawing), scenario-based exercises and small-group discussions. The data gathered consisted of paper-based surveys, diagrams, drawings, written text and photographs.

Research materials were supplied in English. Where required, the staff of country offices translated materials into local languages before administering workshops. All non-English content generated by participants was translated into English by the staff of participating offices. Analysts had access to both the translated and original versions.

All the data were digitized by participating offices and uploaded to secure digital repositories. The data were then collated and analysed by the WSU team, both manually and using analysis software.

Thematic analysis was applied as the primary technique for understanding the data.

During data entry, individual researchers categorized relevant data blocks (e.g., phrases, quotes and sentences) according to the existing themes, and also derived new themes generated by the data. The team then reviewed and discussed relevant data and individual analyses, checking and refining their interpretations. Analyses were summarized and presented using quotes and images from participants, synopses (i.e., core insights and ideas derived from the data), and charts and graphics depicting key concepts and general trends.

Companion reports containing more extensive results and analysis from the workshops will be published in 2020.

Dietary coding

The evidence-based dietary guidelines of the governments of the United States and Australia respectively were used to code the data.[1, 2] These guidelines provide a grouping of foods that are recommended for daily consumption (core foods) for nutritional adequacy and growth, and additional food groups identified as being suitable for occasional consumption (non-core foods) to prevent diet-related chronic diseases.

A point of difference from these dietary guidelines in our coding is the separation of animal-based and plant-based protein. This separation was to specifically explore where and when participants did or did not have access to animal-based protein. With an association shown between children who do not consume adequate amounts of egg, meat and dairy and higher risks of stunting, the identification of this distinction in protein sources is important.[3]

Workshop themes

Adolescents	Mothers
Diet and nutritional intake	Children's dietary intake
Health and body imagew	Mothers' dietary intake
Food marketing	Influences on mothers' feeding decisions
Food influences and environments: school	Feeding outside the home
Food influences and environments: home	Information sources for feeding
Barriers to healthy eating	Barriers faced by mothers feeding their babies
Food culture and special occasions	Feeding toddlers
Food sourcing and preparation	Sourcing and preparing family meals

Core Foods
Grains (e.g. breads, breakfast cereals, grains, noodles, pasta)
Animal protein (e.g. lean meats, lean poultry, fish, seafood, eggs)
Plant protein (e.g. nuts, seeds, legumes, beans, tofu)
Dairy (e.g. milks, yoghurt, cheese)
Vegetables (e.g. dark green or cruciferous, root, tubular and bulb vegetables, legumes, beans)
Fruits (e.g. citrus, pome, tropical, berries, stone, figs, grapes, lychees)
Unsaturated fats (polyunsaturated fats, mono-unsaturated fats)

Non-core Foods
Higher added sugars (e.g. honey, jams, marmalade, sugar, sugar confectionary, syrups)
Higher saturated fat and sodium (e.g. bacon, cream, commercially fried foods, commercial burgers)
Higher saturated fat and added sugars/sodium (e.g. biscuits, cakes, chocolate)

Drinks	
Soft drinks	Fruit juices, cordials
Caffeine	Water
Alcoholic drinks	Energy drinks

Note on figures

Figure A.1: Children not growing well
Children not growing well represents the percentage of children in one of the five categories: stunted, wasted, overweight, stunted and overweight, or stunted and wasted; the first three categories are often available in survey reports, but the last two categories require analysis of microdata. Estimates are based on 441 data sources included in the 2019 edition of the Joint Malnutrition Estimates (JME) where microdata was available for analysis. For countries without microdata, regional adjustment factors were applied based on the sub-regional aggregates of the overlap of stunting and wasting and stunting and overweight to generate country estimates of the five categories. Global and regional aggregates are based on the methodology described in de Onis M, Blössner M, Borghi E, Frongillo EA, Morris R. Estimates of global prevalence of childhood underweight in 1990 and 2015. JAMA. 2004 Jun 2;291(21):2600-6. PubMed PMID: 15173151.

Figure 1.4: Hidden hunger
The prevalence of hidden hunger is based on estimates of iron and vitamin A deficiency among children under-5 years, by UN sub-region. Prevalence of iron deficiency anemia (IDA) is based on Black et al. (2013).[1] A conversion factor of 2.0[2, 3] was applied to calculate the prevalence of iron deficiency. Prevalence of vitamin A deficiency is based on Stevens et al. (2015).[4] Sub-regions with missing data were conservatively assigned a prevalence of 0. For each sub-region, and assuming a 50 per cent overlap between deficiencies, the prevalence (P) of hidden hunger was calculated as P(hidden hunger)= P(a) + 0.5*P(b), where P(a) and P(b) are the maximum and minimum values, respectively, when comparing iron and vitamin A prevalence estimates. Drawing on sub-region-specific estimates of under-5 population sizes, the global number of children <5 years affected was calculated and a weighted global prevalence estimate of hidden hunger was generated.[5]

'What are young children eating? The importance of first foods' (pp. 74–75)The regional and global estimates were generated using the most recent data available for each country between 2013 and 2018. UNICEF regional and global estimates are population weighted averages using the 2018 estimates from the World Population Prospects, 2019 revision as weights.

Statistical tables

The statistical tables in this volume present the most recent key statistics on child survival, development and protection for the world's countries, areas and regions. They support UNICEF's focus on progress and results towards internationally agreed-upon goals and compacts relating to children's rights and development.

General note on the data

Data sources

Data presented in the following statistical tables are derived from the UNICEF global databases and are accompanied by definitions, sources and, where necessary, additional footnotes. The indicator data draw on inter-agency estimates and nationally representative household surveys such as Multiple Indicator Cluster Surveys (MICS) and Demographic and Health Surveys (DHS). In addition, data from administrative sources and other United Nations organizations have been used. More detailed information on the data sources is provided at the end of each table.

The demographic indicators and many of the population-related indicators in these tables were based on the latest population estimates and projections from *World Population Prospects: The 2019 revision* and *World Urbanization Prospects: The 2018 revision* (United Nations Department of Economic and Social Affairs, Population Division). Data quality is likely to be adversely affected for countries that have recently suffered disasters or conflicts, especially where basic country infrastructure has been fragmented or where major population movements have occurred.

In particular, UNICEF assists countries in collecting and analysing data for monitoring the situation of children and women through its international household survey initiative, the Multiple Indicator Cluster Surveys (MICS). Since 1995, as many as 322 surveys have been completed in more than 116 countries and areas. MICS was a major source of data for monitoring progress on the Millennium Development Goals (MDG) indicators and continues to be a major data source during the 2030 Sustainable Development Agenda to measure SDG indicators. More information is available at <mics.unicef.org>.

Regional and global aggregates

Unless otherwise mentioned, regional and global aggregates for indicators were generated as population weighted averages using data from *World Population Prospects: The 2019 revision*. They accord with the relevant age and sex group for each indicator (e.g. total live births for unweighted at birth and number of females aged 15–49 years for maternal anaemia). Again, unless otherwise noted, global and regional estimates are only reported for indicators with a population-level data coverage of at least 50 per cent.

Data comparability

Efforts have been made to maximize the comparability of statistics across countries and time. Nevertheless, data used at the country level may differ in terms of the methods used to collect data or arrive at estimates, and in terms of the populations covered. Furthermore, data presented here are subject to evolving methodologies, revisions of time series data (e.g., immunization, maternal mortality ratios), and changing regional classifications. Also, data comparable from one year to the next are unavailable for some indicators. It is therefore not advisable to compare data from consecutive editions of *The State of the World's Children*.

Further methodological information

Data presented in the following statistical tables generally reflect information compiled and updated from January through August 2019, with specific cutoff time associated with individual indicators described in the 'Main data sources' section underneath each table. The 'last updated' time stamp reflects the time the data were compiled and updated, as part of country consultation or inter-agency processes that are specific to individual topics.

Interested readers are encouraged to visit <data.unicef.org> for methodological details of the indicators and the statistics.

Data presented in the tables are available online at <www.unicef.org/sowc> and via <www.data.unicef.org>. Please refer to these websites for the latest data and for any updates or corrigenda subsequent to printing.

Child mortality estimates

Under-five mortality is used as the principal indicator of progress in child well-being.
www.childmortality.org

Under-five mortality rate (deaths per 1,000 live births)

UNICEF Region	1980	1985	1990	1995	2000	2005	2010	2015	2018
East Asia and Pacific	73	62	57	49	40	29	22	17	15
Europe and Central Asia	44	37	31	27	21	16	12	10	9
Eastern Europe and Central Asia	66	54	46	45	36	26	19	15	13
Western Europe	16	13	10	8	6	5	4	4	4
Latin America and Caribbean	84	68	55	43	33	25	24	18	16
Middle East and North Africa	123	86	65	53	42	34	27	23	22
North America	15	12	11	9	8	8	7	7	6
South Asia	172	150	130	112	94	77	62	49	42
Sub-Saharan Africa	201	188	180	172	153	125	101	85	78
Eastern and Southern Africa	185	172	164	156	136	107	82	64	57
West and Central Africa	217	205	197	188	170	143	120	105	97
Least developed countries	211	192	175	159	137	110	89	71	64
World	**118**	**102**	**93**	**87**	**76**	**63**	**51**	**42**	**39**

Under-five deaths (thousands)

UNICEF Region	1980	1985	1990	1995	2000	2005	2010	2015	2018
East Asia and Pacific	2,622	2,416	2,302	1,706	1,259	910	696	542	462
Europe and Central Asia	571	483	387	305	218	164	135	111	96
Eastern Europe and Central Asia	474	410	329	263	188	138	112	92	78
Western Europe	97	74	57	41	30	26	23	20	18
Latin America and Caribbean	948	786	641	501	377	282	262	190	172
Middle East and North Africa	902	708	547	420	325	271	246	235	220
North America	55	50	47	40	35	35	32	29	27
South Asia	5,585	5,258	4,743	4,191	3,570	2,934	2,279	1,716	1,475
Sub-Saharan Africa	3,396	3,613	3,857	4,087	4,045	3,696	3,304	3,007	2,869
Eastern and Southern Africa	1,631	1,727	1,827	1,908	1,834	1,590	1,322	1,107	1,024
West and Central Africa	1,765	1,886	2,031	2,179	2,212	2,107	1,982	1,900	1,845
Least developed countries	3,580	3,619	3,605	3,558	3,330	2,895	2,508	2,136	1,992
World	**14,080**	**13,314**	**12,524**	**11,250**	**9,831**	**8,292**	**6,955**	**5,828**	**5,322**

Regional classifications

Aggregates presented at the end of each of the 16 statistical tables are calculated using data from countries and areas as classified below.

East Asia and the Pacific
Australia; Brunei Darussalam; Cambodia; China; Cook Islands; Democratic People's Republic of Korea; Fiji; Indonesia; Japan; Kiribati; Lao People's Democratic Republic; Malaysia; Marshall Islands; Micronesia (Federated States of); Mongolia; Myanmar; Nauru; New Zealand; Niue; Palau; Papua New Guinea; Philippines; Republic of Korea; Samoa; Singapore; Solomon Islands; Thailand; Timor-Leste; Tokelau; Tonga; Tuvalu; Vanuatu; Viet Nam

Europe and Central Asia
Eastern Europe and Central Asia; Western Europe

Eastern Europe and Central Asia
Albania; Armenia; Azerbaijan; Belarus; Bosnia and Herzegovina; Bulgaria; Croatia; Georgia; Kazakhstan; Kyrgyzstan; Montenegro; Republic of Moldova; Romania; Russian Federation; Serbia; Tajikistan; North Macedonia; Turkey; Turkmenistan; Ukraine; Uzbekistan

Western Europe
Andorra; Austria; Belgium; Cyprus; Czechia; Denmark; Estonia; Finland; France; Germany; Greece; Holy See; Hungary; Iceland; Ireland; Italy; Latvia; Liechtenstein; Lithuania; Luxembourg; Malta; Monaco; Netherlands; Norway; Poland; Portugal; San Marino; Slovakia; Slovenia; Spain; Sweden; Switzerland; United Kingdom

Latin America and the Caribbean
Anguilla; Antigua and Barbuda; Argentina; Bahamas; Barbados; Belize; Bolivia (Plurinational State of); Brazil; British Virgin Islands; Chile; Colombia; Costa Rica; Cuba; Dominica; Dominican Republic; Ecuador; El Salvador; Grenada; Guatemala; Guyana; Haiti; Honduras; Jamaica; Mexico; Montserrat; Nicaragua; Panama; Paraguay; Peru; Saint Kitts and Nevis; Saint Lucia; Saint Vincent and the Grenadines; Suriname; Trinidad and Tobago; Turks and Caicos Islands; Uruguay; Venezuela (Bolivarian Republic of)

Middle East and North Africa
Algeria; Bahrain; Egypt; Iran (Islamic Republic of); Iraq; Israel; Jordan; Kuwait; Lebanon; Libya; Morocco; Oman; Qatar; Saudi Arabia; State of Palestine; Syrian Arab Republic; Tunisia; United Arab Emirates; Yemen

North America
Canada; United States

South Asia
Afghanistan; Bangladesh; Bhutan; India; Maldives; Nepal; Pakistan; Sri Lanka

Sub-Saharan Africa
Eastern and Southern Africa; West and Central Africa

Eastern and Southern Africa
Angola; Botswana; Burundi; Comoros; Djibouti; Eritrea; Eswatini; Ethiopia; Kenya; Lesotho; Madagascar; Malawi; Mauritius; Mozambique; Namibia; Rwanda; Seychelles; Somalia; South Africa; South Sudan; Sudan; Uganda; United Republic of Tanzania; Zambia; Zimbabwe

West and Central Africa
Benin; Burkina Faso; Cabo Verde; Cameroon; Central African Republic; Chad; Congo; Côte d'Ivoire; Democratic Republic of the Congo; Equatorial Guinea; Gabon; Gambia; Ghana; Guinea; Guinea-Bissau; Liberia; Mali; Mauritania; Niger; Nigeria; Sao Tome and Principe; Senegal; Sierra Leone; Togo

Least developed countries/areas
[Classified as such by the United Nations High Representative for the Least Developed Countries, Landlocked Developing Countries and Small Island Developing States (UNOHRLLS)].

Afghanistan; Angola; Bangladesh; Benin; Bhutan; Burkina Faso; Burundi; Cambodia; Central African Republic; Chad; Comoros; Democratic Republic of the Congo; Djibouti; Eritrea; Ethiopia; Gambia; Guinea; Guinea-Bissau; Haiti; Kiribati; Lao People's Democratic Republic; Lesotho; Liberia; Madagascar; Malawi; Mali; Mauritania; Mozambique; Myanmar; Nepal; Niger; Rwanda; Sao Tome and Principe; Senegal; Sierra Leone; Solomon Islands; Somalia; South Sudan; Sudan; Timor-Leste; Togo; Tuvalu; Uganda; United Republic of Tanzania; Vanuatu; Yemen; Zambia

Notes on specific tables

TABLE 1. DEMOGRAPHICS

The demographics table contains selected indicators on the most important demographic information of each population, including the total population and population by age, as well as annual population growth rates. Annual number of births is a function of both population size and current fertility. Total fertility rate allows for comparison of fertility levels, internationally. A total fertility level of 2.1 is called 'replacement level' and represents a level at which, in the long term, the population would remain the same size. Life expectancy at birth is a measure of the health status and the development of a population and continues to increase in almost all countries in the world. The dependency ratio is the ratio of the not-working-age population (i.e., the economically 'dependent' population) to the working-age population (15–64 years) and can be divided into child dependency ratio (ratio of children under 15 to working-age population) and old-age dependency ratio (ratio of population 65 and older to working-age population). Total dependency ratio is usually U-shaped over time and development: high fertility leads to a large share of the child population and consequently to a high dependency ratio which then decreases with decreasing fertility before increasing again due to increasing life expectancy and an increasing older population share. The proportion of the urban population and the annual urban population growth rate describe the status and dynamic of the urbanization process. The net migration rate refers to the difference between the number of immigrants and the number of emigrants; a country/area with more immigrants than emigrants shows a positive value, while a country with less immigrants than emigrants shows a negative value.

All demographic indicators are based on *World Population Prospects: The 2019 revision*. Except for total population size, most demographic indicators are published only for countries/areas with a population greater than 90,000.

TABLE 2. CHILD MORTALITY

Each year, in *The State of the World's Children*, UNICEF reports a series of mortality estimates for children. These figures represent the best estimates available at the time of printing and are based on the work of the United Nations Inter-agency Group for Child Mortality Estimation (UN IGME), which includes UNICEF, the World Health Organization (WHO), the World Bank group and the United Nations Population Division. UN IGME mortality estimates are updated annually through a detailed review of all newly available data points, which often results in adjustments to previously reported estimates. As a result, consecutive editions of *The State of the World's Children* should not be used for analysing mortality trends over time. Comparable global and regional under-five mortality estimates for the period 1990–2018 are presented below. Country-specific mortality indicators, based on the most recent UN IGME estimates, are presented in Table 2 and are available at <data.unicef.org/child-mortality/under-five> and www.childmortality.org, along with methodological notes.

TABLE 3. MATERNAL AND NEWBORN HEALTH

The maternal and newborn health table includes a combination of demographic and intervention coverage indicators. The demographic indicators consist of life expectancy for females, adolescent birth rate, and maternal mortality estimates including number of maternal deaths, maternal mortality ratio, and lifetime risk of maternal death.

The life expectancy and adolescent birth rate indicators come from the United Nations Population Division. The maternal mortality data are estimates generated by the United Nations Maternal Mortality Estimation Inter-Agency group (UN MMEIG), which includes the World Health Organization (WHO), UNICEF, United Nations Population Fund (UNFPA), the World Bank Group, and the United Nations Population Division. UN MMEIG mortality estimates are updated regularly through a detailed review of all newly available data points. This process often results in adjustments to previously reported estimates. As a result, consecutive editions of *The State of the World's Children* should not be used for analysing maternal mortality trends over time.

Intervention coverage indicators encompass indicators for family planning, antenatal care, delivery care and postnatal care for mother and baby. The data for these indicators come from national household survey programmes such as the DHS and MICS and other reproductive health surveys. Regional and global estimates are calculated by using a weighted average method. The variables used for weighting are indicator-specific and applied to each country. They accord with the appropriate target population for each indicator (the denominator) and are derived from the latest edition of the *World Population Prospects*. Only the most recent data points from 2013–2018 for each country were used to calculate regional and global aggregates. India and China were included in the calculation of the regional and global estimates for all indicators with available data.

The maternal and newborn health table also includes some age disaggregations to provide information on adolescent reproductive and maternal health. Specifically, demand for family planning satisfied with modern methods, antenatal care of at least four visits, and skilled attendant at birth are disaggregated for the 15–19 year age group. The disaggregated data for antenatal care of at least four visits and skilled attendant at birth come from the Federal University of Pelotas, International Center for Equity in Health, Brazil. The total and disaggregated data for demand for family planning satisfied with modern methods come from the United Nations Department of Economic and Social Affairs Population Division. Regional and global estimates are calculated with the same methodology described above for the intervention coverage indicators.

TABLE 4. CHILD HEALTH

The child health table includes a set of indicators which capture information on the coverage of effective interventions delivered to children under the age of five years and at the household level. These include a range of immunization indicators (described below), and indicators on interventions for the prevention or treatment of pneumonia, diarrhoea and malaria (the three leading killers of young children). The main data sources for the indicators on prevention and treatment of childhood illnesses are nationally representative household surveys such as the DHS and MICS. Regional and global estimates are calculated by using a weighted average method. Variables used for weighting are indicator-specific and applied to each country. They accord with the appropriate target population for each indicator (the denominator) and are derived from the latest edition of the *World Population Prospects*. Only the most recent data points from 2013–2018 for each country were used to calculate regional and global estimates. For indicators that capture information about households, total population was used. India and China were included in the calculation of the regional and global estimates for all indicators with available data.

Immunization

The child health table presents the WHO and UNICEF estimates of national immunization coverage. Since 2000, these estimates have been updated annually in July, following a consultation process during which countries are provided with draft reports for review and comment. As new empirical data are incorporated into the process for generating the estimates, the revised estimates supersede prior data releases. Coverage levels from earlier revisions are not comparable. A more detailed explanation of the process can be found at <data.unicef.org/child-health/immunization>.

Regional averages for the reported antigens are computed as follows:

> For BCG, regional averages include only those countries where BCG is included in the national routine immunization schedule.

> For DTP, polio, measles, HepB, Hib, PCV and rotavirus vaccines, regional averages include all countries, as these vaccines are universally recommended by WHO.

> For protection at birth (PAB) from tetanus, regional averages include only the countries where maternal and neonatal tetanus is endemic.

TABLE 5 and 6. HIV/AIDS

In 2019, the Joint United Nations Programme on HIV/AIDS (UNAIDS) released new global, regional and country-level HIV and AIDS estimates for 2018 that reflect the most up-to-date epidemiological estimates, as well as coverage data for antiretroviral therapy (ART), prevention of mother-to-child transmission (PMTCT) and early infant diagnosis for HIV. The estimates are based on the most current available science and WHO programme guidelines, which have resulted in improvements in assumptions of the probability of HIV transmission from mother-to-child, fertility among women by age and HIV serostatus, net survival rates for children living with HIV and more. Based on the refined methodology, UNAIDS has retrospectively generated new estimates of HIV prevalence, the number of people living with HIV and those needing treatment, AIDS-related deaths, new HIV infections, and other important trends in the HIV epidemic.

Key indicators on the HIV response for children are divided into two tables: Table 5. HIV/AIDS epidemiology and Table 6. HIV/AIDS interventions.

TABLE 5. HIV/AIDS: EPIDEMIOLOGY

Table 5 includes key indicators that are used to measure trends in the HIV epidemic. Data are disaggregated by 10-year age groups, as children living with HIV under age 10 are all assumed to be infected through mother-to-child transmission. Children aged 10–19 living with HIV additionally include new HIV infections that occur through sexual transmission and injection drug use, depending on the country context. Due to significant gender disparity among adolescents evident in HIV epidemic trends and programmatic response, disaggregates by sex are now included for all HIV/AIDS epidemiology indicators. For better comparison between countries and regions, the indicator on the number of new HIV infections has been replaced with HIV incidence per 1,000 uninfected population. Similarly, the number of AIDS-related deaths has been replaced with AIDS-related mortality per 100,000 population. These two indicators provide relative measures of new HIV infections and AIDS-related deaths and more accurately demonstrate the impact of the HIV response.

TABLE 6. HIV/AIDS: INTERVENTIONS

Table 6 includes indicators on essential interventions in the HIV response for children. These coverage indicators have been revised from previous editions of *The State of the World's Children* to better reflect progress in current HIV/AIDS programmes and policy. For example, the indicator for early infant HIV diagnosis captures information on what percentage of HIV-exposed infants received an HIV test within two months of birth. All coverage indicators are calculated from the most recent and reliable data available from population-based surveys and programme service statistics.

Each coverage indicator is aggregated regionally or globally using a population-weighted average. Due to sometimes sparse data, indicators from population-based surveys are only aggregated if the data in that area represent at least 50 per cent of the adolescent population.

TABLES 7 and 8. NUTRITION

Table 7 encompasses nutrition at birth and feeding practices for infants and young children and Table 8 comprises estimates of malnutrition among pre-school-aged children, school-aged children and women of reproductive age as well as intervention coverage of key micronutrient programmes.

Indicators of low birthweight, thinness and overweight among school-aged children, and maternal underweight and anaemia are modelled estimates and therefore may be different from survey-reported estimates. For all other indicators, when raw data were available, the country-level estimates were re-analysed to conform to standard analysis methods and may therefore differ from survey-reported values.

Low birthweight: Estimates are based on new methods; therefore country, regional and global estimates may not be comparable with those published in previous editions of *The State of the World's Children*.

Unweighted at birth: A new indicator representing the percentage of births without a birthweight in the data source.

Infant and young child feeding: A total of 8 indicators are presented, including the following with recent definitional changes or which are new: (i) Continued breastfeeding (12–23 months) replaces 2 previous indicators of continued breastfeeding at 1 year (12–15 months) and 2 years (20–23 months); (ii) Minimum Dietary Diversity (MDD) (6–23 months) is now defined as the percentage of children 6–23 months of age who received foods from at least 5 out of 8 defined food groups during the previous day (the older version of this indicator reflected consumption of at least 4 out of 7 defined food groups during the previous day); (iii) Minimum Acceptable Diet (MAD) (6–23 months) is revised to align with the change to the MDD definition and (iv) Zero vegetable or fruit consumption (6–23 months) is a new indicator. The indicator definition of Minimum Meal Frequency (MMF) (6–23 months) was also revised in 2018, but related changes to MMF and MAD estimates have not yet been reflected in these tables.

Stunting, wasting and overweight: UNICEF, WHO and the World Bank have continued a process to harmonize anthropometric data used for computation and estimation of regional and global averages and trend analysis. As part of this process, regional and global averages for stunting, wasting and overweight prevalence are derived from a model described in M. de Onis et al (2004), 'Methodology for Estimating Regional and Global Trends of Child Malnutrition' (*International Journal of Epidemiology*, 33, pp. 1260–1270). New global and regional estimates are released every year, which supersede all previous estimates and should not be compared.

Vitamin A supplementation: Emphasizing the importance for children of receiving two annual doses of vitamin A (spaced 4–6 months apart), this report presents only full coverage of vitamin A supplementation. In the absence of a direct method to measure this indicator, full coverage is reported as the lower coverage estimate from semester 1 (Jan–June) and semester 2 (July–Dec), in a given year. The regional and global aggregates only contain the 82 countries indicated as priority countries for national-level programmes. Hence the regional aggregates are published where at least 50 per cent of the population coverage for the priority countries in each region has been met. In other words, East Asia and Pacific estimates are presented despite there being no data for China.

Malnutrition among school-aged children: Indicators under this title reflect the importance of ending malnutrition among children of all ages. Country estimates for malnutrition among school-aged children are based on the NCD Risk Factor Collaboration (NCD-RisC) (2017), 'Worldwide trends in body-mass index, underweight, overweight, and obesity from 1975 to 2016: a pooled analysis of 2416 population-based measurement studies in 128.9 million children, adolescents, and adults', *The Lancet*, 390(10113), pp. 2627–2642.

Underweight women 18+ years: This indicator reflects the importance of maternal malnutrition if malnutrition among children is to be eliminated. Country estimates for underweight women are based on the NCD Risk Factor Collaboration (NCD-RisC) (2017), 'Worldwide trends in body-mass index, underweight, overweight, and obesity from 1975 to 2016: a pooled analysis of 2416 population-based measurement studies in 128.9 million children, adolescents, and adults', *The Lancet*, 390(10113), pp. 2627–2642.

Anaemia women 15–49 years: This indicator reflects the importance of maternal malnutrition if malnutrition among children is to be eliminated. Country estimates for anaemia are based on WHO (2017), Global Health Observatory (GHO). In: World Health Organization [online]. Geneva, Switzerland. [Cited 1 August 2019] http://apps.who.int/gho/data/node. imr.PREVANEMIA?lang=en; data for adult obesity are based on WHO (2017), Global Health Observatory (GHO).

Iodized salt: The definition of the indicator presented in this report has changed from the past, when it was about households consuming adequately iodized salt. Now it is about salt with any iodine, and therefore global and regional average prevalence estimates are not comparable to the averages published in previous editions of The State of the World's Children.

TABLE 9. EARLY CHILDHOOD DEVELOPMENT

Early childhood, which spans the period up to eight years of age, is critical for cognitive, social, emotional and physical development. Optimal brain development requires a stimulating environment, adequate nutrients and social interaction with attentive caregivers. The early childhood development table presents data on some specific indicators with comparable and nationally representative data on the quality of care at home, access to learning materials at home, and access to early childhood care and education. The information in this table is best interpreted alongside data on other areas vital to early childhood development such as nutrition and protection.

Early stimulation and responsive care by adults: Data on this indicator from the DHS were recalculated according to the MICS methodology for comparability. Therefore, the recalculated data presented here will differ from estimates in DHS national reports.

Early stimulation and responsive care by father: Data from the third and fourth rounds of MICS (MICS3 and MICS4) refer to father's engagement in one or more activities to promote learning and school readiness, while the definition was changed in the fifth round (MICS5) to reflect father's engagement in four or more activities. Therefore, estimates of early stimulation and responsive care by fathers from MICS3 and MICS4 are lower than those based on results beginning with MICS5. Data on this indicator from the DHS were recalculated according to the MICS methodology for comparability. Therefore, the recalculated data presented here will differ from estimates in DHS national reports.

Learning materials at home: Playthings: Changes in the definition of this indicator were made between the third and fourth round of MICS (MICS3 and MICS4). In order to allow for comparability with MICS4 and subsequent rounds of MICS, data from MICS3 were recalculated according to the MICS4 indicator definition.

Therefore, the recalculated data presented here will differ from estimates reported in MICS3 national reports.

Children with inadequate supervision: This indicator was previously referred to as 'children left in inadequate care' but has been renamed to more accurately reflect the nature of the underlying construct.

TABLE 10: EDUCATION

This table contains a set of indicators on the following aspects of education of children: equitable access, school completion and learning outcomes.

In particular, indicators on school completion measure children or young people aged 3–5 years above the intended age for the last grade of each level of education who have completed that grade. Completion rate indicates how many school-age children in a given age group have completed the relevant level of education. By choosing an age group which is slightly older than the theoretical age group for completing each level of education, the indicator measures how many children and adolescents enter school more or less on time and progress through the education system without excessive delays.

This table also includes a set of indicators to monitor equitable learning outcomes, which is a target (4.1) of Sustainable Development Goal 4. The minimum proficiency level is the benchmark of basic knowledge in a domain (i.e., mathematics and reading) measured through learning assessment. The indicator shows data published by national governments as well as agencies and organizations specialized in cross-national learning assessments.

Detailed information on the indicators included in this table can be found in UNESCO Institute for Statistics, July 2017. Metadata for the global and thematic indicators for the follow-up and review of SDG4 and Education 2030.

TABLE 11. CHILD PROTECTION

Child protection refers to prevention and response to violence, exploitation and abuse of children in all contexts. There are many different child protection violations that children can be subjected to but the lack of comparable data limits reporting on the full spectrum. In view of this, the child protection table presents data on a few issues for which comparable and nationally representative data are available. This includes two manifestations of harmful traditional practices, some forms of violence and exploitation as well as the official recording of births.

Birth registration: Changes in the definition of birth registration were made from the second and third rounds of MICS (MICS2 and MICS3) to the fourth round (MICS4). In order to allow for comparability with later rounds, data from MICS2 and MICS3 on birth registration were recalculated according to the MICS4 indicator definition. Therefore, the recalculated data presented here may differ from estimates included in MICS2 and MICS3 national reports.

Child labour: This indicator has been replaced by the one used for SDG reporting on indicator 8.7.1 and reflects the proportion of children engaged in economic activities and/or household chores at or above age-specific hourly thresholds (general production boundary basis):

Child labour for the 5 to 11 age range: children working at least 1 hour per week in economic activity and/or involved in unpaid household services for more than 21 hours per week;

Child labour for the 12 to 14 age range: children working for at least 14 hours per week in economic activity and/or involved in unpaid household services for more than 21 hours per week;

Child labour for the 15 to 17 age range: children working for more than 43 hours per week in economic activity. No hourly threshold is set for unpaid household services for ages 15–17.

Country estimates compiled and presented in the global SDG database and reproduced in SOWC have been re-analysed by UNICEF and ILO in accordance with the definitions and criteria detailed above. This means that the country data values will differ from those published in national survey reports.

Child marriage: While the practice is more widespread among girls, marriage in childhood is a rights violation for both sexes. Therefore, the prevalence of child marriage is shown among both males and females. For males, only marriage before age 18 is shown, as marriage before age 15 is exceedingly rare. For females, the global aggregate is calculated as a population-weighted average of the prevalence in each region; for more details about special considerations and assumptions used in these calculations, refer to *Child Marriage: Latest trends and future prospects*, UNICEF, New York, 2018.

Female genital mutilation (FGM): Data on the prevalence of FGM among girls aged 0–14 years were recalculated for technical reasons and may differ from those presented in original DHS and MICS country reports. Beginning with this edition of SOWC, attitudes towards the practice are shown as the share of the population opposing (rather than supporting) FGM, and this measure is now shown among both males and females. Regional estimates on the prevalence of FGM and attitudes towards the practice are based on available data only from practising countries with nationally representative data and therefore reflect the situation among those living in these affected countries within the region, and not the region as a whole, as there are some non-practising countries in each region as well.

Justification of wife-beating among adolescents: Beginning with this edition of SOWC, the age group used for reporting on this indicator has been revised to refer to adolescents aged 15–19.

Violent discipline: Estimates used in UNICEF publications and in MICS country reports prior to 2010 were calculated using household weights that did not take into account the last-stage selection of children for the administration of the child discipline module in MICS surveys. (A random selection of one child within the reference age group is undertaken for the administration of the child discipline module.) In January 2010, it was decided that more accurate estimates are produced by using a household weight that takes the last-stage selection into account. MICS3 data were recalculated using this approach. Additionally, the reference age group for this indicator was revised beginning with MICS5 to children aged 1–14. Therefore, estimates from MICS3 and MICS4 are not directly comparable since they refer to children aged 2–14.

TABLE 12. SOCIAL PROTECTION AND EQUITY

This table provides information about social protection coverage and the magnitude of income inequality, both of which impact the context in which children live. Social protection indicators include *Mothers with newborns receiving cash benefits, Proportion of children covered by social protection* and *Distribution of Social Protection Benefits* (1st quintile, 5th quintile, bottom 40%). While the first two indicators capture the coverage of social protection, the third indicator reflects both incidence and distribution across quintiles. The table gives an overview of the social safety net that households – children in particular – have access to within each country.

Inequality indicators include *Share of household income* (1st quintile, 5th quintile, bottom 40%), *Gini index, Palma index* and *GDP per capita*. The first indicator captures the share of national income each quintile earns within a country. It illustrates the *structure* of income distribution per country while the *Gini coefficient* expresses the *extent* of inequality and how it deviates from a perfectly equal income distribution. In contrast, the *Palma index* concentrates on the income difference between the share of the richest 10 per cent and the poorest 40 per cent of a population. This indicator is more sensitive to the tails of distribution and extreme inequalities. Because changes in income inequality are mainly driven by changes in the income of the richest 10 per cent and the poorest 40 per cent, the Palma index offers insights on distributional changes of income inequality. GDP per capita complements those indicators as it measures the average standard of living of each country.

The Social Protection and Equity indicators data have an annual frequency and are extracted from the *World Bank's World Development Indicators, the Atlas of Social Protection* – Indicators of Resilience and Equity and the ILO's *World Social Protection Report*.

TABLE 13. WASH

This table contains a set of indicators on access to basic water, sanitation and hygiene services in households, schools and health care facilities. The drinking water, sanitation and hygiene estimates in this report come from the WHO/UNICEF Joint Monitoring Programme for Water Supply, Sanitation and Hygiene (JMP). Full details of the JMP indicator definitions, data sources and methods used to produce national, regional and global estimates can be found at <www.washdata.org>. New estimates are released every two years which supersede all previous estimates and should not be compared.

TABLE 14. ADOLESCENTS

The adolescent table presents a selection of indicators on the well-being of adolescents across various domains of their lives: Health, Protection, Education and learning and Transition to work. While adolescent well-being is broad and cannot be exhaustively captured in a small selection of indicators, the measures in Table 14 are meant to serve as an illustrative sample, and to complement adolescent-relevant indicators which appear throughout the other statistical tables in this publication. The indicators are drawn from the Adolescent Country Tracker, a multi-stakeholder framework grounded in the Sustainable Development Goals which was developed to track adolescent well-being across countries and over time.

NEET and Unemployment: Data on the degree to which adolescents are able to effectively transition to work, illustrated through the measures of those not in employment, education or training (NEET) and the unemployment rate among adolescents aged 15 to 19 years, are drawn from the International Labour Organization (ILO). Metadata and further notes on interpretation of these indicators are available through the 'Metadata' section of <ilo.org/ilostat>.

TABLE 15. ECONOMIC INDICATORS

This table presents a macroeconomic overview of the context affecting children's well-being and development. The indicators included in the table have two descriptive purposes: they reflect the government's fiscal space to finance welfare programmes – as captured by the *Government Revenue and Official Development Assistance (ODA) inflows*; and they display the government expenditure's allocation on key sectors such as health, education, social protection, and foreign aid for DAC member countries. Government expenditure is given in proportion to each country's GDP and overall public budget. This distinction highlights the relative importance and size of each sector for social policy. A similar distinction is operated for ODA between inflows/outflows in million US$ and inflows/outflows in proportion to each country's Gross National Income.

The Economic Indicators data have an annual frequency and are extracted from the World Bank's World Development Indicators, with the exception of ODA (inflows and outflows). The data for this indicator come from the OECD. Due to a lack of data coverage, *government expenditure on social protection as a percentage of government budget* is calculated by the authors. It represents the ratio of *government expenditure on social protection as a percentage of GDP over government revenue as a percentage of GDP*.

TABLE 16. WOMEN'S ECONOMIC EMPOWERMENT

This table has been added in 2019 in recognition of the beneficial effects of women's economic empowerment on the well-being of children as well as to reflect the intrinsic importance of women's economic empowerment as articulated in Sustainable Development Goal 5: Achieve Gender Equality and Empower all Women and Girls.

Social Institutions and Gender Index (SIGI): The SIGI, a composite measure of gender discrimination in social institutions produced by the Organisation for Economic Co-operation and Development, is based on qualitative and quantitative data through information on formal and informal laws, attitudes and practices. Discriminatory laws, attitudes and practices affect the life course of women and girls, restricting their ability to accumulate human, social and productive assets and to exercise agency and voice over choices that affect their well-being.

Legal frameworks that promote, enforce and monitor gender equality in employment and economic benefits: Equality and non-discrimination on the basis of sex are core principles under the international legal and policy framework, including the Convention on the Elimination of All Forms of Discrimination against Women (CEDAW) and the Beijing Platform for Action. Removing discriminatory laws and putting in place legal frameworks that advance gender equality in employment and economic benefits are prerequisites to increasing women's paid work and decent working conditions and, in turn, their economic empowerment. The term 'legal frameworks' is defined broadly to encompass laws, mechanisms and policies/plans to promote, enforce and monitor gender equality. Data derived for this indicator, SDG 5.1.1, are from an assessment of a country's legal frameworks completed by National Statistical Offices and/or National Women's Machinery, and legal practitioners/researchers on gender equality.

Maternity/paternity leave benefits: Parental leave benefits are critical for supporting the health and well-being of children and women's economic empowerment, including infants' survival and healthy development and increased labour force participation and earnings for women. ILO Convention No. 183 provides for 14 weeks of paid maternity benefit to women to whom the instrument applies. While no ILO standard exists specifically on paternity leave, paternity benefits permit working fathers to be more involved in the care of their children and the sharing of household responsibilities. It is important to note, however, that even in countries with legal rights to parental leave, not all workers will have access, such as those employed part-time or employed in the informal economy.

Demand for family planning satisfied with modern methods: Access to and use of an effective means to prevent pregnancy helps enable women and their partners to exercise their rights to decide freely and responsibly the number and spacing of children. As measured by SDG Indicator 3.7.1, modern methods of contraception include female and male sterilization, the intra-uterine device (IUD), the implant, injectables, oral contraceptive pills, male and female condoms, vaginal barrier methods (including the diaphragm, cervical cap and spermicidal foam, jelly, cream and sponge), lactational amenorrhea method (LAM), emergency contraception and other modern methods not reported separately (e.g., the contraceptive patch or vaginal ring). To foster cross-country comparability, information for married or in-union women is reported since not all countries collect the information for all women, irrespective of marital status.

Educational attainment: While primary education provides children with the foundation for a lifetime of learning, secondary education equips them with the knowledge and skills needed to become economically empowered adults. Compared to girls with only a primary education, girls with secondary education are less likely to marry as children and become pregnant as adolescents. And while women with primary education earn only marginally more than women with no education, women with secondary education earn twice as much, on average, than women who have not gone to school (see Wodon et al (2018), 'Missed Opportunities: The High Cost of Not Educating Girls', *The Cost of Not Educating Girls Notes Series*. The World Bank, Washington DC).

Labour force participation and unemployment rates: Equal access to the labour market is critical for women's economic empowerment. The labour force participation rate is calculated by expressing the number of persons in the labour force during a given reference period as a percentage of the working-age population (usually aged 15 and above) in the same reference period. The unemployment rate conveys the percentage of persons (usually persons aged 15 and above) in the labour force who are unemployed, reflecting the inability of an economy to generate employment for those persons who want to work but are not doing so even though they are available for employment and actively seeking work. Information on unemployment by sex highlights the greater difficulty, in many cases, that women have in entering the labour market, which can be directly or indirectly linked to a country's gender norms.

Mobile phone ownership: Mobile phone ownership provides individuals with access to information, financial services, employment opportunities and social networks and, as such, is an important asset for fostering women's economic empowerment as recognized under Goal 5 of the 2030 Agenda. As measured by SDG Indicator 5.b.1, an individual owns a mobile cellular phone if he/she has a mobile cellular phone device with at least one active SIM card for personal use. Mobile cellular phones supplied by employers that can be used for personal reasons (to make personal calls, access the Internet, etc.) are included. Individuals who have only active SIM card(s) and not a mobile phone device are excluded. Individuals who have a mobile phone for personal use that is not registered under his/her name are also included. An active SIM card is a SIM card that has been used in the last three months.

Financial inclusion: Measuring women's access to financial services, such as savings, insurance, payments, credit and remittances, is essential for understanding their economic empowerment. Access to financial services can also increase women's bargaining power in the household, with potential benefits for the well-being of children. As measured by SDG Indicator 8.10.2, an account at a financial institution includes respondents who report having an account at a bank or at another type of financial institution, such as a credit union, microfinance institution, cooperative, or the post office (if applicable), or having a debit card in their own name. In addition, it includes respondents who report receiving wages, government transfers, or payments for agricultural products into an account at a financial institution in the past 12 months; paying utility bills or school fees from an account at a financial institution in the past 12 months; or receiving wages or government transfers into a card in the past 12 months. Mobile money account includes respondents who report personally using GSM Association (GSMA) Mobile Money for the Unbanked (MMU) services in the past 12 months to pay bills or to send or receive money. In addition, it includes respondents who report receiving wages, government transfers, or payments for agricultural products through a mobile phone in the past 12 months.

Number of under-five deaths and under-five mortality by country in 2018

Table ordered by the number of unrounded number of deaths. Lower and Upper bound refer to the lower and upper bound of 90% uncertainty intervals

HIGHEST BURDEN OF DEATH AMONG CHILDREN UNDER-5

Countries and areas	Annual number of under–5 deaths (thousands)	Under–5 mortality rate (deaths per 1,000 live births) Median	Lower bound	Upper bound
India	882	37	33	40
Nigeria	866	120	97	151
Pakistan	409	69	56	85
Democratic Republic of the Congo	296	88	59	129
Ethiopia	191	55	45	69
China	146	9	8	10
Indonesia	121	25	22	29
United Republic of Tanzania	107	53	41	69
Angola	94	77	36	144
Bangladesh	89	30	27	33
Niger	83	84	56	125
Sudan	80	60	46	79
Mozambique	79	73	53	104
Mali	75	98	81	117
Chad	75	119	92	150
Afghanistan	74	62	50	75
Uganda	74	46	37	59
Somalia	73	122	65	233
Côte d'Ivoire	70	81	66	99
Cameroon	66	76	60	96
Philippines	63	28	22	36
Kenya	60	41	31	55
Burkina Faso	56	76	55	105
Egypt	55	21	16	29
Yemen	47	55	35	84
Madagascar	45	54	40	71
Guinea	44	101	81	128
Myanmar	43	46	33	62
Brazil	42	14	13	17
Ghana	41	48	40	58
South Africa	40	34	30	38
South Sudan	38	99	44	186
Benin	38	93	82	106
Zambia	36	58	44	76
Viet Nam	33	21	17	25
Malawi	30	50	35	70
Iraq	29	27	21	34
Mexico	28	13	12	13
Sierra Leone	26	105	85	128
United States	25	7	6	7
Burundi	25	58	40	85
Algeria	24	23	22	25
Senegal	23	44	34	57
Iran (Islamic Republic of)	22	14	9	23
Zimbabwe	21	46	32	65
Central African Republic	19	116	70	192
Nepal	18	32	25	41
Togo	18	70	53	92
Haiti	17	65	51	84

Countries and areas	Annual number of under–5 deaths (thousands)	Under–5 mortality rate (deaths per 1,000 live births) Median	Lower bound	Upper bound
Morocco	15	22	17	29
Uzbekistan	15	21	17	27
Turkey	14	11	9	12
Rwanda	13	35	21	59
Russian Federation	13	7	6	8
Venezuela (Bolivarian Republic of)	13	25	21	29
Liberia	11	71	50	102
Guatemala	11	26	21	34
Papua New Guinea	11	48	38	60
Mauritania	11	76	40	143
Colombia	10	14	11	19
Cambodia	10	28	15	50
Tajikistan	10	35	24	51
Congo	9	50	31	83
Peru	8	14	11	19
Lao People's Democratic Republic	8	47	36	61
Argentina	8	10	10	11
Syrian Arab Republic	7	17	13	25
Bolivia (Plurinational State of)	7	27	21	34
Thailand	7	9	8	12
Democratic People's Republic of Korea	6	18	14	23
Turkmenistan	6	46	19	101
Dominican Republic	6	29	21	41
Guinea-Bissau	5	81	53	121
Gambia	5	58	34	98
Ecuador	5	14	13	15
Lesotho	5	81	57	113
Eritrea	4	42	26	67
Saudi Arabia	4	7	6	9
Malaysia	4	8	7	8
Kazakhstan	4	10	10	10
Ukraine	4	9	8	10
Azerbaijan	4	22	14	32
Honduras	4	18	12	26
Equatorial Guinea	4	85	51	134
Jordan	3	16	13	21
Tunisia	3	17	16	18
United Kingdom	3	4	4	5
France	3	4	4	4
Kyrgyzstan	3	19	18	20
Gabon	3	45	29	69
State of Palestine	3	20	15	28
Paraguay	3	20	11	38
Germany	3	4	3	4
Namibia	3	40	25	65
Sri Lanka	3	7	6	9
Nicaragua	2	18	17	19
Japan	2	2	2	3

About 15,000 children under 5 years old still die every day

LOWEST BURDEN OF DEATH AMONG CHILDREN UNDER-5

Countries and areas	Annual number of under–5 deaths (thousands)	Under–5 mortality rate (deaths per 1,000 live births)			Countries and areas	Annual number of under–5 deaths (thousands)	Under–5 mortality rate (deaths per 1,000 live births)		
		Median	Lower bound	Upper bound			Median	Lower bound	Upper bound
Botswana	2	36	16	73	Denmark	0	4	4	5
Canada	2	5	5	5	Ireland	0	4	3	5
Comoros	2	67	34	142	Vanuatu	0	26	17	42
Chile	2	7	6	9	North Macedonia	0	10	8	12
Timor-Leste	2	46	28	74	Cabo Verde	0	19	16	25
Poland	2	4	4	5	Sao Tome and Principe	0	31	20	49
Eswatini	2	54	35	82	Mauritius	0	16	14	17
El Salvador	2	14	9	21	Suriname	0	19	9	40
Libya	2	12	8	18	Qatar	0	7	6	8
Italy	1	3	3	3	Croatia	0	5	4	5
Romania	1	7	6	9	Kiribati	0	53	32	86
Mongolia	1	16	10	25	Bosnia and Herzegovina	0	6	5	7
Republic of Korea	1	3	3	4	Bahrain	0	7	6	9
Spain	1	3	3	3	Norway	0	3	2	3
Djibouti	1	59	37	94	Singapore	0	3	2	3
Panama	1	15	9	28	Lithuania	0	4	4	5
Australia	1	4	4	4	Belize	0	13	12	15
Oman	1	11	11	12	Finland	0	2	2	2
Lebanon	1	7	4	14	Latvia	0	4	3	5
United Arab Emirates	1	8	7	9	Micronesia (Federated States of)	0	31	13	75
Jamaica	1	14	9	25	Samoa	0	16	11	22
Netherlands	1	4	4	4	Brunei Darussalam	0	12	10	13
Republic of Moldova	1	16	12	21	Maldives	0	9	7	11
Israel	1	4	4	4	Bahamas	0	10	8	13
Costa Rica	1	9	8	10	Marshall Islands	0	33	22	50
Cuba	1	5	4	6	Slovenia	0	2	2	3
Georgia	1	10	8	12	Tonga	0	16	9	26
Armenia	1	12	9	16	Barbados	0	12	9	17
Fiji	0	26	24	28	Estonia	0	3	2	3
Guyana	0	30	19	48	Saint Lucia	0	17	13	22
Serbia	0	6	5	6	Dominica	0	36	28	46
Kuwait	0	8	7	9	Cyprus	0	2	2	3
Belgium	0	4	3	4	Malta	0	7	6	9
Bulgaria	0	7	7	8	Grenada	0	15	13	19
Solomon Islands	0	20	14	29	Saint Vincent and the Grenadines	0	16	13	20
Hungary	0	4	4	5	Seychelles	0	14	11	18
Belarus	0	3	3	4	Montenegro	0	3	2	3
Bhutan	0	30	19	44	Luxembourg	0	2	2	3
Czechia	0	3	3	4	Antigua and Barbuda	0	6	5	9
Greece	0	4	4	5	Nauru	0	32	18	55
Uruguay	0	8	7	8	Iceland	0	2	2	3
Switzerland	0	4	4	5	Saint Kitts and Nevis	0	12	9	16
New Zealand	0	6	5	7	Tuvalu	0	24	14	44
Trinidad and Tobago	0	18	8	43	Palau	0	18	10	34
Sweden	0	3	3	3	Andorra	0	3	2	5
Slovakia	0	6	5	6	Cook Islands	0	8	5	13
Austria	0	4	3	4	Monaco	0	3	2	5
Portugal	0	4	4	4	Niue	0	24	10	56
Albania	0	9	8	9	San Marino	0	2	1	4

TABLE 1. DEMOGRAPHICS

Countries and areas	Population (thousands) 2018 total	under 18	under 5	Annual population growth rate (%) 2000–2018	2018–2030°	Annual number of births (thousands) 2018	Total fertility (live births per woman) 2018	Life expectancy at birth (years) 1970	2000	2018	Dependency ratio (%) 2018 total	child	old age	Proportion of urban population (%) 2018	Annual growth rate of urban population (%) 2000–2018	2018–2030°	Net migration rate (per 1,000 population) 2015–2020
Afghanistan	37,172	18,745	5,601	3.2	2.1	1,207	4.5	37	56	64	84	79	5	25	4.0	3.4	-1.7
Albania	2,883	635	173	-0.5	-0.3	34	1.6	67	74	78	46	26	20	60	1.6	0.9	-4.9
Algeria	42,228	14,416	4,951	1.7	1.5	1,023	3.0	50	71	77	58	47	10	73	2.8	2.1	-0.2
Andorra	77	–	–	0.9	0.1	–	–	–	–	–	–	–	–	88	0.6	0.1	–
Angola	30,810	16,457	5,553	3.5	3.1	1,257	5.5	41	47	61	96	92	4	66	5.0	4.0	0.2
Anguilla	15	–	–	1.5	0.6	–	–	–	–	–	–	–	–	100	1.5	0.6	–
Antigua and Barbuda	96	26	7	1.3	0.7	1	2.0	66	74	77	45	32	13	25	-0.2	0.8	0.0
Argentina	44,361	13,103	3,748	1.0	0.8	755	2.3	66	74	77	56	39	17	92	1.2	1.0	0.1
Armenia	2,952	710	211	-0.2	0.0	41	1.8	70	71	75	47	30	17	63	-0.3	0.4	-1.7
Australia	24,898	5,664	1,627	1.5	1.0	318	1.8	71	80	83	53	29	24	86	1.6	1.2	6.4
Austria	8,891	1,539	434	0.5	0.3	88	1.5	70	78	81	50	21	28	58	0.4	0.8	7.4
Azerbaijan	9,950	2,708	872	1.1	0.6	167	2.1	63	67	73	42	33	9	56	1.6	1.4	0.1
Bahamas	386	106	26	1.4	0.8	5	1.8	66	72	74	42	32	10	83	1.5	1.0	2.6
Bahrain	1,569	353	108	4.8	2.1	22	2.0	63	74	77	28	25	3	89	4.8	2.2	31.1
Bangladesh	161,377	54,163	14,517	1.3	0.9	2,935	2.0	47	65	72	49	41	8	37	3.7	2.7	-2.3
Barbados	287	61	15	0.3	0.1	3	1.6	69	77	79	50	26	24	31	-0.2	0.5	-0.3
Belarus	9,453	1,855	566	-0.2	-0.2	111	1.7	71	67	75	46	25	22	79	0.4	0.3	0.9
Belgium	11,482	2,336	637	0.6	0.3	125	1.7	71	78	81	56	27	29	98	0.7	0.3	4.2
Belize	383	140	39	2.4	1.7	8	2.3	66	69	74	54	47	7	46	2.5	2.2	3.2
Benin	11,485	5,631	1,842	2.9	2.6	417	4.8	42	55	61	84	78	6	47	4.0	3.7	-0.2
Bhutan	754	237	63	1.4	0.9	13	2.0	40	61	71	47	38	9	41	4.0	2.4	0.4
Bolivia (Plurinational State of)	11,353	4,209	1,192	1.7	1.3	247	2.7	46	62	71	62	50	12	69	2.3	1.8	-0.8
Bosnia and Herzegovina	3,324	593	142	-0.7	-0.5	27	1.3	66	74	77	45	21	24	48	0.0	0.4	-6.4
Botswana	2,254	901	272	1.8	1.7	56	2.9	54	51	69	62	55	7	69	3.2	2.6	1.3
Brazil	209,469	54,592	14,654	1.0	0.6	2,915	1.7	59	70	76	43	31	13	87	1.4	0.8	0.1
British Virgin Islands	30	–	–	2.1	0.5	–	–	–	–	–	–	–	–	48	2.9	1.4	–
Brunei Darussalam	429	119	34	1.4	0.8	6	1.8	63	73	76	39	32	7	78	1.9	1.1	0.0
Bulgaria	7,052	1,212	313	-0.7	-0.8	63	1.6	71	72	75	55	23	33	75	-0.2	-0.4	-0.7
Burkina Faso	19,751	10,220	3,345	3.0	2.7	751	5.2	39	50	61	90	85	5	29	5.7	4.7	-1.3
Burundi	11,175	5,789	1,984	3.1	2.9	437	5.4	44	49	61	91	87	4	13	5.7	5.4	0.2
Cabo Verde	544	186	53	1.3	1.0	11	2.3	53	69	73	50	43	7	66	2.5	1.6	-2.5
Cambodia	16,250	5,944	1,774	1.6	1.2	365	2.5	42	58	70	56	49	7	23	2.9	3.0	-1.9
Cameroon	25,216	12,415	4,003	2.7	2.4	893	4.6	47	51	59	83	78	5	56	3.9	3.4	-0.2
Canada	37,075	7,060	1,954	1.1	0.8	386	1.5	73	79	82	49	24	26	81	1.2	1.0	6.6
Central African Republic	4,666	2,418	727	1.4	2.0	166	4.7	42	44	53	89	84	5	41	1.9	3.2	-8.6
Chad	15,478	8,375	2,815	3.4	2.8	654	5.7	41	48	54	98	94	5	23	3.8	4.2	0.1
Chile	18,729	4,450	1,203	1.1	0.3	231	1.6	62	76	80	46	29	17	88	1.2	0.4	6.0
China	1,427,648	304,793	85,912	0.6	0.2	16,824	1.7	59	71	77	40	25	15	59	3.3	1.7	-0.2
Colombia	49,661	14,032	3,730	1.3	0.6	736	1.8	62	73	77	46	34	12	81	1.7	1.0	4.2
Comoros	832	382	122	2.4	2.0	27	4.2	46	59	64	74	69	5	29	2.6	3.0	-2.4
Congo	5,244	2,522	805	2.9	2.4	173	4.4	51	52	64	80	75	5	67	3.6	3.1	-0.8
Cook Islands	18	–	–	-0.1	0.0	–	–	–	–	–	–	–	–	75	0.7	0.3	–
Costa Rica	4,999	1,287	354	1.3	0.7	70	1.8	66	77	80	45	31	14	79	2.9	1.4	0.8
Côte d'Ivoire	25,069	12,228	3,973	2.3	2.5	898	4.6	44	50	57	81	76	5	51	3.2	3.4	-0.3
Croatia	4,156	723	189	-0.4	-0.6	37	1.4	68	75	78	54	22	31	57	0.0	0.1	-1.9
Cuba	11,338	2,233	608	0.1	-0.1	115	1.6	70	77	79	46	24	22	77	0.2	0.0	-1.3
Cyprus	1,189	243	65	1.3	0.6	12	1.3	73	78	81	44	24	20	67	1.1	0.7	4.2
Czechia	10,666	1,943	545	0.2	0.1	110	1.6	70	75	79	54	24	30	74	0.2	0.3	2.1
Democratic People's Republic of Korea	25,550	6,309	1,744	0.6	0.4	355	1.9	60	65	72	42	29	13	62	0.8	0.8	-0.2
Democratic Republic of the Congo	84,068	44,282	15,185	3.2	3.0	3,468	5.9	44	50	60	97	91	6	44	4.5	4.2	0.3
Denmark	5,752	1,149	293	0.4	0.4	61	1.8	73	77	81	57	26	31	88	0.6	0.5	2.6
Djibouti	959	338	101	1.6	1.3	21	2.7	49	57	67	52	45	7	78	1.7	1.5	0.9
Dominica	72	–	–	0.2	0.2	–	–	–	–	–	–	–	–	70	0.6	0.6	–
Dominican Republic	10,627	3,552	1,009	1.3	0.9	207	2.3	58	69	74	54	43	11	81	2.8	1.5	-2.8
Ecuador	17,084	5,724	1,653	1.7	1.2	336	2.4	58	73	77	54	43	11	64	2.0	1.6	2.2
Egypt	98,424	38,430	12,972	2.0	1.7	2,591	3.3	52	69	72	64	55	9	43	2.0	2.1	-0.4
El Salvador	6,421	2,107	578	0.5	0.5	117	2.0	55	69	73	55	42	13	72	1.6	1.2	-6.3
Equatorial Guinea	1,309	556	191	4.3	3.0	44	4.5	40	53	58	65	61	4	72	6.4	3.6	12.4
Eritrea	3,453	1,659	483	2.3	1.7	105	4.1	43	55	66	86	78	8	40	4.6	3.2	-11.6
Estonia	1,323	253	68	-0.3	-0.3	14	1.6	70	70	79	56	26	31	69	-0.4	0.0	3.0
Eswatini	1,136	510	143	0.7	1.1	30	3.0	48	47	59	73	66	7	24	0.9	2.0	-7.4
Ethiopia	109,224	52,244	16,339	2.8	2.4	3,537	4.2	43	52	66	79	73	6	21	4.7	4.5	0.3
Fiji	883	305	91	0.5	0.7	19	2.8	62	66	67	54	45	8	56	1.4	1.6	-7.0

TABLE 1. DEMOGRAPHICS

Countries and areas	Population (thousands) 2018			Annual population growth rate (%)		Annual number of births (thousands) 2018	Total fertility (live births per woman) 2018	Life expectancy at birth (years)			Dependency ratio (%) 2018			Proportion of urban population (%) 2018	Annual growth rate of urban population (%)		Net migration rate (per 1,000 population) 2015–2020
	total	under 18	under 5	2000–2018	2018–2030[a]			1970	2000	2018	total	child	old age		2000–2018	2018–2030[a]	
Finland	5,523	1,068	279	0.3	0.1	51	1.5	70	78	82	61	26	35	85	0.6	0.2	2.5
France	64,991	14,005	3,734	0.5	0.2	729	1.9	72	79	83	61	29	32	80	0.9	0.5	0.6
Gabon	2,119	898	311	3.0	2.2	67	4.0	47	58	66	68	62	6	89	3.7	2.5	1.6
Gambia	2,280	1,159	393	3.0	2.7	88	5.2	38	56	62	88	83	5	61	4.4	3.7	-1.4
Georgia	4,003	922	279	-0.5	-0.3	54	2.1	67	70	74	53	30	23	59	0.1	0.4	-2.5
Germany	83,124	13,774	3,869	0.1	0.0	779	1.6	71	78	81	54	21	33	77	0.3	0.2	6.6
Ghana	29,767	13,045	4,104	2.4	2.0	876	3.9	49	57	64	69	63	5	56	3.8	3.0	-0.3
Greece	10,522	1,796	427	-0.3	-0.5	81	1.3	71	79	82	56	22	34	79	0.2	-0.1	-1.5
Grenada	111	31	9	0.4	0.3	2	2.1	66	73	72	50	35	14	36	0.5	0.9	-1.8
Guatemala	17,248	7,106	2,049	2.2	1.7	424	2.9	53	68	74	65	57	8	51	2.8	2.6	-0.5
Guinea	12,414	6,331	2,020	2.3	2.6	453	4.7	37	51	61	88	82	5	36	3.2	3.8	-0.3
Guinea-Bissau	1,874	915	298	2.5	2.3	66	4.5	41	50	58	82	77	5	43	3.5	3.2	-0.8
Guyana	779	266	76	0.2	0.4	16	2.5	62	65	70	53	43	10	27	-0.2	1.0	-7.7
Haiti	11,123	4,385	1,269	1.5	1.1	271	2.9	46	57	64	62	54	8	55	4.0	2.5	-3.2
Holy See	1	–	–	0.1	-0.1	–	–	–	–	–	–	–	–	100	0.1	-0.1	–
Honduras	9,588	3,670	1,003	2.1	1.5	207	2.5	53	71	75	57	50	7	57	3.4	2.5	-0.7
Hungary	9,708	1,690	448	-0.3	-0.3	92	1.5	69	72	77	51	22	29	71	0.3	0.1	0.6
Iceland	337	79	21	1.0	0.6	4	1.8	74	80	83	53	30	23	94	1.1	0.6	1.1
India	1,352,642	441,501	116,379	1.4	0.9	24,164	2.2	48	63	69	50	41	9	34	2.5	2.3	-0.4
Indonesia	267,671	85,121	24,350	1.3	0.9	4,834	2.3	53	66	72	48	39	9	55	2.8	2.0	-0.4
Iran (Islamic Republic of)	81,800	23,295	7,442	1.2	1.0	1,536	2.1	51	70	76	44	35	9	75	2.1	1.6	-0.7
Iraq	38,434	17,211	5,404	2.7	2.2	1,115	3.7	58	69	70	72	66	6	70	2.9	2.6	0.2
Ireland	4,819	1,212	329	1.3	0.7	62	1.8	71	77	82	54	33	21	63	1.7	1.2	4.9
Israel	8,382	2,733	846	1.9	1.5	170	3.0	72	79	83	66	46	20	92	2.0	1.6	1.2
Italy	60,627	9,797	2,442	0.4	-0.2	457	1.3	72	80	83	56	21	36	70	0.6	0.2	2.5
Jamaica	2,935	845	236	0.6	0.3	47	2.0	68	74	74	48	35	13	56	1.0	1.0	-3.9
Japan	127,202	19,591	5,051	0.0	-0.4	947	1.4	72	81	84	67	21	46	92	0.8	-0.3	0.6
Jordan	9,965	4,031	1,116	3.7	0.6	216	2.8	60	72	74	62	55	6	91	4.5	0.8	1.1
Kazakhstan	18,320	5,847	1,964	1.1	1.0	384	2.7	63	63	73	56	44	12	57	1.3	1.4	-1.0
Kenya	51,393	23,965	6,993	2.6	2.1	1,479	3.5	53	51	66	73	69	4	27	4.3	3.9	-0.2
Kiribati	116	47	15	1.8	1.5	3	3.6	52	63	68	65	59	7	54	3.0	2.7	-6.9
Kuwait	4,137	1,022	302	3.9	1.1	57	2.1	66	73	75	32	28	3	100	4.0	1.1	9.8
Kyrgyzstan	6,304	2,335	788	1.4	1.4	155	3.0	60	66	71	58	51	7	36	1.5	2.4	-0.6
Lao People's Democratic Republic	7,061	2,726	788	1.6	1.3	166	2.7	46	59	68	58	51	6	35	4.2	3.0	-2.1
Latvia	1,928	360	107	-1.2	-1.0	21	1.7	70	70	75	56	25	31	68	-1.2	-0.7	-7.6
Lebanon	6,859	2,149	617	3.2	-0.8	117	2.1	66	75	79	49	39	10	89	3.4	-0.7	-4.5
Lesotho	2,108	822	252	0.2	0.8	56	3.1	51	48	54	60	52	8	28	2.2	2.4	-4.8
Liberia	4,819	2,305	721	2.9	2.3	160	4.3	39	52	64	80	74	6	51	3.7	3.3	-1.0
Libya	6,679	2,223	642	1.2	1.1	126	2.2	56	71	73	49	42	7	80	1.5	1.4	-0.3
Liechtenstein	38	–	–	0.7	0.3	–	–	–	–	–	–	–	–	14	0.4	1.0	–
Lithuania	2,801	495	149	-1.2	-1.0	29	1.7	71	71	76	53	23	30	68	-1.2	-0.6	-11.6
Luxembourg	604	116	33	1.8	1.1	6	1.4	70	78	82	43	23	20	91	2.2	1.3	16.3
Madagascar	26,262	12,455	3,934	2.8	2.5	860	4.1	45	58	67	77	72	5	37	4.6	4.2	-0.1
Malawi	18,143	9,228	2,835	2.7	2.6	621	4.2	40	45	64	87	82	5	17	3.5	4.4	-0.9
Malaysia	31,528	9,191	2,606	1.7	1.1	528	2.0	65	73	76	44	35	10	76	2.8	1.7	1.6
Maldives	516	120	37	3.4	0.1	7	1.9	44	70	79	31	26	5	40	5.4	1.1	22.8
Mali	19,078	10,368	3,460	3.1	2.9	795	5.9	32	48	59	100	95	5	42	5.3	4.5	-2.1
Malta	439	75	22	0.6	0.2	4	1.5	71	79	82	53	22	31	95	0.7	0.2	2.1
Marshall Islands	58	–	–	0.8	0.9	–	–	–	–	–	–	–	–	77	1.4	1.3	–
Mauritania	4,403	2,040	669	2.9	2.5	148	4.6	50	61	65	76	71	6	54	4.8	3.8	1.2
Mauritius	1,267	283	66	0.4	0.0	13	1.4	63	71	75	41	25	16	41	0.1	0.3	0.0
Mexico	126,191	40,251	11,139	1.4	0.9	2,220	2.1	61	74	75	51	40	11	80	1.7	1.3	-0.5
Micronesia (Federated States of)	113	43	12	0.3	1.0	3	3.1	59	65	68	56	49	6	23	0.4	1.8	-5.4
Monaco	39	–	–	1.0	0.6	–	–	–	–	–	–	–	–	100	1.0	0.6	–
Mongolia	3,170	1,092	380	1.6	1.3	76	2.9	55	63	70	53	46	6	68	2.6	1.6	-0.3
Montenegro	628	138	37	0.1	0.0	7	1.7	70	73	77	50	27	22	67	0.9	0.4	-0.8
Montserrat	5	–	–	0.1	-0.4	–	–	–	–	–	–	–	–	9	8.2	0.3	–
Morocco	36,029	11,581	3,433	1.2	1.1	682	2.4	53	69	76	52	41	11	62	2.1	1.8	-1.4
Mozambique	29,496	15,238	4,944	2.8	2.8	1,110	4.9	41	49	60	91	85	6	36	4.0	4.2	-0.2
Myanmar	53,708	17,238	4,518	0.8	0.7	943	2.2	49	60	67	47	39	9	31	1.5	1.8	-3.1
Namibia	2,448	1,049	332	1.7	1.7	70	3.4	53	52	63	68	62	6	50	4.1	3.3	-2.0
Nauru	11	–	–	0.2	0.2	–	–	–	–	–	–	–	–	100	0.2	0.2	–
Nepal	28,096	10,483	2,719	0.9	1.4	563	1.9	41	62	70	57	48	9	20	3.0	3.5	1.5
Netherlands	17,060	3,362	873	0.4	0.2	172	1.7	74	78	82	55	25	30	91	1.4	0.5	0.9

TABLE 1. DEMOGRAPHICS

Countries and areas	Population (thousands) 2018			Annual population growth rate (%)		Annual number of births (thousands) 2018	Total fertility (live births per woman) 2018	Life expectancy at birth (years)			Dependency ratio (%) 2018			Proportion of urban population (%) 2018	Annual growth rate of urban population (%)		Net migration rate (per 1,000 population) 2015–2020
	total	under 18	under 5	2000–2018	2018–2030[a]			1970	2000	2018	total	child	old age		2000–2018	2018–2030[a]	
New Zealand	4,743	1,112	301	1.1	0.7	60	1.9	71	78	82	55	30	24	87	1.2	0.8	3.2
Nicaragua	6,466	2,316	664	1.4	1.1	133	2.4	54	70	74	55	47	8	59	1.7	1.6	-3.3
Niger	22,443	12,732	4,503	3.8	3.7	1,037	6.9	36	50	62	111	105	5	16	3.9	4.7	0.2
Nigeria	195,875	98,709	32,917	2.6	2.5	7,433	5.4	41	46	54	87	82	5	50	4.7	3.8	-0.3
Niue	2	–	–	-0.9	0.3	–	–	–	–	–	–	–	–	45	0.8	1.6	–
North Macedonia	2,083	418	116	0.1	-0.1	23	1.5	66	73	76	43	24	20	58	0.1	0.5	-0.5
Norway	5,338	1,127	301	0.9	0.8	59	1.7	74	79	82	53	27	26	82	1.4	1.2	5.3
Oman	4,829	1,205	440	4.2	1.7	91	2.9	50	72	78	33	29	3	85	5.1	2.4	18.6
Pakistan	212,228	87,938	27,291	2.2	1.8	5,999	3.5	53	63	67	66	58	7	37	2.8	2.7	-1.1
Palau	18	–	–	-0.4	0.3	–	–	–	–	–	–	–	–	80	0.4	0.8	–
Panama	4,177	1,342	389	1.8	1.4	79	2.5	66	75	78	54	42	13	68	2.3	1.9	2.7
Papua New Guinea	8,606	3,629	1,084	2.1	1.8	233	3.6	46	59	64	65	59	6	13	2.1	3.0	-0.1
Paraguay	6,956	2,446	693	1.5	1.1	143	2.4	65	71	74	56	46	10	62	2.1	1.7	-2.4
Peru	31,989	9,782	2,757	1.1	1.0	573	2.3	54	71	77	51	39	12	78	1.4	1.3	3.1
Philippines	106,651	39,276	11,035	1.7	1.2	2,191	2.6	63	69	71	56	48	8	47	1.8	1.9	-0.6
Poland	37,922	6,745	1,843	-0.1	-0.2	371	1.4	70	74	79	48	22	26	60	-0.2	0.0	-0.8
Portugal	10,256	1,699	413	0.0	-0.3	80	1.3	67	77	82	55	21	34	65	1.0	0.5	-0.6
Qatar	2,782	440	134	8.6	1.5	26	1.9	68	77	80	18	16	2	99	8.8	1.5	14.7
Republic of Korea	51,172	8,182	2,060	0.4	0.0	377	1.1	61	76	83	38	18	20	81	0.6	0.1	0.2
Republic of Moldova	4,052	765	210	-0.2	-0.3	41	1.3	65	67	72	38	22	16	43	-0.5	0.2	-0.3
Romania	19,506	3,626	930	-0.7	-0.5	189	1.6	68	70	76	51	23	28	54	-0.6	-0.1	-3.8
Russian Federation	145,734	30,223	9,497	0.0	-0.1	1,842	1.8	69	65	72	48	27	22	74	0.1	0.2	1.3
Rwanda	12,302	5,710	1,801	2.4	2.3	391	4.0	45	49	69	75	70	5	17	3.2	3.4	-0.7
Saint Kitts and Nevis	52	–	–	1.0	0.5	–	–	–	–	–	–	–	–	31	0.6	1.0	–
Saint Lucia	182	42	11	0.8	0.3	2	1.4	64	73	76	40	26	14	19	-1.4	1.0	0.0
Saint Vincent and the Grenadines	110	30	8	0.1	0.2	2	1.9	64	71	72	47	33	14	52	0.9	1.0	-1.8
Samoa	196	87	28	0.7	1.0	5	3.9	60	69	73	76	67	8	18	-0.4	0.5	-14.3
San Marino	34	–	–	1.2	0.2	–	–	–	–	–	–	–	–	97	1.4	0.3	–
Sao Tome and Principe	211	104	31	2.2	2.0	7	4.3	55	61	70	83	78	5	73	3.9	2.8	-8.0
Saudi Arabia	33,703	9,799	3,007	2.7	1.3	598	2.3	53	73	75	40	35	5	84	3.0	1.5	4.1
Senegal	15,854	7,853	2,557	2.7	2.6	548	4.6	39	58	68	86	80	6	47	3.5	3.6	-1.3
Serbia	8,803	1,691	422	-0.4	-0.5	83	1.5	68	72	76	52	24	28	56	-0.1	-0.1	0.5
Seychelles	97	27	8	1.0	0.5	2	2.4	66	71	73	45	34	11	57	1.7	1.2	-2.1
Sierra Leone	7,650	3,655	1,134	2.8	1.9	256	4.3	36	39	54	79	73	5	42	3.8	3.0	-0.6
Singapore	5,758	872	236	2.0	0.7	50	1.2	68	78	83	31	16	15	100	2.0	0.7	4.7
Slovakia	5,453	1,000	282	0.1	-0.1	57	1.5	70	73	77	45	22	23	54	-0.2	0.2	0.3
Slovenia	2,078	366	104	0.2	-0.1	20	1.6	69	76	81	53	23	30	55	0.6	0.5	1.0
Solomon Islands	653	304	101	2.5	2.3	21	4.4	56	67	73	78	72	6	24	4.8	4.0	-2.5
Somalia	15,008	8,056	2,673	2.9	2.9	629	6.1	41	51	57	98	92	6	45	4.6	4.1	-2.7
South Africa	57,793	19,702	5,796	1.4	1.1	1,184	2.4	53	56	64	52	44	8	66	2.2	1.8	2.5
South Sudan	10,976	5,316	1,702	3.2	1.9	387	4.7	36	49	58	83	76	6	20	4.1	3.7	-15.9
Spain	46,693	8,162	2,025	0.7	-0.1	394	1.3	72	79	83	52	22	29	80	1.0	0.2	0.9
Sri Lanka	21,229	6,132	1,690	0.7	0.3	336	2.2	64	71	77	53	37	16	18	0.7	1.4	-4.6
State of Palestine	4,863	2,202	690	2.3	2.2	143	3.6	56	71	74	73	67	5	76	2.6	2.6	-2.2
Sudan	41,802	19,758	6,158	2.4	2.3	1,347	4.4	52	58	65	79	72	6	35	2.7	3.5	-1.2
Suriname	576	187	53	1.1	0.8	11	2.4	63	68	72	52	41	10	66	1.1	1.0	-1.7
Sweden	9,972	2,067	591	0.6	0.5	119	1.9	74	80	83	60	28	32	87	0.9	0.8	4.0
Switzerland	8,526	1,523	444	1.0	0.6	88	1.5	73	80	84	50	22	28	74	1.0	0.8	6.1
Syrian Arab Republic	16,945	6,273	1,797	0.2	3.8	426	2.8	59	73	72	56	49	7	54	0.4	4.9	-24.1
Tajikistan	9,101	3,829	1,329	2.1	2.0	280	3.6	54	62	71	66	61	5	27	2.2	3.0	-2.2
Thailand	69,428	14,537	3,692	0.5	0.1	718	1.5	59	71	77	41	24	17	50	3.1	1.4	0.3
Timor-Leste	1,268	571	169	2.0	1.8	37	4.0	40	59	69	73	65	7	31	3.3	3.0	-4.3
Togo	7,889	3,781	1,189	2.6	2.3	262	4.3	47	53	61	79	74	5	42	3.9	3.6	-0.3
Tokelau	1	–	–	-0.9	0.8	–	–	–	–	–	–	–	–	0	–	–	–
Tonga	103	43	12	0.3	0.9	3	3.6	64	70	71	71	60	10	23	0.3	1.2	-7.7
Trinidad and Tobago	1,390	337	92	0.5	0.1	18	1.7	65	69	73	45	30	16	53	0.2	0.4	-0.6
Tunisia	11,565	3,266	1,036	1.0	0.8	203	2.2	51	73	77	48	36	12	69	1.4	1.3	-0.3
Turkey	82,340	24,377	6,749	1.5	0.7	1,313	2.1	52	70	77	50	37	13	75	2.3	1.2	3.5
Turkmenistan	5,851	2,092	696	1.4	1.2	139	2.8	58	64	68	54	48	7	52	2.1	2.2	-0.9
Turks and Caicos Islands	38	–	–	3.5	1.2	–	–	–	–	–	–	–	–	93	4.0	1.4	–
Tuvalu	12	–	–	1.1	1.1	–	–	–	–	–	–	–	–	62	2.8	2.1	–
Uganda	42,729	23,085	7,538	3.3	2.8	1,627	5.0	49	46	63	96	92	4	24	5.9	5.0	4.0
Ukraine	44,246	8,152	2,250	-0.5	-0.7	421	1.4	71	67	72	48	23	24	69	-0.4	-0.4	0.2

TABLE 1. DEMOGRAPHICS

Countries and areas	Population (thousands) 2018			Annual population growth rate (%)		Annual number of births (thousands) 2018	Total fertility (live births per woman) 2018	Life expectancy at birth (years)			Dependency ratio (%) 2018			Proportion of urban population (%) 2018	Annual growth rate of urban population (%)		Net migration rate (per 1,000 population) 2015–2020
	total	under 18	under 5	2000–2018	2018–2030ᵃ			1970	2000	2018	total	child	old age		2000–2018	2018–2030ᵃ	
United Arab Emirates	9,631	1,637	503	6.2	0.8	100	1.4	61	74	78	19	17	1	87	6.7	1.1	4.2
United Kingdom	67,142	14,042	3,977	0.7	0.4	775	1.8	72	78	81	56	28	29	83	1.1	0.7	3.9
United Republic of Tanzania	56,313	28,558	9,316	2.9	2.8	2,071	4.9	47	51	65	88	83	5	34	5.2	4.7	-0.7
United States	327,096	73,857	19,512	0.8	0.6	3,912	1.8	71	77	79	53	29	24	82	1.1	0.8	2.9
Uruguay	3,449	860	239	0.2	0.3	48	2.0	69	75	78	55	32	23	95	0.4	0.4	-0.9
Uzbekistan	32,476	10,824	3,407	1.5	1.2	696	2.4	62	67	72	49	43	7	50	2.0	1.4	-0.3
Vanuatu	293	131	40	2.5	2.2	9	3.8	54	67	70	74	68	6	25	3.4	2.9	0.4
Venezuela (Bolivarian Republic of)	28,887	9,527	2,545	1.0	1.3	524	2.3	65	72	72	54	43	11	88	1.0	1.3	-22.3
Viet Nam	95,546	26,017	7,831	1.0	0.7	1,598	2.0	60	73	75	44	33	10	36	3.1	2.5	-0.8
Yemen	28,499	13,183	4,084	2.7	2.0	868	3.8	37	61	66	74	69	5	37	4.6	3.6	-1.1
Zambia	17,352	9,033	2,869	2.8	2.8	629	4.6	50	44	64	89	85	4	44	4.1	4.1	-0.5
Zimbabwe	14,439	7,082	2,196	1.1	1.6	443	3.6	57	45	61	83	78	5	32	0.8	2.2	-8.2

SUMMARY

East Asia and Pacific	2,363,341	558,204	156,967	0.7	0.4	30,995	1.8	59	71	76	44	28	15	59	2.7	1.5	-0.2
Europe and Central Asia	918,905	195,798	55,923	0.4	0.1	10,973	1.8	68	72	78	52	27	25	72	0.6	0.5	1.7
Eastern Europe and Central Asia	423,215	103,675	31,140	0.4	0.2	6,107	2.0	64	66	73	49	31	18	67	0.6	0.6	0.7
Western Europe	495,690	92,122	24,782	0.4	0.1	4,866	1.6	71	78	82	55	24	31	77	0.6	0.4	2.6
Latin America and Caribbean	642,217	190,134	52,278	1.2	0.8	10,517	2.0	60	72	75	49	37	13	81	1.5	1.1	-0.8
Middle East and North Africa	447,891	155,634	49,579	2.0	1.5	10,121	2.8	52	70	74	54	46	8	65	2.6	2.0	-0.5
North America	364,296	80,943	21,472	0.9	0.6	4,300	1.8	71	77	79	52	28	24	82	1.1	0.8	3.3
South Asia	1,814,014	619,317	168,297	1.5	1.0	35,224	2.4	48	63	69	52	43	9	34	2.7	2.4	-0.7
Sub-Saharan Africa	1,080,429	530,744	171,759	2.7	2.5	38,074	4.7	44	50	61	84	78	5	40	4.0	3.7	-0.3
Eastern and Southern Africa	560,914	268,016	84,514	2.6	2.4	18,407	4.2	47	51	64	80	74	6	35	3.8	3.7	-0.3
West and Central Africa	519,515	262,728	87,245	2.8	2.6	19,667	5.2	42	49	58	88	83	5	46	4.3	3.8	-0.4
Least developed countries	1,009,691	464,454	145,152	2.4	2.2	31,786	4.0	44	55	65	75	69	6	34	4.0	3.7	-1.0
World	**7,631,091**	**2,330,774**	**676,276**	**1.2**	**0.9**	**140,204**	**2.5**	**57**	**66**	**72**	**53**	**39**	**14**	**55**	**2.2**	**1.7**	**0.0**

For a complete list of countries and areas in the regions, subregions and country categories, see page 182 or visit <data.unicef.org/regionalclassifications>.

It is not advisable to compare data from consecutive editions of *The State of the World's Children*.

DEFINITIONS OF THE INDICATORS

Annual population growth rate – Average exponential rate of growth of the population over one year. It is calculated as ln(Pt/P0)/t where t is the length of the period. It is expressed as a percentage.

Total fertility – The average number of live births a hypothetical cohort of women would have at the end of their reproductive period if they were subject during their whole lives to the fertility rates of a given period and if they were not subject to mortality. It is expressed as live births per woman.

Dependency ratios – The total dependency ratio is the ratio of the sum of the population aged 0-14 and that aged 65+ to the population aged 15-64. The child dependency ratio is the ratio of the population aged 0-14 to the population aged 15-64. The old-age dependency ratio is the ratio of the population aged 65 years or over to the population aged 15-64. All ratios are presented as number of dependants per 100 persons of working age (15-64).

Life expectancy at birth – Number of years newborn children would live if subject to the mortality risks prevailing for the cross section of population at the time of their birth.

Proportion of urban population – Urban population as a percentage of the total population.

Net migration rate – The number of immigrants minus the number of emigrants over a period, divided by the person-years lived by the population of the receiving country over that period. It is expressed as net number of migrants per 1,000 population.

MAIN DATA SOURCES

All demographic data – United Nations, Department of Economic and Social Affairs, Population Division (2019). World Population Prospects 2019, Online Edition. Rev. 1. Proportion of urban population for regions and growth rates for total and urban population calculated by UNICEF.

NOTES

– Data not available.

α Based on medium-fertility variant projections.

Regional and global values are based on more countries and areas than listed here. Therefore, country values don't add up to the corresponding regional values and global value.

TABLE 2. CHILD MORTALITY

Countries and areas	Under-5 mortality rate (deaths per 1,000 live births)			Annual rate of reduction in under-5 mortality rate (%) 2000–2018	Under-5 mortality rate by sex (deaths per 1,000 live births) 2018		Infant mortality rate (deaths per 1,000 live births)		Neonatal mortality rate (deaths per 1,000 live births)			Probability of dying among children aged 5–14 (deaths per 1,000 children aged 5)		Annual number of under-5 deaths (thousands) 2018	Annual number of neonatal deaths (thousands) 2018	Neonatal deaths as proportion of all under-5 deaths (%) 2018	Number of deaths among children aged 5–14 (thousands) 2018
	1990	2000	2018		male	female	1990	2018	1990	2000	2018	1990	2018				
Afghanistan	179	129	62	4.1	66	59	121	48	75	61	37	16	5	74	45	60	5
Albania	41	26	9	6.0	9	8	35	8	13	12	7	7	2	0	0	74	0
Algeria	50	40	23	2.9	25	22	42	20	23	21	15	9	4	24	15	62	3
Andorra	11	6	3	4.4	3	3	9	3	6	3	1	7	1	0	0	50	0
Angola	223	206	77	5.4	83	71	132	52	54	51	28	46	16	94	36	38	15
Anguilla	–	–	–	–	–	–	–	–	–	–	–	–	–	–	–	–	–
Antigua and Barbuda	28	16	6	5.0	7	6	24	5	15	9	3	5	1	0	0	50	0
Argentina	29	20	10	3.8	11	9	25	9	15	11	6	3	2	8	5	64	2
Armenia	49	31	12	5.1	14	11	42	11	23	16	6	3	2	1	0	52	0
Australia	9	6	4	2.9	4	3	8	3	5	4	2	2	1	1	1	62	0
Austria	10	6	4	2.5	4	3	8	3	5	3	2	2	1	0	0	60	0
Azerbaijan	96	75	22	6.9	24	19	76	19	33	34	11	5	3	4	2	51	0
Bahamas	24	16	10	2.4	11	9	20	8	13	8	5	4	2	0	0	53	0
Bahrain	23	13	7	3.2	7	7	20	6	15	5	3	4	2	0	0	43	0
Bangladesh	144	87	30	5.9	32	28	100	25	64	42	17	26	4	89	50	57	12
Barbados	18	15	12	1.2	13	11	16	11	12	9	8	3	2	0	0	65	0
Belarus	15	13	3	7.3	4	3	12	3	8	6	1	4	1	0	0	38	0
Belgium	10	6	4	2.6	4	3	8	3	5	3	2	2	1	0	0	56	0
Belize	38	24	13	3.3	14	12	31	11	19	12	9	5	3	0	0	67	0
Benin	175	139	93	2.2	99	87	106	61	46	40	31	45	22	38	13	35	7
Bhutan	127	78	30	5.3	32	27	89	25	43	32	16	20	7	0	0	56	0
Bolivia (Plurinational State of)	121	75	27	5.7	29	24	84	22	41	29	14	13	5	7	4	54	1
Bosnia and Herzegovina	18	10	6	2.9	6	5	16	5	11	7	4	3	1	0	0	69	0
Botswana	51	87	36	4.8	40	33	39	30	25	26	24	17	6	2	1	67	0
Brazil	63	35	14	4.9	16	13	53	13	25	18	8	5	2	42	24	57	7
British Virgin Islands	–	–	–	–	–	–	–	–	–	–	–	–	–	–	–	–	–
Brunei Darussalam	13	10	12	-0.6	12	11	10	10	6	5	5	4	2	0	0	47	0
Bulgaria	18	18	7	5.0	8	6	15	6	8	8	4	4	2	0	0	51	0
Burkina Faso	199	179	76	4.7	81	72	99	49	46	41	25	40	20	56	19	33	11
Burundi	174	156	58	5.5	63	54	105	41	40	37	22	62	23	25	9	38	8
Cabo Verde	61	36	19	3.3	21	18	47	17	20	17	12	6	2	0	0	59	0
Cambodia	116	107	28	7.4	31	25	85	24	40	35	14	35	5	10	5	52	2
Cameroon	137	149	76	3.8	81	71	85	51	40	35	27	35	32	66	24	36	22
Canada	8	6	5	1.2	5	5	7	4	4	4	3	2	1	2	1	68	0
Central African Republic	180	172	116	2.2	123	110	117	84	52	49	41	32	15	19	7	36	2
Chad	212	186	119	2.5	125	112	112	71	52	44	34	53	28	75	22	30	13
Chile	19	11	7	2.3	8	7	16	6	9	5	5	3	1	2	1	67	0
China	54	37	9	8.1	9	8	42	7	29	21	4	8	2	146	73	50	40
Colombia	35	25	14	3.1	16	13	29	12	18	13	8	5	2	10	6	55	2
Comoros	125	102	67	2.3	73	62	88	51	50	41	32	18	9	2	1	48	0
Congo	90	114	50	4.6	54	46	59	36	27	31	20	37	7	9	3	41	1
Cook Islands	24	18	8	4.6	9	7	20	7	13	10	4	5	2	0	0	50	0
Costa Rica	17	13	9	2.2	10	8	14	8	9	8	6	3	2	1	0	67	0
Côte d'Ivoire	155	145	81	3.2	89	73	105	59	49	47	34	31	25	70	30	43	17
Croatia	13	8	5	3.2	5	4	11	4	8	6	3	3	1	0	0	55	0
Cuba	13	9	5	3.0	5	4	11	4	7	4	2	4	2	1	0	41	0
Cyprus	11	7	2	5.7	3	2	10	2	6	4	1	2	1	0	0	57	0
Czechia	12	5	3	2.7	4	3	10	3	7	3	2	2	1	0	0	52	0
Democratic People's Republic of Korea	43	60	18	6.6	20	16	33	14	22	27	10	8	4	6	3	53	1
Democratic Republic of the Congo	186	161	88	3.3	95	81	119	68	42	39	28	41	29	296	98	33	70
Denmark	9	5	4	1.5	5	4	7	4	4	3	3	2	0	0	0	74	0
Djibouti	118	101	59	3.0	64	54	92	50	50	44	32	26	13	1	1	54	0
Dominica	16	15	36	-4.9	38	33	13	33	10	11	28	3	3	0	0	79	0
Dominican Republic	60	41	29	1.9	32	26	46	24	24	24	19	8	3	6	4	67	1
Ecuador	54	29	14	4.4	16	13	42	12	23	14	7	8	3	5	2	51	1
Egypt	86	47	21	4.4	22	20	63	18	33	23	11	11	4	55	29	53	9
El Salvador	60	33	14	4.9	15	12	46	12	23	15	7	7	4	2	1	49	0
Equatorial Guinea	179	157	85	3.4	91	79	121	63	48	45	30	38	18	4	1	36	1
Eritrea	153	86	42	4.0	47	36	94	31	35	27	18	45	9	4	2	44	1
Estonia	18	11	3	7.9	3	2	14	2	10	5	1	5	1	0	0	47	0
Eswatini	71	126	54	4.7	59	49	54	43	21	23	17	11	13	2	1	32	0
Ethiopia	202	142	55	5.2	61	49	120	39	59	49	28	78	12	191	99	52	34
Fiji	29	23	26	-0.7	28	23	24	22	12	9	11	10	5	0	0	42	0
Finland	7	4	2	5.1	2	2	6	1	4	2	1	2	1	0	0	55	0

TABLE 2. CHILD MORTALITY

Countries and areas	Under-5 mortality rate (deaths per 1,000 live births)			Annual rate of reduction in under-5 mortality rate (%) 2000–2018	Under-5 mortality rate by sex (deaths per 1,000 live births) 2018		Infant mortality rate (deaths per 1,000 live births)		Neonatal mortality rate (deaths per 1,000 live births)			Probability of dying among children aged 5–14 (deaths per 1,000 children aged 5)		Annual number of under-5 deaths (thousands) 2018	Annual number of neonatal deaths (thousands) 2018	Neonatal deaths as proportion of all under-5 deaths (%) 2018	Number of deaths among children aged 5–14 (thousands) 2018
	1990	2000	2018		male	female	1990	2018	1990	2000	2018	1990	2018				
France	9	5	4	1.6	4	4	7	3	4	3	3	2	1	3	2	62	1
Gabon	93	85	45	3.5	49	40	60	33	31	29	21	19	14	3	1	48	1
Gambia	167	115	58	3.8	63	54	82	39	49	40	26	36	13	5	2	46	1
Georgia	48	37	10	7.3	11	9	41	9	25	23	6	7	2	1	0	59	0
Germany	9	5	4	2.1	4	3	7	3	3	3	2	2	1	3	2	60	1
Ghana	127	99	48	4.1	52	43	80	35	42	36	24	27	12	41	21	51	9
Greece	10	6	4	2.0	5	4	9	4	6	4	3	2	1	0	0	56	0
Grenada	22	16	15	0.1	17	14	18	14	12	7	10	3	5	0	0	64	0
Guatemala	80	52	26	3.8	29	23	59	22	28	21	12	12	4	11	5	47	2
Guinea	236	166	101	2.8	105	96	139	65	62	47	31	49	21	44	14	32	8
Guinea-Bissau	223	175	81	4.2	88	75	132	54	64	55	37	40	16	5	2	46	1
Guyana	60	47	30	2.4	34	26	47	25	31	27	18	6	5	0	0	60	0
Haiti	144	103	65	2.6	70	59	100	49	39	30	26	31	12	17	7	40	3
Holy See	–	–	–	–	–	–	–	–	–	–	–	–	–	–	–	–	–
Honduras	58	37	18	4.1	19	16	45	15	22	18	10	9	5	4	2	55	1
Hungary	17	10	4	4.8	5	4	15	4	11	6	2	3	1	0	0	53	0
Iceland	6	4	2	4.0	2	2	5	2	3	2	1	2	1	0	0	50	0
India	126	92	37	5.1	36	37	89	30	57	45	23	21	6	882	549	62	143
Indonesia	84	52	25	4.1	28	22	62	21	31	23	13	15	6	121	62	51	28
Iran (Islamic Republic of)	56	34	14	4.8	15	14	44	12	26	19	9	8	3	22	14	62	3
Iraq	54	44	27	2.8	29	24	42	22	26	24	15	9	7	29	17	58	7
Ireland	9	7	4	3.7	4	3	8	3	5	4	2	2	1	0	0	61	0
Israel	12	7	4	3.4	4	3	10	3	6	4	2	2	1	1	0	52	0
Italy	10	6	3	3.4	3	3	8	3	6	3	2	2	1	1	1	64	0
Jamaica	30	22	14	2.4	16	13	25	12	20	17	10	5	3	1	0	33	0
Japan	6	5	2	3.3	2	2	5	2	3	2	1	2	1	2	1	59	1
Jordan	36	27	16	2.9	18	15	30	14	20	16	9	5	3	3	2	59	1
Kazakhstan	52	43	10	8.1	11	9	44	9	22	21	6	6	3	4	2	56	1
Kenya	107	106	41	5.3	45	37	68	31	28	28	20	18	10	60	29	48	14
Kiribati	95	71	53	1.7	57	48	69	41	36	29	23	16	9	0	0	44	0
Kuwait	18	12	8	2.5	9	7	15	7	10	7	4	5	2	0	0	56	0
Kyrgyzstan	65	49	19	5.3	21	17	54	17	24	20	13	6	3	3	2	69	0
Lao People's Democratic Republic	153	107	47	4.5	52	42	105	38	47	38	23	44	9	8	4	48	1
Latvia	17	14	4	7.2	4	4	13	3	8	7	2	6	1	0	0	51	0
Lebanon	32	20	7	5.5	8	7	27	6	20	12	4	8	2	1	1	59	0
Lesotho	90	118	81	2.1	88	74	72	66	39	40	35	17	9	5	2	43	0
Liberia	262	187	71	5.4	76	65	175	53	59	45	24	33	17	11	4	35	2
Libya	42	28	12	4.8	13	11	35	10	21	15	6	8	6	2	1	52	1
Liechtenstein	–	–	–	–	–	–	–	–	–	–	–	–	–	–	–	–	–
Lithuania	15	11	4	5.4	4	4	12	3	8	5	2	4	1	0	0	50	0
Luxembourg	9	5	2	3.8	3	2	7	2	4	2	1	2	0	0	0	60	0
Madagascar	159	107	54	3.9	58	49	97	38	39	31	21	41	12	45	18	39	8
Malawi	239	173	50	6.9	54	45	139	35	50	40	22	40	14	30	14	46	7
Malaysia	17	10	8	1.5	8	7	14	7	8	5	4	5	3	4	2	55	1
Maldives	86	39	9	8.4	9	8	63	7	39	22	5	12	2	0	0	55	0
Mali	230	188	98	3.6	103	92	120	62	67	51	33	44	26	75	26	34	15
Malta	11	8	7	0.4	8	6	10	6	8	5	5	2	1	0	0	67	0
Marshall Islands	49	41	33	1.1	37	29	39	27	20	18	15	9	6	0	0	46	0
Mauritania	117	114	76	2.3	81	70	71	52	46	43	33	21	8	11	5	45	1
Mauritius	23	19	16	1.0	17	14	20	14	15	12	9	4	2	0	0	59	0
Mexico	45	26	13	4.0	14	11	36	11	22	13	8	5	2	28	17	59	6
Micronesia (Federated States of)	55	54	31	3.1	34	27	43	26	26	25	16	10	6	0	0	53	0
Monaco	8	5	3	2.6	4	3	6	3	4	3	2	2	1	0	0	50	0
Mongolia	108	64	16	7.6	19	13	77	14	30	24	9	10	4	1	1	53	0
Montenegro	17	14	3	9.5	3	2	15	2	11	9	2	2	1	0	0	63	0
Montserrat	–	–	–	–	–	–	–	–	–	–	–	–	–	–	–	–	–
Morocco	79	49	22	4.4	25	20	62	19	36	27	14	10	3	15	9	61	2
Mozambique	241	171	73	4.7	78	68	161	54	60	46	28	60	17	79	31	39	14
Myanmar	115	89	46	3.6	51	42	82	37	48	37	23	31	5	43	22	50	5
Namibia	74	77	40	3.7	43	36	50	29	28	23	16	16	12	3	1	40	1
Nauru	60	42	32	1.5	35	29	46	26	29	25	20	11	6	0	0	60	0
Nepal	140	81	32	5.1	34	30	97	27	58	40	20	29	6	18	11	62	3
Netherlands	8	6	4	2.6	4	3	7	3	5	4	3	3	1	0	0	61	0
New Zealand	11	7	6	1.4	6	5	9	5	4	3	3	2	1	0	0	61	0

TABLE 2. CHILD MORTALITY

Countries and areas	Under-5 mortality rate (deaths per 1,000 live births)			Annual rate of reduction in under-5 mortality rate (%) 2000–2018	Under-5 mortality rate by sex (deaths per 1,000 live births) 2018		Infant mortality rate (deaths per 1,000 live births)		Neonatal mortality rate (deaths per 1,000 live births)			Probability of dying among children aged 5–14 (deaths per 1,000 children aged 5)		Annual number of under-5 deaths (thousands) 2018	Annual number of neonatal deaths (thousands) 2018	Neonatal deaths as proportion of all under-5 deaths (%) 2018	Number of deaths among children aged 5–14 (thousands) 2018
	1990	2000	2018		male	female	1990	2018	1990	2000	2018	1990	2018				
Nicaragua	66	37	18	3.8	20	16	51	16	23	16	9	8	4	2	1	51	1
Niger	329	226	84	5.5	87	80	133	48	54	43	25	68	37	83	26	32	26
Nigeria	211	185	120	2.4	127	113	125	76	50	48	36	41	20	866	267	31	110
Niue	13	24	24	0.0	26	21	12	20	7	13	12	4	5	0	0	0	0
North Macedonia	36	16	10	2.6	11	9	33	9	17	9	7	3	1	0	0	74	0
Norway	9	5	3	3.6	3	2	7	2	4	3	1	2	1	0	0	59	0
Oman	39	16	11	2.0	12	10	32	10	17	7	5	6	2	1	0	45	0
Pakistan	139	112	69	2.7	74	65	106	57	65	60	42	14	10	409	251	62	46
Palau	35	29	18	2.6	20	16	30	17	19	15	9	7	4	0	0	50	0
Panama	31	26	15	2.9	17	14	26	13	17	15	8	8	3	1	1	56	0
Papua New Guinea	87	72	48	2.3	52	44	64	38	31	29	22	15	9	11	5	47	2
Paraguay	45	34	20	2.9	22	18	36	17	22	18	11	7	3	3	2	53	0
Peru	81	39	14	5.5	16	13	57	11	28	16	7	11	3	8	4	52	2
Philippines	57	38	28	1.6	31	25	40	22	19	17	14	14	5	63	30	47	12
Poland	17	9	4	4.1	5	4	15	4	11	6	3	3	1	2	1	61	0
Portugal	15	7	4	3.6	4	3	12	3	7	3	2	4	1	0	0	54	0
Qatar	21	12	7	3.3	7	6	18	6	11	7	4	4	1	0	0	53	0
Republic of Korea	15	7	3	4.7	3	3	13	3	7	3	1	5	1	1	1	46	0
Republic of Moldova	33	31	16	3.8	18	14	28	14	19	21	12	5	2	1	0	74	0
Romania	31	22	7	6.1	8	7	24	6	15	10	3	5	2	1	1	46	0
Russian Federation	22	19	7	5.5	8	6	18	6	11	10	3	5	2	13	6	44	4
Rwanda	154	183	35	9.1	38	32	94	27	40	41	16	72	10	13	6	46	3
Saint Kitts and Nevis	31	23	12	3.7	13	11	25	10	19	15	8	5	2	0	0	63	0
Saint Lucia	22	18	17	0.4	18	15	19	15	12	11	12	4	2	0	0	75	0
Saint Vincent and the Grenadines	24	23	16	1.8	18	15	20	15	13	13	10	4	5	0	0	58	0
Samoa	30	21	16	1.6	17	14	25	14	16	11	8	6	4	0	0	53	0
San Marino	13	6	2	6.3	2	2	12	2	7	3	1	2	1	0	0	–	0
Sao Tome and Principe	108	85	31	5.5	34	28	69	24	26	23	14	20	8	0	0	45	0
Saudi Arabia	45	22	7	6.4	7	7	36	6	22	12	4	7	2	4	2	53	1
Senegal	139	131	44	6.1	48	39	71	32	40	38	21	37	13	23	11	48	6
Serbia	28	13	6	4.6	6	5	24	5	17	8	3	3	1	0	0	61	0
Seychelles	17	14	14	-0.3	16	13	14	12	11	9	9	4	3	0	0	61	0
Sierra Leone	263	234	105	4.4	111	99	156	78	53	51	33	53	21	26	8	32	4
Singapore	8	4	3	1.8	3	3	6	2	4	2	1	2	1	0	0	38	0
Slovakia	15	10	6	3.1	6	5	13	5	9	5	3	3	1	0	0	49	0
Slovenia	10	6	2	5.2	2	2	9	2	6	3	1	2	1	0	0	55	0
Solomon Islands	39	30	20	2.3	22	18	31	17	15	13	8	8	4	0	0	42	0
Somalia	179	172	122	1.9	127	115	108	77	45	44	38	38	24	73	24	32	11
South Africa	59	74	34	4.3	37	31	46	28	20	17	11	8	6	40	13	32	6
South Sudan	254	183	99	3.4	103	93	150	64	65	57	40	52	20	38	15	41	6
Spain	9	5	3	3.2	3	3	7	3	5	3	2	2	1	1	1	56	0
Sri Lanka	22	17	7	4.4	8	7	19	6	13	10	4	6	2	3	2	60	1
State of Palestine	44	30	20	2.2	22	18	36	17	22	16	11	6	3	3	2	54	0
Sudan	132	104	60	3.0	65	55	82	42	43	37	29	29	8	80	38	48	9
Suriname	48	34	19	3.3	21	17	41	17	23	18	10	7	3	0	0	53	0
Sweden	7	4	3	2.3	3	2	6	2	4	2	2	1	1	0	0	56	0
Switzerland	8	6	4	1.7	4	4	7	4	4	3	3	2	1	0	0	72	0
Syrian Arab Republic	37	23	17	1.9	17	15	30	14	17	12	9	9	12	7	4	51	4
Tajikistan	102	84	35	4.9	39	31	81	30	31	28	15	12	5	10	4	44	1
Thailand	37	22	9	4.9	10	8	30	8	20	12	5	9	5	7	4	55	4
Timor-Leste	174	108	46	4.8	50	42	131	39	55	37	20	27	8	2	1	45	0
Togo	145	120	70	3.0	75	64	90	47	43	36	25	37	21	18	6	36	4
Tokelau	–	–	–	–	–	–	–	–	–	–	–	–	–	–	–	–	–
Tonga	22	18	16	0.6	14	12	19	13	10	8	7	5	3	0	0	40	0
Trinidad and Tobago	30	29	18	2.5	20	17	27	16	20	18	12	4	2	0	0	63	0
Tunisia	55	30	17	3.2	18	15	43	15	29	20	11	7	3	3	2	67	1
Turkey	74	38	11	7.1	11	10	55	9	33	19	5	9	2	14	7	52	3
Turkmenistan	85	81	46	3.2	52	40	68	39	28	30	21	7	4	6	3	46	0
Turks and Caicos Islands	–	–	–	–	–	–	–	–	–	–	–	–	–	–	–	–	–
Tuvalu	53	41	24	2.9	27	22	42	21	28	25	16	10	5	0	0	71	0
Uganda	185	148	46	6.4	51	42	109	34	39	32	20	32	15	74	32	44	19
Ukraine	19	18	9	4.1	10	8	17	7	12	11	5	4	2	4	2	58	1
United Arab Emirates	17	11	8	2.2	8	7	14	7	8	6	4	5	2	1	0	53	0
United Kingdom	9	7	4	2.4	5	4	8	4	4	4	3	2	1	3	2	60	1

TABLE 2. CHILD MORTALITY

Countries and areas	Under-5 mortality rate (deaths per 1,000 live births)			Annual rate of reduction in under-5 mortality rate (%)	Under-5 mortality rate by sex (deaths per 1,000 live births) 2018		Infant mortality rate (deaths per 1,000 live births)		Neonatal mortality rate (deaths per 1,000 live births)			Probability of dying among children aged 5–14 (deaths per 1,000 children aged 5)		Annual number of under-5 deaths (thousands)	Annual number of neonatal deaths (thousands)	Neonatal deaths as proportion of all under-5 deaths (%)	Number of deaths among children aged 5–14 (thousands)
	1990	2000	2018	2000–2018	male	female	1990	2018	1990	2000	2018	1990	2018	2018	2018	2018	2018
United Republic of Tanzania	166	130	53	5.0	57	49	101	38	40	34	21	30	13	107	44	41	20
United States	11	8	7	1.4	7	6	9	6	6	5	4	2	1	25	14	54	6
Uruguay	23	17	8	4.5	8	7	20	6	12	8	5	3	2	0	0	60	0
Uzbekistan	72	63	21	6.0	24	18	60	19	31	29	12	6	3	15	8	54	2
Vanuatu	36	29	26	0.5	28	24	29	22	17	13	12	7	5	0	0	44	0
Venezuela (Bolivarian Republic of)	30	22	25	-0.7	26	23	25	21	13	11	15	4	3	13	8	61	2
Viet Nam	51	30	21	2.0	24	17	37	16	24	15	11	12	3	33	17	51	4
Yemen	126	95	55	3.0	59	51	88	43	43	37	27	30	12	36	15	42	6
Zambia	186	162	58	5.7	63	53	111	40	37	35	23	30	12	36	15	42	6
Zimbabwe	80	105	46	4.5	51	42	52	34	24	23	21	14	13	21	9	45	5
SUMMARY																	
East Asia and Pacific	57	40	15	5.4	16	14	43	12	27	20	8	10	3	462	230	50	103
Europe and Central Asia	31	21	9	5.0	10	8	25	8	14	10	5	4	2	96	50	52	17
Eastern Europe and Central Asia	46	36	13	5.7	14	11	37	11	21	17	6	6	2	78	39	51	13
Western Europe	10	6	4	2.8	4	3	9	3	6	3	2	2	1	18	11	60	4
Latin America and Caribbean	55	33	16	3.8	18	15	43	14	23	16	9	6	3	172	95	55	30
Middle East and North Africa	65	42	22	3.7	23	20	50	18	28	21	12	10	4	220	122	56	37
North America	11	8	6	1.4	7	6	9	5	6	5	3	2	1	27	15	55	6
South Asia	130	94	42	4.5	43	41	92	35	59	47	26	20	6	1,475	909	62	211
Sub-Saharan Africa	180	153	78	3.8	83	72	107	53	46	41	28	40	18	2,869	1,054	37	518
Eastern and Southern Africa	164	136	57	4.8	62	52	101	40	43	38	24	39	13	1,024	441	43	189
West and Central Africa	197	170	97	3.1	103	90	115	64	48	44	31	40	23	1,845	613	33	330
Least developed countries	175	137	64	4.2	69	59	108	46	52	42	26	39	14	1,992	821	41	371
World	**93**	**76**	**39**	**3.8**	**41**	**36**	**65**	**29**	**37**	**31**	**18**	**15**	**7**	**5,322**	**2,476**	**47**	**923**

For a complete list of countries and areas in the regions, subregions and country categories, see page 182 or visit <data.unicef.org/regionalclassifications>.

It is not advisable to compare data from consecutive editions of *The State of the World's Children.*

DEFINITIONS OF THE INDICATORS

Under-5 mortality rate – Probability of dying between birth and exactly 5 years of age, expressed per 1,000 live births.

Infant mortality rate – Probability of dying between birth and exactly 1 year of age, expressed per 1,000 live births.

Neonatal mortality rate – Probability of dying during the first 28 days of life, expressed per 1,000 live births.

Probability of dying among children aged 5–14 – Probability of dying at age 5–14 years expressed per 1,000 children aged 5.

MAIN DATA SOURCES

Under-5, infant, neonatal and age 5–14 mortality rates – United Nations Inter-agency Group for Child Mortality Estimation (UNICEF, World Health Organization, United Nations Population Division and the World Bank Group). Last update: September 2019.

Under-5 deaths, neonatal deaths and deaths aged 5–14 – United Nations Inter-agency Group for Child Mortality Estimation (UNICEF, World Health Organization, United Nations Population Division and the World Bank Group). Last update: September 2019.

NOTES

– Data not available.

TABLE 3. MATERNAL AND NEWBORN HEALTH

Countries and areas	Life expec-tancy: female 2018	Demand for family planning satisfied with modern methods (%) 2013–2018* Women aged 15–49	Women aged 15–19	Adoles-cent birth rate 2013–2018*	Births by age 18 (%) 2013–2018*	Antenatal care (%) 2013–2018* At least one visit	At least four visits Women aged 15–49	Women aged 15–19	Delivery care (%) 2013–2018* Skilled birth attendant Women aged 15–49	Women aged 15–19	Institu-tional delivery	C-section	Postnatal health check(%)+ 2013–2018* For new-borns	For mothers	Maternal mortality† 2017 Number of maternal deaths	Maternal mortality ratio	Lifetime risk of maternal death (1 in X)
Afghanistan	66	42	21	77	20	59	18	16	51	54	48	3	9	40	7,700	638	33
Albania	80	5	5	17	3	88	78	72	100	100	99	31	86	88	5	15	3,800
Algeria	78	77	–	10	1	93	67	–	97	–	97	16	–	–	1,200	112	270
Andorra	–	–	–	3	–	–	–	–	–	–	–	–	–	–	–	–	–
Angola	64	30	15	163	38	82	61	56	50	50	46	4	21	23	3,000	241	69
Anguilla	–	–	–	40 x	–	–	–	–	–	–	–	–	–	–	–	–	–
Antigua and Barbuda	78	–	–	67 x	–	100 x	100	–	100	–	–	–	–	–	1	42	1,200
Argentina	80	–	–	65	12 x	98 x	90 x	85 x	100	–	99	29 x	–	–	290	39	1,100
Armenia	78	37	–	24	1	100	96	93	100	100	99	18	98	97	11	26	2,000
Australia	85	–	–	10	–	98 x	92 x	–	–	–	99	31 x	–	–	20	6	8,200
Austria	84	–	–	7	–	–	–	–	99	–	99	24 x	–	–	4	5	13,500
Azerbaijan	75	22 x	13 x	53	4 x	92 x	66 x	40 x	100	93 x	93 x	20 x	–	83 x	44	26	1,700
Bahamas	76	–	–	32 x	–	98 x	85	–	98	–	–	–	–	–	4	70	820
Bahrain	78	–	–	14	–	100 x	100	–	100	–	98 x	–	–	–	3	14	3,000
Bangladesh	74	73	68	78	36	64	31	32	42	42	37	23	32	36	5,100	173	250
Barbados	80	70 x	–	50 x	7 x	93	88 x	–	99	–	100 x	21 x	98 x	97 x	1	27	2,400
Belarus	79	74 x	–	16	3 x	100 x	100 x	95 x	100	100 x	100 x	25 x	100 x	100 x	3	2	23,800
Belgium	84	–	–	6	–	–	–	–	–	–	–	18 x	–	–	6	5	11,200
Belize	78	66	47	64	17	97	93	92	97	97	96	34	96	96	3	36	1,100
Benin	63	26	13	94	19	83	52	52	78	77	84	5	64	66	1,600	397	49
Bhutan	72	85 x	–	28 x	15 x	98 x	85	66 x	75 x	40 x	74 x	12 x	30 x	41 x	24	183	250
Bolivia (Plurinational State of)	74	50	–	71	20 x	96	86	69 x	85 x	76 x	88	33	–	–	380	155	220
Bosnia and Herzegovina	80	22 x	–	11	–	87 x	84 x	–	100	–	100 x	14 x	–	–	3	10	8,200
Botswana	72	–	–	50	–	94 x	73 x	–	99 x	–	100	–	–	–	81	144	220
Brazil	79	89 x	–	59	–	97	91	–	99	–	99	56	–	–	1,700	60	940
British Virgin Islands	–	–	–	27 x	–	–	–	–	–	–	–	–	–	–	–	–	–
Brunei Darussalam	77	–	–	11	–	99 x	93 x	–	100	–	100 x	–	–	–	2	31	1,700
Bulgaria	79	–	–	38	5	–	–	–	100	–	94	36	–	–	6	10	7,000
Burkina Faso	62	56	51	132	28 x	93	47	32 x	80	75 x	82	4	33	74	2,400	320	57
Burundi	63	38	55	58	13	99	49	52	85	91	84	4 x	8 x	51	2,400	548	33
Cabo Verde	76	73 x	68 x	80 x	22 x	98 x	72 x	–	92	–	76 x	11 x	–	–	6	58	670
Cambodia	72	57	46	57	7	95	76	71	89	91	83	6	79	90	590	160	220
Cameroon	60	47	39	119	28	83	59	51	65	66	61	2	69	65	4,700	529	40
Canada	84	–	–	8	–	100 x	99 x	–	100 x	–	98 x	26 x	–	–	40	10	6,100
Central African Republic	55	29 x	–	229 x	45 x	68 x	38 x	32 x	40 x	46 x	53 x	5 x	–	–	1,400	829	25
Chad	55	20	9	179	51	55	31	33	20	27	22	1	5	16	7,300	1,140	15
Chile	82	–	–	33	–	–	–	–	100	–	100	50 x	–	–	29	13	4,600
China	79	97 x	–	9	–	100	81	–	100	–	100	41	63	64	4,900	29	2,100
Colombia	80	87	72	75	20	97	90	86	99	96	99	46	7 x	1	610	83	630
Comoros	66	29 x	20 x	70 x	17 x	92 x	49 x	38 x	82 x	82 x	76 x	10 x	14 x	49 x	72	273	83
Congo	66	43	28	111	26	94	79	77	94	92	92	5	86	80	650	378	58
Cook Islands	–	–	–	67	–	100 x	–	–	100 x	–	100 x	–	–	–	–	–	–
Costa Rica	83	89 x	–	53	13	98 x	90 x	88 x	99	98 x	99	22	–	–	19	27	1,900
Côte d'Ivoire	59	39	–	123	25	93	51	47	74	76	70	3	83	80	5,400	617	34
Croatia	81	–	–	10	–	–	98	–	100	–	–	24	–	–	3	8	9,100
Cuba	81	89	73	52	6	99	98	99	99	97	100	40	98	99	42	36	1,800
Cyprus	83	–	–	4	–	99 x	–	–	–	–	97	–	–	–	1	6	11,000
Czechia	82	86 x	–	12	–	–	–	–	100 x	–	100	20 x	–	–	4	3	17,900
Democratic People's Republic of Korea	76	90	–	1	–	100	94	–	100	–	92	13	99	98	310	89	620
Democratic Republic of the Congo	62	19	12	138 x	27	88	48	50	80	81	80	5	8	44	16,000	473	34
Denmark	83	–	–	3	–	–	–	–	–	–	–	21 x	–	–	2	4	16,200
Djibouti	69	–	–	21 x	–	88 x	23 x	–	87 x	–	87 x	11 x	–	–	51	248	140
Dominica	–	–	–	48 x	–	100 x	–	–	100	–	–	–	–	–	–	–	–
Dominican Republic	77	82	67	90	21	98	93	90	98	99	98	58	95	95	200	95	410
Ecuador	80	79 x	–	111 x	–	84 x	58 x	–	96	–	93	46	–	–	200	59	640
Egypt	74	80	64	56	7	90	83	88	92	93	87	52	14	82	960	37	730
El Salvador	78	80	70	69 x	18	96	90	90	98	99	98	32	97	94	54	46	960
Equatorial Guinea	60	21 x	20 x	176 x	42 x	91 x	67 x	–	68 x	–	67 x	7 x	–	–	130	301	67
Eritrea	68	21 x	6 x	76 x	19 x	89 x	57 x	–	34 x	–	34 x	3 x	–	5 x	510	480	46
Estonia	83	–	–	11	–	–	97	–	100 x	–	99	–	–	–	1	9	6,900
Eswatini	64	83	–	87	17	99	76	68	88	89	88	12	90	88	130	437	72
Ethiopia	68	62	–	80	21	62	32	30	28	39	26	2	0 x	17	14,000	401	55

TABLE 3. MATERNAL AND NEWBORN HEALTH

Countries and areas	Life expectancy: female 2018	Demand for family planning satisfied with modern methods (%) 2013–2018* Women aged 15–49	Women aged 15–19	Adolescent birth rate 2013–2018*	Births by age 18 (%) 2013–2018*	Antenatal care (%) 2013–2018* At least one visit	At least four visits Women aged 15–49	Women aged 15–19	Delivery care (%) 2013–2018* Skilled birth attendant Women aged 15–49	Women aged 15–19	Institutional delivery	C-section	Postnatal health check(%)+ 2013–2018* For newborns	For mothers	Maternal mortality† 2017 Number of maternal deaths	Maternal mortality ratio	Lifetime risk of maternal death (1 in X)
Fiji	69	–	–	40	–	100 x	94	–	100	–	99	–	–	–	6	34	1,000
Finland	85	–	–	6	–	100 x	–	–	–	–	100	16 x	–	–	2	3	20,900
France	85	96 x	–	5	–	100 x	99 x	–	–	–	–	–	–	–	56	8	7,200
Gabon	68	44 x	23 x	91 x	28 x	95 x	78 x	76 x	89 x	91 x	90 x	10 x	25 x	60 x	170	252	93
Gambia	63	27	11	86 x	19	98 x	88	74	57	64	63	2	6	76	520	597	31
Georgia	78	53 x	–	44	6 x	100 x	99	–	100	–	100	41	–	–	14	25	1,900
Germany	84	–	–	9	–	100 x	99	–	–	–	99	29 x	–	–	53	7	9,400
Ghana	65	46	–	75	17	91	87	81	71	76	73	13	23	81	2,700	308	82
Greece	85	–	–	9	–	–	–	–	–	–	–	–	–	–	2	3	26,900
Grenada	75	–	–	36	–	100 x	–	–	99	–	–	–	–	–	0	25	1,700
Guatemala	77	66	50	92	20	91	86	85	66	70	65	26	8	78	400	95	330
Guinea	62	22	14	120	37	81	35	48	55	60	53	3	64	49	2,600	576	35
Guinea-Bissau	60	56	20	106 x	28	92	65	65	45	55	44	4	55	48	440	667	32
Guyana	73	52	17	74	16	91	87	86	86	94	93	17	95	93	26	169	220
Haiti	66	43	31	55	14	91	67	55	42	37	39	5	38	31	1,300	480	67
Holy See	–	–	–	–	–	–	–	–	–	–	–	–	–	–	–	–	–
Honduras	77	76 x	67 x	103	22 x	97 x	89 x	87 x	83 x	87 x	83 x	19 x	81 x	85 x	130	65	560
Hungary	80	–	–	25	–	–	–	–	99 x	–	–	31 x	–	–	11	12	6,200
Iceland	84	–	–	7	–	–	–	–	–	–	–	17 x	–	–	0	4	14,400
India	71	67	27	11	9	79	51	53	81	86	79	17	27	65	35,000	145	290
Indonesia	74	78	72	48 x	7	98	77	65	94	87	74	17	79	87	8,600	177	240
Iran (Islamic Republic of)	78	69 x	–	36	5 x	97 x	94 x	–	96 x	–	95 x	46 x	–	–	250	16	2,600
Iraq	72	55	–	82 x	14	88	68	76	96	97	87	33	78	83	870	79	320
Ireland	84	–	–	7	–	100 x	–	–	100 x	–	100	25 x	–	–	3	5	11,300
Israel	84	–	–	9	–	–	–	–	–	–	–	–	–	–	5	3	10,800
Italy	85	–	–	5	–	99 x	68 x	–	–	–	100	40 x	–	–	7	2	51,300
Jamaica	76	79 x	–	46 x	15 x	98 x	86 x	85 x	99 x	97 x	99 x	21 x	–	–	38	80	600
Japan	88	–	–	4	–	–	–	–	–	–	100	–	–	–	44	5	16,700
Jordan	76	57	31	27	5	98	92	93	100	100	98	26	86	83	100	46	730
Kazakhstan	77	79	–	25	2	99	95	98	99	99	99	15	99	98	37	10	3,500
Kenya	69	76	68	96	23	94	58	49	62	65	61	9	36	53	5,000	342	76
Kiribati	72	36 x	0 x	49 x	9 x	88 x	71 x	–	98 x	–	66 x	10 x	–	–	3	92	290
Kuwait	76	–	–	6	–	100 x	–	–	99 x	–	99	–	–	–	7	12	4,200
Kyrgyzstan	75	66	41	34	4	98	95	93	98	98	98	7	99	98	95	60	480
Lao People's Democratic Republic	69	72	48 x	83	18	78	62	52	64	56	65	6	47	47	310	185	180
Latvia	80	–	–	15	–	92 x	–	–	100 x	–	98	–	–	–	4	19	3,100
Lebanon	81	–	–	17 x	–	96 x	–	–	98 x	–	100 x	–	–	–	34	29	1,600
Lesotho	57	79	55	94	14	95	74	70	78	85	77	10	18	62	310	544	58
Liberia	65	41	22	150	37	96	78	78	61	67	56	4	35	77	1,000	661	32
Libya	76	24	–	11	–	93 x	–	–	–	–	100	–	–	–	92	72	590
Liechtenstein	–	–	–	4	–	–	–	–	–	–	–	–	–	–	2	8	7,500
Lithuania	81	–	–	13	–	100 x	–	–	100 x	–	–	–	–	–	0	5	14,300
Luxembourg	84	–	–	5	–	–	97 x	–	100 x	–	100 x	29 x	–	–	0	5	14,300
Madagascar	68	61	–	152	36	82	51	47 x	44	40 x	38	2	–	–	2,800	335	66
Malawi	67	74	62	138	31	98	51	46	90	92	91	6	60	42	2,100	349	60
Malaysia	78	–	–	10	–	97	–	–	99	–	99	–	–	–	150	29	1,600
Maldives	80	43 x	18 x	10	1	99	82	87	100	100	95	40	82	80	4	53	840
Mali	60	35	21	174	33	80	43	38	67	42	67	2	63	58	4,400	562	29
Malta	84	–	–	13	–	100 x	–	–	–	–	100	–	–	–	0	6	10,200
Marshall Islands	–	81 x	40 x	85 x	21 x	81 x	77 x	–	90 x	–	85 x	9 x	–	–	–	–	28
Mauritania	66	30	–	84	22	87	63	56	69	67	69	5	58	57	1,100	766	28
Mauritius	78	41	–	24	–	–	–	–	100	–	98 x	–	95	–	8	61	1,200
Mexico	78	80	64	71	21	99	94	93	98	98	97	41	95	95	740	33	1,300
Micronesia (Federated States of)	69	–	–	44 x	–	80 x	–	–	100 x	–	87 x	11 x	–	–	2	88	370
Monaco	–	–	–	–	–	–	–	–	–	–	–	–	–	–	–	–	–
Mongolia	74	65	42	30	3	99	90	81	100	97	98	23	99	95	35	45	710
Montenegro	79	43	–	10	3	92	87	–	–	–	99	20	99	95	0	6	9,900
Montserrat	–	–	–	54 x	–	–	–	–	–	–	–	–	–	–	–	–	–
Morocco	78	69	–	32 x	8 x	89	54	30 x	87	70 x	86	21	–	–	480	70	560
Mozambique	63	56	34	194	40 x	87	52	55	65	68	55 x	4 x	28	–	3,100	289	67
Myanmar	70	75	73	36	5	81	59	47	60	61	37	17	36	71	2,400	250	190
Namibia	66	80	47	64	15	97	63	58	88	88	87	14	20	69	140	195	140
Nauru	–	43 x	–	94	22 x	95 x	40 x	–	97 x	–	99 x	8 x	–	–	–	–	–

TABLE 3. MATERNAL AND NEWBORN HEALTH

Countries and areas	Life expectancy: female 2018	Demand for family planning satisfied with modern methods (%) 2013–2018*		Adolescent birth rate 2013–2018*	Births by age 18 (%) 2013–2018*	Antenatal care (%) 2013–2018*			Delivery care (%) 2013–2018*				Postnatal health check(%)† 2013–2018*		Maternal mortality† 2017		
		Women aged 15–49	Women aged 15–19			At least one visit	At least four visits		Skilled birth attendant		Institutional delivery	C-section	For newborns	For mothers	Number of maternal deaths	Maternal mortality ratio	Lifetime risk of maternal death (1 in X)
							Women aged 15–49	Women aged 15–19	Women aged 15–49	Women aged 15–19							
Nepal	72	56	25	88	16	84	69	72	58	69	57	9	58	57	1,100	186	230
Netherlands	84	–	–	3	–	–	–	–	–	–	–	14 x	–	–	9	5	11,900
New Zealand	84	–	–	15	–	–	–	–	–	–	97	23 x	–	–	5	9	6,100
Nicaragua	78	93 x	87 x	92 x	28 x	95 x	88 x	–	88 x	–	71	30 x	–	–	130	98	380
Niger	63	46	28	146	48 x	83 x	38	32 x	40	36 x	59	1 x	13 x	37 x	5,100	509	27
Nigeria	55	43	15	120	31	67	57	47	43	32	39	3	12	42	67,000	917	21
Niue	–	–	–	20 x	–	100 x	–	–	100 x	–	–	–	–	–	–	–	–
North Macedonia	78	22 x	–	16	2 x	99 x	94 x	–	100	–	100	25 x	–	–	2	7	9,000
Norway	84	–	–	4	–	–	–	–	–	–	99	16 x	–	–	1	2	25,700
Oman	80	40	–	14	2	99	94	–	99	–	99	19	98	95	17	19	1,600
Pakistan	68	49	23	46	7	86	51	44	69	70	66	22	64	62	8,300	140	180
Palau	–	–	–	27	–	90 x	81 x	–	100	–	100 x	–	–	–	–	–	–
Panama	82	73	37	79	–	93	88	84	94	89	91	28	93	92	41	52	750
Papua New Guinea	66	41 x	–	65 x	14 x	76	49	–	53 x	–	55	–	–	46	340	145	190
Paraguay	76	79	83	72	–	99	94	92	96	97	93	46	8	94	180	129	290
Peru	79	67	65	44	16	97	96	93	92	90	91	32	96	61	500	88	480
Philippines	75	53	47	47	11	94	87	80	84	86	78	13	86	86	2,700	121	300
Poland	82	–	–	12	–	–	–	–	100 x	–	100	21 x	–	–	8	2	30,300
Portugal	85	–	–	8	–	100 x	–	–	100 x	–	99	31 x	–	–	6	8	10,700
Qatar	82	69 x	–	10	–	91 x	85 x	–	100	–	99 x	20 x	–	–	2	9	5,000
Republic of Korea	86	–	–	1	–	–	97 x	–	–	–	100	32 x	–	–	43	11	8,300
Republic of Moldova	76	60 x	–	24	4 x	99 x	95 x	–	100	–	99 x	16 x	–	–	8	19	3,900
Romania	79	47 x	–	37	–	76	76 x	–	95	–	95	34	–	–	36	19	3,600
Russian Federation	78	72 x	–	24	–	–	–	–	100 x	–	99 x	13 x	–	–	320	17	3,100
Rwanda	71	63	84	41	6	98	44	39	91	94	91	13	19	43	960	248	94
Saint Kitts and Nevis	–	–	–	46 x	–	100 x	–	–	100	–	–	–	–	–	–	–	–
Saint Lucia	77	72 x	–	43 x	–	97 x	90 x	–	99 x	–	100 x	19 x	100 x	90 x	3	117	580
Saint Vincent and the Grenadines	75	–	–	64	–	100 x	100 x	–	99	–	–	–	–	–	1	68	750
Samoa	75	39	11	39 x	6	93	73	–	83	–	82	5	–	63	2	43	590
San Marino	–	–	–	0 x	–	–	–	–	–	–	–	–	–	–	–	–	–
Sao Tome and Principe	73	52	38	92	27	98	84	81	93	94	91	6	91	87	9	130	170
Saudi Arabia	77	–	–	7 x	–	97 x	–	–	98	–	–	–	–	–	100	17	2,300
Senegal	70	51	25	78	16	97	57	53	68	69	78	5	78	77	1,700	315	65
Serbia	78	39	–	15	1	98	94	95	98	98	98	29	–	–	10	12	5,800
Seychelles	77	–	–	66	–	–	–	–	99 x	–	–	–	–	–	1	53	790
Sierra Leone	55	45	32	101	30	97	78	77	82	82	77	3	92	90	2,900	1,120	20
Singapore	86	–	–	3	–	–	–	–	–	–	100	–	–	–	4	8	9,900
Slovakia	81	–	–	26	–	97 x	–	–	99 x	–	–	24 x	–	–	3	5	12,600
Slovenia	84	–	–	4	–	100 x	–	–	100 x	–	100 x	–	–	–	1	7	9,300
Solomon Islands	75	38	13	78	15	89	69	–	86	–	85	6	16	69	22	104	200
Somalia	59	–	–	123 x	–	26 x	6 x	–	9 x	–	9 x	–	–	–	5,100	829	20
South Africa	67	78	–	71	15 x	94	76	77	97	97	96	26	–	84	1,400	119	330
South Sudan	59	6 x	–	158 x	28 x	62	17 x	21 x	19 x	25 x	12 x	1 x	–	–	4,500	1,150	18
Spain	86	–	–	8	–	–	–	–	–	–	–	26 x	–	–	14	4	21,500
Sri Lanka	80	74	58	21	4 x	99	93 x	–	100	–	100	32	–	99	120	36	1,300
State of Palestine	76	65	35	48	22	99	96	96	100	100	99	20	94	91	39	27	880
Sudan	67	30	19	87	22	79	51	49	78	77	28	9	28	27	3,900	295	75
Suriname	75	73 x	–	60	–	91 x	67 x	68 x	90 x	93 x	92 x	19 x	–	–	13	120	330
Sweden	84	–	–	4	–	100 x	–	–	–	–	–	–	–	–	5	4	12,600
Switzerland	85	–	–	3	–	–	–	–	–	–	–	30 x	–	–	4	5	13,900
Syrian Arab Republic	78	53 x	31 x	54 x	9 x	88 x	64 x	–	96 x	–	78 x	26 x	–	–	130	31	1,000
Tajikistan	73	45	18	54	1	92	64	67	95	96	88	5	90	92	46	17	1,400
Thailand	81	89	83	43	9	98	91	89	99	99	99	33	–	–	270	37	1,900
Timor-Leste	71	37	22	42	7	84	77	74	56	58	49	4	31	35	52	142	170
Togo	62	37	15	89	8	52	57	52	45	58	73	7	35	71	1,000	396	56
Tokelau	–	–	–	30 x	–	–	–	–	–	–	–	–	–	–	–	–	–
Tonga	73	48 x	–	30 x	2 x	99 x	70 x	–	96 x	–	98 x	17 x	–	–	1	52	540
Trinidad and Tobago	76	58 x	61 x	38 x	–	95 x	100	–	100	–	98 x	22 x	–	92 x	12	67	840
Tunisia	79	73 x	–	7 x	1 x	98 x	85 x	–	74 x	–	99 x	27 x	98 x	92 x	90	43	970
Turkey	80	60	30	23	6	97	89	57 x	97	98	97	48	72	88	220	17	2,800
Turkmenistan	72	76	11	28	1	100	96	98	100	100	100	6	100	100	10	7	4,400
Turks and Caicos Islands	–	–	–	41 x													

TABLE 3. MATERNAL AND NEWBORN HEALTH

Countries and areas	Life expectancy: female 2018	Demand for family planning satisfied with modern methods (%) 2013–2018* Women aged 15–49	Women aged 15–19	Adolescent birth rate 2013–2018*	Births by age 18 (%) 2013–2018*	Antenatal care (%) 2013–2018* At least one visit	At least four visits Women aged 15–49	Women aged 15–19	Delivery care (%) 2013–2018* Skilled birth attendant Women aged 15–49	Women aged 15–19	Institutional delivery	C-section	Postnatal health check(%)+ 2013–2018* For newborns	For mothers	Maternal mortality† 2017 Number of maternal deaths	Maternal mortality ratio	Lifetime risk of maternal death (1 in X)
Tuvalu	–	41 x	–	28 x	3 x	97 x	67 x	–	93 x	–	93 x	7 x	–	–	–	–	–
Uganda	65	54	–	132	28	97	60	59	74	80	73	5 x	11 x	54	6,000	375	49
Ukraine	77	68 x	–	23	4 x	99 x	87 x	87 x	99 x	99 x	99 x	12 x	99 x	96 x	83	19	3,700
United Arab Emirates	79	–	–	5	–	100 x	–	–	100 x	–	100 x	–	–	–	3	3	17,900
United Kingdom	83	–	–	14	–	–	–	–	–	–	–	26 x	–	–	52	7	8,400
United Republic of Tanzania	67	54	35	139	22	98	62	48	64	70	63	6	42	34	11,000	524	36
United States	81	77	–	19	–	–	97 x	–	–	–	99	31 x	–	–	720	19	3,000
Uruguay	81	–	–	36	–	97	77	44 x	100	100 x	100	30	–	–	8	17	2,900
Uzbekistan	74	–	–	30 x	2 x	99	–	–	100	–	100	14	–	–	200	29	1,200
Vanuatu	72	51	–	78 x	13	76	52	–	89	–	89	12	–	–	6	72	330
Venezuela (Bolivarian Republic of)	76	–	–	95 x	24	98	84	–	100	–	99	52	–	–	670	125	330
Viet Nam	79	70	60	30	5	96	74	55	94	87	94	28	89	90	700	43	1,100
Yemen	68	38	22	67 x	17	60	25	30	45	52	30	5	11	20	1,400	164	150
Zambia	66	62	57	141 x	31	96	56	52	63	73	67	4	16	63	1,300	213	93
Zimbabwe	63	85	77	78	22	93	76	73	78	81	77	6	73	57	2,100	458	55

SUMMARY

	Life expectancy: female 2018	Women aged 15–49	Women aged 15–19	Adolescent birth rate 2013–2018*	Births by age 18 (%) 2013–2018*	At least one visit	At least four visits Women aged 15–49	Women aged 15–19	Skilled birth attendant Women aged 15–49	Women aged 15–19	Institutional delivery	C-section	For newborns	For mothers	Number of maternal deaths	Maternal mortality ratio	Lifetime risk of maternal death (1 in X)
East Asia and Pacific	79	86	–	21	–	97	80	–	96	–	91	32	69	72	21,000	69	790
Europe and Central Asia	81	77	–	17	–	–	–	–	99	–	98	–	–	–	1,400	13	4,300
Eastern Europe and Central Asia	78	69	–	26	–	96	–	–	99	–	97	28	–	–	1,200	19	2,600
Western Europe	84	83	–	8	–	–	–	–	99	–	99	–	–	–	260	5	11,900
Latin America and Caribbean	79	83	–	63	–	97	91	–	94	–	94	44	–	–	7,800	74	630
Middle East and North Africa	76	68	–	40	9	87	68	–	89	–	82	32	–	–	5,800	57	570
North America	82	83	–	19	–	–	–	–	99	–	–	–	–	–	760	18	3,100
South Asia	71	67	–	26	12	79	49	49	77	78	72	18	34	62	57,000	163	240
Sub-Saharan Africa	63	53	–	103	26	81	53	50	59	61	57	5	30	46	200,000	533	38
Eastern and Southern Africa	66	62	–	92	25	85	53	49	62	67	56	7	34	40	70,000	384	58
West and Central Africa	59	41	–	115	28	78	54	51	57	54	58	4	28	52	131,000	674	28
Least developed countries	72	58	–	91	25	80	47	44	61	60	54	7	31	42	130,000	415	56
World	**75**	**76**	**–**	**44**	**15**	**86**	**65**	**56**	**81**	**76**	**76**	**21**	**45**	**61**	**295,000**	**211**	**190**

For a complete list of countries and areas in the regions, subregions and country categories, see page 182 or visit <data.unicef.org/regionalclassifications>.

It is not advisable to compare data from consecutive editions of *The State of the World's Children.*

DEFINITIONS OF THE INDICATORS

Life expectancy at birth – Number of years newborn female children would live if subject to the mortality risks prevailing for the cross section of population at the time of their birth.

Demand for family planning satisfied with modern methods – Percentage of women (15–19 and 15–49) who have their need for family planning satisfied with modern methods.

Adolescent birth rate – Number of births per 1,000 adolescent girls aged 15–19.

Births by age 18 – Percentage of women aged 20-24 who gave birth before age 18. The indicator refers to women who had a live birth in a recent time period, generally two years for MICS and five years for DHS.

Antenatal care (at least one visit) – Percentage of women (aged 15–49) attended at least once during pregnancy by skilled health personnel (typically a doctor, nurse or midwife).

Antenatal care (at least four visits) – Percentage of women (aged 15-19 and 15-49) attended by any provider at least four times.

Skilled birth attendant – Percentage of births from mothers aged 15-19 and 15-49, attended by skilled heath personnel (typically a doctor, nurse or midwife).

Institutional delivery – Percentage of women (aged 15–49) who gave birth in a health facility.

C-section – Percentage of births delivered by Caesarean section. NB: C-section rates between 5 per cent and 15 per cent are expected with adequate levels of emergency obstetric care.

Postnatal health check for newborn – Percentage of last live births in the last 2 years who received a health check within 2 days after delivery. NB: For MICS, health check refers to a health check while in facility or at home following delivery or a postnatal visit.

Postnatal health check for mother – Percentage of women (aged 15–49) who received a health check within 2 days after delivery of their most recent live birth in the last 2 years. NB: For MICS, health check refers to a health check while in facility or at home following delivery or a postnatal visit.

Number of maternal deaths – Number of deaths of women from pregnancy-related causes.

Maternal mortality ratio – Number of deaths of women from pregnancy-related causes per 100,000 live births during the same time period.

Lifetime risk of maternal death – Lifetime risk of maternal death takes into account both the probability of becoming pregnant and the probability of dying as a result of that pregnancy, accumulated across a woman's reproductive years.

MAIN DATA SOURCES

Life expectancy – United Nations Population Division, World Population Prospects 2019. Last update: July 2019.

Demand for family planning satisfied with modern methods – United Nations, Department of Economic and Social Affairs, Population Division, United Nations Population Fund (UNFPA), based on Demographic and Health Surveys (DHS), Multiple Indicator Cluster Surveys (MICS), Reproductive Health Surveys, other national surveys, and National Health Information Systems (HIS). Last Update: March 2019.

Demand for family planning satisfied with modern methods (women 15–19) – United Nations, Department of Economic and Social Affairs, Population Division, based on Demographic and Health Surveys (DHS), Multiple Indicator Cluster Surveys (MICS), Reproductive Health Surveys, other national surveys, and National Health Information Systems (HIS). Last Update: February 2019.

Adolescent birth rate – United Nations Population Division, 2019. Last update: July 2019.

Births by age 18 – DHS, MICS and other national household surveys. Last update: May 2019.

Antenatal care (at least one visit) – DHS, MICS and other national household surveys. Last update: May 2019.

Antenatal care, at least four visits (women 15-19) – International Center for Equity in Health, Federal University of Pelotas, Brazil, based on Demographic and Health Surveys (DHS), Multiple Indicator Cluster Surveys (MICS) and other national surveys. Last update: August 2019.

Skilled birth attendant – Joint UNICEF/WHO SBA database, based on DHS, MICS and other national household surveys as well as national administrative data. Last update: February 2019.

Skilled birth attendant (women 15-19) – International Center for Equity in Health, Federal University of Pelotas, Brazil, based on Demographic and Health Surveys (DHS), Multiple Indicator Cluster Surveys (MICS) and other national surveys. Last update: August 2019.

Institutional delivery – DHS, MICS and other national household surveys. Last update: May 2019.

C-section – DHS, MICS and other national household surveys. Last update: May 2019.

Postnatal health check for newborn and mother – DHS, MICS and other national household surveys. Last update: May 2019.

Number of maternal deaths – United Nations Maternal Mortality Estimation Inter-agency Group (WHO, UNICEF, UNFPA, the World Bank and the United Nations Population Division). Last Update: September 2019.

Maternal mortality ratio – United Nations Maternal Mortality Estimation Inter-agency Group (WHO, UNICEF, UNFPA, The World Bank and the United Nations Population Division). Last update: September 2019.

Lifetime risk of maternal death – United Nations Maternal Mortality Estimation Inter-agency Group (WHO, UNICEF, UNFPA, the World Bank and the United Nations Population Division). Last Update: September 2019.

Country data on SDG indicators included in this table (demand for family planning satisfied with modern methods, adolescent birth rate, skilled birth attendant and maternal mortality ratio) refer to the most recent year available as reported in the SDG global database 2019 version.

NOTES

– Data not available.

x Data refer to years or periods other than those specified in the column heading. Such data are not included in the calculation of regional and global averages. Estimates from data years prior to 2000 are not displayed.

+ Data collection method for this indicator varies across surveys and may affect comparability of the coverage estimates. For detailed explanation see General Note on the Data, page 180.

† Maternal mortality estimates are from the 2019 United Nations inter-agency maternal mortality estimates. Periodically, the United Nations Maternal Mortality Estimation Inter-agency Group (WHO, UNICEF, UNFPA, the World Bank and the United Nations Population Division) produces internationally comparable sets of maternal mortality data that account for the well-documented problems of under-reporting and misclassification of maternal deaths, including also estimates for countries with no data. Please note that owing to an evolving methodology, these values are not comparable with previously reported maternal mortality ratio 'adjusted' values.

* Data refer to the most recent year available during the period specified in the column heading.

TABLE 4. CHILD HEALTH

Countries and areas	Intervention coverage																
	Immunization for vaccine preventable diseases (%) 2018[β]										Pneumonia 2013–2018*	Diarrhoea 2013–2018*	Malaria 2013–2018*		
	BCG	DTP1	DTP3	Polio3	MCV1	MCV2'	HepB3	Hib3	Rota	PCV3	Protection at birth (PAB) against tetanus[Λ]	Care seeking for children with symptoms of Acute Respiratory Infection (ARI)(%)	Treatment with oral rehydration salts (ORS)(%)	Care seeking for children with fever (%)	Children sleeping under ITNs (%)	Households with at least one ITN (%)
Afghanistan	78	73	66	73	64	39	66	66	60	65	68	62	46	63	5	26
Albania	99	99	99	99	94	96	99	99	–	98	95	82	35	60	–	–
Algeria	99	96	91	91	80	77	91	91	–	91	98	66	25	–	–	–
Andorra	–	99	99	99	99	95	98	99	–	94	–	–	–	–	–	–
Angola	86	67	59	56	50	35	59	59	65	67	78	49	43	51	22	31
Anguilla	–	–	–	–	–	–	–	–	–	–	–	–	–	–	–	–
Antigua and Barbuda	–	99	95	94	96	95	95	95	–	–	–	–	–	–	–	–
Argentina	93	91	86	84	94	89	86	86	80	88	–	94 x	18 x	–	–	–
Armenia	99	96	92	92	95	96	92	92	93	92	–	57 x	37	71	–	–
Australia	–	98	95	95	95	93	95	94	87	95	–	–	–	–	–	–
Austria	–	90	85	85	94	84	85	85	61	–	–	–	–	–	–	–
Azerbaijan	97	96	95	96	96	96	95	95	–	95	–	36 x	11 x	–	1 x	–
Bahamas	–	94	90	90	89	69	90	90	70	90	100	–	–	–	–	–
Bahrain	–	99	99	99	99	99	99	99	98	98	98	–	–	–	–	–
Bangladesh	99	99	98	98	97	93	98	98	–	97	98	42	77	55	–	–
Barbados	–	96	95	94	85	74	95	95	–	89	–	–	–	–	–	–
Belarus	98	97	97	98	97	98	98	9	–	–	–	93 x	45 x	–	–	–
Belgium	–	99	98	98	96	85	97	97	87	94	–	–	–	–	–	–
Belize	99	97	96	96	97	91	96	96	–	–	91	67	55	71	–	–
Benin	89	84	76	75	71	–	76	76	–	73	85	46	22	53	70	85
Bhutan	99	98	97	97	97	91	97	97	–	–	89	74 x	61 x	–	–	–
Bolivia (Plurinational State of)	90	89	83	83	89	38	83	83	87	83	87	62 x	22 x	–	–	–
Bosnia and Herzegovina	95	89	73	73	68	76	80	62	–	–	–	87 x	36 x	–	–	–
Botswana	98	98	95	96	97	74	95	95	87	91	93	14 x	43 x	75 x	31 x	53 x
Brazil	90	87	83	85	84	69	83	83	80	84	94	50 x	–	–	–	–
British Virgin Islands	–	–	–	–	–	–	–	–	–	–	–	–	–	–	–	–
Brunei Darussalam	99	99	99	99	99	98	99	99	–	–	96	–	–	–	–	–
Bulgaria	96	94	92	92	93	87	85	92	31	88	–	–	–	–	–	–
Burkina Faso	98	95	91	91	88	71	91	91	91	91	92	52	40	74	54	75
Burundi	91	94	90	90	88	77	90	90	92	90	90	63	36	70	40	46
Cabo Verde	96	99	98	98	99	88	99	99	–	–	92	–	–	–	–	–
Cambodia	93	94	92	90	84	70	92	92	–	84	93	69	35	61	4 x	5 x
Cameroon	88	86	79	78	71	–	79	79	78	79	85	28	16	33	55	71
Canada	–	95	91	91	90	87	71	91	79	81	–	–	–	–	–	–
Central African Republic	74	69	47	47	49	–	47	47	–	47	60	30 x	16 x	–	36 x	47 x
Chad	59	55	41	44	37	–	41	41	–	–	78	26	20	23	36	77
Chile	96	99	95	95	93	93	95	95	–	93	–	–	–	–	–	–
China	99	99	99	99	99	99	99	–	–	–	–	–	–	–	–	–
Colombia	89	92	92	92	95	88	92	92	90	94	95	64 x	54 x	54 x	–	3 x
Comoros	94	96	91	94	90	–	91	91	–	–	85	38 x	38 x	45 x	41 x	59 x
Congo	81	79	75	75	75	–	75	75	72	73	85	28	27	51	61	66
Cook Islands	99	99	99	99	99	99	99	99	–	–	–	–	–	–	–	–
Costa Rica	92	95	94	94	94	93	98	94	–	96	–	77 x	40 x	–	–	–
Côte d'Ivoire	98	95	82	82	71	–	82	82	59	81	85	44	17	45	60	76
Croatia	98	98	93	94	93	95	93	94	–	–	–	–	–	–	–	–
Cuba	99	99	99	99	99	99	99	99	–	–	–	93	61	93	–	–
Cyprus	–	99	99	97	90	88	97	97	–	81	–	–	–	–	–	–
Czechia	–	98	96	94	96	84	94	94	–	–	–	–	–	–	–	–
Democratic People's Republic of Korea	96	99	97	99	98	99	97	97	–	–	98	86	74	–	–	–
Democratic Republic of the Congo	83	82	81	79	80	–	81	81	–	81	85	42	39	55	56	70
Denmark	–	97	97	97	95	90	–	97	–	96	–	–	–	–	–	–
Djibouti	93	91	84	84	86	81	84	84	87	84	98	94 x	94 x	–	20 x	32 x
Dominica	95	99	94	94	84	81	94	94	–	–	–	–	–	–	–	–
Dominican Republic	99	99	94	89	95	31	92	90	82	70	99	73	48	65	–	–
Ecuador	90	86	85	85	83	74	85	85	85	85	88	–	46 x	–	–	–
Egypt	95	96	95	95	94	94	95	95	–	–	86	68	28	68	–	–
El Salvador	81	82	81	83	81	85	81	81	82	75	92	80	70	–	–	–
Equatorial Guinea	63	44	25	27	30	–	25	25	–	–	70	54 x	40 x	62 x	23 x	38 x
Eritrea	97	97	95	95	99	–	95	95	96	95	99	45 x	43 x	–	20 x	71 x
Estonia	92	93	92	92	87	88	93	92	85	–	–	–	–	–	–	–
Eswatini	98	96	90	90	89	75	90	90	90	88	88	60	84	63	2 x	10 x
Ethiopia	85	85	72	67	61	–	72	72	79	67	93	31	30	35	45	64

TABLE 4. CHILD HEALTH

Countries and areas	Immunization for vaccine preventable diseases (%) 2018[β]										Protection at birth (PAB) against tetanus[λ]	Pneumonia 2013–2018* Care seeking for children with symptoms of Acute Respiratory Infection (ARI)(%)	Diarrhoea 2013–2018* Treatment with oral rehydration salts (ORS) (%)	Malaria 2013–2018*		
	BCG	DTP1	DTP3	Polio3	MCV1	MCV2[¹]	HepB3	Hib3	Rota	PCV3				Care seeking for children with fever (%)	Children sleeping under ITNs (%)	Households with at least one ITN (%)
Fiji	99	99	99	99	94	94	99	99	99	99	96	–	–	–	–	–
Finland	–	99	91	91	96	93	–	91	82	88	–	–	–	–	–	–
France	–	99	96	96	90	80	90	95	–	92	–	–	–	–	–	–
Gabon	87	78	70	64	59	–	70	70	–	–	85	68 x	26 x	67 x	39 x	36 x
Gambia	94	94	93	93	91	71	93	93	93	93	92	68	59	83	62	79
Georgia	97	99	93	93	98	96	93	93	79	81	–	74 x	40 x	–	–	–
Germany	–	98	93	93	97	93	87	92	68	84	–	–	–	–	–	–
Ghana	98	97	97	98	92	83	97	97	94	96	89	56	49	77	52	68
Greece	–	99	99	99	97	83	96	99	20	96	–	–	–	–	–	–
Grenada	–	98	96	96	84	74	96	96	–	–	–	–	–	–	–	–
Guatemala	88	94	86	85	87	76	86	86	87	85	90	52	49	50	–	–
Guinea	72	63	45	45	48	–	45	45	–	–	80	83	55	62	27	44
Guinea-Bissau	91	89	88	89	86	–	88	88	88	88	83	34	35	51	81	90
Guyana	99	99	95	94	98	84	95	95	91	91	99	84	43	71	7	5
Haiti	83	84	64	64	69	38	64	64	58	1	81	37	39	40	18	31
Holy See	–	–	–	–	–	–	–	–	–	–	–	–	–	–	–	–
Honduras	94	94	90	90	89	94	90	90	91	90	99	64 x	60 x	62 x	–	–
Hungary	99	99	99	99	99	99	–	99	–	99	–	–	–	–	–	–
Iceland	–	97	91	91	93	95	–	91	–	90	–	–	–	–	–	–
India	92	92	89	89	90	80	89	89	35	6	90	78	51	73	5	1
Indonesia	81	85	79	80	75	67	79	79	–	8	85	92	36	90	3 x	3 x
Iran (Islamic Republic of)	99	99	99	99	99	98	99	99	–	–	95	76 x	61 x	–	–	–
Iraq	95	92	84	71	83	81	84	84	60	32	75	44	25	75	–	–
Ireland	–	98	94	94	92	–	94	94	89	90	–	–	–	–	–	–
Israel	–	99	98	98	98	96	97	98	81	94	–	–	–	–	–	–
Italy	–	98	95	95	93	89	95	94	19	92	–	–	–	–	–	–
Jamaica	93	99	97	98	89	82	97	98	–	–	90	82 x	64 x	–	–	–
Japan	99	99	99	97	97	93	–	99	–	98	–	–	–	–	–	–
Jordan	94	98	96	92	92	96	96	96	93	–	90	72	44	68	–	–
Kazakhstan	95	99	98	98	99	98	98	98	–	95	–	81 x	62 x	–	–	–
Kenya	95	97	92	81	89	45	92	92	78	81	88	66	54	72	56	59
Kiribati	89	98	95	93	84	79	95	95	97	94	–	81 x	62 x	27 x	–	–
Kuwait	99	99	99	99	99	99	99	99	3	99	99	–	–	–	–	–
Kyrgyzstan	97	98	94	92	96	96	92	92	–	92	–	60	33	56	–	–
Lao People's Democratic Republic	79	73	68	67	69	57	68	68	–	56	90	40	56	58	50	61
Latvia	95	97	96	96	98	94	96	96	79	82	–	–	–	–	–	–
Lebanon	–	96	83	81	82	63	80	85	–	82	–	74 x	44 x	–	–	–
Lesotho	98	98	93	90	90	82	93	93	70	93	85	63	53	61	–	–
Liberia	92	99	84	84	91	–	84	84	74	84	89	51	60	78	44	62
Libya	99	98	97	97	97	96	97	97	97	96	–	–	–	–	–	–
Liechtenstein	–	–	–	–	–	–	–	–	–	–	–	–	–	–	–	–
Lithuania	96	95	92	92	92	92	93	92	1	82	–	–	–	–	–	–
Luxembourg	–	99	99	99	99	90	96	99	89	96	–	–	–	–	–	–
Madagascar	70	81	75	76	62	–	75	75	78	75	78	41	15	46	73	80
Malawi	92	96	92	91	87	72	92	92	90	92	89	78	65	54	68	82
Malaysia	98	99	99	99	96	99	99	99	–	–	92	–	–	–	–	–
Maldives	99	99	99	99	99	99	99	99	–	–	99	22 x	75	86	–	–
Mali	83	82	71	73	70	–	71	71	55	68	85	71	21	53	73	85
Malta	–	99	97	97	96	95	98	97	–	–	–	–	–	–	–	–
Marshall Islands	98	97	81	80	83	61	84	72	42	67	–	–	38 x	63 x	–	–
Mauritania	90	89	81	81	78	–	81	81	76	77	80	34	25	35	18	49
Mauritius	99	98	97	98	99	99	97	97	95	96	95	–	–	–	–	–
Mexico	96	90	88	88	97	99	55	88	77	88	96	73	61	–	–	–
Micronesia (Federated States of)	80	97	75	75	73	48	83	59	52	67	–	–	–	–	–	–
Monaco	89	99	99	99	87	79	99	99	–	–	–	–	–	–	–	–
Mongolia	99	99	99	99	99	98	99	99	–	26	–	70	42	–	–	–
Montenegro	83	95	87	87	58	83	73	87	–	–	–	89 x	16 x	74	–	–
Montserrat	–	–	–	–	–	–	–	–	–	–	–	–	–	–	–	–
Morocco	99	99	99	99	99	99	99	99	99	99	88	70 x	22 x	–	–	–
Mozambique	95	90	80	80	85	59	80	80	80	80	86	57	46	69	73	82
Myanmar	90	95	91	91	93	87	91	91	–	91	90	58	62	65	19	27
Namibia	94	94	89	84	82	50	89	89	92	61	88	68	72	63	6	24

TABLE 4. CHILD HEALTH

Countries and areas	\multicolumn{11}{c}{Intervention coverage}															
	\multicolumn{10}{c}{Immunization for vaccine preventable diseases (%) 2018β}										Pneumonia 2013–2018*		Diarrhoea 2013–2018*	\multicolumn{3}{c}{Malaria 2013–2018*}		
	BCG	DTP1	DTP3	Polio3	MCV1	MCV2¹	HepB3	Hib3	Rota	PCV3	Protection at birth (PAB) against tetanus▲	Care seeking for children with symptoms of Acute Respiratory Infection (ARI)(%)	Treatment with oral rehydration salts (ORS) (%)	Care seeking for children with fever (%)	Children sleeping under ITNs (%)	Households with at least one ITN (%)
Nauru	99	99	90	90	99	94	90	90	–	–	–	69 x	23 x	51 x	–	–
Nepal	96	96	91	91	91	69	91	91	–	82	89	85	37	80	–	–
Netherlands	–	97	93	93	93	89	92	93	–	93	–	–	–	–	–	–
New Zealand	–	95	93	93	92	90	93	92	86	96	–	–	–	–	–	–
Nicaragua	98	99	98	99	99	95	98	98	98	98	90	58 x	65 x	–	–	–
Niger	87	91	79	79	77	48	79	79	79	79	81	59	41	75	96	87
Nigeria	53	70	57	57	65	–	57	57	–	57	60	73	40	72	49	65
Niue	99	99	99	99	99	99	99	99	99	99	–	–	–	–	–	–
North Macedonia	97	97	91	91	83	97	91	91	–	–	–	93 x	62 x	–	–	–
Norway	–	99	96	96	96	93	–	96	93	94	–	–	–	–	–	–
Oman	99	99	99	99	99	99	99	99	–	99	99	56	59	–	–	–
Pakistan	86	83	75	75	76	67	75	75	58	79	85	84	37	81	0	4
Palau	–	99	95	98	90	75	98	92	93	89	–	–	–	–	–	–
Panama	99	96	88	88	98	99	88	88	95	92	–	82	52	–	–	–
Papua New Guinea	69	67	61	67	61	–	61	61	–	43	70	63	30	48	–	69
Paraguay	91	91	88	88	93	83	88	88	91	94	95	89	28	86	–	–
Peru	81	90	84	83	85	66	84	84	85	82	95	62	32	61	–	–
Philippines	75	66	65	66	67	40	65	65	–	43	90	67	45	55	–	–
Poland	92	98	95	87	93	92	91	95	–	60	–	–	–	–	–	–
Portugal	–	99	99	99	99	96	98	99	–	98	–	–	–	–	–	–
Qatar	99	99	98	98	99	95	98	98	95	98	–	–	–	–	–	–
Republic of Korea	98	98	98	98	98	97	98	98	–	97	–	–	–	–	–	–
Republic of Moldova	96	96	93	94	93	96	94	92	75	94	–	79 x	42 x	–	–	–
Romania	96	94	86	86	90	81	93	86	–	–	–	–	–	–	–	–
Russian Federation	95	97	97	96	98	97	97	–	–	82	–	–	–	–	–	–
Rwanda	97	98	97	97	99	96	97	97	98	97	95	54	28	56	68	84
Saint Kitts and Nevis	97	99	97	97	96	96	98	98	–	–	–	–	–	–	–	–
Saint Lucia	99	99	95	95	86	68	95	95	–	–	–	–	–	–	–	–
Saint Vincent and the Grenadines	99	99	97	99	99	99	97	97	–	–	–	–	–	–	–	–
Samoa	62	56	34	31	31	13	34	34	–	–	–	78	63	59	–	–
San Marino	–	94	90	93	89	84	78	91	–	58	–	–	–	–	–	–
Sao Tome and Principe	96	97	95	95	95	76	95	95	95	95	99	69	49	66	61	78
Saudi Arabia	98	96	96	98	98	97	97	96	97	98	–	–	–	–	–	–
Senegal	83	83	81	81	82	63	82	82	80	81	95	60	28	51	61	84
Serbia	98	98	96	96	92	90	91	96	–	48	–	90 x	36 x	–	–	–
Seychelles	97	99	99	99	96	97	99	99	99	16	100	–	–	–	–	–
Sierra Leone	90	98	90	90	80	55	90	90	92	90	90	74	78	70	60	71
Singapore	98	98	96	96	95	84	96	96	–	82	–	–	–	–	–	–
Slovakia	–	99	96	96	96	97	96	96	–	96	–	–	–	–	–	–
Slovenia	–	97	93	93	93	94	–	93	–	60	–	–	–	–	–	–
Solomon Islands	83	86	85	85	93	54	85	85	–	84	85	79	37	62	70	86
Somalia	37	52	42	47	46	–	42	42	–	–	67	13 x	13 x	–	11 x	12 x
South Africa	70	81	74	74	70	50	74	74	70	73	90	88	51	68	–	–
South Sudan	52	58	49	50	51	–	49	49	–	–	68	48 x	39 x	57	46	66
Spain	–	97	93	93	97	94	94	94	–	93	–	–	–	–	–	–
Sri Lanka	99	99	99	99	99	99	99	99	–	–	99	52	54	92	3 x	6
State of Palestine	99	99	99	99	99	99	99	99	99	96	–	77	32	–	–	–
Sudan	88	97	93	93	88	72	93	93	94	93	80	48	20	–	30 x	25 x
Suriname	–	95	95	95	98	39	95	95	–	–	93	76 x	42 x	–	43 x	61 x
Sweden	26	99	97	97	97	95	92	97	–	97	–	–	–	–	–	–
Switzerland	–	97	96	96	96	89	72	95	–	85	–	–	–	–	–	–
Syrian Arab Republic	79	67	47	53	63	54	47	48	–	–	91	77 x	50 x	–	–	–
Tajikistan	99	98	96	96	98	97	96	96	96	–	–	69	62	44	1 x	2 x
Thailand	99	99	97	97	96	87	97	–	–	98	–	80	73	76	–	–
Timor-Leste	95	92	83	83	77	54	83	83	–	–	83	71	70	58	55	64
Togo	83	92	88	66	85	–	88	88	89	88	83	49	19	56	70	85
Tokelau	–	–	–	–	–	–	–	–	–	–	–	–	–	–	–	–
Tonga	88	86	81	83	85	85	81	81	–	–	–	–	–	64 x	–	–
Trinidad and Tobago	–	99	99	99	90	92	99	99	–	99	–	74 x	45 x	–	–	–
Tunisia	92	98	97	97	96	99	97	97	–	–	96	60 x	65 x	–	–	–
Turkey	96	99	98	98	96	87	98	98	–	97	95	–	–	–	–	–
Turkmenistan	98	99	99	99	99	99	99	99	–	–	–	59	47	59	–	–
Turks and Caicos Islands	–	–	–	–	–	–	–	–	–	–	–	–	–	–	–	–

TABLE 4. CHILD HEALTH

Countries and areas	Intervention coverage															
	Immunization for vaccine preventable diseases (%) 2018β											Pneumonia 2013–2018*	Diarrhoea 2013–2018*	Malaria 2013–2018*		
	BCG	DTP1	DTP3	Polio3	MCV1	MCV2	HepB3	Hib3	Rota	PCV3	Protection at birth (PAB) against tetanus^	Care seeking for children with symptoms of Acute Respiratory Infection (ARI)(%)	Treatment with oral rehydration salts (ORS) (%)	Care seeking for children with fever (%)	Children sleeping under ITNs (%)	Households with at least one ITN (%)
Tuvalu	99	99	89	89	88	81	89	89	–	–	–	–	44 x	79 x	–	–
Uganda	88	99	93	88	86	–	93	93	36	92	85	80	47	81	62	78
Ukraine	90	65	50	48	91	90	52	39	–	–	–	92 x	59 x	–	–	–
United Arab Emirates	95	99	99	99	99	99	99	99	99	99	–	–	–	–	–	–
United Kingdom	–	98	94	94	92	88	–	94	91	92	–	–	–	–	–	–
United Republic of Tanzania	99	99	98	91	99	84	98	98	98	98	90	55	45	75	55	78
United States	–	97	94	93	92	94	91	92	73	92	–	–	–	–	–	–
Uruguay	98	96	91	91	97	91	91	91	–	93	–	91	–	–	–	–
Uzbekistan	96	99	98	98	96	99	98	98	84	96	–	68 x	28 x	–	–	–
Vanuatu	94	93	85	85	75	–	85	85	–	–	78	72	48	57	51	83
Venezuela (Bolivarian Republic of)	92	84	60	53	74	39	60	60	–	–	70	72 x	38 x	–	–	–
Viet Nam	95	78	75	90	97	90	75	75	–	–	94	81	51	–	9 x	10 x
Yemen	64	75	65	59	64	46	65	65	64	64	70	34	25	33	–	–
Zambia	91	94	90	90	94	65	90	90	91	90	85	70	64	75	41	68
Zimbabwe	95	94	89	89	88	78	89	89	90	89	87	51	41	50	9	48
SUMMARY																
East Asia and Pacific	93	93	91	92	92	87	88	35	1	14	89**	–	–	–	–	–
Europe and Central Asia	93	97	94	93	95	91	84	76	24	77	–	–	–	–	–	–
Eastern Europe and Central Asia	96	96	93	93	96	94	94	61	16	72	–	–	–	–	–	–
Western Europe	69	98	95	94	94	88	71	94	35	84	–	–	–	–	–	–
Latin America and Caribbean	91	90	85	85	89	78	78	85	73	79	92	–	–	–	–	–
Middle East and North Africa	93	94	90	88	89	87	90	90	32	39	87	59	28	–	–	–
North America	–	97	94	93	92	93	89	92	74	91	–	–	–	–	–	–
South Asia	91	91	87	87	87	78	87	87	36	29	89	75	50	73	4	2
Sub-Saharan Africa	79	84	76	74	74	26	76	76	50	72	81	57	38	60	53	68
Eastern and Southern Africa	86	88	81	78	77	40	81	81	74	77	86	56	40	60	51	67
West and Central Africa	73	79	70	70	71	12	70	70	28	67	76	58	36	61	55	70
Least developed countries	86	87	80	79	78	40	80	80	50	76	86	51	42	57	51	64
World	**89**	**90**	**86**	**85**	**86**	**69**	**84**	**72**	**35**	**47**	**86****	**68**	**44**	**67**	**–**	**–**

For a complete list of countries and areas in the regions, subregions and country categories, see page 182 or visit <data.unicef.org/regionalclassifications>.
It is not advisable to compare data from consecutive editions of *The State of the World's Children*.

DEFINITIONS OF THE INDICATORS

BCG – Percentage of live births who received bacilli Calmette-Guérin (vaccine against tuberculosis).

DTP1 – Percentage of surviving infants who received the first dose of diphtheria, pertussis and tetanus vaccine.

DTP3 – Percentage of surviving infants who received three doses of diphtheria, pertussis and tetanus vaccine.

Polio3 – Percentage of surviving infants who received three doses of the polio vaccine.

MCV1 – Percentage of surviving infants who received the first dose of the measles-containing vaccine.

MCV2 – Percentage of children who received the second dose of measles-containing vaccine as per national schedule.

HepB3 – Percentage of surviving infants who received three doses of hepatitis B vaccine.

Hib3 – Percentage of surviving infants who received three doses of Haemophilus influenzae type b vaccine.

Rota – Percentage of surviving infants who received the last dose of rotavirus vaccine as recommended.

PCV3 – Percentage of surviving infants who received three doses of pneumococcal conjugate vaccine.

Protection at birth (PAB) – Percentage of newborns protected at birth against tetanus with tetanus toxoid.

Care seeking for children with symptoms of Acute Respiratory Infection (ARI) – Percentage of children under age 5 with symptoms of pneumonia (cough and fast or difficult breathing due to a problem in the chest) for whom advice or treatment was sought from a health facility or provider.

Diarrhoea treatment with oral rehydration salts (ORS) – Percentage of children under age 5 who had diarrhoea in the two weeks preceding the survey and who received oral rehydration salts (ORS packets or pre-packaged ORS fluids).

Care seeking for children with fever – Percentage of children under five years of age with fever for whom advice or treatment was sought from a health facility or provider. Excludes drug vendor, stores, shops and traditional healer. In some countries, particularly non-malaria endemic countries, pharmacies have also been excluded from the calculation.

Children sleeping under ITNs – Percentage of children under age 5 who slept under an insecticide-treated mosquito net the night prior to the survey.

Households with at least one ITN – Percentage of households with at least one insecticide-treated mosquito net.

MAIN DATA SOURCES

Immunization – WHO and UNICEF estimates of national immunization coverage, 2018 revision. Last update: July 2019.

Care seeking for children with symptoms of Acute Respiratory Infection (ARI) – DHS, MICS and other national household surveys. Last update: May 2019.

Diarrhoea treatment with oral rehydration salts (ORS) – DHS, MICS and other national household surveys. Last update: May 2019.

Care seeking for children with fever – DHS, MICS, MIS and other national household surveys. Last update: May 2019.

Children sleeping under ITNs – DHS, MICS, MIS and other national household surveys. Last update: May 2019.

Households with at least one ITN – DHS, MICS, MIS and other national household surveys. Last update: May 2019.

NOTES

– Data not available or vaccine not in the national schedule.

x Data refer to years or periods other than those specified in the column heading. Such data are not included in the calculation of regional and global averages. Estimates from data years prior to 2000 are not displayed.

β For the calculation of regional and global vaccination coverage, the national coverage is considered to be 0% for the countries that did not introduce the vaccine in their national schedule or did not report coverage, with the exception of BCG that is only recommended in countries or settings with a high incidence of tuberculosis or high leprosy burden. World Population Prospects (2019 revision) estimates of target populations were used in the calculation of global and regional aggregates.

^ Generally, the second dose of measles-containing vaccine (MCV2) is recommended for administration during the second year of life; however, in many countries, MCV2 is scheduled after the second year. World Population Prospects (2019 revision) estimates of the second year of life target population were used to calculate regional and global aggregates.

λ WHO and UNICEF employ a complex process employing administrative data, surveys (routine and supplemental), serosurveys, and information on other vaccines to calculate the percentage of births that can be considered as protected against tetanus because pregnant women were given two doses or more of tetanus toxoid (TT) vaccine. The complete methodology can be found at <http://who.int/immunization/monitoring_surveillance/data/en/>.

* Data refer to the most recent year available during the period specified in the column heading.

** Excludes China.

TABLE 5. HIV/AIDS: EPIDEMIOLOGY

Countries and areas	HIV incidence per 1,000 uninfected population 2018				AIDS-related mortality per 100,000 population 2018				Number of children living with HIV 2018			
	Children 0–14	Adolescents 10–19	Adolescent girls 10–19	Adolescent boys 10–19	Children 0–14	Adolescents 10–19	Adolescent girls 10–19	Adolescent boys 10–19	Children 0–14	Adolescents 10–19	Adolescent girls 10–19	Adolescent boys 10–19
Afghanistan	0.01	<0.01	<0.01	<0.01	0.28	0.07	0.07	0.06	<500	<200	<100	<100
Albania	–	–	–	–	–	–	–	–	–	–	–	–
Algeria	0.01	0.02	0.02	0.01	0.14	0.02	<0.01	<0.01	<500	<200	<200	<100
Andorra	–	–	–	–	–	–	–	–	–	–	–	–
Angola	1.35	1.10	1.91	0.30	36.66	9.91	10.88	8.93	38,000	21,000	14,000	7,200
Anguilla	–	–	–	–	–	–	–	–	–	–	–	–
Antigua and Barbuda	0.12	0.11	0.23	0.23	3.94	<0.01	<0.01	<0.01	<100	<100	<100	<100
Argentina	0.03	0.06	0.05	0.08	0.07	0.08	0.09	0.08	1,800	2,300	1,100	1,200
Armenia	–	–	–	–	–	–	–	–	–	–	–	–
Australia	<0.01	<0.01	<0.01	0.01	<0.01	<0.01	<0.01	<0.01	<100	<100	<100	<100
Austria	–	–	–	–	–	–	–	–	–	–	–	–
Azerbaijan	–	–	–	–	–	–	–	–	–	–	–	–
Bahamas	0.79	0.26	0.23	0.22	21.03	9.72	7.94	7.61	<200	<200	<100	<100
Bahrain	–	–	–	–	–	–	–	–	–	–	–	–
Bangladesh	<0.01	<0.01	<0.01	<0.01	0.07	0.01	0.01	0.01	<500	<200	<200	<100
Barbados	–	–	–	–	–	–	–	–	–	–	–	–
Belarus	0.05	0.08	0.12	0.04	0.69	<0.01	<0.01	<0.01	<500	<200	<100	<100
Belgium	–	–	–	–	–	–	–	–	–	–	–	–
Belize	0.64	1.55	1.74	1.36	14.87	3.82	2.57	2.52	<200	<500	<200	<200
Benin	0.26	0.34	0.50	0.18	7.39	4.80	4.63	4.90	4,600	3,800	2,100	1,600
Bhutan	–	–	–	–	–	–	–	–	–	–	–	–
Bolivia (Plurinational State of)	0.04	0.06	0.06	0.06	1.10	0.85	0.82	0.88	620	680	<500	<500
Bosnia and Herzegovina	–	–	–	–	–	–	–	–	–	–	–	–
Botswana	1.27	5.58	9.30	1.99	71.79	85.42	84.91	85.92	14,000	17,000	9,600	7,500
Brazil	–	–	–	–	–	–	–	–	–	–	–	–
British Virgin Islands	–	–	–	–	–	–	–	–	–	–	–	–
Brunei Darussalam	–	–	–	–	–	–	–	–	–	–	–	–
Bulgaria	–	–	–	–	–	–	–	–	–	–	–	–
Burkina Faso	0.21	0.15	0.22	0.09	5.55	6.41	5.40	7.38	9,100	8,700	4,600	4,100
Burundi	0.41	0.11	0.18	0.03	12.62	12.65	11.79	13.61	11,000	9,300	4,900	4,400
Cabo Verde	–	–	–	–	–	–	–	–	–	–	–	–
Cambodia	0.06	0.03	0.04	0.02	0.71	0.74	0.65	0.82	3,300	3,100	1,600	1,600
Cameroon	1.18	1.30	2.25	0.37	35.35	22.46	22.42	22.51	43,000	35,000	21,000	14,000
Canada	–	–	–	–	–	–	–	–	–	–	–	–
Central African Republic	1.46	0.94	1.31	0.57	43.69	31.89	27.71	35.97	11,000	8,300	4,500	3,800
Chad	0.78	0.79	1.05	0.54	20.59	11.70	11.47	11.93	16,000	12,000	6,600	5,400
Chile	0.02	0.12	0.08	0.15	0.46	0.08	0.08	0.08	<500	<500	<200	<500
China	–	–	–	–	–	–	–	–	–	–	–	–
Colombia	0.14	0.05	0.03	0.08	–	–	–	–	3,600	3,100	1,400	1,600
Comoros	–	–	–	–	–	–	–	–	–	–	–	–
Congo	1.43	1.26	2.30	0.23	40.11	15.89	16.29	15.50	7,700	5,400	3,500	1,900
Cook Islands	–	–	–	–	–	–	–	–	–	–	–	–
Costa Rica	–	–	–	–	–	–	–	–	–	–	–	–
Côte d'Ivoire	0.68	0.61	1.07	0.16	22.72	17.82	16.12	19.51	31,000	26,000	14,000	11,000
Croatia	–	–	–	–	–	–	–	–	–	–	–	–
Cuba	0.01	0.08	0.06	0.09	0.33	0.08	0.17	0.16	<100	<200	<100	<100
Cyprus	–	–	–	–	–	–	–	–	–	–	–	–
Czechia	–	–	–	–	–	–	–	–	–	–	–	–
Democratic People's Republic of Korea	–	–	–	–	–	–	–	–	–	–	–	–
Democratic Republic of the Congo	0.42	0.25	0.43	0.07	9.85	7.00	7.07	6.92	64,000	44,000	25,000	20,000
Denmark	–	–	–	–	–	–	–	–	–	–	–	–
Djibouti	0.86	0.38	0.53	0.23	20.97	16.23	15.88	16.57	810	690	<500	<500
Dominica	–	–	–	–	–	–	–	–	<100	<100	<100	<100
Dominican Republic	0.09	0.35	0.38	0.31	2.14	1.30	1.36	1.23	1,400	2,300	1,300	1,100
Ecuador	0.03	0.07	0.07	0.07	0.42	0.13	0.13	0.13	660	620	<500	<500
Egypt	0.01	0.02	0.02	0.02	0.22	0.02	0.02	0.01	<500	<500	<200	<200
El Salvador	0.10	0.21	0.17	0.25	2.68	0.79	0.81	0.94	610	830	<500	<500
Equatorial Guinea	4.89	2.86	4.13	1.60	110.08	36.17	31.55	40.69	5,300	2,500	1,400	1,100
Eritrea	0.22	0.16	0.28	0.04	6.17	3.94	3.91	3.97	1,300	1,000	570	<500
Estonia	–	–	–	–	–	–	–	–	–	–	–	–
Eswatini	5.66	11.16	22.56	0.52	76.48	74.46	85.87	63.11	11,000	12,000	7,700	3,800
Ethiopia	0.18	0.27	0.47	0.08	4.63	3.43	3.40	3.47	36,000	36,000	21,000	15,000
Fiji	–	–	–	–	–	–	–	–	–	–	–	–
Finland	–	–	–	–	–	–	–	–	–	–	–	–

TABLE 5. HIV/AIDS: EPIDEMIOLOGY

Countries and areas	HIV incidence per 1,000 uninfected population 2018				AIDS-related mortality per 100,000 population 2018				Number of children living with HIV 2018			
	Children 0–14	Adolescents 10–19	Adolescent girls 10–19	Adolescent boys 10–19	Children 0–14	Adolescents 10–19	Adolescent girls 10–19	Adolescent boys 10–19	Children 0–14	Adolescents 10–19	Adolescent girls 10–19	Adolescent boys 10–19
France	<0.01	0.05	0.05	0.06	0.13	0.01	0.02	0.02	<500	600	<500	<500
Gabon	1.43	1.22	2.28	0.19	37.50	18.93	19.59	18.78	3,200	2,200	1,400	840
Gambia	0.77	0.33	0.56	0.09	17.64	7.04	6.68	7.78	1,900	920	520	<500
Georgia	–	–	–	–	–	–	–	–	–	–	–	–
Germany	<0.01	0.02	0.01	0.02	0.04	0.01	<0.01	<0.01	<200	<200	<100	<200
Ghana	0.81	0.69	1.26	0.16	24.53	14.97	13.61	16.27	30,000	21,000	13,000	8,400
Greece	–	–	–	–	–	–	–	–	–	–	–	–
Grenada	0.09	0.11	<0.01	0.21	3.19	<0.01	<0.01	<0.01	<100	<100	<100	<100
Guatemala	0.11	0.07	0.08	0.05	2.86	1.36	1.41	1.31	2,000	1,900	990	930
Guinea	0.62	0.63	1.06	0.21	17.30	8.32	8.56	8.08	10,000	7,800	4,800	3,100
Guinea-Bissau	2.46	0.93	1.31	0.56	57.90	33.74	31.39	36.08	5,700	3,000	1,600	1,400
Guyana	0.37	0.31	0.42	0.20	8.18	2.08	1.40	1.37	<500	<500	<200	<100
Haiti	0.69	0.80	1.38	0.22	14.38	6.28	6.14	6.33	8,700	8,300	5,100	3,200
Holy See	–	–	–	–	–	–	–	–	–	–	–	–
Honduras	0.07	0.15	0.12	0.18	1.98	0.75	0.71	0.79	890	1,300	610	710
Hungary	–	–	–	–	–	–	–	–	–	–	–	–
Iceland	–	–	–	–	–	–	–	–	–	–	–	–
India	–	–	–	–	–	–	–	–	–	–	–	–
Indonesia	0.14	0.27	0.20	0.33	3.45	0.63	0.59	0.67	18,000	18,000	6,900	11,000
Iran (Islamic Republic of)	0.01	0.02	0.02	0.02	0.23	0.16	0.15	0.17	880	660	<500	<500
Iraq	–	–	–	–	–	–	–	–	–	–	–	–
Ireland	<0.01	0.02	0.02	0.02	<0.01	<0.01	<0.01	<0.01	<100	<100	<100	<100
Israel	<0.01	0.03	0.02	0.03	0.08	<0.01	<0.01	<0.01	<100	<100	<100	<100
Italy	0.02	0.03	0.03	0.03	0.35	0.02	0.04	0.03	<500	<500	<200	<200
Jamaica	0.11	0.42	0.41	0.42	1.14	0.41	0.42	0.40	<500	<500	<500	<500
Japan	–	–	–	–	–	–	–	–	–	–	–	–
Jordan	–	–	–	–	–	–	–	–	–	–	–	–
Kazakhstan	0.03	0.04	0.05	0.03	0.45	0.04	<0.01	<0.01	<500	<200	<200	<100
Kenya	1.12	1.45	2.33	0.56	27.56	26.64	25.31	27.94	120,000	130,000	71,000	57,000
Kiribati	–	–	–	–	–	–	–	–	–	–	–	–
Kuwait	–	–	–	–	–	–	–	–	–	–	–	–
Kyrgyzstan	0.03	0.02	0.03	0.02	0.48	0.09	<0.01	<0.01	<500	<200	<100	<100
Lao People's Democratic Republic	0.09	0.08	0.09	0.07	2.11	0.61	0.69	0.53	700	<500	<500	<200
Latvia	–	–	–	–	–	–	–	–	–	–	–	–
Lebanon	–	–	–	–	–	–	–	–	–	–	–	–
Lesotho	6.31	8.10	14.00	2.52	95.13	51.44	53.65	48.77	12,000	13,000	8,300	4,800
Liberia	0.40	0.58	0.90	0.26	14.66	12.33	10.60	13.99	3,700	3,300	1,900	1,400
Libya	0.04	0.03	0.03	0.03	1.06	0.27	0.18	0.17	<500	<200	<100	<100
Liechtenstein	–	–	–	–	–	–	–	–	–	–	–	–
Lithuania	–	–	–	–	–	–	–	–	–	–	–	–
Luxembourg	–	–	–	–	–	–	–	–	–	–	–	–
Madagascar	0.11	0.47	0.37	0.57	2.51	0.94	0.82	1.01	1,900	3,800	1,600	2,200
Malawi	1.20	2.64	4.75	0.56	31.39	24.90	25.00	24.79	74,000	75,000	44,000	31,000
Malaysia	<0.01	0.28	0.01	0.56	0.06	0.25	0.07	0.43	<500	2,500	<500	2,200
Maldives	–	–	–	–	–	–	–	–	–	–	–	–
Mali	1.03	1.15	1.85	0.47	24.84	9.30	9.43	9.17	19,000	14,000	8,800	5,300
Malta	–	–	–	–	–	–	–	–	–	–	–	–
Marshall Islands	–	–	–	–	–	–	–	–	–	–	–	–
Mauritania	0.06	0.01	0.01	0.01	1.37	0.78	0.68	0.88	<500	<200	<100	<100
Mauritius	0.15	0.19	0.23	0.14	2.97	1.60	1.09	1.05	<100	<100	<100	<100
Mexico	0.02	0.03	0.02	0.05	–	–	–	–	2,300	2,400	1,000	1,400
Micronesia (Federated States of)	–	–	–	–	–	–	–	–	–	–	–	–
Monaco	–	–	–	–	–	–	–	–	–	–	–	–
Mongolia	–	–	–	–	–	–	–	–	–	–	–	–
Montenegro	–	–	–	–	–	–	–	–	–	–	–	–
Montserrat	–	–	–	–	–	–	–	–	–	–	–	–
Morocco	0.02	0.05	0.05	0.05	0.14	0.07	0.07	0.06	560	700	<500	<500
Mozambique	3.05	7.16	11.63	2.84	62.88	37.24	39.24	35.29	140,000	130,000	86,000	43,000
Myanmar	0.18	0.43	0.41	0.45	2.75	1.59	1.58	1.61	9,800	11,000	5,500	5,300
Namibia	1.24	3.32	4.97	1.68	35.75	32.44	35.15	30.11	11,000	11,000	5,900	4,700
Nauru	–	–	–	–	–	–	–	–	–	–	–	–
Nepal	0.03	0.02	0.02	0.01	0.48	0.20	0.22	0.21	1,400	1,000	520	500
Netherlands	–	–	–	–	–	–	–	–	–	–	–	–
New Zealand	–	–	–	–	–	–	–	–	–	–	–	–
Nicaragua	0.02	0.03	0.03	0.03	0.53	0.24	0.17	0.16	<500	<200	<100	<100

TABLE 5. HIV/AIDS: EPIDEMIOLOGY

Countries and areas	HIV incidence per 1,000 uninfected population 2018				AIDS-related mortality per 100,000 population 2018				Number of children living with HIV 2018			
	Children 0–14	Adolescents 10–19	Adolescent girls 10–19	Adolescent boys 10–19	Children 0–14	Adolescents 10–19	Adolescent girls 10–19	Adolescent boys 10–19	Children 0–14	Adolescents 10–19	Adolescent girls 10–19	Adolescent boys 10–19
Niger	0.09	0.05	0.06	0.03	2.01	1.46	1.36	1.56	2,500	2,200	1,100	1,000
Nigeria	0.79	0.90	1.30	0.53	17.04	7.05	6.87	7.25	140,000	120,000	70,000	51,000
Niue	–	–	–	–	–	–	–	–	–	–	–	–
North Macedonia	–	–	–	–	–	–	–	–	–	–	–	–
Norway	–	–	–	–	–	–	–	–	–	–	–	–
Oman	–	–	–	–	–	–	–	–	–	–	–	–
Pakistan	0.05	0.06	0.06	0.05	1.15	0.10	0.11	0.09	5,500	3,000	1,700	1,300
Palau	–	–	–	–	–	–	–	–	–	–	–	–
Panama	0.05	0.16	0.16	0.17	0.80	0.14	0.29	0.28	<500	<500	<200	<200
Papua New Guinea	0.24	0.19	0.28	0.12	–	–	–	–	2,900	2,400	1,300	1,100
Paraguay	0.05	0.31	0.24	0.36	1.46	0.74	0.76	0.73	<500	860	<500	<500
Peru	0.04	0.05	0.04	0.06	0.77	0.24	0.25	0.24	1,600	1,300	600	650
Philippines	0.01	0.30	0.04	0.55	0.14	0.31	0.07	0.54	<500	6,700	<500	6,200
Poland	–	–	–	–	–	–	–	–	–	–	–	–
Portugal	<0.01	0.04	0.03	0.05	0.07	<0.01	<0.01	<0.01	<100	<100	<100	<100
Qatar	–	–	–	–	–	–	–	–	–	–	–	–
Republic of Korea	–	–	–	–	–	–	–	–	–	–	–	–
Republic of Moldova	0.17	0.09	0.12	0.06	3.91	0.71	0.98	0.91	<500	<200	<100	<100
Romania	<0.01	0.02	0.03	0.02	0.07	0.09	0.10	0.09	<100	<500	<500	<500
Russian Federation	–	–	–	–	–	–	–	–	–	–	–	–
Rwanda	0.20	0.34	0.59	0.08	5.91	8.46	8.01	8.91	12,000	13,000	7,200	6,000
Saint Kitts and Nevis	–	–	–	–	–	–	–	–	<100	<100	<100	<100
Saint Lucia	–	–	–	–	–	–	–	–	<100	<100	<100	<100
Saint Vincent and the Grenadines	–	–	–	–	–	–	–	–	<100	<100	<100	<100
Samoa	–	–	–	–	–	–	–	–	–	–	–	–
San Marino	–	–	–	–	–	–	–	–	–	–	–	–
Sao Tome and Principe	0.06	0.12	0.08	0.16	3.11	3.66	3.68	3.64	<100	<100	<100	<100
Saudi Arabia	–	–	–	–	–	–	–	–	–	–	–	–
Senegal	0.16	0.09	0.15	0.03	5.38	2.78	2.64	2.92	4,500	3,200	1,700	1,400
Serbia	–	–	–	–	–	–	–	–	–	–	–	–
Seychelles	–	–	–	–	–	–	–	–	–	–	–	–
Sierra Leone	0.59	1.22	1.79	0.65	17.90	10.29	9.96	10.62	6,600	6,500	4,000	2,500
Singapore	–	–	–	–	–	–	–	–	–	–	–	–
Slovakia	–	–	–	–	–	–	–	–	–	–	–	–
Slovenia	–	–	–	–	–	–	–	–	–	–	–	–
Solomon Islands	–	–	–	–	–	–	–	–	–	–	–	–
Somalia	0.05	0.01	0.03	<0.01	1.79	1.36	1.33	1.38	1,300	940	<500	<500
South Africa	2.48	8.61	15.70	1.87	26.80	24.01	28.58	19.50	260,000	310,000	200,000	110,000
South Sudan	1.34	1.23	1.73	0.74	35.91	13.63	13.68	13.59	16,000	11,000	6,100	4,500
Spain	<0.01	0.03	0.02	0.05	–	–	–	–	<100	<500	<100	<200
Sri Lanka	–	–	–	–	–	–	–	–	–	–	–	–
State of Palestine	–	–	–	–	–	–	–	–	–	–	–	–
Sudan	0.13	0.07	0.09	0.05	3.04	0.67	0.69	0.66	4,200	2,000	1,100	850
Suriname	0.08	0.27	0.35	0.23	1.32	<0.01	<0.01	<0.01	<100	<100	<100	<100
Sweden	–	–	–	–	–	–	–	–	–	–	–	–
Switzerland	–	–	–	–	–	–	–	–	–	–	–	–
Syrian Arab Republic	–	–	–	–	–	–	–	–	–	–	–	–
Tajikistan	0.04	0.02	0.02	0.02	0.55	0.06	0.11	0.11	540	<200	<100	<100
Thailand	0.01	0.22	0.18	0.27	0.73	1.45	1.31	1.60	3,200	9,100	4,400	4,700
Timor-Leste	–	–	–	–	–	–	–	–	–	–	–	–
Togo	1.07	0.51	0.85	0.17	30.51	18.69	17.00	20.48	12,000	8,700	4,800	4,000
Tokelau	–	–	–	–	–	–	–	–	–	–	–	–
Tonga	–	–	–	–	–	–	–	–	–	–	–	–
Trinidad and Tobago	–	–	–	–	–	–	–	–	–	–	–	–
Tunisia	–	–	–	–	–	–	–	–	–	–	–	–
Turkey	–	–	–	–	–	–	–	–	–	–	–	–
Turkmenistan	–	–	–	–	–	–	–	–	–	–	–	–
Turks and Caicos Islands	–	–	–	–	–	–	–	–	–	–	–	–
Tuvalu	–	–	–	–	–	–	–	–	–	–	–	–
Uganda	1.03	1.73	3.08	0.41	29.02	20.76	20.15	21.36	100,000	90,000	54,000	35,000
Ukraine	0.02	0.09	0.07	0.10	0.76	0.22	0.20	0.24	850	1,000	510	520
United Arab Emirates	–	–	–	–	–	–	–	–	–	–	–	–
United Kingdom	–	–	–	–	–	–	–	–	–	–	–	–
United Republic of Tanzania	0.95	1.91	2.79	1.01	22.45	15.77	15.44	16.08	92,000	93,000	54,000	39,000
United States	–	–	–	–	–	–	–	–	–	–	–	–

TABLE 5. HIV/AIDS: EPIDEMIOLOGY

Countries and areas	HIV incidence per 1,000 uninfected population 2018				AIDS-related mortality per 100,000 population 2018				Number of children living with HIV 2018			
	Children 0–14	Adolescents 10–19	Adolescent girls 10–19	Adolescent boys 10–19	Children 0–14	Adolescents 10–19	Adolescent girls 10–19	Adolescent boys 10–19	Children 0–14	Adolescents 10–19	Adolescent girls 10–19	Adolescent boys 10–19
Uruguay	0.03	0.13	0.10	0.15	0.73	0.20	<0.01	<0.01	<200	<200	<100	<100
Uzbekistan	0.30	0.03	0.04	0.03	3.93	0.43	0.43	0.44	6,000	1,500	750	720
Vanuatu	–	–	–	–	–	–	–	–	–	–	–	–
Venezuela (Bolivarian Republic of)	–	–	–	–	–	–	–	–	–	–	–	–
Viet Nam	0.04	0.03	0.04	0.02	0.50	0.13	0.16	0.10	5,000	3,000	1,600	1,400
Yemen	0.02	0.07	0.03	0.10	0.38	0.11	0.06	0.12	<500	680	<200	<500
Zambia	1.68	4.31	6.79	1.82	36.43	24.50	24.69	24.16	62,000	64,000	39,000	25,000
Zimbabwe	2.02	3.67	5.94	1.42	53.17	49.51	49.01	50.21	84,000	81,000	46,000	36,000
SUMMARY												
East Asia and Pacific	0.04	0.10	0.07	0.13	0.84	0.27	0.25	0.29	50,000	62,000	25,000	36,000
Europe and Central Asia	–	–	–	–	–	–	–	–	–	–	–	–
Eastern Europe and Central Asia	–	–	–	–	–	–	–	–	–	–	–	–
Western Europe	–	–	–	–	–	–	–	–	–	–	–	–
Latin America and Caribbean	0.08	0.12	0.13	0.12	1.68	0.63	0.63	0.62	42,000	48,000	25,000	23,000
Middle East and North Africa	0.01	0.03	0.02	0.03	0.23	0.06	0.05	0.06	3,500	3,300	1,500	1,800
North America	–	–	–	–	–	–	–	–	–	–	–	–
South Asia	0.03	0.05	0.05	0.04	0.54	0.15	0.15	0.15	64,000	61,000	30,000	31,000
Sub-Saharan Africa	0.85	1.42	2.33	0.52	19.69	12.48	12.53	12.45	1,550,000	1,460,000	880,000	580,000
Eastern and Southern Africa	1.03	2.14	3.57	0.72	22.65	15.72	16.08	15.35	1,110,000	1,120,000	680,000	440,000
West and Central Africa	0.67	0.67	1.04	0.32	16.76	9.19	8.86	9.52	440,000	340,000	200,000	140,000
Least developed countries	0.20	0.36	0.58	0.15	13.04	7.37	7.38	7.36	810,000	720,000	430,000	290,000
World	**0.25**	**0.33**	**0.51**	**0.16**	**5.18**	**2.69**	**2.76**	**2.64**	**1,730,000**	**1,650,000**	**970,000**	**680,000**

For a complete list of countries and areas in the regions, subregions and country categories, see page 182 or visit <data.unicef.org/regionalclassifications>.
It is not advisable to compare data from consecutive editions of The *State of the World's Children*.

DEFINITIONS OF THE INDICATORS

HIV incidence per 1,000 uninfected population –
Estimated number of new HIV infections per 1,000 uninfected population at risk of HIV infection.

AIDS-related mortality per 100,000 population – Estimated number of AIDS-related deaths per 100,000 population.

Number of children living with HIV – Estimated number of children living with HIV.

MAIN DATA SOURCES

HIV incidence per 1,000 uninfected population – UNAIDS 2019 estimates. Last update: July 2019.

AIDS-related mortality per 100,000 population – UNAIDS 2019 estimates. Last update: July 2019.

Number of children living with HIV – UNAIDS 2019 estimates. Last update: July 2019.

NOTES

– Data not available.

Due to rounding of the estimates, disaggregates may not add up to the total.

TABLE 6. HIV/AIDS: INTERVENTION COVERAGE

Countries and areas	Pregnant women living with HIV receiving ARVs for PMTCT (%) 2018	Early infant HIV diagnosis (%) 2018	Children living with HIV receiving ART (%) 2018		Comprehensive knowledge of HIV among adolescents age 15–19 (%) 2012–2018*		Condom use among adolescents age 15–19 with multiple partners (%) 2012–2018*		Adolescents age 15–19 tested for HIV in the last 12 months and received results (%) 2012–2018*	
			children 0–14	adolescents 10–19	male	female	male	female	male	female
Afghanistan	11.1	1.2	17.2	34.5	4.3 y	0.6 y	–	–	0.0 y	1.2 y
Albania	–	–	–	–	19.6	35.3	–	–	0.1	1.0
Algeria	74.1	46.7	>95	>95	–	6.8	–	–	–	0.7
Andorra	–	–	–	–	–	–	–	–	–	–
Angola	38.2	1.4	12.9	–	29.4	31.1	39.1	30.5	4.2	15.7
Anguilla	–	–	–	–	–	–	–	–	–	–
Antigua and Barbuda	–	–	<1	–	55.1 x	40.2 x	100 x	53.8 x	–	–
Argentina	>95	70.6	92.1	–	–	35.7	–	–	–	–
Armenia	–	–	–	–	8.9	14.7	–	–	0.2	0.6
Australia	–	–	–	–	–	–	–	–	–	–
Austria	–	–	–	–	–	–	–	–	–	–
Azerbaijan	–	–	–	–	2.1 x	3.1 x	–	–	–	–
Bahamas	–	–	21.1	31.0	–	–	–	–	–	–
Bahrain	–	–	–	–	–	–	–	–	–	–
Bangladesh	28.3	25.2	32.9	77.5	–	12 y	–	–	–	–
Barbados	–	–	–	–	–	65.6	–	–	–	9.7
Belarus	90.3	92.3	88.1	–	52.8	50.8	–	–	14.7	15.1
Belgium	–	–	–	–	–	–	–	–	–	–
Belize	43.9	–	33.9	–	43.5	39.7	68.7	–	7.0	12.9
Benin	>95	64.9	44.1	–	14.4	14.1	26.2	38.7	3.5	6.3
Bhutan	–	–	–	–	–	21.9 x	–	–	–	3.4 x
Bolivia (Plurinational State of)	>95	–	40.1	–	23.8 x	20.0 x	44.2 x	–	1.4 x	–
Bosnia and Herzegovina	–	–	–	–	41	42.3	–	–	0.0	0.0
Botswana	>95	76.5	37.9	63.3	–	–	–	–	–	–
Brazil	–	–	–	–	–	–	–	–	–	–
British Virgin Islands	–	–	–	–	–	–	–	–	–	–
Brunei Darussalam	–	–	–	–	–	–	–	–	–	–
Bulgaria	–	–	–	–	–	–	–	–	–	–
Burkina Faso	>95	16.7	21.0	–	30.8 x	29 px	76.4 x	57.3 x	4.0 x	7.9 x
Burundi	79.7	–	30.4	–	50.2	46.3	–	–	8.0	13.2
Cabo Verde	–	–	–	–	–	–	–	–	–	–
Cambodia	85.1	45.7	91.6	–	42.4	32.7	–	–	2.9	6.7
Cameroon	80.0	61.3	23.8	26.6	29.8 x	25.7 x	69.6 x	52 x	1.9 x	3 x
Canada	–	–	–	–	–	–	–	–	–	–
Central African Republic	70.7	24.3	23.4	87.8	26.4 x	17.1 x	49.8 x	28.1 x	6.8 x	14.6 x
Chad	55.8	–	16.3	–	11.6	10.2	–	53.6 p	1.5	5.3
Chile	>95	81.2	55.5	–	–	–	–	–	–	–
China	–	–	–	–	–	–	–	–	–	–
Colombia	21.3	30.7	40.6	–	25.9	27.7	65.9	44.7	–	8.1 x
Comoros	–	–	–	–	20.6	17.8	50.7	–	2.5	1.8
Congo	25.0	1.9	25.5	–	41.9	26	54.7	48.9	3.8	7.4
Cook Islands	–	–	–	–	–	–	–	–	–	–
Costa Rica	–	–	–	–	–	29.1 x	–	58.6 px	–	9.4 x
Côte d'Ivoire	89.8	56.3	40.0	–	31.5	24.4	72.7	30.4	7.9	16.3
Croatia	–	–	–	–	–	–	–	–	–	–
Cuba	>95	>95	33.8	>95	47.9	59.2	–	79.2 p	15.5	18.7
Cyprus	–	–	–	–	–	–	–	–	–	–
Czechia	–	–	–	–	–	–	–	–	–	–
Democratic People's Republic of Korea	–	–	–	–	–	–	–	–	–	–
Democratic Republic of the Congo	43.9	19.7	24.9	–	20.3	17.1	17.3	12.1	1.4	4.5
Denmark	–	–	–	–	–	–	–	–	–	–
Djibouti	29.6	3.4	10.1	24.0	–	–	–	–	–	–
Dominica	–	–	<1	–	39.3 x	49.2 x	73.5 x	85.7 x	–	–
Dominican Republic	84.2	67.7	54.6	–	39.2	39.4	67.4	40.3	5.3	11.6
Ecuador	>95	–	82.3	–	–	–	–	–	–	–
Egypt	16.3	12.7	39.0	–	–	2.8 y	–	–	–	–
El Salvador	39.7	37.1	24.3	–	25.1	25.1	–	30.9 p	–	7.5
Equatorial Guinea	50.1	–	14.4	–	–	–	–	–	–	–
Eritrea	47.9	20.2	37.2	–	31.9 x	22.3 x	–	–	–	–
Estonia	–	–	–	–	–	–	–	–	–	–
Eswatini	79.2	78.0	75.7	83.6	44.4	44.5	92.4 px	–	30.4	40.8
Ethiopia	91.7	60.8	59.3	–	37.6	24.0	56.9 p	–	8.9	12.4

TABLE 6. HIV/AIDS: INTERVENTION COVERAGE

Countries and areas	Pregnant women living with HIV receiving ARVs for PMTCT (%) 2018	Early infant HIV diagnosis (%) 2018	Children living with HIV receiving ART (%) 2018		Comprehensive knowledge of HIV among adolescents age 15–19 (%) 2012–2018*		Condom use among adolescents age 15–19 with multiple partners (%) 2012–2018*		Adolescents age 15–19 tested for HIV in the last 12 months and received results (%) 2012–2018*	
			children 0–14	adolescents 10–19	male	female	male	female	male	female
Fiji	–	–	–	–	–	–	–	–	–	–
Finland	–	–	–	–	–	–	–	–	–	–
France	–	–	–	–	–	–	–	–	–	–
Gabon	71.6	17.4	57.1	–	34.8	28.8	77.3	58.3	6.1	20.4
Gambia	67.6	28.2	29.5	–	26.5	21.9	–	–	1.9	5.9
Georgia	–	–	–	–	–	–	–	–	–	1.6 x
Germany	–	–	–	–	–	–	–	–	–	–
Ghana	78.9	58.2	19.9	–	24.5	18.1	24.4 x	21.6 p	1.3	4.5
Greece	–	–	–	–	–	–	–	–	–	–
Grenada	>95	>95	36.4	–	66.7 x	58.5 x	80.0 x	92.3 x	–	–
Guatemala	34.5	23.5	36.4	38.6	17.5	19.8	66.3	38 p	2.3	4.8
Guinea	65.0	15.0	20.3	–	27.2	14.0	46.2 p	17.9	0.9	4.7
Guinea-Bissau	47.7	26.7	6.1	–	19.3	20.3	59.5	40.9	1.8	4.8
Guyana	89.3	61.2	37.5	–	33.2	47.6	82.6 p	–	10.1	15.8
Haiti	83.4	46.1	39.5	39.7	33.5	36.2	72.5	42.3	6.2	12.2
Holy See	–	–	–	–	–	–	–	–	–	–
Honduras	58.7	44.5	40.5	–	–	–	72.6	38.9	2.8	9.6
Hungary	–	–	–	–	–	–	–	–	–	–
Iceland	–	–	–	–	–	–	–	–	–	–
India	–	–	–	–	28.2	18.5	29.9	35.3 p	0.7	1.9
Indonesia	15.4	1.2	22.1	–	4.0 py	9.4	–	–	–	–
Iran (Islamic Republic of)	80.9	39.8	58.3	28.8	–	–	–	–	–	–
Iraq	–	–	–	–	–	5.1	–	–	–	0.7
Ireland	–	–	–	–	–	–	–	–	–	–
Israel	–	–	–	–	–	–	–	–	–	–
Italy	–	–	–	–	–	–	–	–	–	–
Jamaica	>95	–	50.9	62.6	33.7	39.1	75.2	55.9 p	20.0	34.7
Japan	–	–	–	–	–	–	–	–	–	–
Jordan	–	–	–	–	7.7 y	1.9 y	–	–	–	–
Kazakhstan	59.4	51.5	>95	>95	29.5	19.6	93.6 px	–	13.8 x	10.9
Kenya	91.2	67.3	60.7	–	57.7	49.0	64.1	26.1 p	26.6	35.3
Kiribati	–	–	–	–	–	–	–	–	–	–
Kuwait	–	–	–	–	–	–	–	–	–	–
Kyrgyzstan	88.1	82.1	>95	>95	18.3	17.0	–	–	0.9	10.5
Lao People's Democratic Republic	35.4	12.7	39.7	–	21.2	19.1	57.2	27.4 p	0.5	1.0
Latvia	–	–	–	–	–	–	–	–	–	–
Lebanon	–	–	–	–	–	–	–	–	–	–
Lesotho	77.2	69.5	70.0	–	29.7	34.8	79.7	57.9 p	24.9	40.5
Liberia	93.2	14.7	18.2	–	19.0	34.6	21.6 p	27.1	3.6	13.1
Libya	62.7	45.1	32.6	–	–	–	–	–	–	–
Liechtenstein	–	–	–	–	–	–	–	–	–	–
Lithuania	–	–	–	–	–	–	–	–	–	–
Luxembourg	–	–	–	–	–	–	–	–	–	–
Madagascar	25.0	–	4.7	–	24	20.9	5.2	5.5 p	0.8	2.0
Malawi	>95	>95	61.0	–	43.1	38.9	59.1	44	22	31.9
Malaysia	>95	>95	93.9	–	–	–	–	–	–	–
Maldives	–	–	–	–	21.3	26.9	–	–	1.8	2.7
Mali	23.7	13.8	18.0	–	26.7	20.7	47.0	25.7	1.6	5.0
Malta	–	–	–	–	–	–	–	–	–	–
Marshall Islands	–	–	–	–	–	–	–	–	–	–
Mauritania	37.5	–	54.3	66.5	7.4	7.0	–	–	1.0	2.4
Mauritius	>95	75.3	44.9	–	–	–	–	–	–	–
Mexico	–	–	–	>95	–	27.6	–	36.3 p	–	6.9
Micronesia (Federated States of)	–	–	–	–	–	–	–	–	–	–
Monaco	–	–	–	–	–	–	–	–	–	–
Mongolia	–	–	–	–	17.3	17.5	77.8 p	–	4.6	6.5
Montenegro	–	–	–	–	35.2	42.3	64.4 p	–	0.0	0.4
Montserrat	–	–	–	–	–	–	–	–	–	–
Morocco	61.0	–	>95	–	–	12.2 x	–	–	–	–
Mozambique	>95	66.4	60.2	–	28.0	27.7	38.6	43.2 p	10.1	25.3
Myanmar	79.7	25.0	80.1	–	14.3	13.4	–	–	2.0	0.9
Namibia	>95	–	77.9	>95	61.0	55.9	75.1 p	61.4 p	13.9	28.5
Nauru	–	–	–	–	–	–	–	–	–	–

TABLE 6. HIV/AIDS: INTERVENTION COVERAGE

Countries and areas	Pregnant women living with HIV receiving ARVs for PMTCT (%) 2018	Early infant HIV diagnosis (%) 2018	Children living with HIV receiving ART (%) 2018		Comprehensive knowledge of HIV among adolescents age 15–19 (%) 2012–2018*		Condom use among adolescents age 15–19 with multiple partners (%) 2012–2018*		Adolescents age 15–19 tested for HIV in the last 12 months and received results (%) 2012–2018*	
			children 0–14	adolescents 10–19	male	female	male	female	male	female
Nepal	50.7	70.8	91.2	–	24.3	18.3	–	–	3.0	2.5
Netherlands	–	–	–	–	–	–	–	–	–	–
New Zealand	–	–	–	–	–	–	–	–	–	–
Nicaragua	90.4	77.2	54.7	–	–	16.4 x	–	–	–	–
Niger	57.7	7.7	52.5	40.3	20.3	11.2	–	–	1.5	4.1
Nigeria	43.6	18.1	35.0	34.2	24.8	28.1	62.0	42.7	7.3	7.9
Niue	–	–	–	–	–	–	–	–	–	–
North Macedonia	–	–	–	–	–	–	–	–	–	–
Norway	–	–	–	–	–	–	–	–	–	–
Oman	–	–	–	–	–	–	–	–	–	–
Pakistan	10.0	1.9	11.2	9.6	0.2 y	1.0 y	–	–	0.0 py	0.2 y
Palau	–	–	–	–	–	–	–	–	–	–
Panama	92.1	90.1	75.8	>95	–	–	–	–	–	–
Papua New Guinea	78.6	74.6	49.2	–	–	–	–	–	–	–
Paraguay	87.5	59.8	43.0	27.7	–	24.9	–	61.0	–	9
Peru	84.6	82.2	47.6	>95	–	–	–	–	–	–
Philippines	18.5	3.6	20.3	5.8	–	15.7	34.3 px	–	–	0.3
Poland	–	–	–	–	–	–	–	–	–	–
Portugal	–	–	–	–	–	–	–	–	–	–
Qatar	–	–	–	–	22.8	9.7	–	–	–	–
Republic of Korea	–	–	–	–	–	–	–	–	–	–
Republic of Moldova	72.6	74.2	40.4	59.8	25.6	35.2	–	–	6.4	9.9
Romania	>95	–	>95	–	–	–	–	–	–	–
Russian Federation	–	–	–	–	–	–	–	–	–	–
Rwanda	>95	82.5	63.2	–	59.5	61.6	–	–	21.9	27.4
Saint Kitts and Nevis	50.0	–	<1	25.0	55.2 x	54.4 x	53.8 x	50.0 x	–	–
Saint Lucia	–	71.4	5.6	–	–	57.7	–	–	–	11.9
Saint Vincent and the Grenadines	–	–	36.4	–	–	–	–	–	–	–
Samoa	–	–	–	–	–	–	–	–	–	–
San Marino	–	–	–	–	–	–	–	–	–	–
Sao Tome and Principe	–	>95	62.2	30.8	42.0	40.5	78.5	–	8.0	22.1
Saudi Arabia	–	–	–	–	–	–	–	–	–	–
Senegal	65.1	23.8	30.7	–	25.7	20.3	49.1 p	–	1.5	6.1
Serbia	–	–	–	–	43.0 x	52.9 x	62.8 x	–	1.3 x	1.3 x
Seychelles	–	–	–	–	–	–	–	–	–	–
Sierra Leone	–	–	16.9	–	26.0	24.8	8.8	11.5	3.0	7.4
Singapore	–	–	–	–	–	–	–	–	–	–
Slovakia	–	–	–	–	–	–	–	–	–	–
Slovenia	–	–	–	–	–	–	–	–	–	–
Solomon Islands	–	–	–	–	–	–	–	–	–	–
Somalia	19.4	–	14.3	–	–	–	–	–	–	–
South Africa	86.5	88.7	63.0	–	35.5	38.3	87.9	54.8	28.7	38.4
South Sudan	56.0	5.7	8.9	–	–	8.3 x	–	6.1 px	–	3.2 x
Spain	–	–	–	–	–	–	–	–	–	–
Sri Lanka	–	–	–	–	–	–	–	–	–	–
State of Palestine	–	–	–	–	–	4.7	–	–	–	–
Sudan	5.1	–	14.7	–	9.8	7.7	–	–	–	0.6
Suriname	>95	–	71.6	>95	–	40.3 x	–	–	–	11.4 x
Sweden	–	–	–	–	–	–	–	–	–	–
Switzerland	–	–	–	–	–	–	–	–	–	–
Syrian Arab Republic	–	–	–	–	–	–	–	–	–	–
Tajikistan	46.5	29.1	>95	–	9.4 x	8.5	–	–	–	2.1
Thailand	>95	>95	82.6	84.8	45.0	46.5	–	–	3.5	6.3
Timor-Leste	–	–	–	–	12.7	5.9	–	–	0.3	0.0
Togo	80.3	46.0	33.6	–	27.9	22.8	–	46.5 px	6.7	11.2
Tokelau	–	–	–	–	–	–	–	–	–	–
Tonga	–	–	–	–	–	–	–	–	–	–
Trinidad and Tobago	–	–	–	–	–	55.3 x	–	–	–	10.0 x
Tunisia	–	–	–	–	12.2	13.0	–	–	0.0	0.3
Turkey	–	–	–	–	–	–	–	–	–	–
Turkmenistan	–	–	–	–	–	18.6	–	–	–	4.8
Turks and Caicos Islands	–	–	–	–	–	–	–	–	–	–
Tuvalu	–	–	–	–	–	–	–	–	–	–

TABLE 6. HIV/AIDS: INTERVENTION COVERAGE

Countries and areas	Pregnant women living with HIV receiving ARVs for PMTCT (%) 2018	Early infant HIV diagnosis (%) 2018	Children living with HIV receiving ART (%) 2018		Comprehensive knowledge of HIV among adolescents age 15–19 (%) 2012–2018*		Condom use among adolescents age 15–19 with multiple partners (%) 2012–2018*		Adolescents age 15–19 tested for HIV in the last 12 months and received results (%) 2012–2018*	
			children 0–14	adolescents 10–19	male	female	male	female	male	female
Uganda	92.9	44.8	65.7	–	40.2	40.7	52.1	26.0	28.4	39.4
Ukraine	>95	65.0	>95	–	36.6	42.6	89.8	–	9.9	6.9
United Arab Emirates	–	–	–	–	–	–	–	–	–	–
United Kingdom	–	–	–	–	–	–	–	–	–	–
United Republic of Tanzania	93.3	46.9	65.0	56.2	41.9	36.8	45.2	37.7	13.1	20.8
United States	–	–	–	–	–	–	–	–	–	–
Uruguay	>95	75.0	63.9	–	–	36.4	–	66.8 p	–	7.2
Uzbekistan	35.4	31.3	92.8	>95	–	–	–	–	–	–
Vanuatu	–	–	–	–	–	–	–	–	–	–
Venezuela (Bolivarian Republic of)	–	–	–	–	–	–	–	–	–	–
Viet Nam	81.0	50.8	91.7	–	–	50.5	–	–	–	3.8
Yemen	12.8	–	33.0	–	–	–	–	–	–	–
Zambia	>95	71.4	78.7	–	42.3	38.9	37.7	33	14.9	28.8
Zimbabwe	93.9	63.0	76.4	88.9	48.7	51.4	71.1	–	19.9	29.1
SUMMARY										
East Asia and Pacific	55.0	36.9	60.8	–	–	–	–	–	–	–
Europe and Central Asia	–	–	–	–	–	–	–	–	–	–
Eastern Europe and Central Asia	–	–	–	–	–	–	–	–	–	–
Western Europe	–	–	–	–	–	–	–	–	–	–
Latin America and Caribbean	78.6	48.5	46.0	–	–	–	–	–	–	–
Middle East and North Africa	53.2	35.5	73.1	–	–	–	–	–	–	–
North America	–	–	–	–	–	–	–	–	–	–
South Asia	56.2	30.8	91.1	–	23.6	15.2	29.9	35.3	0.6	1.7
Sub-Saharan Africa	84.4	60.4	52.0	–	31.1	28.0	51.3	32.9	10.3	15.0
Eastern and Southern Africa	91.5	68.8	61.2	–	37.6	33.0	53.6	33.2	15.8	21.9
West and Central Africa	58.8	29.3	28.4	–	23.6	22.2	48.6	32.6	4.5	7.1
Least developed countries	88.5	49.8	51.0	–	27.7	21.5	41.4	–	7.2	11.6
World	**82.4**	**58.7**	**54.2**	**–**	**24.1**	**20.3**	**–**	**–**	**–**	**6.7**

For a complete list of countries and areas in the regions, subregions and country categories, see page 182 or visit <data.unicef.org/regionalclassifications>.
It is not advisable to compare data from consecutive editions of *The State of the World's Children*.

DEFINITIONS OF THE INDICATORS

Pregnant women living with HIV receiving ARVs for PMTCT – Percentage of the estimated number of pregnant women living with HIV who received effective regimens (excluding single-dose nevirapine) of antiretroviral medicines (ARVs) for prevention of mother-to-child transmission (PMTCT) of HIV.

Early infant HIV diagnosis – Percentage of HIV-exposed infants who received a virologic test for HIV within two months of birth.

Children living with HIV receiving ART – Percentage of children living with HIV who received antiretroviral therapy (ART).

Comprehensive knowledge of HIV among adolescents age 15–19 – Percentage of adolescents aged 15–19 who correctly identify the two ways of preventing the sexual transmission of HIV, who know that a healthy-looking person can be HIV-positive and who reject the two most common misconceptions about HIV transmission.

Condom use among adolescents age 15–19 with multiple partners – Percentage of adolescents aged 15-19 who had more than one sexual partner in the past 12 months reporting the use of a condom during their last sexual intercourse.

Adolescents age 15–19 tested for HIV in the last 12 months and received results – Percentage of adolescents aged 15-19 who have been tested for HIV in the last 12 months and received the result of the last test.

MAIN DATA SOURCES

Pregnant women living with HIV receiving ARVs for PMTCT – Global AIDS Monitoring and UNAIDS 2019 estimates. Last update: July 2019.

Early infant HIV diagnosis – Global AIDS Monitoring and UNAIDS 2019 estimates. Last update: July 2019.

Children living with HIV receiving ART – Global AIDS Monitoring and UNAIDS 2019 estimates. Last update: July 2019.

Comprehensive knowledge of HIV among adolescents age 15–19 – Nationally representative population-based surveys, including MICS, DHS, AIS, and other household surveys 2012-2018. Last update: April 2019.

Condom use among adolescents age 15–19 with multiple partners – Nationally representative population-based surveys, including MICS, DHS, AIS, and other household surveys 2012-2018. Last update: April 2019.

Adolescents age 15–19 tested for HIV in the last 12 months and received results – Nationally representative population-based surveys, including MICS, DHS, AIS, and other household surveys 2012-2018. Last update: April 2019.

NOTES

– Data not available.

x Data refer to years or periods other than those specified in the column heading. Such data are not included in the calculation of regional and global averages. Estimates from years prior to 2000 are not displayed.

p Based on small denominators (typically 25–49 unweighted cases). No data based on fewer than 25 unweighted cases are displayed.

y Data differ from the standard definition or refer to only part of a country. If they fall within the noted reference period, such data are included in the calculation of regional and global averages.

* Data refer to the most recent year available during the period specified in the column heading.

TABLE 7. NUTRITION: NEWBORNS, INFANTS AND YOUNG CHILDREN

Countries and areas	Weight at birth — Low birthweight (%) 2015	Weight at birth — Unweighed at birth (%) 2010–2018*	Early initiation of breastfeeding (%)	Exclusive breastfeeding (<6 months) (%)	Introduction to solid, semi-solid or soft foods (6–8 months) (%)	Continued breastfeeding (12–23 months) (%) — All children	Continued breastfeeding — Poorest 20%	Continued breastfeeding — Richest 20%	Minimum diet diversity (6–23 months) (%)	Minimum meal frequency (6–23 months) (%)	Minimum acceptable diet (6–23 months) (%)	Zero vegetable or fruit consumption (6–23 months) (%)
Afghanistan	–	86	63	58	61	74	80	70	22	51	15	59
Albania	5	13	57	37	89	43	38	37	52	51	29	26
Algeria	7	11	36 x	25 x	77 x	36 x	35 x	34 x	–	52 x	–	–
Andorra	7	14	–	–	–	–	–	–	–	–	–	–
Angola	15	45	48	37	79	67	74	53	29	33	13	36
Anguilla	–	–	–	–	–	–	–	–	–	–	–	–
Antigua and Barbuda	9	–	–	–	–	–	–	–	–	–	–	–
Argentina	7	4	53 x	32 x	97 x	39 x	49 x	33 x	–	68 x	–	–
Armenia	9	0	41	44	90	29	32	24	36	72	24	22
Australia	7	1	–	–	–	–	–	–	–	–	–	–
Austria	7	0	–	–	–	–	–	–	–	–	–	–
Azerbaijan	7	3	20	12	77	26 x	24 x	15 x	35 x	–	–	38 x
Bahamas	13	16	–	–	–	–	–	–	–	–	–	–
Bahrain	12	2	–	–	–	–	–	–	–	–	–	–
Bangladesh	28	68	51	55	65	92	94	85	27	64	23	53
Barbados	–	2	40 x	20 x	90 x	41 x	– x,p	– x,p	–	61 x	–	–
Belarus	5	0	53 x	19 x	95 x	17 x	26 x	19 x	–	74 x	–	–
Belgium	7	4	–	–	–	–	–	–	–	–	–	–
Belize	9	1	68	33	79	47	59	37	58	68 x	–	30
Benin	17	40	54	41	56	69	77	52	26	45	15	54
Bhutan	12	28	78	51	87	80 x	88 x	76 x	–	63 x	–	–
Bolivia (Plurinational State of)	7	17	55	58	81 x	55	74 x,r	53 x,r	64 x	–	–	20 x
Bosnia and Herzegovina	3	2	42 x	18 x	76 x	12 x	16 x	10 x	–	72 x	–	–
Botswana	16	5	53	30	73	15	–	–	–	–	–	–
Brazil	8	3	43 x	39 x	94 x	–	–	–	–	–	–	–
British Virgin Islands	–	–	–	–	–	–	–	–	–	–	–	–
Brunei Darussalam	11	4	–	–	–	–	–	–	–	–	–	–
Bulgaria	10	6	–	–	–	–	–	–	–	–	–	–
Burkina Faso	13	36	56	48	75	90 x	93 x	77 x	5 x	57	3 x	75 x
Burundi	15	20	85	82	86	89	92	84	18	39	10	9
Cabo Verde	–	–	73 x	60 x	–	–	–	–	–	–	–	–
Cambodia	12	9	63	65	82	58	65	39	40	72	30	35
Cameroon	12	40	31	28	83	46	75	16	23	60	16	42
Canada	6	1	–	–	–	–	–	–	–	–	–	–
Central African Republic	15	39	53	29	94 x	66 x	74 x	57 x	27 x	20 x	9 x	22 x
Chad	–	88	23	<1.0	59	79	82	68	9	37	6	70
Chile	6	0	–	–	–	–	–	–	–	–	–	–
China	5	0	29	21	83	–	–	–	35	69	25	–
Colombia	10	18	72	36	78	45 x	49 x	33 x	–	61	–	–
Comoros	24	33	34 x	11 x	80 x	65 x	68 x	69 x	22 x	30 x	6 x	52 x
Congo	12	10	25	33	84	32	54	20	14	32	5	51
Cook Islands	3	–	–	–	–	–	–	–	–	–	–	–
Costa Rica	7	2	60 x	33 x	90 x	40 x	50 x	13 x	–	79 x	–	–
Côte d'Ivoire	15	25	37	23	65	63	76	36	23	49	14	44
Croatia	5	–	–	–	–	–	–	–	–	–	–	–
Cuba	5	5	48	33	91	31	–	–	70	79	56	27
Cyprus	–	27	–	–	–	–	–	–	–	–	–	–
Czechia	8	0	–	–	–	–	–	–	–	–	–	–
Democratic People's Republic of Korea	–	0	43	71	78	–	–	–	47	75	29	–
Democratic Republic of the Congo	11	24	52	47	79	82	87	67	17	35	8	29
Denmark	5	4	–	–	–	–	–	–	–	–	–	–
Djibouti	–	–	52 x	12 x	–	–	–	–	–	–	–	–
Dominica	–	–	–	–	–	–	–	–	–	–	–	–
Dominican Republic	11	4	38	5	81	20	27	14	51	80	43	35
Ecuador	11	19	55 x	40 x	74 x	–	–	–	–	–	–	–
Egypt	–	39	27	40	75	50	58	43	35	60	23	45
El Salvador	10	7	42	47	90	67	71	57	73	87	65	16
Equatorial Guinea	–	30	–	7 x	–	31 x	47 x,r	34 x,r	–	39 x	–	–
Eritrea	–	65	93 x	69 x	44 x	86 x	–	–	–	–	–	–
Estonia	4	0	–	–	–	–	–	–	–	–	–	–
Eswatini	10	9	48	64	90	28	29	19	48	85	38	–
Ethiopia	–	86	73	57	60	85	84	83	12	45	7	69

TABLE 7. NUTRITION: NEWBORNS, INFANTS AND YOUNG CHILDREN

Countries and areas	Weight at birth		Infant and Young Child Feeding (0–23 months) 2013–2018*									
	Low birthweight (%) 2015	Unweighed at birth (%) 2010–2018*	Early initiation of breastfeeding (%)	Exclusive breastfeeding (<6 months) (%)	Introduction to solid, semi-solid or soft foods (6–8 months) (%)	Continued breastfeeding (12–23 months) (%)			Minimum diet diversity (6–23 months) (%)	Minimum meal frequency (6–23 months) (%)	Minimum acceptable diet (6–23 months) (%)	Zero vegetable or fruit consumption (6–23 months) (%)
						All children	Poorest 20%	Richest 20%				
Fiji	–	11 x	57 x	40 x	–	–	–	–	–	–	–	–
Finland	4	6	–	–	–	–	–	–	–	–	–	–
France	7	0	–	–	–	–	–	–	–	–	–	–
Gabon	14	9	32 x	5 x	82 x	23 x	34 x	19 x	18 x	–	–	52 x
Gambia	17	41	52	47	55	78	81	69	10	58	8	76
Georgia	6	0	69 x	55 x	85 x	30 x	31 x	31 x	–	–	–	–
Germany	7	2	–	–	–	–	–	–	–	–	–	–
Ghana	14	40	56	52	73	76	92	71	24	43	13	51
Greece	9	4	–	–	–	–	–	–	–	–	–	–
Grenada	–	–	–	–	–	–	–	–	–	–	–	–
Guatemala	11	6	63	53	80	72	85	48	59	82	52	27
Guinea	–	49	34	33	54	78	91 r	53 r	6	24	2	85
Guinea-Bissau	21	56	34	53	57	77	83	57	10	57	8	44
Guyana	16	11	49	21	81	46	64	25	40	63	28	33
Haiti	–	67	47	40	91	52	59	43	19	39	11	55
Holy See	–	–	–	–	–	–	–	–	–	–	–	–
Honduras	11	17	64 x	31 x	86 x	59 x	76 x	42 x	61 x	86 x	55 x	36 x
Hungary	9	0	–	–	–	–	–	–	–	–	–	–
Iceland	4	8	–	–	–	–	–	–	–	–	–	–
India	– z	22	41	55	46	80	88	69	20	36	10	55
Indonesia	10	10	58	51	86	67	74	56	54	72	40	18
Iran (Islamic Republic of)	–	–	69 x	53 x	76 x	–	–	–	–	–	–	–
Iraq	–	28	32	26	85	35	47	32	45	78	35	25
Ireland	6	4	–	–	–	–	–	–	–	–	–	–
Israel	8	0	–	–	–	–	–	–	–	–	–	–
Italy	7	2	–	–	–	–	–	–	–	–	–	–
Jamaica	15	4	65 x	24 x	64 x	38 x	39 x	29 x	–	42 x	–	–
Japan	9	5	–	–	–	–	–	–	–	–	–	–
Jordan	14	5	67	25	83	26	28	33	35	62	23	41
Kazakhstan	5	1	83	38	66	41	40	45	49	77	38	21
Kenya	11	34	62	61	80	75	79	69	36	51	22	29
Kiribati	–	24 x	80 x	66 x	70 x	85 x	92 x	80 x	27 x	–	–	–
Kuwait	10	30	–	–	–	–	–	–	–	–	–	–
Kyrgyzstan	6	0	81	46	91	47	53	36	60	76	44	14
Lao People's Democratic Republic	17	33	50	44	87	43	66	19	36	70	27	36
Latvia	5	0	–	–	–	–	–	–	–	–	–	–
Lebanon	9	0	41 x	–	–	14 x	–	–	–	–	–	–
Lesotho	15	17	65	67	83	53	74	26	17	61	11	50
Liberia	–	77	61	55	47	69	76	53	10	30	5	39
Libya	–	–	–	–	–	–	–	–	–	–	–	–
Liechtenstein	–	–	–	–	–	–	–	–	–	–	–	–
Lithuania	5	7	–	–	–	–	–	–	–	–	–	–
Luxembourg	7	0	–	–	–	–	–	–	–	–	–	–
Madagascar	17	60 x	66 x	42 x	90 x	79 x	79 x	77 x	22 x	–	–	33 x
Malawi	14	16	76	59	85	84	87	78	23	29	8	23
Malaysia	11	1	–	40	–	–	–	–	–	–	–	–
Maldives	12	11	67	63	97	73	79	– p	71	70	51	15
Mali	–	63	53	40	42	79	82 r	73 r	11	23	3	70
Malta	6	0	–	–	–	–	–	–	–	–	–	–
Marshall Islands		10	61	43	64	36	25	– p	34	61	16	46
Mauritania	–	64	68	40	74	70	75	61	28	39	14	51
Mauritius	17	6	–	–	–	–	–	–	–	–	–	–
Mexico	8	2	51	30	82	36	52	16	59	81	48	18
Micronesia (Federated States of)	–	–	–	–	–	–	–	–	–	–	–	–
Monaco	5	0	–	–	–	–	–	–	–	–	–	–
Mongolia	5	1	84	59	97	64	66	58	45	92	41	37
Montenegro	5	1	14	17	95	15	27	11	69	90	61	9
Montserrat	–	–	–	–	–	–	–	–	–	–	–	–
Morocco	17	27	43	35	84 x	35 x	45 x	19 x	–	–	–	–
Mozambique	14	49	69	41	95	75 x	80 x	53 x	28 x	41 x	13 x	36 x
Myanmar	12	55	67	51	75	78	84	66	21	58	16	56
Namibia	16	14	71	48	80	47	55	27	25	41	13	52
Nauru	–	4	76 x	67 x	–	67 x	–	–	–	–	–	–

TABLE 7. NUTRITION: NEWBORNS, INFANTS AND YOUNG CHILDREN

Countries and areas	Weight at birth		Infant and Young Child Feeding (0–23 months) 2013–2018*									
	Low birthweight (%) 2015	Unweighed at birth (%) 2010–2018*	Early initiation of breastfeeding (%)	Exclusive breastfeeding (<6 months) (%)	Introduction to solid, semi-solid or soft foods (6–8 months) (%)	Continued breastfeeding (12–23 months) (%)			Minimum diet diversity (6–23 months) (%)	Minimum meal frequency (6–23 months) (%)	Minimum acceptable diet (6–23 months) (%)	Zero vegetable or fruit consumption (6–23 months) (%)
						All children	Poorest 20%	Richest 20%				
Nepal	22	39	55	65	84	94	97	91	45	71	36	38
Netherlands	6	6	–	–	–	–	–	–	–	–	–	–
New Zealand	6	8	–	–	–	–	–	–	–	–	–	–
Nicaragua	11	8	54 x	32 x	89 x	52 x	64 x	28 x	–	–	–	–
Niger	–	77	53 x	23 x	62 x	78 x	85 x	71 x	8 x	51 x	6 x	67 x
Nigeria	–	75	33	25	66	51	80 r	48 r	34	46	15	32
Niue	–	–	–	–	–	–	–	–	–	–	–	–
North Macedonia	9	4	21 x	23 x	87 x	27 x	25 x	26 x	–	65 x	–	–
Norway	4	3	–	–	–	–	–	–	–	–	–	–
Oman	11	0	82	23	95	–	–	–	–	65	–	–
Pakistan	–	84	20	47	65	63	75	52	15	63	13	61
Palau	–	–	–	–	–	–	–	–	–	–	–	–
Panama	10	9	47	21	78	41	57	18	–	64	–	–
Papua New Guinea	–	–	–	56 x	–	–	–	–	–	–	–	–
Paraguay	8	2	50	30	87	33	41	43	52	75	40	16
Peru	9	5	50	66	95	65	69	53	83	–	–	7
Philippines	20	16	57	33 x	89 x	60	68	49	54 x	–	–	22 x
Poland	6	0	–	–	–	–	–	–	–	–	–	–
Portugal	9	0	–	–	–	–	–	–	–	–	–	–
Qatar	7	2	34 x	29 x	74 x	47 x	–	–	–	49 x	–	–
Republic of Korea	6	2	–	–	–	–	–	–	–	–	–	–
Republic of Moldova	5	1	61 x	36 x	75 x	27 x	44 x	22 x	70 x	49 x	–	10 x
Romania	8	2	58 x	16 x	–	–	–	–	–	–	–	–
Russian Federation	6	0	25 x	–	–	–	–	–	–	–	–	–
Rwanda	8	8	80	87	57	91	94	81	28	47	18	25
Saint Kitts and Nevis	–	–	–	–	–	–	–	–	–	–	–	–
Saint Lucia	–	0	50 x	3 x	– x,p	29 x	– x,p	– x,p	–	50 x	–	–
Saint Vincent and the Grenadines	–	–	–	–	–	–	–	–	–	–	–	–
Samoa	–	24	81	70	74	73	–	–	–	–	–	–
San Marino	3	2	–	–	–	–	–	–	–	–	–	–
Sao Tome and Principe	7	7	38	72	74	51	65	46	37	60	23	27
Saudi Arabia	–	–	–	–	–	–	–	–	–	–	–	–
Senegal	18	40	34	42	67	70	77	61	20	31	8	52
Serbia	5	2	51	13	97	15	20	18	77	96	70	3
Seychelles	12	0	–	–	–	–	–	–	–	–	–	–
Sierra Leone	14	52	56	47	68	61	71	33	18	43	9	41
Singapore	10	17	–	–	–	–	–	–	–	–	–	–
Slovakia	8	2	–	–	–	–	–	–	–	–	–	–
Slovenia	6	4	–	–	–	–	–	–	–	–	–	–
Solomon Islands	–	14	79	76	–	71	–	–	–	–	–	–
Somalia	–	96 x	23 x	5 x	17 x	43 x	61 x	23 x	–	–	–	–
South Africa	14	19	67	32	83	34	47	25	40	52	23	37
South Sudan	–	–	50 x	45 x	42 x	62 x	67 x	58 x	–	12 x	–	–
Spain	8	4	–	–	–	–	–	–	–	–	–	–
Sri Lanka	16	0	90	82	88	91	–	–	–	–	–	–
State of Palestine	8	0	41	38	90	31	33	29	50	79	39	27
Sudan	–	89	69	55	61	73	72	74	24	42	15	67
Suriname	15	19	45 x	3 x	79 x	17 x	16 x	15 x	–	64 x	–	–
Sweden	2	5	–	–	–	–	–	–	–	–	–	–
Switzerland	6	0	–	–	–	–	–	–	–	–	–	–
Syrian Arab Republic	–	52 x	46 x	43 x	44 x	45 x	57 x	42 x	–	–	–	–
Tajikistan	6	9	62	36	63	57	63	53	23	40	9	58
Thailand	11	1	40	23	85	24	35	11	63	85	54	22
Timor-Leste	–	47	75	50	63	52	61	44	28	46	13	35
Togo	16	40	61	57	67	82	92	69	18	46	12	45
Tokelau	–	–	–	–	–	–	–	–	–	–	–	–
Tonga	–	6	79 x	52 x	–	41 x	–	–	–	–	–	–
Trinidad and Tobago	12	19	46 x	21 x	56 x	34 x	45 x	– x,p	–	70 x	–	–
Tunisia	7	3	32	14	97	30	39	28	–	88	55	20
Turkey	11	0	50	30	75	50	–	–	–	–	–	–
Turkmenistan	5	1	73	58	82	44	54	24	82	93	77	9
Turks and Caicos Islands	–	–	–	–	–	–	–	–	–	–	–	–
Tuvalu	–	3 x	15 x	35 x	–	53 x	–	–	–	–	–	–

TABLE 7. NUTRITION: NEWBORNS, INFANTS AND YOUNG CHILDREN

Countries and areas	Weight at birth		Infant and Young Child Feeding (0–23 months) 2013–2018*									
	Low birthweight (%) 2015	Unweighed at birth (%) 2010–2018*	Early initiation of breastfeeding (%)	Exclusive breastfeeding (<6 months) (%)	Introduction to solid, semi-solid or soft foods (6–8 months) (%)	Continued breastfeeding (12–23 months) (%)			Minimum diet diversity (6–23 months) (%)	Minimum meal frequency (6–23 months) (%)	Minimum acceptable diet (6–23 months) (%)	Zero vegetable or fruit consumption (6–23 months) (%)
						All children	Poorest 20%	Richest 20%				
Uganda	–	33	66	65	81	67	77	53	26	42	15	44
Ukraine	6	3	66 x	20 x	75 x	31 x	31 x	30 x	–	64 x	–	–
United Arab Emirates	13	3	–	–	–	–	–	–	–	–	–	–
United Kingdom	7	4	–	–	–	–	–	–	–	–	–	–
United Republic of Tanzania	10	36	51	59	92	72	75	70	21	40	9	29
United States	8	2	–	35	–	13	–	–	–	–	–	–
Uruguay	8	6	77	–	–	–	–	–	–	–	–	–
Uzbekistan	5	1 x	67 x	24 x	47 x	57 x	66 x	52 x	–	–	–	–
Vanuatu	11	13	85	73	72	58	–	–	–	–	–	–
Venezuela (Bolivarian Republic of)	9	–	–	–	–	–	–	–	–	–	–	–
Viet Nam	8	6	26	24	91	43	55	29	59	91	55	14
Yemen	–	92	53	10	69	63	73	56	21	59	15	66
Zambia	12	34	66	70	82	63	87 r	48 r	18	42	10	35
Zimbabwe	13	18	58	47	91	55	61	45	23	36	8	32
SUMMARY												
East Asia and Pacific	8	6	38	30	84	60 q	68 q	47 q	40	71	30	23 q
Europe and Central Asia	7	2	–	–	–	–	–	–	–	–	–	–
Eastern Europe and Central Asia	7	2	57 q	33 q	75 q	47 q	–	–	–	–	–	–
Western Europe	7	3	–	–	–	–	–	–	–	–	–	–
Latin America and Caribbean	9	7	54 q	38 q	84 q	45 q	57 q	28 q	60 q	75 q	–	21 q
Middle East and North Africa	11	35	36	30	78	47	55	42	36	65	26	42
North America	8	2	–	35	–	13	–	–	–	–	–	–
South Asia	27	39	40	54	52	78	86	67	20	44	12	55
Sub-Saharan Africa	14	52	52	44	72	67	79	59	24	43	12	42
Eastern and Southern Africa	14	48	65	55	77	72	77	65	24	43	13	44
West and Central Africa	14	54	41	34	68	64	82	53	25	42	12	40
Least developed countries	16	54	58	51	72	78	82	69	21	45	13	49
World	**15**	**29**	**44**	**42**	**69**	**65**	**78**	**58**	**29**	**53**	**19**	**44**

For a complete list of countries and areas in the regions, subregions and country categories, see page 182 or visit <data.unicef.org/regionalclassifications>.

It is not advisable to compare data from consecutive editions of *The State of the World's Children*.

DEFINITIONS OF THE INDICATORS

Low birthweight – Percentage of infants weighing less than 2,500 grams at birth.

Unweighed at birth – Percentage of births without a birthweight in the data source; Note that (i) estimates from household surveys include live births among women age 15–49 years in the survey reference period (e.g. last 2 years) for which a birthweight was not available from an official document (e.g. health card) or could not be recalled by the respondent at the time of interview and may have been recalculated to count birthweights <250g and >5500g as missing and (ii) estimates from administrative sources (e.g. Health Management Information Systems) were calculated using numerator data from the country administrative source and denominator data were the number of annual births according to the United Nations Population Division World Population Prospects, 2017 edition. These estimates include unweighed births and weighed births not recorded in the system.

Early initiation of breastfeeding – Percentage of children born in the last 24 months who were put to the breast within one hour of birth.

Exclusive breastfeeding (<6 months) – Percentage of infants 0–5 months of age who were fed exclusively with breastmilk during the previous day.

Continued breastfeeding (12–23 months) – Percentage of children 12–23 months of age who were fed with breastmilk during the previous day.

Introduction of solid, semi-solid or soft foods (6–8 months) – Percentage of infants 6–8 months of age who were fed with solid, semi-solid or soft food during the previous day.

Minimum Diet Diversity (6–23 months) – Percentage of children 6-23 months of age who received foods from at least 5 out of 8 defined food groups during the previous day.

Minimum Meal Frequency (6–23 months) – Percentage of children 6–23 months of age who received solid, semi-solid, or soft foods (but also including milk feeds for non-breastfed children) the minimum number of times or more during the previous day.

Minimum Acceptable Diet (6–23 months) – Percentage of children 6–23 months of age who received a minimum acceptable diet during the previous day.

Zero vegetable or fruit consumption (6–23 months) – Percentage of children 6–23 months of age who did not consume any vegetables or fruits during the previous day.

MAIN DATA SOURCES

Low birthweight – Modelled estimates from UNICEF and WHO. Last update: May 2019.

Unweighed at birth – Demographic and Health Surveys (DHS), Multiple Indicator Cluster Surveys (MICS), other national household surveys, data from routine reporting systems. Last update: June 2019.

Infant and young child feeding (0–23 months) – DHS, MICS and other national household surveys. Last update: June 2019.

NOTES

–   Data not available.

x   Data refer to years or periods other than those specified in the column heading. Such data are not included in the calculation of regional and global averages. Estimates from years prior to 2000 are not displayed.

p   Based on small denominators (typically 25-49 unweighted cases). No data based on fewer than 25 unweighted cases are displayed.

q   Regional estimates for East Asia and Pacific exclude China, Latin America and the Caribbean exclude Brazil, Eastern Europe and Central Asia exclude the Russian Federation.

r   Disaggregated data are from different sources than the data presented for all children for the same indicator.

z   The estimate is based on partial data for the most recent survey, therefore modeled estimates are not shown for the individual country but have been used in regional and global estimates.

*   Data refer to the most recent year available during the period specified in the column heading.

TABLE 8. NUTRITION: PRESCHOOL/SCHOOL AGE CHILDREN, WOMEN AND HOUSEHOLDS

Countries and areas	Malnutrition among preschool-aged children (0–4 years of age) 2013–2018*						Vitamin A supplementation, full coverage (%) 2017	Malnutrition among school-aged children (5–19 years of age) 2016		Malnutrition among women 2016		Percentage of households consuming iodized salt 2013–2018*
	Stunted (%) (moderate and severe)			Wasted (%)		Overweight (%)		Thinness (%)	Overweight (%)	Underweight 18+ years (%)	Anaemia 15–49 years (%)	
	all children	poorest 20%	richest 20%	severe	moderate and severe	moderate and severe		thin and severely thin	overweight and obese	BMI <18.5 kg/m²	mild, moderate and severe	
Afghanistan	41	49	31	4	10	5	95 f	17	9	16	42	57
Albania	11	17	9	1	2	16	–	1	25	2	25	65
Algeria	12	13 x	11 x	1 x	4 x	12 x	–	6	31	4	36	81
Andorra	–	–	–	–	–	–	–	1	36	1	14	–
Angola	38	47	20	1	5	3	3 f	8	11	11	48	82
Anguilla	–	–	–	–	–	–	–	–	–	–	–	–
Antigua and Barbuda	–	–	–	–	–	–	–	3	27	4	22	–
Argentina	8 x	–	–	<1 x	1 x	10 x	–	1	37	1	19	–
Armenia	9	12	6	2	4	14	–	2	19	3	29	99
Australia	2 x	–	–	<1 x	<1 x	8 x	–	1	34	2	9	–
Austria	–	–	–	–	–	–	–	2	27	3	17	–
Azerbaijan	18	28	16	1	3	14	41 f,w	3	19	3	38	93
Bahamas	–	–	–	–	–	–	–	3	36	3	23	–
Bahrain	–	–	–	–	–	–	–	6	35	4	42	–
Bangladesh	36	49	20	3	14	2	99 f	18	9	22	40	68
Barbados	8	8 x	3 x	2 x	7 x	12 x	–	4	28	3	22	37 x
Belarus	4 x	10 x	2 x	1 x	2 x	10 x	–	2	23	2	23	–
Belgium	–	–	–	–	–	–	–	1	24	2	16	–
Belize	15	26	5	1	2	7	–	3	29	3	22	85
Benin	32	46	18	1	5	2	99 f	7	11	9	47	85
Bhutan	34 x	41 x	21 x	2 x	6 x	8 x	– f	16	10	11	36	–
Bolivia (Plurinational State of)	16	32 x,r	9 x,r	1	2	10	31 f	1	28	2	30	86
Bosnia and Herzegovina	9	10 x	10 x	2 x	2 x	17 x	–	2	21	2	29	–
Botswana	31 x	–	–	3 x	7 x	11 x	83 f	6	18	7	30	83 x
Brazil	7 x	–	–	<1 x	2 x	6 x	–	3	28	3	27	98 x
British Virgin Islands	–	–	–	–	–	–	–	–	–	–	–	–
Brunei Darussalam	20 x	–	–	<1 x	3 x	8 x	–	6	27	6	17	–
Bulgaria	9 w,x	–	–	1 w,x	3 w,x	14 w,x	–	2	29	2	26	92 x,y
Burkina Faso	21	42 x,r	19 x,r	2	9	2	0 f	8	8	13	50	92 x
Burundi	56	69	31	1	5	1	79 f	7	10	12	27	89
Cabo Verde	–	–	–	–	–	–	–	7	12	8	33	97 x,y
Cambodia	32	42	19	2	10	2	73 f	11	11	14	47	68
Cameroon	32	42	14	1	5	7	9 f	6	13	7	41	86
Canada	–	–	–	–	–	10 x,y	–	1	32	2	10	–
Central African Republic	40	45 x	30 x	2 x	8 x	2 x	0 f	8	11	13	46	84 x
Chad	40	41	31	4	13	3	67 f	8	9	14	48	77
Chile	2	–	–	–	<1	9	–	1	35	1	15	–
China	8	–	–	1 x	2	9	–	3	29	6	26	96 b,y
Colombia	13 x	19 x	6 x	<1 x	1 x	5 x	–	2	24	3	21	–
Comoros	31	39 x	24 x	4 x	11 x	11 x	21 f	7	12	9	29	82 x
Congo	21	30	14	3	8	6	12 f	7	11	12	52	91
Cook Islands	–	–	–	–	–	–	–	<1	63	<1	–	–
Costa Rica	6 x	–	–	–	1 x	8 x	–	2	32	2	15	–
Côte d'Ivoire	22	30	9	1	6	1	94 f	6	13	8	53	80
Croatia	–	–	–	–	–	–	–	1	28	2	27	–
Cuba	7 x	–	–	–	2 x	–	–	3	30	4	25	–
Cyprus	–	–	–	–	–	–	–	1	33	2	25	–
Czechia	3 x	–	–	1 x	5 x	4 x	–	2	28	1	26	–
Democratic People's Republic of Korea	19	–	–	1	3	2	90 f	5	23	8	32	–
Democratic Republic of the Congo	43	49	23	3	8	4	1 f	9	10	14	41	82
Denmark	–	–	–	–	–	–	–	1	25	3	16	–
Djibouti	34	41 x	23 x	9 x	22 x	8 x	– f	6	17	8	33	4 x
Dominica	–	–	–	–	–	–	–	3	33	3	24	–
Dominican Republic	7	12	4	1	2	8	–	3	33	4	30	30 x
Ecuador	24	37 x,r	14 x,r	1	2	8	–	1	28	2	19	–
Egypt	22	25	24	5	9	16	– f	3	37	1	29	93
El Salvador	14	24	5	<1	2	6	–	2	30	3	23	–
Equatorial Guinea	26 x	28 x	19 x	2 x	3 x	10 x	5 f	8	11	10	44	57 x
Eritrea	52 x	59 x	29 x	4 x	15 x	2 x	– f,z	8	11	17	38	86 x
Estonia	–	–	–	–	–	–	–	2	21	2	26	–
Eswatini	26	30	9	<1	2	9	33 f	4	17	6	27	90

TABLE 8. NUTRITION: PRESCHOOL/SCHOOL AGE CHILDREN, WOMEN AND HOUSEHOLDS

Countries and areas	Malnutrition among preschool-aged children (0–4 years of age) 2013–2018*						Vitamin A supplemen-tation, full coverage (%) 2017	Malnutrition among school-aged children (5–19 years of age) 2016		Malnutrition among women 2016		Percentage of households consuming iodized salt 2013–2018*
	Stunted (%) (moderate and severe)			Wasted (%)		Overweight (%)		Thinness (%)	Overweight (%)	Underweight 18+ years (%)	Anaemia 15–49 years (%)	
	all children	poorest 20%	richest 20%	severe	moderate and severe	moderate and severe		thin and severely thin	overweight and obese	BMI <18.5 kg/m²	mild, moderate and severe	
Ethiopia	38	45	26	3	10	3	77 f	10	9	15	23	86
Fiji	8 x	–	–	2 x	6 x	5 x	–	4	34	2	31	–
Finland	–	–	–	–	–	–	–	1	27	1	16	–
France	–	–	–	–	–	–	–	1	30	3	18	–
Gabon	17	31 x	6 x	1 x	3 x	8 x	0 f	6	16	7	59	89 x
Gambia	25	29	15	4	11	3	32 f	7	12	10	58	69
Georgia	11 x	22 x	8 x	1 x	2 x	20 x	–	3	20	3	27	>99 x,y
Germany	1 x	–	–	<1 x	1 x	4 x	–	1	26	1	16	–
Ghana	19	25	8	1	5	3	50 f	6	11	7	46	64
Greece	–	–	–	–	–	–	–	1	37	1	16	–
Grenada	–	–	–	–	–	–	–	4	26	4	23	–
Guatemala	47	66	17	<1	1	5	26 f,w	1	29	2	16	88 x
Guinea	32	39	18	3	8	4	64 f	7	10	11	51	73
Guinea-Bissau	28	31	15	1	6	2	95 f	7	11	9	44	26
Guyana	11	20	7	2	6	5	–	5	25	5	32	43
Haiti	22	34	9	1	4	3	17 f	4	28	6	46	8
Holy See	–	–	–	–	–	–	–	–	–	–	–	–
Honduras	23	42 x	8 x	<1 x	1 x	5 x	–	2	27	3	18	–
Hungary	–	–	–	–	–	–	–	2	28	2	26	–
Iceland	–	–	–	–	–	–	–	1	28	2	16	–
India	38	51	22	8	21	2	– f,z	27	7	24	51	93
Indonesia	36	48	29	7	14	12	62 f	10	15	12	29	92 b,y
Iran (Islamic Republic of)	7 x	–	–	1 x	4 x	–	–	9	26	4	30	–
Iraq	22 x	24 x	21 x	3 x	6 x	11 x	–	5	32	3	29	68
Ireland	–	–	–	–	–	–	–	1	31	1	15	–
Israel	–	–	–	–	–	–	–	1	35	1	16	–
Italy	–	–	–	–	–	–	–	1	37	1	17	–
Jamaica	6	–	–	1	4	8	–	2	30	4	23	–
Japan	7 x	–	–	<1 x	2 x	2 x	–	2	14	10	22	–
Jordan	8	14 x	2 x	1 x	2 x	5 x	– f	4	31	4	31	88 b,x,y
Kazakhstan	8	10	6	1	3	9	–	2	20	4	31	94
Kenya	26	36	14	1	4	4	44 f	8	11	10	27	95
Kiribati	–	–	–	–	–	–	37 f	<1	55	1	26	–
Kuwait	5	–	–	1	3	8	– x,y	4	42	1	24	–
Kyrgyzstan	13	18	11	1	3	7	– f	3	16	4	36	99
Lao People's Democratic Republic	44 x	61 x	20 x	2 x	6 x	2 x	57 f	9	14	12	40	94
Latvia	–	–	–	–	–	–	–	2	22	2	25	–
Lebanon	17 x	–	–	3 x	7 x	17 x	–	5	33	3	31	95 x
Lesotho	33	46	13	1	3	7	18 f	5	15	5	27	85
Liberia	32	36	20	2	6	3	97 f	7	10	8	35	91
Libya	21 x	–	–	3 x	7 x	22 x	–	6	33	2	33	69 x
Liechtenstein	–	–	–	–	–	–	–	–	–	–	–	–
Lithuania	–	–	–	–	–	–	–	3	21	1	26	–
Luxembourg	–	–	–	–	–	–	–	1	26	2	16	–
Madagascar	49	39	47	1	8	1	87 f	7	11	15	37	68 x
Malawi	37	46	25	1	3	5	91 f	6	11	9	34	78
Malaysia	21	–	–	–	12	6	–	7	27	7	25	28 x,y
Maldives	19 x	22 x	15 x	3 x	11 x	6 x	69 f	14	17	9	43	97 x
Mali	30	41	15	3	13	2	9 f	8	11	10	51	90
Malta	–	–	–	–	–	–	–	1	37	1	16	–
Marshall Islands	35	44	20	1	4	4	– f	<1	59	1	27	–
Mauritania	28	36	19	4	15	1	0 f	8	13	8	37	8
Mauritius	–	–	–	–	–	–	–	2	15	7	25	–
Mexico	10	16	7	<1	2	5	– f	2	35	2	15	–
Micronesia (Federated States of)	–	–	–	–	–	–	– f	<1	51	2	23	–
Monaco	–	–	–	–	–	–	–	<1	<1	<1	–	–
Mongolia	7	14	3	<1	1	12	83 f	2	18	3	19	80
Montenegro	9	5	9	1	3	22	–	2	25	2	25	–
Montserrat	–	–	–	–	–	–	–	–	–	–	–	–
Morocco	15 x	28 x	7 x	1 x	2 x	11 x	99 f,w	6	27	3	37	43 x
Mozambique	43 x	51 x	24 x	2 x	6 x	8 x	61 f	4	13	10	51	42 x
Myanmar	29	38	16	1	7	2	89 f	13	12	14	46	81

TABLE 8. NUTRITION: PRESCHOOL/SCHOOL AGE CHILDREN, WOMEN AND HOUSEHOLDS

Countries and areas	Malnutrition among preschool-aged children (0–4 years of age) 2013–2018* Stunted (%) (moderate and severe) all children	poorest 20%	richest 20%	Wasted (%) severe	moderate and severe	Overweight (%) moderate and severe	Vitamin A supplemen-tation, full coverage (%) 2017	Malnutrition among school-aged children (5–19 years of age) 2016 Thinness (%) thin and severely thin	Overweight (%) overweight and obese	Malnutrition among women 2016 Underweight 18+ years (%) BMI <18.5 kg/m²	Anaemia 15–49 years (%) mild, moderate and severe	Percentage of households consuming iodized salt 2013–2018*
Namibia	23	31	9	3	7	4	27 f	8	15	9	23	74
Nauru	24 x	52 x	18 x	<1 x	1 x	3 x	–	<1	65	<1	–	–
Nepal	36	48	18	2	10	1	81 f	16	8	17	35	94
Netherlands	–	–	–	–	–	–	–	1	25	2	16	–
New Zealand	–	–	–	–	–	–	–	<1	40	2	12	–
Nicaragua	17	35 x	6 x	1 x	2 x	8 x	– f	2	29	3	16	–
Niger	41	47 x,r	35 x,r	2	10	1	53 f	10	8	13	49	59
Nigeria	44	63	18	3	11	2	83 f	10	8	10	50	93 x
Niue	–	–	–	–	–	–	–	<1	59	1	–	–
North Macedonia	5 x	7 x	2 x	<1 x	2 x	12 x	–	2	26	2	23	–
Norway	–	–	–	–	–	–	–	1	27	2	15	–
Oman	14	–	–	2	8	4	–	7	32	5	38	88
Pakistan	38	56	22	2	7	3	92 f	19	10	15	52	69 x,y
Palau	–	–	–	–	–	–	–	<1	64	1	–	–
Panama	19 x	–	–	<1 x	1 x	10 x	–	2	29	3	23	–
Papua New Guinea	49 x	–	–	6 x	14 x	14 x	– f	1	32	3	37	60 x
Paraguay	6	12	1	<1	1	12	–	2	28	3	23	93 x
Peru	13	29	5	<1	1	8	–	1	27	2	18	89
Philippines	33	49	15	2 x	7	4	– f	10	13	14	16	52 y
Poland	3	–	–	–	–	–	–	2	26	2	26	–
Portugal	–	–	–	–	–	–	–	1	32	1	18	–
Qatar	–	–	–	–	–	–	–	5	39	2	28	–
Republic of Korea	3 x	–	–	<1 x	1 x	7 x	–	1	27	5	23	–
Republic of Moldova	6	11 x	3 x	<1 x	2 x	5 x	–	3	18	2	27	58 x
Romania	13 x	–	–	1 x	4 x	8 x	–	3	25	2	27	–
Russian Federation	–	–	–	–	–	–	–	2	21	2	23	–
Rwanda	37 w	49	21	<1 w	2 w	6	98 f	6	11	8	22	90
Saint Kitts and Nevis	–	–	–	–	–	–	–	4	28	3	–	–
Saint Lucia	2	5 x	– x,p	1 x	4 x	6 x	–	4	23	4	22	75 x
Saint Vincent and the Grenadines	–	–	–	–	–	–	–	3	29	4	25	–
Samoa	5	6	3	1	4	5	–	<1	53	1	31	96
San Marino	–	–	–	–	–	–	–	<1	<1	<1	–	–
Sao Tome and Principe	17	25	7	1	4	2	23 f	5	13	8	46	91
Saudi Arabia	9 x	–	–	5 x	12 x	6 x	–	8	36	3	43	70 x,y
Senegal	17	27	6	1	9	1	58 f	9	10	11	50	62
Serbia	6	14	4	1	4	14	–	2	27	2	27	–
Seychelles	8	–	–	1 x	4 x	10 x	–	6	23	5	22	–
Sierra Leone	38	42	29	4	9	9	98 f	7	11	10	48	85
Singapore	4 x	–	–	1 x	4 x	3 x	–	2	22	8	22	–
Slovakia	–	–	–	–	–	–	–	1	23	2	27	–
Slovenia	–	–	–	–	–	–	–	1	27	2	24	–
Solomon Islands	32	37	25	4	8	5	–	1	23	2	39	88
Somalia	25 x	52 x	25 x	5 x	15 x	3 x	11 f	7	13	10	44	7 x
South Africa	27	36	13	1	2	13	47 f	5	25	3	26	91
South Sudan	31 x	31 x	27 x	12 x	24 x	6 x	51 f	<1	<1	<1	34	60 x
Spain	–	–	–	–	–	–	–	1	34	1	17	–
Sri Lanka	17	25	12	3	15	2	93 f	15	13	13	33	95 y
State of Palestine	7	7	6	<1	1	8	–	–	–	–	–	88
Sudan	38	44	21	5	17	3	20 f	<1	<1	<1	31	34
Suriname	9 x	13 x	6 x	2 x	6 x	4 x	–	4	31	3	24	–
Sweden	–	–	–	–	–	–	–	1	24	2	15	–
Switzerland	–	–	–	–	–	–	–	<1	22	3	18	–
Syrian Arab Republic	28 x	33 x	22 x	5 x	12 x	18 x	91 f	6	28	3	34	65 x
Tajikistan	18	22	17	2	6	3	–	4	15	5	31	91
Thailand	11	13	12	1	5	8	–	8	22	8	32	85
Timor-Leste	51	59	39	2	11	1	66 f	11	13	19	41	83
Togo	28	33	11	1	7	2	87 f	6	10	9	49	77
Tokelau	–	–	–	–	–	–	–	–	–	–	–	–
Tonga	8	7 x	10 x	2 x	5 x	17 x	–	<1	58	<1	21	–
Trinidad and Tobago	9 x	9 x	15 x	2 x	6 x	11 x	–	6	25	3	24	63 x
Tunisia	10	16 x	8 x	2 x	3 x	14 x	–	7	25	3	31	–
Turkey	10	19	5	<1	2	11	–	5	30	2	31	85 x

TABLE 8. NUTRITION: PRESCHOOL/SCHOOL AGE CHILDREN, WOMEN AND HOUSEHOLDS

Countries and areas	Malnutrition among preschool-aged children (0–4 years of age) 2013–2018*						Vitamin A supplemen-tation, full coverage (%) 2017	Malnutrition among school-aged children (5–19 years of age) 2016		Malnutrition among women 2016		Percentage of households consuming iodized salt 2013–2018*
	Stunted (%) (moderate and severe)			Wasted (%)		Overweight (%)		Thinness (%)	Overweight (%)	Underweight 18+ years (%)	Anaemia 15–49 years (%)	
	all children	poorest 20%	richest 20%	severe	moderate and severe	moderate and severe		thin and severely thin	overweight and obese	BMI <18.5 kg/m²	mild, moderate and severe	
Turkmenistan	11	16	11	1	4	6	– f	3	18	4	33	>99
Turks and Caicos Islands	–	–	–	–	–	–	–	–	–	–	–	–
Tuvalu	10 x	8 x	13 x	1 x	3 x	6 x	–	<1	58	1	–	–
Uganda	29	32	17	1	3	4	27 f	6	10	10	29	91
Ukraine	23 x	–	–	4 x	8 x	27 x	–	5	36	3	28	36 x
United Arab Emirates	–	–	–	–	–	–	–	1	31	2	15	–
United Kingdom	–	–	–	–	–	–	–	7	12	10	37	76
United Republic of Tanzania	34	40	19	1	5	4	87 f	1	42	2	13	–
United States	4	–	–	<1	<1	9	–	2	33	1	21	–
Uruguay	11 x	–	–	<1 x	1 x	7 x	–	3	17	4	36	82 x
Uzbekistan	20 x	21 x	16 x	1	4	5	99 f	2	31	3	24	63
Vanuatu	29	39	16	1	4	5	–	2	34	2	24	–
Venezuela (Bolivarian Republic of)	13 x	–	–	–	4	6 x	–	2	34	2	24	–
Viet Nam	25	41 x,r	6 x,r	1	6	5	99 f,w	14	10	18	24	61 x
Yemen	46	59	26	5	16	2	– f	14	20	9	70	49
Zambia	40	47	28	2	6	6	99 f	6	13	9	34	88
Zimbabwe	27	33	17	1	3	6	43 f	6	15	6	29	93
SUMMARY												
East Asia and Pacific	8	44 q	22 q	1	3	6	74	6	23	8	27	92
Europe and Central Asia	–	–	–	–	–	–	–	2	26	2	23	–
Eastern Europe and Central Asia	9 e	18 q	8 q	1 e	2 e	15 e	–	3	23	2	28	–
Western Europe	–	–	–	–	–	–	–	1	30	2	18	–
Latin America and Caribbean	9	24 q	7 q	<1	1	7	–	2	30	3	22	–
Middle East and North Africa	15	–	–	3	8	11	–	6	31	3	34	–
North America	3 d	–	–	<1 d	<1 d	9 d	–	1	41	2	13	–
South Asia	34	51	22	5	15	3	66	25	8	23	50	89
Sub-Saharan Africa	33	46	20	2	8	4	55	7	10	10	39	80
Eastern and Southern Africa	34	42	22	2	6	4	57	7	11	9	31	82
West and Central Africa	34	50	18	2	6	4	53	9	10	10	48	76
Least developed countries	32	45	22	2	8	4	58	10	10	14	40	74
World	**22**	**45**	**20**	**2**	**7**	**6**	**62**	**11**	**18**	**9**	**33**	**88**

For a complete list of countries and areas in the regions, subregions and country categories, see page 182 or visit <data.unicef.org/regionalclassifications>.
It is not advisable to compare data from consecutive editions of *The State of the World's Children*.

DEFINITIONS OF THE INDICATORS

Stunting (preschoolers) – Moderate and severe: Percentage of children aged 0–59 months who are below minus two standard deviations from median height-for-age of the WHO Child Growth Standards.

Wasting (preschoolers) – Moderate and severe: Percentage of children aged 0–59 months who are below minus two standard deviations from median weight-for-height of the WHO Child Growth Standards.

Wasting (preschoolers) – Severe: Percentage of children aged 0–59 months who are below minus three standard deviations from median weight-for-height of the WHO Child Growth Standards.

Overweight (preschoolers) – Moderate and severe: Percentage of children aged 0–59 months who are above two standard deviations from median weight-for-height of the WHO Child Growth Standards (includes severe overweight).

Vitamin A supplementation, full coverage – The estimated percentage of children aged 6–59 months reached with 2 doses of vitamin A supplements approximately 4–6 months apart in a given calendar year.

Thinness (school-age children) – Percentage of children aged 5–19 years with BMI < −2 SD of the median according to the WHO growth reference for school-age children and adolescents.

Overweight (school-age children) – Percentage of children aged 5–19 years with BMI > 1 SD of the median according to the WHO growth reference for school-age children and adolescents.

Underweight (women 18+) – Percentage of women 18+ years of age with a body mass index (BMI) less than 18.5 kg/m².

Anaemia (women 15–49 years) – Percentage of women aged 15–49 years with a haemoglobin concentration less than 120 g/L for non-pregnant women and lactating women, and less than 110 g/L for pregnant women, adjusted for altitude and smoking.

Households consuming salt with iodine – Percentage of households consuming salt with any iodine (>0 ppm).

MAIN DATA SOURCES

Stunting, overweight, wasting and severe wasting (preschool children) – DHS, MICS, and other national household surveys. Last update: March 2019.

Vitamin A supplementation – UNICEF. Last Update: February 2019.

Thinness and overweight (school-age children), and underweight (women 18+) – NCD Risk Factor Collaboration (NCD-RisC), based on Worldwide trends in body mass index, underweight, overweight and obesity from 1975 to 2016: a pooled analysis of 2416 population-based measurement studies in 128.9 million children, adolescents, and adults. The Lancet 2017, 390 (10113): 2627–2642. Last update: August 2019.

Underweight (women 18+) – Global Health Observatory, WHO. Last update: August 2019.

Anaemia (women 15–49 years) – Global Health Observatory, WHO. Last update: August 2019.

Iodized salt consumption – DHS, MICS, other national household surveys, and school-based surveys. Last update: June 2019.

NOTES

– Data not available.

a Full coverage with vitamin A supplements is reported as the lower percentage of 2 annual coverage points (i.e., lower point between semester 1 (January–June) and semester 2 (July–December) of 2017. Data are only presented for VAS priority countries; thus aggregates are only based on and representative of these priority countries.

b Cannot be confirmed whether the reported value includes households without salt or not.

c Global and regional averages for stunting (moderate and severe), overweight (moderate and severe),wasting (moderate and severe) and wasting (severe) are estimated using statistical modelling data from the UNICEF-WHO-World Bank Group Joint Child Malnutrition Estimates, March 2019 Edition. For more information see <data.unicef.org/malnutrition>. Disaggregations for stunting (moderate and severe) are population-weighted, which means using the most recent estimate for each country with data between 2013 and 2018; therefore disaggregations may not coincide with total estimates at the global and regional level presented in this table.

d For stunting, wasting and severe wasting estimates, the Northern America regional average is based only on United States data; the Australia and New Zealand regional estimates for stunting and overweight are based only on Australian data.

e Consecutive low population coverage, interpret with caution.

f Identifies countries which are designated 'priority'. Priority countries for national vitamin A supplementation programmes are identified as having high under-five mortality rates (over 70 per 1,000 live births), and/or evidence of vitamin A deficiency among this age group, and/or a history of vitamin A supplementation programmes.

p Based on small denominators (typically 25-49 unweighted cases). No data based on fewer than 25 unweighted cases are displayed.

q Regional estimates for East Asia and Pacific exclude China, Latin America and the Caribbean exclude Brazil, Eastern Europe and Central Asia exclude the Russian Federation.

r Disaggregated data are from different sources than the data presented for all children for the same indicator.

w Reduced age range. For vitamin A supplementation, this identifies countries with national vitamin A supplementation programmes targeted towards a reduced age range. Coverage figure is reported as targeted.

x Data refer to years or periods other than those specified in the column heading. Such data are not included in the calculation of regional and global averages. Estimates from data years prior to 2000 are not displayed.

y Data differ from the standard definition or refer to only part of a country. If they fall within the noted reference period, such data are included in the calculation of regional and global averages.

z Identifies countries for which the national estimate is not displayed but for which the national estimate has been used for regional and all priority country estimates.

* Data refer to the most recent year available during the period specified in the column heading.

TABLE 9. EARLY CHILDHOOD DEVELOPMENT

Countries and areas	Attendance in early childhood education 2010–2018*					Early stimulation and responsive care by adults+ 2010–2018*					Early stimulation and responsive care by father+ 2010–2018*	Learning materials at home 2010–2018*						Children with inadequate supervision 2010–2018*				
												Children's books			Playthings+							
	total	male	female	poorest 20%	richest 20%	total	male	female	poorest 20%	richest 20%		total	poorest 20%	richest 20%	total	poorest 20%	richest 20%	total	male	female	poorest 20%	richest 20%
Afghanistan	1	1	1	0	4	73	74	73	72	80	62 y	2	1	5	53	52	57	40	42	39	43	27
Albania	73	73	73	62	88	78	75	80	57	88	14	32 x	16 x	52 x	53 x	57 x	48 x	7	7	6	9	3
Algeria	17	17	16	7	31	78	79	78	64	92	79 y	11	3	23	35	32	36	6	6	5	6	6
Andorra	–	–	–	–	–	–	–	–	–	–	–	–	–	–	–	–	–	–	–	–	–	–
Angola	–	–	–	–	–	–	–	–	–	–	–	–	–	–	–	–	–	–	–	–	–	–
Anguilla	–	–	–	–	–	–	–	–	–	–	–	–	–	–	–	–	–	–	–	–	–	–
Antigua and Barbuda	–	–	–	–	–	–	–	–	–	–	–	–	–	–	–	–	–	–	–	–	–	–
Argentina	63	61	66	46	85	84	83	85	73	95	57 y	61	40	83	61	58	63	8	9	8	10	5
Armenia	–	–	–	–	–	–	–	–	–	–	–	–	–	–	–	–	–	–	–	–	–	–
Australia	–	–	–	–	–	–	–	–	–	–	–	–	–	–	–	–	–	–	–	–	–	–
Austria	–	–	–	–	–	–	–	–	–	–	–	–	–	–	–	–	–	–	–	–	–	–
Azerbaijan	–	–	–	–	–	–	–	–	–	–	–	–	–	–	–	–	–	–	–	–	–	–
Bahamas	–	–	–	–	–	–	–	–	–	–	–	–	–	–	–	–	–	–	–	–	–	–
Bahrain	–	–	–	–	–	–	–	–	–	–	–	–	–	–	–	–	–	–	–	–	–	–
Bangladesh	13	13	14	12	18	78	78	78	64	94	10	9	2	23	60	57	60	12	11	12	14	12
Barbados	90	88	91	90 p	97 p	97	97	97	100 p	100 p	46 y	85	83	89	76	68	77	1	2	1	0	3
Belarus	88	86	89	75	91	96	94	97	90	99	68 y	92	83	96	79	77	79	4	4	4	4	5
Belgium	–	–	–	–	–	–	–	–	–	–	–	–	–	–	–	–	–	–	–	–	–	–
Belize	55	52	58	29	72	88	89	86	80	94	24	44	23	73	68	70	66	13	15	11	15	11
Benin	19 y	18 y	20 y	5 y	49 y	39 y	39 y	39 y	32 y	56 y	4 y	2 y	0 y	7 y	55 y	39 y	70 y	29 y	28 y	30 y	36 y	22 y
Bhutan	10	10	10	3	27	54	52	57	40	73	51 y	6	1	24	52	36	60	14	13	15	17	7
Bolivia (Plurinational State of)	–	–	–	–	–	–	–	–	–	–	–	–	–	–	–	–	–	–	–	–	–	–
Bosnia and Herzegovina	13	12	14	2	31	95	95	96	87	100	76 y	56	39	73	56	58	60	2	2	2	3	1
Botswana	18 x	–	–	–	–	–	–	–	–	–	–	–	–	–	–	–	–	–	–	–	–	–
Brazil	70 y	–	–	–	–	–	–	–	–	–	–	–	–	–	–	–	–	–	–	–	–	–
British Virgin Islands	–	–	–	–	–	–	–	–	–	–	–	–	–	–	–	–	–	–	–	–	–	–
Brunei Darussalam	–	–	–	–	–	–	–	–	–	–	–	–	–	–	–	–	–	–	–	–	–	–
Bulgaria	–	–	–	–	–	–	–	–	–	–	–	–	–	–	–	–	–	–	–	–	–	–
Burkina Faso	3 y	3 y	3 y			14 x	14 x	14 x	12 x	26 x	24 x,y	–	–	–	–	–	–	–	–	–	–	–
Burundi	7 y	7 y	7 y	1 y	31 y	58 y	58 y	59 y	56 y	67 y	3 y	0 y	0 y	0 y	35 y	29 y	52 y	42 y	42 y	42 y	43 y	30 y
Cabo Verde	–	–	–	–	–	–	–	–	–	–	–	–	–	–	–	–	–	–	–	–	–	–
Cambodia	15 y	12 y	17 y	7 y	38 y	59 y	57 y	62 y	48 y	73 y	8 y	4 y	1 y	12 y	34 y	20 y	53 y	10 y	10 y	10 y	16 y	4 y
Cameroon	28	27	29	2	66	44	45	44	50	52	4	4	0	17	53	47	65	34	34	35	52	23
Canada	–	–	–	–	–	–	–	–	–	–	–	–	–	–	–	–	–	–	–	–	–	–
Central African Republic	5	5	6	2	17	74	74	74	70	78	42 y	1	0	3	49	41	51	61	60	62	58	60
Chad	3 y	3 y	3 y	1 y	11 y	47 y	47 y	46 y	41 y	51 y	1 y	1 y	1 y	2 y	41 y	33 y	52 y	47 y	50 y	45 y	43 y	46 y
Chile	–	–	–	–	–	–	–	–	–	–	–	–	–	–	–	–	–	–	–	–	–	–
China	–	–	–	–	–	–	–	–	–	–	–	–	–	–	–	–	–	–	–	–	–	–
Colombia	37 y	–	–	–	–	–	–	–	–	–	–	–	–	–	–	–	–	–	–	–	–	–
Comoros	–	–	–	–	–	–	–	–	–	–	–	–	–	–	–	–	–	–	–	–	–	–
Congo	36	36	37	7	77	59	59	58	47	77	6	3	0	10	51	42	51	42	42	41	54	30
Cook Islands	–	–	–	–	–	–	–	–	–	–	–	–	–	–	–	–	–	–	–	–	–	–
Costa Rica	18	17	18	8	40	68	69	66	54	88	52 y	37	13	70	73	68	74	4	4	4	6	3
Côte d'Ivoire	14	14	15	2	51	29	29	29	18	61	5	1	0	7	45	35	53	20	20	19	20	18
Croatia	83 y	74 y	83 y	–	–	–	–	–	–	–	–	–	–	–	–	–	–	–	–	–	–	–
Cuba	76	75	77	–	–	89	89	90			18	48	–	–	78	–	–	4	4	4	–	–
Cyprus	–	–	–	–	–	–	–	–	–	–	–	–	–	–	–	–	–	–	–	–	–	–
Czechia	–	–	–	–	–	–	–	–	–	–	–	–	–	–	–	–	–	–	–	–	–	–
Democratic People's Republic of Korea	73	73	73	–	–	95 y	94 y	95 y			21 y	50	–	–	59	–	–	16	17	16	–	–
Democratic Republic of the Congo	7 y	7 y	7 y	1 y	20 y	52 y	55 y	48 y	45 y	64 y	3 y	1 y	0 y	2 y	27 y	18 y	49 y	49 y	50 y	48 y	57 y	29 y
Denmark	–	–	–	–	–	–	–	–	–	–	–	–	–	–	–	–	–	–	–	–	–	–
Djibouti	14 x	12 x	16 x	–	–	37 y	38 y	35 y			28 y	15 x	–	–	24 x	–	–	8	8	8	–	–
Dominica	–	–	–	–	–	–	–	–	–	–	–	–	–	–	–	–	–	–	–	–	–	–
Dominican Republic	40	39	40	16	72	58	58	59	38	73	6	10	2	28	57	57	58	5	5	5	7	3
Ecuador	–	–	–	–	–	–	–	–	–	–	–	–	–	–	–	–	–	–	–	–	–	–
Egypt	47 y	48 y	47 y	34 y	50 y	–	–	–	–	–	–	–	–	–	–	–	–	4	4	4	7	2
El Salvador	25	24	26	19	44	59	57	62	45	78	8	18	6	44	62	62	58	4	4	3	4	4
Equatorial Guinea	–	–	–	–	–	–	–	–	–	–	–	–	–	–	–	–	–	–	–	–	–	–
Eritrea	–	–	–	–	–	–	–	–	–	–	–	–	–	–	–	–	–	–	–	–	–	–
Estonia	–	–	–	–	–	–	–	–	–	–	–	–	–	–	–	–	–	–	–	–	–	–
Eswatini	30	26	33	28	48	39	33	44	25	59	2	6	2	19	67	56	78	17	16	17	18	15
Ethiopia	–	–	–	–	–	–	–	–	–	–	–	–	–	–	–	–	–	–	–	–	–	–
Fiji	–	–	–	–	–	–	–	–	–	–	–	–	–	–	–	–	–	–	–	–	–	–

TABLE 9. EARLY CHILDHOOD DEVELOPMENT

Countries and areas	Attendance in early childhood education 2010–2018*					Early stimulation and responsive care by adults† 2010–2018*					Early stimulation and responsive care by father† 2010–2018*	Learning materials at home 2010–2018* — Children's books			Learning materials at home 2010–2018* — Playthings†			Children with inadequate supervision 2010–2018*				
	total	male	female	poorest 20%	richest 20%	total	male	female	poorest 20%	richest 20%		total	poorest 20%	richest 20%	total	poorest 20%	richest 20%	total	male	female	poorest 20%	richest 20%
Finland	–	–	–	–	–	–	–	–	–	–	–	–	–	–	–	–	–	–	–	–	–	–
France	–	–	–	–	–	–	–	–	–	–	–	–	–	–	–	–	–	–	–	–	–	–
Gabon	–	–	–	–	–	–	–	–	–	–	–	–	–	–	–	–	–	–	–	–	–	–
Gambia	18	17	19	12	32	48	49	47	50	55	21 y	1	0	4	42	28	50	21	22	19	25	18
Georgia	62 y	–	–	–	–	83	82	84	85	82	35 y	58 y	40 y	74 y	38 x	41 x	41 x	6 y	6 y	7 y	6 y	8 y
Germany	–	–	–	–	–	–	–	–	–	–	–	–	–	–	–	–	–	–	–	–	–	–
Ghana	68	65	72	42	97	40	38	42	23	78	30 y	6	1	23	41	31	51	21	21	21	27	15
Greece	–	–	–	–	–	–	–	–	–	–	–	–	–	–	–	–	–	–	–	–	–	–
Grenada	–	–	–	–	–	–	–	–	–	–	–	–	–	–	–	–	–	–	–	–	–	–
Guatemala	–	–	–	–	–	–	–	–	–	–	–	–	–	–	–	–	–	–	–	–	–	–
Guinea	9	9	9	3	32	31	33	30	22	51	4	0	0	1	32	17	54	34	36	33	38	36
Guinea-Bissau	13	13	14	3	46	34	41	28	33	51	0	1	0	3	31	24	46	31	31	31	27	38
Guyana	61	63	59	45	76	87	85	90	82	94	16	47	25	76	69	65	70	5	5	5	10	1
Haiti	63 y	63 y	63 y	31 y	84 y	54 y	52 y	57 y	34 y	79 y	7 y	8 y	1 y	20 y	48 y	33 y	58 y	22 y	23 y	22 y	28 y	15 y
Holy See	–	–	–	–	–	–	–	–	–	–	–	–	–	–	–	–	–	–	–	–	–	–
Honduras	19	17	21	13	28	39	38	39	20	64	17	11	1	34	78	74	81	4	5	4	8	2
Hungary	–	–	–	–	–	–	–	–	–	–	–	–	–	–	–	–	–	–	–	–	–	–
Iceland	–	–	–	–	–	–	–	–	–	–	–	–	–	–	–	–	–	–	–	–	–	–
India	–	–	–	–	–	–	–	–	–	–	–	–	–	–	–	–	–	–	–	–	–	–
Indonesia	17	16	18	–	–	–	–	–	–	–	–	–	–	–	–	–	–	–	–	–	–	–
Iran (Islamic Republic of)	20 y	19 y	22 y	–	–	70 y	69 y	70 y	–	–	60 y	36 y	–	–	67 y	–	–	15 y	15 y	15 y	–	–
Iraq	2	2	3	1	5	44 y	44 y	45 y	31 y	53 y	10 y	3	1	9	47	52	43	10	10	10	12	12
Ireland	–	–	–	–	–	–	–	–	–	–	–	–	–	–	–	–	–	–	–	–	–	–
Israel	–	–	–	–	–	–	–	–	–	–	–	–	–	–	–	–	–	–	–	–	–	–
Italy	–	–	–	–	–	–	–	–	–	–	–	–	–	–	–	–	–	–	–	–	–	–
Jamaica	92	92	91	88	100	88	86	90	76	86	28 y	55	34	73	61	64	56	2	2	2	2	1
Japan	–	–	–	–	–	–	–	–	–	–	–	–	–	–	–	–	–	–	–	–	–	–
Jordan	13 y	12 y	14 y	5 y	35 y	92 y	92 y	91 y	85 y	99 y	32 y	16 y	6 y	32 y	71 y	69 y	66 y	16 y	17 y	16 y	16 y	21 y
Kazakhstan	55	53	58	45	70	86	84	87	83	95	7	51	35	73	60	63	61	5	4	6	8	3
Kenya	–	–	–	–	–	–	–	–	–	–	–	–	–	–	–	–	–	–	–	–	–	–
Kiribati	–	–	–	–	–	–	–	–	–	–	–	–	–	–	–	–	–	–	–	–	–	–
Kuwait	–	–	–	–	–	–	–	–	–	–	–	–	–	–	–	–	–	–	–	–	–	–
Kyrgyzstan	23	23	23	12	50	72	74	70	63	73	3	27	15	54	59	63	54	5	5	4	6	5
Lao People's Democratic Republic	32	30	34	13	69	30 y	29 y	30 y	21 y	49 y	7 y	4	0	18	61	51	63	12	13	12	17	6
Latvia	–	–	–	–	–	–	–	–	–	–	–	–	–	–	–	–	–	–	–	–	–	–
Lebanon	62 x	63 x	60 x	–	–	56 x,y	58 x,y	54 x,y	–	–	74 x,y	29 x	–	–	16 x,y	–	–	9 x	8 x	10 x	–	–
Lesotho	–	–	–	–	–	–	–	–	–	–	–	–	–	–	–	–	–	–	–	–	–	–
Liberia	–	–	–	–	–	–	–	–	–	–	–	–	–	–	–	–	–	–	–	–	–	–
Libya	–	–	–	–	–	–	–	–	–	–	–	–	–	–	–	–	–	–	–	–	–	–
Liechtenstein	–	–	–	–	–	–	–	–	–	–	–	–	–	–	–	–	–	–	–	–	–	–
Lithuania	–	–	–	–	–	–	–	–	–	–	–	–	–	–	–	–	–	–	–	–	–	–
Luxembourg	–	–	–	–	–	–	–	–	–	–	–	–	–	–	–	–	–	–	–	–	–	–
Madagascar	39	37	41	26	67	29	29	30	22	44	3	1	0	6	45	35	66	37	37	37	39	28
Malawi	53	52	55	–	–	25	25	24	–	–	–	56	–	–	62	–	–	3	3	3	–	–
Malaysia	–	–	–	–	–	–	–	–	–	–	–	–	–	–	–	–	–	–	–	–	–	–
Maldives	78 y	78 y	79 y	69 y	82 p,y	96 y	96 y	97 y	97 y	–	25 y	59 y	50 y	70 y	48 y	50 y	33 y	12 y	10 y	14 y	11 y	22 y
Mali	5	6	5	1	21	55	55	55	53	65	5	0	0	2	52	42	70	32	32	32	31	27
Malta	–	–	–	–	–	–	–	–	–	–	–	–	–	–	–	–	–	–	–	–	–	–
Marshall Islands	5	5	5	4	11	72	72	73	71	83	2	19	3	44	71	61	82	9	9	10	10	9
Mauritania	12	12	12	3	30	44	46	42	30	65	5	1	0	3	33	24	52	34	35	34	39	26
Mauritius	–	–	–	–	–	–	–	–	–	–	–	–	–	–	–	–	–	–	–	–	–	–
Mexico	60	58	62	58	71	76	71	80	62	94	14	35	15	64	76	74	85	5	5	5	8	3
Micronesia (Federated States of)	–	–	–	–	–	–	–	–	–	–	–	–	–	–	–	–	–	–	–	–	–	–
Monaco	–	–	–	–	–	–	–	–	–	–	–	–	–	–	–	–	–	–	–	–	–	–
Mongolia	68	68	68	36	90	55	55	55	38	71	10	33	13	57	56	57	58	10	9	11	15	8
Montenegro	40	39	42	7	66	98	97	99	93	98	45	73	48	87	60	61	66	3	3	3	2	3
Montserrat	–	–	–	–	–	–	–	–	–	–	–	–	–	–	–	–	–	–	–	–	–	–
Morocco	39 x	36 x	41 x	6 x	78 x	36 y	36 y	36 y	26 y	47 y	65 y	21 x,y	9 x,y	52 x,y	14 x,y	19 x,y	7 x,y	7	–	–	–	–
Mozambique	–	–	–	–	–	47 x	45 x	48 x	48 x	50 x	20 x,y	3 x	2 x	10 x	–	–	–	33 x	33 x	32 x	–	–
Myanmar	23 y	22 y	25 y	11 y	42 y	52 y	51 y	53 y	41 y	73 y	6 y	5 y	1 y	15 y	72 y	64 y	76 y	13 y	14 y	13 y	21 y	5 y
Namibia	–	–	–	–	–	–	–	–	–	–	–	–	–	–	–	–	–	–	–	–	–	–
Nauru	–	–	–	–	–	–	–	–	–	–	–	–	–	–	–	–	–	–	–	–	–	–
Nepal	51	52	49	41	84	67	70	64	51	90	10	5	1	16	59	60	60	21	20	21	30	12
Netherlands	–	–	–	–	–	–	–	–	–	–	–	–	–	–	–	–	–	–	–	–	–	–

TABLE 9. EARLY CHILDHOOD DEVELOPMENT

Countries and areas	Attendance in early childhood education 2010–2018*					Early stimulation and responsive care by adults+ 2010–2018*					Early stimulation and responsive care by father+ 2010–2018*	Learning materials at home 2010–2018*						Children with inadequate supervision 2010–2018*				
												Children's books			Playthings+							
	total	male	female	poorest 20%	richest 20%	total	male	female	poorest 20%	richest 20%		total	poorest 20%	richest 20%	total	poorest 20%	richest 20%	total	male	female	poorest 20%	richest 20%
New Zealand	–	–	–	–	–	–	–	–	–	–	–	–	–	–	–	–	–	–	–	–	–	–
Nicaragua	–	–	–	–	–	–	–	–	–	–	–	–	–	–	–	–	–	–	–	–	–	–
Niger	–	–	–	–	–	–	–	–	–	–	–	–	–	–	–	–	–	–	–	–	–	–
Nigeria	36	36	35	8	78	63	62	63	46	87	11	6	0	19	46	38	60	32	32	31	31	30
Niue	–	–	–	–	–	–	–	–	–	–	–	–	–	–	–	–	–	–	–	–	–	–
North Macedonia	35	–	–	–	–	92	92	91	81	96	71 y	52	18	81	71	70	79	5	5	5	11	1
Norway	–	–	–	–	–	–	–	–	–	–	–	–	–	–	–	–	–	–	–	–	–	–
Oman	29	28	31			81	78	84	–	–	22	25	–	–	75	–	–	45	44	45	–	–
Pakistan	–	–	–	–	–	–	–	–	–	–	–	–	–	–	–	–	–	–	–	–	–	–
Palau	–	–	–	–	–	–	–	–	–	–	–	–	–	–	–	–	–	–	–	–	–	–
Panama	37	38	35	28	67	74	73	74	55	89	45 y	26	7	59	69	67	68	3	3	2	6	1
Papua New Guinea	–	–	–	–	–	–	–	–	–	–	–	–	–	–	–	–	–	–	–	–	–	–
Paraguay	31	30	32	10	61	64	62	65	40	90	17 y	23	3	61	60	55	65	3	2	3	4	2
Peru	77 y	76 y	79 y	70 y	90 y	–	–	–	–	–	–	–	–	–	–	–	–	–	–	–	–	–
Philippines	–	–	–	–	–	–	–	–	–	–	–	–	–	–	–	–	–	–	–	–	–	–
Poland	–	–	–	–	–	–	–	–	–	–	–	–	–	–	–	–	–	–	–	–	–	–
Portugal	–	–	–	–	–	–	–	–	–	–	–	–	–	–	–	–	–	–	–	–	–	–
Qatar	41	41	41	–	–	88	89	88	–	–	85 y	40	–	–	55	–	–	12	12	11	–	–
Republic of Korea	–	–	–	–	–	–	–	–	–	–	–	–	–	–	–	–	–	–	–	–	–	–
Republic of Moldova	71	74	67	50	88	89	86	92	81	95	47 y	68	33	87	68	75	69	6	6	6	9	5
Romania	82 y	82 y	83 y	–	–	–	–	–	–	–	–	–	–	–	–	–	–	–	–	–	–	–
Russian Federation	–	–	–	–	–	–	–	–	–	–	–	–	–	–	–	–	–	–	–	–	–	–
Rwanda	13 y	12 y	14 y	3 y	45 y	44 y	43 y	45 y	32 y	63 y	2 y	1 y	0 y	3 y	30 y	21 y	41 y	35 y	35 y	35 y	38 y	21 y
Saint Kitts and Nevis	–	–	–	–	–	–	–	–	–	–	–	–	–	–	–	–	–	–	–	–	–	–
Saint Lucia	85	87	84	–	–	93	89	96	–	–	50 y	68	–	–	59	–	–	5	5	5	–	–
Saint Vincent and the Grenadines	–	–	–	–	–	–	–	–	–	–	–	–	–	–	–	–	–	–	–	–	–	–
Samoa	–	–	–	–	–	–	–	–	–	–	–	–	–	–	–	–	–	–	–	–	–	–
San Marino	–	–	–	–	–	–	–	–	–	–	–	–	–	–	–	–	–	–	–	–	–	–
Sao Tome and Principe	36	34	39	21	63	63	63	63	48	74	3	6	1	20	65	65	57	16	17	14	26	8
Saudi Arabia	–	–	–	–	–	–	–	–	–	–	–	–	–	–	–	–	–	–	–	–	–	–
Senegal	24 y	23 y	26 y	5 y	56 y	29 y	28 y	31 y	21 y	44 y	1 y	1 y	0 y	4 y	24 y	13 y	31 y	28 y	28 y	28 y	33 y	14 y
Serbia	50	52	49	9	82	96	95	96	87	98	37	72	44	83	75	78	76	1	2	1	3	2
Seychelles	–	–	–	–	–	–	–	–	–	–	–	–	–	–	–	–	–	–	–	–	–	–
Sierra Leone	12	11	12	1	41	19 y	19 y	19 y	13 y	31 y	5 y	2	0	9	41	27	66	30	30	30	32	25
Singapore	–	–	–	–	–	–	–	–	–	–	–	–	–	–	–	–	–	–	–	–	–	–
Slovakia	–	–	–	–	–	–	–	–	–	–	–	–	–	–	–	–	–	–	–	–	–	–
Slovenia	–	–	–	–	–	–	–	–	–	–	–	–	–	–	–	–	–	–	–	–	–	–
Solomon Islands	–	–	–	–	–	–	–	–	–	–	–	–	–	–	–	–	–	–	–	–	–	–
Somalia	2 x	2 x	2 x	1 x	6 x	79 x	80 x	79 x	76 x	85 x	48 x,y	–	–	–	–	–	–	–	–	–	–	–
South Africa	48 y	–	–	–	–	–	–	–	–	–	–	–	–	–	–	–	–	–	–	–	–	–
South Sudan	6	6	6	2	13	–	–	–	–	–	–	–	–	–	–	–	–	–	–	–	–	–
Spain	–	–	–	–	–	–	–	–	–	–	–	–	–	–	–	–	–	–	–	–	–	–
Sri Lanka	–	–	–	–	–	–	–	–	–	–	–	–	–	–	–	–	–	–	–	–	–	–
State of Palestine	26	27	26	21	38	78	77	78	69	87	12	20	13	31	69	64	72	14	14	15	15	12
Sudan	22	22	23	7	59	–	–	–	–	–	–	2	0	7	46	36	55	–	–	–	–	–
Suriname	34	33	35	16	63	73	71	75	56	91	26 y	25	4	61	59	61	60	7	7	7	9	8
Sweden	–	–	–	–	–	–	–	–	–	–	–	–	–	–	–	–	–	–	–	–	–	–
Switzerland	–	–	–	–	–	–	–	–	–	–	–	–	–	–	–	–	–	–	–	–	–	–
Syrian Arab Republic	8 x	8 x	7 x	4 x	18 x	70 x	70 x	69 x	52 x	84 x	62 x,y	30 x	12 x	53 x	52 x	52 x	51 x	17 x	17 x	17 x	22 x	15 x
Tajikistan	6	–	–	–	–	74 x	73 x	74 x	56 x	86 x	23 x,y	17 x	4 x	33 x	46 x	43 x	44 x	13 x	13 x	12 x	15 x	11 x
Thailand	85	84	85	86	84	93	93	92	87	98	34	41	23	73	76	81	67	2	6	6	8	3
Timor-Leste	14 y	13 y	16 y	9 y	16 y	81 y	83 y	79 y	72 y	89 y	15 y	4 y	2 y	9 y	40 y	22 y	61 y	29 y	29 y	30 y	33 y	26 y
Togo	26 y	26 y	26 y	15 y	52 y	26 y	26 y	26 y	22 y	44 y	3 y	1 y	0 y	3 y	34 y	22 y	48 y	29 y	26 y	33 y	36 y	26 y
Tokelau	–	–	–	–	–	–	–	–	–	–	–	–	–	–	–	–	–	–	–	–	–	–
Tonga	–	–	–	–	–	–	–	–	–	–	–	–	–	–	–	–	–	–	–	–	–	–
Trinidad and Tobago	85	85	84	72	93	96	95	96	94	100	57 y	76	63	93	76	75	82	2	2	1	3	1
Tunisia	44	42	47	13	81	71	68	74	44	90	71 y	18	3	40	53	46	56	13	13	14	18	9
Turkey	–	–	–	–	–	–	–	–	–	–	–	–	–	–	–	–	–	–	–	–	–	–
Turkmenistan	43	43	43	17	81	94	94	95	92	98	15	48	30	66	53	59	56	1	0	1	1	1
Turks and Caicos Islands	–	–	–	–	–	–	–	–	–	–	–	–	–	–	–	–	–	–	–	–	–	–
Tuvalu	–	–	–	–	–	–	–	–	–	–	–	–	–	–	–	–	–	–	–	–	–	–
Uganda	37 y	34 y	39 y	15 y	66 y	53 y	51 y	55 y	38 y	74 y	3 y	2 y	0 y	8 y	50 y	39 y	59 y	37 y	37 y	37 y	49 y	21 y
Ukraine	52	54	50	30	68	98	97	98	95	99	71 y	91	92	92	52	61	51	7	6	7	11	5
United Arab Emirates	–	–	–	–	–	–	–	–	–	–	–	–	–	–	–	–	–	–	–	–	–	–
United Kingdom	–	–	–	–	–	–	–	–	–	–	–	–	–	–	–	–	–	–	–	–	–	–

TABLE 9. EARLY CHILDHOOD DEVELOPMENT

Countries and areas	Attendance in early childhood education 2010–2018*					Early stimulation and responsive care by adults+ 2010–2018*					Early stimulation and responsive care by father+ 2010–2018*	Learning materials at home 2010–2018* Children's books			Playthings+			Children with inadequate supervision 2010–2018*				
	total	male	female	poorest 20%	richest 20%	total	male	female	poorest 20%	richest 20%		total	poorest 20%	richest 20%	total	poorest 20%	richest 20%	total	male	female	poorest 20%	richest 20%
United Republic of Tanzania	–	–	–	–	–	–	–	–	–	–	–	–	–	–	–	–	–	–	–	–	–	–
United States	–	–	–	–	–	–	–	–	–	–	–	–	–	–	–	–	–	–	–	–	–	–
Uruguay	81	83	80	–	–	93	94	91	–	–	66 y	59	–	–	75	–	–	3	3	3	–	–
Uzbekistan	32 y	33 y	31 y	–	–	91 x	91 x	90 x	83 x	95 x	54 x,y	43 x	32 x	59 x	67 x	74 x	62 x	5 x	5 x	5 x	6 x	7 x
Vanuatu	–	–	–	–	–	–	–	–	–	–	–	–	–	–	–	–	–	–	–	–	–	–
Venezuela (Bolivarian Republic of)	66 y	–	–	–	–	–	–	–	–	–	–	–	–	–	–	–	–	–	–	–	–	–
Viet Nam	71	74	69	53	86	76	76	76	52	96	15	26	6	58	52	44	54	7	6	8	14	2
Yemen	3 x	3 x	3 x	0 x	8 x	33 x	34 x	32 x	16 x	56 x	37 x,y	10 x	4 x	31 x	49 x	45 x	49 x	34 x	36 x	33 x	46 x	22 x
Zambia	–	–	–	–	–	–	–	–	–	–	–	–	–	–	–	–	–	–	–	–	–	–
Zimbabwe	22	20	23	17	34	43	43	43	35	59	3	3	1	12	62	48	74	19	19	18	25	7
SUMMARY																						
East Asia and Pacific	–	–	–	–	–	–	–	–	–	–	–	–	–	–	–	–	–	–	–	–	–	–
Europe and Central Asia	–	–	–	–	–	–	–	–	–	–	–	–	–	–	–	–	–	–	–	–	–	–
Eastern Europe and Central Asia	–	–	–	–	–	–	–	–	–	–	–	–	–	–	–	–	–	–	–	–	–	–
Western Europe	–	–	–	–	–	–	–	–	–	–	–	–	–	–	–	–	–	–	–	–	–	–
Latin America and Caribbean	61	–	–	–	–	–	–	–	–	–	–	–	–	–	–	–	–	–	–	–	–	–
Middle East and North Africa	28	28	28	20	37	–	–	–	–	–	–	–	–	–	–	–	–	9	9	9	9	6
North America	–	–	–	–	–	–	–	–	–	–	–	–	–	–	–	–	–	–	–	–	–	–
South Asia	–	–	–	–	–	–	–	–	–	–	–	–	–	–	–	–	–	–	–	–	–	–
Sub-Saharan Africa	26	24	25	8	55	51	51	51	40	70	7	3	0	10	42	33	57	35	35	34	38	27
Eastern and Southern Africa	–	–	–	–	–	–	–	–	–	–	–	–	–	–	–	–	–	–	–	–	–	–
West and Central Africa	24	24	24	7	56	52	52	51	41	71	8	3	0	12	41	32	56	35	35	34	38	28
Least developed countries	17	16	17	8	35	56	56	55	47	71	10	3	1	9	46	38	57	31	31	31	36	22
World	–	–	–	–	–	–	–	–	–	–	–	–	–	–	–	–	–	–	–	–	–	–

For a complete list of countries and areas in the regions, subregions and country categories, see page 182 or visit <data.unicef.org/regionalclassifications>.

It is not advisable to compare data from consecutive editions of *The State of the World's Children*.

DEFINITIONS OF THE INDICATORS

Attendance in early childhood education – Percentage of children 36–59 months old who are attending an early childhood education programme.

Early stimulation and responsive care by adults – Percentage of children 36–59 months old with whom an adult has engaged in four or more of the following activities to promote learning and school readiness in the past 3 days: a) reading books to the child, b) telling stories to the child, c) singing songs to the child, d) taking the child outside the home, e) playing with the child, and f) spending time with the child naming, counting or drawing things.

Early stimulation and responsive care by father – Percentage of children 36–59 months old whose father has engaged in four or more of the following activities to promote learning and school readiness in the past 3 days: a) reading books to the child, b) telling stories to the child, c) singing songs to the child, d) taking the child outside the home, e) playing with the child, and f) spending time with the child naming, counting or drawing things.

Learning materials at home: Children's books – Percentage of children 0–59 months old who have three or more children's books at home.

Learning materials at home: Playthings – Percentage of children 0–59 months old with two or more of the following playthings at home: household objects or objects found outside (sticks, rocks, animals, shells, leaves etc.), homemade toys or toys that came from a store.

Children with inadequate supervision – Percentage of children 0–59 months old left alone or in the care of another child younger than 10 years of age for more than one hour at least once in the past week.

MAIN DATA SOURCES

Attendance in early childhood education – Demographic and Health Surveys (DHS), Multiple Indicator Cluster Surveys (MICS), and other national surveys. Last update: August 2019.

Early stimulation and responsive care by adults – DHS, MICS and other national surveys. Last update: August 2019.

Early stimulation and responsive care by father – DHS, MICS and other national surveys. Last update: August 2019.

Learning materials at home: Children's books – DHS, MICS and other national surveys. Last update: August 2019.

Learning materials at home: Playthings – DHS, MICS and other national surveys. Last update: August 2019.

Children with inadequate supervision – DHS, MICS and other national surveys. Last update: August 2019.

NOTES

– Data not available.

p Based on small denominators (typically 25–49 unweighted cases). No data based on fewer than 25 unweighted cases are displayed.

x Data refer to years or periods other than those specified in the column heading. Such data are not included in the calculation of regional and global averages.

y Data differ from the standard definition or refer to only part of a country. If they fall within the noted reference period, such data are included in the calculation of regional and global averages.

+ A more detailed explanation of the methodology and the changes in calculating these estimates can be found in the General Note on the Data, page 180.

* Data refer to the most recent year available during the period specified in the column heading.

TABLE 10. EDUCATION

	Equitable access								Completion						Learning							
	Out-of-school rate 2012–2018*								Completion rate 2012–2018*						Learning outcomes 2010–2018*							
	One year before primary entry age		Primary education		Lower secondary education		Upper secondary education		Primary education		Lower secondary education		Upper secondary education		Proportion of children in grade 2 or 3 achieving minimum proficiency level		Proportion of children at the end of primary achieving minimum proficiency level		Proportion of children at the end of lower secondary achieving minimum proficiency level		Youth (15–24 years) literacy rate (%)	
Countries and areas	male	female	male	female	male	female	male	female	male	female	male	female	male	female	reading	math	reading	math	reading	math	male	female
Afghanistan	–	–	–	–	–	–	46	69	67	40	49	26	32	14	47	52	55	63	–	–	62	32
Albania	10	11	2	4	1	4	17	18	91	93	97	96	43	60	86	–	95	97	48	39	99	99
Algeria	–	–	0	2	–	–	–	–	93	94	57	72	30	47	–	41 x	–	–	21	19	–	–
Andorra	–	–	–	–	–	–	–	–	–	–	–	–	–	–	–	–	–	–	–	–	–	–
Angola	30	38	–	–	–	–	–	–	53	49	41	31	21	15	–	–	–	–	–	–	85	71
Anguilla	–	–	–	–	–	–	–	–	–	–	–	–	–	–	59	38	76	67	–	–	–	–
Antigua and Barbuda	14	12	18	17	16	24	21	22	–	–	–	–	–	–	38	46	50	78	–	–	–	–
Argentina	1	3	0	1	1	1	13	5	95	97	72	81	53	66	62	63	67	59	62	38	99	100
Armenia	–	–	8	8	8	6	–	–	100	99	94	99	91	96	–	–	–	95	–	76	100	100
Australia	12	13	4	3	1	2	2	0	–	–	–	–	–	–	95	96	94	95	82	78	–	–
Austria	2	0	–	–	0	1	7	7	–	–	–	–	–	–	–	–	87	95	84	87	–	–
Azerbaijan	39	39	7	5	0	0	–	–	–	–	–	–	–	–	–	–	82	71	27 x	55 x	100	100
Bahamas	65	60	15	8	11	5	15	10	–	–	–	–	–	–	–	–	–	–	–	–	–	–
Bahrain	23	24	1	1	3	0	7	5	–	–	–	–	–	–	–	72	–	–	–	75	94	95
Bangladesh	–	–	8	2	–	–	37	38	69	79	53	55	31	26	65	39	91	81	87	57	92	94
Barbados	8	12	10	9	4	0	–	–	99	99	98	98	91	97	–	–	87	60	–	–	100	100
Belarus	1	4	4	4	2	1	2	0	100	100	100	100	96	98	–	–	–	–	80	80	–	–
Belgium	0	0	1	1	3	3	1	1	–	–	–	–	–	–	–	–	–	–	80	80	–	–
Belize	16	16	0	1	11	11	38	34	78 x	86 x	40 x	48 x	20 x	25 x	25 x	–	–	–	–	–	–	–
Benin	12	12	–	–	26	43	46	66	51	44	25	13	12	5	10	34	52	40	–	–	64	41
Bhutan	–	–	19	17	20	10	34	27	67 x	71 x	41 x	38 x	25 x	18 x	–	–	–	–	33	51	90	84
Bolivia (Plurinational State of)	8	9	7	8	13	13	17	18	–	–	–	–	–	–	–	–	–	–	–	–	99	99
Bosnia and Herzegovina	–	–	–	–	–	–	–	–	99	100	97	97	92	92	–	–	–	–	–	77 x	100	100
Botswana	67	65	11	10	–	–	–	–	–	–	–	–	–	–	56	61	66	66	79	80	96	99
Brazil	4	1	4	2	3	4	19	16	94	97	73	82	53	64	78	77	97	100	49	30	99	99
British Virgin Islands	–	–	–	–	–	–	–	–	–	–	–	–	–	–	–	–	–	–	–	–	–	–
Brunei Darussalam	5	5	3	4	–	–	20	16	–	–	–	–	–	–	–	–	–	–	–	–	99	100
Bulgaria	5	4	7	7	6	7	8	12	–	–	–	–	–	–	–	–	93	92	59	58	98	98
Burkina Faso	83	83	22	24	48	46	67	68	32 x	29 x	13 x	6 x	6 x	2 x	35	59	57	59	–	–	57	44
Burundi	58	58	4	2	31	27	60	57	46	54	26	19	4	3	79	97	56	87	–	–	85	75
Cabo Verde	21	20	13	14	20	20	37	32	–	–	–	–	–	–	–	–	–	–	–	–	98	99
Cambodia	58	56	9	10	12	14	–	–	68	79	41	39	20	20	–	–	61	–	38	17	92	93
Cameroon	54	54	1	9	31	39	48	57	67	64	46	41	18	14	30	55	49	35	–	–	85	76
Canada	–	–	–	–	0	0	8	8	–	–	–	–	–	–	–	–	–	–	89	86	–	–
Central African Republic	–	–	23	40	44	66	79	90	54 x	33 x	16 x	8 x	8 x	6 x	–	–	–	–	–	–	49	27
Chad	89	90	17	34	51	70	71	88	31	24	18	10	15	6	18	48	16	19	39	33	41	22
Chile	3	3	5	5	8	8	7	6	–	–	–	–	–	–	70	63	94	98	72	63	99	99
China	–	–	–	–	–	–	–	–	97	97	93	93	64	67	82	85	–	–	80	79	100	100
Colombia	13	12	7	6	6	5	17	15	91	95	74	81	69	78	82	82	87	57	89	79	98	99
Comoros	60	62	15	16	30	29	57	55	75	77	47	45	24	32	–	–	66 x	70 x	–	–	74	70
Congo	79	77	16	9	–	–	–	–	78	82	56	45	28	19	38	71	41	29	–	–	86	77
Cook Islands	2	0	2	5	8	7	37	30	–	–	–	–	–	–	–	–	–	–	–	–	–	–
Costa Rica	10	11	3	3	5	6	14	9	94 x	95 x	55 x	71 x	38 x	56 x	89	84	94	95	60	38	99	99
Côte d'Ivoire	78	78	7	15	36	49	57	69	60	53	36	22	17	15	17	34	48	27	–	–	59	47
Croatia	2	7	4	1	3	0	16	12	–	–	–	–	–	–	–	–	99	93	80	68	100	100
Cuba	0	0	3	3	0	0	23	15	99	100	98	98	81	86	–	–	94 x	95 x	–	–	100	100
Cyprus	5	6	2	2	2	2	6	5	–	–	–	–	–	–	87 x	93	–	–	64	78 x	100	100
Czechia	8	8	–	–	–	–	2	2	–	–	–	–	–	–	98	96	–	–	78	78	–	–
Democratic People's Republic of Korea	–	–	–	–	8	8	11	11	100	100	100	100	100	100	94	83	–	–	–	–	–	–
Democratic Republic of the Congo	–	–	–	–	–	–	–	–	71	66	59	49	30	21	–	–	81	85	–	–	91	80
Denmark	3	2	1	1	1	1	14	11	–	–	–	–	–	–	99	96	–	–	85	86	–	–
Djibouti	91	91	39	46	48	56	66	72	–	–	–	–	–	–	–	–	–	–	–	–	–	–
Dominica	29	30	3	1	–	–	10	10	–	–	–	–	–	–	81	50	40	29	–	–	–	–
Dominican Republic	13	12	6	6	7	9	26	23	88	94	76	89	48	66	46	28	65	63	28	9	99	99
Ecuador	4	4	3	1	–	–	16	16	–	–	–	–	–	–	75	78	68	64	72	43	99	99
Egypt	62	62	2	1	8	7	22	22	91	92	79	81	71	69	5	–	–	–	–	47	89	87
El Salvador	19	18	19	18	16	17	34	35	84	89	73	74	34	36	–	23 x	78 x	79 x	–	20 x	98	98
Equatorial Guinea	57	55	56	55	–	–	–	–	–	–	–	–	–	–	–	–	–	–	–	–	98	99
Eritrea	82	83	61	64	53	60	66	71	–	–	–	–	–	–	–	–	–	–	–	–	–	–
Estonia	10	7	7	6	–	–	5	3	–	–	–	–	–	–	–	–	–	–	89	89	100	100

TABLE 10. EDUCATION

Countries and areas	Equitable access — Out-of-school rate 2012–2018*								Completion — Completion rate 2012–2018*						Learning — Learning outcomes 2010–2018*							
	One year before primary entry age		Primary education		Lower secondary education		Upper secondary education		Primary education		Lower secondary education		Upper secondary education		Proportion of children in grade 2 or 3 achieving minimum proficiency level		Proportion of children at the end of primary achieving minimum proficiency level		Proportion of children at the end of lower secondary achieving minimum proficiency level		Youth (15–24 years) literacy rate (%)	
	male	female	male	female	male	female	male	female	male	female	male	female	male	female	reading	math	reading	math	reading	math	male	female
Eswatini	–	–	24	25	13	13	25	30	52	68	38	45	31	33	–	–	99 x	91 x	–	–	92	95
Ethiopia	61	63	11	17	45	49	73	75	51	51	42	36	13	13	–	–	–	–	–	–	–	–
Fiji	–	–	2	2	–	–	30	23	–	–	–	–	–	–	–	–	–	–	–	–	–	–
Finland	2	1	1	1	1	1	5	4	–	–	–	–	–	–	99	97	–	–	89	86	–	–
France	1	0	1	1	2	2	6	5	–	–	–	–	–	–	95	87	–	–	79	77	–	–
Gabon	–	–	–	–	–	–	–	–	57	67	23	26	11	11	–	–	95 x	90 x	–	–	87	89
Gambia	–	–	25	17	–	–	–	–	56	57	50	46	31	29	23	31	33	22	–	–	66	56
Georgia	–	–	2	2	1	2	8	5	–	–	–	–	–	–	86	78	–	–	48	43	100	100
Germany	–	–	–	–	–	–	–	–	–	–	–	–	–	–	–	–	97	96	84	83	–	–
Ghana	13	8	17	15	16	13	31	31	64	68	50	50	42	35	71	55	72	61	–	21	88	83
Greece	12	11	7	7	6	8	10	11	–	–	–	–	–	–	95 x	–	–	–	73	64	99	99
Grenada	14	17	4	3	2	26	17	11	–	–	–	–	–	–	54	43	66	57	–	–	99	100
Guatemala	19	19	12	12	30	36	56	61	83	77	54	46	27	25	50	41	40	45	15	18	95	93
Guinea	57	61	14	29	41	59	59	75	58	49	43	25	29	15	–	–	–	–	–	–	57	37
Guinea-Bissau	–	–	–	–	–	–	–	–	33	26	20	14	11	8	–	–	–	–	–	–	71	50
Guyana	10	6	5	3	7	5	34	25	96	99	80	88	49	64	–	–	–	–	–	–	96	97
Haiti	–	–	–	–	–	–	–	–	49	58	32	38	17	16	–	–	–	–	–	–	–	–
Holy See	–	–	–	–	–	–	–	–	–	–	–	–	–	–	–	–	–	–	–	–	–	–
Honduras	19	18	17	16	37	35	54	48	81	85	42	55	27	33	93	92	84	77	89	61	95	97
Hungary	8	9	3	3	4	4	12	12	–	–	–	–	–	–	–	–	95	92	73	88	99	99
Iceland	2	2	0	1	2	1	18	14	–	–	–	–	–	–	93 x	–	–	–	78	76	–	–
India	–	–	3	2	17	12	47	49	92	91	82	79	46	40	25	28	–	–	17 x	15 x	90	82
Indonesia	6	3	5	10	14	10	17	13	91	92	64	59	40	37	66	49	–	–	45	31	100	100
Iran (Islamic Republic of)	51	52	–	–	2	2	27	23	–	–	–	–	–	–	76	65	–	–	–	63	98	98
Iraq	–	–	–	–	–	–	–	–	78	73	46	47	45	43	–	–	–	–	–	–	57	49
Ireland	2	2	0	0	–	–	2	0	–	–	–	–	–	–	97	97	–	–	90	94	–	–
Israel	2	0	3	2	–	–	4	0	–	–	–	–	–	–	93	–	–	–	73	68	–	–
Italy	1	3	1	2	–	–	5	5	–	–	–	–	–	–	98	93	–	–	79	89	100	100
Jamaica	7	4	–	–	22	17	24	19	99 x	100 x	97 x	97 x	80 x	83 x	87	14	–	–	64	77	94	99
Japan	–	–	2	2	–	–	4	2	–	–	–	–	–	–	–	50	–	–	54	45	99	99
Jordan	–	–	–	–	28	29	53	46	96	97	86	88	49	63	–	–	–	96	59	91	100	100
Kazakhstan	37	35	2	0	–	–	3	0	100	100	100	100	95	96	–	–	–	96	–	–	100	100
Kenya	–	–	19	15	–	–	–	–	77	82	61	69	44	38	60	71	80	77	–	–	87	86
Kiribati	–	–	–	–	–	–	–	–	–	–	–	–	–	–	–	–	–	–	–	–	–	–
Kuwait	25	23	7	7	9	4	20	16	–	–	–	–	–	–	58	33	–	–	–	45	99	100
Kyrgyzstan	6	4	1	2	1	1	30	26	99	99	95	97	82	85	–	–	36	35	17 x	13 x	–	–
Lao People's Democratic Republic	37	36	6	7	21	22	35	41	87	86	57	55	33	31	83	46	–	–	82	79	94	91
Latvia	2	1	4	2	2	1	5	4	–	–	–	–	–	–	98 x	96 x	–	–	82	79	100	100
Lebanon	1	7	9	14	21	26	34	34	–	–	–	–	–	–	–	–	–	–	30	71	–	–
Lesotho	65	63	19	17	29	21	46	39	60	83	29	46	20	27	–	–	79 x	58 x	–	–	80	94
Liberia	13	18	61	64	24	31	24	34	36	33	29	23	18	9	–	–	–	–	–	–	–	–
Libya	–	–	–	–	–	–	–	–	–	–	–	–	–	–	–	–	–	–	88	86	–	–
Liechtenstein	1	0	3	2	2	8	–	–	–	–	–	–	–	–	–	–	–	–	–	–	–	–
Lithuania	1	0	0	0	0	0	4	3	–	–	–	–	–	–	–	–	92	99	75	75	100	100
Luxembourg	2	1	1	1	6	4	20	16	–	–	–	–	–	–	99 x	–	–	–	74	74	–	–
Madagascar	–	–	–	–	–	–	–	–	–	–	–	–	–	–	–	–	79 x	94 x	–	–	78	75
Malawi	–	–	–	–	23	25	59	65	43	52	23	21	15	13	22	51	24	41	–	–	72	73
Malaysia	2	1	2	1	13	11	41	32	–	–	–	–	–	–	86	71	88	47	73	42	97	98
Maldives	1	3	0	0	–	–	–	–	–	–	–	–	–	–	–	–	–	–	–	–	99	99
Mali	48	52	29	37	52	58	68	77	50	41	36	25	23	12	2	3	12	13	–	–	61	39
Malta	4	0	3	0	3	2	16	9	–	–	–	–	–	–	74	87	–	–	64	84	98	99
Marshall Islands	34	35	24	19	23	23	40	28	–	–	–	–	–	–	–	–	–	–	–	–	–	–
Mauritania	–	–	25	22	45	44	72	73	64	56	42	34	14	15	–	–	47 x	38 x	–	–	98	99
Mauritius	8	10	5	3	8	5	22	15	–	–	–	–	–	–	–	–	78	79	77	42	98	99
Mexico	1	0	2	0	10	7	32	29	97	96	88	87	25	22	78	78	50	40	66	35	99	99
Micronesia (Federated States of)	20	27	17	15	20	16	–	–	–	–	–	–	–	–	–	–	–	–	–	–	–	–
Monaco	–	–	–	–	–	–	–	–	–	–	–	–	–	–	–	–	–	–	–	–	–	–
Mongolia	3	5	1	2	–	–	–	–	96	99	88	93	64	78	–	67 x	–	–	–	66 x	98	99
Montenegro	31	32	3	4	4	5	14	14	100	100	99	99	84	87	–	–	–	–	58	48	99	99
Montserrat	–	–	–	–	–	–	–	–	–	–	–	–	–	–	57	54	70	81	–	–	–	–

TABLE 10. EDUCATION

Countries and areas	Equitable access — Out-of-school rate 2012–2018* — One year before primary entry age		Primary education		Lower secondary education		Upper secondary education		Completion — Completion rate 2012–2018* — Primary education		Lower secondary education		Upper secondary education		Learning — Learning outcomes 2010–2018* — Proportion of children in grade 2 or 3 achieving minimum proficiency level		Proportion of children at the end of primary achieving minimum proficiency level		Proportion of children at the end of lower secondary achieving minimum proficiency level		Youth (15–24 years) literacy rate (%)	
	male	female	male	female	male	female	male	female	male	female	male	female	male	female	reading	math	reading	math	reading	math	male	female
Morocco	42	50	3	3	9	14	26	33	–	–	–	–	–	–	21	41	–	–	–	41	95	88
Mozambique	–	–	11	14	40	48	66	74	43 x	37 x	13 x	10 x	8 x	4 x	–	–	78 x	67 x	–	–	79	63
Myanmar	–	–	–	–	25	23	50	43	78	84	43	46	13	18	–	–	–	–	–	–	85	84
Namibia	35	31	4	0	–	–	–	–	75	86	48	62	33	39	–	–	86 x	52 x	–	–	93	95
Nauru	33	16	17	14	21	14	55	60	–	–	–	–	–	–	–	–	–	–	–	–	–	–
Nepal	12	18	4	7	14	8	33	18	79	76	68	65	52	39	–	–	–	–	–	–	90	80
Netherlands	2	1	–	–	1	0	1	1	–	–	–	–	–	–	100	99	–	–	82	83	–	–
New Zealand	4	3	1	1	2	2	4	0	–	–	–	–	–	–	76	84	–	–	83	78	–	–
Nicaragua	–	–	–	–	–	–	–	–	–	–	–	–	–	–	63	45	76	77	–	–	–	–
Niger	78	78	29	38	61	69	83	89	35	24	10	4	4	1	10	28	8	8	–	–	49	32
Nigeria	–	–	–	–	–	–	–	–	81	79	78	72	70	59	75	28	54	18	–	–	–	–
Niue	77	–	–	–	–	–	–	–	–	–	–	–	–	–	–	–	–	–	–	–	–	–
North Macedonia	56	56	8	8	–	–	–	–	100 x	99 x	98 x	97 x	80 x	69 x	66 x	–	–	–	29	30	99	99
Norway	4	3	0	0	0	1	8	7	–	–	–	–	–	–	95	98	–	–	85	83	–	–
Oman	18	15	1	1	10	7	12	12	–	–	–	–	–	–	47	61	–	–	–	52	98	99
Pakistan	–	–	18	29	42	50	57	67	64	55	55	45	43	38	17	15	52	48	73	68	80	66
Palau	–	20	–	–	–	–	–	–	–	–	–	–	–	–	–	–	–	–	–	–	98	99
Panama	28	26	12	13	10	10	35	31	95	96	75	81	57	68	68	54	77	74	35 x	21 x	98	97
Papua New Guinea	26	27	20	25	7	17	39	50	–	–	–	–	–	–	–	–	–	–	–	–	65	71
Paraguay	29	29	11	11	4	15	32	30	89	95	57	54	0	0	71	72	69	69	68	68	98	99
Peru	3	3	1	0	2	1	–	–	95	95	83	83	78	72	94	71	–	–	42	28	99	99
Philippines	21	19	5	4	9	5	24	17	89	95	75	88	54	66	–	34 x	–	–	–	39 x	97	99
Poland	1	1	4	4	5	5	8	7	–	–	–	–	–	–	95	96	–	–	86	83	–	–
Portugal	0	1	3	4	1	1	0	3	–	–	–	–	–	–	98	97	–	–	83	76	99	99
Qatar	9	5	1	2	13	9	43	16	–	–	–	–	–	–	60	64	–	–	48	64	95	97
Republic of Korea	3	4	4	3	6	5	1	1	–	–	–	–	–	–	–	100	–	–	86	85	–	–
Republic of Moldova	7	4	10	10	15	15	36	35	99	100	95	98	63	74	–	–	91 x	88	54	50	99	100
Romania	12	12	10	10	9	10	23	22	–	–	–	–	–	–	86	79	–	–	61	60	99	99
Russian Federation	3	4	3	2	2	1	10	–	–	–	–	–	–	–	–	–	99	98	84	81	100	100
Rwanda	59	58	6	6	–	–	–	–	48	61	25	30	19	16	–	–	–	–	–	–	84	86
Saint Kitts and Nevis	–	–	–	–	–	–	–	–	–	–	–	–	–	–	–	–	–	–	–	–	–	–
Saint Lucia	8	19	–	–	10	14	24	17	99	99	85	98	70	90	68	62	62	46	–	–	–	–
Saint Vincent and the Grenadines	12	10	1	2	–	–	11	14	–	–	–	–	–	–	–	–	–	–	–	–	–	–
Samoa	65	61	4	3	2	2	23	15	–	–	–	–	–	–	–	–	–	–	–	–	99	99
San Marino	6	5	7	7	–	–	–	–	–	–	–	–	–	–	–	–	–	–	–	–	–	–
Sao Tome and Principe	47	45	3	3	12	6	20	18	79	86	32	36	12	12	81	100	–	–	–	–	97	96
Saudi Arabia	63	61	1	0	–	–	9	8	–	–	–	–	–	–	65	43	–	–	–	34	99	99
Senegal	82	80	29	21	52	45	64	62	48	51	28	24	14	10	18	62	61	59	42	16	76	64
Serbia	3	3	2	1	1	2	12	10	99	100	99	99	71	81	–	–	–	91	67	61	100	100
Seychelles	3	7	–	–	–	–	5	4	–	–	–	–	–	–	–	–	88	74	86	79	99	99
Sierra Leone	65	63	1	1	40	40	61	63	63	65	47	42	27	18	–	–	–	–	–	–	65	51
Singapore	–	–	–	–	–	–	–	–	–	–	–	–	–	–	97	99	–	–	89	99	100	100
Slovakia	19	17	–	–	4	5	10	10	–	–	–	–	–	–	–	–	96	88	68	72	–	–
Slovenia	4	6	3	2	1	2	5	4	–	–	–	–	–	–	95	95	–	–	85	84	100	100
Solomon Islands	35	34	31	30	–	–	–	–	–	–	–	–	–	–	–	–	–	–	–	–	–	–
Somalia	–	–	–	–	–	–	–	–	–	–	–	–	–	–	–	–	–	–	–	–	–	–
South Africa	–	–	9	8	–	–	15	19	95	98	85	91	45	52	84	39	92	71	84	34	99	99
South Sudan	80	83	64	72	54	67	61	75	30 x	18 x	23 x	10 x	13 x	4 x	–	–	–	–	–	–	–	–
Spain	4	4	2	1	1	0	2	1	–	–	–	–	–	–	94	93	–	–	84	78	100	100
Sri Lanka	–	–	2	4	1	2	21	16	–	–	–	–	–	–	86	84	–	–	90	68	99	99
State of Palestine	38	38	6	6	12	7	44	26	99	100	80	93	52	73	–	–	–	–	–	52	99	99
Sudan	–	–	37	38	–	–	–	–	71	73	45	43	34	29	–	–	–	–	–	–	–	–
Suriname	10	7	12	8	17	9	42	33	80	90	41	58	19	28	–	–	–	–	–	–	98	97
Sweden	2	1	0	1	5	4	1	3	–	–	–	–	–	–	98	95	–	88	82	82	–	–
Switzerland	1	1	0	0	–	–	17	19	–	–	–	–	–	–	–	–	–	–	80	84	–	–
Syrian Arab Republic	61	62	32	33	42	44	68	67	–	–	–	–	–	–	–	–	–	–	–	43	–	–
Tajikistan	87	88	1	2	–	–	–	–	99	98	95	93	80	63	–	–	–	–	–	–	100	100
Thailand	3	3	–	–	11	11	21	21	98	98	76	88	50	62	–	77	–	–	50	46	98	98
Timor-Leste	67	67	21	18	14	12	30	26	77	85	63	70	49	55	80	–	–	–	–	–	80	79
Togo	–	–	5	11	16	28	47	66	66	59	31	20	20	10	20	41	38	48	–	–	90	78

TABLE 10. EDUCATION

Column groups:
- **Equitable access — Out-of-school rate 2012–2018*** (male/female for: One year before primary entry age; Primary education; Lower secondary education; Upper secondary education)
- **Completion — Completion rate 2012–2018*** (male/female for: Primary education; Lower secondary education; Upper secondary education)
- **Learning — Learning outcomes 2010–2018*** (reading/math for: Proportion of children in grade 2 or 3 achieving minimum proficiency level; Proportion of children at the end of primary achieving minimum proficiency level; Proportion of children at the end of lower secondary achieving minimum proficiency level)
- **Youth (15–24 years) literacy rate (%)** (male/female)

Countries and areas	OOS 1yr before entry M	F	OOS Primary M	F	OOS Lower sec M	F	OOS Upper sec M	F	Compl. Primary M	F	Compl. Lower sec M	F	Compl. Upper sec M	F	Grade 2/3 reading	math	End primary reading	math	End lower sec reading	math	Youth lit. M	F
Tokelau	22	–	–	–	–	–	62	80	–	–	–	–	–	–	15 x	–	–	–	–	–	99	100
Tonga	–	–	5	3	13	9	48	38	–	–	–	–	–	–	78	–	76	63	58	48	100	100
Trinidad and Tobago	–	–	–	–	–	–	–	–	94	97	68	80	40	57	–	–	–	34	28	25	97	96
Tunisia	–	–	–	–	–	–	–	–	–	–	–	–	–	–	–	–	–	–	–	–	100	99
Turkey	33	36	5	6	9	10	15	16	99	98	94	90	58	48	–	–	72 x	81	60	70	100	100
Turkmenistan	–	–	–	–	–	–	–	–	100	100	93	91	83	80	–	–	70	–	–	–	100	100
Turks and Caicos Islands	–	–	–	–	–	–	–	–	–	–	–	–	–	–	–	–	70	–	–	–	–	–
Tuvalu	6	–	–	–	–	–	58	46	–	–	–	–	–	–	–	–	–	–	–	–	–	–
Uganda	–	–	10	8	–	–	–	–	33	36	24	21	16	14	60	72	52	53	–	–	86	82
Ukraine	–	–	8	6	3	3	6	4	100	99	100	100	97	97	–	–	79 x	–	–	81	100	100
United Arab Emirates	12	11	2	4	1	2	13	19	–	–	–	–	–	–	64	70	–	–	60	74	–	–
United Kingdom	0	0	0	0	1	1	3	2	–	–	–	–	–	–	–	–	–	–	82	78	–	–
United Republic of Tanzania	49	47	20	18	–	–	85	88	75	84	31	27	32	27	56	35	97 x	87 x	–	–	87	85
United States	10	8	4	4	3	1	7	6	–	–	–	–	–	–	69	95	–	–	81	71	–	–
Uruguay	3	2	2	2	2	1	23	16	92	95	52	70	45	28	81	75	90	94	61	48	99	99
Uzbekistan	63	64	1	2	4	5	16	17	–	–	–	–	–	–	–	–	–	–	–	–	100	100
Vanuatu	–	–	14	12	1	1	43	46	–	–	–	–	–	–	–	–	–	–	–	–	95	96
Venezuela (Bolivarian Republic of)	17	18	14	14	18	17	32	24	–	–	–	–	–	–	–	–	–	–	58 x	40 x	98	99
Viet Nam	0	1	–	–	–	–	–	–	96	97	81	87	50	61	–	–	99	87	86	81	–	–
Yemen	95	96	12	22	23	35	46	68	70	55	55	39	37	23	–	9	–	–	–	–	–	–
Zambia	–	–	16	12	–	–	–	–	73	75	54	48	34	23	1	9	56 x	33 x	–	–	91	87
Zimbabwe	64	63	16	14	8	11	52	55	87	89	66	74	15	11	–	–	81 x	73 x	–	–	88	93
SUMMARY																						
East Asia and Pacific	14	12	4	4	9	8	23	15	96	96	82	83	56	59	79	77	–	–	72	68	99	99
Europe and Central Asia	13	14	3	3	3	4	10	10	–	–	–	–	–	–	–	–	–	–	76	78	100	100
Eastern Europe and Central Asia	22	23	4	4	4	5	14	14	–	–	–	–	67	61	–	–	89	–	70	75	100	100
Western Europe	3	3	2	2	2	2	7	6	–	–	–	–	–	–	96	93	–	–	81	81	–	–
Latin America and Caribbean	6	4	5	4	7	7	24	21	94	95	75	80	45	50	76	72	75	70	58	38	99	99
Middle East and North Africa	51	53	5	7	12	15	31	36	87	85	66	68	52	53	37	–	–	–	–	46	89	86
North America	7	6	4	4	1	1	5	5	–	–	–	–	–	–	69	95	–	–	82	72	–	–
South Asia	·	·	6	7	18	17	47	49	88	88	75	71	44	38	29	28	–	–	–	–	88	80
Sub-Saharan Africa	57	57	19	24	34	37	54	61	64	64	48	42	35	29	52	42	57	45	–	–	80	72
Eastern and Southern Africa	56	57	19	20	32	37	54	60	60	63	41	38	28	25	–	–	–	–	–	–	86	83
West and Central Africa	56	57	19	27	37	40	53	61	69	65	54	46	41	33	50	35	53	37	–	–	73	60
Least developed countries	56	57	17	20	29	34	53	59	60	60	41	36	26	20	–	–	–	–	–	–	81	73
World	**31**	**31**	**8**	**10**	**15**	**16**	**36**	**36**	**83**	**83**	**71**	**69**	**47**	**43**	**54**	**53**	**–**	**–**	**–**	**61**	**92**	**88**

For a complete list of countries and areas in the regions, subregions and country categories, see page 182 or visit <data.unicef.org/regionalclassifications>.

It is not advisable to compare data from consecutive editions of The *State of the World's Children*.

DEFINITIONS OF THE INDICATORS

Out-of-school rate for children one year before the official primary entry age – Number of children of one year before primary entry age who are not enrolled in pre-primary or primary schools, expressed as a percentage of the population of one year before the official primary entry age.

Out-of-school rate for children of primary school age – Number of children of official primary school age who are not enrolled in primary or secondary school, expressed as a percentage of the population of official primary school age.

Out-of-school rate for children of lower secondary school age – Number of children of lower secondary school age who are not enrolled in primary or secondary school, expressed as a percentage of the population of official lower secondary school age.

Out-of-school rate for children of upper secondary school age – Number of children of official upper secondary school age who are not enrolled in primary or secondary school or higher education, expressed as a percentage of the population of official upper secondary school age.

Completion rate for primary education – Number of children or young people aged 3 -5 years above the intended age for the last grade of primary education who have completed the last grade of primary school.

Completion rate for lower secondary education – Number of children or young people aged 3 -5 years above the intended age for the last grade of lower secondary education who have completed the last grade of lower secondary.

Completion rate for upper secondary education – Number of children or young people aged 3 -5 years above the intended age for the last grade of upper secondary education who have completed the last grade of upper secondary.

Proportion of children and young people (a) in grade 2/3; (b) at the end of primary education; and (c) at the end of lower secondary education achieving at least a minimum proficiency in (i) reading and (ii) mathematics – Percentage of children and young people in Grade 2 or 3 of primary education, at the end of primary education and the end of lower secondary education achieving at least a minimum proficiency level in (a) reading and (b) mathematics.

Youth literacy rate – Number of literate persons aged 15–24 years, expressed as a percentage of the total population in that group.

MAIN DATA SOURCES

Out of school rate – UNESCO Institute for Statistics (UIS). Last update: February 2019.

Completion rate – Demographic and Health Surveys (DHS), Multiple Indicator Cluster Surveys (MICS), other national household surveys, data from routine reporting systems. Last update: June 2019.

Proportion of children and young people (a) in grade 2/3; (b) at the end of primary education; and (c) at the end of lower secondary education achieving at least a minimum proficiency in (i) reading and (ii) mathematics – United Nations Statistics Division database. Last update: April 2019.

Youth literacy – UNESCO Institute for Statistics (UIS). Last update: February 2019.

NOTES

–   Data not available.

x   Data refer to years or periods other than those specified in the column heading. Such data are not included in the calculation of regional and global averages.

*   Data refer to the most recent year available during the period specified in the column heading.

All data refer to official International Standard Classifications of Education (ISCED) for the primary and lower secondary education levels and thus may not directly correspond to a country-specific school system.

TABLE 11. CHILD PROTECTION

Countries and areas	Child labour (%)+ 2010–2018* total	male	female	Child marriage (%)+ 2012–2018* female married by 15	female married by 18	male married by 18	Birth registration (%)+ 2010–2018* total	male	female	Female genital mutilation (%)+ 2010–2018* prevalence women[a]	girls[b]	attitudes want the practice to stop[c] male	female	Justification of wife-beating among adolescents (%)+ 2012–2018* male	female	Violent discipline (%)+ 2012–2018* total	male	female	Sexual violence in childhood 2012–2018* male	fem
Afghanistan	21	23	20	9	35	7	42	43	42	–	–	–	–	71 y	78 y	74 x,y	75 x,y	74 x,y	–	1
Albania	3 y	4 y	3 y	1	12	1	98	99	98	–	–	–	–	11	5	48 y	49 y	45 y	–	
Algeria	4 y	5 y	4 y	0	3	–	100	100	100	–	–	–	–	–	55 y	86 y	88 y	85 y	–	
Andorra	–	–	–	–	–	–	100 v	100 v	100 v	–	–	–	–	–	–	–	–	–	–	
Angola	19	17	20	8	30	6	25	25	25	–	–	–	–	24	25	–	–	–	–	5
Anguilla	–	–	–	–	–	–	–	–	–	–	–	–	–	–	–	–	–	–	–	
Antigua and Barbuda	–	–	–	–	–	–	–	–	–	–	–	–	–	–	–	–	–	–	–	
Argentina	–	–	–	–	–	–	100 y	100 y	100 y	–	–	–	–	–	2	72 y	74 y	71 y	–	
Armenia	4	5	3	0	5	0	99	100	99	–	–	–	–	25	9	69	71	67	–	
Australia	–	–	–	–	–	–	100 v	100 v	100 v	–	–	–	–	–	–	–	–	–	–	
Austria	–	–	–	–	–	–	100 v	100 v	100 v	–	–	–	–	–	–	–	–	–	–	
Azerbaijan	–	–	–	2 x	11 x	0 x	94 x	93 x	94 x	–	–	–	–	–	24 x	77 x,y	80 x,y	74 x,y	–	0
Bahamas	–	–	–	–	–	–	–	–	–	–	–	–	–	–	–	–	–	–	–	
Bahrain	–	–	–	–	–	–	–	–	–	–	–	–	–	–	–	–	–	–	–	
Bangladesh	–	–	–	22	59	4 x	20	20	20	–	–	–	–	–	29 y	82	83	82	–	3
Barbados	1 y	2 y	1 y	1	11	–	99	99	99	–	–	–	–	–	5	75 y	78 y	72 y	–	
Belarus	1 y	1 y	1 y	0	3	1	100 y	100 y	100 y	–	–	–	–	3	3	65 y	67 y	62 y	–	
Belgium	–	–	–	–	–	–	100 v	100 v	100 v	–	–	–	–	–	–	–	–	–	–	
Belize	3	4	3	6	34	22	96	95	96	–	–	–	–	8	6	65	67	63	–	
Benin	41	42	41	7	26	5	85	85	84	9	0	89	86	17	29	91	92	90	–	
Bhutan	4 y	3 y	4 y	6 x	26 x	–	100	100	100	–	–	–	–	–	70 x	–	–	–	–	
Bolivia (Plurinational State of)	–	–	–	3	20	5	92 y	–	–	–	–	–	–	–	17 x	–	–	–	–	
Bosnia and Herzegovina	–	–	–	0	4	0	100 x	100 x	99 x	–	–	–	–	5	1	55 y	60 y	50 y	–	
Botswana	–	–	–	–	–	–	88 y	87 y	88 y	–	–	–	–	–	–	–	–	–	–	
Brazil	–	–	–	6 x	26 x	–	96	–	–	–	–	–	–	–	–	–	–	–	–	
British Virgin Islands	–	–	–	–	–	–	–	–	–	–	–	–	–	–	–	–	–	–	–	
Brunei Darussalam	–	–	–	–	–	–	–	–	–	–	–	–	–	–	–	–	–	–	–	
Bulgaria	–	–	–	–	–	–	100 y	100 y	100 y	–	–	–	–	–	–	–	–	–	–	
Burkina Faso	42 y	44 y	40 y	10 x	52 x	4 x	77	77	77	76	13	87	90	40 x	39 x	83 x,y	84 x,y	82 x,y	–	
Burundi	31	30	32	3	19	1	84	84	83	–	–	–	–	48	63	90	91	89	0	4
Cabo Verde	–	–	–	3 x	18 x	3 x	91	–	–	–	–	–	–	24 x	23 x	–	–	–	–	
Cambodia	13	12	14	2	19	4	73	74	73	–	–	–	–	26 y	46 y	–	–	–	–	2
Cameroon	39	40	38	10	31	4	66	67	65	1 x	1 x,y	85 x	84 x	45	37	85	85	85	4 x	16
Canada	–	–	–	–	–	–	100 v	100 v	100 v	–	–	–	–	–	–	–	–	–	–	
Central African Republic	30 y	29 y	32 y	29 x	68 x	28 x	61	61	62	24	1	–	75	83 x	79 x	92 x,y	92 x,y	92 x,y	–	
Chad	39	37	41	30	67	8	12	12	12	38	10	49 x	45	54	69	71	72	71	–	2
Chile	6	7	5	–	–	–	99 y	–	–	–	–	–	–	–	–	–	–	–	–	
China	–	–	–	–	–	–	–	–	–	–	–	–	–	–	–	–	–	–	–	
Colombia	4	4	3	5	23	7	97	97	97	–	–	–	–	–	–	–	–	–	0	2
Comoros	28 y	25 y	32 y	10	32	12	87	87	87	–	–	–	–	29	43	–	–	–	–	3
Congo	14	13	15	7	27	6	96	96	96	–	–	–	–	45	56	83	83	82	–	
Cook Islands	–	–	–	–	–	–	100 y	100 y	100 y	–	–	–	–	–	–	–	–	–	–	
Costa Rica	2	2	2	7 x	21 x	–	100 y	–	–	–	–	–	–	–	3 x	46 x,y	52 x,y	39 x,y	–	
Côte d'Ivoire	29 y	27 y	31 y	7	27	4	72	73	71	37	10	82	79	29	43	87	88	85	–	
Croatia	–	–	–	–	–	–	100 y	100 y	100 y	–	–	–	–	–	–	–	–	–	–	
Cuba	–	–	–	5	26	11	100	100	100	–	–	–	–	5 y	4 y	36	37	35	–	
Cyprus	–	–	–	–	–	–	100 v	100 v	100 v	–	–	–	–	–	–	–	–	–	–	
Czechia	–	–	–	–	–	–	100 v	100 v	100 v	–	–	–	–	–	–	–	–	–	–	
Democratic People's Republic of Korea	4	5	4	–	–	–	100 x	100 x	100 x	–	–	–	–	4	4	59	63	55	–	
Democratic Republic of the Congo	27	22	31	10	37	6	25	24	25	–	–	–	–	69	75	82	82	81	–	13
Denmark	–	–	–	–	–	–	100 v	100 v	100 v	–	–	–	–	–	–	–	–	–	–	
Djibouti	–	–	–	2 x	5 x	–	92 x	93 x	91 x	93 x	43	–	51 x	–	–	72 x,y	73 x,y	71 x,y	–	
Dominica	–	–	–	–	–	–	–	–	–	–	–	–	–	–	–	–	–	–	–	
Dominican Republic	7	8	6	12	36	8	88	88	88	–	–	–	–	–	3	63	64	61	–	
Ecuador	–	–	–	3	20	–	82 y	–	–	–	–	–	–	–	–	–	–	–	–	
Egypt	5	6	4	2	17	0 x	99	100	99	87	14 y	28	38	–	46 y	93	93	93	–	
El Salvador	10	9	11	6	26	–	99	99	98	–	–	–	–	–	10	52	55	50	–	
Equatorial Guinea	–	–	–	9 x	30 x	4 x	54	53	54	–	–	–	–	56 x	57 x	–	–	–	–	
Eritrea	–	–	–	13 x	41 x	2 x	–	–	–	83	33	85	82	60 x	51 x	–	–	–	–	
Estonia	–	–	–	–	–	–	100 v	100 v	100 v	–	–	–	–	–	–	–	–	–	–	
Eswatini	8 y	8 y	7 y	1	5	1	54	51	56	–	–	–	–	29	32	88	89	88	–	
Ethiopia	49 y	51 y	46 y	14	40	5	3	3	3	65	16	87	79	33	60	–	–	–	–	5
Fiji	–	–	–	–	–	–	–	–	–	–	–	–	–	–	–	72 x,y	–	–	–	–

TABLE 11. CHILD PROTECTION

Countries and areas	Child labour (%)+ 2010–2018* total	male	female	Child marriage (%)+ 2012–2018* female married by 15	married by 18	male married by 18	Birth registration (%)+ 2010–2018* total	male	female	Female genital mutilation (%)+ 2010–2018* prevalence women[a]	girls[b]	attitudes want the practice to stop[c] male	female	Justification of wife-beating among adolescents (%)+ 2012–2018* male	female	Violent discipline (%)+ 2012–2018* total	male	female	Sexual violence in childhood (%) 2012–2018* male	female
Finland	–	–	–	–	–	–	100 v	100 v	100 v	–	–	–	–	–	–	–	–	–	–	–
France	–	–	–	–	–	–	100 v	100 v	100 v	–	–	–	–	–	–	–	–	–	–	–
Gabon	20 y	19 y	17 y	6	22	5	90	91	88	–	–	–	–	47	58	–	–	–	–	9
Gambia	–	–	–	9	30	1	72	73	71	75	56	–	33	42	58	90 x,y	90 x,y	91 x,y	–	0
Georgia	2	2	1	1 x	14 x	–	100	100	100	–	–	–	–	–	5 x	67 x,y	70 x,y	63 x,y	–	–
Germany	–	–	–	–	–	–	100 v	100 v	100 v	–	–	–	–	–	–	–	–	–	–	–
Ghana	20 y	19 y	21 y	5	21	2	71	71	70	4	1	–	93 x	20	35	94 x,y	94 x,y	94 x,y	–	10 x
Greece	–	–	–	–	–	–	100 v	100 v	100 v	–	–	–	–	–	–	–	–	–	–	–
Grenada	–	–	–	–	–	–	–	–	–	–	–	–	–	–	–	–	–	–	–	–
Guatemala	–	–	–	6	30	10	96 y	–	–	–	–	–	–	12	14	–	–	–	1	4
Guinea	24	24	25	19	51	2	75	75	75	97	45	38	22	–	60	89	90	89	–	–
Guinea-Bissau	36	36	37	6	24	2	24	24	24	45	29	–	81	37	40	82	83	82	–	–
Guyana	11	10	12	4	30	9	89	88	89	–	–	–	–	14	10	70	74	65	–	–
Haiti	36 y	44 y	26 y	2	15	2	85	84	85	–	–	–	–	15	23	83	84	82	–	5
Holy See	–	–	–	–	–	–	–	–	–	–	–	–	–	–	–	–	–	–	–	–
Honduras	–	–	–	8	34	12	94	94	94	–	–	–	–	18	15	–	–	–	–	5
Hungary	–	–	–	–	–	–	100 v	100 v	100 v	–	–	–	–	–	–	–	–	–	–	–
Iceland	–	–	–	–	–	–	100 v	100 v	100 v	–	–	–	–	–	–	–	–	–	–	–
India	–	–	–	7	27	4	80	79	80	–	–	–	–	35	41	–	–	–	–	1
Indonesia	–	–	–	1	11	5	72 y	–	–	–	49 y	–	–	48 y	45	–	–	–	–	–
Iran (Islamic Republic of)	–	–	–	3 x	17 x	–	99 y	99 y	99 y	–	–	–	–	–	–	–	–	–	–	–
Iraq	6 y	6 y	6 y	7	28	–	99	99	99	7	1	–	94	–	31	81	82	80	–	–
Ireland	–	–	–	–	–	–	100 v	100 v	100 v	–	–	–	–	–	–	–	–	–	–	–
Israel	–	–	–	–	–	–	100 v	100 v	100 v	–	–	–	–	–	–	–	–	–	–	–
Italy	–	–	–	–	–	–	100 v	100 v	100 v	–	–	–	–	–	–	–	–	–	–	–
Jamaica	3	3	2	1 x	8 x	–	98	–	–	–	–	–	–	–	17	85 x,y	87 x,y	82 x,y	–	2 y
Japan	–	–	–	–	–	–	100 v	100 v	100 v	–	–	–	–	–	–	–	–	–	–	–
Jordan	2	2	1	0	8	–	99	99	99	–	–	–	–	64 y	63 y	90 y	91 y	89 y	–	–
Kazakhstan	–	–	–	0	7	0 x	100	100	100	–	–	–	–	–	8	53	55	50	–	–
Kenya	–	–	–	4	23	3	67	67	66	21	3	89	93	37	45	–	–	–	2	4
Kiribati	–	–	–	3 x	20 x	5 x	94 x	95 x	93 x	–	–	–	–	65 x	77 x	81 x,y	–	–	–	–
Kuwait	–	–	–	–	–	–	–	–	–	–	–	–	–	–	–	–	–	–	–	–
Kyrgyzstan	16	18	14	1	12	0	98	98	98	–	–	–	–	–	22	57	60	54	–	–
Lao People's Democratic Republic	12	11	14	7	33	11	73	73	73	–	–	–	–	17	30	69	70	68	–	–
Latvia	–	–	–	–	–	–	100 v	100 v	100 v	–	–	–	–	–	–	–	–	–	–	–
Lebanon	–	–	–	1 x	6 x	–	100 x	100 x	100 x	–	–	–	–	–	22 x,y	82 x,y	82 x,y	82 x,y	–	–
Lesotho	–	–	–	1	17	1	43	42	44	–	–	–	–	49	48	–	–	–	–	–
Liberia	14	15	13	9	36	5	25 y	25 y	24 y	44	–	–	55	29	45	90 x,y	90 x,y	90 x,y	–	4 x
Libya	–	–	–	–	–	–	–	–	–	–	–	–	–	–	–	–	–	–	–	–
Liechtenstein	–	–	–	–	–	–	100 v	100 v	100 v	–	–	–	–	–	–	–	–	–	–	–
Lithuania	–	–	–	–	–	–	100 v	100 v	100 v	–	–	–	–	–	–	–	–	–	–	–
Luxembourg	–	–	–	–	–	–	100 v	100 v	100 v	–	–	–	–	–	–	–	–	–	–	–
Madagascar	–	–	–	12	41	13	83	83	83	–	–	–	–	44	47	–	–	–	–	–
Malawi	19	20	19	9	42	7	6 y	6 y	5 y	–	–	–	–	24	21	72	73	72	–	4
Malaysia	–	–	–	–	–	–	–	–	–	–	–	–	–	–	–	71 y	74 y	67 y	–	–
Maldives	–	–	–	0 x	4 x	1 x	93 x	93 x	92 x	–	–	–	–'	33 y	35 y	–	–	–	–	–
Mali	37	40	35	18	50	3	87	88	87	83	73	22 x	14	54	68	73	73	73	–	–
Malta	–	–	–	–	–	–	100 v	100 v	100 v	–	–	–	–	–	–	–	–	–	–	–
Marshall Islands	–	–	–	6 x	26 x	12 x	84	85	82	–	–	–	–	71 x	47 x	–	–	–	–	–
Mauritania	17 y	17 y	18 y	18	37	2	66 y	66 y	66 y	67	51	19 x	50	18	26	80	80	80	–	–
Mauritius	–	–	–	–	–	–	–	–	–	–	–	–	–	–	–	–	–	–	–	–
Mexico	5	6	4	4	26	–	95	96	95	–	–	–	–	–	6	63	63	63	–	–
Micronesia (Federated States of)	–	–	–	–	–	–	–	–	–	–	–	–	–	–	–	–	–	–	–	–
Monaco	–	–	–	–	–	–	100 v	100 v	100 v	–	–	–	–	–	–	–	–	–	–	–
Mongolia	17	18	15	0	5	3	99	99	99	–	–	–	–	9 x	14 x	49	52	46	–	–
Montenegro	9	10	9	1	5	0	99	100	99	–	–	–	–	5	2	69	73	66	–	–
Montserrat	–	–	–	–	–	–	100 y	100 y	100 y	–	–	–	–	–	–	–	–	–	–	–
Morocco	–	–	–	1 x	13 x	–	96 y	–	–	–	–	–	–	–	64 x	91 x,y	92 x,y	90 x,y	–	–
Mozambique	–	–	–	17	53	10	55	54	56	–	–	–	–	21	14	–	–	–	0	2
Myanmar	–	–	–	2	16	5	81	82	81	–	–	–	–	57	53	77 y	80 y	75 y	–	1
Namibia	–	–	–	2	7	1	78 y	–	–	–	–	–	–	30	28	–	–	–	–	1
Nauru	–	–	–	2 x	27 x	12 x	96	–	–	–	–	–	–	–	–	–	–	–	–	–
Nepal	22	20	23	7	40	10	56	57	55	–	–	–	–	31	33	82	83	81	–	3

TABLE 11. CHILD PROTECTION

Countries and areas	Child labour (%)+ 2010–2018* total	male	female	Child marriage (%)+ 2012–2018* female married by 15	female married by 18	male married by 18	Birth registration (%)+ 2010–2018* total	male	female	Female genital mutilation (%)+ 2010–2018* prevalence women[a]	girls[b]	attitudes want the practice to stop[c] male	female	Justification of wife-beating among adolescents (%)+ 2012–2018* male	female	Violent discipline (%)+ 2012–2018* total	male	female	Sexual violence in childhood 2012–2018* male	fem
Netherlands	–	–	–	–	–	–	100 v	100 v	100 v	–	–	–	–	–	–	–	–	–	–	–
New Zealand	–	–	–	–	–	–	100 v	100 v	100 v	–	–	–	–	–	–	–	–	–	–	–
Nicaragua	–	–	–	10	35	19	85	–	–	–	–	–	–	–	19 x,y	–	–	–	–	–
Niger	34 y	34 y	34 y	28	76	6	64	65	62	2	2 y	91	82	41	54	82 y	82 y	81 y	–	–
Nigeria	31	32	31	18	44	3	47	47	47	18	13	*62*	68	25	30	85	86	84	–	4
Niue	–	–	–	–	–	–	–	–	–	–	–	–	–	–	–	–	–	–	–	–
North Macedonia	8 y	8 y	7 y	1 x	7 x	–	100	100	100	–	–	–	–	–	14 x	69 x,y	71 x,y	67 x,y	–	–
Norway	–	–	–	–	–	–	100 v	100 v	100 v	–	–	–	–	–	–	–	–	–	–	–
Oman	–	–	–	1	4	–	100 y	100 y	100 y	–	–	–	–	–	10	–	–	–	–	–
Pakistan	–	–	–	3	21	3	34	34	33	–	–	–	–	58 p,y	51 y	–	–	–	–	–
Palau	–	–	–	–	–	–	–	–	–	–	–	–	–	–	–	–	–	–	–	–
Panama	–	–	–	7	26	–	96	95	96	–	–	–	–	–	9	45	47	43	–	3
Papua New Guinea	–	–	–	2 x	21 x	5 x	–	–	–	–	–	–	–	–	–	–	–	–	–	–
Paraguay	18	20	13	4	22	–	69 y	69 y	69 y	–	–	–	–	–	7	52	55	49	–	–
Peru	15	14	15	3	19	–	98 y	–	–	–	–	–	–	–	–	–	–	–	–	–
Philippines	–	–	–	2	17	3 x	92	92	91	–	–	–	–	–	12	–	–	–	–	2
Poland	–	–	–	–	–	–	100 y	100 y	100 y	–	–	–	–	–	–	–	–	–	–	–
Portugal	–	–	–	–	–	–	100 v	100 v	100 v	–	–	–	–	–	–	–	–	–	–	–
Qatar	–	–	–	0	4	1	100 y	100 y	100 y	–	–	–	–	22	6 y	50 y	53 y	46 y	–	–
Republic of Korea	–	–	–	–	–	–	–	–	–	–	–	–	–	–	–	–	–	–	–	–
Republic of Moldova	–	–	–	0	12	1	100	99	100	–	–	–	–	14	13	76 y	77 y	74 y	–	5
Romania	–	–	–	–	–	–	–	–	–	–	–	–	–	–	–	–	–	–	–	–
Russian Federation	–	–	–	–	–	–	100 v	100 v	100 v	–	–	–	–	–	–	–	–	–	–	–
Rwanda	19 y	17 y	21 y	0	7	1	56	56	56	–	–	–	–	24	45	–	–	–	0	10
Saint Kitts and Nevis	–	–	–	–	–	–	–	–	–	–	–	–	–	–	–	–	–	–	–	–
Saint Lucia	3 y	5 y	2 y	1	8	–	92	91	93	–	–	–	–	–	15	68 y	71 y	64 y	–	–
Saint Vincent and the Grenadines	–	–	–	–	–	–	–	–	–	–	–	–	–	–	–	–	–	–	–	–
Samoa	–	–	–	1	11	2	59	59	58	–	–	–	–	28	34	–	–	–	–	–
San Marino	–	–	–	–	–	–	100 v	100 v	100 v	–	–	–	–	–	–	–	–	–	–	–
Sao Tome and Principe	18	17	19	8	35	3	95	96	95	–	–	–	–	19	24	80	80	79	–	3
Saudi Arabia	–	–	–	–	–	–	–	–	–	–	–	–	–	–	–	–	–	–	–	–
Senegal	23	27	19	8	29	1	77	79	76	24	14	79	81	43	48	–	–	–	–	2
Serbia	7	8	6	0	3	1 x	99	99	100	–	–	–	–	–	2	43	44	42	–	–
Seychelles	–	–	–	–	–	–	–	–	–	–	–	–	–	–	–	–	–	–	–	–
Sierra Leone	39 y	39 y	38 y	13	30	7	81	82	81	86	8	*40*	27	29	44	87	87	86	0	2
Singapore	–	–	–	–	–	–	–	–	–	–	–	–	–	–	–	–	–	–	–	–
Slovakia	–	–	–	–	–	–	100 y	100 y	100 y	–	–	–	–	–	–	–	–	–	–	–
Slovenia	–	–	–	–	–	–	100 v	100 v	100 v	–	–	–	–	–	–	–	–	–	–	–
Solomon Islands	18 y	17 y	19 y	6	21	4	88	87	89	–	–	–	–	60	78	86 y	86 y	85 y	–	–
Somalia	–	–	–	8 x	45 x	–	3	3	3	98 x	46 x,y	–	33 x	–	75 x,y	–	–	–	–	–
South Africa	4 y	4 y	3 y	1 x	6 x	–	89 y	–	–	–	–	–	–	14	7	–	–	–	–	–
South Sudan	–	–	–	9 x	52 x	–	35	35	36	–	–	–	–	–	72 x	–	–	–	–	–
Spain	–	–	–	–	–	–	100 v	100 v	100 v	–	–	–	–	–	–	–	–	–	–	–
Sri Lanka	–	–	–	1	10	–	97 x	97 x	97 x	–	–	–	–	–	54 x,y	–	–	–	–	–
State of Palestine	9 y	10 y	8 y	1	15	–	96	–	–	–	–	–	–	–	–	92	93	92	–	–
Sudan	18	20	16	12	34	–	67	69	66	87	30	*64*	53	–	36	64	65	63	–	–
Suriname	4 y	4 y	4 y	5 x	19 x	–	99	99	99	–	–	–	–	–	19 x	86 x,y	87 x,y	85 x,y	–	–
Sweden	–	–	–	–	–	–	100 v	100 v	100 v	–	–	–	–	–	–	–	–	–	4 y	13
Switzerland	–	–	–	–	–	–	100 v	100 v	100 v	–	–	–	–	–	–	–	–	–	–	–
Syrian Arab Republic	–	–	–	3 x	13 x	–	96 x	96 x	96 x	–	–	–	–	–	–	89 x,y	90 x,y	88 x,y	–	–
Tajikistan	–	–	–	0	9	–	96	96	96	–	–	–	–	–	44	69	70	68	–	0
Thailand	–	–	–	4	23	10	100 y	100 y	100 y	–	–	–	–	9	9	75	77	73	–	–
Timor-Leste	–	–	–	3	15	1	60	60	61	–	–	–	–	48	69	–	–	–	–	3
Togo	23	23	22	6	22	3	78	79	77	5	0	96	95	19	26	81	81	80	–	4
Tokelau	–	–	–	–	–	–	–	–	–	–	–	–	–	–	–	–	–	–	–	–
Tonga	–	–	–	0	6	6	93	94	93	–	–	–	–	29	27	–	–	–	–	–
Trinidad and Tobago	1 y	1 y	1 y	3 x	11 x	–	97	97	97	–	–	–	–	–	8 x	77 x,y	79 x,y	75 x,y	–	25
Tunisia	2 y	3 y	1 y	0	2	–	99	99	100	–	–	–	–	–	27	93 y	94 y	92 y	–	–
Turkey	–	–	–	1	15	–	99 y	99 y	99 y	–	–	–	–	–	10	–	–	–	–	–
Turkmenistan	0	0	0	0	6	–	100	100	100	–	–	–	–	–	17	37 y	39 y	34 y	–	–
Turks and Caicos Islands	–	–	–	–	–	–	–	–	–	–	–	–	–	–	–	–	–	–	–	–
Tuvalu	–	–	–	0 x	10 x	0 x	50 x	49 x	51 x	–	–	–	–	83 x	69 x	–	–	–	–	–
Uganda	18	17	19	7	34	6	32	32	32	0	*1*	–	83	53	58	85	85	85	1	5

TABLE 11. CHILD PROTECTION

Countries and areas	Child labour (%)[+] 2010–2018[*]			Child marriage (%)[+] 2012–2018[*]			Birth registration (%)[+] 2010–2018[*]			Female genital mutilation (%)[+] 2010–2018[*]				Justification of wife-beating among adolescents (%)[+] 2012–2018[*]		Violent discipline (%)[+] 2012–2018[*]			Sexual violence in childhood (%) 2012–2018[*]	
				female		male				prevalence		attitudes want the practice to stop[c]								
	total	male	female	married by 15	married by 18	married by 18	total	male	female	women[a]	girls[b]	male	female	male	female	total	male	female	male	female
Ukraine	3 y	3 y	3 y	0	9	4	100	100	100	–	–	–	–	2	2	61 y	68 y	55 y	–	2 x
United Arab Emirates	–	–	–	–	–	–	100 y	100 y	100 y	–	–	–	–	–	–	–	–	–	–	–
United Kingdom	–	–	–	–	–	–	100 v	100 v	100 v	–	–	–	–	–	–	–	–	–	–	–
United Republic of Tanzania	24	25	24	5	31	4	26	28	25	10	0	89 x	95	50	59	–	–	–	–	7
United States	–	–	–	–	–	–	100 v	100 v	100 v	–	–	–	–	–	–	–	–	–	–	–
Uruguay	4	5	3	1	25	–	100	100	100	–	–	–	–	–	3	55 y	58 y	51 y	–	–
Uzbekistan	–	–	–	0 x	7 x	1 x	100 x	100 x	100 x	–	–	–	–	63 x	63 x	–	–	–	–	–
Vanuatu	16 y	15 y	16 y	3	21	5	43 y	44 y	43 y	–	–	–	–	63	56	84 y	83 y	84 y	–	–
Venezuela (Bolivarian Republic of)	–	–	–	–	–	–	81 y	–	–	–	–	–	–	–	–	–	–	–	–	–
Viet Nam	13	13	14	1	11	3 x	96	96	96	–	–	–	–	–	28	68	72	65	–	–
Yemen	–	–	–	9	32	–	31	31	30	19	15	–	75	–	49	79 y	81 y	77 y	–	–
Zambia	23	23	23	6	31	2	11	12	11	–	–	–	–	41	49	–	–	–	–	5
Zimbabwe	–	–	–	4	32	1	38	–	–	–	–	–	–	49	54	63	63	62	–	6
SUMMARY																				
East Asia and Pacific	–	–	–	1	7	–	–	–	–	–	–	–	–	–	–	–	–	–	–	–
Europe and Central Asia	–	–	–	–	–	–	100	100	100	–	–	–	–	–	–	–	–	–	–	–
Eastern Europe and Central Asia	–	–	–	1	11	–	99	99	99	–	–	–	–	–	11	–	–	–	–	–
Western Europe	–	–	–	–	–	–	100	100	100	–	–	–	–	–	–	–	–	–	–	–
Latin America and Caribbean	–	–	–	4	25	–	94	–	–	–	–	–	–	–	–	–	–	–	–	–
Middle East and North Africa	5	5	4	4	18	–	92	92	92	–	–	–	–	–	44	87	88	86	–	–
North America	–	–	–	–	–	–	100	100	100	–	–	–	–	–	–	–	–	–	–	–
South Asia	–	–	–	8	30	4	65	65	65	–	–	–	–	39	42	–	–	–	–	2
Sub-Saharan Africa	29	29	29	12	37	4	46	45	44	35	13	–	73	36	44	81	82	81	–	6
Eastern and Southern Africa	27	27	26	9	34	5	40	36	35	42	11	–	81	35	44	–	–	–	–	5
West and Central Africa	31	30	31	15	40	4	53	53	52	29	15	68	66	37	45	83	84	82	–	6
Least developed countries	29	29	29	12	39	6	40	40	40	–	–	–	–	43	48	80	81	79	–	5
World	–	–	–	5	21	–	73	75	74	–	–	–	–	37	38	–	–	–	–	–

For a complete list of countries and areas in the regions, subregions and country categories, see page 182 or visit <data.unicef.org/regionalclassifications>.

It is not advisable to compare data from consecutive editions of *The State of the World's Children.*

DEFINITIONS OF THE INDICATORS

Child labour – Percentage of children 5–17 years old involved in child labour at the moment of the survey. A child is considered to be involved in child labour under the following conditions: (a) children 5–11 years old who, during the reference week, did at least one hour of economic activity and/or more than 21 hours of unpaid household services, (b) children 12–14 years old who, during the reference week, did at least 14 hours of economic activity and/or more than 21 hours of unpaid household services, (c) children 15–17 years old who, during the reference week, did at least 43 hours of economic activity.

Child marriage – Percentage of women 20–24 years old who were first married or in union before they were 15 years old; percentage of women 20–24 years old who were first married or in union before they were 18 years old; percentage of men 20–24 years old who were first married or in union before they were 18 years old.

Birth registration – Percentage of children under age 5 who were registered at the moment of the survey. The numerator of this indicator includes children reported to have a birth certificate, regardless of whether or not it was seen by the interviewer, and those without a birth certificate whose mother or caregiver says the birth has been registered.

Female genital mutilation (FGM) – (a) Women: percentage of women 15–49 years old who have undergone FGM; (b) girls: percentage of girls 0–14 years old who have undergone FGM (as reported by their mothers); (c) want the practice to stop: percentage of women and men 15–49 years old who have heard about FGM and think the practice should stop.

Justification of wife-beating among adolescents – Percentage of girls and boys 15–19 years old who consider a husband to be justified in hitting or beating his wife for at least one of the specified reasons, i.e., if his wife burns the food, argues with him, goes out without telling him, neglects the children or refuses sexual relations.

Violent discipline – Percentage of children 1–14 years old who experience any violent discipline (psychological aggression and/or physical punishment) in the past month.

Sexual violence in childhood – Percentage of women and men 18–29 years old who experienced sexual violence by age 18.

MAIN DATA SOURCES

Child labour – Demographic and Health Surveys (DHS), Multiple Indicator Cluster Surveys (MICS) and other national surveys. Last update: March 2019.

Child marriage – DHS, MICS and other national surveys. Last update: (female) March 2019; (male) August 2019.

Birth registration – DHS, MICS, other national surveys, censuses and vital registration systems. Last update: March 2019.

Female genital mutilation – DHS, MICS and other national surveys. Last update: (a) March 2019; (b, c) August 2019.

Justification of wife-beating among adolescents – DHS, MICS and other national surveys. Last update: August 2019.

Violent discipline – DHS, MICS and other national surveys. Last update: March 2019.

Sexual violence in childhood – DHS and other national surveys. Last update: March 2019.

NOTES

– Data not available.

p Based on small denominators (typically 25–49 unweighted cases). No data based on fewer than 25 unweighted cases are displayed.

v Estimates of 100% were assumed given that civil registration systems in these countries are complete and all vital events (including births) are registered. Source: United Nations, Department of Economic and Social Affairs, Statistics Division, last update December 2017.

x Data refer to years or periods other than those specified in the column heading. Such data are not included in the calculation of regional and global averages.

y Data differ from the standard definition or refer to only part of a country.

If they fall within the noted reference period, such data are included in the calculation of regional and global averages.

+ A more detailed explanation of the methodology and the changes in calculating these estimates can be found in the General Note on the Data, page 180.

* Data refer to the most recent year available during the period specified in the column heading.

Italicized data are from older sources than data presented for other indicators on the same topic within this table. Such discrepancies may be due to an indicator being unavailable in the latest data source, or to the databases for each indicator having been updated as of different dates.

TABLE 12. SOCIAL PROTECTION AND EQUITY

Countries and areas	Mothers with newborns receiving cash benefit (%) 2010–2018*	Proportion of children covered by social protection 2010–2018*	Distribution of social protection benefits (%, 2010–2016*)			Share of household income (%, 2010–2018*)			Gini coefficient 2010–2018*	Palma index of income inequality 2010–2018*	GDP per capita (current US$) 2010–2018*
			bottom 40%	top 20%	bottom 20%	bottom 40%	top 20%	bottom 20%			
Afghanistan	–	–	–	–	–	–	–	–	–	–	556.3
Albania	–	–	28.2	30.3	13.5	–	37.8	8.9	29.0	–	4532.9
Algeria	11.2	–	–	–	–	–	37.2	9.4	27.6	–	4048.3
Andorra	–	–	–	–	–	–	–	–	–	–	39134.4
Angola	–	–	–	–	–	–	–	–	–	2.2	4095.8
Anguilla	–	–	–	–	–	–	–	–	–	–	–
Antigua and Barbuda	40.0	–	–	–	–	–	–	–	–	–	15824.7
Argentina	34.0	84.6	16.7	39.6	6.7	15.3	46.0	5.2	40.6	2.4	14591.9
Armenia	61.0	21.4	37.7	23.1	17.8	20.8	42.4	8.4	33.6	1.2	3914.5
Australia	–	100.0	–	–	–	18.8	43.0	6.8	35.8	–	54093.6
Austria	100.0	100.0	–	–	–	21.1	38.4	7.9	30.5	–	47380.8
Azerbaijan	14.0	–	29.4	32.4	17.3	–	–	–	–	–	4147.1
Bahamas	–	–	–	–	–	–	–	–	–	–	31857.9
Bahrain	–	–	–	–	–	–	–	–	–	–	23715.5
Bangladesh	20.9	29.4	20.0	52.7	8.7	21.0	41.4	8.6	32.4	1.3	1564.0
Barbados	–	–	–	–	–	–	–	–	–	–	16327.6
Belarus	–	–	37.3	21.8	16.9	24.1	35.5	9.9	25.4	0.9	5761.7
Belgium	100.0	100.0	–	–	–	22.6	36.5	8.6	27.7	–	43507.2
Belize	–	–	40.4	32.5	18.9	–	–	–	–	–	4956.8
Benin	–	–	–	–	–	–	52.1	3.2	47.8	–	827.4
Bhutan	–	–	16.5	41.1	1.3	–	44.4	6.7	37.4	1.8	3390.7
Bolivia (Plurinational State of)	51.5	65.0	29.3	37.3	14.5	–	–	–	–	–	3351.1
Bosnia and Herzegovina	–	–	27.8	29.0	11.8	–	40.7	7.5	33.0	–	5394.6
Botswana	–	5.5	28.5	28.6	12.8	–	58.5	3.9	53.3	–	7893.7
Brazil	45.0	96.8	12.6	51.7	4.2	–	57.8	3.2	53.3	4.3	9880.9
British Virgin Islands	–	–	–	–	–	–	–	–	–	–	–
Brunei Darussalam	–	–	–	–	–	–	–	–	–	–	28572.1
Bulgaria	100.0	48.6	–	–	–	17.8	43.9	6.0	37.4	–	8228.0
Burkina Faso	0.4	–	3.8	69.5	1.5	–	44.3	8.3	35.3	1.9	642.0
Burundi	–	–	–	–	–	–	46.3	6.9	38.6	–	293.0
Cabo Verde	–	31.5	–	–	–	–	–	–	–	–	3295.3
Cambodia	1.5	–	8.7	46.9	0.1	–	–	–	–	1.5	1385.3
Cameroon	0.6	0.4	2.9	59.4	0.7	–	51.7	4.5	46.6	–	1421.6
Canada	100.0	39.7	–	–	–	18.9	40.7	6.6	34.0	–	45069.9
Central African Republic	–	1.0	–	–	–	–	–	–	–	–	471.6
Chad	–	–	15.2	45.7	1.6	–	48.8	4.9	43.3	–	664.3
Chile	44.0	93.1	17.1	48.8	7.6	–	52.9	5.2	46.6	3.5	15037.4
China	64.9	2.2	9.2	51.1	3.0	17.0	45.4	6.4	38.6	2.1	8759.0
Colombia	–	27.3	6.7	71.7	3.0	12.4	54.8	4.1	49.7	4.5	6375.9
Comoros	–	–	–	–	–	–	50.4	4.5	45.3	–	1312.4
Congo	–	–	–	–	–	–	53.7	4.2	48.9	–	1702.6
Cook Islands	–	–	–	–	–	–	–	–	–	–	–
Costa Rica	–	17.7	13.1	61.2	5.3	12.8	54.0	4.4	48.3	3.3	11752.5
Côte d'Ivoire	–	–	16.3	52.8	6.6	–	47.8	5.7	41.5	–	1557.2
Croatia	100.0	–	29.1	30.5	13.1	20.4	38.4	7.3	31.1	–	13383.7
Cuba	–	–	–	–	–	–	–	–	–	–	8541.2
Cyprus	100.0	60.3	–	–	–	20.0	42.1	7.9	34.0	–	25760.8
Czechia	100.0	–	–	–	–	24.4	35.9	9.7	25.9	–	20379.9
Democratic People's Republic of Korea	–	–	–	–	–	–	–	–	–	–	–
Democratic Republic of the Congo	–	1.3	8.2	63.9	3.4	–	48.4	5.5	42.1	–	467.1
Denmark	100.0	100.0	–	–	–	23.3	37.7	9.4	28.2	–	57218.9
Djibouti	–	–	22.3	43.3	10.3	–	47.6	5.4	41.6	–	1953.9
Dominica	–	–	–	–	–	–	–	–	–	–	6951.3
Dominican Republic	–	–	20.4	44.6	8.5	13.9	51.5	4.9	45.7	2.7	7222.6
Ecuador	–	6.7	14.0	61.6	6.7	14.1	50.1	4.7	44.7	3.1	6213.5
Egypt	100.0	–	15.6	53.5	7.2	21.9	41.5	9.1	31.8	–	2440.5
El Salvador	–	–	7.2	70.9	2.4	17.4	44.7	6.4	38.0	3.0	3902.2
Equatorial Guinea	–	–	–	–	–	–	–	–	–	–	9738.4
Eritrea	–	–	–	–	–	–	–	–	–	–	811.4
Estonia	100.0	100.0	–	–	–	20.0	40.4	7.5	32.7	–	20200.4
Eswatini	–	–	24.7	36.9	13.7	–	–	–	–	3.5	3941.9
Ethiopia	–	–	–	–	–	17.6	46.7	6.6	39.1	1.4	768.0
Fiji	–	–	22.8	34.3	9.5	–	44.7	7.5	36.7	2.2	6006.4
Finland	100.0	100.0	–	–	–	23.4	36.7	9.4	27.1	–	45804.7

TABLE 12. SOCIAL PROTECTION AND EQUITY

Countries and areas	Mothers with newborns receiving cash benefit (%) 2010–2018*	Proportion of children covered by social protection 2010–2018*	Distribution of social protection benefits (%, 2010–2016*)			Share of household income (%, 2010–2018*)			Gini coefficient 2010–2018*	Palma index of income inequality 2010–2018*	GDP per capita (current US$) 2010–2018*
			bottom 40%	top 20%	bottom 20%	bottom 40%	top 20%	bottom 20%			
France	100.0	100.0	–	–	–	20.7	40.9	7.9	32.7	–	38679.1
Gabon	–	–	–	–	–	–	44.4	6.0	38.0	–	7212.5
Gambia	–	–	7.6	58.7	3.4	19.0	43.6	7.4	35.9	–	672.8
Georgia	24.0	–	39.8	19.0	20.4	17.4	44.5	6.3	37.9	2.1	4045.4
Germany	100.0	100.0	–	–	–	20.7	39.7	7.8	31.7	–	44681.1
Ghana	41.7	5.6	3.0	48.3	0.7	–	48.6	4.7	43.5	–	2025.9
Greece	100.0	–	–	–	–	17.7	41.8	5.9	36.0	–	18883.5
Grenada	–	–	–	–	–	–	–	–	–	–	10163.6
Guatemala	14.0	3.1	2.3	83.2	1.0	–	53.6	4.5	48.3	–	4470.6
Guinea	–	–	7.6	54.3	4.1	–	41.5	7.6	33.7	–	821.7
Guinea-Bissau	–	–	–	–	–	12.8	56.7	4.5	50.7	–	736.7
Guyana	–	–	–	–	–	–	–	–	–	–	4586.1
Haiti	–	–	0.4	97.3	0.0	–	47.1	5.5	41.1	–	765.6
Holy See	–	–	–	–	–	–	–	–	–	–	–
Honduras	–	–	16.6	61.4	7.6	11.0	54.6	3.2	50.5	5.2	2432.9
Hungary	100.0	100.0	–	–	–	21.1	38.4	7.8	30.4	–	14278.9
Iceland	100.0	–	–	–	–	23.2	37.3	9.4	27.8	–	71314.8
India	41.0	–	42.9	16.5	22.3	–	44.4	8.1	35.7	1.4	1981.5
Indonesia	–	–	63.2	4.1	35.5	17.5	45.2	6.8	38.1	1.7	3836.9
Iran (Islamic Republic of)	14.0	–	–	–	–	–	46.7	6.1	40.0	–	5627.7
Iraq	–	–	21.5	41.5	9.1	–	38.5	8.8	29.5	–	5143.7
Ireland	100.0	100.0	–	–	–	20.9	40.2	8.0	31.8	–	68941.8
Israel	–	–	–	–	–	15.9	44.2	5.2	38.9	–	40543.6
Italy	100.0	–	–	–	–	18.0	41.3	5.9	35.4	–	32155.2
Jamaica	–	–	29.0	34.1	14.6	–	–	–	–	–	5060.5
Japan	–	–	–	–	–	–	–	–	–	–	38332.0
Jordan	–	–	25.1	38.8	12.2	20.3	42.4	8.2	33.7	1.5	4168.6
Kazakhstan	44.6	100.0	23.6	37.9	10.7	23.4	37.4	9.8	27.5	1.1	9030.3
Kenya	–	8.1	30.9	31.3	14.6	–	47.5	6.2	40.8	–	1568.2
Kiribati	–	–	–	–	–	–	–	–	–	–	1625.6
Kuwait	–	–	–	–	–	–	–	–	–	–	29474.5
Kyrgyzstan	23.8	17.8	31.0	30.2	15.5	23.6	37.4	9.9	27.3	1.3	1242.8
Lao People's Democratic Republic	–	–	–	–	–	–	44.6	7.6	36.4	–	2423.8
Latvia	100.0	100.0	35.1	19.5	15.4	19.4	41.5	7.1	34.2	1.4	15684.6
Lebanon	–	–	–	–	–	–	40.0	7.9	31.8	–	7838.3
Lesotho	–	10.4	–	–	–	9.6	58.2	2.8	54.2	–	1232.8
Liberia	–	–	37.5	21.5	20.8	–	42.8	7.2	35.3	–	698.7
Libya	–	–	–	–	–	–	–	–	–	–	5792.1
Liechtenstein	100.0	–	–	–	–	–	–	–	–	–	165028.2
Lithuania	100.0	–	39.9	18.9	20.2	17.7	44.1	6.1	37.4	–	16809.6
Luxembourg	100.0	–	–	–	–	19.3	41.0	7.2	33.8	–	104498.7
Madagascar	–	–	–	–	–	15.7	49.4	5.7	42.6	2.3	448.4
Malawi	–	9.8	22.7	38.5	11.0	16.2	51.7	6.4	44.7	2.3	356.7
Malaysia	–	–	22.9	37.2	10.2	–	47.3	5.8	41.0	2.6	10117.6
Maldives	–	–	37.0	27.3	18.7	–	–	–	–	–	9801.6
Mali	–	5.4	6.1	67.0	0.4	–	–	–	–	1.3	828.6
Malta	100.0	–	–	–	–	21.9	38.1	8.5	29.4	–	27241.1
Marshall Islands	–	–	–	–	–	–	–	–	–	–	3516.7
Mauritania	–	–	18.2	42.7	7.7	–	40.2	7.5	32.6	–	1161.8
Mauritius	–	–	26.6	35.6	12.0	–	43.9	7.4	35.8	–	10484.9
Mexico	9.6	28.4	16.4	58.2	7.7	15.5	50.1	5.7	43.4	2.7	9281.1
Micronesia (Federated States of)	–	–	–	–	–	–	46.0	5.5	40.1	–	3018.4
Monaco	–	–	–	–	–	–	–	–	–	–	166726.1
Mongolia	100.0	100.0	33.0	24.9	15.2	20.4	40.6	8.0	32.3	–	3671.9
Montenegro	–	–	24.1	37.6	10.5	20.8	40.5	8.5	31.9	1.0	7784.1
Montserrat	–	–	–	–	–	–	–	–	–	–	–
Morocco	–	–	–	–	–	–	47.0	6.7	39.5	–	3036.2
Mozambique	0.2	–	13.4	55.6	5.3	–	59.5	4.2	54.0	–	441.6
Myanmar	0.7	–	–	–	–	–	45.7	7.3	38.1	–	1249.8
Namibia	–	–	–	–	–	–	63.7	2.8	59.1	–	5646.5
Nauru	–	–	–	–	–	–	–	–	–	–	8844.4
Nepal	–	–	17.1	47.7	5.9	20.4	41.5	8.3	32.8	1.3	900.6
Netherlands	100.0	100.0	–	–	–	22.8	37.3	8.9	28.2	–	48482.8
New Zealand	–	–	–	–	–	–	–	–	–	–	42260.1

TABLE 12. SOCIAL PROTECTION AND EQUITY

Countries and areas	Mothers with newborns receiving cash benefit (%) 2010–2018*	Proportion of children covered by social protection 2010–2018*	Distribution of social protection benefits (%, 2010–2016*)			Share of household income (%, 2010–2018*)			Gini coefficient 2010–2018*	Palma index of income inequality 2010–2018*	GDP per capita (current US$) 2010–2018*
			bottom 40%	top 20%	bottom 20%	bottom 40%	top 20%	bottom 20%			
Nicaragua	–	–	9.3	56.1	2.5	–	52.1	5.1	46.2	–	2168.2
Niger	–	4.2	12.2	51.6	5.5	–	42.4	7.8	34.3	–	375.9
Nigeria	0.1	–	8.7	68.6	2.2	–	–	–	–	3.0	1968.6
Niue	–	–	–	–	–	–	–	–	–	–	–
North Macedonia	–	–	–	–	–	17.3	41.1	5.6	35.6	2.3	5417.6
Norway	100.0	100.0	–	–	–	23.1	36.5	9.0	27.5	–	75704.2
Oman	–	–	–	–	–	–	–	–	–	–	15170.4
Pakistan	–	–	11.9	58.2	5.1	21.1	42.8	8.9	33.5	–	1466.8
Palau	–	–	–	–	–	–	–	–	–	–	16274.9
Panama	–	37.3	14.3	55.1	5.7	11.5	54.2	3.4	49.9	3.6	15166.1
Papua New Guinea	–	–	33.0	52.4	4.5	–	–	–	–	–	2640.2
Paraguay	3.0	32.8	11.8	61.2	4.6	13.2	54.0	4.6	48.8	3.7	5680.6
Peru	–	–	10.3	63.2	5.4	14.4	48.4	4.7	43.3	2.9	6700.8
Philippines	11.0	13.6	26.1	46.7	12.9	–	47.3	6.6	40.1	2.2	2981.9
Poland	100.0	100.0	26.1	30.0	11.5	21.3	39.5	8.5	30.8	1.3	13861.1
Portugal	100.0	93.1	–	–	–	18.7	42.7	6.7	35.5	–	21291.4
Qatar	–	–	–	–	–	–	–	–	–	–	61264.4
Republic of Korea	–	–	–	–	–	20.3	39.0	7.3	31.6	–	29742.8
Republic of Moldova	–	–	36.5	20.8	15.9	24.1	36.1	10.0	25.9	1.3	2724.5
Romania	100.0	100.0	25.1	32.3	9.6	16.9	40.7	5.1	35.9	1.0	10793.0
Russian Federation	63.0	100.0	28.8	23.8	9.5	18.0	45.3	6.9	37.7	1.9	10750.6
Rwanda	–	–	27.0	42.9	12.7	15.8	50.8	6.0	43.7	3.2	762.5
Saint Kitts and Nevis	–	–	–	–	–	–	–	–	–	–	–
Saint Lucia	–	–	–	–	–	–	–	–	–	–	–
Saint Vincent and the Grenadines	–	–	–	–	–	–	–	–	–	–	7149.6
Samoa	–	–	25.1	42.2	11.0	–	46.4	6.8	38.7	–	4307.8
San Marino	–	–	–	–	–	–	–	–	–	–	48494.6
Sao Tome and Principe	–	–	–	–	–	21.1	39.5	8.4	30.8	–	1811.0
Saudi Arabia	–	–	–	–	–	–	–	–	–	–	20803.7
Senegal	–	4.0	3.2	66.3	1.2	–	46.9	6.1	40.3	1.9	1367.2
Serbia	–	–	30.1	28.0	13.4	22.5	37.7	9.0	28.5	1.1	6284.2
Seychelles	–	–	–	–	–	–	53.0	5.4	46.8	–	15683.7
Sierra Leone	–	–	–	–	–	–	42.4	7.9	34.0	1.5	499.4
Singapore	–	–	–	–	–	–	–	–	–	–	60297.8
Slovakia	100.0	100.0	27.9	18.4	10.5	23.1	35.0	8.5	26.5	0.9	17579.3
Slovenia	96.0	79.4	–	–	–	24.1	35.1	9.6	25.4	–	23449.6
Solomon Islands	–	–	–	–	–	–	44.6	7.0	37.1	–	2077.1
Somalia	–	–	–	–	–	–	–	–	–	–	488.6
South Africa	–	75.1	37.1	31.6	18.5	7.2	68.2	2.4	63.0	7.1	6120.5
South Sudan	–	–	17.1	55.9	3.9	–	–	–	–	–	283.5
Spain	100.0	100.0	–	–	–	17.5	42.1	5.8	36.2	–	28208.3
Sri Lanka	–	–	15.7	49.3	6.0	–	47.6	7.0	39.8	1.6	4104.6
State of Palestine	–	–	39.3	13.1	18.8	19.2	41.1	7.3	33.7	1.5	3254.5
Sudan	–	–	33.0	22.9	18.0	–	–	–	–	1.4	3015.0
Suriname	–	–	–	–	–	–	–	–	–	–	5379.1
Sweden	100.0	100.0	–	–	–	22.1	37.6	8.2	29.2	–	53253.5
Switzerland	100.0	100.0	–	–	–	20.3	40.2	7.8	32.3	–	80333.4
Syrian Arab Republic	–	–	–	–	–	–	–	–	–	–	–
Tajikistan	59.5	6.4	35.3	25.8	17.0	–	41.7	7.4	34.0	1.2	806.0
Thailand	–	18.9	17.5	48.9	8.4	18.4	44.1	7.3	36.5	1.8	6578.2
Timor-Leste	–	30.7	8.8	88.0	5.3	–	38.4	9.4	28.7	–	2000.6
Togo	–	49.0	2.3	86.2	0.0	–	48.6	5.0	43.1	1.8	619.1
Tokelau	–	–	–	–	–	–	–	–	–	–	–
Tonga	–	–	5.0	44.9	0.0	–	45.4	6.8	37.6	–	4217.5
Trinidad and Tobago	–	–	–	–	–	–	–	–	–	–	16076.1
Tunisia	–	48.3	37.3	19.7	19.8	20.1	40.9	7.8	32.8	1.5	3494.3
Turkey	–	–	16.7	38.7	6.1	15.6	48.3	5.7	41.9	1.9	10499.7
Turkmenistan	–	–	–	–	–	–	–	–	–	–	6587.1
Turks and Caicos Islands	–	–	–	–	–	–	–	–	–	–	25933.6
Tuvalu	–	–	–	–	–	17.4	46.4	6.6	39.1	–	3572.6
Uganda	–	–	11.4	68.2	0.9	–	49.8	6.1	42.8	2.3	631.5
Ukraine	100.0	100.0	32.0	25.7	14.0	24.5	35.1	10.1	25.0	0.9	2640.7
United Arab Emirates	–	–	–	–	–	–	–	–	–	–	40325.4
United Kingdom	100.0	100.0	–	–	–	19.7	40.6	7.5	33.2	–	39932.1
United Republic of Tanzania	0.3	–	7.0	70.8	3.1	–	45.8	7.4	37.8	–	1004.8

TABLE 12. SOCIAL PROTECTION AND EQUITY

Countries and areas	Mothers with newborns receiving cash benefit (%) 2010–2018*	Proportion of children covered by social protection 2010–2018*	Distribution of social protection benefits (%, 2010–2016*)			Share of household income (%, 2010–2018*)			Gini coefficient 2010–2018*	Palma index of income inequality 2010–2018*	GDP per capita (current US$) 2010–2018*
			bottom 40%	top 20%	bottom 20%	bottom 40%	top 20%	bottom 20%			
United States	–	–	–	–	–	15.2	46.9	5.0	41.5	–	59927.9
Uruguay	100.0	66.2	11.9	50.7	3.2	16.5	45.8	5.9	39.5	2.5	16437.2
Uzbekistan	16.0	22.0	–	–	–	–	–	–	–	–	1826.6
Vanuatu	–	–	–	–	–	17.8	44.8	6.7	37.6	–	2976.1
Venezuela (Bolivarian Republic of)	–	–	–	–	–	–	–	–	–	–	16054.5
Viet Nam	44.5	–	10.6	54.4	3.7	18.8	42.5	6.9	35.3	–	2365.6
Yemen	–	–	–	–	–	–	44.7	7.3	36.7	–	963.5
Zambia	–	21.1	1.3	75.5	0.3	8.9	61.3	2.9	57.1	4.8	1534.9
Zimbabwe	–	–	7.6	58.7	2.2	–	49.7	5.8	43.2	–	1602.4
SUMMARY											
East Asia and Pacific	57.8	5.4	17.9	44.5	8.2	17.3	45.1	6.6	38.2	2.0	10,092.7
Europe and Central Asia	85.8	93.2	–	–	–	19.7	41.4	7.4	33.7	–	23,451.8
Eastern Europe and Central Asia	62.8	84.1	26.8	29.0	10.5	18.9	43.1	7.3	35.4	1.6	8,000.9
Western Europe	100.0	99.6	–	–	–	20.2	40.1	7.5	32.4	–	36,682.3
Latin America and Caribbean	32.3	62.8	13.3	56.6	5.5	14.5	53.2	4.4	47.8	3.6	9,271.8
Middle East and North Africa	51.6	–	–	–	–	–	42.7	7.9	34.3	–	7,497.5
North America	100.0	39.7	–	–	–	15.6	46.3	5.2	40.7	–	58,411.2
South Asia	38.9	–	–	25.7	18.5	21.0 ‡	43.9	8.2	35.1	1.4	1,864.8
Sub-Saharan Africa	–	–	13.9	56.5	5.6	14.1	49.7	5.8	43.1	2.8	1,625.3
Eastern and Southern Africa	–	–	21.8	47.2	9.9	–	51.3	5.7	44.5	2.8	1,879.2
West and Central Africa	4.7	–	8.5	62.8	2.7	–	47.4	5.8	41.0	2.7	1,365.2
Least developed countries	11.1	17.1	14.2	56.7	5.8	18.5	46.0	6.9	38.5	1.7	1,113.8
World	**47.1**	**33.1**	**24.1**	**39.5**	**11.3**	**18.2**	**45.6**	**6.9**	**38.1**	**2.0**	**10,046.2**

For a complete list of countries and areas in the regions, subregions and country categories, see page 182 or visit <data.unicef.org/regionalclassifications>.

It is not advisable to compare data from consecutive editions of *The State of the World's Children*.

DEFINITIONS OF THE INDICATORS

Mothers with newborns receiving cash benefit (%) – Proportion of women giving birth covered by maternity benefits: ratio of women receiving cash maternity benefits to women giving birth in the same year (estimated based on age-specific fertility rates published in the UN's World Population Prospects or on the number of live births corrected for the share of twin and triplet births).

Proportion of children covered by social protection – Proportion of children covered by social protection benefits: ratio of children/households receiving child or family cash benefits to the total number of children/households with children.

Distribution of social protection benefits – Percentage of benefits going to the 1st quintile, bottom 40% and 5th quintile relative to the total benefits going to the population. Social protection coverage includes: providing social assistance through cash transfers to those who need them, especially children; benefits and support for people of working age in case of maternity, disability, work injury or for those without jobs; and pension coverage for the elderly.

Share of household income – Percentage of income received by the 20 per cent of households with the highest income, by the 40 per cent of households with the lowest income and by the 20 per cent of households with the lowest income.

Gini coefficient – Gini index measures the extent to which the distribution of income (or, in some cases, consumption expenditure) among individuals or households within an economy deviates from a perfectly equal distribution. A Lorenz curve plots the cumulative percentages of total income received against the cumulative number of recipients, starting with the poorest individual or household. The Gini index measures the area between the Lorenz curve and a hypothetical line of absolute equality, expressed as a percentage of the maximum area under the line. Thus a Gini index of 0 represents perfect equality, while an index of 100 implies perfect inequality.

Palma index of income inequality – Palma index is defined as the ratio of the richest 10% of the population's share of gross national income divided by the poorest 40%'s share.

GDP per capita (current US$) – GDP per capita is gross domestic product divided by midyear population. GDP is the sum of gross value added by all resident producers in the economy plus any product taxes and minus any subsidies not included in the value of the products. It is calculated without making deductions for depreciation of fabricated assets or for depletion and degradation of natural resources. Data are in current US dollars.

MAIN DATA SOURCES

Mothers with newborns receiving cash benefit (%) – ILO World Social Protection Report, 2017-2019. Last update: July 2019.

Proportion of children covered by social protection – ILO World Social Protection Report, 2017-2019. Last update: July 2019.

Distribution of social protection benefits – The Atlas of Social Protection: Indicators of Resilience and Equity. Last update: May 2019.

Share of household income – World Development Indicators. Last update: July 2019.

Gini coefficient – World Development Indicators. Last update: July 2019.

Palma index of income inequality – The World Bank. Global Monitor Report, 2014–2015. Last update: 2015.

GDP per capita (current US$) – World Development Indicators. Last update: July 2019.

NOTES

– Data not available.

* Data refer to the most recent year available during the period specified in the column heading.

‡ Excludes India.

TABLE 13. WASH

Countries and areas	Households — At least basic drinking water services (%) 2017			Households — At least basic sanitation services (%) 2017			Households — Basic hygiene facilities (%) 2017			Schools — Basic water services (%) 2016			Schools — Basic sanitation services (%) 2016			Schools — Basic hygiene services (%) 2016			Health care facilities — Basic water services (%) 2016	Health care facilities — Basic sanitation services (%) 2016	Health care facilities — Basic hygiene services (%) 2016	Health care facilities — Basic waste management services (%) 2016
	total	urban	rural	total	urban	rural	total	urban	rural	total	primary	secondary	total	primary	secondary	total	primary	secondary	total	total	total	total
Afghanistan	67	96	57	43	62	37	38	64	29	–	–	–	–	–	–	–	–	–	–	–	–	–
Albania	91	92	90	98	98	97	–	–	–	–	–	–	–	–	–	–	–	–	–	–	–	–
Algeria	94	95	89	88	90	82	84	88	73	93	87	98	99	98	100	99	98	99	–	–	–	–
Andorra	100	100	100	100	100	100	–	–	–	100	100	100	100	100	100	100	100	100	100	–	–	100
Angola	56	71	27	50	64	23	27	34	13	–	–	–	–	–	–	–	–	–	–	–	–	–
Anguilla	97	97	–	97	97	–	–	–	–	–	–	–	–	–	–	–	–	–	–	–	–	–
Antigua and Barbuda	97	–	–	88	–	–	–	–	–	–	–	–	–	–	–	–	–	–	–	–	–	–
Argentina	–	100	–	–	96	–	–	–	–	–	–	–	77	77	–	–	–	–	–	–	–	–
Armenia	100	100	100	94	100	83	94	97	90	–	–	–	–	–	–	–	–	–	97	41	69	97
Australia	100	100	100	100	–	–	–	–	–	100	100	100	100	100	100	100	100	100	–	–	–	–
Austria	100	100	100	100	100	100	–	–	–	–	–	–	–	–	–	–	–	–	–	–	–	–
Azerbaijan	91	99	82	93	96	88	83	–	–	100	100	100	100	100	100	100	100	100	100	48	100	–
Bahamas	99	–	–	95	–	–	–	–	–	–	–	–	–	–	–	–	–	–	–	–	–	–
Bahrain	100	–	–	100	–	–	–	–	–	100	100	100	100	100	100	100	100	100	–	–	–	–
Bangladesh	97	97	97	48	51	47	35	51	26	74	73	87	59	57	67	44	39	58	70	–	–	11
Barbados	98	–	–	97	–	–	–	–	–	100	100	100	100	100	100	100	100	100	–	–	–	–
Belarus	96	96	98	98	98	96	–	–	–	100	100	100	100	100	100	100	100	100	–	–	–	–
Belgium	100	100	100	99	99	99	–	–	–	100	100	100	–	–	–	100	100	100	–	–	–	–
Belize	98	99	97	88	93	83	90	91	90	–	–	–	–	–	–	–	–	–	–	–	–	–
Benin	66	76	58	16	27	8	11	17	6	–	–	–	–	–	–	–	–	–	74	–	–	26
Bhutan	97	98	97	69	73	67	–	–	–	59	58	63	76	75	93	–	–	–	–	–	–	–
Bolivia (Plurinational State of)	93	99	78	61	72	36	25	28	19	–	–	–	–	–	–	–	–	–	–	–	–	–
Bosnia and Herzegovina	96	95	97	95	99	92	–	–	–	–	–	–	–	–	–	–	–	–	–	–	–	–
Botswana	90	97	76	77	89	51	–	–	–	–	–	–	–	–	–	–	–	–	–	–	–	–
Brazil	98	100	90	88	93	60	–	–	–	–	–	–	84	84	–	61	61	65	–	–	–	–
British Virgin Islands	100	–	–	–	–	–	–	–	–	–	–	–	–	–	–	–	–	–	–	–	–	–
Brunei Darussalam	100	–	–	–	–	–	–	–	–	–	–	–	–	–	–	–	–	–	–	–	–	–
Bulgaria	99	99	98	86	87	84	–	–	–	–	–	–	–	–	–	–	–	–	–	–	–	–
Burkina Faso	48	80	35	19	39	11	12	23	8	53	55	42	70	74	52	18	18	–	79	–	–	31
Burundi	61	90	57	46	42	46	6	20	4	42	39	–	48	35	89	19	20	16	73	–	–	84
Cabo Verde	87	93	76	74	80	62	–	–	–	–	–	–	–	–	–	–	–	–	–	–	–	–
Cambodia	79	97	73	59	96	48	66	88	60	–	–	–	39	48	67	41	49	40	–	–	–	–
Cameroon	60	77	39	39	56	18	9	15	3	34	31	–	–	–	–	–	–	–	–	–	–	–
Canada	99	100	99	99	99	99	–	–	–	–	–	–	–	–	–	–	–	–	–	–	–	–
Central African Republic	–	–	–	–	–	–	–	–	–	16	16	–	–	–	–	–	–	–	–	–	–	–
Chad	39	70	29	8	30	2	6	18	2	23	19	–	–	–	–	–	–	–	–	–	–	55
Chile	100	100	100	100	100	100	–	–	–	–	–	–	96	96	–	–	–	–	–	–	–	–
China	93	98	86	85	91	76	–	–	–	–	–	–	–	–	–	–	–	–	91	–	36	–
Colombia	97	100	86	90	93	76	65	73	35	55	–	–	61	–	–	–	–	–	–	–	–	–
Comoros	80	88	77	36	45	32	–	–	–	–	–	–	–	–	–	–	–	–	21	2	–	–
Congo	73	87	46	20	27	6	48	56	32	–	–	–	–	–	–	–	–	–	37	–	–	12
Cook Islands	100	–	–	98	–	–	–	–	–	100	100	100	100	100	100	100	100	100	–	–	–	–
Costa Rica	100	100	100	98	98	96	–	–	–	82	85	78	70	68	76	70	68	76	–	–	–	–
Côte d'Ivoire	73	88	58	32	46	18	19	28	10	–	–	–	–	–	–	–	–	–	57	–	–	–
Croatia	100	100	100	97	98	95	–	–	–	51	–	–	34	–	–	26	–	–	–	–	–	–
Cuba	95	97	90	93	92	95	85	88	76	–	–	–	–	–	–	–	–	–	–	–	–	–
Cyprus	100	100	100	99	100	98	–	–	–	–	–	–	–	–	–	–	–	–	–	–	–	–
Czechia	100	100	100	99	99	99	–	–	–	–	–	–	–	–	–	–	–	–	100	95	100	100
Democratic People's Republic of Korea	95	97	90	83	90	72	–	–	–	–	–	–	–	–	–	–	–	–	–	–	–	–
Democratic Republic of the Congo	43	69	23	20	23	18	4	7	2	–	–	–	–	–	–	–	–	–	–	–	–	12
Denmark	100	100	100	100	100	100	–	–	–	100	100	100	100	100	100	100	100	100	–	–	–	–
Djibouti	76	84	47	64	76	19	–	–	–	–	–	–	–	–	–	–	–	–	–	–	–	35
Dominica	–	–	–	–	–	–	–	–	–	100	100	100	100	100	100	100	100	100	–	–	–	–
Dominican Republic	97	98	90	84	86	74	55	58	42	–	–	–	90	90	–	–	–	–	–	–	–	–
Ecuador	94	100	83	88	91	83	81	84	75	51	40	61	83	83	–	87	80	94	–	–	–	49
Egypt	99	99	99	94	98	91	90	93	88	–	–	–	100	100	100	100	100	100	–	–	–	–
El Salvador	97	99	92	87	91	79	91	92	86	84	80	87	–	–	–	–	–	–	–	–	–	–
Equatorial Guinea	65	78	31	66	70	57	–	–	–	–	–	–	–	–	–	–	–	–	–	–	–	–
Eritrea	–	–	–	–	–	–	–	–	–	–	–	–	–	–	–	–	–	–	–	–	–	–

TABLE 13. WASH

Countries and areas	At least basic drinking water services (%) 2017			At least basic sanitation services (%) 2017			Basic hygiene facilities (%) 2017			Basic water services (%) 2016			Basic sanitation services (%) 2016			Basic hygiene services (%) 2016			Basic water services (%) 2016	Basic sanitation services (%) 2016	Basic hygiene services (%) 2016	Basic waste management services (%) 2016
	total	urban	rural	total	urban	rural	total	urban	rural	total	primary	secondary	total	primary	secondary	total	primary	secondary	total	total	total	total
Estonia	100	100	99	99	99	99	–	–	–	100	100	100	100	100	100	100	100	100	100	–	100	100
Eswatini	69	97	60	58	51	61	24	48	17	–	–	–	–	–	–	–	–	–	–	–	–	–
Ethiopia	41	80	31	7	20	4	8	23	4	–	–	–	–	–	–	6	5	7	30	59	–	64
Fiji	94	98	89	95	95	95	–	–	–	88	–	–	76	–	–	61	–	–	–	–	–	–
Finland	100	100	100	99	99	99	–	–	–	100	100	100	100	100	100	100	100	100	–	–	–	–
France	100	100	100	99	99	99	–	–	–	100	100	100	100	100	100	100	100	100	–	–	–	–
Gabon	86	90	55	47	49	37	–	–	–	–	–	–	–	–	–	–	–	–	–	–	–	–
Gambia	78	87	63	39	45	30	8	12	1	–	–	–	82	83	80	–	–	–	–	–	–	–
Georgia	98	100	96	90	95	83	–	–	–	74	–	–	60	–	–	12	–	–	–	–	–	–
Germany	100	100	100	99	99	99	–	–	–	100	100	100	100	100	100	100	100	100	–	–	–	–
Ghana	81	93	68	18	24	12	41	45	37	–	–	–	–	–	–	–	–	–	71	–	–	51
Greece	100	100	100	99	99	98	–	–	–	–	–	–	–	–	–	–	–	–	–	–	–	–
Grenada	96	–	–	91	–	–	–	–	–	100	100	100	–	–	–	100	100	100	–	–	–	–
Guatemala	94	98	90	65	79	51	77	83	70	–	–	–	76	76	–	–	–	–	–	–	–	–
Guinea	62	86	49	23	34	17	17	26	13	10	10	–	–	–	–	–	–	–	–	–	–	–
Guinea-Bissau	67	84	53	21	37	8	6	9	5	–	–	–	–	–	–	–	–	–	–	–	–	0
Guyana	96	100	94	86	92	84	77	75	78	–	–	–	–	–	–	–	–	–	–	–	–	–
Haiti	65	85	43	35	44	24	23	29	16	–	–	–	–	–	–	–	–	–	–	–	–	6
Holy See	–	–	–	–	–	–	–	–	–	–	–	–	–	–	–	–	–	–	–	–	–	–
Honduras	95	99	89	81	85	76	–	–	–	59	65	52	82	–	–	12	5	21	58	1	–	–
Hungary	100	100	100	98	98	99	–	–	–	100	100	100	92	100	100	99	100	100	–	–	–	–
Iceland	100	100	100	99	99	100	–	–	–	–	–	–	–	–	–	–	–	–	–	–	–	–
India	93	96	91	60	72	53	60	80	49	69	68	75	73	72	79	54	55	53	–	–	–	–
Indonesia	89	95	82	73	80	65	64	72	55	66	65	68	34	31	41	42	43	40	80	–	–	66
Iran (Islamic Republic of)	95	97	89	88	92	79	–	–	–	–	–	–	–	–	–	–	–	–	–	–	–	–
Iraq	97	99	91	94	97	88	95	96	90	–	–	–	–	–	–	–	–	–	–	–	–	–
Ireland	97	97	98	91	89	94	–	–	–	–	–	–	–	–	–	–	–	–	–	–	–	–
Israel	100	100	100	100	100	100	–	–	–	100	100	100	100	100	100	100	100	100	–	–	–	–
Italy	99	99	99	99	99	99	–	–	–	100	100	100	100	100	100	100	100	100	–	–	–	–
Jamaica	91	96	85	87	86	90	–	–	–	83	94	69	83	94	69	83	94	69	–	–	–	–
Japan	99	–	–	100	–	–	–	–	–	–	–	–	–	–	–	–	–	–	–	–	–	–
Jordan	99	99	98	97	97	96	–	–	–	93	–	–	33	–	–	–	–	–	–	–	–	–
Kazakhstan	96	98	92	98	97	99	99	99	99	–	–	–	–	–	–	–	–	–	–	–	–	–
Kenya	59	85	50	29	35	27	25	32	22	–	–	–	–	–	–	–	–	–	66	–	–	33
Kiribati	72	–	–	48	–	–	–	–	–	–	–	–	–	–	–	–	–	–	–	–	–	–
Kuwait	100	–	–	100	–	–	–	–	–	100	100	100	100	100	100	100	100	100	100	100	100	100
Kyrgyzstan	87	97	82	97	92	99	89	93	87	–	–	–	–	–	–	–	–	100	–	–	–	–
Lao People's Democratic Republic	82	94	76	74	95	64	50	67	41	–	–	–	–	–	–	–	–	–	–	–	–	33
Latvia	99	99	98	92	96	83	–	–	–	100	100	100	100	100	100	100	100	100	–	–	–	–
Lebanon	93	–	–	98	–	–	–	–	–	59	60	61	93	92	95	36	34	46	61	16	–	64
Lesotho	69	93	59	43	43	43	2	6	1	–	–	–	43	–	–	50	–	–	–	–	–	–
Liberia	73	84	62	17	28	6	1	2	1	42	–	–	43	–	–	50	–	–	–	3	36	67
Libya	99	–	–	100	–	–	–	–	–	–	–	–	95	–	–	13	–	–	–	–	–	43
Liechtenstein	100	–	–	100	–	–	–	–	–	–	–	–	–	–	–	–	–	–	–	–	–	–
Lithuania	98	100	93	93	97	85	–	–	–	–	–	–	–	–	–	–	–	–	100	–	–	–
Luxembourg	100	100	99	98	97	99	–	–	–	–	–	–	–	–	–	–	–	–	–	–	–	–
Madagascar	54	86	36	11	18	6	–	–	–	–	–	–	–	–	52	–	–	–	–	–	–	–
Malawi	69	86	65	26	34	25	9	15	7	–	–	–	70	72	61	–	–	–	–	–	–	43
Malaysia	97	99	89	100	100	99	–	–	–	100	99	100	100	99	100	100	99	100	–	–	–	–
Maldives	99	98	100	99	99	99	96	97	95	–	–	–	–	–	–	–	–	–	55	15	80	30
Mali	78	92	68	39	53	29	52	70	39	–	–	–	20	17	20	–	–	–	–	–	–	–
Malta	100	100	100	100	100	100	–	–	–	–	–	–	–	–	–	–	–	–	–	–	–	–
Marshall Islands	88	87	94	83	91	59	83	84	77	3	3	–	27	27	–	36	36	–	–	–	–	–
Mauritania	71	89	50	48	75	19	43	55	29	–	–	–	27	27	26	–	–	–	81	–	–	25
Mauritius	100	100	100	96	96	95	–	–	–	100	100	100	100	100	100	100	100	100	–	–	–	–
Mexico	99	100	97	91	93	82	88	90	80	–	–	–	75	75	–	–	–	–	–	–	–	–
Micronesia (Federated States of)	79	–	–	88	–	–	–	–	–	–	–	–	–	–	–	–	–	–	–	–	–	–
Monaco	100	100	–	100	100	–	–	–	–	100	100	100	100	100	100	100	100	100	–	–	–	–
Mongolia	83	96	56	58	66	42	71	81	49	74	73	73	63	70	63	41	44	66	–	–	–	–
Montenegro	97	96	99	98	100	94	–	–	–	–	–	–	–	–	–	–	–	–	100	85	100	100

TABLE 13. WASH

Countries and areas	At least basic drinking water services (%) 2017 total	urban	rural	At least basic sanitation services (%) 2017 total	urban	rural	Basic hygiene facilities (%) 2017 total	urban	rural	Basic water services (%) 2016 total	primary	secondary	Basic sanitation services (%) 2016 total	primary	secondary	Basic hygiene services (%) 2016 total	primary	secondary	Basic water services (%) 2016 total	Basic sanitation services (%) 2016 total	Basic hygiene services (%) 2016 total	Basic waste management services (%) 2016 total
										Schools										**Health care facilities**			
Montserrat	–	–	–	–	–	–	–	–	–	–	–	–	–	–	–	–	–	–	–	–	–	–
Morocco	87	97	71	89	94	79	–	–	–	82	73	91	70	70	–	–	–	–	–	–	–	–
Mozambique	56	84	40	29	52	17	–	–	–	–	–	–	48	48	–	15	15	–	–	–	–	–
Myanmar	82	93	77	64	76	59	79	92	74	71	71	–	–	–	–	–	–	–	–	–	–	3
Namibia	83	96	69	35	51	18	45	62	27	76	–	–	46	–	–	20	–	–	–	–	–	–
Nauru	99	99	–	66	66	–	–	–	–	–	–	–	–	–	–	86	100	66	–	–	–	–
Nepal	89	89	89	62	67	61	48	67	43	47	39	76	–	–	–	–	–	–	–	–	–	1
Netherlands	100	100	100	98	98	100	–	–	–	100	100	100	100	100	100	100	100	100	–	–	–	–
New Zealand	100	100	100	100	100	100	–	–	–	–	–	–	–	–	–	–	–	–	–	–	–	–
Nicaragua	82	98	59	74	84	62	–	–	–	–	–	–	43	43	–	–	–	–	–	–	–	–
Niger	50	84	44	14	44	8	–	–	–	–	–	–	21	18	–	14	14	–	–	–	–	60
Nigeria	71	87	56	39	48	31	42	53	31	–	–	–	–	–	–	–	–	–	50	12	43	43
Niue	98	–	–	97	–	–	–	–	–	100	100	100	100	100	100	100	100	100	–	–	–	–
North Macedonia	93	91	97	99	100	98	–	–	–	–	–	–	–	–	–	–	–	–	–	–	–	–
Norway	100	100	100	98	98	98	–	–	–	100	100	100	100	100	100	100	100	100	–	–	–	–
Oman	92	95	78	100	100	100	97	–	–	92	–	–	–	–	–	–	–	–	–	–	–	–
Pakistan	91	94	90	60	77	50	60	83	46	57	52	81	–	–	–	–	–	–	–	–	–	–
Palau	100	100	100	100	100	100	–	–	–	–	–	–	–	–	–	–	–	–	–	–	–	–
Panama	96	98	93	83	92	65	–	–	–	–	–	–	82	82	–	–	–	–	–	–	–	–
Papua New Guinea	41	86	35	13	48	8	–	–	–	47	46	80	45	44	69	10	10	14	70	–	–	10
Paraguay	100	100	99	90	94	83	80	84	72	–	–	–	77	77	–	–	–	–	85	26	–	6
Peru	91	96	76	74	80	56	–	–	56	73	71	73	68	70	72	–	–	–	46	7	–	28
Philippines	94	98	90	77	78	75	78	85	73	50	49	58	39	33	68	46	49	30	–	–	–	–
Poland	100	100	100	99	99	99	–	–	–	–	–	–	–	–	–	–	–	–	–	–	–	–
Portugal	100	100	100	100	100	100	–	–	–	100	100	100	100	100	100	100	100	100	–	–	–	–
Qatar	100	–	–	100	–	–	–	–	–	100	100	100	100	100	100	100	100	100	–	–	–	–
Republic of Korea	100	–	–	100	–	–	–	–	–	100	100	100	100	100	100	100	100	100	–	–	–	–
Republic of Moldova	89	97	83	76	86	69	–	–	–	100	100	100	94	100	100	100	100	100	–	–	–	–
Romania	100	100	100	84	95	71	–	–	–	–	–	–	–	–	–	–	–	–	–	–	–	–
Russian Federation	97	99	93	90	95	78	–	–	–	–	–	–	–	–	–	–	–	–	–	–	–	–
Rwanda	58	82	53	67	52	70	5	13	3	44	39	51	88	91	84	48	45	51	–	–	–	–
Saint Kitts and Nevis	–	–	–	–	–	–	–	–	–	84	79	100	–	–	–	84	79	100	–	–	–	–
Saint Lucia	98	98	98	88	78	91	–	–	–	99	99	100	99	99	100	99	99	100	–	–	–	–
Saint Vincent and the Grenadines	95	–	–	87	–	–	–	–	–	100	100	100	100	100	100	100	100	100	–	–	–	–
Samoa	97	100	97	98	98	98	–	–	–	–	–	100	–	–	–	–	–	–	–	–	–	–
San Marino	100	–	–	100	–	–	–	–	–	–	–	–	–	–	–	–	–	–	100	–	100	100
Sao Tome and Principe	84	87	77	43	48	31	41	39	47	–	–	–	76	73	100	–	–	–	–	–	–	–
Saudi Arabia	100	–	–	100	–	–	–	–	–	–	–	–	–	–	–	–	–	–	–	–	–	–
Senegal	81	92	70	51	65	40	24	42	9	32	32	–	–	–	–	22	25	10	46	–	–	31
Serbia	86	83	88	98	100	95	–	–	–	72	63	91	74	66	92	73	66	91	96	73	100	100
Seychelles	96	–	–	100	–	–	–	–	–	100	100	100	100	100	100	100	100	100	–	–	–	80
Sierra Leone	61	76	50	16	26	9	19	27	14	62	–	–	12	–	–	–	–	–	–	–	–	17
Singapore	100	100	–	100	100	–	–	–	–	100	100	100	100	100	100	100	100	100	–	–	–	–
Slovakia	100	100	100	98	99	97	–	–	–	100	100	100	100	100	100	100	100	100	–	–	–	–
Slovenia	100	100	99	99	99	99	–	–	–	100	100	100	100	100	100	100	100	100	–	–	–	–
Solomon Islands	68	91	61	34	78	20	36	59	29	17	20	19	27	22	34	17	–	–	–	–	–	–
Somalia	52	83	28	38	61	20	10	12	8	–	–	–	–	–	–	–	–	–	–	–	–	13
South Africa	93	99	81	76	76	75	44	53	27	78	–	–	–	–	–	–	–	–	–	–	–	–
South Sudan	41	65	35	11	37	5	–	–	–	–	–	–	–	–	–	–	–	–	–	–	–	–
Spain	100	100	100	100	100	100	–	–	–	100	100	100	100	100	100	100	100	100	–	–	–	–
Sri Lanka	89	97	88	96	95	96	–	–	–	–	–	–	100	100	100	–	–	–	99	–	–	27
State of Palestine	97	97	96	97	97	96	–	–	–	80	81	86	81	78	86	23	22	29	–	–	–	–
Sudan	60	74	53	37	60	24	23	32	19	–	–	–	–	–	–	–	–	–	–	–	–	–
Suriname	95	98	90	84	89	75	–	–	–	–	–	–	–	–	–	–	–	–	–	–	–	–
Sweden	100	100	100	99	99	100	–	–	–	–	–	–	–	–	–	–	–	–	–	–	–	–
Switzerland	100	100	100	100	100	100	–	–	–	100	100	100	100	100	100	100	100	100	–	–	–	–
Syrian Arab Republic	97	99	95	91	91	91	71	72	69	–	–	–	–	–	–	–	–	–	–	–	–	–
Tajikistan	81	96	76	97	95	98	73	87	67	79	–	–	44	–	–	26	–	–	–	–	–	–
Thailand	100	100	100	99	99	98	84	85	83	–	–	–	–	–	–	–	–	–	–	–	–	–
Timor-Leste	78	98	70	54	76	44	28	43	22	–	–	–	–	–	–	–	–	–	–	–	–	–

TABLE 13. WASH

Countries and areas	Households — At least basic drinking water services (%) 2017			At least basic sanitation services (%) 2017			Basic hygiene facilities (%) 2017			Schools — Basic water services (%) 2016			Basic sanitation services (%) 2016			Basic hygiene services (%) 2016			Health care facilities — Basic water services (%) 2016	Basic sanitation services (%) 2016	Basic hygiene services (%) 2016	Basic waste management services (%) 2016
	total	urban	rural	total	urban	rural	total	urban	rural	total	primary	secondary	total	primary	secondary	total	primary	secondary	total	total	total	total
Togo	65	89	48	16	29	7	10	20	4	–	–	–	23	–	–	–	–	–	58	–	–	30
Tokelau	100	–	100	97	–	97	–	–	–	–	–	–	–	–	–	–	–	–	–	–	–	–
Tonga	100	100	100	93	97	92	–	–	–	–	–	–	–	–	–	–	–	–	–	–	–	–
Trinidad and Tobago	98	–	–	93	–	–	–	–	–	–	–	–	–	–	–	–	–	–	–	–	–	–
Tunisia	96	100	89	91	95	81	79	90	54	70	70	–	99	99	–	–	–	–	–	–	–	–
Turkey	99	99	100	97	100	90	–	–	–	–	–	–	–	–	–	–	–	–	–	–	–	–
Turkmenistan	99	100	98	99	98	99	100	100	100	–	–	–	–	–	–	–	–	–	–	–	–	–
Turks and Caicos Islands	94	–	–	88	–	–	–	–	–	–	–	–	–	–	–	–	–	–	–	–	–	–
Tuvalu	99	100	99	84	83	86	–	–	–	–	–	–	–	–	–	–	–	–	–	–	–	–
Uganda	49	75	41	18	26	16	21	34	17	69	–	–	79	–	–	37	–	–	31	12	–	43
Ukraine	94	91	99	96	97	94	–	–	–	–	–	–	–	–	–	83	69	93	–	–	–	–
United Arab Emirates	98	–	–	99	–	–	–	–	–	–	–	–	–	–	–	–	–	–	–	–	–	–
United Kingdom	100	100	100	99	99	99	–	–	–	–	–	–	–	–	–	–	–	–	–	–	–	–
United Republic of Tanzania	57	86	43	30	43	24	48	63	40	–	–	–	47	47	–	23	23	–	65	5	35	27
United States	99	100	97	100	100	100	–	–	–	100	100	100	100	100	100	100	100	100	–	–	–	–
Uruguay	99	100	95	97	97	97	–	–	–	–	–	–	83	83	–	–	–	–	–	–	–	–
Uzbekistan	98	100	96	100	100	100	–	–	–	90	90	89	92	93	91	89	90	89	–	–	–	–
Vanuatu	91	100	88	34	48	29	25	48	17	–	–	–	–	–	–	–	–	–	–	–	–	–
Venezuela (Bolivarian Republic of)	96	–	–	94	–	–	–	–	–	97	97	–	90	90	–	–	–	–	–	–	–	–
Viet Nam	95	99	93	84	94	78	86	93	82	–	–	–	–	–	–	–	–	–	51	–	–	–
Yemen	63	79	55	59	88	43	50	71	38	36	–	46	25	–	–	8	–	–	–	–	–	13
Zambia	60	84	42	26	36	19	14	26	5	79	76	94	66	–	–	54	52	63	40	–	–	40
Zimbabwe	64	94	50	36	46	31	37	49	31	64	64	65	–	–	–	–	–	–	81	17	58	55
SUMMARY																						
East Asia and Pacific	93	98	86	84	91	75	–	–	–	–	66	–	–	43	–	–	53	–	87	–	36	–
Europe and Central Asia	98	99	97	97	98	93	–	–	–	97	99	98	95	99	99	93	97	98	–	–	–	–
Eastern Europe and Central Asia	96	97	94	94	97	88	–	–	–	–	–	–	–	–	–	–	–	–	98	58	96	–
Western Europe	100	100	100	99	99	99	–	–	–	100	100	100	100	100	100	100	100	100	–	–	–	–
Latin America and Caribbean	97	99	88	87	91	69	–	–	59	–	–	–	78	79	–	61	60	65	–	–	–	–
Middle East and North Africa	94	97	88	91	95	82	80	–	70	73	–	80	81	94	99	75	95	94	–	–	–	–
North America	99	100	97	100	100	100	–	–	–	100	100	100	100	100	100	100	100	100	–	–	–	–
South Asia	92	96	91	59	70	53	57	77	46	68	66	77	71	71	78	53	53	53	–	–	–	–
Sub-Saharan Africa	61	84	46	31	45	22	25	37	17	–	–	–	–	–	–	21	–	–	51	23	–	40
Eastern and Southern Africa	58	85	44	31	49	22	24	38	16	–	–	–	62	–	–	21	18	–	48	33	–	46
West and Central Africa	64	84	48	30	41	21	26	35	19	–	–	–	–	–	–	–	–	–	55	12	43	36
Least developed countries	65	84	55	34	47	28	28	39	22	57	–	–	53	51	62	26	24	38	55	–	–	27
World	**90**	**97**	**81**	**74**	**85**	**59**	**60**	**–**	**46**	**69**	**66**	**75**	**66**	**63**	**72**	**53**	**53**	**55**	**74**	**–**	**–**	**–**

For a complete list of countries and areas in the regions, subregions and country categories, see page 182 or visit <data.unicef.org/regionalclassifications>.
It is not advisable to compare data from consecutive editions of *The State of the World's Children.*

DEFINITIONS OF THE INDICATORS

Population using at least basic drinking water services – Percentage of the population using an improved drinking water source, where collection time is not more than 30 minutes for a round trip including queuing (improved sources include: piped water; boreholes or tubewells; protected dug wells; protected springs; rainwater; and packaged or delivered water).

Population using at least basic sanitation services – Percentage of the population using an improved sanitation facility that is not shared with other households (improved facilities include: flush/pour flush to piped sewerage systems, septic tanks or pit latrines; ventilated improved pit latrines; composting toilets or pit latrines with slabs).

Population with basic hygiene facilities – Percentage of the population with a handwashing facility with water and soap available on premises.

Proportion of schools with basic water services – Percentage of schools with drinking water from an improved source available at the time of the survey.

Proportion of schools with basic sanitation services – Percentage of schools with improved sanitation facilities which are single-sex and usable.

Proportion of schools with basic hygiene services – Percentage of schools with handwashing facilities with water and soap available.

Proportion of health care facilities with basic water services – Percentage of health care facilities with water available from an improved source located on premises.

Proportion of health care facilities with basic sanitation services – Percentage of health care facilities with improved sanitation facilities which are usable with at least one toilet dedicated for staff, at least one sex-separated toilet with menstrual hygiene facilities, and at least one toilet accessible for people with limited mobility.

Proportion of health care facilities with basic hygiene services – Percentage of health care facilities with functional hand hygiene facilities (with water and soap and/or alcohol-based hand rub) available at points of care, and within 5 metres of toilets.

Proportion of health care facilities with basic waste management services – Percentage of health care facilities where waste is safely segregated into at least three bins, and sharps and infectious waste are treated and disposed of safely.

MAIN DATA SOURCES

Basic water, sanitation and hygiene services in schools – WHO/UNICEF Joint Monitoring Programme for Water Supply, Sanitation and Hygiene (JMP). Last update: July 2018.

Basic drinking water, sanitation and hygiene services in households – WHO/UNICEF Joint Monitoring Programme for Water Supply, Sanitation and Hygiene (JMP). Last update: June 2019.

Basic water, sanitation, hygiene and waste management services in health care facilities – WHO/UNICEF Joint Monitoring Programme for Water Supply, Sanitation and Hygiene (JMP). Last update: April 2019.

NOTES

– Data not available.

TABLE 14. ADOLESCENTS

Countries and areas	Adolescent population 2018 Aged 10–19 (thousands) total	Proportion of total population (%) total	Health Alcohol use 2016 total	Health Tobacco use 2013–2017* total	Health Thinness 2016 total	Health Over-weight 2016 total	Protection Intimate partner violence 2010–2018* female	Protection Bullying 2010–2017* male	Protection Bullying 2010–2017* female	Education Proficiency in math male	Education Proficiency in math female	Education Proficiency in reading male	Education Proficiency in reading female	Transition Not in education, employment, or training male	Transition NEET female	Transition Unemployment male	Transition Unemployment female	Transition Engagement in household chores male	Transition Engagement in household chores female
Afghanistan	9,442	25	0	9	17	9	29	42	45	–	–	–	–	17	59	17	20	9	22
Albania	391	14	38	11	1	24	–	–	–	39	40	45	51	21	22	27	17	1	2
Algeria	6,242	15	2	9	6	29	–	48	55	18	21	15	28	–	–	32	38	1	1
Andorra	–	–	64	–	1	34	–	–	–	–	–	–	–	–	–	–	–	–	–
Angola	7,290	24	34	–	8	11	24	–	–	–	–	–	–	5	7	15	12	15	19
Anguilla	–	–	–	–	–	–	–	22	30	–	–	–	–	–	–	–	–	–	–
Antigua and Barbuda	14	15	35	12 x	3	25	–	24 x	27 x	–	–	–	–	–	–	–	–	–	–
Argentina	7,085	16	55	24 x	1	34	–	25	24	41	35	59	65	13	14	24	32	–	–
Armenia	356	12	16	7 x	2	18	–	–	–	74	79	–	–	34	20	–	–	0	1
Australia	3,029	12	69	–	1	33	–	–	–	78	78	77	87	–	–	19	15	–	–
Austria	876	10	68	–	2	26	–	–	–	81	75	79	88	10	5	11	12	–	–
Azerbaijan	1,311	13	13	7 x	3	18	12 x	–	–	58 x	51 x	22 x	32 x	–	–	13	15	–	–
Bahamas	65	17	30	13	3	34	–	25	22	–	–	–	–	–	–	38	46	–	–
Bahrain	172	11	4	19	6	34	–	36	23	70	80	–	–	–	–	10	21	–	–
Bangladesh	31,080	19	1	9	18	8	28 y	27	17	62	52	87	87	10	30	12	18	–	–
Barbados	37	13	38	15	4	26	–	15	11	–	–	–	–	–	–	44	45	0	0
Belarus	896	9	58	10	2	22	–	–	–	–	–	–	–	–	–	–	–	0	0
Belgium	1,285	11	66	–	1	23	–	–	–	81	79	78	83	4	4	19	20	–	–
Belize	78	20	27	12	4	27	–	30	31	–	–	–	–	17	33	13	33	1	3
Benin	2,638	23	15	5	7	11	–	47	52	–	–	–	–	10	20	3	5	18	33
Bhutan	140	19	17	24	15	9	–	31	29	–	–	–	–	–	–	5	7	2	5
Bolivia (Plurinational State of)	2,280	20	31	19 x	1	27	–	32	28	–	–	–	–	4	8	6	5	–	–
Bosnia and Herzegovina	360	11	34	16	2	21	–	–	–	76 x	77 x	–	–	16	15	43	51	–	–
Botswana	453	20	19	24 x	6	16	–	53 x	52 x	75	84	70	87	24 x	32 x	34	51	–	–
Brazil	32,143	15	27	8 y	3	26	–	–	–	33	26	44	53	16	22	34	44	–	–
British Virgin Islands	–	–	–	–	–	–	–	18 x	17 x	–	–	–	–	–	–	–	–	–	–
Brunei Darussalam	67	16	25	10	6	25	–	25	22	–	–	–	–	15	13	41	48	–	–
Bulgaria	654	9	54	29	2	27	–	–	–	57	59	50	68	12	15	–	–	–	–
Burkina Faso	4,730	24	24	–	8	8	5	–	–	–	–	–	–	–	–	5	12	9	29
Burundi	2,526	23	19	19 x	7	10	38	–	–	–	–	–	–	3	3	3	–	20	30
Cabo Verde	100	18	21	13 x	7	12	–	–	–	–	–	–	–	–	–	27	47	–	–
Cambodia	3,041	19	19	2	11	10	7	23	22	14	18	31	44	9	11	1	1	1	5
Cameroon	5,833	23	26	10	6	12	27	–	–	–	–	–	–	9	18	3	5	8	22
Canada	3,974	11	52	–	1	31	–	–	–	86	85	86	92	13	11	17	14	–	–
Central African Republic	1,211	26	24	–	8	10	32 x	–	–	–	–	–	–	–	–	–	–	14	23
Chad	3,803	25	13	19 x	9	8	15	–	–	–	–	–	–	–	–	–	–	15	30
Chile	2,514	13	54	25	1	34	–	16	14	67	59	69	74	13	15	20	29	8	10
China	166,857	12	41	7	4	25	–	84	84	76	81	–	–	–	–	–	–	–	–
Colombia	8,314	17	25	–	2	24	23	–	–	80	77	88	90	13	24	16	27	1	3
Comoros	183	22	2	12	7	12	4	–	–	–	–	–	–	19 x	29 x	–	–	15	28
Congo	1,176	22	37	24 x	8	11	–	–	–	–	–	–	–	17 x	21 x	–	–	8	9
Cook Islands	–	–	36	22	<1	62	6 y	29	32	–	–	–	–	–	–	26	24	–	–
Costa Rica	731	15	24	10 x	2	30	–	18 x	20 x	43	32	56	63	13	15	35	51	0	3
Côte d'Ivoire	5,874	23	25	19 x	6	12	20 y	–	–	–	–	–	–	22	42	–	4	7	18
Croatia	416	10	47	29 x	2	26	–	–	–	70	66	75	85	16	12	–	–	–	–
Cuba	1,288	11	33	17 x	4	28	–	–	–	–	–	–	–	–	–	5 y	13 y	–	–
Cyprus	143	12	55	20 x	1	32	–	73 x	82 x	53	75	6	9	–	–	–	–	–	–
Czechia	1,002	9	65	21	2	26	–	–	–	78	79	73	83	2	3	19	–	–	–
Democratic People's Republic of Korea	3,678	14	27	–	5	22	–	–	–	–	–	–	–	–	–	–	–	–	–
Democratic Republic of the Congo	19,479	23	24	–	10	10	36	–	–	–	–	–	–	12	20	8	6	7	20
Denmark	682	12	64	–	1	24	–	–	–	87	86	82	88	3	2	14	10	–	–
Djibouti	180	19	11	15	6	16	–	44 x	36 x	–	–	–	–	–	–	–	–	–	–
Dominica	–	–	31	25 x	3	31	–	29 x	26 x	–	–	–	–	–	–	–	–	–	–
Dominican Republic	1,935	18	29	19 x	3	31	22	26	22	10	9	23	33	22	27	10	27	2	4
Ecuador	3,115	18	32	–	1	27	–	–	–	44	41	70	74	10	19	6	9	–	–
Egypt	17,670	18	1	14	3	35	17	70	70	45	49	–	–	8	18	16	25	1	5
El Salvador	1,210	19	19	13	2	29	7 y	21	24	24 x	17 x	–	–	14	33	8 y	14 y	7	20
Equatorial Guinea	251	19	59	22 x	8	10	56 p	–	–	–	–	–	–	–	–	–	–	–	–
Eritrea	796	23	12	7 x	8	10	–	–	–	–	–	–	–	–	–	–	–	–	–
Estonia	130	10	62	31 x	2	19	–	–	–	88	90	86	93	3	5	–	–	–	–
Eswatini	270	24	18	12 x	4	16	–	33	31	–	–	–	–	17	24	37	43	2	3
Ethiopia	26,128	24	13	–	10	8	24	–	–	–	–	–	–	5	11	2	3	49	58

TABLE 14. ADOLESCENTS

Countries and areas	Adolescent population 2018 Aged 10–19 (thousands) total	Proportion of total population (%) total	Health Alcohol use 2016 total	Tobacco use 2013–2017* total	Thinness 2016 total	Over-weight 2016 total	Protection Intimate partner violence 2010–2018* female	Bullying 2010–2017* male	female	Education and learning 2010–2017* Proficiency in math male	female	Proficiency in reading male	female	Transition to work 2010–2018* Not in education, employment, or training male	female	Unemployment male	female	Engagement in household chores male	female
Fiji	154	17	10	12	4	33	–	33	26	–	–	–	–	8	13	16	32	–	–
Finland	599	11	62	21 x	1	25	–	–	–	84	89	84	94	5	6	26	25	–	–
France	7,832	12	65	–	1	29	–	–	–	76	77	74	83	8	6	24	29	–	–
Gabon	399	19	52	9	6	15	40	–	–	–	–	–	–	–	–	27	38	6	7
Gambia	526	23	16	–	7	11	5	–	–	–	–	–	–	20	36	6	14	–	–
Georgia	457	11	24	12	3	19	–	–	–	40	46	37	61	–	–	25	31	0	0
Germany	7,973	10	70	–	1	25	–	–	–	85	81	81	86	–	–	8	7	–	–
Ghana	6,384	21	15	13 x	6	10	23 x	–	–	25	17	–	–	9	18	5	7	3	11
Greece	1,072	10	53	16 x	1	35	–	–	–	63	65	66	80	10	10	44	59	–	–
Grenada	16	14	35	10	4	25	–	29 x	26 x	–	–	–	–	–	–	–	–	–	–
Guatemala	3,855	22	17	17	1	27	9	26	20	–	–	–	–	7	40	4	7	–	–
Guinea	3,062	25	13	26 x	7	9	–	–	–	–	–	–	–	4 x	5 x	–	–	11	18
Guinea-Bissau	426	23	17	–	7	10	–	–	–	–	–	–	–	–	–	–	–	5	13
Guyana	151	19	26	15	6	24	–	40	37	–	–	–	–	30	40	26	35	2	3
Haiti	2,322	21	22	–	4	26	28	–	–	–	–	–	–	–	–	7	10	19	13
Holy See	–	–	–	–	–	–	–	–	–	–	–	–	–	–	–	–	–	–	–
Honduras	2,081	22	18	8	2	26	16	13 y	12 y	26	17	–	–	13	38	6	10	–	–
Hungary	974	10	55	25	2	27	–	–	–	90	87	68	77	5	6	23	–	–	–
Iceland	44	13	59	–	1	27	–	–	–	76	77	71	84	4	–	11	–	–	–
India	252,611	19	25	15 x	27	6	18	–	–	14 x	16 x	11 x	21 x	7	32	12	9	–	–
Indonesia	46,369	17	13	13	10	14	–	24	19	30	32	38	51	12	17	20	21	–	–
Iran (Islamic Republic of)	11,349	14	2	27 x	9	25	–	–	–	62	65	–	–	–	–	–	–	–	–
Iraq	8,411	22	2	14	5	30	–	32	22	–	–	–	–	17	56	19	7	1	6
Ireland	636	13	71	–	<1	29	–	–	–	94	94	88	92	10	9	21	22	–	–
Israel	1,352	16	41	–	1	34	–	–	–	68	68	68	78	–	–	9	9	–	–
Italy	5,733	9	51	–	1	34	–	–	–	90	89	76	82	14	14	46	56	–	–
Jamaica	484	16	23	29 x	2	28	11 y	26	25	–	–	–	–	–	–	41	58	0	0
Japan	11,416	9	46	–	2	13	–	–	–	–	–	–	–	–	–	4	3	–	–
Jordan	2,129	21	2	24	4	30	18	46 x	37 x	41	48	37	70	–	–	36	39	0	2
Kazakhstan	2,445	13	26	3	2	19	–	–	–	90	92	55	63	–	–	2	3	–	–
Kenya	12,220	24	14	10	8	11	23	57 x	57 x	–	–	–	–	–	–	5	5	–	–
Kiribati	23	20	7	29 x	<1	54	–	42	32	–	–	–	–	–	–	27	8	–	–
Kuwait	489	12	0	22	4	43	–	36	28	43	46	–	–	–	–	15	27	2	3
Kyrgyzstan	1,044	17	15	8	3	15	3	–	–	14	13 x	12 x	22 x	–	–	15	27	2	3
Lao People's Democratic Republic	1,447	20	26	11	9	13	14 y	15	11	–	–	–	–	31	34	18	16	2	2
Latvia	180	9	65	25	2	20	–	–	–	77	80	76	89	3	2	–	–	–	–
Lebanon	1,182	17	3	60 x	5	31	–	24	12	72	70	28	31	–	–	24 x	37 x	–	–
Lesotho	433	21	10	25 x	6	15	–	–	–	–	–	–	–	–	–	–	–	–	–
Liberia	1,120	23	19	–	7	10	37 x	43	51	–	–	–	–	7	11	–	19	1	5
Libya	1,146	17	0	8 x	6	31	–	40 x	31 x	–	–	–	–	–	–	–	–	–	–
Liechtenstein	–	–	–	–	–	–	–	–	–	89	83	85	90	–	–	–	–	–	–
Lithuania	257	9	71	28	3	19	–	–	–	73	76	68	82	3	2	–	–	–	–
Luxembourg	66	11	86	–	1	25	–	–	–	75	73	71	78	3	–	–	–	–	–
Madagascar	6,110	23	12	23 x	7	10	–	–	–	–	–	–	–	3	3	3	2	–	–
Malawi	4,467	25	14	14 x	6	10	28	43 x	47 x	–	–	–	–	17	28	40	50	5	11
Malaysia	5,262	17	18	17	8	25	–	24	18	73	78	54	70	–	–	–	–	–	–
Maldives	60	12	4	11	14	16	–	30	30	–	–	–	–	20	17	29	16	–	–
Mali	4,642	24	13	17 x	8	10	23 x	–	–	–	–	–	–	24	42	–	–	13	24
Malta	42	10	49	–	1	35	–	–	–	83	86	57	72	8	11	–	–	–	–
Marshall Islands	–	–	–	28	<1	58	27 y	–	–	–	–	–	–	–	–	–	–	–	–
Mauritania	956	22	1	22 x	8	13	–	48	46	–	–	–	–	19	42	10	11	10	20
Mauritius	182	14	20	19	7	14	–	29	22	50 x	49 x	45 x	61 x	14	19	29 y	42 y	–	–
Mexico	22,353	18	29	20 x	2	34	–	46	41	54	63	–	–	8	21	7	8	2	2
Micronesia (Federated States of)	24	21	9	43	<1	50	35 y	–	–	–	–	–	–	14	19	–	29 y	–	–
Monaco	–	–	–	–	<1	<1	–	–	–	–	–	–	–	–	–	56 y	42 y	–	–
Mongolia	466	15	20	14	2	17	8 y	36	25	67 x	64 x	–	–	9	7	14	30	15	19
Montenegro	79	13	41	10	2	24	–	–	–	48	48	51	66	–	–	–	–	0	1
Montserrat	–	–	–	–	–	–	–	32 x	25 x	–	–	–	–	–	–	–	–	–	–
Morocco	5,995	17	1	6	6	26	–	44	32	41	41	–	–	–	–	17	11	–	–
Mozambique	7,169	24	13	5	4	12	10 y	45	46	–	–	–	–	–	–	7	5	–	–
Myanmar	10,059	19	16	14	13	11	22	51	49	–	–	–	–	11	17	5	5	–	–
Namibia	509	21	19	11	8	14	52 p	48	45	–	–	–	–	17	22	37	39	–	–
Nauru	–	–	13	26 x	<1	64	–	40	38	–	–	–	–	21	39	–	–	–	–

TABLE 14. ADOLESCENTS

Countries and areas	Adolescent population 2018 Aged 10–19 (thousands) total	Proportion of total population (%) total	Health Alcohol use 2016 total	Tobacco use 2013–2017* total	Thinness 2016 total	Over-weight 2016 total	Protection Intimate partner violence 2010–2018* female	Bullying 2010–2017* male	female	Education and learning 2010–2017* Proficiency in math male	female	Proficiency in reading male	female	Transition to work 2010–2018* Not in education, employment, or training male	female	Unemployment male	female	Engagement in household chores male	female
Nepal	6,305	22	17	7	16	7	17	56	45	–	–	–	–	28 x	26 x	23	26	7	17
Netherlands	1,990	12	61	–	1	24	–	–	–	83	84	78	86	2	2	9	9	–	–
New Zealand	617	13	64	20 x	<1	38	–	–	–	78	78	78	88	–	–	21	17	–	–
Nicaragua	1,231	19	21	18	2	28	12 y	–	–	–	–	–	–	2	3	6	11	–	–
Niger	5,425	24	12	9 x	10	8	–	–	–	–	–	–	–	6	29	–	–	17	25
Nigeria	44,938	23	37	–	10	8	9	–	–	–	–	–	–	21	24	–	11	7	9
Niue	–	–	21	18 x	<1	58	–	–	–	–	–	–	–	–	–	–	–	–	–
North Macedonia	239	11	39	15	2	25	–	–	–	29	31	22	38	–	–	61	63	1	1
Norway	642	12	69	–	1	27	–	–	–	81	85	79	91	3	2	17	13	–	–
Oman	502	10	3	7	7	30	–	45	39	46	59	–	–	–	–	39	51	–	–
Pakistan	44,454	21	1	11	19	9	–	45 x	35 x	–	–	–	–	7	43	10	6	–	–
Palau	–	–	–	45	<1	62	8 y	–	–	–	–	–	–	21 x	18 x	–	–	–	–
Panama	715	17	33	13 x	2	28	–	–	–	21 x	22 x	28 x	41 x	10	15	10	18	–	–
Papua New Guinea	1,866	22	7	33	1	31	–	–	–	–	–	–	–	21	21	3	2	–	–
Paraguay	1,341	19	23	7	2	27	–	19	15	–	–	–	–	10	23	15	22	4	8
Peru	5,303	17	39	10	1	26	18	47	48	30	26	40	44	17	19	11	9	3	5
Philippines	21,091	20	21	15	10	12	11	53	49	35 x	42 x	–	–	12	15	5	8	–	–
Poland	3,664	10	56	20 x	2	24	–	–	–	84	82	81	91	3	2	–	–	–	–
Portugal	1,042	10	58	17	1	30	–	–	–	77	76	80	86	5	4	31	36	–	–
Qatar	229	8	26	16	5	37	–	49	35	62	66	39	58	–	–	0	1	–	–
Republic of Korea	5,056	10	51	6	2	25	–	–	–	82	87	81	92	–	–	11	7	–	–
Republic of Moldova	420	10	53	10	3	17	15 x	–	–	49	50	43	65	–	–	–	–	–	–
Romania	2,064	11	55	11	3	23	–	–	–	60	60	58	64	11	12	27	–	–	–
Russian Federation	14,358	10	40	15	2	19	–	–	–	82	81	79	88	–	–	28	31	–	–
Rwanda	2,769	23	23	12 x	6	11	–	–	–	–	–	–	–	21	27	18	19	22	31
Saint Kitts and Nevis	–	–	40	9 x	4	27	–	25	20	–	–	–	–	–	–	–	–	–	–
Saint Lucia	26	14	35	21 x	4	22	–	25 x	25 x	–	–	–	–	–	–	–	–	3	1
Saint Vincent and the Grenadines	18	16	32	19 x	4	28	–	31 x	29 x	–	–	–	–	–	–	–	–	–	–
Samoa	41	21	9	41 x	<1	51	–	79	69	–	–	–	–	27	21	34	64	–	–
San Marino	–	–	–	15	<1	<1	–	–	–	–	–	–	–	–	–	34	45	–	–
Sao Tome and Principe	51	24	21	26 x	6	13	28 x	–	–	–	–	–	–	–	–	–	–	12	15
Saudi Arabia	4,792	14	3	15 x	8	35	–	–	–	31	37	–	–	–	–	37	65	–	–
Senegal	3,629	23	12	11	10	9	19	–	–	–	–	–	–	27	36	6	6	6	23
Serbia	1,019	12	47	10 x	2	26	–	–	–	63	60	57	77	12	11	43	48	0	0
Seychelles	13	14	39	21	6	21	–	45	50	–	–	–	–	–	–	20	22	–	–
Sierra Leone	1,788	23	19	–	7	10	31	60	57	–	–	–	–	7	9	13	7	4	5
Singapore	548	10	57	9 x	2	21	–	–	–	99	99	86	92	–	–	4	15	–	–
Slovakia	541	10	57	29 x	1	22	–	–	–	72	72	61	75	7	6	37	36	–	–
Slovenia	190	9	60	21 x	1	25	–	–	–	84	84	79	91	4	3	–	–	–	–
Solomon Islands	142	22	7	40 x	1	24	–	64	68	–	–	–	–	2	2	–	–	6	9
Somalia	3,739	25	0	–	7	12	–	–	–	–	–	–	–	–	–	–	–	–	–
South Africa	10,080	17	20	22 x	4	26	–	–	–	33	36	–	–	13	15	61	69	1	2
South Sudan	2,536	23	–	–	<1	<1	–	–	–	–	–	–	–	–	–	–	–	–	–
Spain	4,614	10	57	–	1	32	–	–	–	80	76	80	87	11	10	50	50	–	–
Sri Lanka	3,347	16	18	8	15	12	–	50	29	63	71	–	–	15	17	23	34	–	–
State of Palestine	1,072	22	–	–	–	–	–	–	–	47	57	–	–	20	18	42	61	1	6
Sudan	9,724	23	1	12	<1	<1	–	–	–	–	–	–	–	–	–	29	33	4	7
Suriname	102	18	28	12	4	30	–	25	25	–	–	–	–	–	–	–	–	2	2
Sweden	1,080	11	62	–	2	23	–	–	–	82	82	76	88	3	3	30	25	–	–
Switzerland	836	10	72	–	<1	21	–	–	–	84	84	76	85	5	5	9	9	–	–
Syrian Arab Republic	3,320	20	1	21 x	6	27	–	–	–	45	41	–	–	–	–	14 x	48 x	–	–
Tajikistan	1,708	19	12	4	4	14	6	7 x	7 x	–	–	–	–	20 x	38 x	15 x	4 x	–	–
Thailand	8,775	13	27	14	8	20	–	38	28	45	47	41	57	9	11	4	5	–	–
Timor-Leste	304	24	13	23	11	11	38	39	25	–	–	–	–	14	13	–	14	–	–
Togo	1,815	23	15	8	7	10	13	–	–	–	–	–	–	5	10	–	–	9	16
Tokelau	–	–	–	–	–	–	–	39	39	–	–	–	–	–	–	–	–	–	–
Tonga	23	22	8	19	<1	57	41 x,y	46	31	–	–	–	–	–	–	–	–	–	–
Trinidad and Tobago	181	13	44	12 x	6	23	–	13	18	43	52	48	67	–	–	7	–	0	0
Tunisia	1,604	14	3	11 x	7	24	–	37 x	24 x	27	24	23	33	15	20	32	28	1	1
Turkey	13,559	16	4	17 x	5	28	18 y	–	–	69	71	54	66	14	25	16	20	–	–
Turkmenistan	969	17	18	0	3	17	–	–	–	–	–	–	–	–	–	–	–	0	0
Turks and Caicos Islands	–	–	–	–	–	–	–	–	–	–	–	–	–	–	–	–	–	–	–
Tuvalu	–	–	8	21	<1	57	–	40	15	–	–	–	–	15	23	–	–	–	–

TABLE 14. ADOLESCENTS

Countries and areas	Adolescent population 2018 Aged 10–19 (thousands) total	Proportion of total population (%) total	Health Alcohol use 2016 total	Tobacco use 2013–2017* total	Thinness 2016 total	Over-weight 2016 total	Protection Intimate partner violence 2010–2018* female	Bullying 2010–2017* male	Bullying female	Education and learning 2010–2017* Proficiency in math male	Proficiency in math female	Proficiency in reading male	Proficiency in reading female	Transition to work 2010–2018* Not in education, employment, or training male	NEET female	Unemployment male	Unemployment female	Engagement in household chores male	Engagement in household chores female
Uganda	10,668	25	24	17 x	6	10	31	50 x	41 x	–	–	–	–	8	13	4	3	7	18
Ukraine	4,188	9	45	19 x	2	20	2 x	–	–	80	82	–	–	–	–	–	–	2	2
United Arab Emirates	816	8	8	12	5	34	–	33	22	70	78	48	70	8	9	27	23	–	–
United Kingdom	7,500	11	62	–	1	30	–	–	–	79	77	79	85	8	8	19	17	–	–
United Republic of Tanzania	13,169	23	24	6	7	11	30	25 y	28 y	–	–	–	–	10	16	3	4	4	7
United States	42,365	13	60	13	1	41	–	26 y	25 y	71	70	77	85	12	11	15 y	11 y	–	–
Uruguay	488	14	57	13	2	32	–	18	20	50	45	55	66	14	16	33	44	1	2
Uzbekistan	5,309	16	12	14	3	16	–	–	–	–	–	–	–	–	–	–	–	–	–
Vanuatu	62	21	7	26 x	2	29	–	60	46	–	–	–	–	–	–	10 x	11 x	1	0
Venezuela (Bolivarian Republic of)	5,171	18	25	9 x	2	33	–	–	–	46 x	36 x	55 x	61 x	12	21	13	18	–	–
Viet Nam	13,324	14	23	4	14	9	16 y	26	26	79	83	81	91	8	9	8	7	2	4
Yemen	6,511	23	0	16	14	18	–	47	33	–	–	–	–	18	58	–	–	–	–
Zambia	4,298	25	17	26 x	6	12	30	63 x	67 x	–	–	–	–	26	34	28	21	8	9
Zimbabwe	3,366	23	10	20	6	14	32	–	–	–	–	–	–	8	17	9	18	–	–
SUMMARY																			
East Asia and Pacific	303,742	13	35	9	6	21	–	–	–	72	71	67	73	–	–	–	–	–	–
Europe and Central Asia	103,867	11	47	–	2	25	–	–	–	78	78	72	81	10	12	19	19	–	–
Eastern Europe and Central Asia	52,241	12	30	12	3	21	–	–	–	72	75	64	75	–	–	19	23	–	–
Western Europe	51,625	10	62	–	1	28	–	–	–	82	80	78	85	8	7	19	18	–	–
Latin America and Caribbean	106,649	17	30	–	2	29	–	–	–	42	37	54	61	13	22	18	27	–	–
Middle East and North Africa	74,983	17	3	13	6	29	–	52	46	45	48	–	–	–	–	21	21	1	4
North America	46,339	13	59	13	1	40	–	26	25	86	71	86	85	12	11	15	12	–	–
South Asia	347,439	19	19	–	24	7	19	–	–	–	–	–	–	8	33	12	13	–	–
Sub-Saharan Africa	249,533	23	21	–	8	10	22	–	–	–	–	–	–	13	20	8	9	13	20
Eastern and Southern Africa	129,278	23	16	–	7	11	26	–	–	–	–	–	–	9	14	8	9	19	25
West and Central Africa	120,255	23	26	–	9	9	18	–	–	–	–	–	–	17	25	–	8	8	16
Least developed countries	228,364	23	13	–	10	9	26	–	–	–	–	–	–	11	23	9	10	15	24
World	**1,232,553**	**16**	**30**	**–**	**11**	**17**	**–**	**–**	**–**	**–**	**–**	**–**	**–**	**10**	**24**	**13**	**14**	**–**	**–**

For a complete list of countries and areas in the regions, subregions and country categories, see page 182 or visit <data.unicef.org/regionalclassifications>.
It is not advisable to compare data from consecutive editions of *The State of the World's Children*.

DEFINITIONS OF THE INDICATORS

Alcohol use – Percentage of adolescents ages 15–19 who had at least one alcoholic drink at any time during the last twelve months.

Tobacco use – Percentage of adolescents ages 13–15 who smoked cigarettes or used smoked or smokeless tobacco products at any time during the last one month.

Thinness – Percentage of adolescents aged 10–19 years with BMI < –2 SD of the median according to the WHO growth reference for school-age children and adolescents.

Overweight – Percentage of adolescents aged 10–19 years with BMI > 1 SD of the median according to the WHO growth reference for school-age children and adolescents.

Intimate partner violence – Percentage of ever-partnered girls aged 15–19 years who have experienced physical and/or sexual violence by a current or former intimate partner during the last twelve months.

Bullying – Percentage of students aged 13–15 years who reported being bullied on one or more days in the past 30 days.

Proficiency in math – Percentage of children and young people at the end of lower secondary achieving at least a minimum proficiency level in math.

Proficiency in reading – Percentage of children and young people at the end of lower secondary achieving at least a minimum proficiency level in reading.

Not in education, employment or training (NEET) – Percentage of adolescents aged 15–19 years not in education, employment or training.

Unemployment – Percentage of adolescents aged 15–19 years in the labour force who are unemployed.

Engagement in household chores – Percentage of adolescents aged 10–14 years who, during the reference week, spent at least 21 hours on unpaid household services.

MAIN DATA SOURCES

Alcohol use – WHO estimates based on international surveys (WHS, STEPS, GENACIS, and ECAS) as well as national surveys. Last update: August 2019.

Tobacco use – School-based surveys, other national surveys, and censuses. Last update: August 2019.

Intimate partner violence – DHS, MICS and other national surveys. Last update: March 2019.

Thinness and overweight – NCD Risk Factor Collaboration (NCD–RisC), based on Worldwide trends in body mass index, underweight, overweight and obesity from 1975 to 2016: a pooled analysis of 2416 population-based measurement studies in 128.9million children, adolescents, and adults. The Lancet 2017, 390 (10113): 2627–2642. Last update: August 2019.

Intimate partner violence – DHS, MICS and other national surveys. Last update: March 2019.

Bullying – Health Behaviour in School-aged Children Study (HBSC) and Global School-based Student Health Surveys (GSHS). Last update: August 2019.

Proficiency in math and reading – United Nations Statistics Division. Last update: April 2019.

NEET – International Labour Organization. Last update: February 2019.

Unemployment – International Labour Organization. Last update: August 2019.

Engagement in household chores – DHS, MICS and other national surveys. Last update: March 2019.

NOTES

– Data not available.

p Based on small denominators (typically 25-49 unweighted cases). No data based on fewer than 25 unweighted cases are displayed.

x Data refer to years or periods other than those specified in the column heading. Such data are not included in the claculation of regional and global averages. Data from years prior to 2000 are not displayed.

y Data differ from the standard definition or refer to only part of a country. If they fall within the noted reference period, such data are included in the calculation of regional and global averages.

* Data refer to the most recent year available during the period specified in the column heading.

TABLE 15. ECONOMIC INDICATORS

Countries and areas	Government revenue as % of GDP 2010–2018*	Government Expenditure 2010–2018*							Official Development Assistance 2010–2018*			
		As % of GDP				As % of government budget						
		Total	On health	On education	On social protection	On health	On education	On social protection	Inflow in millions US$	Inflow as a % of recipient GNI	Outflow in millions US$	Ouflow as a % of donor GNI
Afghanistan	12.2	36.7	0.5	3.2	–	2.0	12.5	–	3804.0	18.1	–	–
Albania	25.7	23.9	2.9	3.4	1.6	9.5	11.3	0.1	157.0	1.2	–	–
Algeria	40.4	29.5	4.9	–	–	10.7	–	–	189.0	0.1	–	–
Andorra	–	–	5.0	3.3	–	15.2	–	–	–	–	–	–
Angola	16.4	16.7	1.4	3.5	2.3	4.6	8.7	0.1	223.0	0.2	–	–
Anguilla	–	–	–	–	–	–	–	–	–	–	–	–
Antigua and Barbuda	19.3	–	3.2	–	–	12.3	–	–	10.0	0.7	–	–
Argentina	19.5	24.3	6.8	5.8	2.1	16.6	14.0	0.1	–5.0	0.0	–	–
Armenia	22.5	22.6	1.6	2.8	1.4	6.1	10.7	0.1	255.0	2.1	–	–
Australia	24.8	26.6	6.4	5.3	–	17.2	14.1	–	–	–	3036.0	0.2
Austria	43.5	44.2	7.5	5.5	–	14.8	10.7	–	–	–	1251.0	0.3
Azerbaijan	35.2	28.0	1.4	3.0	0.8	3.7	7.6	0.0	116.0	0.3	–	–
Bahamas	16.9	19.1	3.0	–	–	15.9	–	–	–	–	–	–
Bahrain	24.0	23.4	3.2	2.7	–	8.8	7.3	–	–	–	–	–
Bangladesh	10.2	9.4	0.4	1.5	0.7	3.4	11.4	0.1	3740.0	1.4	–	–
Barbados	27.5	36.3	3.2	4.7	–	9.1	12.9	–	–	–	–	–
Belarus	29.6	29.3	3.7	4.8	3.1	8.5	11.5	0.1	–253.0	–0.5	–	–
Belgium	39.0	40.2	8.4	6.6	–	15.7	12.2	–	–	–	2196.0	0.5
Belize	29.0	27.2	4.1	6.7	–	11.4	21.2	–	34.0	2.0	–	–
Benin	16.7	–	0.8	4.4	3.0	3.2	17.5	–	676.0	7.3	–	–
Bhutan	–	17.9	2.7	7.4	0.3	10.0	26.4	0.0	119.0	5.1	–	–
Bolivia (Plurinational State of)	–	–	4.4	7.3	2.2	9.8	16.8	–	947.0	2.6	–	–
Bosnia and Herzegovina	38.8	34.4	6.6	–	3.9	15.2	–	0.1	441.0	2.4	–	–
Botswana	31.1	26.1	3.3	–	1.7	8.8	–	0.1	102.0	0.6	–	–
Brazil	27.2	34.9	3.8	6.2	1.4	9.9	16.2	0.0	265.0	0.0	–	–
British Virgin Islands	–	–	–	6.3	–	–	–	–	–	–	–	–
Brunei Darussalam	–	–	2.3	4.4	–	5.9	11.4	–	–	–	–	–
Bulgaria	32.4	32.3	4.2	–	1.4	10.3	11.4	0.0	–	–	–	–
Burkina Faso	19.2	21.1	1.7	4.2	2.0	7.2	18.0	0.1	885.0	7.1	–	–
Burundi	14.5	17.0	2.5	6.4	2.3	9.1	24.2	0.1	428.0	12.3	–	–
Cabo Verde	–	28.4	3.6	5.3	2.5	11.4	16.7	0.1	123.0	7.3	–	–
Cambodia	18.6	14.3	1.3	1.9	0.9	6.6	8.8	0.1	843.0	4.1	–	–
Cameroon	–	10.9	0.7	2.8	0.0	3.3	13.2	0.0	1213.0	3.5	–	–
Canada	17.8	17.3	7.6	5.3	–	19.2	12.2	–	–	–	4305.0	0.3
Central African Republic	–	7.8	0.6	1.2	2.8	4.3	7.8	0.4	508.0	26.0	–	–
Chad	–	–	1.1	2.9	0.7	5.8	12.5	–	648.0	6.6	–	–
Chile	21.1	22.4	4.9	4.9	3.5	19.6	19.6	0.2	69.0	0.0	–	–
China	15.7	8.6	2.9	–	0.8	9.4	–	0.1	–1045	0.0	–	–
Colombia	22.7	25.3	3.8	4.5	3.0	12.8	15.1	0.1	845.0	0.3	–	–
Comoros	–	–	1.0	4.3	0.7	3.8	15.3	–	67.0	10.2	–	–
Congo	43.8	20.1	1.6	4.6	0.1	2.9	8.0	0.0	108.0	1.4	–	–
Cook Islands	–	–	–	–	–	–	–	–	19.0	–	–	–
Costa Rica	24.4	26.4	5.8	7.1	0.7	29.9	–	0.0	99.0	0.2	–	–
Côte d'Ivoire	16.5	20.6	1.1	4.8	–	5.0	21.2	–	827.5	2.1	–	–
Croatia	39.8	38.6	5.6	4.6	3.4	11.7	9.5	0.1	–	–	–	–
Cuba	–	–	11.5	12.8	–	18.2	–	–	718.0	–	–	–
Cyprus	38.3	36.1	2.9	6.4	–	7.1	16.3	–	–	–	–	–
Czechia	31.8	32.1	6.0	5.8	–	14.3	13.9	–	–	–	304.0	0.2
Democratic People's Republic of Korea	–	–	–	–	–	–	–	–	133.0	–	–	–
Democratic Republic of the Congo	14.3	8.4	0.7	2.2	0.7	4.0	11.7	0.1	2280.0	6.3	–	–
Denmark	38.9	37.5	8.6	7.6	–	15.8	13.8	–	–	–	2448.0	0.7
Djibouti	–	–	2.4	4.5	0.2	4.1	12.3	–	134.0	7.3	–	–
Dominica	26.3	–	3.6	3.4	–	10.6	10.5	–	19.0	3.5	–	–
Dominican Republic	16.0	16.9	2.5	–	1.2	14.0	–	0.1	118.0	0.2	–	–
Ecuador	–	–	4.2	5.0	1.5	10.8	12.6	–	203.0	0.2	–	–
Egypt	21.0	30.2	1.6	–	0.2	5.0	–	0.0	–114.0	–0.1	–	–
El Salvador	25.3	24.9	4.4	4.0	0.8	20.8	16.6	0.0	152.0	0.7	–	–
Equatorial Guinea	17.2	9.8	0.6	–	–	1.4	–	–	7.0	0.1	–	–
Eritrea	–	–	0.4	–	–	1.2	–	–	79.0	–	–	–
Estonia	35.0	35.2	4.9	5.2	2.6	12.1	13.0	0.1	–	–	–	–
Eswatini	29.2	–	5.0	7.1	1.7	14.9	24.9	–	147.0	3.3	–	–
Ethiopia	9.6	11.2	1.0	4.7	1.0	5.9	27.1	0.1	4117.0	5.1	–	–
Fiji	28.7	26.5	2.3	3.9	1.1	7.0	14.3	0.0	146.0	3.0	–	–

TABLE 15. ECONOMIC INDICATORS

Countries and areas	Government revenue as % of GDP 2010–2018*	Government Expenditure 2010–2018* As % of GDP				As % of government budget			Official Development Assistance 2010–2018*			
		Total	On health	On education	On social protection	On health	On education	On social protection	Inflow in millions US$	Inflow as a % of recipient GNI	Outflow in millions US$	Ouflow as a % of donor GNI
Finland	36.9	38.2	7.6	7.1	–	13.3	12.4	–	–	–	1084.0	0.4
France	44.8	47.5	8.8	5.5	–	15.5	9.6	–	–	–	11331.0	0.4
Gabon	–	17.1	1.6	2.7	0.2	7.0	11.2	0.0	106.0	0.8	–	–
Gambia	–	–	0.8	3.1	–	2.8	10.4	–	270.0	27.3	–	–
Georgia	25.0	24.8	2.8	3.8	7.0	9.6	13.0	0.3	446.0	3.1	–	–
Germany	28.3	27.9	9.3	4.8	–	21.3	11.0	–	–	–	25005.0	0.7
Ghana	17.5	30.5	2.1	5.9	0.6	8.6	23.8	0.0	1257.0	2.8	–	–
Greece	46.7	47.4	4.7	–	–	8.8	–	–	–	–	314.0	0.2
Grenada	20.4	20.0	1.9	10.3	2.0	7.4	42.8	0.1	6.0	0.5	–	–
Guatemala	11.0	11.8	1.9	3.0	0.2	15.7	24.1	0.0	367.0	0.5	–	–
Guinea	–	–	0.4	2.5	1.6	2.0	11.6	–	457.0	4.4	–	–
Guinea-Bissau	–	12.6	2.2	2.1	0.0	9.4	16.2	0.0	113.0	8.4	–	–
Guyana	–	–	2.3	5.3	–	7.8	17.8	–	51.0	1.4	–	–
Haiti	–	–	0.9	3.2	–	4.0	14.4	–	980.0	11.6	–	–
Holy See	–	–	–	–	–	–	–	–	–	–	–	–
Honduras	23.4	22.0	3.0	6.4	0.8	11.4	24.6	0.0	441.0	2.1	–	–
Hungary	39.9	42.1	4.7	4.6	3.1	9.4	9.1	0.1	–	–	149.0	0.1
Iceland	32.2	29.9	6.7	7.7	–	15.9	18.2	–	–	–	68.0	0.3
India	–	14.9	0.9	3.8	1.5	3.1	14.1	0.1	3094.0	0.1	–	–
Indonesia	12.2	14.3	1.2	3.6	0.8	6.9	20.5	0.1	234.0	0.0	–	–
Iran (Islamic Republic of)	–	–	4.0	2.8	–	22.6	18.6	–	140.0	0.0	–	–
Iraq	26.9	26.0	0.7	–	2.6	1.7	–	0.1	2907.0	1.5	–	–
Ireland	24.8	24.4	5.3	3.8	–	18.4	13.0	–	–	–	838.0	0.3
Israel	33.6	36.7	4.6	5.9	–	11.6	15.0	–	–	–	–	–
Italy	38.0	41.5	6.7	4.1	–	13.3	8.1	–	–	–	5858.0	0.3
Jamaica	29.3	26.6	3.6	5.5	–	12.9	20.1	–	59.0	0.4	–	–
Japan	12.8	16.4	9.1	3.5	–	23.2	9.1	–	–	–	11463.0	0.2
Jordan	30.0	26.1	3.6	3.6	0.7	12.0	12.5	0.0	2921.0	7.3	–	–
Kazakhstan	16.6	19.5	1.9	2.8	1.6	8.4	12.2	0.1	59.0	0.0	–	–
Kenya	21.9	26.2	1.7	5.3	0.4	6.3	16.7	0.0	2475.0	3.3	–	–
Kiribati	100.5	77.4	6.9	–	0.7	6.3	–	0.0	77.0	22.2	–	–
Kuwait	38.6	52.0	3.4	–	0.8	6.2	–	0.0	–	–	–	–
Kyrgyzstan	28.5	26.0	2.7	6.0	3.1	7.3	15.8	0.1	461.0	6.3	–	–
Lao People's Democratic Republic	14.5	–	0.9	2.9	0.2	3.8	–	–	476.0	3.0	–	–
Latvia	41.0	42.6	3.3	5.3	0.8	8.5	14.1	0.0	–	–	–	–
Lebanon	19.8	25.8	3.9	2.5	1.0	14.3	8.6	0.0	1306.0	2.5	–	–
Lesotho	33.8	35.2	5.4	–	7.1	11.3	13.8	0.2	147.0	5.0	–	–
Liberia	–	16.5	1.1	4.1	2.6	3.1	7.2	0.2	622.0	33.5	–	–
Libya	–	–	–	–	–	0.0	–	–	432.0	0.8	–	–
Liechtenstein	–	–	–	2.6	–	–	–	–	–	–	–	–
Lithuania	31.2	31.2	4.3	4.2	0.5	12.3	12.3	0.0	–	–	–	–
Luxembourg	42.0	39.8	5.1	3.9	–	12.2	9.4	–	–	–	424.0	1.0
Madagascar	–	–	2.4	–	0.2	15.6	19.0	–	780.0	7.0	–	–
Malawi	18.5	18.8	2.7	5.6	1.5	9.7	21.6	0.1	1515.0	24.6	–	–
Malaysia	16.3	16.0	2.1	5.0	0.7	8.2	19.8	0.0	–29	0.0	–	–
Maldives	25.7	25.1	6.4	4.5	1.2	18.2	12.9	0.0	42.0	1.0	–	–
Mali	17.4	12.5	1.0	3.8	0.6	4.7	18.2	0.0	1356.0	9.1	–	–
Malta	39.5	34.9	5.7	5.3	–	14.2	13.2	–	–	–	–	–
Marshall Islands	39.3	63.2	11.6	–	1.1	20.2	–	0.0	72.0	27.4	–	–
Mauritania	–	–	1.8	2.6	2.5	5.5	9.3	–	284.0	5.7	–	–
Mauritius	22.3	23.0	2.4	4.9	3.5	9.5	19.5	0.2	12.0	0.1	–	–
Mexico	20.1	20.4	3.0	5.2	1.7	10.9	19.0	0.1	737.0	0.1	–	–
Micronesia (Federated States of)	34.2	24.2	3.2	12.5	–	5.8	22.3	–	98.0	25.1	–	–
Monaco	–	–	1.6	–	–	8.1	–	–	–	–	–	–
Mongolia	21.1	23.8	2.0	4.2	2.0	6.0	12.4	0.1	764.0	7.7	–	–
Montenegro	–	–	–	–	1.8	–	–	–	117.0	2.4	–	–
Montserrat	–	–	–	–	–	–	–	–	36.0	–	–	–
Morocco	32.7	24.5	2.4	–	1.1	7.7	–	0.0	1885.0	1.8	–	–
Mozambique	25.1	18.4	0.4	6.5	1.3	1.2	19.0	0.1	1776.0	14.9	–	–
Myanmar	15.8	16.8	1.1	2.2	0.3	4.9	9.4	0.0	1543.0	2.3	–	–
Namibia	34.2	34.8	5.3	3.1	3.2	12.4	7.6	0.1	187.0	1.4	–	–
Nauru	–	85.0	5.3	–	–	5.0	–	–	26.0	17.8	–	–
Nepal	23.2	19.6	1.0	3.7	1.3	5.1	17.0	0.1	1258.0	5.1	–	–

TABLE 15. ECONOMIC INDICATORS

Countries and areas	Government revenue as % of GDP 2010–2018*	Government Expenditure 2010–2018*							Official Development Assistance 2010–2018*			
		As % of GDP				As % of government budget						
		Total	On health	On education	On social protection	On health	On education	On social protection	Inflow in millions US$	Inflow as a % of recipient GNI	Outflow in millions US$	Ouflow as a % of donor GNI
Netherlands	39.2	37.8	8.4	5.4	–	18.8	12.3	–	–	–	4958.0	0.6
New Zealand	32.6	30.5	7.4	6.3	–	22.1	16.4	–	–	–	450.0	0.2
Nicaragua	17.8	16.4	4.5	4.1	2.2	17.9	–	0.1	563.0	4.2	–	–
Niger	–	–	1.5	6.0	0.7	4.6	18.5	–	1207.0	15.2	–	–
Nigeria	5.0	–	0.6	–	0.3	5.3	–	–	3359.0	0.9	–	–
Niue	–	–	–	–	–	–	–	–	15.0	–	–	–
North Macedonia	26.5	28.1	4.1	–	–	12.8	–	–	–	–	–	–
Norway	45.4	38.8	8.6	7.6	–	17.7	15.7	–	–	–	4125.0	1.0
Oman	49.5	34.6	3.8	6.7	–	7.6	15.3	–	–	–	–	–
Pakistan	–	17.6	0.7	2.7	0.6	3.7	13.2	0.0	2283.0	0.7	–	–
Palau	26.6	41.7	4.5	–	–	13.3	–	–	22.0	7.9	–	–
Panama	–	–	4.2	3.2	1.5	11.6	13.0	–	41.0	0.1	–	–
Papua New Guinea	15.4	16.9	1.7	–	0.0	8.2	–	0.0	532.0	2.6	–	–
Paraguay	17.3	15.6	4.2	4.5	–	10.9	–	–	143.0	0.5	–	–
Peru	17.0	20.3	3.2	4.0	1.4	14.5	17.6	0.1	-8.0	0.0	–	–
Philippines	15.6	14.3	1.4	–	0.7	7.3	–	0.0	160.0	0.0	–	–
Poland	33.6	34.2	4.4	4.8	2.0	10.7	11.6	0.1	–	–	679.0	0.1
Portugal	37.8	41.7	5.9	4.9	–	12.3	10.2	–	–	–	381.0	0.2
Qatar	34.2	18.7	2.6	2.9	–	6.3	8.9	–	–	–	–	–
Republic of Korea	27.8	25.4	4.2	5.3	–	12.9	–	–	–	–	2201.0	0.1
Republic of Moldova	32.2	26.8	4.6	–	1.3	12.2	18.3	0.0	241.0	2.8	–	–
Romania	28.6	31.6	3.9	3.1	1.1	10.8	9.1	0.0	–	–	–	–
Russian Federation	24.4	30.6	3.1	3.8	1.9	8.8	10.9	0.1	–	–	–	–
Rwanda	20.0	18.9	2.2	3.8	1.5	7.9	12.5	0.1	1225.0	13.7	–	–
Saint Kitts and Nevis	28.0	24.4	2.1	2.8	–	6.6	8.6	–	–	–	–	–
Saint Lucia	22.3	19.4	2.2	4.4	0.5	8.6	16.5	0.0	13.0	0.8	–	–
Saint Vincent and the Grenadines	27.5	26.6	2.6	5.8	–	9.2	19.0	–	7.0	0.9	–	–
Samoa	27.0	22.9	4.5	4.1	0.8	11.5	10.5	0.0	130.0	15.6	–	–
San Marino	39.8	42.2	5.5	2.4	–	13.3	10.6	–	–	–	–	–
Sao Tome and Principe	16.0	18.2	1.7	3.9	–	4.9	11.3	–	40.0	10.2	–	–
Saudi Arabia	–	28.0	4.1	–	0.7	10.1	–	0.0	–	–	–	–
Senegal	17.2	18.0	1.7	7.1	1.0	5.8	23.8	0.1	910.0	5.8	–	–
Serbia	34.9	36.9	5.4	4.0	2.0	12.3	8.9	0.1	1688.0	4.4	–	–
Seychelles	36.4	33.3	3.2	4.4	2.6	10.0	11.7	0.1	19.0	1.4	–	–
Sierra Leone	9.8	11.8	1.6	4.6	0.9	7.9	19.9	0.1	538.0	14.7	–	–
Singapore	21.4	14.5	2.2	2.9	–	12.4	20.0	–	–	–	–	–
Slovakia	37.5	38.9	5.4	4.6	2.4	12.0	10.3	0.1	–	–	119.0	0.1
Slovenia	37.9	38.0	6.1	4.9	2.6	12.7	11.2	0.1	–	–	76.0	0.2
Solomon Islands	32.7	33.6	3.5	9.9	–	7.3	17.5	–	187.0	15.3	–	–
Somalia	–	0.0	–	–	0.2	–	–	1422.8	1760.0	24.0	–	–
South Africa	30.9	34.4	4.4	6.0	3.3	13.3	18.7	0.1	1014.0	0.3	–	–
South Sudan	–	–	–	1.4	10.1	–	3.3	–	2183.0	–	–	–
Spain	15.6	18.7	6.5	4.3	–	14.9	9.8	–	–	–	2560.0	0.2
Sri Lanka	13.8	16.4	1.7	2.2	0.7	8.4	11.0	0.0	297.0	0.4	–	–
State of Palestine	6.9	8.3	–	5.1	2.3	–	–	0.3	2111.0	12.8	–	–
Sudan	–	10.5	2.1	–	1.0	18.1	–	0.1	840.0	0.8	–	–
Suriname	25.7	22.4	4.0	–	–	12.7	–	–	20.0	0.6	–	–
Sweden	33.1	31.3	9.2	7.6	–	18.5	15.5	–	–	–	5563.0	1.0
Switzerland	18.4	17.4	7.5	5.1	–	22.1	15.5	–	–	–	3138.0	0.5
Syrian Arab Republic	–	–	–	–	–	0.0	–	–	10361.0	–	–	–
Tajikistan	–	–	1.9	5.2	0.6	6.1	16.4	–	304.0	3.7	–	–
Thailand	19.2	18.4	2.8	4.1	0.5	15.3	19.1	0.0	250.0	0.1	–	–
Timor-Leste	32.4	36.4	2.3	2.7	6.5	4.5	6.8	0.2	232.0	8.9	–	–
Togo	18.8	15.4	1.3	5.2	0.2	4.2	16.7	0.0	345.0	6.9	–	–
Tokelau	–	–	–	–	–	–	–	–	7.0	–	–	–
Tonga	–	31.4	2.7	–	–	6.8	–	–	80.0	18.6	–	–
Trinidad and Tobago	39.4	35.8	3.2	–	–	8.3	–	–	–	–	–	–
Tunisia	31.4	35.5	4.0	6.6	0.8	13.9	22.9	0.0	776.0	2.0	–	–
Turkey	29.7	31.9	3.2	4.3	1.1	9.7	12.8	0.0	3142.0	0.4	–	–
Turkmenistan	–	–	1.5	3.0	–	8.7	20.8	–	29.0	0.1	–	–
Turks and Caicos Islands	–	–	–	3.3	–	–	–	–	–	–	–	–
Tuvalu	–	–	13.2	–	–	10.3	–	–	27.0	45.3	–	–
Uganda	14.6	13.3	1.0	2.8	0.8	5.1	12.1	0.1	2008.0	7.9	–	–

TABLE 15. ECONOMIC INDICATORS

Countries and areas	Government revenue as % of GDP 2010–2018*	Government Expenditure 2010–2018* As % of GDP				As % of government budget			Official Development Assistance 2010–2018*			
		Total	On health	On education	On social protection	On health	On education	On social protection	Inflow in millions US$	Inflow as a % of recipient GNI	Outflow in millions US$	Ouflow as a % of donor GNI
Ukraine	32.6	33.6	2.9	5.0	4.4	6.6	12.4	0.1	1166.0	1.0	–	–
United Arab Emirates	3.5	4.1	2.6	–	–	7.9	–	–	–	–	–	–
United Kingdom	35.7	36.4	7.9	5.6	–	18.5	13.8	–	–	–	18103.0	0.7
United Republic of Tanzania	16.4	15.7	1.3	3.5	0.5	7.3	17.3	0.0	2584.0	5.0	–	–
United States	19.7	22.4	13.8	5.0	–	36.6	13.6	–	–	–	34732.0	0.2
Uruguay	32.6	34.1	6.2	4.4	1.2	19.0	14.9	0.0	41.0	0.1	–	–
Uzbekistan	21.8	15.0	3.0	7.1	–	9.0	21.1	–	638.0	1.3	–	–
Vanuatu	25.0	27.9	2.0	5.5	0.3	4.9	13.0	0.0	132.0	15.5	–	–
Venezuela (Bolivarian Republic of)	–	–	2.0	–	–	4.1	–	–	87.0	–	–	–
Viet Nam	21.5	21.6	2.4	5.7	1.0	7.9	18.5	0.0	2376.0	1.1	–	–
Yemen	–	–	0.6	–	–	2.2	–	–	3234.0	–	–	–
Zambia	16.9	20.8	2.1	–	0.3	7.4	–	0.0	1023.0	4.1	–	–
Zimbabwe	17.4	26.6	4.0	7.5	0.4	15.9	30.0	–	726.0	4.6	–	–
SUMMARY												
East Asia and Pacific	15.9	11.8	2.9	4.0 **	0.8	9.9	16.6 **	0.1	–497.8	0.2	7908.9 **	0.2 **
Europe and Central Asia	31.0	32.7	5.4	4.7	–	12.7	11.8	–	1461.6	1.1	9847.3	0.4
Eastern Europe and Central Asia	27.2	29.4	3.1	4.3	2.0	8.8	12.5	0.1	1461.6	1.1	–	–
Western Europe	34.2	35.4	7.4	5.1	–	16.0	11.2	–	–	–	9847.3	0.4
Latin America and Caribbean	22.7	26.6	3.8	5.5	1.7	11.8	17.0	0.1	386.9	0.4	–	–
Middle East and North Africa	27.4	27.9	2.8	–	0.9	9.4	–	0.0	1346.5	0.9	–	–
North America	19.5	21.9	13.2	5.0	–	34.8	13.5	–	–	–	31625.9	0.2
South Asia	12.3 ‡	15.3	0.8	3.5	1.3	3.3	13.7	0.1	3007.2	0.7	–	–
Sub-Saharan Africa	14.5	16.9	1.5	4.3	1.0	7.0	17.7	29.9	2018.1	5.2	–	–
Eastern and Southern Africa	17.6	17.9	2.0	4.6	1.4	8.9	19.0	43.8	1993.3	5.6	–	–
West and Central Africa	11.3	15.1	0.9	3.8	0.7	5.1	15.9	–	2043.5	4.8	–	–
Least developed countries	14.2	14.0	1.1	3.2	1.0	5.8	15.3	27.4	2196.7	6.6	–	–
World	**17.9**	**18.8**	**2.9**	**4.1**	**1.2**	**9.1**	**15.2**	**4.6**	**1447.8**	**1.3**	**11263.6**	**–**

For a complete list of countries and areas in the regions, subregions and country categories, see page 182 or visit <data.unicef.org/regionalclassifications>.

It is not advisable to compare data from consecutive editions of *The State of the World's Children*.

DEFINITIONS OF THE INDICATORS

Government revenue as % of GDP – Revenue is cash receipts from taxes, social contributions, and other revenues such as fines, fees, rent, and income from property or sales. Grants are also considered as revenue but are excluded here.

Government expenditure – General government final consumption expenditure (formerly general government consumption) includes all government current expenditures for purchases of goods and services (including compensation of employees). It also includes most expenditures on national defence and security, but excludes government military expenditures that are part of government capital formation.

Government expenditure expressed as a % of GDP – Total government expenditure as well as the specific expenditures on health, education, and social protection.

Government expenditure expressed as a % of Total government expenditure – Specific expenditures on health, education, and social protection.

ODA (Net official development assistance) – Official development assistance flows are defined as those flows to countries and territories on the DAC List of ODA Recipients and to multilateral development institutions which are: (a) provided by official agencies, including state and local governments, or by their executive agencies; (b) each transaction of which is administered with the promotion of the economic development and welfare of developing countries as its main objective; and (c) is concessional in character.

ODA (Net official development assistance) for donor countries – expressed as an outflow of resources (in US dollars and as % of Gross National Income).

ODA (Net official development assistance) for recipient countries – expressed as an intflow of resources (in US dollars and as % of Gross National Income).

MAIN DATA SOURCES

ODA – Organisation for Economic Co-operation and Development. Last update: February 2019.

Government revenue as % of GDP – World Development Indicators. Last update: June 2019.

Government Expenditure – World Development Indicators. Last update: June 2019.

NOTES

– Data not available.

* Data refer to the most recent year available during the period specified in the column heading.

** Excludes China.

‡ Excludes India.

TABLE 16. WOMEN'S ECONOMIC EMPOWERMENT

Countries and areas	Social Institutions and Gender Index (SIGI) 2019	Legal frameworks on gender equality in employment 2018	Maternity leave benefits 2018	Paternity leave benefits 2018	Demand for family planning satisfied with modern methods (%) 2013–2018*	Educational attainment 2010–2017* upper secondary male	female	Labour force participation rate 2010–2018* male rural	male urban	male total	female rural	female urban	female total	Unemployment rate 2010–2018* male rural	male urban	male total	female rural	female urban	female total	Mobile phone ownership 2014–2017* male	female	Financial inclusion 2014–201* male	fem
Afghanistan	Very high	–	No	Yes	42	–	–	74	71	73	23	16	21	10	12	10	9	36	14	–	–	23	
Albania	Low	0.7	Yes	Yes	5	46	44	–	–	–	–	–	–	–	–	–	–	–	–	–	–	42	
Algeria	–	–	Yes	Yes	77	28 x	23 x	65	57	60	10	15	13	–	–	–	–	–	–	–	–	56	
Andorra	–	–	–	–	–	48	47	–	–	–	–	–	–	–	–	–	–	–	–	–	–	–	
Angola	–	–	No	No	30	20	12	89	73	80	90	63	75	2	12	7	1	15	8	78	80	36	
Anguilla	–	–	–	–	–	–	–	–	–	–	–	–	–	–	–	–	–	–	–	–	–	–	
Antigua and Barbuda	–	–	No	No	–	–	–	–	–	–	–	–	–	–	–	–	–	–	–	–	–	–	
Argentina	–	–	Yes	No	Yes	40 x	44 x	–	–	–	–	–	–	–	–	–	–	–	–	–	–	46	
Armenia	Low	0.8	Yes	No	37	92	92	74	68	71	61	48	53	8	25	18	7	25	17	–	–	56	
Australia	Very low	1.0	Yes	Yes	–	78	75	67	72	71	57	61	60	–	–	–	–	–	–	–	–	100	
Austria	Very low	–	Yes	No	–	86	73	67	67	67	57	55	56	2	7	5	3	6	5	–	–	98	
Azerbaijan	Low	–	Yes	No	22 x	92	85	–	–	–	–	–	–	–	–	–	–	–	–	88	80	29	
Bahamas	–	–	–	–	–	81 x	82 x	–	–	–	–	–	–	–	–	–	–	–	–	–	–	–	
Bahrain	–	–	No	Yes	–	39	47	–	–	–	–	–	–	–	–	–	–	–	–	100	100	86	
Bangladesh	Very high	0.2	Yes	No	73	34	24	80	81	81	39	31	36	3	3	3	6	9	7	54	31	65	
Barbados	–	0.4	No	No	70 x	23 x	25 x	–	–	–	–	–	–	–	–	–	–	–	–	–	–	–	
Belarus	Low	0.5	Yes	No	74 x	88 x	82 x	–	–	–	–	–	–	–	–	–	–	–	–	91	95	81	
Belgium	Very low	–	Yes	Yes	–	69	65	61	59	59	52	49	50	4	7	6	4	6	6	–	–	98	
Belize	–	–	Yes	No	66	36	37	81	77	79	41	57	49	4	5	5	12	8	10	–	–	44	
Benin	Medium	–	Yes	Yes	26	–	–	78	70	74	73	65	70	1	4	2	2	4	3	–	–	49	
Bhutan	–	–	No	Yes	85 x	8	3	70	75	71	60	46	56	–	–	–	–	–	–	–	–	39	
Bolivia (Plurinational State of)	Low	–	No	Yes	50	46	39	91	76	80	77	58	64	1	5	3	1	5	4	–	–	55	
Bosnia and Herzegovina	Low	–	Yes	Yes	22 x	75	51	53	53	53	27	37	31	16	19	17	21	19	20	–	–	63	
Botswana	–	–	No	No	–	–	–	71 x	69 x	70 x	53 x	57 x	56 x	12 x	14 x	13 x	19 x	20 x	20 x	–	–	56	
Brazil	Low	0.8	Yes	Yes	89 x	42	46	82	77	78	55	56	56	2 x	7 x	6 x	5 x	12 x	11 x	83	84	73	
British Virgin Islands	–	–	–	–	–	–	–	–	–	–	–	–	–	–	–	–	–	–	–	–	–	–	
Brunei Darussalam	–	–	No	No	–	–	–	68	69	69	53	58	56	9	9	9	12	9	10	99	99	–	
Bulgaria	Low	1.0	Yes	Yes	–	77	74	55	65	62	38	54	49	10	4	6	9	3	5	–	–	71	
Burkina Faso	Medium	–	Yes	Yes	56	4	2	77	69	75	59	55	58	3	6	4	9	9	9	–	–	51	
Burundi	–	–	No	No	38	5	2	79	69	78	83	55	80	1	10	2	0	10	1	16	7	8	
Cabo Verde	–	0.7	No	Yes	73 x	20	20	66	55	63	55	36	49	31	–	31	30	–	32	75	74	–	
Cambodia	Low	–	No	No	57	47	29	89	85	88	78	70	76	1	1	1	1	1	1	–	–	22	
Cameroon	Very high	0.4	Yes	Yes	47	25	11	80	74	78	74	58	67	1	6	3	1	9	4	–	–	39	
Canada	Very low	–	Yes	No	–	83	83	67	70	70	59	62	61	6	6	6	5	6	6	–	–	100	1
Central African Republic	High	–	Yes	No	29 x	–	–	–	–	–	–	–	–	–	–	–	–	–	–	–	–	18	
Chad	High	–	Yes	Yes	20	10 x	2 x	–	–	–	–	–	–	–	–	–	–	–	–	–	–	29	
Chile	Medium	0.8	Yes	Yes	–	58	56	72	70	71	42	50	49	5	7	7	7	8	8	87	97	78	
China	–	–	Yes	Yes	97 x	25	19	–	–	–	–	–	–	–	–	–	–	–	–	–	–	84	
Colombia	Very low	0.8	Yes	Yes	87	46	48	86	79	80	46	60	57	3	9	7	8	12	12	72	74	49	
Comoros	–	–	Yes	No	29 x	–	–	52 x	48 x	51 x	34 x	29 x	33 x	4 x	6 x	4 x	4 x	7 x	5 x	–	–	26	
Congo	–	–	Yes	No	43	–	–	77 x	64 x	69 x	80 x	58 x	67 x	6 x	27 x	18 x	7 x	34 x	21 x	–	–	31	
Cook Islands	–	–	–	–	–	–	–	–	–	–	–	–	–	–	–	–	–	–	–	–	–	–	
Costa Rica	Low	0.6	Yes	No	89 x	37	39	75	73	74	39	49	46	7	8	8	14	12	12	87	87	75	
Côte d'Ivoire	High	0.8	Yes	Yes	39	15	7	77	66	66	52	46	46	1	3	3	1	4	4	81	47	47	3
Croatia	Very low	1.0	Yes	No	–	79	63	56	58	57	41	48	46	8	7	8	12	8	9	–	–	90	
Cuba	–	–	–	–	89	58	57	–	–	–	–	–	–	–	–	–	–	–	–	–	–	–	
Cyprus	Low	–	Yes	No	–	73	70	63	69	68	51	59	57	9	8	8	9	9	9	100	99	87	
Czechia	Very low	–	Yes	No	86 x	94	86	68	69	69	52	53	53	2	2	2	3	3	3	97	97	84	
Democratic People's Republic of Korea	Low	–	–	–	90	–	–	–	–	–	–	–	–	–	–	–	–	–	–	–	–	–	
Democratic Republic of the Congo	Medium	–	Yes	Yes	19	39	17	76	61	70	75	44	63	2	11	5	1	10	4	–	–	27	2
Denmark	Very low	0.9	Yes	Yes	–	78	79	64	69	67	55	60	58	4	5	5	4	6	5	82	83	100	1
Djibouti	–	–	Yes	Yes	–	–	–	–	–	–	–	–	–	–	–	–	–	–	–	61	52	17	
Dominica	–	–	No	No	–	11 x	10 x	–	–	–	–	–	–	–	–	–	–	–	–	–	–	–	
Dominican Republic	Very low	0.9	Yes	Yes	82	31	38	79	76	76	40	51	49	3	5	4	5	9	8	70	69	58	5
Ecuador	Low	–	No	Yes	79 x	43	42	85	77	79	61	52	55	1	4	3	2	6	4	59	58	60	4
Egypt	–	–	No	No	80	–	–	68	65	67	22	22	22	7	10	8	19	29	23	99	97	39	
El Salvador	Low	0.9	Yes	Yes	80	31	28	82	75	77	35	52	46	4	5	5	3	4	4	81	78	38	
Equatorial Guinea	–	–	Yes	Yes	21 x	–	–	–	–	–	–	–	–	–	–	–	–	–	–	–	–	–	
Eritrea	–	–	No	No	21 x	–	–	–	–	–	–	–	–	–	–	–	–	–	–	–	–	–	
Estonia	Very low	–	Yes	Yes	–	84	90	67	74	71	55	59	57	5	6	5	5	5	5	–	–	98	

TABLE 16. WOMEN'S ECONOMIC EMPOWERMENT

Countries and areas	Social Institutions and Gender Index (SIGI) 2019	Legal frameworks on gender equality in employment 2018	Maternity leave benefits 2018	Paternity leave benefits 2018	Demand for family planning satisfied with modern methods (%) 2013–2018*	Educational attainment 2010–2017* upper secondary male	female	Labour force participation rate 2010–2018* male rural	urban	total	female rural	urban	total	Unemployment rate 2010–2018* male rural	urban	total	female rural	urban	total	Mobile phone ownership 2014–2017* male	female	Financial inclusion 2014–2017* male	female
Eswatini	–	–	No	No	83	–	–	51	71	56	42	63	47	24	15	21	26	22	24	–	–	30	27
Ethiopia	Low	–	No	No	62	13	6	88	73	85	79	61	75	–	–	–	–	–	–	–	–	41	29
Fiji	–	0.6	No	No	–	39 x	40 x	82	72	77	38	39	39	2	5	4	5	6	6	–	–	–	–
Finland	Very low	1.0	Yes	Yes	–	73	75	59	65	63	53	57	56	6	8	7	7	8	7	95	103	100	100
France	Very low	0.9	Yes	Yes	96 x	73	67	59	61	60	52	51	52	7	10	9	8	10	9	–	–	97	91
Gabon	High	–	Yes	No	44 x	–	–	–	–	–	–	–	–	–	–	–	–	–	–	–	–	64	54
Gambia	–	–	Yes	Yes	27	–	–	67	70	69	52	49	50	4	9	7	11	14	13	–	–	–	–
Georgia	Low	–	Yes	No	53 x	94	93	82	68	75	71	49	58	6	24	15	4	21	13	89	81	58	64
Germany	Very low	1.0	Yes	No	–	88	79	68	67	67	57	56	56	2	4	4	2	3	3	–	–	99	99
Ghana	Medium	–	No	No	46	27	15	53	64	59	50	60	55	2	6	4	2	6	4	–	–	62	54
Greece	Low	1.0	Yes	Yes	–	57	52	59	61	60	41	46	44	13	16	15	20	26	24	–	–	86	85
Grenada	–	–	No	No	–	–	–	–	–	–	–	–	–	–	–	–	–	–	–	–	–	–	–
Guatemala	Low	0.6	No	Yes	66	26	27	89	81	85	30	47	39	1	3	2	3	4	4	–	–	46	42
Guinea	Very high	–	Yes	No	22	–	–	73 x	55 x	66 x	70 x	45 x	63 x	2 x	15 x	6 x	2 x	11 x	4 x	–	–	27	20
Guinea-Bissau	–	–	No	No	56	–	–	–	–	–	–	–	–	–	–	–	–	–	–	–	–	–	–
Guyana	–	–	No	No	52	29 x	33 x	68	71	69	40	52	44	10	10	10	15	15	15	–	–	–	–
Haiti	Medium	–	No	No	43	–	–	80	67	74	59	49	54	5	19	11	10	22	16	–	–	35	30
Holy See	–	–	–	No	–	–	–	–	–	–	–	–	–	–	–	–	–	–	–	–	–	–	–
Honduras	Low	–	No	No	76 x	23	26	92	77	84	37	52	46	1	5	3	3	7	6	–	–	50	41
Hungary	Low	–	Yes	Yes	–	81	72	67	65	66	49	49	49	4	3	3	4	4	4	–	–	78	72
Iceland	–	–	Yes	Yes	–	67 x	55 x	87	85	86	79	78	78	2	3	3	1	3	3	–	–	–	–
India	Medium	0.3	Yes	No	67	34	19	80	76	79	26	18	23	2	3	2	3	7	4	–	–	83	77
Indonesia	High	–	No	Yes	78	38	30	85	79	82	55	50	52	3	6	4	3	5	4	65	54	46	51
Iran (Islamic Republic of)	Very high	–	Yes	Yes	69 x	48	49	66	63	64	16	15	15	–	–	–	–	–	–	77	55	96	92
Iraq	Very high	0.6	Yes	No	55	34	24	74	72	72	7	13	11	6	8	7	4	16	12	83	57	26	20
Ireland	Very low	–	Yes	Yes	–	68	73	67	70	69	53	58	56	5	6	6	5	6	6	83	83	95	95
Israel	–	–	Yes	No	–	82	81	70	68	68	64	59	60	–	–	–	–	–	–	–	–	92	94
Italy	Very low	–	Yes	Yes	–	50	48	59	60	59	40	41	41	9	10	10	11	12	12	93	90	96	92
Jamaica	Low	–	No	No	79 x	–	–	76	71	73	59	62	61	–	–	–	–	–	–	96	97	79	78
Japan	Low	–	Yes	No	–	82	79	–	–	–	–	–	–	–	–	–	–	–	–	90	87	98	98
Jordan	Very high	0.2	No	No	57	43	40	–	–	–	–	–	–	–	–	–	–	–	–	–	–	56	27
Kazakhstan	Low	–	Yes	No	79	86 x	85 x	–	–	–	–	–	–	–	–	–	–	–	–	87	87	57	60
Kenya	Medium	0.9	No	Yes	76	26	18	76	80	78	74	68	71	1	5	3	1	7	3	46	44	86	78
Kiribati	–	–	No	No	36 x	–	–	–	–	–	–	–	–	–	–	–	–	–	–	–	–	–	–
Kuwait	–	–	No	No	–	26	36	–	–	–	–	–	–	–	–	–	–	–	–	–	–	83	73
Kyrgyzstan	Low	–	Yes	No	66	90 x	87 x	75	75	75	50	43	46	2	9	4	3	8	4	–	–	41	39
Lao People's Democratic Republic	Low	–	Yes	Yes	72	–	–	39	59	45	30	49	37	14	7	11	11	4	8	–	–	26	32
Latvia	Very low	–	Yes	Yes	–	87	91	65	70	68	52	58	56	9	8	8	8	6	6	–	–	94	93
Lebanon	Very high	0.5	No	No	–	33 x	33 x	–	–	–	–	–	–	–	–	–	–	–	–	–	–	57	33
Lesotho	Medium	–	No	No	79	13 x	14 x	–	–	–	–	–	–	–	–	–	–	–	–	–	–	45	46
Liberia	High	–	Yes	No	41	–	–	91	75	82	84	63	72	1	7	4	1	4	2	–	–	44	28
Libya	–	–	Yes	No	24	–	–	–	–	–	–	–	–	–	–	–	–	–	–	–	–	71	60
Liechtenstein	–	–	–	–	–	81 x	63 x	–	–	–	–	–	–	–	–	–	–	–	–	–	–	–	–
Lithuania	Very low	1.0	Yes	Yes	–	89	84	64	70	68	50	60	57	10	5	7	8	4	5	97	97	85	81
Luxembourg	–	–	Yes	Yes	–	83	76	61	66	64	54	57	56	4	6	5	5	7	6	–	–	99	98
Madagascar	High	0.4	Yes	No	61	–	–	92	80	89	87	72	84	1	5	2	1	7	2	–	–	20	16
Malawi	High	–	No	No	74	–	–	56	75	60	47	65	50	24	13	21	37	36	37	52	33	38	30
Malaysia	–	0.3	No	No	–	58	59	83	79	80	49	56	54	–	–	–	–	–	–	97	94	88	82
Maldives	–	–	No	Yes	43 x	6 x	4 x	77	80	78	46	48	47	–	–	–	–	–	–	–	–	–	–
Mali	High	–	Yes	Yes	35	8	3	84	75	81	59	46	55	1	4	1	0	4	1	–	–	45	26
Malta	Low	–	Yes	Yes	–	39	37	70	70	70	54	49	49	5	4	4	7	4	4	–	–	98	97
Marshall Islands	–	–	No	No	81 x	72	68	–	–	–	–	–	–	–	–	–	–	–	–	–	–	–	–
Mauritania	–	–	Yes	No	30	–	–	63	63	63	29	26	28	4	14	8	5	23	12	–	–	26	15
Mauritius	–	–	Yes	Yes	41	48	40	–	–	–	–	–	–	–	–	–	–	–	–	78	71	93	87
Mexico	Low	0.8	No	Yes	80	34	32	81	76	77	31	47	43	2	4	3	2	4	3	73	70	41	33
Micronesia (Federated States of)	–	–	No	No	–	–	–	–	–	–	–	–	–	–	–	–	–	–	–	–	–	–	–
Monaco	–	–	–	–	–	–	–	–	–	–	–	–	–	–	–	–	–	–	–	–	–	–	–
Mongolia	Low	–	Yes	No	65	64	71	76	60	66	67	48	54	4	9	7	4	7	6	–	–	91	95
Montenegro	–	–	Yes	No	43	80	65	–	–	–	–	–	–	–	–	–	–	–	–	–	–	69	68
Montserrat	–	–	–	–	–	–	–	–	–	–	–	–	–	–	–	–	–	–	–	–	–	–	–

TABLE 16. WOMEN'S ECONOMIC EMPOWERMENT

Countries and areas	Social Institutions and Gender Index (SIGI) 2019	Legal frameworks on gender equality in employ-ment 2018	Mater-nity leave bene-fits 2018	Pater-nity leave bene-fits 2018	Demand for family planning satisfied with modern methods (%) 2013–2018*	Educational attainment 2010–2017* upper secondary male	female	Labour force participation rate 2010–2018* male rural	urban	total	female rural	urban	total	Unemployment rate 2010–2018* male rural	urban	total	female rural	urban	total	Mobile phone ownership 2014–2017* male	female	Financ... inclusio... 2014–201... male	fe...
Morocco	Very high	–	Yes	Yes	69	–	–	80	70	74	36	18	25	–	–	–	–	–	–	92	92	41	
Mozambique	Low	0.7	No	Yes	56	11	8	84	73	80	87	62	78	1	7	3	1	12	4	–	–	51	
Myanmar	High	–	Yes	Yes	75	–	–	79	72	77	49	46	48	1	2	1	2	3	2	–	–	26	
Namibia	Low	–	No	No	80	19 x	16 x	54	70	63	49	61	55	16	24	21	13	22	19	–	–	81	
Nauru	–	–	–	–	43 x	–	–	–	–	–	–	–	–	–	–	–	–	–	–	–	–	–	
Nepal	Medium	–	No	No	56	25	10	48	60	54	21	32	26	12	9	10	13	13	13	–	–	50	
Netherlands	Very low	1.0	Yes	Yes	–	74	66	69	70	70	58	59	59	2	4	4	3	4	4	86	82	99	
New Zealand	Very low	–	Yes	No	–	72	68	81	76	76	70	65	65	–	–	–	–	–	–	–	–	99	
Nicaragua	Very low	–	No	Yes	93 x	–	–	90	78	83	35	56	48	1	6	4	5	6	6	–	–	37	
Niger	–	–	Yes	Yes	46	5	2	90	70	86	68	40	63	0	2	1	–	3	0	77	55	20	
Nigeria	High	0.3	No	No	43	51 x	39 x	58	54	56	48	49	49	5	8	6	4	10	7	49	32	51	
Niue	–	–	–	–	–	–	–	–	–	–	–	–	–	–	–	–	–	–	–	–	–	–	
North Macedonia	–	–	Yes	Yes	22 x	–	–	72	66	67	45	42	43	17	23	21	18	21	20	–	–	80	
Norway	Very low	–	Yes	No	–	78	77	65	68	66	59	64	62	3	5	4	3	4	4	–	–	99	
Oman	–	–	No	No	40	45	63	81	89	88	21	33	30	–	–	–	–	–	–	94	87	84	
Pakistan	Very high	0.0	No	No	49	34	21	82	78	80	28	12	22	4	5	4	3	10	5	–	–	35	
Palau	–	–	No	No	–	88	88	–	–	–	–	–	–	–	–	–	–	–	–	–	–	–	
Panama	–	0.7	Yes	Yes	73	40	46	80	74	76	45	52	50	2	4	3	4	6	5	–	–	51	
Papua New Guinea	–	–	No	No	41 x	–	–	48	57	49	47	52	48	3	13	4	1	8	1	–	–	–	
Paraguay	Medium	1.0	Yes	Yes	79	36	37	87	83	84	55	62	59	4	6	5	7	8	8	–	–	51	
Peru	Low	1.0	Yes	Yes	67	61	51	92	80	83	86	64	69	0	4	3	0	5	4	69	65	51	
Philippines	Very high	0.9	No	Yes	53	57	60	74	71	72	43	48	45	2	3	2	2	3	3	–	–	30	
Poland	Very low	–	Yes	Yes	–	87	83	65	65	65	46	50	48	4	4	4	4	3	4	–	–	85	
Portugal	Very low	–	Yes	Yes	–	35	38	63	65	64	50	56	54	6	7	7	7	8	7	–	–	94	
Qatar	–	–	No	No	69 x	37	59	–	96	96	–	59	59	–	–	–	–	–	–	100	100	69	
Republic of Korea	–	–	–	Yes	–	83	70	76	73	74	56	53	53	3	4	4	3	4	4	96	93	95	
Republic of Moldova	Low	–	Yes	Yes	60 x	76	74	45	47	46	42	39	41	2	5	3	1	4	2	–	–	43	
Romania	Very low	–	Yes	Yes	47 x	72	61	65	65	65	43	47	46	5	4	5	4	3	3	–	–	62	
Russian Federation	Low	–	Yes	No	72 x	86	83	67	73	71	50	58	56	7	4	5	7	4	5	–	–	75	
Rwanda	Low	–	No	Yes	63	11	7	58	70	61	41	57	44	15	16	16	19	20	19	–	–	56	
Saint Kitts and Nevis	–	–	No	No	–	–	–	–	–	–	–	–	–	–	–	–	–	–	–	–	–	–	
Saint Lucia	–	–	No	No	72 x	38	43	–	–	–	–	–	–	–	–	–	–	–	–	–	–	–	
Saint Vincent and the Grenadines	–	–	No	No	–	–	–	–	–	–	–	–	–	–	–	–	–	–	–	–	–	–	
Samoa	–	–	No	Yes	39	70	75	54	60	55	29	42	31	11	10	11	24	14	21	–	–	–	
San Marino	–	–	Yes	No	–	–	–	–	–	–	–	–	–	–	–	–	–	–	–	–	–	–	
Sao Tome and Principe	–	–	Yes	No	52	–	–	–	–	–	–	–	–	–	–	–	–	–	–	–	–	–	
Saudi Arabia	–	–	No	Yes	–	51	46	–	–	–	–	–	–	–	–	–	–	–	–	96	92	81	
Senegal	Medium	–	Yes	Yes	51	17	5	62	55	58	33	36	35	3	10	6	3	11	7	–	–	47	
Serbia	Very low	1.0	Yes	Yes	39	77	66	66	61	63	46	47	47	10	14	12	12	15	14	92	91	73	
Seychelles	–	–	Yes	Yes	–	48 x	44 x	–	–	–	–	–	–	–	–	–	–	–	–	–	–	–	
Sierra Leone	High	–	No	No	45	–	–	49	62	58	46	62	56	12	3	6	7	3	4	–	–	25	
Singapore	Low	–	Yes	Yes	–	74	68	–	–	–	–	–	–	–	–	–	–	–	–	91	88	100	
Slovakia	Very low	–	Yes	No	–	92	83	67	68	68	50	54	52	8	5	6	9	6	7	–	–	85	
Slovenia	Very low	0.9	Yes	Yes	–	87	77	64	64	64	54	54	54	4	5	5	5	6	6	–	–	98	
Solomon Islands	–	–	No	No	38	–	–	–	–	–	–	–	–	–	–	–	–	–	–	–	–	–	
Somalia	–	–	–	–	–	–	–	–	–	–	–	–	–	–	–	–	–	–	–	–	–	44	
South Africa	Low	–	Yes	Yes	78	67	63	48	69	62	35	55	48	29	24	25	32	28	29	117	57	68	
South Sudan	–	–	No	No	6 x	16 x	11 x	–	–	–	–	–	–	–	–	–	–	–	–	–	–	13	
Spain	Very low	1.0	Yes	Yes	–	49	48	59	65	64	46	53	52	13	14	14	18	17	17	–	–	96	
Sri Lanka	High	–	No	No	74	60	63	76	73	75	37	30	36	3	3	3	7	6	7	–	–	74	
State of Palestine	–	0.4	No	No	65	40	40	–	–	–	–	–	–	–	–	–	–	–	–	82	65	34	
Sudan	–	–	No	No	30	–	–	73	66	70	30	25	28	12	14	12	24	42	31	70	54	20	
Suriname	–	–	No	No	73 x	23	26	–	–	–	–	–	–	–	–	–	–	–	–	–	–	–	
Sweden	Very low	1.0	Yes	Yes	–	76	75	73	76	76	69	72	71	6	7	6	5	7	6	–	–	99	
Switzerland	Very low	–	Yes	No	–	89	81	75	74	74	67	62	63	3	5	4	3	6	5	–	–	98	
Syrian Arab Republic	–	–	Yes	No	53 x	25 x	19 x	–	–	–	–	–	–	–	–	–	–	–	–	–	–	27	
Tajikistan	Medium	–	Yes	No	45	85	76	57 x	54 x	56 x	29 x	28 x	29 x	6 x	8 x	7 x	3 x	7 x	4 x	–	–	52	
Thailand	Medium	–	No	No	89	34	32	77	76	77	59	61	60	1	1	1	1	1	1	82	81	84	
Timor-Leste	–	–	No	Yes	37	–	–	75	65	73	65	50	61	2	9	3	4	18	6	–	–	–	
Togo	High	–	Yes	Yes	37	17	3	53	45	49	69	53	61	1	5	3	2	4	2	49	39	53	
Tokelau	–	–	–	–	–	–	–	–	–	–	–	–	–	–	–	–	–	–	–	–	–	–	

TABLE 16. WOMEN'S ECONOMIC EMPOWERMENT

Countries and areas	Social Institutions and Gender Index (SIGI) 2019	Legal frameworks on gender equality in employment 2018	Maternity leave benefits 2018	Paternity leave benefits 2018	Demand for family planning satisfied with modern methods (%) 2013–2018*	Educational attainment 2010–2017* male	female	Labour force participation rate 2010–2018* male rural	urban	total	female rural	urban	total	Unemployment rate 2010–2018* male rural	urban	total	female rural	urban	total	Mobile phone ownership 2014–2017* male	female	Financial inclusion 2014–2017* male	female
Tonga	–	–	No	No	48 x	53	55	–	–	–	–	–	–	–	–	–	–	–	–	–	–	–	–
Trinidad and Tobago	Low	0.8	Yes	No	58 x	57 x	57 x	–	–	–	–	–	–	–	–	–	–	–	–	–	–	88	74
Tunisia	High	–	No	Yes	73 x	50	39	73	69	70	18	29	26	14	13	13	22	23	23	–	–	46	28
Turkey	Low	–	Yes	Yes	60	40	29	–	–	–	–	–	–	–	–	–	–	–	–	–	–	83	54
Turkmenistan	–	–	–	–	76	–	–	–	–	–	–	–	–	–	–	–	–	–	–	–	–	46	36
Turks and Caicos Islands	–	–	–	–	–	–	–	–	–	–	–	–	–	–	–	–	–	–	–	–	–	–	–
Tuvalu	–	–	–	–	41 x	–	–	–	–	–	–	–	–	–	–	–	–	–	–	–	–	–	–
Uganda	High	0.8	No	Yes	54	14	6	57	77	62	39	60	45	2	5	3	3	12	4	–	–	66	53
Ukraine	Low	0.5	Yes	No	68 x	78 x	71 x	67	70	69	54	58	57	–	–	–	–	–	–	–	–	65	61
United Arab Emirates	–	0.1	No	No	–	43 x	60 x	–	–	–	–	–	–	–	–	–	–	–	–	99	99	93	76
United Kingdom	Very Low	0.9	Yes	Yes	–	76	73	64	69	68	55	58	58	3	4	4	3	4	4	–	–	97	96
United Republic of Tanzania	High	0.8	No	Yes	54	5	2	91	83	88	86	72	80	1	3	2	1	6	3	–	–	52	42
United States	Very low	–	No	No	77	89	90	64	70	69	53	58	57	4	4	4	4	4	4	–	–	94	93
Uruguay	Low	–	Yes	Yes	–	26	33	77	72	72	51	56	56	2	7	7	7	10	10	78	80	68	61
Uzbekistan	–	–	Yes	No	–	94	91	–	–	–	–	–	–	–	–	–	–	–	–	–	–	38	36
Vanuatu	–	–	No	No	51	–	–	82 x	68 x	78 x	63 x	51 x	60 x	2 x	10 x	4 x	2 x	15 x	5 x	–	–	–	–
Venezuela (Bolivarian Republic of)	–	–	–	–	–	59	65	76	69	69	32	46	45	–	–	–	–	–	–	–	–	77	70
Viet Nam	Low	0.7	Yes	Yes	70	30 x	21 x	85	74	81	77	63	72	2	3	2	1	3	2	–	–	31	30
Yemen	Very high	–	–	–	38	–	–	65	66	65	5	8	6	13	10	12	25	29	26	–	–	11	2
Zambia	Medium	–	No	No	62	–	–	34	59	45	20	36	28	12	10	11	10	15	13	–	–	52	40
Zimbabwe	Medium	–	Yes	No	85	19	12	90	70	82	95	87	92	1	12	5	1	19	6	–	–	59	52

SUMMARY

East Asia and Pacific	–	–	–	–	86	35	29	–	–	78 **	–	–	55 **	–	–	3 **	–	–	3 **	–	–	75	71
Europe and Central Asia	–	–	–	–	77	74	69	–	–	66	–	–	53	–	–	6	–	–	7	–	–	84	79
Eastern Europe and Central Asia	–	–	–	–	69	76	71	–	–	69	–	–	53	–	–	6	–	–	6	–	–	68	62
Western Europe	–	–	–	–	83	72	68	–	–	65	–	–	53	–	–	7	–	–	7	–	–	95	93
Latin America and Caribbean	–	–	–	–	83	42	44	–	–	78	–	–	52	–	–	5	–	–	8	–	–	59	52
Middle East and North Africa	–	–	–	–	68	43	40	–	–	68	–	–	19	–	–	–	–	–	–	–	–	59	43
North America	–	–	–	–	83	88	89	–	–	69	–	–	58	–	–	4	–	–	4	–	–	94	93
South Asia	–	–	–	–	67	34	20	–	–	79	–	–	25	–	–	3	–	–	4	–	–	75	64
Sub-Saharan Africa	–	–	–	–	53	30	20	–	–	70	–	–	59	–	–	6	–	–	8	–	–	47	35
Eastern and Southern Africa	–	–	–	–	62	24	18	–	–	75	–	–	63	–	–	7	–	–	10	–	–	49	41
West and Central Africa	–	–	–	–	41	35	22	–	–	64	–	–	54	–	–	5	–	–	5	–	–	44	28
Least developed countries	–	–	–	–	58	23	13	–	–	75	–	–	52	–	–	4	–	–	7	–	–	41	28
World	–	–	–	–	76	44	38	–	–	74	–	–	44	–	–	4	–	–	5	–	–	72	65

For a complete list of countries and areas in the regions, subregions and country categories, see page 182 or visit <data.unicef.org/regionalclassifications>.

It is not advisable to compare data from consecutive editions of *The State of the World's Children*.

DEFINITIONS OF THE INDICATORS

Social Institutions and Gender Index (SIGI) – Level of gender discrimination in social institutions defined as discrimination in the family, restricted physical integrity, restricted access to reproductive and financial resources, and restricted liberties.

Legal frameworks that promote, enforce and monitor gender equality in employment and economic benefits – Measures as a percentage of achievement from 0 to 100 with 100 being best practice, government efforts to put in place legal frameworks that promote, enforce and monitor gender equality in the area of employment and economic benefits.

Maternity leave benefits – Whether the law provides for 14 weeks or more of paid maternity leave in accordance with the International Labour Organization standards.

Paternity leave benefits – Whether the law provides for paid paternity leave (of any length).

Demand for family planning satisfied with modern methods – Percentage of women of reproductive age (15–49 years) who have their need for family planning satisfied with modern methods.

Educational attainment – Percentage of the population aged 25 years and older that completed at least upper secondary education (ISCED 3).

Labour force participation rate – The proportion of a country's working-age population that engages actively in the labour market, either by working or looking for work.

Unemployment rate – The percentage of persons in the labour force who are unemployed.

Mobile phone ownership – Proportion of individuals who own a mobile telephone.

Financial inclusion – Percentage of adults (ages 15+) who report having an account (by themselves or together with someone else) at a bank or another type of financial institution or personally using a mobile money service in the past 12 months.

MAIN DATA SOURCES

Social Institutions and Gender Equality Index (SIGI) – Organisation for Economic Co-operation and Development (OECD). Last update: March 2019.

Legal frameworks that promote, enforce and monitor gender equality in employment and economic benefits – UN Women, World Bank Group, OECD Development Centre. Last update: July 2019.

Maternity leave benefits – World Bank Women Business and the Law. Last update: February 2019.

Paternity leave benefits – World Bank Women Business and the Law. Last update: February 2019.

Demand for family planning satisfied with modern methods – United Nations, Department of Economic and Social Affairs, Population Division, United Nations Population Fund (UNFPA), based on Demographic and Health Surveys (DHS), Multiple Indicator Cluster Surveys (MICS), Reproductive Health Surveys, other national surveys, and National Health Information Systems (HIS). Last Update: March 2019.

Educational attainment – UNESCO Institute for Statistics (UIS). Last update: June 2019.

Labour force participation rate – International Labour Organization (ILO). Last update: August 2019.

Unemployment rate – International Labour Organization (ILO). Last update: August 2019.

Mobile phone ownership – International Telecommunication Union (ITU). Last update: March 2019.

Financial inclusion – World Bank. Last update: July 2019.

Country data on SDG indicators included in this table (legal frameworks on gender equality in employment, demand for family planning satisfied with modern methods, mobile phone ownership, and financial inclusion) refer to the most recent year available as reported in the SDG Global Database 2019 version.

NOTES

– Data not available.

x Data refer to years or periods other than those specified in the column heading. Such data are not included in the calculation of regional and global averages. Estimates from data years prior to 2000 are not displayed.

* Data refer to the most recent year available during the period specified in the column heading.

** Excludes China.